italy

FODOR'S TRAVEL PUBLICATIONS
NEW YORK • TORONTO • LONDON • SYDNEY • AUCKLAND

WWW.FODORS.COM

Contents

KEY TO SYMBOLS

- Map reference
- Address
- Telephone number
- Opening times
- Admission prices
- Metro station
- Bus number
- Train station
- Ferry/boat
- Tours
- Guidebook
- Restaurant
- Café
- Bar
- Shop
- Lavatories
- Number of rooms
- Parking
- Air-conditioning
- No smoking
- Swimming pool
- Gym
- Place to eat
- Place to stay

Eating and Staying
331–398

Planning
399–420

Maps
421–451

Index
452–459

UNDERSTANDING ITALY

Italy is so varied, it is worth planning your trip and deciding what you want to see before you leave home. The country is divided into 20 regions and it would be hard to cover them all satisfactorily in a single trip, so it's probably a good idea to concentrate on one region or a few of the major tourist areas. The big art cities of Rome, Florence and Venice are very popular, outdoor enthusiasts will also find plenty to do throughout the year in the mountainous north, and beach-lovers can choose from numerous glitzy resorts, empty beaches and secluded coves along the country's sinuous coastline. City life throughout Italy has an attractive style and ease, drawing visitors tempted by a vibrant arts scene and some of the best shopping in Europe.

The 14th-century Castello degli Challand, on a lofty outcrop in the Alpine foothills near the Valle d'Aosta town of Verres (left); a view over the resort of Limone Sul Garda on Lake Garda (right)

LANDSCAPE

Italy is a mountainous Mediterranean country extending south from the Alps, with two major off-shore islands, Sicily and Sardinia, and several groups of smaller islands. It covers an area of 294,020sq km (113,530 sq miles) and has a coastline running for 7,600km (4,723 miles). It is over 1,500km (930 miles) long, a contrast to the width, which you can drive across in 3–4 hours.

The chain of the Apennine Mountains runs down the country from Genoa in the north to Reggio di Calabria in the south, covered in huge tracts of forest. North of Genova lie the flat plains of the Po Valley, immensely fertile and intensively farmed. These mist-laden plains are backed by the Alps, stretching eastward from the border at Ventimiglia through to Slovenia, with the most scenic ranges, the Ortles and Dolomites, in the east. The stereotypical classic rolling hill landscape dotted with vines and lined with cypress trees is confined to central Italy, seen at its best in Tuscany and Umbria.

ECONOMY

Despite the dichotomy between the north and south, Italy is a modern industrialized nation. Business and commerce revolve around Milan in the north, but the deep south remains one of Europe's most economically depressed areas.

Apart from natural gas, the country has few natural resources, with no substantial deposits of oil, iron or coal. Much of the land is unsuited to agriculture and Italy is a net food importer. Its economic strength lies in the processing and manufacturing of goods, primarily in small-to-medium-sized, family-owned firms. The major industries are car and precision machinery manufacture, textiles, clothing and footwear, ceramic and chemical production and food processing. Sixty-two per cent of the population is employed in tourism and the service industries. Major trading partners include the US and countries within the European Union, with car and fashion industries exporting worldwide.

POLITICS

The Republic of Italy was created in 1948; since then there have been well over 50 governments. The head of state is the president, chosen by an electoral college drawn from the houses of parliament and regional representatives. Decision-making lies with the lower house, the Chamber of Deputies, directly elected by universal suffrage. The upper house, the Senate, is made up of six representatives from each region, plus a number of senators-for-life. The complicated proportional representation electoral system has been responsible for a series of coalition governments, many of which have been suspected of corruption at the highest level. The *Mani Pulite* (Clean Hands) investigation in the 1990s extinguished the *tangentopoli* (bribetown) climate, leading to the downfall of some of the old established parties. Scandals continue, but there is a genuine feeling that Italy is moving forward.

THE NORTHWEST

Lombardy is heavily industrialized, but it also has beautiful valleys and Alpine foothills and some splendid historic towns. Among these are medieval Pavia, Cremona, famous as the birthplace of Stradivari and Amati violins, the great Gonzaga stronghold of Mantua, and Bergamo. To the north lie the lakes—Orta, Iseo, Garda and Como, popular destinations for Italians and visitors alike.

Piedmont, at the foot of the Alps, borders France and is renowned for its winter skiing and summer walking, found at their best in the Parco Nazionale di Gran Paradiso, Italy's oldest national park. For culture there's Alba, a lovely mix of narrow streets and medieval, Renaissance and baroque buildings. This region is known for its stuffed pastas, and connoisseurs will enjoy the renowned red wine, Barolo, and the world-famous white truffles.

Liguria is Italy's Riviera, a tiny region between the Alps and the sea, tucked around the Gulf of Genoa and curving northwest toward France. The rugged coast, scattered with chic, glitzy resorts famous for their seafood, contrasts with the unspoiled and largely unknown interior. To sample the best of both, head for the Cinque Terre and Lerici, south of Genoa, or switch off for a few days in Portofino or Rapallo, both on the Riviera di Levante, east of the city.

The village of Baschi in Umbria (left); the morning haze over the lush vineyards of the Chianti district, famed for its production of fine red wine (right)

VENICE, THE NORTHEAST AND EMILIA-ROMAGNA

The Veneto is a rich and developed region spreading from the flatlands and lagoon northward into the Dolomites. Its cities include thriving Padua, with its medieval core, centuries-old university and tempting shopping; the Palladian delights of Vicenza, Europe's textile capital, and rich, historic Verona, but **Venice** is the main draw. Smaller towns worth exploring are Asolo, a medieval walled town in the foothills of the Dolomites, and Conegliano, a pleasing old town in the middle of the wine-growing area.

Friuli-Venezia-Giulia has mountain ranges in the north, spiritual retreats in the east and Adriatic lagoon land to the south. The ancient past is preserved in towns like Aquileia, with its 11th-century basilica and Roman remains, and Cividale del Friuli, home to some exceptional Lombard treasures. Trieste is the regional capital, its grandiose architecture balanced by the airiness of Udine.

Trentino-Alto-Adige is a German-Italian region in the far northeast, created in 1919. The Alto-Adige is German, while Trentino is distinctly Italian, a contrast of cultures evident in the region's main towns. Bolzano (Bozen), the trim capital of the Alto Adige, Bressanone (Brixen) and Merano (Meran) are markedly German in character, while Trento, with its castle, is undoubtedly Italian.

Emilia-Romagna is famous for its artistic towns and cuisine. Prosperous Bologna is the capital, and culture lovers will find plenty to admire—the Byzantine mosaics of Ravenna, Parma's Lombard-Romanesque duomo and baptistery, and Ferrara's huge castle, fine palaces and museums. Lower-key delights lie in Piacenza and Pavarotti's home town of Modena.

FLORENCE, TUSCANY AND UMBRIA

Tuscany has an abundance of artistic towns, attracting huge numbers of visitors each year, but leave time for the rural pleasures in the wooded hills of Chianti, famous for its wine, and the rolling honey-coloured landscape, dotted with cypress trees. **Florence,** renowned as the cradle of the Renaissance, has long been on the tourist map. Topping the list of bigger towns is Siena, with its shell-shaped Campo and medieval architecture, closely followed by Pisa with its tower.

Umbria is Italy's only land-locked region, whose capital is Perugia. Orvieto, with its famous cathedral, far in the west, is the other main town, while to the east lies Spoleto, a quiet, historic town that comes alive during its summer arts festival. Between these is a clutch of smaller towns: medieval Gubbio, Assisi, St. Francis's birthplace, laid-back Spello and Montefalco. Umbria also has blue waters at Lago di Trasimeno, dramatic gorges in the Valnerina and the towering mountains of the Sibillini.

ROME, LAZIO AND THE MARCHE

Lazio is a quiet and low-key region with a gentle landscape. Rome is close to many of the key sights—the stunning baroque gardens at Tivoli, the towns of the Alban Hills known as the Castelli Romani, and the ancient Roman port of Ostia. The Etruscan settlements of Cerveteri and Tarquinia are older still, and medieval Viterbo is culturally fascinating. **Rome,** Italy's compelling capital, has a staggering wealth of monuments, museums, galleries and architecture spanning almost 3,000 years. There are outstanding examples of baroque sculpture and countless Renaissance masterpieces on display in its galleries and museums. Above all Rome is a vibrant modern capital, where life continues to buzz through the patchwork of its ancient, medieval and modern streets.

The Marche is tucked away inconspicuously in the east on the calf of Italy, across the Apennines. This is an unspoiled region with historic towns, long stretches of coastline and a green, hilly interior. The main attraction is Urbino, a classic Renaissance ducal town, but don't miss compact Ascoli Piceno in the eastern valley and the tiny fortress town of San Leo. There are plenty of family resorts to choose from—Pesaro is the most notable, with its old town and well-groomed, sandy beaches.

Naples from Castel San Elmo (left); Taormina, with the snowcapped peak of Mount Etna in the background (middle); and clear turquoise water near Capriccioni on the Costa Smeralda (right)

THE SOUTH

Campania has a vibrant capital—Naples—a coastline dotted with picturesque villages between Sorrento and Amalfi, the jewel-like islands of Ischia and Capri, and a wealth of archaeological sites: Pompei, Herculaneum and Paestum.

Molise is remote and undiscovered; nearby, **Abruzzo**, is better known, chiefly for its superb Parco Nazionale d'Abruzzo, Italy's third-largest park. The Gran Sasso massif is a magnet for outdoor enthusiasts and wilderness lovers. L'Aquila is the region's bustling and prosperous capital.

Basilicata has superb mountain scenery, seen at its best in the Parco Nazionale del Pollino. Enjoy the coastline on both the Mar Tirenno and Golfo di Taranto, delve back in time in Matera to the east, an ancient settlement peppered with cave houses, or travel south for archaeology at Metaponto.

Calabria, Italy's toe, is an undeveloped region with a long coastline and mountains inland. The Sila range, with its rolling plateaux and dense woodlands, shouldn't be overlooked. Reggio di Calabria is the main ferry port for Sicily and its chief attraction is its outstanding archaeological museum.

Puglia, the heel, is more prosperous than other regions in the south. Highlights include the port of Bari, with its labyrinthine old town and Norman cathedral, exuberant Lecce, one of Italy's finest baroque towns, and Castel del Monte, a 13th-century, isolated Swabian castle. More relaxing is the Gargano peninsula, the spur of the boot, a limestone promontory dotted with fishing villages.

SICILY AND SARDINIA

Sicily, to the southwest of the toe of Italy, has enough to keep you busy for weeks. Palermo is the capital, its vitality rivalled only by grimy Catania and the ancient Greek settlement of Siracusa. There's more of archaeological interest at Greek Agrigento, Selinunte and Segesta. Taormina's main attraction is Mount Etna, one of the world's largest active volcanoes. Quieter, but equally attractive, are Noto, a superb baroque town built after the 1693 earthquake, the inland town of Enna and the north-coast fishing port of Cefalù, with its beaches and Norman cathedral.

Sardinia, 200km (124 miles) to the west of the mainland, is renowned for its idyllic coastline, clear waters, classy resorts and wild interior. Walled Cagliari is the capital, and Nora is the island's premier archaeological site with Phoenician, Carthaginian and Roman remains. There is an abundance of coastal resorts too—the Costa Smeralda in the northeast, the Riviera di Corallo in the northwest, and Cala Gonone, with mountainous cliffs and sea caves, in the east.

ITALY'S REGIONS

FL · CH · A · TRENTINO-ALTO-ADIGE · FRIULI-VENEZIA-GIULA · SLO · VALLE D'AOSTA · LOMBARDIA · VENETO · HR · F · PIEMONTE · EMILIA-ROMAGNA · LIGURIA · MC · TOSCANA · MARCHE · UMBRIA · ABRUZZO · LAZIO · MOLISE · CAMPANIA · PUGLIA · BASILICATA · SARDEGNA · CALABRIA · SICILIA

THE BEST ART CITIES

Florence (p. 115–134) Buildings and art collections that provide an insight into the revolutionary Renaissance.

Naples (p. 198–201) A variety of architecture, from Gothic to Baroque, and the city's classical art collections are among the finest in the country.

Ravenna (p. 110) Some of the world's finest Byzantine mosaics.

Rome (p. 157–180) Artistic delights spanning two thousand years, encompassing architecture, sculpture, painting and mosaics.

Siena (p. 152–153) A perfectly preserved medieval city with an artistic heritage and cityscape focused on the Italian Gothic.

Venice (p. 81–102) A city built on water, crammed with treasures covering over a thousand years of art history.

THE BEST COASTAL AREAS

The Amalfi Coast (p. 318–319) A stretch of coast south of Naples, with towering cliffs, steep, green mountains and fabulous views over the azure sea.

Cinque Terre (p. 279–281) 'The Five Lands'—a string of higgledy-piggledy fishing and holiday villages, where cliffs, covered in terraced vineyards, lead down to hidden beaches.

Costa Smeralda (p. 220) Sardinia's Emerald Coast, where natural beauty and clear waters combine with chic resorts.

Gargano Peninsula (p. 322–323) The spur of the 'boot'—a limestone peninsula fringed with turquoise water, relaxed fishing villages and small resorts.

Riviera de Levante (p. 80) A beautiful area south of Genova, renowned for its up-market resorts and dramatic cliffs.

THE NORTHWEST

The Parco Nazionale del Gran Paradiso (p. 76) Some excellent walking in majestic mountain scenery.

Milan (p. 72–75) Explore the art and architecture and indulge in some of the world's best retail therapy.

Finestre Sul Po, Turin (p. 345) Sit back and relax in this long-established riverside restaurant that serves unforgettable food in beautiful surroundings.

Bellagio (p. 69) Tour around Lake Como by car or ferry from here.

Grand Hotel Villa Serbelloni, Bellagio (p. 340) Blow the budget and stay at one of Italy's most beautiful lakeside hotels on Lake Como.

The Via dell'Amore, Cinque Terre (p. 279) Walk along this cliff-side path in the Cinque Terre, particularly dramatic between Manarola and Riomaggiore.

Isole Barromee (p. 70) Take a boat trip to these idyllic islands in Lago Maggiore.

Mantua (p. 77) Survey some of the 500 rooms of the vast complex of the Palazzo Ducale, once the home of the Gonzagas.

When it comes to shopping for the latest styles, there's plenty of choice in Milan (left)

The marina in Bellagio (above)

VENICE

The Canal Grande (p. 84) Take the *vaporetto* No. 1 down this famous waterway for a panoramic presentation of elegant architecture.

The Basilica di San Marco (p. 82–83) Appreciate this mind-blowing overview of Venetian art and history.

The Accademia Bridge (p. 88–89) Admire the view down the Canal Grande towards the great church of the Salute.

Antiche Carampane (p. 347) Track down the Antiche Carampane, an off-the-beaten-track restaurant in the heart of Venice, for the best fish in the city.

Burano, Murano and Torcello (p. 86, 91, 102) Spend a day exploring the lagoon islands.

The Scuola Grande di San Rocco (p. 102) Take in Tintoretto's great cycle of paintings.

Rialto (p. 97) Make a morning visit to the Rialto food markets and admire the fruit and vegetables piled high and the sparklingly fresh fish and seafood.

Pensione Accademia Villa Maravege (p. 351) Stay in the Pensione Accademia in Dorsoduro, the perfect Venetian base—but be sure to book ahead.

Shopping (p. 240) Browse among the shops for handmade Venetian products—vibrant carnival masks and Murano glass.

Ca' Rezzonico (p. 86) Visit this palace for a glimpse of the ostentation and grandiose style that characterized 18th-century Venetian life.

A vaporetto on the Canal Grande in Venice (above); Murano glassware by Stefano Toso (left)

The Roman Amphitheatre in Verona (below)

THE NORTHEAST AND EMILIA-ROMAGNA

Bologna (p. 105) Spend time strolling through the arcaded streets—don't miss the Strada Maggiore.

Verona (p. 112–113) Admire the Roman Arena before exploring the area around the Piazza delle Erbe.

The Grande Strada dei Dolomiti (p. 290–291) Drive along this route past mountain views, high passes and picturesque villages.

Villa Madruzzo, Trento (p. 356) Drink in the mountain air while staying in country house comfort at the Villa Madruzzo.

Parma (p. 109) Shop for *prosciutto di Parma* (Parma ham) and Parmigiano Reggiano (Parmesan cheese) before taking in the city's artistic treasures.

Ferrara (p. 106) Take a tour of this historical town, once the Este powerbase—don't miss the Castello Estense.

Parmigiano Reggiano (right)

FLORENCE

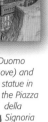

The Duomo, Campanile and Battistero (p. 116–119) Appreciate this harmonious trio of Renaissance church buildings.

The Galleria degli Uffizi (p. 122–123) Trace the development of Italian painting and admire the treasures.

The Piazza della Signoria (p. 131) Sit and enjoy a coffee while overlooking the Palazzo Vecchio and the statues, the heart of historic Florence and a great place for people-watching.

Il Latini (p. 360) Enjoy a meal at this restaurant, famous for its traditional Florentine cooking.

The Galleria Palatina, Palazzo Pitti (p. 128–129) Admire the superb Renaissance pictures and then relax with a picnic in the Giardino di Boboli.

Shopping (p. 247) Try the Via de Tornabuoni and the Via della Vigna Nuova for high fashion, or track down Florentine products such as ceramics, leather and marbled paper goods.

San Lorenzo (p. 134) Visit the Medici family church, and the Biblioteca Laurenziana nextdoor, before moving on to the Cappelle Medicee with its superlative sculpture by Michelangelo.

Fiesole (p. 141) Take an evening trip here for a quiet dinner and great views of Florence lit up at night.

Soggiorno Antica Torre (p. 364) Stay in the heart of the city in this quintessentially Florentine hotel.

The Duomo (above) and a statue in the Piazza della Signoria (left) in Florence

TUSCANY AND UMBRIA

Siena (p. 152–153) Wander around one of Italy's most perfect medieval cities.

Southern Tuscany (p. 302–304) Drive through this classic landscape of rolling hills, olive groves, vines and cypresses, dropping in on historic towns along the way.

Granaro del Monte (p. 368) Sample the very best of Umbrian cooking in the heart of the Sibillini Mountains at the Granaro del Monte in Norcia.

Montalcino and Montepulciano (p. 143, 144) Sample the great red wines of Montalcino and Montepulciano in their place of origin.

Assisi (p. 137) Follow the pilgrim trail to this lovely Umbrian town that is famously the birthplace of St. Francis.

Norcia (p. 144–145) Drive up the Valnerina to Norcia to eat some of Italy's finest pork products and pasta dishes rich in truffles.

Orvieto (p. 146) Admire the fine façade of Orvieto's Duomo before shopping for ceramics in vibrant colours.

Grand Hotel Continental (p. 372) Stay the night a couple of minutes' walk from Siena's glorious Campo.

Orvieto's Duomo (above)

ROME

The Basilica di San Pietro (p. 158–159) Marvel at the overwhelming opulence of this famous Roman Catholic landmark.

The Musei Vaticani (p. 168–171) Don't miss one of the world's greatest museums, home to Michelangelo's Sistine Chapel.

The Colosseo (p. 162–163) See this ancient arena lit up at night.

The Piazza di Spagna (p. 172) Stroll through the piazza before climbing the Spanish Steps for great views across the city.

The Galleria Borghese (p. 166) Spend a morning or afternoon viewing this wonderful art collection, in verdant surroundings.

Antonio al Pantheon (p. 374) Mix with the local clientele and sample Roman cuisine as it used to be at Antonio al Pantheon.

The Campo dei Fiori (p. 160) Enjoy a taste of everyday Roman life at this morning market.

Trastevere Explore the maze of streets and relax in one of the many cafés.

The Pantheon (p. 173) Step inside this impressive example of the grandeur of ancient Rome.

Lancelot (p. 378) Retreat to the cool space and warm welcome of the Hotel Lancelot at the end of a day's sightseeing.

The Pantheon in Rome (above)

LAZIO AND THE MARCHE

Tivoli (p. 189) Take time out surrounded by the shade and rushing water of the Villa d'Este gardens.

Ascoli Piceno (p. 182) Drive down the Tronto Valley to this relatively undiscovered jewel with its beguiling piazza.

La Vecchia Urbino (p. 384) Eat the very best of the Marche's regional dishes in Urbino's top restaurant.

Sirene (p. 383) Spend a night in magical Tivoli at the Hotel Sirene and be first at the Villa d'Este in the morning.

Piazza del Popolo in Ascoli Piceno (above)

THE SOUTH

Naples (p. 198–201) Explore the treasures and streets of this vibrant city, where life is theatrical and emotions run high.

Pompei (p. 204–207) Step back in time into a Roman town preserved by the eruption of Vesuvius in AD79.

The Amalfi Coast (p. 209) Drive along the corniche road south of Naples, punctuated by pretty villages.

Caravella (p. 385) Discover the secrets of modern southern Italian cooking at the renowned Caravella in Amalfi.

Pensione Continental (p. 390) Use the Continental, with its verdant gardens and beautiful views, as a base for exploring the Amalfi coast.

There are plenty of seafood restaurants to choose from along the Amalfi Coast (left)

SICILY AND SARDINIA

Palermo (p. 215) Experience this brash fusion of architecture, art and culture with a chequered history and fascinating cityscape.

Monreale (p. 214) Visit the Norman cathedral famed for its Greek, Byzantine and Sicilian mosaics.

Ristorante da Lorenzo, Taormina (p. 397) Have a romantic summer meal on the terrace.

Stromboli (p. 213) Climb the slopes on the Aeolian island and get close to an active volcano.

Agrigento (p. 212) Watch the night draw in around the magnificent Greek temples.

Hotel Moderno, Erice (p. 395) Stay in one of Sicily's most picturesque villages.

Palermo's narrow streets buzz with activity (below)

TOP 10 EXPERIENCES

Visit Rome for artistic delights spanning 2,000 years, encompassing architecture, sculpture, painting and mosaics (p. 157–180).

Stroll out in the early evening anywhere in Italy and join the locals for the *passeggiata*.

Head for Venice, crammed with palaces, churches, museums and galleries built on the water; a unique visual experience (p. 81–102).

Sample some of the local dishes—Italian cooking is regional, seasonal and fresh, and there is always something local on the menu (p. 331–398).

Visit Florence, a city whose buildings and art collections are a product of the Renaissance at its most revolutionary (p. 115–134).

Head for a bar and enjoy an excellent cup of coffee.

Shop for the best of Italian style or seek out sumptuous textiles, sophisticated stationery and a wide range of handmade gifts (p. 222–224).

Take a walk in the country—from north to south there are beautiful areas waiting to be explored (p. 277–330).

Browse in a food market, a feast of colour and scent and an inspiration for all cooks and food lovers (p. 222).

Swim in clear warm sea off sandy beaches or rocky coasts.

A marble copy of David—4m *(13ft) high—by Michelangelo in Piazzale Michelangelo in Florence (left). The original (1501–1504) stands in the Galleria dell'Accademia in Florence*

Living Italy

A farm worker wrestling with a bucket full of juicy grapes during harvest time in the Chianti region

A villa surrounded by vineyards in the steep hillsides near Camigliano (above)

Hen pecking in the mountainous Parco Nazionale d'Abruzzo (left), sunflowers in the the the Valle Umbra (above) and Stromboli erupting in 1998 (below)

Nature and Landscape

Black Runs

Italians love their volcanoes, so much so that they live and farm on their fertile slopes (asparagus is particularly popular) and even holiday on them. Plucky skiers can whiz down Etna, Europe's tallest and most active volcano and the focus for some well-managed ski resorts. The most popular among locals is Piano Provenzana, as the slopes on the northern side of Etna receive more snow. The other main ski town is Linguaglossa, which means 'big tongue of lava'. Of course the resorts face unique problems—the last eruption destroyed ski lifts and cable cars—but passes are cheap and you get the added bonus of some great views of the sea, with a literal whiff of danger thrown in.

Italy covers an area of 301,323sq km (116,350sq miles) and is surprisingly mountainous, with the Alps forming a natural northern barrier and the Apennines running from the French border down the middle of the country to Sicily. South of the Alps is the Po Valley, the country's largest flat, fertile area, intensively farmed and irrigated. The central regions of Tuscany, Umbria and Lazio are hilly rather than mountainous, ideal for grape and olive cultivation. Farther south and on the islands of Sicily and Sardinia the climate is dryer and harsher and the soil generally poorer, making agricultural production difficult. Although 1.4 million people are employed in farming, only 28 per cent of Italy is arable and most farms are small, with the average being only 7ha (17 acres).

Visitors to the major cities quickly become familiar with the problems of air pollution and over-aggressive housebuilding—seen at its worst in the villas constructed within the Agrigento archaeological park— and yet, there are signs that Italy is becoming eco-friendlier. The country has had a decent sprinkling of green MPs and senators—and even a couple of ministers—over the last 20 years. Millennium celebrations inspired a big clean-up operation, especially in Rome, and the national parks are working hard to educate people about the importance of the countryside and endangered habitats.

A European grey wolf—*Canis lupus* (left), a marble quarry in the Apuan mountains in the Carrara region of Tuscany (above) and the Positano coastline (below)

Ripening olives in the Tuscan countryside (above) and freshly harvested corn in the Veneto (below)

Crying Wolf

Once hated and killed by villagers and shepherds alike, the Apennine wolf has been nursed back from near extinction in the 1970s. There are now around 400 European wolves living in Italy and numbers are growing by about 7 per cent a year. If they continue to thrive, environmentalists believe that they could spread throughout the Alps and cross over into neighbouring countries. Success is most evident in the Abruzzo National Park, where Operation St. Francis has educated locals about the wolf population, encouraging them away from hunting and leading to the establishment of a wolf museum in the park village of Civitella Alfedena (p. 202). This has also increased visitor numbers to the area and transformed the economy of a once decaying village—a striking example of the powers of ecotourism.

High Seas

The rising waters around Venice tend to hog the headlines, but Italy, a country surrounded by water, could lose 4,500sq km (1,740sq miles) of land to flooding and rising seas by the end of the century. Rapid development and erratic weather conditions in vulnerable areas have accelerated coastal erosion. The sunny southern beaches are most at risk, with the largest losses predicted between the toe and the heel of Italy around the Gulf of Taranto. Government officials will soon be forced to act if they want to preserve the beaches and profitable tourist industry. Large-scale investment is needed and there are plans to build dikes to protect areas at risk, but in the long term they may have to accept that some beautiful parts of Italy will return to the sea.

Alpine Assistance

To get close to the great Italian outdoors, head for a Via Ferrata, a network of metal ladders, pegs, bridges and ropes, cemented onto the mountainsides to help walkers reach otherwise inaccessible areas of the Dolomites without specialist climbing equipmet. They are not for the faint-hearted though—some sections are vertical and you will need a good head for heights. Climbing aids were first introduced around 100 years ago, used by soldiers during the two World Wars, but only became popular with climbers from the 1930s onwards when the Bochette Way was opened. Today there are dozens of routes, maintained mostly by the Club Alpino Italiano—the Italian Alpine Club (www.cai.it).

Olive Branch

Italian olive trees have become a victim of their own beauty, a work of art to be treasured—and consequently stolen and sold on to private 'collectors' to decorate their gardens, both abroad and in the north of Italy. The practice of uprooting ancient olive trees is particularly prevalent in the south where thieves and farmers use mechanical diggers to prize up the precious specimens. Unlike Spain, which has a similar problem, Italy does have legislation to protect the trees and farmers are supposed to obtain permission before moving their trees, but the law is clearly being disregarded on a huge scale. The real tragedy is that many of the replanted trees die within 12 months.

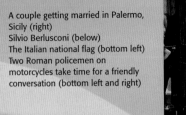

A couple getting married in Palermo, Sicily (right)
Silvio Berlusconi (below)
The Italian national flag (bottom left)
Two Roman policemen on motorcycles take time for a friendly conversation (bottom left and right)

Society and
Politics

Italy has some of the most densely populated areas in Europe, as Italians gravitate towards the cities for economic reasons, leaving their native regions behind. Women's roles are evolving, particularly in the north, with many continuing with their careers after marriage. Over the last 20 years the birth rate has fallen alarmingly, while the divorce rate has rocketed, affecting traditional patterns. Despite this, family and community ties remain strong. The impression of the family gathering to eat together regularly is still a very real one (51 per cent of Italians live within 15 minutes of their mother's home). The concept of family underpins all Italian relationships, whether it's between actual blood relations or simply in the construction of a familiar world of personal ties. Despite past political turmoil, the Italian way of life remains enviable—southern Italians in particular work fewer hours, have more holidays and enjoy a lower cost of living than their frenetic northern European counterparts.

Mamma's Children

These days, the image of a prosperous, pasta-serving *mamma* surrounded by a house full of kids is way off the mark. Italy has one of the lowest birth rates in the world, at 9.1 per 1,000 inhabitants, and one of the lowest fertility rates, with 1.2 children born per adult woman (compared with 1.7 in the UK and 2.0 in the US). But parents continue to play a key role in their children's lives. At the last count 56 per cent of 25- to 29-year-olds still lived at home and the number is increasing. According to the Italian statistical institute, Eurispes, the figures are connected: 'Young people are getting married less, and until they do marry they prefer to live at home'.

Two men chatting animatedly in Piazza Navona, Rome (below left)

A cyclist navigating the busy streets of Milan, Italy's business capital (below middle)

Emanuele Filiberto, his father Prince Vittorio Emanuele and his mother Princess Marina Doria attending Mass in May 2003 in the Pantheon in Rome (left)

A protester publicizing his cause by attaching himself to the Italian flag (below right)

Berlusconi's Blunders

In June 2003 the Italian parliament approved a law granting the Italian Prime Minister Silvio Berlusconi, media magnate turned centre-right political crusader, immunity from prosecution, positioning him above the law and immediately halting his trial where he faced charges of bribing judges. Lawyers used the same law in July 2003 to stop an inquiry into tax fraud involving two of his TV corporations. In the same month he made a dramatic entrance as European President when, during an argument with German MEP Martin Schulz, he suggested he play a guard in a film about a Nazi concentration camp, stunning the European Union. His current term began in June 2001 and he looks set to stay in power for the foreseeable future if he can continue to rein in his talent for gaffes.

New Men

The role of husbands is beginning to change with the establishment of the Italian Association of Househusbands in the town of Pietrasanta in Tuscany. While working opportunities for women in Italy have improved, females still tend to do the majority of the household tasks. This is where the Association comes in, teaching men how to do housework, cook, clean, and even enjoy it. At the moment it has 2,000 members—mainly those who have chosen to leave the workplace or whose wives are the main breadwinners—and there is growing interest from around the country. Best of all, like Italian housewives, they can also claim pension benefits relating to their work at home.

New Women

In the 21st century, it seems that the historically male-dominated Italian Mafia is adjusting to the modern world. Erminia Giuliano is one of the growing number of 'godmothers' in the business. No ordinary housewife, she became the head of one of Naples's leading Mafia families after all her brothers (Guglielmo, Carmine 'The Lion', and 'Little Luigi' Giuliano) were jailed, and she even made it onto Italy's most-wanted list. Police finally caught her in 2001 when they discovered she was operating the business from a secret room behind a kitchen cupboard in her house. More chillingly, in 2002, the glass ceiling was firmly smashed when women in the rival Cava and Graziano clans just outside Naples were both the victims and killers in a horrific shootout.

Royalty

If you thought the British Royal Family was having a rough time, pity the former Italian sovereigns. Exiled 50 years ago to Geneva after rather too fulsome support for Mussolini, the royals have long argued for their right to return home. Following a change of heart by the Italian parliament, they have made something of a comeback. Vittorio Emanuele, the son of Italy's last king Umberto II and just nine years old when he left, has recently returned to Italy (albeit briefly) to have a chat with the Pope and swear allegiance to the Republic. Though the family has categorically denied any possibility of wearing a crown again, this hasn't stopped Vittorio's son Emanuele Filiberto appearing in a television commercial for olives that make you 'feel like a king'.

A banner advertizing the fashion designer Versace in Piazza di Spagna, Rome (right) Shop for the latest fashions in Salvatore Ferragamo (below left)

A woman laden down with designer shopping bags in Milan (right), a sign for one of Buccellati's luxurious jewellery shops on Via dei Condotti in Rome (below right) and the Fiat 500, a compact style icon designed to cope with narrow streets and tight city parking (bottom)

High Style

Is It Art?

Could Prada be the new Palladio? Or Gucci the new Giotto? Perhaps it's not too fanciful to say that Italian fashion is the new art. After all, the iconic Giorgio Armani had an entire exhibition at the Guggenheim Museum in New York in 2001 devoted to the development of his work, which was treated in exactly the same way as the work of a classical Renaissance artist. Elsewhere, Gianni Versace's creations were on show in the same city's Metropolitan Museum of Art in spring 2003. Italy itself has also recognized the skills of its native sons, with the Palazzo Pitti in Florence exhibiting more than 60 Gianfranco Ferre outfits for its grand reopening.

There's a long-established Italian tradition of craftsmanship and luxurious living, dating right back to the glittering Renaissance courts. With this background, the native sense of style and the cult of the *bella figura*, it's not surprising that fashion and design are booming. Italians seem to infuse everything with elegance, whether it's gorgeous clothes or cars, interior or exterior building design, washing machines or typewriters (Olivetti's Lettera 22 and Lexikon 80 models are even part of the permanent collection of New York's Museum of Modern Art). The sense of style spills over into the media and the creative arts, too, evident in the cutting-edge sharpness of Italian magazines and the distinctive and unmistakable films of Italian-born Federico Fellini and Michelangelo Antonioni. Enterprising and creative Milan is one of the world's genuine style capitals, a hotbed for must-have fashion items and accessories—Gucci, Armani, Prada, Missoni, Versace—as well as affordable, zappy wardrobes from Max Mara and the super-giant Benetton. Refreshingly, there is no pigeonholing of designers according to industry: Donatella Versace has overseen every lifestyle element of the Italian-themed Palazzo Versace hotel in Australia, for example. Italian style is famous worldwide: The rich and stylish cruise the roads in Italian cars by Ferrari, Lamborghini and Maserati, and deck their houses with functional and sleek furniture, fabrics and gadgets.

An impressive lineup of shining vintage Lancias parked on the waterfront in Portofino (above) Giorgio Armani showing off his 2004 autumn Emporio Armani collection on the catwalks of Milan in March 2003 (left)

A woman zipping around the streets of Milan on a scooter (right) and a window display of gloves in Florence (below)

Pininfarina

The Pininfarina company was founded in 1930 by Battista Pininfarina, who was inspired by a meeting with Henry Ford and the entrepreneurial culture of America. His cars came to embody the idea of democracy in car design—an international approach, extremely unusual in Italy at that time, which marked him out as a unique designer. The company's down-to-earth approach means that it has been happy to work on 'normal' cars such as the Peugeot 205 and the Austin-Morris 1100 (its 1952 Ambassador also revolutionized the design of small cars in the US as well as the more exciting and sporty names such as Ferrari, Alfa Romeo and the two-seater sports car. Enjoy, winner at the Geneva Motor Show 2003.

Benetton—A Success Story

Luciano Benetton is said to have sold his accordion to buy his sister a knitting machine, setting the ball rolling for the development of one of the retailing world's great success stories. Today, there are over 7,000 Benetton stores in more than 120 countries, selling affordable and stylish knitwear and much more besides. The company owns huge tracts of Argentina, where some of their 280,000 sheep are raised, and the wool from these animals only provides about 10 per cent of the company's annual requirements. On a global scale, Benetton has had far more impact than big Italian fashion names such as Armani, Missoni, Pucci, Gucci et al. Lines differ from country to country—and the Italian stores definitely have the cutting edge.

La Bella Figura

The concept of *bella figura* means many things—keeping up a good front, not making a fool of yourself, and above all, looking good. It's a little bit presence, and a little bit self-respect, and a little bit being careful not to let the side down. The opposite is *brutta figura*, as in the expression *fare una brutta figura*, to show oneself up. Around 60 per cent of Italian women buy a new wardrobe twice a year, their choice dictated by the latest shades and styles. When the seasons change, it is common for women to take a day of work just to rearrange their wardrobe. Italians spend up to 50 per cent of their disposable income on clothes and fashion, and designer wear is considered an option for all. It's not what you've got, but what you project that's important.

Little Stinger

The Vespa was built and named by Enrico Piaggio—'Sembra una vespa' ('It looks like a wasp')—to meet postwar needs for an affordable means of getting around for the general public, both men and women, that kept their clothes clean (Piaggio now produces a range of clothes and accessories, too). The scooter owes its revolutionary construction to the aeronautic background of its designer, Corradino d'Ascanio. From humble beginnings it became a cult icon, its elegantly simple look coming to symbolize a sense of freedom and independence for each new generations thanks to careful image adjustments. Consequently it has been a scene stealer in films from Fellini's *La Dolce Vita* right through to Austin Powers' *Goldmember*.

Restoration
of Giotto's
frescoes,
in the
Scrovegni
Chapel, Padova
(top)
A fresco in the Villa
Imperiale, Sicily
(left)
The Roman ruins in
Herculaneum (right)
The Leaning Tower of Pisa
(below)

Living with History

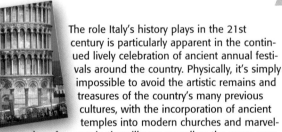

The role Italy's history plays in the 21st century is particularly apparent in the continued lively celebration of ancient annual festivals around the country. Physically, it's simply impossible to avoid the artistic remains and treasures of the country's many previous cultures, with the incorporation of ancient temples into modern churches and marvellous frescoes in tiny villages as well as the more monumental grandeur of the capital. With 31 Unesco World Heritage Sites, Italy stands at the top of the international list for cultural importance. The artistic heritage spans over 4,000 years, comprising archaeological sites, monuments, churches and works of art. In the last 50 years Italy has made outstanding achievements in the field of restoration, preserving important treasures nationwide and rising superbly to challenges such as the aftermath of the 1997 earthquake in Umbria. However, the ongoing process of decay is still frightening. Many regions contain nearly abandoned towns and villages, churches have been looted and stand empty, and often the scaffolding around historic buildings remains in place for years. Until recently over 15,000 objects vanished from churches, palaces and museums annually, while archaeological sites have been ruthlessly pillaged. There's no easy answer in a country with so many top-flight treasures, but it's generally agreed there could be a better balance between the money poured into the major attractions and the neglect of a broad conservation infrastructure.

Fragile Frescoes

In terms of restoration, there's probably more to do with regard to preserving frescoes than anything else. Buildings and stonework also require urgent restoration, but, with frescoes, time is of the essence. Fresco technique involves applying pigment to wet plaster, the drying process causing a chemical reaction that fixes the image permanently into the plaster. The condition of centuries-old frescoes deteriorates for a number of reasons; some problems go as far back as the artist's original application of the pigments, while others arise through damp, previous restoration attempts and pollution. New techniques are being developed all the time, ensuring that, with proper attention, frescoes will survive indefinitely.

The ruins at Selinunte in Sicily (above)
Neptune having a wash in Rome (below)
Canal Grande in Venice (far right)

Fresco fragments from the octagonal Baptistery in Parma (left) and the Cattedrale di San Francesco in Assisi (below)

Going Underground

Underneath modern Rome is a buried, hidden city encountered by building developers who constantly unearth new remains whenever they start to dig. St. Peter's Basilica sits on top of a massive Roman necropolis, but to get a closer look at Rome's history head for the 12th-century Basilica of San Clemente near the Colosseum, below which you can see the original 4th-century and even earlier 1st-century buildings including a temple dedicated to the ancient god Mithras. So extensive are the remains that guided visits are now offered by several specialized tour operators, including Roma Sotteranea, an association devoted to the underbelly of the capital; it has an excellent website at www.underome.com, which is full of pictures.

Can You Spot a Fake?

If you fancy a masterwork but have no millions to spare, you could commission a genuine fake from artist-to-the-stars Daniele Donde, whose client list includes the Pope and the late Princess Diana. Donde is the latest in a long line of fine Italian copyists, including Alceo Dossena (1878–1937) from northern Italy. A sculptor and stonemason, Dossena was so good that unscrupulous dealers started to sell his work as the real thing, and experts and museums simply couldn't tell the difference. When the artist found out what was going on, he blew the whistle on the charade and took his dealer to court, claiming that he had been cheated out of thousands of lire. It is believed that many of his pieces are still collected and exhibited unwittingly as genuine originals today.

Sensitive Statues

Michelangelo's *David*, in the Galleria degli Uffizi in Florence, has been getting some pampering—financed partly by big names such as Sting and Mel Gibson—in time for his 500th birthday in 2004. As always, his restoration is dogged by controversy. Early efforts included inserting metal pins in his broken left arm in the 16th century, cleaning by concentrated hydrochloric acid in the 19th century and the addition of a new toe in the 20th century when it was accidentally chiselled off. Modern restorers are more sensitive: The most recent walked out after an argument about the use of water-soaked poultices rather than careful dry brushing.

Acqua Alta

Venice has been battling against water for 1,500 years—it has sunk more than 23cm (9in) over the last 100 years—and scientists now estimate that unless dramatic action is taken, the city will be destroyed by the end of this century. Dedicated groups such as Venice in Peril (www.veniceinperil.org) and Save Venice (www.savevenice.org) raise awareness and international support, and the latest move by the Italian government is to install huge flood control barriers, a series of 78 mobile gates that can be used during high tides. The Moses Project, as it is known, is not without its critics: Environmentalists claim it will cause irreparable damage to the area's ecosystem.

The Vilo Per Grango Easter Parade in Gargano (far left)
Detail of Annibale Carracci's *Assumption of the Virgin* in the church of Santa Maria del Popolo, Rome (left)
Crowds gathered outside the Basilica di San Pietro in Rome, waiting to catch a glimpse of the Pope (below)
Detail of a fresco by Ghirlandaio in the church of Santa Trinità in Florence (bottom)

Catholic Italy

Mass Appeal

The hottest thing on Italian television is not Big Brother or scantily clad lovelies, but religion. From the Bible to St. Francis of Assisi, the dramatized lives of the holy are getting massive ratings on the small screen, and a biopic about the current pope is in development. One of the most popular of these shows has been the 2003 made-for-television film story of the celebrated 12-year-old martyr St. Maria Goretti, played by 13-year-old Martina Pinto. It was shot in just one month on location in Tuscany, and Maria's deathbed scene—in which she forgives her killer who had attempted to rape her—held a third of Italian households spellbound.

Although church and state are theoretically separate in Italy, the Catholic Church is so well established that its position of strength seems unassailable. Around 85 per cent of native-born Italians are still nominally Roman Catholic, and celebrations such as First Communion remain a major event. Still important, too, is the tradition of *onomastico*, celebrating your saint's day as you would your own birthday (the saint who shares your first name). The Catholic Church is making some effort to move with the times with the Pope introducing a 'thought for the day' SMS text messaging service and a Trieste priest successfully opening his church on Saturday nights until 2am to attract young clubbers. And yet young Italians take divorce, birth control and abortion for granted and cracks are appearing—over 95 per cent of Italians are baptized, but less than 10 per cent attend Mass regularly.

Italian Catholics can now even get unchristened—and the 21st century will bring further challenges. Not least of these is growing immigration from Africa, Asia and the Middle East, resulting in increased numbers of practising Buddhists and Muslims in the country, which is bringing about political and social conflict as seen in Prime Minister Berlusconi's divisive comments about Islam following the terrorist attacks of September 11 in 2001. But the Church thinks in centuries, not decades, and continues to view modern apathy with equanimity.

A statue of the Madonna and Child outside a building in Burano, Venice (left)
The Turin Shroud (right)
Pope John Paul II in Vatican City (below left)
A ceramic panel depicting St. Francis on Asissi's external walls (lower left)
A mosaic crucifix in the church of San Clemente, Rome (lower right)
A Swiss Guard (far right)

Superstitions

Despite 2,000 years of Christian teaching, some Italians can be very superstitious. Seeing a nun is supposedly unlucky, and you should either touch iron if you see one or say 'Your nun' to shunt the bad luck onto somebody else. Then there's the Evil Eye. If you think you're suffering because of it, stick out your index and small fingers, fold your middle fingers back under your thumb, and point the whole hand downwards. Most cures simply promote general good luck, such as putting new coins heads up on the windowsill on New Year's Eve, but others are quite specific, such as the Sicilian tradition of burying a statue of St. Joseph upside down in your front garden to help you sell your house.

John Paul II—The Saintmaker

While Pope John Paul II will be remembered as a loved and admired if often conservative leader and teacher, he will certainly go down in history as the pontiff who has canonized the most saints, nearly 500 (plus the same number of beatifications)—more than all his predecessors put together. Among them are Padre Pio, who had the stigmata, and Spanish priest Josemaría Escrivá, founder of the Opus Dei movement. One reason for the increased numbers is an easing of requirements (one less proven miracle), but also John Paul has canonized groups from China, Spain and Vietnam, as well as 'role models' such as the first married couple, Luigi and Maria Beltrame-Quattrocchi. By canonizing more lay people living ordinary lives, the Pope wants to show that holiness is achievable in the modern world.

Nazareth House

Italy has many pilgrimage sites, most holding saints' relics. But pilgrims to the town of Loreto come to see the Virgin Mary's house (p. 184). According to pious legend, this humble cottage—scene of the Annunciation and Jesus' family home—was miraculously transported by angels from Nazareth to Loreto in the late 13th century. Recent investigations indicate that, after the Crusades, a noble Byzantine family called Angeli shipped the stones of the Holy House to Italy, where it was rebuilt. It has only three walls; the fourth side formed by a grotto dug out of the rock in Nazareth, a common arrangement for houses of that time. Technical comparisons show the Loreto house and the Nazareth grotto to be contiguous.

The Vatican Online

The Vatican may be a male-dominated organization, but one branch at least is in female hands. Sister Judith Zoebelein, an American Franciscan nun, is the driving force behind the Holy See's website. Brought over in 1991 to expand the Vatican's rudimentary computer network, she soon became involved in setting up the website (www.vatican.va), which was launched in earnest over Easter 1997. The three computers that initially handled the Internet traffic were called Michael, Gabriel and Raphael, after the three archangels. After a million hits in the first three days, the amount of visitors settled down to the present average of 50,000 per day. Available in six languages, the Vatican website provides access to over 25,000 Holy See documents, including some in the Vatican Secret Archives.

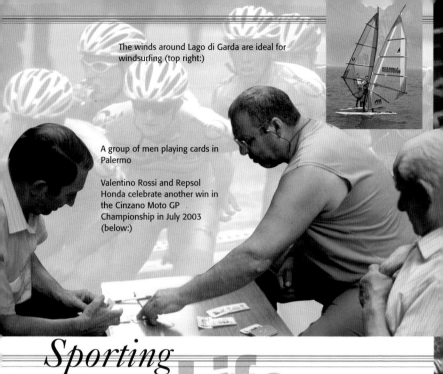

The winds around Lago di Garda are ideal for windsurfing (top right:)

A group of men playing cards in Palermo

Valentino Rossi and Repsol Honda celebrate another win in the Cinzano Moto GP Championship in July 2003 (below:)

Sporting Life

Holy Team Spirit

Is football (soccer) the new religion in Italy? Pope John Paul II is a fan and was a handy goalkeeper in his youth. Indeed, as an example of how fundamental a role the sport plays in Italian society, look no further than the Vatican itself, which has run its own internal five-a-side-league for the last 30 years. Rather than teams packed with international stars, the league consists of job-themed sides, firemen taking on archivists, postmen pitting their skills against Swiss Guards. Best of all, in contrast to the clichéd image of shirt-tugging, diving, complaining Italian footballers, the Vatican teams play the cleanest game in the world, with no dissent or professional fouls. Could we see an international Vatican side entering European competitions?

Sport is part of daily life in Italy, a country that has its own daily newspapers devoted entirely to the subject—*La Gazzetta dello Sport* (the pink paper) and the *Corriere dello Sport.* The Italian Olympic Committee's president, Gianni Petrucci, has stressed the importance of promoting all sports within the country, but football (soccer) is the undisputed king by some distance (though when it comes to actually taking part, cycling probably has the edge). The national side has an impressive reputation in world football, sometimes edging towards the mercurial, summed up by the loss against South Korea in the 2002 World Cup and the subsequent gnashing of teeth and crying foul by many Italians. Despite this, Petrucci is right: There is interest in other sports, notably cycling and motor racing. The Italians' obvious ability in ball games extends to basketball, handball, volleyball and tennis, not to mention rugby (the national side is now firmly established in the prestigious Six Nations tournament) and, perhaps more surprisingly, cricket. The country also has a passion for skiing. But football continues to dominate the headlines, whether it's pay-TV negotiations delaying the start of the league, financial mismanagement at some major clubs, or the return to Europe of its leading sides AC Milan, Juventus and Inter Milan.

Paragliding in Spello in Umbria (left)
Cyclists exploring tne Italian Lakes near Lago d'Iseo (right)

Medieval football in front of Florence's Santa Croce during the Calcio Storico (left)

The fast-paced bareback horseracing of the Palio in Siena (left)

Sardinian Stampede

There is plenty of horsemanship, historic costumes and partying at the dangerous downhill race the L'Ardia di San Costantino in Sedilo, Sardinia (5–7 July). Though the origins of the race are probably pagan, the race is said to commemorate Constantine's—and consequently Christianity's—victory in AD312 at the battle of Ponte Milvio (Milvio Bridge), the race recreating its historic battle charge. The riders and their horses meet up on a hill just outside the town's sanctuary and after various speeches and prayers for safety, they gallop at top speed down the slope, past the sanctuary and towards the finishing post in town (a dry fountain), with the man representing Constantine at the front—it's a safe bet who's going to win each year!

Driving Skills

With his film-star looks and likeable manner, Giancarlo Fisichella is the toast of Italian Formula 1 Grand Prix motor racing. It helps that he is a fast and stylish driver, especially in tricky wet conditions, admired so much by his peers that they voted him driver of the year in 2002. But his is a talent largely unfulfilled, and until his controversial win in the 2002 Brazilian Grand Prix he was well on the way to becoming the finest driver never to have won an F1 race. This is partly as a result of driving for teams who have thus far failed to match the technical skill of the top constructors, but with his native Ferrari team lined up for 2004, his luck may change.

Packs of Cards

Bridge players will know that the Italians are keen on their cards, but if you observe a card game in Italy, the deck and game may look strange. In place of clubs, hearts, spades and diamonds many areas also have coins, cups, swords and clubs. Packs—which have a marvellous medieval design and no Queen—also vary regionally in their shape (Trento's are long, Naples' are small) and number (most games use 40, some use 52), and while some games like Scopa—a complicated capture game—are nationally popular, there are regional playoffs such as *madrasso* (similar to bridge) in Venice and *coteccio*, a trick-taking game, in Trieste.

Gladiator School

Russell Crowe is far from the last word in modern Italian gladiators. For the last 10 years the fun-loving Gruppo Storico Romano, based at the appropriately historical address of Via Appia Antica in Rome, has been running regular gladiator training classes with frighteningly authentic swordplay and in full gladiatorial regalia. The range of courses corresponds to your level of interest, from introductory training, two months of twice-weekly sessions (after which you can specialize in various weapons and styles), to total-immersion courses that last three days. Rather like the craze for replacing a trip to the gym with toned-down fighting techniques, the idea of keeping fit and relieving stress is as strong among its members as their proud interest in Roman history.

Orvieto wine (left), a masked figure during Carnevale in Venice (right), Caffè del Greco in Milan (below) and a sign advertising the local wine in San Gimignano (bottom left)

The opening of Calcio Storico in Piazza Signoria, Florence (above), a child dressed up for the Carnevale in Venice (left) and the poster from Fellini's film La Dolce Vita (below)

La Dolce Vita

For centuries, visitors to Italy have found something invigorating about the country, whether it be the cultural aspects beloved of the Grand Tourists or the personal growth outlined in E. M. Forster's *A Room with a View*. Family life, sociability, food and drink, civic pride and cultural interests all play their part in shaping the concept of *la dolce vita*—the sweet life—as does the obsession with style and design. *La dolce vita* is a double-edged attitude, though, as outlined in Fellini's famous film, which did much to internationalize the philosophy: Fellini shows a post-war Italy enjoying a period of relative peace and stability wallowing in a haze of decadence. But elements of the sweet lifestyle are on the wane, with increasing European homogenization threatening the survival of the traditional siesta and the *passeggiata*, the early evening stroll. Yet there is no doubt that Italians are pleasure people; a recent poll by Censis shows that more than a quarter of Italians are not happy with their sweet life.

The Perfect Espresso

Whether it's made in a one-cup pot at home or comes from a gleaming machine in a bar, all Italian coffee is made by the espresso method. In bars, freshly ground coffee is put into a filter, compressed, and attached to the machine. Hot, not boiling, water is forced through, producing an intense, aromatic brew with a distinctive *crema* (cream) on top. Milk is frothed with steam from a separate nozzle and added for the perfect cappuccino. The roast varies from region to region, becoming increasingly potent the further south you go, but Romans claim to make the best coffee because their water is so good.

Slow Food

The essence of Italian cooking is good ingredients, but no less important is the way meals are prepared, eaten and appreciated. To this end, the Slow Food movement was born in 1986 and has now grown into an international lobby, promoting the enjoyment of eating. It also campaigns to preserve endangered ingredients threatened by the destruction of the environment, industrial standardization and strict hygiene and retail legislation. Members regard themselves as 'eco-gastronomes' whose main priority is to counter what they see as shabby eating habits: Junk food is a particular bugbear. It promotes its ideals around the world through events and festivals and publishes *The Ark of Taste*, a catalogue listing products and dishes around the world close to extinction (www.slowfood.com).

The Story of Italy

Greeks, Carthaginians, Etruscans

Surrounded by water and cut off from the European landmass by a mountain barrier, the boot-shaped peninsula of modern Italy was destined to develop into a exceptionally individual country. Despite being isolated from the north by the Alps, its shores were easily reached by eastern and southern invaders, the great early civilizations of the Phoenicians, who settled Carthage, and the Greeks. From their colonies in present-day Sicily and Sardinia, the Phoenicians established trade routes with Carthage, while the Greeks set up a new and magnificent empire in the south, totally assimilating the native people.

Farther north, the enigmatic Etruscans, whose history and language have barely been penetrated, were the dominant civilization. They lived in an area between the Tiber and Arno rivers and established a confederation of 12 sophisticated city-states, which traded with the Greek colonies in the south. As their power grew, they edged out the other northern indigenous peoples, the Ladini, the Ligurians and the Sabines. With the emergence of Rome, their civilization waned and their culture and influence were eclipsed by the growing Empire.

A wall painting in the Etruscan tombs at Monterozzi (right)

Magna Graecia

In the eighth century BC, the Greeks colonized southern Italy and Sicily, establishing hugely prosperous colonies (Magna Graecia). The cities of Siracusa, Sybaris, Metapontum and Tarentum became richer than many cities in Greece. By 400BC the Romans had moved in and sacked the most important, but some superb examples remain: Paestum, south of Salerno, Metapontum, with its archaeological museum, the theatres in Taormina (p. 217) and Siracusa (p. 216), and the temples at Segesta, Selinunte (p. 214) and Agrigento (p. 212) in Sicily.

1200BC

An Etruscan plate in the Museum of Ancient Tuscany in Chiusi (above left); A Carthaginian coin (above right); The amphitheatre at Segesta in Sicily (right)

The Etruscans

Much of what we know about the Etruscans comes from discoveries made in their necropoli, huge stone cities of the dead found at the sites of their main settlements in central Italy. Their cities of wood have long since gone, but the stone cemeteries remain. The tombs were lavish; some, as at Cerveteri and Orvieto, take the form of miniature houses lining paved streets, others, like Tarquinia, are beautifully decorated underground chambers. Elsewhere there are apartments full of funerary niches, known as *colombari*. These tombs for the afterlife were often filled with statues, jewellery and vases, and decorated with religious scenes and people hunting, fishing, playing games and dancing.

The Phoenicians

The Phoenicians came from modern-day Lebanon, emerging in the 12th century BC as what was to become the greatest trading nation of the ancient world. The Greeks called them Phoenicians after the valuable purple dye derived from molluscs that they exportedl over the world. They were middlemen as much as anything, buying in and selling on goods from all over the Mediterranean. The early Italian civilizations were good customers, and the Phoenicians, from their western power base of Carthage, established trading settlements in Sicily and southern Italy. To the north, the Etruscans were eager for luxury goods, particularly purple-dyed fabrics and Greek pottery, which were traded for Etruscan items such as jewellery and mirrors.

The Ladini

The far northern valleys of the Dolomites, where the regions of Trentino, Alto-Adige and the Veneto meet, is still home to one of Italy's oldest peoples. The Ladini, a distinct ethnic group with their own language and culture, have lived here since 4000BC. Their epics portray a history of battles, triumphs, disasters and treachery. Threatened by the Germanic tribes from the north and marauders from the south, the Ladini were constantly at war, invoking their primitive divinities for help. When Christianity arrived, they blended the new religion with the old, investing Christian saints with their gods' powers. Ladino is still spoken in the area around the Sella Mountains, and the people preserve much of their culture and customs today.

Prehistoric Buildings and Bronzes

Little is known about the first Sardinians or where they came from. These prehistoric tribes that dominated the island between 1500 and 500BC are known as the Nuraghi, the same name given to their temples and necropoli that are scattered all over the island. For years the peasants believed they were the tombs of a race of giants from whom they were descended. Enigmatic structures, they are mainly round, with a vaulted interior, connected to an upper terrace by stairs and corridors. Equally mysterious are the hundreds of eighth-century BC statuettes that have also been found on the island—bizarre bronzes of gods, people and animals.

A detail of a Phoenician sarcophagus (left); The farewell of Admetos and Alketis, a scene on an Etruscan vase found at Vulci (right)

An Etruscan vase (left)

600BC

The Etruscan barrow tombs within the necropolis that surrounds the medieval town of Cerveteri (above)

The Hellenistic Greek theatre near Taormina, rebuilt by the Romans (above);
A 6th-century Etruscan bronze of Romulus and Remus in the Musei Capitolini in Rome (left)

Roman Empire

The Roman Empire prospered at the expense of the Etruscans, who were absorbed into Roman culture and finally displaced. The Romans went on to defeat the Carthaginians in the Mediterranean, winning large parts of north Africa and Spain along the way. After conquering Italy they spread out over the rest of the Mediterranean. As the generals, troops and administrators fanned out over Europe, their ideas and inventions formed the bedrock for much that is familiar in today's society. Fundamental concepts of law and order, justice, democracy, literature and philosophy that were pioneered by the Greeks, were adopted and developed by the Romans. They also gave those they conquered a taste for good plumbing, warm houses, paved roads and luxurious living. The Roman era lasted almost a thousand years, evolving from a high-minded republic to a hedonistic empire. Periods of expansion and prosperity were tempered by civil unrest, and from AD300 the Empire was divided into east and west. By AD400, the emperors were reliant on the support of disenchanted mercenaries in their conquered territories and the frontiers collapsed. The barbarians moved in and a dark veil descended over Italy.

Julius Caesar
Soldier, orator, first consul of Rome and financier, Julius Caesar looked fate in the eye in 49BC, when he left the battlefields of Gaul to challenge his rival Pompey for control of the Empire. He took his troops with him, and as he approached the river Rubicon, the boundary with Rome, he was faced with a major decision. It was a heinous crime to enter Roman territory with an army without informing the Senate. He vacillated, unable to decide whether or not to risk all. Then came his famous words, 'Let the die be cast' and he crossed the river to march on Rome. By 44BC, he had been appointed ruler for life; a few months later he was dead, assassinated on the Ides of March.

Items from the Roman Toilet (left); Julius Caesar (102–44BC)

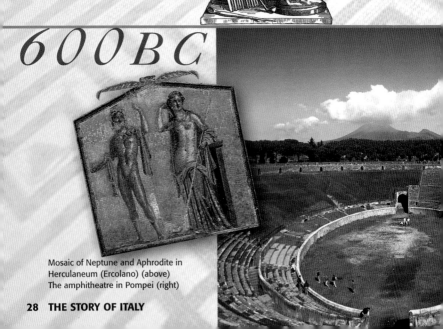

6 0 0 B C

Mosaic of Neptune and Aphrodite in Herculaneum (Ercolano) (above)
The amphitheatre in Pompei (right)

What the Romans Did for Us

Superbly practical, the Romans' inventions made life easier and more comfortable. Good road networks were essential to travel their huge Empire. Some still exist, others are the foundation for today's highways. Aqueducts efficiently brought fresh water over long distances to prosperous cities. Bathing was now a feasible option and people benefited from hot and cold running water, steam baths and clean lavatories. The latter were often communal—a great place to catch up on the gossip. Cold winters were made bearable by central heating, with hot air being circulated under the floors by a flue system. The Romans also invented dozens of small gadgets—reliable water clocks, cooking utensils, brushes, combs, mirrors, and comfortable chairs and beds.

Hannibal and the Elephants

Even before the great Carthaginian general Hannibal arrived at the foothills of the Alps to invade Rome, his battle elephants had had an adventurous trip from their starting point in Spain. They had to cross the River Rhone, deep and fast, and evade the Roman sentries. The river was too deep for the elephants to wade through, so Hannibal had water wings made for them from inflated bladders, and floated them across. Thirty-seven elephants made it to the Alps and the crossing took 19 days, trudging through late snow and struggling on the slopes. The descent into Italy was too steep for many of the elephants, and most perished, while only a few of the remainder made it through the following winter.

Vestal Virgins

The Vestal Virgins were the custodians of the sacred fire, a perpetual flame of great religious significance. This cult involved the safety of the state, and the smoke emerging from the circular marble Temple of Vesta, goddess of the hearth, was a sign that all was well. There were six Vestals, girls of unblemished character recruited from irreproachable families. They served the goddess for 30 years: 10 learning their duties, 10 performing them, and 10 passing on their knowledge. Sacred to Vesta, they enjoyed incredible privileges, but led circumscribed lives, constantly watched by the chief priest and his spies. If a Vestal slipped, the punishments were severe. Breaking the vow of chastity was seen as betraying the faith of Rome and the offender was buried alive.

Rome in Flames

According to legend, Emperor Nero played the fiddle and watched while Rome burned around him in AD64, having set fire to the city to see how Troy had looked in flames. It's a notorious tale, but fails to stand up to scrutiny, as violins were not invented for another 1,500 years. Two-thirds of the city did burn that year, though: Nero considered much of the city ugly and wanted to rebuild on a grand scale and rumours were rife that the fires had been started as his orders. To see the results, head for the ruins of Nero's Golden House, near the Colosseum in Rome, one of the largest and most ostentatious palaces in the world in its heyday.

Nero reigned for 13 years, 7 months and 28 days before he killed himself in AD68 (below)

Hannibal, the famous Carthaginian General (247–182BC, left)

Detail of a fresco in a Pompei garden (above left)

Hubert Robert's (1733–1808) painting *The Fire of Rome, 18 July AD64* (above)

The Atrium Vestae in the Foro Romano, where the six Vestal Virgins lived for 30 years and kept the sacred flame burning at the temple of Vesta, the symbol of Rome's continuity (above)

Dark Times

For the next 500 years chaos whirled through Italy. Ostrogoths, Visigoths and the ferocious Huns moved south, as the remnants of the Roman Empire were bitterly contested. The Ostrogoths under Theodoric emerged triumphant in the west, while the Byzantines held the east. The Ostrogoths continued moving west and in AD552 established a presence in southern Italy and Sardinia that was to last 500 years. To the north, the Lombards moved south into Italy, gradually extending their power. Franks eased east from Gaul, advantageously allying themselves with the emergent papacy, a crafty move that led to the Frankish ruler Charlemagne being crowned Emperor of the Holy Roman Empire by Pope Leo III in AD800. This empire covered central and northern Italy; to the south, the Byzantines had been joined by Arabs and Greeks. No dynasty or ruler was stable, nothing endured. Charlemagne's empire collapsed, and by 1000 Italy had no official ruler. Into the void swept the Normans, synthesizing their culture with the half-Arab, half-Byzantine south. The power of the papacy grew, the Holy Roman Empire rose again, and time was ripe for the start of two centuries of conflict on the issue of papal versus imperial supremacy. The Guelphs supported the pope, the Ghibellines the emperor, and Italy was torn between the two.

The Sack of Rome

By 410 the writing was on the wall for the tottering Western Empire. The Visigoth chief, Alaric, had blockaded Rome for two years, hoping for loot and prestige. The Western Roman Emperor, Honorius, now based in Ravenna, refused his demands, and Alaric, his patience finally snapping, let his troops loose on the already dying city. For three days, the Visigoths plundered, killed, raped and looted, finally moving south and devastating Rome. Alaric died shortly afterwards, and myth has him buried, together with a hoard of treasure, in a diverted riverbed in Calabria. The great Roman cities and civic buildings gradually decayed, but they were still used, and Latin continued to be widely spoken. The might of Rome collapsed, not with a bang but a whimper.

Atilla, King of the Huns (right inset), and a Byzantine mosaic of Emperor Justinian I (AD483–565) in the Basilica San Vitale in Ravenna (right)

400

The Fall of Rome (AD410), illustrating the death of Alaric after the sack of Rome (below)

Cultural U-Turn

The Lombards, a Germanic barbarian tribe, moved south into Italy in the 6th century. They arrived with barbaric customs, such as drinking out of their enemies' skulls, and set up their capital in Cividale del Friuli in the far northeast. Within a century they had moved farther south under the ruthless King Aistulf, taking Ravenna, and embraced Christianity and its culture. They left some of the most beautiful and serene artworks of the Dark Ages, gently smiling saints and charming reliefs, while their excavated tombs have yielded fabulous gold jewellery, crosses, swords and shield-holds. The designs are sinuous and intricate, the workmanship sophisticated. The Lombards were defeated by the Franks in 774, leaving a fascinating artistic legacy behind.

Larger-Than-Life Ladies

Roman and Byzantine Ravenna produced two remarkable women, both captured in the city's stunning mosaics. Galla Placidia was half-sister to the 5th-century Roman Emperor Honorius, and was kidnapped by the Goths, creating a major scandal when she married one of her abductors and fought beside him in battle. The other leading lady was Theodora, wife of Emperor Justinian, who lived in the 6th century. Her previous professions as circus entertainer, sex-show performer and prostitute made tongues wag. Aristocratic Romans were horrified when the sagacious Justinian married her and she embarked on a consortship of bad conduct, marked by acquisitiveness, corruption and venality.

Red Hair and Food for the Gods

Sweeping into southern Italy and Sicily in the 11th century, the Normans created one of the Mediterranean's most vibrant cultures. They intermarried among the dark-skinned southerners, leaving a genetic legacy that's still alive and well in Sicily. Carrot-coloured hair, straight Norman noses and startlingly blue eyes are found in even remote villages, and some Sicilian dialects still contain substantial numbers of French words and phrases. The Arab inheritance appeals more to the tastebuds. Rice and oranges, extra-sweet desserts and pastries stuffed with nuts and candied fruit, and fish served with couscous are all Arab imports. Street food vendors sell dishes that wouldn't seem out of place in a souk, while combinations of sweet and savoury in meat and fish dishes reflect North African cuisine.

Charlemagne (right)

The Coronation of Charlemagne

Charlemagne (747–814), king of the Franks and de facto ruler of Western Europe, came south in the winter of 800 to help Pope Leo III deal with the Lombards. On Christmas Day he attended Mass in Rome, and while he was kneeling in prayer the Pope picked up a crown and set it on Charlemagne's head, declaring him Emperor of Western Europe, apparently to Charlemagne's surprise. The story's probably apocryphal, and it's more likely that Pope and would-be Emperor cooked up the plan between them beforehand. The coronation was a boost to them both; it enhanced Charlemagne's reputation, while stressing the power of the papacy to make kings, increasing their temporal and spiritual clout.

Empress Placidia and her son depicted on an ivory diptych in Monza (left) and an icon of the canonized Byzantine Empress Theodora (above)

1280

A market stall in Pompei (left); the Basilica San Vitale in Ravenna (below)

A Byzantine mosaic (c. AD547) of Empress Theodora with her court of two ministers and seven women in the Basilica San Vitale, Ravenna (left)

Northern Prosperity

Confusion continued into the 13th century, with the south and Sicily hotly contested by the French and the Aragonese, the papacy fleeing to Avignon, and the political power of the major rulers under pressure all over the country. But times were changing, and no more so than in central and northern Italy. By 1300, some 300 virtually independent city-states had emerged, with a concept of citizenship radically different from that of the traditional lord-and-vassal relationship. Growing wealth from commerce and trade provided a good breeding ground for the birth of a ruling class in many of these cities, but one where the ruling class constantly feuded among itself for a place in the sun. Fed up with the bloodshed and perpetual vendettas, by the 15th century many cities had opted for rule by a single overlord strong enough to maintain order. The day of the signore had arrived. These despotic rulers oiled up to the papacy, obtaining official titles to bolster their power, so that by the second half of the 15th century most city-states were under princely, rather than republican, rule. Italy was well on the way to taking the political shape it was to maintain up until unification in the 19th century.

The Marketplace in Naples during the Plague of 1656 (1672) by Carlo Coppola (left)

The Black Death of 1348

The Black Death, which wiped out between 25 and 50 per cent of Europe's population over four years, arrived in Italy from China via a Genoese ship returning from the Black Sea in spring 1348. Most people contracted the bubonic strain, transmitted by infected fleas carried by rats. The first symptom was the appearance of the dreaded buboes, pus-filled swellings around the neck, armpits or groin. Death followed within a week. With no defence and no understanding of the cause of the plague, people panicked and law and order broke down. It was at this time that the Florentine writer Giovanni Boccaccio wrote his great work *The Decameron*, documenting individual accounts of suffering.

1280

The Cappella Colleoni in Bergamo (above)

A marble statue of Dante with an eagle at his feet in Florence's vast Piazza Santa Croce (right), cypress trees adorn an otherwise bare hillside near Mount Amata (middle)

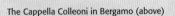

Condottiere— Medieval Mercenaries

The city-states were constantly battling it out for territorial, commercial and political advantage. Their populations were small, their citizens too busy for campaigns and sieges. The solution was the *condottiere*, a mercenary leader who offered himself, and his men, to the highest bidder. Attracted to the richer contracts, they amassed huge wealth and prestige, their deeds and deaths celebrated. Bartolomeo Colleoni, better known as 'The Invincible', was born in 1400. He fought for the Venetians and became their captain general, leaving behind the beautiful Colleoni chapel in Bergamo and donating his wealth to the city of Venice, where he is commemorated by Verocchio's great equestrian statue.

The Language of Literature

After the fall of Rome, Latin was still widely spoken throughout Italy, but a Latin that was constantly evolving as the waves of invaders introduced new words from their own languages. During the more prosperous times of the 13th and 14th centuries, scholarship and literature once more found a place, and the earliest of the new writers all spoke the Tuscan dialect, rich in Latin roots. Dante, Boccaccio and Petrarch wrote in Tuscan, which became established as Italy's literary language and later became the country's official language. The other dialects clung on; many are still spoken today, though mass communication is eroding them fast, and there are few modern Italians who cannot speak in 'pure' Italian as well as their local dialect.

Marco Polo

In 1295 Marco Polo returned to Venice after 25 years in China. He had learned many Eastern languages on his travels, but returned to find himself a stranger and a little rusty in his native tongue. He came to fame when he was captured in 1298 during the Battle of Curzola and imprisoned in Genova, where he shared a cell with the writer Rustichello di Pisa. Enthralled by Marco's tales, Rustichello turned them into a book, *Divisament dou Monde* (Description of the World). A bestseller, it was translated from French into dozens of languages, and revealed the wonderful wealth of the Orient. The book soon became known as *Il Milioni*, while Marco earned the nickname of Messer Marco Milioni, for the millions of tall tales he told.

St. Francis of Assisi

St. Francis was born to wealthy parents in 1182, spending his youth drinking and womanizing. His bad conduct continued until a spell in prison turned him to God. In 1209 he decided to dedicate his life to preaching. His message was simple— do away with material goods, love God in poverty, chastity and obedience, and see the Lord's hand in the beauty of the world. He loved nature, and is famous for blessing birds and animals—beautifully depicted by Giotto in a fresco in Assisi (p. 137). He attracted 12 followers and obtained papal permission to found a religious order, the Franciscans. In 1224, he received the stigmata, the wounds of Christ, on his hands, feet and in his side, and died two years later. He was canonized in 1228.

The Italian writer Giovanni Boccaccio (1313–75) from a print by Cornelius Van Dalen (right)

Francis Petrarch (1304–74), one of the earliest modern lyric poets (left middle) Marco Polo (left)

1450

The equestrian statue of Bartolomeo Colleoni (1400–75) in Venice

Frescoes by Ghirlandaio depicting the life of St. Francis of Assisi in Florence's Santa Trinità church (above)

Renaissance *Italy*

Booming economies and relatively stable governments were fertile ground for the flowering of the Renaissance—the 're-birth' of scholarship, architecture and the visual arts. The dynastic families and autocratic rulers of the most important states—Florence, the Papal States, Milan, Venice and Naples—were in competition to establish glittering courts, finance building schemes and patronize the finest minds and artists of the day. Smaller centres, such as Siena, Modena, Mantova, Ferrara and Urbino, were hot on their tails, resulting in an explosion of creativity all over the country.

The Renaissance started as an intellectual movement with the rediscovery of classical manuscripts and texts, which gave rise to the philosophical movement known as Neoplatonism. This influenced new architecture, new styles of painting and a new approach to sculpture inspired by the classical delight in human beauty. The restrictions that earlier thinking had imposed disappeared, leaving the way open for huge strides in every field, science and medicine in particular. No longer constrained by Aristotle's model of the universe, astronomers and cartographers re-examined existing theories of the universe and made more accurate maps. This provided the impetus for a wave of exploration and discovery.

David by Michelangelo in the Galleria dell'Accademia in Florence (right)

Patrons and Artists

The Renaissance artist certainly didn't see himself as an inspired genius, seeking to express himself. His patrons paid him to do a job. Summoned to the great man's presence, artists would be confronted with a complete brief for the proposed commission, down to the last angel in the top right-hand corner. If the painting was secular, every figure in the complicated composition had an iconographical meaning, carefully configured by the philosophers—a mere artist was not deemed capable of working out the deeper significance of a piece. Pigments were expensive, so exact amounts of different tones were specified. Blue, derived from lapis lazuli, was the most expensive of them all; lots of blue means lots of money.

Leonardo da Vinci (1452–1519)

1450

Botticelli's *Birth of Venus* (c.1485) in the Galleria Uffizi in Florence

Detail of a fresco in the elegant Renaissance Villa Farnesina (1511) in Rome (right middle)

Galileo Galilei

Galileo, astronomer and mathematician, made huge contributions to our understanding of the solar system. Born in Pisa in 1564, he pioneered 'experimental scientific method' and was the first to use a refracting telescope to make important discoveries. He supported Copernicus's theory that the Earth and planets moved around the sun, rejecting Aristotle's Earthcentric model. Galileo's Inquisition opponents prevailed over his supporters, and he was told to suppress his opinions—which he did not. At the age of 69, he again faced the authorities, who made him kneel and deny the Copernician theory. He spent his last years in Florence under house arrest, and wrote his greatest work. His dying words supposedly were: 'But it does move'.

Italian Explorers and Foreign Financiers

Christoforo Colombo was born in 1451, and lived in Genova until his sea-faring career took him to Portugal and Spain, whose monarchs financed his discoveries. During his four voyages to the Caribbean (1492–1504) he unintentionally discovered the New World while searching for a sea route to Cathay (China). He died in 1506, convinced he had found the 'Indies'. The Florentine Amerigo Vespucci (1454–1512) was less naïve. He studied navigation, which allowed him to calculate the geographical location of Columbus's Indies more accurately, and on a Spanish expedition west in 1499 he observed that the land masses of North and South America were actually separate from Asia.

Niccolò Machiavelli

Machiavelli was born in Florence in 1469. A true patriot, he dreamed of a career in politics and began work as a diplomatic secretary for the Florentine republic, meeting important contemporary political figures. Once the Medici returned to power in 1512, he was out of a job, and turned to writing in the hope of attracting patronage. In 1513 he wrote *Principe* (*The Prince*), an intensely practical guide to the exercise of raw political power over a Renaissance principality. It cut no ice with the Medici, and the book's reputation continued to haunt him after they fell from power; he never again held public office. He died in 1527, his theories so twisted by public opinion that his name has become synonomous with political corruption.

Michelangelo and the Sistine Ceiling

In 1508 Pope Julius II commissioned Michelangelo to decorate the ceiling of the Sistine Chapel in the Vatican. It was a huge task; the incentive was the sum of 3,000 ducats. The surface area is over 500sq m (5,500sq ft), all of which is painted with stories from the Book of Genesis, prophets and sibylls, and enclosed within a *trompe l'oeil* architectural framework. Executed in all temperatures as the artist lay or crouched on a scaffold some 20m (65ft) above the floor, it was physically gruelling work that took him 4 years to complete. He hated the task, which took him away from his sculpture, writing, 'I am attending to work as much as I can...I don't have a penny...I am unhappy and not in too good health…'.

Galileo Galilei
(1564–1642)

Christoforo Colombo
(1451–1506)

Niccoló Machiavelli
(1469–1527)

1600

The Creation of Adam in the Sistine Chapel in the Vatican City (above right); a delicate Madonna by Filippo Lippi, in the Galleria Uffizi in Florence (opposite); an altarpiece by Giovanni Bellini (c.1430–1516) in San Zaccaria in Venice (below)

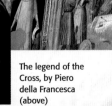

The legend of the Cross, by Piero della Francesca (above)

Foreign Domination

The Italian states didn't stay rich and independent for long. As early as 1494 the Duke of Milan made the fatal mistake of asking for French help, and the other European super-powers soon had considerably more than a foot in the door. Spain controlled Naples, Sardinia, Sicily, Milan and parts of Tuscany, the French were on the move in the north and only the Papal States and Venice remained independent. Great chunks of Italy were bartered between the French and Spanish as alliances changed. Spain hung on for nearly 200 years, only to be replaced by Austrian domination as a result of the War of the Spanish Succession. The Austrians were perhaps the most progressive occupiers, preparing the way in the north for early industrialization.

With Napoleon's arrival on the scene it was all change once more, and by 1810 he was in command of the whole peninsula, setting up family members and trusted supporters as his puppet rulers. Napoleon introduced political reforms, such as representative assemblies, which were to have far-reaching consequences for the emerging middle class. After Waterloo, the Vienna Settlement attempted to re-establish the old order, but protest against oppression and occupation grew increasingly in the first half of the 19th century.

Earthquake in Sicily

In January 1639, the southeast corner of Sicily was devastated by a series of earthquakes. The shocks continued for three days, accompanied by a blood-red moon, fissures in the land and catastrophic tidal waves. Over 60,000 people perished and churches, civic buildings and houses were destroyed. The quake's epicentre was the Val di Noto to the southeast of Catania and Siracusa, which were extensively damaged. In the years that followed, many towns in the area were rebuilt, almost entirely in the baroque style. Today, they are considered to be the final flowering of baroque art in Europe—an innovative new approach to town planning and urban building, Noto being the finest example.

1600

Raphael's *Marriage of the Virgin* and *The Virgin in Prayer* by Sassoferrato (1609–85, right); A baroque façade in Noto, rebuilt after the 1683 earthquake (below)

The Austrian Legacy

The Austrians were big players in northern Italy throughout the 18th century and into the 19th century, their grip only loosening in 1859 following the war engineered by Count Camillo Cavour and Napoleon III. They hung on longer in the far northern South Tirol region, which only became part of Italy in 1919, when Mussolini renamed it the Alto-Adige. It's still almost completely Austrian in character. German is the first language, the towns and villages are sprinkled with onion-domed churches and traversed by arcaded streets, and all the street signs are in German. The food, in particular, is heavily teutonic, with sauerkraut, knödel (dumplings) and strudel on the menu, and scarcely a whiff of pasta.

Napoleon and the Popes

The conqueror of Europe kept the Papacy well under control during his years of power. In 1798, French troops invaded Rome, demanding the abdication of the 82-year-old Pius VI; he refused, and was promptly deported to die in France. Five years later, Napoleon summoned Pius VII to Paris to officiate at his coronation. In 1809, Napoleon proclaimed the Papal States part of the French Empire and the Pope merely the Bishop of Rome. Pius excommunicated Napoleon, who retaliated by sending his troops to seize the pontiff and hustle him away to exile. He and his Cardinal of State left in such a hurry the Pope forgot his spectacles and the two venerable churchmen had less than 5 scudos (€2) between them.

Paolina Borghese

Napoleon's sister, Pauline, was married to Prince Borghese when she was 23, and became Princess Paolina. Beautiful, selfish and spoiled, she was famed in Roman society for her looks, lovers and style. Her wedding present to her husband was a near-nude statue of herself posing as Venus, sculpted by Canova. Rome buzzed with Paolina stories—her clothes and jewels, the huge black servant who carried her to her bath, and the use of ladies-in-waiting as footstools. Her lovers were numerous; artists, actors, musicians and handsome young army officers. Generally disliked, she had one redeeming feature, her love for her brother. She shared his exile on Elba and gave him her jewels to help fund the Waterloo campaign.

The Grand Tour

Backpackers of the 21st century exploring the sights and delights of Italy are not the first visitors to fall for Italian pleasures. In the 18th century it was fashionable for young English gentlemen to go on the Grand Tour of Europe, including an Italian jaunt to enrich the mind. In practice it was a glorious excuse for profligate living, late nights and debauchery. The days were spent sightseeing with the tutors, while the nights were given over to drinking, gambling and whoring. Shopping was a serious pursuit, and many of the statues, prints and paintings found in large country houses were brought home from the Tour. Artists were kept busy churning out portraits of the young gentry. With Joshua Reynolds charging over £150 in London, Roman portraits were a snip at £25.

Count Camillo Cavour (1810–61), Napoleon Bonaparte (1808–73), Pope Pius VII (in office 1800–1823) and Byron (1788–1824) (left to right)

1860

The Duomo in Milan (left); a regatta in Venice from Giacomo Franco's *Habiti d'Houmeni et Donne Venetiane* (right)

The reclining Paolina Borghese (Canova, 1804) in the Galleria Borghese

From Unification to World War II

Between 1848 and 1860 the movement to oust the occupiers and reform and unite the country grew. It was known as the Risorgimento, the new arising, and its key players were Giuseppe Mazzini, Giuseppe Garibaldi and Count Emilio Cavour. As ever in Italy, the story is complicated, but by 1860 Piemonte, Tuscany and Emilia were united. Garibaldi took Sicily and Naples, while a referendum secured Umbria and the Papal States. In 1861, the Kingdom of Italy was proclaimed, albeit without Rome and Venice. It took until 1871 for Unification to be complete.

The 1880s saw the start of the new nation's colonial expansion into North Africa, which brought Abyssinia (present-day Ethiopia), Eritrea and Libya under Italian control. World War I was seen as a chance to get even with Austria for past wrongs, gaining Trieste and Trentino Alto-Adige at vast cost. Disillusioned with this, the middle classes turned to the Fascists and their leader, Benito Mussolini. He became dictator in 1925, ruling by the adage 'Everything within the State, nothing outside the State, nothing against the State'. Allied with Nazi Germany, Italy entered World War II in 1940. As the Nazis' dominance began to falter in Europe, Italy signed an armistice with the Allies in 1943 and Mussolini was finally captured from the Germans and executed in 1945.

Garibaldi and the Thousand

A guerrilla fighter and a man of the people, with a gift for motivating and enthusing the masses, Giuseppe Garibaldi (1807–82) was a key instigator in the Unification of Italy. He arrived in Sicily in 1860 with 1,000 soldiers, brightly clad in red shirts, and proclaimed himself dictator in the name of Vottorio Emanuele II. He defeated the Neapolitans and, helped by a popular uprising, captured Palermo. Crossing to the mainland. He then took Naples, handing both Sicily and Naples over to Vittorio Emanuele.

Giuseppe Garibaldi (above)

1860

Posters showing the Allies' flight towards the heel of Italy, and Hitler and Mussolini working together to erect a monument dedicated to peace, civilization and work (1938)

Austrian Italy

Before Unification, a big chunk of northeastern Italy, much of it German-speaking, belonged to the Austrian Empire. Some areas, such as the Veneto and Friuli were soon acquired by Italy, but the South Tirol in particular, proud of its Austrian links and traditions, continued to look firmly towards Vienna, and was loath to change. Politicians in Rome, determined on a fully united Italy, felt differently, and put the reacquisition of the Austrian areas of the country at the top of its list of World War I objectives. At the cost of a huge war debt, 650,000 dead, and a million casualties, the politicians got their way in 1919 when the frontier was moved north to the Brenner Pass, and the South Tirol and Trentino became part of Italy.

The Prisoner of the Vatican

Right up to Italian Unification, the Papal States sprawled across central Italy, successive popes hanging on to their temporal power. As elsewhere, the natives were restless and the Pope needed outside help to retain control. Garibaldi invaded twice during the Risorgimento, but the Pope, Pius IX, somehow hung on to Rome itself. Finally, in 1870, King Vittorio Emanuele seized the city and Rome became the capital of a united Italy. Furious, Pius refused to accept the loss of his holdings and retreated into the Vatican, declaring himself a prisoner. Later popes followed his example, never setting foot outside from election until death. The question was only settled by Mussolini's Lateran Treaty of 1929, which established Vatican City as the world's smallest independent state.

Vittorio Emanuele III, King of Italy in 1901 (left)
Summer holidays at the Hotel Excelsior in Venice in 1931 (below)

Resistance

Southern Tuscany was one of Italy's strongest partisan regions during World War II, with anti-Fascist and anti-Nazi feeling running high. In 1943, as the Allies moved north from Monte Cassino, Resistance groups in the Val d'Orcia harried the Nazis incessantly, destroying whatever they could. The penalty was death, as it was for sheltering or feeding Allied soldiers on the run. In Florence, the Resistance was protected by the anti-Nazi German consul, but many farmers and peasants risked their lives and were imprisoned, transported or executed. Memorials can be found in many of the region's hill-top towns.

Monte Cassino monastery

Mussolini's End

By April 1945, the Allies were uncomfortably close to Mussolini's puppet Republic of Salò on Lake Garda, and the ex-Duce, together with his mistress, Claretta Petacci, tried to flee to Switzerland. They were caught at Lake Como by partisans and shot on 28 April. The next day the bodies were taken to the Piazzale Loreto in Milan and strung by their feet from the girders of a gas station, to be kicked, shot at and spat upon by a furious crowd. After a year's interment in Milan's municipal cemetery, Mussolini's body was stolen by surviving Fascists. It was finally returned to his widow in 1957 and buried at his birthplace, Predappio in Emilia, which became a magnet for Fascists.

1945

A giant figure towering above the Fiat Factory in Turin, lending a hand with construction (1917, below)

A photograph of Hitler and Mussolini with Goering (left) and Count Ciano (right), the Italian Foreign Minister, at the Four Power Conference in Munich on 30 September 1938 (left)

Post-World War II

The years since 1945 have seen successive governments come and go, political scandal on a large scale, corruption in high places and terrorism. Despite this, Italy has boomed economically, establishing itself as a front-rank industrialized nation and a key player in influencing style across Europe, but the gulf between north and south remains.

Politics and the Mafia

In the early 2000s evidence emerged linking top politicians with the Mafia during the 1990s, in particular Prime Minister Silvio Berlusconi and Giulio Andreotti, the symbol of postwar Christian Democratic power. The most important super-grass was Antonino Giuffre, whose collaboration with the Palermo magistrates in early 2003 helped fill in the political background to the murders in Sicily in 1992 of the anti-Mafia magistrates Giovanni Falcone and Paolo Borsellino and the Uffizi bombing in Florence the following year. Giuffre gave evidence that these outrages occurred at a time when the Mafia was withdrawing its support from the Christian Democrats, infiltrating the emergent Forza Italia and negotiating with Berlusconi and his representatives. Forza Italia, he said, had given guarantees that the Mafia's legal problems would be resolved within 10 years.

The Sicily Bridge

After years of discussion, construction is due to start in 2005 on a suspension bridge that will cross the Straits of Messina between Sicily and mainland Italy. The project should be completed in 2011, at a cost of €4.4 billion. It will carry two railway lines and a 12-lane expressway and is designed to resist earthquakes of up to 7.1 on the Richter scale and wind speeds of 200kph (125mph). But officials are concerned that it will also bridge the gap between the Mafia and the Calabrian gangsters.

The Uffizi Bombing

At 1am on 27 May 1993, 100kg (220 pounds) of TNT, hidden in a car, exploded on the west side of the Uffizi Gallery in Florence, killing five people, demolishing one building, causing structural damage to the gallery and destroying paintings. Blame was initially laid on the Mafia, but some Florentines were convinced that responsibility lay with Italy's political and military establishment. Threatened by new parties and the emerging forces of separatism, the establishment was perceived to be employing tactics of destabilization to ensure the public's loyalty to the threatened state. Opinion is still divided and no one has been charged for the crime.

1945 to the present

Silvio Berlusconi (top), sophisticated women in Rome (above), big names in Italian fashion design (above) and a swarm of scooters in Rome (right)

On the Move

ARRIVING

By Air

A large percentage of visitors to Italy arrive by air, the numbers increasing steadily with the growing popularity of short breaks and the choice of budget airlines.

If you're arriving from another continent you will almost certainly fly into either Roma Leonardo da Vinci Fiumicino, the main airport for the capital, or Milano Malpensa, serving Italy's economic capital and the Lakes. These are both large, busy, state-of-the-art airports with an aura of style that's discernibly Italian, and an excellent range of facilities. Rome and Milan each have another airport: Roma Ciampino and Milano Linate.

Italy's third busiest airport is Venice, not only the internal gateway to the buzzing Veneto, but a good arrival point for northeastern Italy and beyond. Most visitors heading for Florence will find themselves landing at Pisa, an hour or so from the city, but Florence does have its own small airport, mainly served by internal flights and popular with people visiting the country on business. Naples is the south's busiest international airport, though by no means as frenetic as its northern counterparts.

Rome Leonardo Da Vinci Fiumicino (FCO), usually called Fiumicino, is 32km (20 miles) west of central Rome. The airport has three terminals: A for domestic flights, B for domestic and international, and C, with a satellite connected to the terminal by monorail, for international flights only. All three terminals are big, so allow plenty of time for connections; follow the signs *corrispondenza/flight connections*. Fiumicino has airport information desks, a tourist information office, a hotel reservation desk, car rental desks, shops, banks, restaurants, a lost-luggage office and left-luggage facilities. There are interactive touch-screen information points in both the arrival and departure areas.

Rome Ciampino (CIA) is 15km (9 miles) southeast of Rome on the Via Appia Nuova, a short distance from the city ring road (GRA), which feeds into the north/south and east/west motorway (expressway) system. There are three passenger terminals—arrivals, departures (used for both)—all of which have information desks, bars and shops. Other services include car rental desks, banks and left luggage facilities.

GETTING INTO CITIES FROM THE AIRPORT		
AIRPORT (CODE)	**ROME FIUMICINO (FCO)**	**ROME CIAMPINO (CIA)**
DISTANCE TO CITY	32km (20 miles)	15km (9 miles)
TAXI	Price: €45 Time: 30–45 min	Price: €45 Time: 30–45 min
TRAINS/ BOATS	Fiumicino to Termini Frequency: First train 7.37am, then hourly from 8am–10pm Price: €8.80 Journey time: 30 min Fiumicino to Trastevere, Tiburtina, Ostiense, then metro to Termini Frequency: Every 20 min from 6.27am–11.27am Price: €5 Journey time: 30–45 min	Bus to Ciampino town station, from where trains run to Termini Frequency: Every 15 min 6.30am–11pm Price: €2.40 Journey time: 20 min Anagnina Metro (Line A) to Termini Frequency: Buses run from the airport to Anagnina every 60 min Price: €1.10 Journey time: 20 min
BUS	CO.TRAL buses from Fiumicino to Tiburtina Frequency: Every 90 min during the night Price: €3.60 Journey time: 45 min	There is a free shuttle bus available for disabled and elderly people. Reserve in advance, tel 06 6991 0000 There is no direct route into central Rome from Ciampino. The choice is either a combination of bus and metro or bus and train
CAR	Take Fiumicino–Rome motorway and travel eastwards	Take the Via Appia Nuova northwest into the centre

Pisa Galileo Galilei (PSA) is Florence's main entry point for most overseas visitors, 91km (57 miles) west of Florence. It has good road and train connections to Tuscany's capital and handles internal and European flights. The one spacious terminal has information desks, a train ticket office and adjoining railway station, banks, bureau de change, left-luggage facilities and car rental desks. There is a bar and restaurant, but only a limited number of shops.

Milan Malpensa (MXP), Italy's main international gateway in the north, has two terminals and is 50km (31 miles) northwest of the city. Terminal 1 handles domestic, international and intercontinental flights and is the larger and busier of the two terminals; Terminal 2 is mainly for short to medium-haul flights and charters. Both terminals have airport information, tourist information, hotel reservation and car rental desks, bars, restaurants, shops, banks and left-luggage.

Milan Linate (LIN), 7km (4 miles) from the city centre, handles Italian domestic and European flights from its one terminal, and classes itself as a city airport. It has a full range of airport services, including tourist information and car rental .

Firenze Amerigo Vespucci (FLR) city airport is 4km (2.5 miles) northwest of the city centre. It handles mainly internal flights, with a limited number of daily departures to other European cities. The one small

GETTING INTO CITIES FROM THE AIRPORT			
PISA (FLORENCE) (PSA)	**MILAN MALPENSA (MXP)**	**NAPLES (NAP)**	**VENICE MARCO POLO (VCE)**
91km (57 miles) to Florence; 2km (1 mile) to Pisa	50km (31 miles)	8km (5 miles)	By water 7km (4 miles); overland 12km (7.5 miles)
Price: €120–150 to Florence; €6–8 to Pisa Time: 60–80 min to Florence; 10–20 min to Pisa	Price: €60–75 Time: 35–60 min	Price: €15–20 Time: 20–30 min	**Land taxi price:** €15–18 Time: 15–25 min **Water taxi price:** €70–90 Time: 20–35 min
Pisa Aeroporto–Firenze Santa Maria Novella Frequency: Every 60 min to Florence, stopping at Pisa Centrale Price: €4.85 Journey time: 75 min For Siena change at Empoli	Malpensa to Milano Nord Frequency: Every 30 min between 6.30am and1.30am Price: €8 (discounted tickets for Alitalia passengers) Journey time: 40 min	N/A	**Boat Alilaguna service** Airport to city centre via Murano and the Lido Frequency: Every 60 min Price: €10 Journey time: 30 min to Murano, 55 min to the Lido, 1 hour 10 min to city centre
CPT No.3 from Pisa airport to Pisa city centre Frequency: Every 15 min Price: 50c Journey time: 10–15 min	Malpensa to Stazione Centrale Frequency: Every 20 min 5.20am–10.30pm Price: €7 Journey time: 45–60 min	Airport CLP bus from outside airport to Piazza Garibaldi and Piazza Municipio; No. 14 or No. 15 from outside airport to Piazza Garibaldi Frequency: CLP every 30 min; No. 14 and No. 15 every 15 min Price: CLP €1.55; No. 14 and No. 15 77c Journey time: 20–30 min	Airport bus (ATVO) to Piazzale Roma, ACTV bus No. 5 to Piazzale Roma Frequency: Airport bus (ATVO) every 20 min, ACTV bus No . 5 every 30 min Price: ATVO €2.70, ACTV 77c Journey time: ATVO 20 min, ACTV 20 min
From the airport follow the motorway Pisa–Firenze east to Florence	Take the link motorway southeast to the A8 (E62) and follow signs to the city centre	Driving into Naples is not recommended	N/A

terminal has tourist information and car rental desks, banking services, a cafébar and left-luggage facilities. Shopping is very limited.

Naples Capodichino (NAP) lies 8km (5 miles) northeast of the city centre. This rapidly expanding airport handles domestic and international European scheduled flights and charter flights to a large number of destinations. The airport has a

Inside the light and spacious terminal building at Venice Marco Polo Airport

MAJOR AIRPORTS AND PORTS

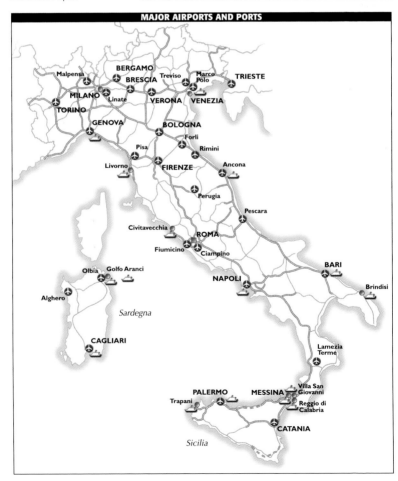

Malpensa
BERGAMO
BRESCIA
Treviso
Marco Polo
TRIESTE
MILANO
Linate
VERONA
VENEZIA
TORINO
GENOVA
BOLOGNA
Forlì
Pisa
Rimini
Livorno
FIRENZE
Ancona
Perugia
Pescara
Civitavecchia
ROMA
Fiumicino
Ciampino
BARI
Olbia
Golfo Aranci
Brindisi
Alghero
NAPOLI
Sardegna
CAGLIARI
Lamezia Terme
Villa San Giovanni
PALERMO
MESSINA
Trapani
Reggio di Calabria
CATANIA
Sicilia

good range of services, including tourist information, post office, banking services, ATMs, left-luggage facilities, hotel booking desk, car rental desks, bars, restaurants and shops.

Venice Marco Polo (VCE) is on the northern edge of the Venetian lagoon, 7km (4 miles) from the city by water and 12km (7.5 miles) by road. Serving the prosperous northeast of Italy, this is a busy airport popular with business commuters as well as visitors from abroad. Its well-designed terminal is on three levels (ground floor for arrivals, first floor for check-in and departures, second floor for VIP lounges) handling mainly domestic and European flights and one daily flight to the USA. There is a full range of services, including airport information, hotel reservation and car rental desks, banks, bars, restaurants, left-luggage facilities and an excellent airside shopping complex. Frequent and efficient water taxi and ferry services run from the airport to the heart of Venice.

Some charter and budget airlines use Treviso San Angelo (TSF), a small, but convenient airport 30km (18.5 miles) north of the city.

Book your rental car before you leave home, by phone or on-line. These are major international rental groups.

Alamo
tel 0870 400 4562 (UK)
tel 1 800 462 5266 (US)
www.alamo.com

Budget
tel 01442 276266 (UK)
tel 1 800 527 0700 (US)
www.budget.com

Avis
tel 0870 606 0100 (UK)
tel 1 800 230 4898 (US)
www.avis.com

Hertz
tel 0800 317540 (UK)
tel 1 800 654 3131 (US)
www.hertz.com

National
tel 1 800 CAR RENT
www.nationalcar.com

CAR RENTAL
The major chains are all represented and have offices at airports, train stations and downtown in the major cities. You will get a better deal if you shop around before you leave home and book from your own country. Smaller, local companies will often have airport pickup points, but you may be unable to book them in advance from home. If you book with a specialist tour operator, it will be able to arrange car rental in advance.

Before you leave, check your insurance and see if you will need any additional cover. You will need your credit card as a deposit when you pick up the car, and it's rare to pay additional charges for car rental with anything other than a credit card.

Drivers of rental cars must be over 21/25 (depending on the individual hire company) and should have a valid driver's licence. If there is to be more than one driver, you must specify this when you collect the car. Any additional drivers may also have to sign the rental agreement. If you intend to go off public roads, check that the insurance covers this. You will be offered the choice of returning the car filled with fuel; it is cheaper to fill it up yourself just before you return it. Before driving off, be sure to thoroughly check both inside and outside the vehicle for any damage. If you find any, report it at once and get a company representative to make a note.

ON THE MOVE

AIRPORTS
General www.worldairportguide.com
Florence tel 055 306 1300 www.adr.it
Naples tel 081 789 6111 www.gesac.it
Milan Malpensa tel 02 748 5220
www.sea-aeroportimilano.it
Milan Linate tel 02 748 5220
www.sea-aeroportimilano.it
Pisa tel 050 849300
www.pisa-airport.com
Rome Ciampino tel 06 794941
www.adr.it
Rome Fiumicino tel 06 65951
www.adr.it
Treviso tel 0422 315111
www.veniceairport.it
Venice tel 041 260 9260
www.veniceairport.it

AIRLINES
UK
Alitalia tel 0870 544 8259
www.alitalia.co.uk
British Airways tel 0870 850 9850,
(UK); 199 712266 (ITA) www.ba.com
BMI Baby tel 0870 264 2229
www.bmibaby.com
Easyjet tel 0871 750 0100
www.easyjet.com
Flybe tel 0870 567 6676
www.flybe.com
Meridiana tel 020 7839 2222
www.meridiana.it
MyTravelLite tel 0870 1564564
www.mytravellite.com
Ryanair tel 0870 156 9569
www.ryanair.com

Volare Airlines tel 0870 000 2468
www.volare-airlines.com

US
Alitalia tel 800 223 5730
www.alitaliausa.com
American Airlines tel 800 433 7300
www.aa.com
Continental tel 800 231 0856
www.continental.com
Delta tel 800 241 4141 www.delta-air.com
Northwest Airlines tel 800 225 2525
www.nwa.com
United tel 800 5382929
www.ual.com
US Airways tel 800 4284322
www.usairways.com

ON THE MOVE

By Ferry

If you are planning a trip to Sicily or Sardinia, or onwards to Greece, you may want to travel by ferry. With the exception of the short hop across the Straits of Messina to Sicily, it's best to book a crossing in advance. You need to arrive at the departure port anything between 2 and 6 hours before sailing; individual companies will provide details when you book. The major ferry ports are clearly marked by road signs with a ship symbol, the name of the destination port and the word *traghetti* (ferries). Overnight ferries have cabins available; these, too, should be reserved in advance. Comfort and facilities vary between different operators' ships, ranging from adequate to excellent, and safety standards are up to international requirements.

For faster links to the main islands there's also the hydrofoil, though these services tend to be greatly reduced or even suspended outside the peak summer season. Prices vary considerably according to factors such as number of passengers, size of car and time of year, but

A ferry at Civitavecchio in Rome

booking well in advance may get you a good deal. The best way to research Italian ferries is through www.traghettionline.net/eng, a portal site linking virtually all the major ferry and hydrofoil operators, with an online booking facility. For ferries to Greece, use www.ferries.gr.

By Rail

From Britain you can travel by train to Italy, routing, via the Channel Tunnel, through either Brussels or Paris. The journey

time via Brussels is longer, but if you choose the Paris option, you have to change from the Gare du Nord to the Gare de Lyon. Direct trains run to **Rome, Florence, Milan, Turin** and **Venice.**

The choice of routes and fares is highly complex, but it's best to use the **Eurostar** as far as **Paris** or **Brussels** from where trains south are fast and frequent. The old train and ferry route is now little used, and consequently badly timetabled.

Eurostar trains depart from Waterloo Station and link London with Paris and Brussels in under 3 hours. You must check in 30

FERRY INFORMATION AND TICKETS

SICILY

Operator N.G.I., tel 090 679039, www.cormorano.net/ngi
Departure port Reggio di Calabria
Arrival port Messina
Frequency Every 20–40 min
Duration of crossing 40 min

Operator Caronte, tel 090 371851, fax 090 51422, www.traghettionline.net/eng
Departure port Villa San Giovanni (Caronte)
Arrival port Messina
Frequency Every 20–40 min
Duration of crossing 25 min

Operator Tirrenia/Snav, tel 010 582080, www.traghettionline.net/eng
Departure port Naples
Arrival port Palermo

Frequency 1 daily
Duration of crossing 11 hours

Operator Grandi Navi Veloci, tel 010 582080, www.traghettionline.net/eng
Departure port Genoa
Arrival port Palermo
Frequency 1 daily
Duration of crossing 20 hours

SARDINIA

Operator Tirrenia, tel 010 582080, www.traghettionline.net/eng
Departure ports Civitavecchia, Genoa, Livorno
Arrival ports Cagliari, Olbia, Golfo Aranci
Frequency From Civitavecchia 1 daily to Cagliari, 1–2 daily to Olbia; from Genoa Jul–Sep 2 weekly to Cagliari, 3–7 weekly to Olbia; from Naples 1–2 weekly; from Palermo 1 weekly

Duration of crossing Civitavecchia to Cagliari 15–17 hours, Civitavecchia to Olbia 9 hours; Genoa to Cagliari 21 hours, Genoa to Olbia 14 hours; Naples to Cagliari 17 hours; Palermo to Cagliari 14 hours

GREECE

Operators Superfast, Minoan, Blue Star (www.superfast.com, www.bluestarferries.com, www.minoan.com,)
Departure ports Ancona, Bari, Venice (Blue Star)
Arrival port Patras, Igoumenitsa, Corfu (Blue Star)
Frequency Ancona 3 daily; Bari 1 daily; Venice 2 daily
Duration of crossing Ancona 19 hours; Bari 16 hours 30 min; Venice 22 hours

TRAIN INFORMATION AND TICKETS

RAIL

Eurostar tel 0870 518 6186, www.eurostar.com

Rail Europe tel 0870 584 8848, www.raileurope.co.uk

Eurostar EPS House, Waterloo Station, London SE1 8SE, tel 0870 518186 www.eurostar.com

Italian State Railways (Trenitalia) tel 020 7724 0011, www.trenitalia.com

Rail Europe 179 Piccadilly, London W1V 0BA; International Rail Centre,

Victoria Station, London W1V 1JY tel 0870 584 8848, www.raileurope.co.uk

Venice-Simplon-Orient-Express Ltd Sea Containers House, 20, Upper Ground, London SE1 9PF, tel 020 7805 5100, www.orient-express.com

MOTORAIL

Railsavers @4 All Hallows Rd, Bispham, Lancashire FY2 0AS, tel 0870 750 7070, www.railsavers.com

French Motorail tel 08702 415415

minutes before departure and you are allowed two suitcases and one item of hand baggage. Label all bags clearly with your name, address and seat number. You need your passport to clear immigration and customs.

• The total journey time from Waterloo to Italian destinations varies from 11 to 15 hours.

• Return ticket prices range from around €250–€300.

Both Eurostar and other fast European trains have facilities which include:

• 1st- and 2nd-class seating.
• Bar/restaurant cars.
• Trolley service on day trains.
• Baby-changing facilities on day trains.
• Air-conditioning.
• Telephone kiosks.
• Lavatories in each carriage including some that are accessible to wheelchairs.

Sleepers are available from Paris on direct routes to Rome, Milan, Florence and Venice. Accommodation varies from 3-, 4- and 6-berth couchettes to single and double sleepers with integral shower and lavatory.

The Orient Express, the ultimate luxury train ride to Italy, runs from London to Venice. The journey time is 31 hours, and a one-way ticket costs around €1,770.

Motorail has a weekly (Friday) direct service between April and September from Denderleeuw (25km/16 miles from Brussels) to Bologna (€900

including car, 4-bed couchette, ferry/Eurotunnel crossings from the UK and breakfast).

RAIL PASSES

See also p. 57.

• **Interail Passes** are valid for 1 month's unlimited train travel within a specific zone; Italy is in Zone G together with Turkey, Greece and Slovenia. You have to be a European citizen or have lived in Europe for 6 months to be eligible. The full fare is around €315 for adults and €275 for those under 26. The ticket gives discounts on the cross-Channel services, including Eurostar, and is valid on the Brindisi–Patras–Corfu ferry.

• **Eurailpasses** are available for North American visitors. They allow several days consecutive travel, or a certain number of days in a fixed time period in up to 17 countries. There are many combinations to choose from; see www.raileurope.com.

• **Trenitalia Passes,** valid from 4 to 10 days, allow unlimited rail travel during a 2-month period (adult €360, child €180). There is also a Saver Pass available for groups of 2–5 people travelling together (10 days–adult €300, child €150).

• **Rail Europe Senior Cards** are available if you hold a senior citizen railcard. They cost €7 and give 30 per cent discount on rail fares through Europe, including Italy.

Before you invest in a pass, bear in mind that train travel in

Italy is cheap—a return ticket from Venice to Florence costs around €40—so if you're only planning to go on one or two train journeys during your stay, it might work out cheaper to buy individual tickets.

By Bus

International buses to Italy from the UK are run by National Express Eurolines (tel 0875 808080, www.eurolines.co.uk). Services run between 3 and 5 times a week depending on the time of year and the destination in Italy; you may have to change.

Destinations: Bologna, Florence, Genoa, Milan, Naples, Parma, Rome, Siena, Turin, Venice, Verona.

Journey time: Milan 22 hours, Florence 28 hours, Rome 32 hours, Naples 36 hours.

Tickets: Eurolines issues 30- and 60-day travel passes valid for 48 European cities (€360 for 30 days, €400 for 60).

By Car

Driving to Italy, you will need the following documents: valid driver's licence, original vehicle registration document, motor insurance certificate (at least third-party insurance is compulsory) and passport.

From the UK, you can cross the Channel either by ferry or through the Channel Tunnel. The main routes south from the Channel to Italy run through France, Switzerland and Germany. All cross the Alps; the main passes are the St. Gotthard, the Great St. Bernard, Frejus and the Mont Blanc tunnel. The St. Gotthard tunnel is free, the others range from €15–€25. To reach these from Calais take the E15 and E17 to Reims, then pick up the motorways towards the different passes.

There are toll roads (turnpikes) all along the route (p. 52). You should allow between 11 and 14 hours driving time to reach the north Italian border.

GETTING AROUND

Getting Around in Rome

ATAC run Rome's public transport system, which includes the bus, tram and metro network, all frequent, cheap and reliable. You can navigate the city easily by using just a few lines.

INFORMATION

● The ATAC office is at Piazza dei Cinquecento (tel 800 431784, daily 7.30–7). Transport details, ticket information and free transport maps are available.
● On-line at www.atac.roma.it

TICKETS

Buy tickets before boarding at *tabacchi*, shops and bars displaying the ATAC logo. Main stops and some metro stations have automatic ticket machines. Shops and metro stations often run out of tickets so try to buy enough for your entire stay when you first arrive.
● *Biglietto integrato a tempo* (BIT) 77c—valid for 75 minutes for unlimited bus and tram travel plus one metro trip.
● *Biglietto integrato giorlaliera* (BIG) €3.10—valid up to midnight on the day of use for unlimited travel on buses, trams, metro, CO>TRAL and FS trains.
● *Carta integrata settimanale* (CIS) €12.40—valid for a week.
● **Validate** your ticket the first time it's used. The machines are inside buses and trams and just before escalators on the metro. BIT tickets must be validated again if you are using the BIT on the metro. The fine for not validating your ticket is €51 and is strictly enforced—no excuses.

BUSES

Standard single-decker buses cover most routes, with the narrow streets of the historic centre served by small electric minibuses (routes 116, 117, 119). There are few seats and buses can be very crowded. Be wary of pickpockets.
● **Bus stops** (*fermata*) show the route number, the *capitolinea* (headstop where the service originates) and list the intermediate stops for buses using the stop. The stop where you are is circled.
● Board through the rear doors (*salita*) and **validate** your ticket. Exit through the middle doors (*uscita*).

Night Buses

Services start at midnight and drop off at stops marked with a blue owl logo. Tickets are available on board.

METRO (LA METROPOLITANA)

There are **two lines**, A and B, which intersect at Termini, the main railway station.
● **Trains** run between 5.30am and 11.30pm.
● **Entrances** are marked with a large white M on a red background.
● **Ticket machines** are below street level; validate your ticket before you use the escalators.
● **Information boards** are at the bottom of the escalator. They indicate the direction of travel and identify your platform.
● The metro is always very crowded. Use the **route maps** (though these are sometimes inaccurate) displayed in the carriages to find out which side the doors will open at your stop, and start working your way towards the door well before the train stops. Otherwise, you may find that you are unable to leave the train.

TRAMS

Trams are good for getting to the outskirts. The following routes are great for sightseeing:
3—Villa Borghese, Villa Giulia, modern art museum, zoo and Trastevere
8—Trastevere
19—Piazza del Risorgimento for San Pietro. Also serves Villa Borghese, Villa Giulia, the modern art museum and the zoo.

DISCOUNTS

● Children under 10 travel free.
● No concessions for senior citizens (unless resident).
● Reductions for students holding ISIC cards.

SIGHTSEEING TOURS OF ROME		TIPS–BUSES

ATAC 110 City Tour Every 30 min. Hop on and off (stop 'n' go) ticket €12.91, complete circuit €7.75.
ATAC Archeobus From Piazza Venezia hourly. Circuit of archaeological sights including the Via Appia Antica and the catacombs, 2 hours, €7.75.
Appian Line Piazza Esquilino 6/7,

tel 06 4878 6604, fax 06 481 9712.
Green Line Tours Via del Viminale, tel 06 462 0651/06 482 8647/ 06 4877 2253, fax: 06 4782 3335 www.greenlinetours.com.
Stop 'n' Go CSR, Via Barberini 86, 00187 Roma, tel 06 4782 6379, fax 06 4890 5780, www.romecitytours.com €12.

● Outward and return journeys may follow different routes.
● If the bus is very busy, pass your ticket through the crowd and someone will stamp it.
● Be aware of pickpockets, who tend to be children or teenagers.

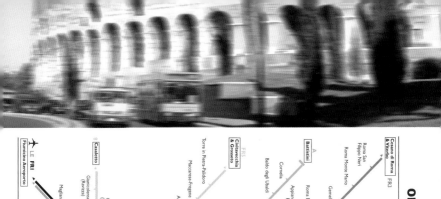

ROME METRO AND TRAMS

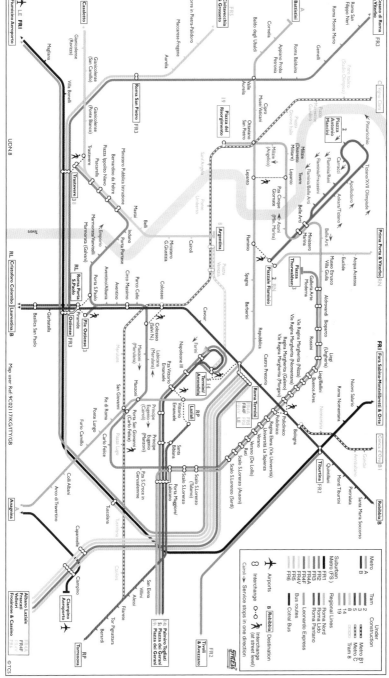

Getting Around in Other Major Cities

The metro, buses and trams are easy to use, but knowing some key words makes things easier (p. 417–420). Information is provided on all services, and safety standards are high.

MILAN

www.atm-mi.it

Milan has an efficient integrated transport system comprising trams, buses and a metro. The metro is the easiest and fastest option, though you may have to combine it with a bus or tram.

Metro: 4 lines: red MM1, green MM2, yellow MM3 and blue *passante ferroviario*. These intersect at the hub stations of Stazione Centrale, Duomo, Cadorna and Loreto.

Buses and trams: Routes cover the whole city and the follow the metro routes overground.

Tickets: A single (€1) is valid for 75 min from validation and can be used on the entire system for as many bus and tram trips as you want and one metro journey. A book of 10 tickets costs €9.20, and 1- and 2-day travel cards (€3 and €5.50) are also available. Tickets are sold at *tabacchi*, bars, newsstands and metro stations. The network runs 6am–12.30am, with night buses continuing until 1.30am.

FLORENCE

www.ATAF.net

Florence is largely pedestrianized and the historic heart can be crossed on foot in 30 min, so you're unlikely to have to use the bus system. It is useful if you're

A Eurotram on line 14 in Milan

staying on the outskirts.

Buses: Most lines either originate at or pass the railway station, a 15–20 min walk from the Piazza della Signoria. They run 6am–midnight.

Tickets: 77c for 1hour, €1.30 for 3 hours, €3.10 for 24 hours. Tickets are sold at *tabacchi*, bars and newsstands displaying ATAF signs.

VENICE

www.actv.it

Walking and taking the *vaporetti* (water buses) are the quickest ways to get around.

Water buses: There are two types of boats, *vaporetti* (bigger and slower) and *motoscafi* (smaller and faster). All are numbered on the side and follow set routes. They leave from *pontile*, floating piers, marked with the stop name, service numbers and a route map. The same numbers sometimes go in two directions, so check you are heading the right way before you board; busy routes have separate boarding points for each direction.

Tickets: Sold at many *pontile* or at shops (single €1.80) showing the ACTV sticker. You can save money by buying a 24-hour (€10.50) or 72-hour (€22) ticket. Validate your ticket at the yellow machine on the *pontile* before boarding. There is a limited night service on most routes. ACTV produces a booklet, available at ticket booths (*orario*) containing routes,

services, and timetables.

Traghetti: These are gondola ferries that cross and recross the Canal Grande at seven points. The Canal only has three bridges, so they can save time and your feet. Follow the yellow street signs to the boarding points and watch your balance, as it is customary to stand up.

Tickets: Pay the gondolier (50c) on boarding.

NAPLES

www.campaniatrasporti.it

Naples is a big, congested city where the best option is to walk. You'll have to use the public transport system to reach outlying areas and the Bay of Naples, though. There are several integrated options run by ANM— buses, the Metropolitana, funiculars within the city and three suburban rail systems.

Buses: The best option for short journeys, though they can be very slow.

The Metropolitana: Expanding to cover more of the city.

Funiculars: These run up the hill of the Vomero.

Out-of-town trains: The Circumvesuviana runs around the bay to Sorrento; the Ferrovia Cumana runs west to Pozzuoli and Baia; the Circumflegrea goes to Cuma.

Tickets: Single tickets (77c) are valid for 90 min and allow any combination of bus and tram rides plus unlimited travel on two additional forms of transport. Tickets are sold at *tabacchi*, stations and the ANM booth on Piazza Garibaldi, which has timetables and route maps. A 24-hour pass is available (€2.32).

Driving

Italy's road system is comprehensive, with motorways (expressways) covering the entire peninsula from north to south and trans-Apennine links at regular intervals. In addition, all regions have dual-carriageway (divided highway) and main-road alternatives and rural villages are connected by minor roads. Civil engineering is excellent, with bridges soaring over ravines and well-lit tunnels going through mountains. Given the country's north/south economic divide, the road network is at its best in the north, but even in the south, driving is easy and a pleasure. However, driving in the cities, particularly in Rome, should be avoided.

Driving is an ideal form of transport if you are concentrating on smaller towns and cities and rural areas. Although it's not for the faint-hearted, you can enjoy panoramic views from the road, famously along the Amalfi coast (p. 318–319 and through the Dolomites (p. 290–293).

Italian driving belies its fearsome reputation; once you grasp their rationale, you'll find Italian drivers less erratic and on the whole safer than many other nationalities.

The best bet is to steer clear of cities. One-way systems, narrow streets, lack of parking, traffic congestion and occasional aggression make city driving stressful. Be prepared for traffic jams in August when all of Italy is on holiday and everyone heads for the roads and motorways, particularly on weekends.

BRINGING YOUR OWN CAR

Before you leave:

● Have headlights adjusted for driving on the right.
● Contact your motor insurer or broker at least 1 month before taking your car to Italy.
● Have your car serviced.
● Check the tyres.
● If you don't have a rear-view mirror on the left side, fit one before you go.
● Ensure you have adequate breakdown assistance cover (AA Five Star 0800 444500 , www.theAA.com).

You will need:

● A valid driving licence.
● The original vehicle registration document.
● A motor insurance certificate; at least third-party insurance is compulsory.
● A first aid kit, fire extinguisher and spare bulbs.
● It is compulsory to carry a warning triangle and display a nationality sticker (unless you have Euro-plates).
● If you're driving in winter you may need winter tyres or snow chains.

A vigile urbano (traffic policeman) in Piazza Venezia, Rome

DOCUMENTS

Carry documents with you whenever you are driving; if you are stopped by the *polizia stradale* or *carabinieri* they will want to see them. Both UK and US driver's licences are valid in Italy, but you should also carry a translation. In the UK, the new licences with photographs and the pink, EU-style ones include a translation, but if you hold an older, green licence, you can either update the licence or apply for an International Driving Permit. Holders of US driver's licences should also apply for an International Driving Permit. These permits are not compulsory, but can smooth out problems and act as another form of identification. Permits can be obtained from the Italian State Tourist Offices or through national motoring organizations such as the AA and AAA.

HOW TO NAVIGATE A ROUNDABOUT

This sign indicates that there is a roundabout (traffic circle) ahead. You must give way to traffic approaching from the left. If road markings allow you to approach without giving way, proceed, but look left before joining. Always look forward before moving onto the roundabout to check traffic is moving.

1. To take the first exit, signal right, approach in the right-hand lane, keep right and continue signalling right.
2. To take the intermediate exit, select the appropriate lane, signalling as necessary, stay in this lane and signal right after you pass the exit before the one you want.
3. To take the last exit or go full circle, sign a left, approach in the left-hand lane, keep left until you need to exit and signal right after you pass the exit before the one you want.

RULES OF THE ROAD

- Drivers must be at least 18 and hold a full driver's licence.
- Drive on the right and give way to traffic approaching from the left unless directed otherwise.
- Seat belts must be worn in the front of a vehicle and (where fitted) in the back.
- Children under 4 must have a suitable restraint system. Children aged between 4 and 12 cannot travel in the front of the car without a fitted restraint system.
- Speed limits: built-up areas—50kph (31mph); outside built-up areas—110kph (68mph); motorways (autostrade)—130kph (81mph) (if your car is over 1100cc).
- Use dipped headlights in non-urban areas during the day and in towns or cities at night. These

are compulsory when driving in tunnels, even if they are well-lit.
- There are severe penalties for drinking and driving. The legal level is below 0.05 per cent of alcohol in the bloodstream.
- Italy uses international road signs.

MOTORWAYS AND TOLL ROADS (EXPRESSWAYS AND TURNPIKES)

As you approach the autostrada take the ticket from the automatic box on the left-hand side of the car or press the red button to get one. The barrier will lift. Keep your ticket safe, as you will need it to pay when you leave the autostrada. Cash payment is normally made to the official in the booth; the amount is displayed on a screen outside the pay window. If you are using a pass or paying by

Autostrada *toll booths*

credit card, follow the signs into the Viacard booth.

Slip roads onto and off Italian autostrade are short. You may have to stop and wait for traffic to pass before you can join the motorway.

Italians are fast, disciplined drivers on the motorway. Only use the outer lanes for overtaking and be prepared to move continuously between lanes to allow faster drivers behind you to overtake; they often drive up close behind you. Use the indicator before you pull out and while you are overtaking.

Autostrade have regularly spaced service areas (area di servizio) with filling stations, bar/restaurant, shops and lavatories. There are also occasional pull-off areas with

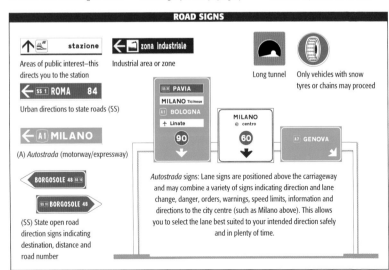

ROAD SIGNS

stazione
Areas of public interest—this directs you to the station

zona industriale
Industrial area or zone

Long tunnel

Only vehicles with snow tyres or chains may proceed

SS 1 ROMA 84
Urban directions to state roads (SS)

A1 MILANO
(A) Autostrada (motorway/expressway)

SS 35 PAVIA
MILANO Ticinese
A1 BOLOGNA
Linate
90

MILANO @ centro
60

A7 GENOVA

BORGOSOLE 48 SS 18
SS 18 BORGOSOLE 48
(SS) State open road direction signs indicating destination, distance and road number

Autostrada signs: Lane signs are positioned above the carriageway and may combine a variety of signs indicating direction and lane change, danger, orders, warnings, speed limits, information and directions to the city centre (such as Milano above). This allows you to select the lane best suited to your intended direction safely and in plenty of time.

shady trees and picnic tables, some with lavatories.

The Italian *autostrada* network is run by several different companies, which means that both price and frequency of tolls vary greatly. On the whole, northern motorways tend to be more expensive, and you may find a *pedaggio* (toll station) coming up every few kilometres. South of Naples, the A1 (*Autostrada del Sole*) is state-subsidized and free. Motorcycles under 150cc are not allowed on the motorway.

PROBLEMS

If your car breaks down turn on your hazard warning lights and place the warning triangle 50m (164ft) behind the vehicle.

If you're driving your own car, obtain assistance from the Automobile Club d'Italia (ACI) by calling 116 and telling the operator where you are, the make of car and the registration number. This is not a free service, so it might be better to arrange breakdown cover with a motoring organization before you leave home.

If your rental car breaks down, call the rental company on the emergency number, included with the car's paperwork.

If you have an accident call the police (113), but do not admit liability. Witnesses should remain to make statements, exchange details (name, address, car details, insurance company's name and address).

If you are stopped by the police (the *carabinieri*, the *polizia stradale* or the *polizia municipale*) they will want to see your papers. They may give no reason for stopping you, in which case it is likely to be a random spot check and once they realize you are a non-national they will probably wave you on. The commonest offence is speeding, for which there is a hefty on-the-spot fine. The police are legally obliged to issue fined drivers with a receipt.

The chart below gives the distances in kilometres (green) and duration in hours and minutes (blue) of a car journey between key towns. The times are based on average driving speeds using the fastest roads. They do not allow for delays or rest breaks.

	Ancona	Aosta	Bologna	Bolzano	Firenze	Genova	Lecce	Milano	Napoli	Padova	Perugia	Pisa	Ravenna	Reggio di Calabria	Roma	Siena	Torino	Trento	Trieste	Venezia	Verona
Ancona		608	222	501	333	512	611	424	459	323	209	400	150	909	314	327	534	428	520	345	344
Aosta			404	445	455	236	1158	200	919	411	608	401	450	1345	731	525	120	412	604	430	328
Bologna	612			257	129	309	812	220	553	125	242	156	104	1019	405	159	331	224	322	148	140
Bolzano	215	395			357	427	1051	313	821	227	511	425	343	1248	633	427	430	042	420	246	142
Firenze	498	465	281			242	831	320	455	231	144	109	215	921	307	106	420	324	428	254	240
Genova	323	472	103	369			1043	146	706	353	356	148	354	1133	518	312	201	354	547	413	310
Lecce	510	245	293	425	227			1014	441	913	735	909	740	523	609	819	1124	1018	1110	935	934
Milano	613	1214	817	1100	849	1079			744	239	434	255	306	1211	556	350	145	240	432	258	156
Napoli	428	183	211	294	298	147	1030			655	346	533	527	503	233	430	844	748	852	718	704
Padova	482	947	578	844	472	702	442	774			345	259	157	1122	507	301	356	154	213	039	103
Perugia	326	407	116	190	216	367	928	236	692			222	203	809	200	129	533	438	542	407	354
Pisa	157	621	252	518	146	376	746	447	369	365			242	959	345	128	326	352	456	321	308
Ravenna	391	410	171	437	78	165	925	285	548	285	222			1038	344	245	416	310	341	207	226
Reggio di Calabria	163	480	83	366	190	377	765	295	554	169	185	256			659	851	1310	1214	1318	1144	1130
Roma	934	1419	1050	1316	944	1174	478	1246	491	1164	840	1017	1086			246	656	600	704	530	516
Siena	301	757	388	654	282	512	604	584	227	502	169	355	354	698			450	354	458	324	310
Torino	258	539	170	436	69	294	806	365	429	283	109	108	257	900	229			357	549	415	313
Trento	549	112	332	420	395	168	1151	138	871	362	544	333	416	1342	671	462			348	214	109
Trieste	444	410	227	58	314	376	1046	239	790	178	463	380	311	1261	590	381	366			159	257
Venezia	525	602	315	385	416	562	1127	431	891	199	565	481	307	1362	691	483	557	373			123
Verona	362	438	152	221	252	399	964	267	728	36	401	318	143	1199	528	319	394	210	179		
	360	332	143	152	230	292	962	161	706	78	379	296	227	1177	506	297	287	98	273	110	

SAFETY

For peace of mind, keep car doors locked while you are driving. In large cities, particularly in the south, keep windows shut.

Never leave anything visible in the car when you're not using it. Italians usually detach their radios and take them with them.

If you're taking your own car, lower the aerial and tuck in the wing mirrors when you leave the vehicle.

In the countryside watch out for APEs (three-wheeler all-purpose mini-pickups) as their drivers rarely signal their intentions. Be aware of animals, slow-moving agricultural vehicles, soft roadsides and unsurfaced roads, which can be lethal in long spells of drought or heavy rain.

PARKING

Parking in Italy is difficult as its ancient and picturesque towns and villages are not built to accommodate vehicles.

● Invest in a parking dial; these are used in permitted parking areas and are displayed in your windscreen to indicate when you arrived. Rental cars are normally equipped with one; they are also available at tourist offices.

● Many cities have parking zones: Blue zones (with blue lines) have a maximum stay of 1–2 hours. Pay the attendant or at the meter. White zones (with white lines) are free and unlimited in some cities, but reserved for residents in others. Yellow zones (with yellow lines)

are generally for residents only.

● Pedestrianized historic towns allow cars in to deposit luggage—you may have to obtain a permit first from your hotel.

● City centre car parks are expensive.

● If you arrive at night, check that your chosen parking street does not have a market the following day. If it does, your car will be towed away well before dawn.

● A *zona di rimozione* is a tow-away zone.

BUYING FUEL

Italian service stations may not self-service. If there is an attendant, he will fill your tank, check water, oil, tyre pressures and clean the windscreen if requested. Pay him direct; you will have to ask for a receipt (*una ricevuta*). If they check the tyres it's customary to give a small tip (50c–€1).There are two grades of unleaded petrol (*senza piombo*), 95 and 98 octane, diesel (*gasolio*) and LPG. Leaded petrol is virtually nonexistent and you will have to buy lead-substitute additive. Fuel prices are generally similar to UK prices and considerably higher

A scooter—the fastest way to get around Rome's congested streets

than US prices. Motorway service areas and filling stations in major towns accept credit cards.

If you need fuel at night, you will need to find a filling station with a 24-hour (24 *ore*) automatic pump. These take €5, €10 and €20 notes. Feed the money into the slot in the machine. The fuel stops automatically when the money runs out. These can be temperamental and often reject old notes.

SCOOTERS

In the land of the Vespa, it's tempting to hire a scooter (*motorino*). Most large towns and holiday resorts have scooter rental outlets—ask at a tourist office for details. To rent a scooter you must be over 21 and hold a full driver's licence. You need to leave your passport and/or a credit card as a deposit. Crash helmets are compulsory.

Scooters are not for the faint-hearted, and if you've never ridden one in a big city Italy is not the place to start. But if you're having a seaside holiday or staying in a quiet rural area, they're economical, fun and easier to park than a car. Italian scooter drivers weave in and out of the traffic. Unless you are experienced, do not be tempted to emulate them.

TRANSLATIONS OF ITALIAN ROAD SIGNS

Accendere Switch on lights	**Parcheggio** Parking
Accendere i fari Switch on headlights	**Parcheggio autorizzato** Parking allowed
Banchina non Keep off hard shoulder	**Passaggio a livello** Level crossing
Caduta massi Falling rocks	**Pericolo** Danger
Crocevia Crossroads (intersection)	**Rallentare** Slow down
Curva pericolosa Dangerous bend	**Senso unico** One way
Discesa pericolosa Dangerous downhill	**Senso vietato** No entry
Divieto di accesso No entry	**Sosta autorizzata** Parking permitted
Divieto di sorpasso No overtaking	**Svolta** Bend
Divieto di sosta No parking	**Uscita** Exit
Entrata Entry	**Vietata ingresso veicoli** No entry
Incrocio Crossroads	for vehicles

CYCLING

Cycling is popular both as a sport and as a way of getting around, particularly in the northern plains. Tourist offices will be able to give you details of local rental companies and maps of routes in and around towns. If you rent a bike you will need to leave your passport or credit card as a deposit. There are few cycle paths, so you will need to keep your wits about you. It is now compulsory to wear a helmet, but they are recommended.

Buses

Italy has no national long-distance bus company. Buses are operated by myriad different companies, mainly running services within their own region, though there are a few that operate outside their own immediate area. With the low cost of rail travel, longer journeys are more efficient and cheaper when made by train.

If you are planning to use buses to get around a particular region, you can get **timetables and information** from the company office or the tourist information office.

● **Bus stations** are often next to the railway station. In small towns and villages, buses stop in the main piazza. Bus stations in larger towns tend to have lavatories, a newsstand, bar and lost-property office.

● **Tickets** are available from bus station ticket offices or on board.

● **Seat reservations** are not generally available.

● **Air-conditioning** is generally not available.

● **Smoking** is not permitted.

RURAL BUSES

Rural buses link outlying small towns and villages with the main regional centres or the larger local towns.

● **Timetables and information** are available from the bus company office (normally in the major towns of

the region) or from tourist information offices.

● **Tickets** are available from the bus office or on board.

● Buses stop at **designated stops,** either at points along the route or in the main piazzas of the villages.

● Services are geared to the local population's needs, so many buses operate to suit working and school hours and are drastically reduced on weekends and during school holidays.

Taxis

Taxis are available in all towns and cities. Government regulated vehicles are either white or yellow. Always check that the taxi is registered and that the meter is running—avoid taxis without a meter, as they may not be insured. All charges should be listed on a rate card displayed inside the vehicle. It can be difficult to hail a cab, so it is often better to go to a rank or book over the phone. Supplements are added for telephone booking, luggage and additional passengers. Rates are higher at night and on Sundays and public holidays. Many city taxis have set rates from the airport to the city centre. Confirm the price before you begin your journey.

TAXIS					
	ROME	**MILAN**	**FLORENCE**	**VENICE**	**NAPLES**
COLOUR	Yellow or white	Yellow	White with yellow graphics	A boat with a white cabin	White with yellow Neapolitan emblem
RANKS	Termini, Piazza Venezia, Piazza San Silvestro, Piazza di Spagna, Piazza Sonnino (Trastevere)	Stazione Centrale, Piazza Duomo, Largo Cairoli, Piazza San Babile	Piazza della Repubblica, Santa Maria Novella, Piazza della Stazione, Piazza del Duomo, Piazza San Marco, Piazza Santa Croce, Piazza di Santa Trinità	San Marco, Piazzale Roma, Aeroporto Venezia Marco Polo	Piazza Garibaldi, Piazza Plebiscito, Piazza Municipio, Piazza della Repubblica, Piazza de Nicola, Piazza Dante
RADIO TAXI TELEPHONE NUMBERS	06 3570 06 4989 06 41571	02 6969	055 4390 055 4798 055 4242 055 4386	041 522 2303	081 552 5252 081 551 5151 081 556 4444 081 570 7070
NUMBER OF PASSENGERS	4	4	4/5	6/8	4
PRICE	Moderate	Moderate	Expensive	Extremely expensive	Moderate

Trains

Italy has one of Europe's cheapest and most efficient rail networks, and if you're planning to cover a lot of ground without a car, trains are the best option. They run on time and carriages are clean and comfortable. Trenitalia, the state railway system, covers the whole country. This is supplemented by a number of privately run lines, which run from separate stations but operate in the same way and use an identical fare structure to the state service. With its extensive choice of routes, trains and tickets, rail travel can get you virtually anywhere you want to go in Italy.

DIFFERENT TYPES OF TRAIN

● **Eurostar Italia (ES)** A super-fast (250kph/155mph) service connecting the main Italian cities. A first-class ticket price includes newspapers and refreshments. All trains have a restaurant car and trolley service. Prebooked business coaches with PC facilities and mobile phone chargers are available. A supplement of 30 per cent on the normal fare is payable and reservations are compulsory (€3, tel 892021 in Italy, book on-line, at stations or via FS agents).

● **Intercity (IC)** High-speed trains connecting the main Italian cities and important regional towns. Almost all trains have restaurant/trolley facilities. Advance booking is advisable (€3, tel 892021, book on-line, at stations or via Trenitalia agents).

● **Intercity Notte (ICN)** Overnight domestic long-distance trains made up of a combination of ordinary carriages, Wagons-Lits

and couchette (4-berth) coaches. Advance booking for seats and sleepers is essential. There is a supplement to pay for sleepers, which is non-refundable and varies from around €11 for a *cuccetta* to €38 for a Wagons-Lit berth. (Book on-line, at stations or via FS agents).

● **Treni Espressi (E)** Long-distance express trains connecting major cities and towns all over Italy. Espressi services include overnight trains, and seats and sleeping compartments can be reserved in advance. (Book on-line, at

Passengers boarding at Termini railway station in Rome

stations or via Trenitalia agents).

● **Diretti (D)** Similar to Treni Espressi, they call at larger stations. No seat reservations.

● **Regionale (R)** Local trains operating within 100km (62 miles) of their departure station. They stop at every station and can be very slow. There are no seat reservations available and smoking is not permitted.

Trenitalia also operates **Interregionali** services,

WHERE TO BUY TRENITALIA PASSES	
Trenitalia agents in your country or in Italy	● Napoli Centrale
At the following stations in Italy:	● Palermo Centrale
● Bari	● Fiumicino Aeroporto
● Bologna Centrale	● Roma Termini
● Brindisi	● Torino Porta Nuova
● Firenze SMN	● Venezia Santa Lucia
● Genova PP	● Venezia Mestre
● Milano Centrale	● Verona

connecting coastal resorts and holiday areas with the major cities. A range of international trains provides direct connections to France, Austria, Switzerland, Germany and Spain.

TICKETING AND FARES

● Italian trains have first- and second-class tickets, which can be purchased on-line (www.trenitalia.com), at railway stations or through an FS agent.
● Train fares are calculated by the kilometre. A single second-class Rome–Milan fare works out around €40.
● Supplements are payable on the faster services such as Eurostar, Intercity and Espressi. You are issued with a separate ticket for the supplement.
● There is no reduction for return (round-trip) journeys.
● Children aged 4–12 travel at 50 per cent of the normal fare; children under 4, not occupying a seat, travel free.
● Tickets are valid for up to 2 months, but must be used within 6 hours of being validated (p. 58).

RAIL PASSES AND DISCOUNTS

● **Trenitalia Pass (for European foreigners)** If you're going to be using the train a lot in Italy, the best discount pass for non-nationals is the Trenitalia Pass. This is valid for 4–10 days' travel within a 2-month period and is issued for first- and second-class travel. It can be purchased through Trenitalia in your own country up to 6 months in advance, or up to 2 months in advance once you arrive in Italy. You must specify the number of days' travel required when you buy the pass, which also gives reductions on the journey to Italy and ferries to the main islands and Greece. If you travel on Eurostar trains, reserve a seat or take a sleeper, a supplement is payable. Before your pass is used for the first time, it must be validated at any Italian station ticket window or information office. The staff will stamp it and write the first and last day of validity and your passport or ID number on the ticket. Remember that you are not allowed to validate the pass yourself.
● **Italy Flexi Rail Cards** are available for US and Canadian visitors. They allow 4 days of rail travel in a 2-month period for US$191 (half price for children under 12). You can also buy a **Eurail Pass** valid for train and

*A timetable information board on a platform (*binario*) at Termini station in Rome*

ferry travel on Eurail group transport for periods of 15 or 21 days and 1, 2 or 3 months. Useful if you're coming to Europe for a long trip and plan to do a lot of moving around. The similar **Eurail Flexipass** is valid for 15 or 21 days within a 2-month period.
Visit www.raileurope.com

DISCOUNT PASSES

There are two passes you can buy in Italy that are each valid for one year. The Cartaverde gives a 20 per cent discount for those under 26 and the Carta d'Argento gives a 20 per cent discount for those over 65.

TRAIN TIMETABLES

There are several ways to obtain train and timetable information:
● **On-line** at www.fs-on-line.com
● **Travel agents** displaying the FS (Ferrovie dello Stato) logo have up-to-date timetables and you can also book tickets here.
● **Stations** display departure and arrival times in the entrance foyer. In addition there are timetables for arrivals and departures from that station displayed on boards on every platform; *partenze* for departures, *arrivi* for arrivals.
● Take note of timetabling variations beside different trains: *Si effetua dal… al …* specifies

dates between which this service runs.

Periodico...................seasonal
Feriale............weekday service
Festivi...Sunday/holiday service

● You can buy a full timetable for the whole of Italy at newsstands and station bookstalls; ask for **Tutt'Italia** (€16), though it's generally known as the ***pozzorario.***

TICKETS

● Large stations have separate ticket windows for advance booking, and sometimes for first- and second-class travel. Major city stations may also have a travel centre for enquiries and advance bookings.

● Ask for either *andata* (one way) or *andata e tornata* (round trip). The kilometres and price are displayed on an electronic

Biglietteria/Tickets

A train ticket machine

board next to the booking clerk. Specify which train you are taking in case there is a **supplement** to pay. This can be paid directly to the ticket inspector on the train, but it is cheaper to pay it in advance. Payment can be made in cash or by credit card, though the latter is often not accepted for low-cost tickets.

● Once you have purchased your

ticket it must be **validated** before you board the train. Do this by inserting your ticket into the yellow boxes found at various points in the station and on the platforms. If you fail to do this, you are liable to an **on-the-spot fine** of around €16. Your ticket is inspected during your journey.

● On long journeys with changes, you may be issued with **several travel documents,** which will represent tickets for different trains and their supplements. Keep them together as inspectors may want to see them all.

POINTS TO REMEMBER

● For **lost property** call the station at either your departure or arrival point.

● If you have a **connection** to make, head for the timetable board on the platform where your train has pulled in. Find your connection by looking for either the train number, its final destination, or its departure time from this station. The platform will be listed under *binario.* Using the underpass, transfer to the relevant platform.

● Except for the smallest, all Italian stations have a ticket

The chart on the left gives the duration in hours and minutes of a train journey between major towns in Italy by the fastest route. It is a general guide and does not allow for delays.

	Ancona	Bari (Centrale)	Bologna (Centrale)	Bolzano (Novarese)	Firenze (S.M.N.)	Genova (Piazza Principe)	Milano (Centrale)	Napoli (Centrale)	Padova	Perugia	Piacenza	Pisa (Centrale)	Ravenna	Reggio di Calabria	Roma (Termini)	Siena	Trento	Torino (Porta Susa)	Venezia (Santa Lucia)	Verona (Porta Nuova)	Trieste
	403																				
	152	601																			
	653	1250	444																		
	316	647	053	447																	
	455	906	302	343	231																
	344	753	146	141	247	131															
	508	403	432	831	326	717	620														
	341	753	115	433	217	413	207	613													
	230	652	304	721	148	608	507	414	410												
	308	719	116	253	219	128	039	623	252	411											
	453	817	222	607	049	146	341	457	357	303	317										
	209	618	100	456	217	422	255	619	207	423	243	357									
	951	640	915	1315	809	1202	1219	421	1058	907	1109	935	1125								
	308	439	241	631	135	418	430	134	400	204	418	247	406	615							
	518	811	246	723	119	358	434	506	430	319	423	143	424	955	301						
	435	845	221	445	319	424	235	708	158	553	331	502	408	1142	505	543					
	502	913	324	202	420	137	123	817	403	604	152	328	435	1347	602	545	436				
	414	825	147	507	249	447	240	645	029	441	326	409	242	1126	432	449	230	148			
	332	814	118	336	216	316	118	605	046	450	214	359	255	1039	402	434	053	314	119		
	609	1021	337	717	441	646	424	843	230	719	518	606	425	1318	624	648	431	631	203	303	

ITALY'S MAJOR RAIL ROUTES

Bolzana (Bozen)
Trento
TRIESTE
MILANO
PADOVA
VERONA
VENEZIA
TORINO
Piacenza
GENOVA
BOLOGNA
Ravenna
Pisa
FIRENZE
Siena
Ancona
Perugia
ROMA
BARI
NAPOLI
Sardegna
Reggio di Calabria
Sicilia

office, bookstall, bar, lavatories and left luggage.

● Station bars sell **food** to take away; in larger stations there are also trolleys selling drinks, water, sandwiches and biscuits. Ask for what you want … *da portare via* (to take away).

● **Luggage trolleys (baggage carts)** are few and far between even at major stations. There are **porters** at Rome, Milan, Venice, Turin, Naples, Genoa and Bologna.

● **Announcements** are clear, but are in Italian only, except for airport train announcements at Rome and Florence, which are also in English.

● There are occasional **platform changes**—check the departure board before boarding. Boards at the end of the platforms show the next train to leave.

● Train doors automatically close 30–60 seconds before departure.

● Intercity, Eurostar and Espressi trains have **on-board catering** and **air-conditioning.**

● Eurostar and Intercity have **on-board telephones.**

● All trains have **on-board toilets.**

● There are **smoking carriages** on all trains except *regionale*.

GETTING AROUND 59

Domestic Flights

The main Italian cities and regional capitals all have their own airports, with daily connecting flights between the Italian airports and international gateways.

Italy's national carrier, Alitalia, runs regular flights between all the major cities. In addition, there are a number of regional airlines, useful for accessing more out-of-the-way places if you're planning a long trip. Internal flights within Italy make sense if you want to see a lot fast, and are particularly useful for travelling to Sicily and Sardinia from outside the country; the hub airports all have regular connections.

● With the advent of on-line booking, you can use the web to book and purchase tickets on the regional airlines, as well as with Alitalia. If you don't have access to the internet, your travel agent can do this for you.

● Tickets for internal flights are relatively expensive

Air One livery

INTERNAL AIRLINES			
AIRLINE	**BASE**	**WEBSITE**	**DESTINATIONS**
AIR DOLOMITI	Trieste	www.airdolomiti.it	Alghero, Ancona, Bari, Bologna, Cagliari, Genoa, Milan, Olbia, Naples, Rimini, Pisa, Trieste, Verona, Venice
AIR EUROPE	Milan	www.aireurope.it	Bari , Milan, Naples, Palermo, Rome, Verona, Venice
AIR ONE	Pescara	www.air-one.it	Alghero, Bari, Bologna, Brindisi, Cagliari, Catania, Crotone, Florence, Genoa, Lamezia Terme, Milan, Naples, Olbia, Palermo, Pescara, Pisa, Reggio di Calabria, Rome, Turin, Venice (seasonal: Lampedusa, Pantelleria)
AIR VALLEE	Aosta	www.airvallee.com	Ancona, Bari, Bologna, Brindisi, Catania, Cagliari, Florence, Genoa
ALITALIA	Rome	www.alitalia.it	Lamezia Terme, Milan, Naples, Palermo, Perugia, Pisa, Reggio di Calabria, Rome, Trieste, Turin, Venice, Verona
ALPIEAGLES	Venice	www.alpieagles.com	Cagliari, Catania, Lamezia Terme, Milan, Naples, Olbia, Palermo, Rome, Verona, Venice
AZZURRA AIR	Bergamo	www.azzurraair.it	Bergamo, Rome
GANDALF	Milan	www.gandalf.it	Brescia, Milan, Pisa, Rome, Verona
MERIDIANA	Olbia	www.meridiana.it	Bergamo, Bologna, Cagliari, Catania, Florence, Milan, Naples, Olbia, Palermo, Pisa, Rome, Turin, Venice, Verona
VOLARE	Vicenza	www.volare-airlines.com	Bari, Catania, Milan, Naples, Palermo, Rome, Venice

(eg Naples–Milan around €160, Rome–Venice around €135), but advance booking may secure you one of the limited number of cheap seats available on each flight. The popular routes tend to sell out more quickly. If you fly to Italy with Alitalia, you are eligible for its Visit Italy Pass, which allows you to take three internal flights for around €125, useful if you're going south.

• Check-in times vary from 1–2 hours. Security can be very slow, so allow plenty of time for this.

• You may need documentation; Italians have to carry their identity cards with them at all times; a passport will serve this purpose.

• Most domestic flights are one class.

• Domestic flights are non-smoking.

• On short hops you are offered a drink; on longer flights a light snack is served.

• Regional airports are generally well-equipped with the usual range of facilities and services, albeit on a small scale.

AIRPORTS NEAR POPULAR AREAS

To save time you may want to take advantage of Italy's internal flight network. Below is a list of popular sightseeing and holiday destinations and the airports that best serve them:

Adriatic Riviera—Ancona Raffaello Sanzio (AOI).
Calabria—Lamezia Terme (SUF).

The terminal building at Venice Marco Polo Airport

Alitalia planes at Trieste Airport

Cinque Terre—Genova Cristoforo Colombo (GOA).
Dolomites—Verona Valerio Catullo (VRN) or Venice Marco Polo (VCE).
Florence—Firenze Amerigo Vespucci (FLR) is 4km (2.5 miles) northwest of the city, and Pisa Galileo Galilei (PSA) is 80km (50 miles) west of the city.
Lake Como—Bergamo Orio al Serio (BGY).
Lake Garda—Verona Valerio Catullo (VRN), Brescia (Verona) (VBS), Milan Linate (LIN), Milan Malpensa (MXP), Milano Orio al Serio (BGY).
Lampedusa island—Lampedusa (LMP).
Milan—Milan Linate (LIN), Milan Malpensa (MXP).

Naples, Sorrento and the Amalfi Coast—Naples Capodichino (NAP) is 6km (3.8 miles) north of the city of Naples.
The Northeast and Emilia-Romagna—Bologna Guglielmo Marconi (BLQ), Trieste International (TRS).
Pantelleria island—Pantelleria (PNL).
Puglia—Bari Palese (BRI).
Riviera di Levante—Genova Cristoforo Colombo (GOA).
Riviera di Ponente—Genova Cristoforo Colombo (GOA).
Rome—Rome Ciampino (CIA) is 16km (10 miles) southeast of the city, and Rome Leonardo da Vinci Fiumicino (FCO) is 36km (22 miles) southwest of the city.
Sardinia—Cagliari Mario Mameli (CAG) in the south and Alghero Fertilia (AHO) in the northwest.
Sicily—Catania (CTA) in the east and Palermo Punta Raisi (PMO) in the northwest.
Turin and the Italian/French Alps—Torino Caselle (TRN) is 18km (11 miles) north of Turin and (48km) 30 miles from the Italian/French Alps.
Tuscany—Pisa Galileo Galilei (PSA).
Umbria—Perugia International (PEG).
Venice—Venice Marco Polo (VCE) is 13km (8 miles) away from the city on the northern mainland.

Domestic Ferries

ISLAND FERRIES

Besides the main islands of Sardinia and Sicily, Italy has a number of smaller islands. Italians have gone to these destinations for years, but now foreign visitors are beginning to discover their charms and the pleasures of their laid-back, low-key resorts. All are regularly served by ferries from the mainland, often with a choice of departure ports. Caremar is the main operator providing services to Ischia and Capri, but there are several others, all operating from the Molo Beverello in Naples. It is essential to book ferries and accommodation in advance in peak season (July and August). Out-of-season services are drastically reduced, or even, in the case of the more remote islands, nonexistent.

Sicily—p. 46
www.traghettionline.net
Sardinia—p. 46
www.traghettionline.net

VENICE

ACTV runs a comprehensive service between the lagoon islands and the city (p. 50)

The Garda Express ferries passengers across Lake Garda

FERRIES TO ITALY'S ISLANDS					
	ELBA	**GIGLIO**	**ISOLE PONZIANE**	**ISCHIA**	**CAPRI**
MAINLAND PORT	Piombino	Porto Santo Stefano	Anzio, Formia and others (Terracina, Naples)	Naples, Pozzuoli, Procida	Naples, Sorrento
ARRIVAL PORT	Portoferraio	Giglio Porto	Ponza	Ischia Porto	Marina Grande
JOURNEY TIME	1 hour	1 hour	From Anzio 2 hours, Formia 2 hours 30 min, Terracina 2 hours 30 min	From Naples 1 hour 20 min; from Pozzuoli 1 hour 40 min	From Naples 1 hour min, from Sorrento min
FERRY COMPANY	**Moby** Nuova Stazione Marittima, Piombino tel 0565 225211 Via Ninci 1, Portoferraio tel 0565 9361 www.mobylines.it **Toremar** Nuova Stazione Marittima, Piombino tel 0565 31100 Calata Italia 23, Portoferraio tel 0565 918080 www.toremar-elba.it	**Maregiglio** Porto Santo Stefano tel 0564 812920 www.maregiglio.it **Toremar** Porto Santo Stefano tel 0564 810803 www.toremar.it	**Caremar** Via Ardeatina 114, Anzio tel 06 9860 0083 Molo Musco, Ponza tel 0771 80656/ 081 317 2999 (overseas callers)/199 123199 (call centre from Italy) www.gruppotirrenia.it/ caremar **Caremar** Banchina Azzurra, Formia, tel 0771 227 102 3800	**Caremar** Molo Beverello, Napoli tel 081 551 3882 Banchina Redentore e Olimpia, Ischia tel 081 984818 Banchina Emporio Pozzuoli tel 081 526271/199 123199 (call centre from Italy) www.gruppotirrenia.it/ caremar	**Caremar** Molo Beverello, Nap tel 081 5513882 Angelina srl, Marin Grande Capri tel 081 8370700 Dott Raniero Morel Piazza Marinai d'Ita Sorrento tel 081 8073077/19 123199 (call centre from Italy)
ADVANCE BOOKING	Yes	Yes	Yes	Foot passengers no, cars yes	No

LAKE FERRIES

Italy's most scenically beautiful lakes are in the north, and are one of the country's most popular holiday destinations. The big names—Como, Garda and Maggiore—draw crowds throughout the summer, the majority of whom use the lake ferries to enjoy waterborne views. Ferries link the lakeside towns and are as much a useful form of transport as excursion boats. Further south, the two central Italian lakes of Bolsena and Trasimeno run pleasure boats to their islands.

COMO, MAGGIORE, GARDA

Services on Lakes Como, Garda, Maggiore and smaller Iseo are all run by Navigazione Laghi. The service on Lake Como links Cadenabbia, Menaggio, Varenna and Bellagio, a cluster of

attractive resort villages in the central part of the lake. Maggiore and Garda have a comprehensive service, with boats making stops at numerous villages on either side of the length of the lakes. The boats

People boarding at Orta San Giulio on Lake Orta

on Lake Maggiore cross the border and run into Switzerland. In addition, there are many cruises (including night-time) and excursions to the islands. Tickets are sold in the villages or on board; timetable information is displayed at the landing stages.
Contact:
Navigazione Laghi
Via L. Ariosto 21, 20145 Milano
800 551801/02 467 6101
www.navigazionelaghi.it

LAGO TRASIMENO
Excursions run from Castiglione del Lago and Passignano to Isola Maggiore.

LAGO DI BOLSENA
Excursions run from Capodimonte and Bolsena to Isola Bizantina.

FERRIES TO ITALY'S ISLANDS				
ISOLE EOLIE	**ISOLE EGADI**	**PANTELLERIA**	**ISOLE PELAGIE**	**ISOLE TREMITI**
Milazzo	Trápani	Trápani	Porto Empédocle	Vieste (Jun–Sep)
...rto di Levante, Vulcano	Favignana	Pantelleria	Linosa, Lampedusa	San Nicola
1 hour 30 min	1 hour	5 hours 30 min	To Linosa 5 hours 45 min, to Lampedusa 7 hours 30 min	From Manfredonia 2 hours (hydrofoil); from Vieste 1 hour (hydrofoil)
Siremar ...Allia srl, Via dei Mille ...alazzo Sta Rita), Milazzo tel 090 928 3424 ...lcano Viaggi srl, Piazza ...cano Levante 3, Porto di Levante tel 090 985 2149/199 ...23199 (call centre from Italy) ...ww.gruppotirrenia.it/ siremar **N.G.I.,** tel 090 928 4091 ...ww.cormorano.net/ngil	**Siremar** Terminal Aliscafo, Stazione Marittima Molo Dogana, Trápani tel 0923 545455 Catalano Viaggi, Molo S Leonardo, Favignana tel 0923 921363/199 123199 (call centre from Italy) www.gruppotirrenia.it/ siremar	**Siremar** Terminal Aliscafo, Stazione Marittima Molo Dogana, Trápani tel 0923 545455 Agenzia Rizzo, Via Borgo Italia 22, Pantelleria tel 0923 911120/199 123199 (call centre from Italy) www.gruppotirrenia.it/ siremar	**Siremar** Tricoli e Nuara, Via Molo 13 tel 0922 636683 Porto Empédocle Gaetano Cavallaro, Via Principe Umberto tel 0922 972062 Linosa, Sebastiano Strazzera, Longomare L Rizzo, Lampedusa tel 0922 970003/199 123199 (call centre from Italy) www.gruppotirrenia.it/ siremar	**Adriatica** Gargano Viaggi, Piazza Roma 7, Vieste tel 0884 708501 Dita Cafiero Emilio, Via degli Abbati 10, Tremiti tel 0882 663008 www.adriatica.it
Foot passengers no, cars yes	Foot passengers no, cars yes	Yes	Yes	Yes

ON THE MOVE WITH A DISABILITY

As in so many other countries, the overall picture of disabled facilities in Italy is mixed. The major problems are often not with transport, accommodation or public buildings, but in the layout and nature of the cities and towns themselves. The historic interest and architectural beauty of many of the main tourist attractions in Italy inevitably make disabled access a challenge. Things are progressing, particularly with regard to public transport and access to museums and galleries, but visitors with disabilities will often find that it's not easy getting there in the first place. Italians are generally helpful, but, with some key exceptions, disabled facilities have not yet caught up with those in northern European countries and North America.

● If you have a disability, plan carefully, aim to travel with able-bodied friends or consider booking your holiday with a specialist tour operator.

● You should contact your airline in advance of your date of travel They will let the airports know what assistance you will need.

An electric lift organized by Regency San Marino Travel Agency

USEFUL CONTACTS

ATAC DISABLED SERVICES
tel 06 4695 4887/06 4695 4286
open daily 8–2.30
ATAC manages and provides information on Rome's public transport system.

INFORMAHANDICAP
Viale Garibaldi 155, 30174 Venezia
Mestre tel 041 534 1700, fax 041 534 2257, e-mail
informahandicap@comune.venezia.it
Informahandicap can give you help and advice if you are planning to visit Venice.

CO.IN SOCIALE (COOPERATIVE INTEGRATE ONLUS)
Via Enrico Giglioli 54, Roma
tel 06 712 9011
www.coinsociale.it
CO.IN plans and promotes the building of accessible public spaces in Rome and produces a list of sights that have disabled access.

UNIONE ITALIANA DEI CIECHI (ITALIAN BLIND SOCIETY)
Unione Italiana dei Ciechi, Via Borgognona 38, 00187 Roma
tel 06 699881, fax 06 678 6815
www.uiciechi.it

SATH (SOCIETY FOR ACCESSIBLE TRAVEL AND HOSPITALITY)
www.sath.org
Lots of useful travel tips for holidaymakers who are visually impaired or have a disability.

ACCESSIBLE ITALY (REGENCY SAN MARINO SRL)
Via C. Manetti 34, 47891 Dogana Borgomaggiore
Repubblica di San Marino 47031
tel 0549 941108, fax 0549 907189
www.accessibleitaly.com
An Italian travel company that run tours for visitors with disabilities. Local contacts give the the company the edge over many foreign operators.

● Trains sometimes have wheelchair access, and this is indicated on the timetable by a wheelchair symbol. If you need assistance at the station, contact them 24 hours in advance.

● Taxis can take wheelchairs folded and stored in the boot, but Italian taxis are saloon (sedan)-type cars and getting in and out may be difficult.

● If you are driving, you can use your blue Disabled Person's Parking Badge in Italy.

● Be aware that many streets in historic towns are cobbled and can be very steep.

● Major pedestrian crossings in cities have a sound signal for the visually impaired.

● An increasing number of public places and some museums have information in braille.

● Book well in advance and be specific about your requirements when reserving accommodation.

● For a more relaxed Italian holiday, steer clear of the major cities and use a car to explore rural areas and the smaller artistic towns and villages.

VENICE

Venice poses particular problems for wheelchair users, but, with judicious planning, you will be able to see plenty. *Vaporetti* (p. 50) can take wheelchairs, and some of the major sights are accessible from the *vaporetto* stops without having to negotiate bridges. Facilities inside some museums and galleries are good, and there are hotels and restaurants where you will have no problems. The tourist office publishes a map with routes suitable for wheeelchairs, and four main bridges in the *sestiere* of San Marco have automated ramps; access keys are available from the tourist office. For more information contact Informahandicap (see above for contact information).

This chapter is divided geographically into nine sections. Places of interest are listed alphabetically within each area. The major sites are listed at the front of each regional section.

The Sights

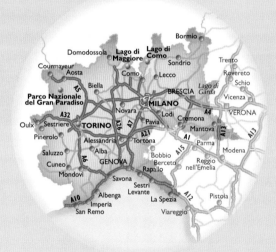

THE NORTHWEST

This is an area of diversity, from the scenic splendour of Lago di Como, Lago Maggiore and the towering Alps to stylish Milano, Italy's economic powerhouse. The smaller historic cities, such as Mantova and Cremona, are crammed with artistic treasures, while the coast has beaches, picturesque villages and the vibrant port of Genova.

MAJOR SIGHTS

Towers surrounding the central Piazza Risorgimento in Alba

Children enjoying the cool water in the Piazza Duomo, Bergamo

ALBA

⊞ 432 C5 ⓘ Piazza Medford 3, 12051 Alba, tel 0173 35833 ⓡ Alba
www.langheroero.it

Prized for its wines and white truffles *(tartufi bianchi)*, the medieval town of Alba, 62km (39 miles) from Turin, is the main town in the Langhe, a beautiful region of vine-clad slopes and hills crowned by ancient castles. Here gastronomy reigns supreme: Delicatessens are piled high with hams, wild boar, home-made pastas, *funghi* and bottles of Barolo and Barberesco.

The old town is compact and its cobbled streets, arcades, red-brick medieval towers and historic monuments have been well-preserved. The Piazza del Risorgimento, or Piazza del Duomo as it is known, is overlooked by the town hall and the redbrick Duomo di San Lorenzo *(Mon–Sat 9–noon, 3–5.30, Sun and holidays 9–1, 3–5.30)*. The 15th-century duomo has beautifully carved and inlaid choir stalls. From the square you can see the tallest and best-preserved of the town's medieval towers; there were originally 100 in the town.

ASTI

⊞ 432 C5 ⓘ Piazza Alfieri 29, 14100 Asti, tel 0141 530357 ⓡ Asti

Asti is the home of, and synonymous with, Spumante, the sweet sparkling wine. This large town, 60km (37 miles) east of Turin, is predominantly industrial, but its medieval past is evident in the historic buildings and churches that are scattered throughout the old centre.

In medieval times Asti was the largest town in Piedmont and a rival city to Milan. The town's *palio* (bareback horse-race, similar to Siena's) is the oldest in Italy, dating from the late 13th

century. Asti once had 125 towers, but 12 survive.

The main cultural attraction is the medieval complex of the 15th-century Church of San Pietro in Consavia, a Gothic cloister with a small circular baptistery dating from the 10th to 12th century and an archaeology museum *(Tue–Sun 10–1, 4–7, summer; 10–1, 3–6, rest of year)*. The large Gothic church of San Secondo on the piazza of the same name has a Romanesque bell tower and an altarpiece by Gaudenzio Ferrari (1471/81–1546) *(Mon–Sat 8–noon, 3.30–6, Sun 3.30–5.30)*.

BERGAMO

⊞ 431 E3 ⓘ (Lower Town) Viale Vittorio Emanuele 20, 24100 Bergamo, tel 035 210204 ⓘ (Upper Town) Vicolo dell'Aquila Nera 2, 24100 Bergamo, tel 035 232730 ⓡ Bergamo

Northeast of Milan in the southern foothills of the Alps, Bergamo could not be more different from Italy's business capital. The city is divided into the medieval Citti Alta (Upper Town) and the relatively dull, modern Citti Bassa (Lower Town).

The arches of the Palazzo della Ragione lead to the glorious Piazza del Duomo and the Cappella Colleoni (1470–76). Built as a mausoleum for Bartolomeo Colleoni, the famous Venetian *condottiere* (mercenary soldier), it has a pink and white marble façade covered with statues, reliefs and stuccowork, topped with a large rose window above the portal *(Daily 9–12.30, 2–6.30, Mar–Oct; Tue–Sun 9–12.30, 2–4.3, rest of year)*. To the right of the chapel is a copy of the 14th-century octagonal baptistery, complete with a red marble gallery. Inside are Flemish and Florentine tapestries, 15th- to 17th-century frescoes,

Donizetti's tomb and a splendid wooden choir stall (1522–55) with inlaid panels designed by Lorenzo Lotti depicting scenes from the Old Testament *(Sun 3–6 or on request, tel 035 210223)*.

BRESCIA

⊞ 434 F4 ⓘ Corso Zanardelli 34, 25121 Brescia, tel 030 43418 ⓡ Brescia
www.bresciaholiday.com

Brescia may lack the charm of its neighbour Bergamo, but it is an ancient city with a strong cultural heritage. The most appealing of its three squares is the Venetian-style Piazza Loggia, where you will find the richly decorated Palazzo della Loggia (the town hall), with its arcade and cupola. An archway on the south side leads to the controversial Victory Square, built in a Fascist style during Mussolini's rule. The archway brings you to Piazza Paolo VI, the religious heart of the city, overlooked by the great green cupola of the Duomo Nuovo *(Mon–Sat 7.30–12, 4–7, Sun 8–1, 4–7.30)*. This towering, modern baroque cathedral dwarfs its older and more interesting neighbour, the Duomo Vecchio, a rare example of a Romanesque cathedral with a circular plan—hence its nickname, La Rotonda *(Tue–Sun 9–noon, 3–7, Apr–Oct; Tues–Sun 9–noon, 3–6, rest of year)*.

The remains of the Capitoline Temple around Piazza del Foro are a legacy of the Roman colony of Brixia, established here in AD73 by Emperor Vespasian. Archaeological remains from the site are housed in the Museo della Città, in the nearby 16th-century Monastery of Santa Giulia. The highlight is a bronze *Winged Victory* discovered in 1826 *(Tue–Sun 10–6)*.
Don't Miss The Capitoline Temple.

THE SIGHTS

The white houses of Vernazza clinging to the coast

Genova, Italy's most important commercial port

THE SIGHTS

CINQUE TERRE

⊞ 433 E6 ⓘ Via Seggino, 19016 Monterosso, tel 0187 817506; daily 9–12, 3–6 Jun–Sep only 🚆 La Spezia–Monterosso line 🚢 Apr–Oct Navigazione Golfo dei Poeti operates a regular boat service linking all the villages except Corniglia. Summer ferries and catamarans from Genova to the Cinque Terre
www.aptcinqueterre.sp.it

The ravishing coastline of the Cinque Terre (Five Lands) is named after the five little fishing villages that cling precariously to the cliffs northwest of La Spezia. From here to Levanto the landscape is characterized by mountains cloaked in woods, terraces of vines and cliffs providing spectacular views over the turquoise sea. Tourism is growing rapidly here, but the area is a protected national park and the locals are encouraged to maintain their traditional occupations of fishing and viticulture. Grapes grown on the steep slopes produce the fragrant and fruity white Cinque Terre wine and the rarer, stronger and sweeter Sciacchetri. The villages most easily reached by road, and hence the best-equipped and least charming are Monterossa and Riomaggiore. Vernazza is arguably the most beautiful of the five villages, a huddle of painted houses, narrow alleys and arcades. Genoese fortifications here include medieval bastions and a watchtower. Manarola is another highly photogenic village, with a cluster of pastel-washed houses, steep cobbled streets, a quaint harbour and the only sandy beach in the Cinque Terre. Corniglia, the smallest of the five villages, clings to a ridge, with steps leading down to the sea. The clear blue waters and rocky coastline are home to a huge variety of fish and thriving underwater gardens making this a popular destination for divers.

CREMONA

⊞ 433 E4 ⓘ Piazza del Comune 5, 26100 Cremona, tel 0372 23233 🚆 Cremona
www.aptcremona.it

This is the birthplace of the Stradivarius. The first modern violin, as opposed to the medieval fiddle, was made here by Andrea Amati in 1566, and Antonio Stradivari, the great violin-maker, was born here in 1644. His life and work are commemorated in the Museo Stradivariano, where many of his tools are on display *(Mon–Sat 9–6, Sun and holidays 10–6)*. The Sala dei Violini in the Palazzo Comune also has a collection of historic violins, including examples by Amati and Stradivarius.

This little market town on the north banks of the River Po, 95km (59 miles) southeast of Milan, revolves around the Piazza del Comune with its ensemble of medieval monuments. The Romanesque and Gothic cathedral (1107–1332) has an ornately sculpted marble façade with a fine rose window. The frescoes inside by the Cremona school are the highlight. Particularly notable is Pordenone's *Crucifixion* (1520–21), prized for its bold spatial effects *(Tue–Sat 7.30–noon, 3.30–7, Sun and holidays 7.30–1, 3.30–7)*. The 14th-century Lombard-Gothic church of Sant'Agostino (1339–45) is also worth visiting to see its serene altarpiece by Perugino, *The Madonna and Saints,* in the fifth chapel on the south side *(Daily 9–noon, 4–6.30)*. **Don't miss** The Romanesque and Gothic cathedral.

GENOVA (GENOA)

⊞ 433 D5 ⓘ Porto Antico, Ponte Spinola, 17121 Genova, tel 010 2530671 🚆 Genova
www.apt.genova.it

Its outskirts are unattractive, but Genova has a rich heritage and a wealth of historical palaces, churches and museums to explore. It was, and still is, Italy's principal seaport and was famously the birthplace of Christopher Columbus in 1451. Genova enjoyed a major facelift when Renzo Piano revamped the harbour in preparation for EXPO 92. Its *carruggi* (narrow alleys) and lavishly decorated mansions and palazzi, especially along Via Garibaldi and Via Balbi, further soften its rough exterior.

The Galleria Nazionale di Palazzo Spinola on Via San Luca, an opulent 16th- to 18th-century palace, has original furnishings, frescoed ceilings and an art collection that includes works by Van Dyck, Antonello da Messina, Rubens and Pisano *(Tue–Sat 8.30–7.30, Sun 1–8)*. The Museo Civico di Palazzo Bianco, housed in a 16th-century palace on Via Garibaldi, also has an exceptional collection of paintings by Genoese and other European artists, including works by Rubens, Van Dyck, Antonello da Messina, Caravaggio and Murillo *(Closed for restoration)*. The early 13th-century Cattedrale di San Lorenzo in the piazza of the same name has a Gothic black-and-white striped marble façade *(Mon–Sat 9–11.30, 3–5.30)*. Opened for EXPO 92, the Acquario di Genova is the second biggest aquarium in Europe. It was built to commemorate the fifth centenary of Columbus' discovery of the New World *(Mon–Fri 9.30–7.30, Sat–Sun and holidays 9.30–8.30, last entrance 2 hours before closing; 9.30–11pm July–Aug)*. **Don't miss** The Galleria Nazionale di Palazzo Spinola; the Museo Civico di Palazzo Bianco; the Cattedrale di San Lorenzo; the Acquario di Genova.

LAGO DI COMO

**Its temperate climate and lavish villas make Como the most romantic of the three major Italian lakes.
Enjoy boat trips, walks in the mountains, visits to lakeshore villas and gardens and the wonderful panoramas.**

Surrounded by high mountains and rugged hills, Lake Como has inspired writers, artists and musicians from Pliny the Younger in Roman times to 19th-century Romantics such as French novelists Stendhal and Flaubert and the Italian composer Rossini. The first steamboat was launched from here in 1826 and visitors have been taking boat trips to enjoy the views of the lakeside ever since.

Como is smaller than Lakes Maggiore and Garda but it has the longest perimeter (over 170km/106 miles) and at its deepest point, between Argegno and Nesso, it measures 410m (1,345ft), making it the deepest lake in Italy.

THE THREE LAKES
The sunny and gentle west coast of the Como branch of the lake is typified by patrician villas, elegant hotels, harbours and villages often presided over by an ancient campanile. The shadier Lecco branch, between the High Brianza to the west and the Grigna to the east, is less accessible, with fewer villages and harbours. At the southern tip, Lecco developed into a large industrial centre in the 19th century. The northern section of the lake, often referred to as Alto Lario, is different again. Here the lake widens and campsites dot both shores. In the north, Monte Legnone (2,609m/8,560ft) towers above Culico, south of which lies the main attraction along the coast—Piona's ancient abbey, on the tip of a peninsula. The 'three lakes' meet at the Punta Sparivento (the Point That Divides the Wind).

LAKESIDE TOWNS AND VILLAS
At this central headland is Bellagio, known as the pearl of the lake for its charming setting and beautiful villas. Isolated on the map, it has excellent boat connections, which make it popular for daytrips. Against a backdrop of high mountains, the lively resort of Menaggio has some excellent walking, windsurfing, swimming, trekking and rock-climbing opportunities. Villa d'Este at Cernobbio (p. 285) is the most famous of Como's villas. Built in the 16th century, it is now a sumptuous hotel. In a glorious setting on a wooded peninsula, Villa del Balbianello in Lenno, is full of unusual treasures, including mementos collected by the eccentric explorer who lived here.

RATINGS				
Good for food	●	●	●	●
Good for kids	●	●	●	●
Historic interest	●	●	●	
Photo stops	●	●	●	●

TIP

● Spring and autumn are the best times to visit as in peak season the main resorts and the narrow winding coastal roads are uncomfortably crowded.

BASICS

✚ 431 D3

Tourist information office
Piazza Cavour 17, 22100 Como
☎ 031 3300111
🕐 Mon–Sat 9–1, 2–6
🚉 Como town 🛳 The centre of the lake has a car ferry service linking Menaggio, Varenna, Bellagio and Cadenabbia

www.lakecomo.com
A stylish website providing ferry information and links to tour guides and hotels. English version.

A view of Bellagio on the shores of Lago di Como

LAGO MAGGIORE

An area of natural beauty that is best admired from the water. Famous for its gardens, Borromean Islands and elegant resorts.

Maggiore is the second largest and the most westerly of the three main lakes. Piedmont in the west, Lombardy in the east and the Ticon canton in Switzerland, in the north, all converge on its shores. With its southern tip approximately 55km (35 miles) northwest of Milan, the lake is 65km (40 miles) long, averages 2km (1.25 miles) across and has a perimeter of 170km (106 miles). The surface area is 212sq km (82sq miles) and the deepest point, in the Gulf of Borromeo, is 372m (1,220ft). The scenery ranges from wild, mountainous landscapes in the north to gentle Mediterranean views further south. Gardens flourish in the spring when camellias, rhododendrons and azaleas brighten up the shores.

EARLY TOURISM
Maggiore has long been a popular holiday destination. In the 17th century, the illustrious Borromeo family of Milan built opulent palaces and gardens on Isola Bella and Isola Madre. The Lombard aristocracy followed in the 18th and 19th centuries with their splendid villas between Stresa and Arona and, thanks to the mild climate and fertile soil, their gardens flourished. Grand hotels were opened to accommodate wealthy Europeans, and Stresa became a stop on the Grand Tour. The shores also provided inspiration for musicians such as the Italian conductor Arturo Toscanini, and literati, including John Ruskin, Charles Dickens, Lord Byron and Percy Bysshe Shelley from Britain, Gustave Flaubert and Stendhal from France. Queen Victoria and Sir Winston Churchill stayed in Baveno, and the Hotel Des Iles Borromees in Stresa was a popular choice with royalty.

STRESA AND THE BORROMEAN ISLANDS
In Stresa, Baveno and Pallanza, flower-filled promenades have delightful views of the Borromean Islands (Isola Bella, Isola Madre and Isola dei Pescatori). Rising above Stresa and accessible by cable car or toll road, the snowcapped peak of Monte Mottarone commands stunning views, while from the west-shore road between Arona and Stresa, known as The Riviera, you can see across to the eastern shore.

Don't miss The towering fortress of the Rocca Borromeo in Angera; the islands and majestic mountains of the Gulf of Borromeo.

RATINGS				
Good for food	●	●	●	
Good for kids	●	●	●	●	●
Historic interest	●	●	●	●	
Photo stops	●	●	●	●	●

TIP
● The best places to stay are Stresa, Baveno and Pallanza. The resorts further north are quiet but unexciting and, in comparison to the western shore, the eastern shore is scenically dull.

BASICS
➕ 431 D3

Tourist information
Piazza Marconi 16, PO Box 17, 28838 Stresa ☎ 0323 31308 or 0323 30150
🕐 Daily 10–12.30, 3–6.30 summer; Mon–Sat 10–12.30, 3–6 winter

🚆 Trains from Milan 🚌 Buses from Verona 🚤 Boats run to the Borromean Islands every 30 minutes in high season. Ferries to and from other lakeside destinations (Angera, Stresa, Pallanza, Intra)

Statues overlooking the coast of Isola Bella on Lago Maggiore

View overlooking the town of Malcesine on Lago di Garda

Boats moored on Lago d'Iseo

People enjoying refreshment in Orta San Giulio

LAGO DI GARDA

⊞ 434 F4 🛈 Lungolago Regina Adelaide 3, 37016 Garda, tel 045 6270384 📅 Mar–Oct
www.aptgardaveneto.com

The largest and most visited of the Italian lakes, Garda stretches between the Dolomites and the Lombardy Plain, with the regions of Trentino Alto-Adige, the Veneto and Lombardy converging on its shores. The landscape is remarkably diverse: In the north, narrow and fjord-like with dramatic rocks dropping sheer into the deep water; in the south; sea-like, with beaches lining the huge expanse of water. From the early Middle Ages, ruling dynasties identified the strategic importance of the lake, building splendid defences that are visible along its shores today. Although picturesque villages still dot the shorelines and medieval castles rise from the waters, the south in particular has become commercialized.

Lake Garda is 51km (32 miles) long and 17km (11 miles) across at its widest point. Its waters are renowned for their clarity and are warm enough for summer swimming. The daily Ora del Garda wind ensures superb windsurfing and sailing conditions, particularly in the north. Mediterranean flora flourishes in the warm climate, including olive and citrus trees, and the lakeside promenades are lined with palms and pines. A cable car runs up to Monte Baldo. Rising above the eastern shore, the mountain is known as the Garden of Europe.

LAGO D'ISEO

⊞ 431 E3 🛈 Lungolago Marconi 2C/D, 25049 Iseo, tel 030 980209; closed Sat pm and Sun winter 🚉 Iseo 🚢 Seasonal ferry linking Sarnico with Lovere, stopping at towns, villages and Monte Isola
www.bresciaholiday.com

With its wild, mountainous scenery and peaceful villages, Lago d'Iseo—or Sebino, as it is sometimes still called—is a quiet alternative to the larger, more commercialized lakes. Between the provinces of Bergamo to the east and Brescia to the west, Iseo is the seventh largest Italian lake. It is 24km (15 miles) long, averages 2.4km (1.5 miles) across and has the largest lake island (Monte Isola) in Italy. An Ice Age glacier created its characteristic S shape, and the Oglio River feeds it from its source at Passo Gavia in the Camonica Valley.

The attractive hilly region of Franciacorta in the south, renowned for its champagne-style wines, lies between the lake and Brescia. The main town of Iseo, in the south, has a medieval centre, a long, pleasant, tree-shaded promenade, a lido with good sports facilities and the best choice of shops, hotels and campsites on the lake. Clusane, to the west, is a fishing village famous for *tinca ripiena* (stuffed tench), while Sarnico is a popular for sports. Lovere, in the north, is the most appealing town and Pisogne, across the lake, is also worth a detour for the 16th-century frescoes of Girolamo Romanino in the Church of Santa Maria della Neve.

At the hamlet of Zone (turn off the eastern shore road at Marone) is the Riserva Naturale Piramidi di Zone, an extraordinary landscape of erosion pillars, created by weather-beaten debris from glaciers. Tapering at the top, these strange natural formations look like pinnacles, some spectacularly high and others with huge boulders on top. Cislano is the best place from which to admire them.
Don't miss The Riserva Naturale Piramidi di Zone.

LAGO D'ORTA

⊞ 430 C3 🛈 Via Panoramica, Orta San Giulio, 28016, tel 0322 905614 🚉 Orta San Giulio 🚢 Ferry service links the main towns: Easter to mid-Oct; weekends only, rest of year
www.orta.net

Separated from Lago Maggiore by the Mottarone peak, Orta is the westernmost lake in the northwest. With its island and beautifully preserved medieval village of Orta San Giulio, it is arguably the most enchanting of all the pre-Alpine lakes. Legend has it that in the fourth century St. Julius drove away the dragons and serpents from the island in the middle of the lake and founded a church there. From here he preached to the fishermen and the island became the religious heart of the lake, a role that it maintains today.

Measuring 14km (9 miles) in length and around 3km (2 miles) at its broadest point, Orta is tiny compared to the lakes further east. The largest town on the lake is Omegna, in the north. Known chiefly for manufacturing, it still preserves some of its old quarter around Piazza XXIV Aprile. The village of Quarno Sotto, 7km (4 miles) west of Omegna, stands 809m (2,654ft) above sea level and has spectacular views of the lake. In the 19th century the village was renowned worldwide for making wind instruments, some of which can be seen in the local Museo Etnografico e dello Strumento Musicale a Fiato. 20km (12 miles) west is Varallo, a predominantly industrial town dominated by the Sacro Monte, the prototype for the Orta San Giulio's Sacro Monte. This huge complex consists of 45 chapels, over 800 statues and 4,000 paintings of scenes from the life of Christ.
Don't miss The Orta San Giulio's Sacro Monte.

Milano (Milan)

**Italy's most dynamic city, the powerhouse of the country's economy.
One of Europe's richest cities, with chic shopping and cutting-edge style in its galleries, shops and restaurants.
An abundance of historical and artistic heritage and a thriving contemporary cultural scene.**

The magnificent marble façade of Milan's Duomo

A close-up view of the duomo's exterior (above) and the glass-roofed shopping complex of the Galleria Vittorio Emanuele II (right)

RATINGS	
Historic interest	●●●○
Shopping	●●●●●
Specialist shopping	●●●●●
Value for money	●●●○

BASICS

✠ 431 D4

Tourist information
✠ 74 C3 • Via Marconi 1, 20123 Milano
☎ 02 72524301/2/3
⏰ Mon–Sat 8.45–1, 2–6, Sun 9–1, 2–5

🚉 Milano Centrale, Milano Garibaldi, Milano Lambrate, Milano Porta Genova, Milano Nord ✈ Milan Malpensa and Milan Linate

www.milanoinfotourist.com
Crammed with information: extensive accommodation, restaurant, entertainment and shopping listings; full information on museums and public monuments; transport details; up-to-date information on what's going on and how to get the most out of your visit; in English and Italian.

One of the Duomo's many statues

SEEING MILAN

Booming Milan lies in the flat country 48km (30 miles) south of the Alps and 3 hours 30 minutes by fast train northwest of Rome. It is a northern, grey city, with a fast pace of life and efficient infrastructure. Milan is not immediately beguiling, but its architecture reflects its diversity. There are a few medieval and Renaissance buildings, but the style is predominantly neoclassical, art nouveau and modern, and the streets are wide and busy. The historic core lies within three concentric ring roads, and most of the major sights are within the Cerchia dei Navigli, which follows the path of the medieval walls. The Piazza del Duomo is the heart of Milan: it's a good place to get your initial bearings, and most sights are within walking distance. For farther-flung sights, simply hop on a bus, tram or take the metro (p. 50).

HIGHLIGHTS

DUOMO
✠ 74 C2 • Piazza del Duomo, 20123 Milano ☎ 02 86463456 ⏰ Daily 9–7
Milan's duomo is the hub of the city, the world's largest Gothic cathedral and the third largest church in Europe. Building began in 1386 under Duke Gian Galeazzo Visconti and finally finished nearly 500 years later, eight years after Napoleon had himself crowned here. The façade, built of marble from the Lake Maggiore area, is a strange mix of Gothic and baroque. The brass strip on the pavement near the entrance is part of Europe's largest sundial, laid out in 1786. Above the chancel, the crucifix has a nail from Christ's cross, while the nearby crypt contains the remains of St. Charles Borromeo, who worked with Milan's poor in the 16th century. The highlight is the roof itself, a forest of pinnacles and statues with views as far as the Alps.

PINACOTECA DI BRERA
✠ 74 C1 • Via Brera 28, 20123 Milano ☎ 02 722631 ⏰ Tue–Sat 8.30–7.30 🎫 €6.20
Right in the heart of the smart Brera district, the Pinacoteca di

La Scala and Museo la Scala

✚ 74 C2 • Corso Magenta, 20123
Milano ☎ 02 4691528 ⏲ Daily 9–6
(closed for restoration) 🎫 €5

La Scala is one of the world's
most famous opera houses,
designed by Piermarini in 1778,
with an opulent gilt and velvet
interior that can seat over 2,000
people. It remains the social and
cultural focus for the city's rich,
but is under restoration until at
least 2005.

Sant'Ambrogio

✚ 74 A3 • Piazza Sant'Ambrogio 15,
20123 Milano ☎ 02 86450895
⏲ Daily 7–12, 2.30–7

An outstanding Lombard-
Romanesque church, founded in
the fourth century by St.
Ambrose, patron of Milan, whose
remains lie in the crypt. The simple structure, replete with relics,
carving and mosaics, is reached
through a superlative colonnaded
courtyard; outside is Bramante's
Cortile della Canonica.

Brera is Milan's most prestigious art gallery, originally founded by
Napoleon to display loot from churches, convents and displaced aris-
tocrats. The collection is huge, with over 600 works exhibited in 40
rooms, so be selective. The emphasis is on Italian Renaissance painting, and in particular the Venetian schools. Early Renaissance Venetian
works include pictures by Carpaccio and Giovanni and Gentile Bellini,
and there is a striking *Dead Christ* by Bellini's brother-in-law, Andrea
Mantegna, viewed from a vantage point at the soles of Jesus' feet.
There is a lively Veronese *Supper in the House of Simon*, and a more
spiritual *Deposition* by Tintoretto, painted in the 1560s. For a serene
contrast to Venetian drama, don't miss Piero della Francesca's
Madonna with Saints and Federigo di Montefeltro, all harmony and
pellucid greys, and Raphael's sumptuously languid *Marriage of the
Virgin.* For something different again, there is the 17th-century realism
of Caravaggio and Il Pitochetto, a Lombard artist who specialized in
depicting the poor.

SANTA MARIA DELLE GRAZIE

✚ 74 A2 • Piazza Santa Maria delle Grazie, Corso Magenta, 20123 Milano ☎ 02
89421146 ⏲ Tue–Sun 8–7.30; book at least 2 days in advance; visits restricted to 25
people for 15 minutes 🎫 €8

The church of Santa Maria delle Grazie was begun in Gothic style in
the mid-15th century, and altered considerably by Bramante in 1492
when he added the beautiful tribune, serene cloister and massive
dome. What draws the crowds, however, is Leonardo da Vinci's fragile
fresco of the *Last Supper* on one wall of the Old Refectory in the
adjoining monastery. This huge work portrays the scene at the Last
Supper when Christ announces that one of his disciples will betray
him. Da Vinci applied the tempera and oil to dry plaster, rather than

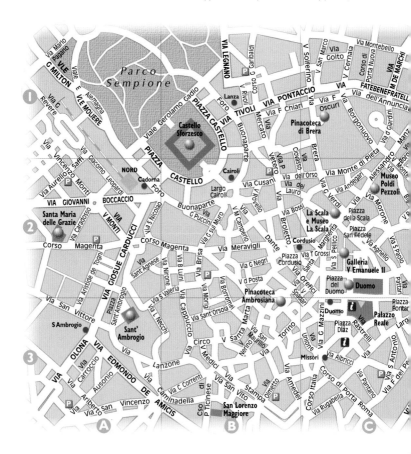

using the more stable, wet-plaster technique, so his work began to deteriorate five years after it was completed. Napoleonic troops used the fresco for target practice and the building was bombed in 1943, but amazingly the fresco survived. The work is fading fast despite continuous restoration, but against the odds, the brilliance of the artist's hand continues to shine through.

CASTELLO SFORZESCO

🗺 74 B1 • Piazza Castello, Milano ☎ 02 6208 3940; Museo 02 88463701 🕐 Tue–Sun 9–5.30 💲 Free

The Castello Sforzesco, built originally by the ruling Visconti family in the 15th century, is one of Milan's major landmarks. Destroyed in the 1440s, it was rebuilt by the Sforzas and, under their patronage, became the heart of one of Europe's most powerful and cultured courts. It was used as a barracks from the 15th century, when the

Galleria Vittorio Emanuele II

🗺 74 C2 • Galleria Vittorio Emanuele II, 20123 Milano

A monumental glass-roofed shopping arcade, built in 1867, which links the Piazza del Duomo with the Piazza della Scala. The central mosaic shows the symbols of the cities of the newly united Italy. It is considered good luck to stand on the testicles of Turin's bull. Lined with expensive bars, cafés and shops, its is a great place for people-watching.

The Museo Nazionale della Scienza e della Tecnica (left) and outside La Scala opera house (right)

Sforzas fell, until it was converted into a museum complex in the 19th century. Artistic highlights include Michelangelo's unfinished *Rondanini Pietà*, sculpted at the end of his life, works by Bellini and Mantegna, and Arcimboldo's 16th-century surrealistic portrait of *Primavera*, an image composed entirely of flowers.

BACKGROUND

Mediolanum fell to Rome in 222BC. It became the seat of the rulers of the Western Empire in AD286, and it was here that Constantine gave his approval to Christianity in AD313. From the 13th to the 16th century, Milan was ruled by dynastic families. Under the rule of the Viscontis, the city became powerful through marriage with other European royal houses, and under the Sforza's, art and culture flourished, enriching the city with some of its finest monuments. The late 16th century saw the start of 300 years of foreign rule by the French, Spanish and Austrians, an era when Milan developed into Italy's economic capital. The city was bombed extensively during World War II, and much of the city has been rebuilt since 1945.

Pinacoteca Ambrosiana

🗺 74 B3 • Piazza Pio XI 2, 20123 Milano ☎ 02 806921 🕐 Tue–Sun 10–5.30 💲 €7.50

Cardinal Federico Borromeo founded this art gallery in the early 17th century. Highlights include Leonardo da Vinci's *Portrait of a Musician,* Raphael's cartoon for the *School of Athens* in the Vatican and Caravaggio's *Basket of Fruit*—purportedly Italy's first still life.

Museo Poldi-Pezzoli

🗺 74 C2 • Via Alessandro Manzoni 12, 20123 Milano ☎ 02 794889 🕐 Tue–Sun 10–6 💲 €6.20

The museum has a fine collection of paintings, jewellery, clocks and *objets d'art*, bequeathed to the city by the 19th-century collector Gian Giacomo Poldo Pezzoli. There are some good Renaissance pictures here, including Pollaiuolo's *Portrait of a Young Woman* and *San Nicola da Tolentino* by Piero della Francesca.

RATINGS

Value for money	● ● ●
Good for kids	● ●
Historic interest	● ● ● ● ●
Photo stops	● ● ● ● ●

BASICS

✚ 430 B3

Tourist information offices
Via Umberto I, 100080 Noasca • Near the town hall ☎ 0124 901070 ⊙ Daily 9–12.30, 2–7

☛ For guided tours tel 0124 901070

🚉 Aosta and Pont Canavese have railway stations

www.parks.it/parco.nazionale.gran.paradiso
The English version of this website picks out points of interest in the park and places to stay and provides itineraries and information on the park's visitor centres, up and coming events and environmental education schemes.

TIP

● In summer the visitor centres organize activities, show films and run trips for children.

A view overlooking Cogne and Valnontey with the Gran Paradiso mountains in the background (above)

PARCO NAZIONALE DEL GRAN PARADISO

Once a hunting reserve of the House of Savoy, now Italy's premier national park.
Spectacular panoramas of mountains and glaciers.

The Parco Nazionale del Gran Paradiso was established in 1922, the first national park in Italy. Surrounding the Gran Paradiso massif, the park extends over some 70,000ha (173,000 acres), shared between the Valle d'Aosta and Piedmont and linked to the Vanoise National Park across the French border. At the heart of the park, the Gran Paradiso massif rises to 4,084m (13,400ft). The scenery is extremely varied: snowcapped mountain peaks and glaciers, flower-filled slopes, high pastures, waterfalls, fast-flowing streams, and forests of larch, pine and fir in the valleys.

THE PARK'S RESORTS

Two of the most popular resorts are Valsavarenche, the main village in the valley of the same name and a starting point for the climb of Gran Paradiso and Grivola (3,969m/13,022ft), and Cogne, the main resort on the Aosta side of the park and another good base for excursions. The park has 450km (280 miles) of tracks. The most popular takes you from Valnontey, near Cogne, up a steep path to the Rifugio Vittorio Sella (2,599m/8,527ft), then on to the Rifugio Sella Herbetet and the head of the valley (full day).

FLORA AND FAUNA

The number of ibex in the park declined drastically in the 1940s, but careful protection has seen numbers rise to around 3,500, and they have now been reintroduced to other parts of the Alps. They are normally seen well above the tree line; one of the best places to observe them is from the pastureland of the Gran Piano di Noasca in the Piedmont section of the park (a beautiful path, with fine views of the Orco Valley, connects Nivolet and the Gran Piano). There are around 6,000 chamois in the park, as well as Alpine marmot and rare birds such as the bearded vulture, which disappeared from here in 1912 and is now returning, thanks to a reintroduction project. Many rare species of Alpine flora can be seen in the Giardino Alpino Paradiso at Valnontey near Cogne. Established in 1955, this garden now supports around 2,000 species of Alpine flora, including the mountain lily (*paradisea liliastrum*). Late spring is the best time to visit to see the flowers, while winter is ideal for cross-country skiing.

The colonnaded portico of the Palazzo Ducale in Mantova

The compact rows of tall, brightly painted houses that line the waterfront of the ancient fortified coastal town of Portovenere

LERICI

✚ 433 E6 🛈 Via Biaggini 6, 19033 Lerici, tel 0187 967346

Surrounded by steep terraced slopes, Lerici is an attractive resort with a seafront lined with elegant villas, gardens, pines, palms and pebble beaches. A former fishing village, its sheltered cove and bay, in the Golfo dei Poeti, was immortalized by the 19th-century English romantic poets Lord Byron and Percy Bysshe Shelley. Byron famously swam from Portovenere across the gulf to visit Shelley, who rented a house in the village of San Terenzo, 2km (1.25 miles) north of Lerici. In 1822, while returning from Livorno to his home on San Terenzo, Shelley drowned (aged 30) when his yacht capsized in a storm near Viareggio.

MANTOVA (MANTUA)

✚ 434 F4 🛈 Piazza Mantegna 6, 46100 Mantova, tel 0376 328253/4 🚉 Mantova www.aptmantova.it

In the heart of the featureless Lombard plain, Mantova's uninspiring outskirts belie a beautifully preserved medieval city which, under the Gonzaga family (1328–1708), grew to be one of the greatest Renaissance courts in Europe.

Life here revolves around three squares. The spacious cobbled Piazza Sordello is flanked on one side by the formidable redbrick walls of the Palazzo Ducale. Home of the Gonzagas, this is a vast complex of buildings, courtyards and gardens between Piazza Sordello and Lake Inferiore. The palace's history spans four centuries, from the end of 13th century to the early 17th century. The oldest parts are the Palazzo del Capitano and the adjacent Magna Domus,

founded by the Bonacolsi family who ruled Mantova from 1271 to 1328. There are over 500 rooms, the most famous being the Camera degli Sposi (Bridal Chamber), decorated with a cycle of frescoes (1474) by Mantegna, glorifying the Gonzaga family *(Tue–Sun 8.45–7.15; ticket office closes 6.30).* Opposite the Palazzo Ducale stand the Palazzo Bianchi (Archbishop's Palace) and the duomo (Cattedrale di San Pietro), whose Romanesque tower is all that remains of the original church *(Daily 7–noon, 3–7).* The interior was rebuilt by Giulio Romano in 1545 after a fire and was richly decorated with 16th- and late 17th-century works of art.

PAVIA

✚ 433 D4 🛈 Via Fabio Filzi 2, 27100, tel 0382 27238/22156 🚉 Pavia and Certosa di Pavia

Fine Romanesque and medieval buildings grace Pavia, but it is the nearby Certosa di Pavia, one of the most extravagant religious complexes in northern Italy, that draws the crowds. In medieval times Charlemagne and Frederick Barbarossa were crowned here and in the 14th century it was taken by the Viscontis of Milan, who built the castle and founded both the university and the Certosa. Pavia's rich heritage of art and architecture is reflected in its Renaissance cathedral, whose architects include Leonardo da Vinci, Bramante and Amadeo, several fine medieval churches and the Visconti castle. The Certosa as it is known, lies 8km (5 miles) north of Pavia, set in former hunting grounds. This monastery was originally founded as a mausoleum by Gian Galeazzo Visconti in 1396. The church's exuberant façade

(1400s–1560) in marble has a profusion of sculpture. Notable works include the frescoes by Bergognone in the transept, chapels and roof vaults and the polyptych by Perugino (1499) in the second chapel on the left *(Tue–Sun 9–11.30, 2.30–4.30; later in summer).*

PORTOVENERE

✚ 433 E6 🛈 Piazza Bastreri 7, 19025 Portovenere, tel 0187 790691 🚢 Catamarans link Genoa and Portovenere (summer). www.waptcinqueterre.sp.it

Almost as picturesque as Portofino, and very much cheaper, Portovenere has an old town and magnificent views to the offshore islets. Its tall, pastel painted houses, built in defensive form, are wedged along the seafront and main street. The steep narrow stairways lead up from the port to the cobbled streets and alleys of the old town, home to the Romanesque church of San Lorenzo. Its prized possession is a revered Madonna Bianca (White Madonna), reputedly washed up on the shores of Lerici.

On the cliff top are the ruins of the Genoese 12th-century Castello di San Lorenzo, worth visiting if only for the magnificent views across the Cinque Terre. San Pietro, the windswept sanctuary on the tip of the promontory, is said to stand on the site of an ancient temple dedicated to Venus. It was built in 1277 in the local style with black and white marble bands.

Boat trips run from Portovenere to the Cinque Terre and the offshore islands: Isola Palmaria, visited for its Blue Grotto; the Isola del Tino, with ruins of a Romanesque abbey; and the tiny Isola del Tinetto, home to the remains of an ancient monastery.

Torino (Turin)

**Splendid baroque architecture, elegant shops and excellent museums.
An important cultural hub with many contemporary art museums and galleries
hosting major exhibitions.**

The racetrack on top of the Lingotto Fiat factory   *The roof tops of Turin*   *Café Torino in Turin*

RATINGS	
Cultural interest	●●●●○
Shopping	●●●○○
Historic interest	●●●●○
Photo stops	●●●○○

TIP
● The Turin card (€15 for 48 hours, €17 for 72 hours) covers 120 museums, monuments, castles and palaces in Turin and Piedmont, plus urban and suburban transport and river trips. It also gives 15–50 per cent reductions on services such as guided tours, car rental and theatre tickets.

SEEING TORINO

Turin lies between the River Po and the foothills of the Alps, a handsome city of palatial baroque residences, fine piazzas, wide boulevards and 18km (11 miles) of arcades. Associated primarily with industry, Turin is often overlooked, but there are plenty of cultural sights and it is excellent for shopping. Besides designer labels, you will find artisan workshops, gastronomic delicacies, antiques and flea markets. Numerous historic cafés serve *gelati* (ice cream), Turin chocolates and *bicerin* (the local drink made of coffee, chocolate and cream), while excellent *trattorie* serve rich Piedmont dishes and wines. Be sure to visit Via Po, off Piazza Castello, with its long arcades and historic palaces and cafés.

HIGHLIGHTS

THE MUSEO EGIZIO AND THE GALLERIA SABAUDA

Palazzo dell'Accademia, Via Accademia delle Scienze 6, 10100 Torino
☎ 011 5617776 ● Tue–Sun 8.30–7.30 ● Museo Egizio €6.50; Galleria Sabauda €4; combined ticket €8

Housed in a vast baroque palace, this is the world's third most important Egyptian museum after those in Cairo and London. Among the great treasures are a black granite statue of Ramses II, the tomb of the architect Kha, and the reconstructed temple of Ellesija. The Galleria Sabauda, in the same building, has an exceptional collection of paintings, begun by the Dukes of Savoy, with works of art by Piedmontese, Tuscan, Lombard and Venetian masters, and a major Flemish and Dutch collection (Van Eyck, Memling, Rembrandt). The museum adjoins Piazza San Carlo, known as the 'the drawing room of Turin'—a baroque square flanked at the far end by the twin churches of San Carlo and Santa Cristina.

PALAZZO CARIGNANO

Piazza San Carlo, 10100 Torino ☎ 011 5621147 ● Museum: Tue–Sun 8.30–7.30
● €6.50

The nearby Palazzo Carignano, designed by Guarino Guarini (1679), was the birthplace of Vittorio Emanuele II in 1820 and the seat of the Subalpine parliament. The Unification of Italy was proclaimed here in

A statue of the Cavaliere d'Italia in Piazza Castello

1861. It is now home to the Museo del Risorgimento. You can also wander around the royal apartments and the outstanding Royal Armoury (separate entrance) of the Palazzo Reale, built by the princess of the House of Savoy *(Royal apartments Tue–Sun 8.30–9.30; garden daily 9–7).*

GALLERIA CIVICA D'ARTE MODERNA E CONTEMPORANEA

Via Magenta 31, 20100 Torino ☎ 011 5629911 ⏰ Tue–Sun 9–7 🎫 Adult €5.50, child (10–25) €3, child (under 10) free

If you like modern art, seek out the Galleria Civica d'Arte Moderna e Contemporanea (GAM), northwest of the station. It has 15,000 works of art, mainly by Italian artists, including pieces by Modigliani, De Chirico, Paul Klee and Andy Warhol.

MOLE ANTONELLIANA

Via Montebello 20, 10100 Torino ☎ 011 8125658 ⏰ Tue–Sun 9–8, Sat 9–11 🎫 Museum: Adult €5.20, child (under 10) free. Lift: Adult €3.62, child (under 10) free. Combined ticket: Adult €6.80, child (10–16) €5.20, child (under 10) free

Turin's answer to Paris's Eiffel Tower is 167m (548ft) high. Built between 1798 and 1888, it now houses an outstanding museum tracing the history of cinema. Displays include stage sets, dramatic lighting effects and film projections. A panoramic lift takes you up to the top.

BACKGROUND

In 1574, the House of Savoy made Torino its capital and remained here for the next eight centuries, shaping the baroque palaces, wide boulevards and splendid squares visible today. After Italian Unification, Torino-born Vittorio Emanuele II was proclaimed the first king of Italy in 1861 and ruled until 1865. Giovanni Agnelli founded Fiat here in 1899, and the Lingotto, the ex-Fiat car factory designed in 1914–16, has been transformed by Renzo Piano into a vast conference, exhibition and shopping space with an art gallery, the Pinacoteca Giovanni e Marella Agnelli, on top. Turin will host the winter Olympic Games in 2006, prompting the development of a new metro network in the town.

BASICS

✚ 432 C4

Tourist information office
Piazza Castello 161, 10021 ☎ 011 535181/53590 ⏰ Mon–Sat 9.30–7, Sun 9.30–5

🎫 Guided tours for individuals or groups tel 011 535181/535901

Ⓜ A metro line is under construction
🚌 The city is served by a network of buses, trams and a funicular. Tickets are sold at stations, tabacchi, etc. A tourist bus takes visitors around the city with a guide (departs from Piazza Castello)
🚆 The city is a major rail terminus. Regular trains run to and from Milan (1 hour 15 minutes)
✈ Torino Caselle Airport is 16km (10 miles) north of the city centre, accessible by a regular bus service

www.comune.torino.it
This website run by the city of Turin has a great deal of information in English and other European languages including accommodation listings, pointers on transport to and from Turin and getting around the city, visitor itineraries, guided tours, stuff for children and useful contacts.

Rapallo's palm-fringed bay

The Romanesque bell tower (1113) of the Santa Orso rising up above the Collegiata (collegiate church) in Aosta

THE SIGHTS

RAPALLO

➕ 433 D6 ℹ️ Lungomare Via Veneto 7, 16034 Rapallo, tel 0185 230346; daily 9.30–12.30, 3–7.30 summer 🚉 Rapallo

Rapallo's bay overlooks the Gulf of Tigullio and is protected by the surrounding mountains. Its temperate climate and natural beauty attracted the wealthy here in the early part of the last century, and in the 1920s it became a haunt of the literati. Authors D. H. Lawrence and Ernest Hemingway stayed here briefly and the American poet Ezra Pound lived here for 20 years, working on *A Draft of XXX Cantos*.

At the end of a promenade, lined with palm trees, orange trees and open-air cafés, stands the 16th-century castle. Built to protect the town against the Saracens, it is now an exhibition centre. In the hills behind Rapallo, overlooking the valley and bay, the Santuario di Montallegro was built in the 16th century to protect a Byzantine icon of the Madonna that miraculously appeared here in 1557 (*Daily 7–12.30, 2.30–6 (8 in summer*).

RIVIERA DI LEVANTE

➕ 433 D6 ℹ️ Piazza Matteotti 9, 17121 Genova, tel 010 5308201 🚉 Santa Margherita Ligure www.turismo.liguriainrete.it

This stretch of coastline between Genova and La Spezia is bordered by rugged mountains and hills cloaked in pine, olives and vines. Subtropical trees and flowers, form a lush backdrop to the resorts and tiny fishing villages that cling to the cliffs.

The most attractive section of the Riviera is the Cinque Terre (p. 69), whose fishing villages have kept their picturesque charm. East of Genova most of the rugged Portofino promontory is a

national park. A retreat for the rich and famous, Portofino has an idyllic natural harbour, with pastel-washed houses and a piazza overlooked by chic but notoriously pricey cafés, restaurants and designer boutiques. Down the road from Portofino is Santa Margherita Ligure, a fashionable, but slightly more affordable resort. La Spezia in the far east, the largest naval base in the country, is worth a visit for its Pinacoteca Civica Amedeo Lia, a Franciscan convent converted into an art gallery with works by Bellini, Titian, Tintoretto, Veronese and other great Italian masters (*Tue–Sun 10–6*).

SACRA DI SAN MICHELE

➕ 432 B4 • Abbazia Sacra di San Michele, 10651 Avigliana ☎ 011 939130 🕐 Mon–Fri 9–12, 3–6, Sat and Sun 12–1, 2-7; closed Sat–Sun in winter 💶 Adult €2.50, child (under 14) €1.50 🚉 Avigliana (26km/16 miles and 30 minutes west of Turin). www.sacradisanmichele.com

This ancient monastery perches spectacularly on a spur halfway up Monte Pirchiriano at 962m (3,156ft), 18km (11 miles) from the ancient town of Avigliana. Founded as a small church in 983–986 by Hughes de Montboissier from Auvergne, the monastery was entrusted to five Benedictine monks. It was enlarged in the 12th century with the addition of a five-apsed church and soon became a pilgrimage church for worshippers en route to Rome. The complex began to decline in the 14th century and suffered French attacks in the 17th century, but it has undergone major renovations since. The fortress-like church is accessed via 154 steps cut into the rock, gruesomely named Scalone dei Morti (Stairway of the Dead) after restorers discovered skeletons of monks in the

walls. Inside, the church has a high altar by the Piedmontese artist Defendente Ferrari and a fresco of *The Assumption* (1505) in the left aisle, painted mainly by Secondo del Bosco di Poirino.

TORINO

p. 78–79

VALLE D'AOSTA

➕ 430 B3 ℹ️ Piazza Chanoux 2, 11100 Aosta, tel 0165 236627 www.regione.vda.it/turismo

The Aosta Valley, dominated by Alpine peaks, is a region of finely preserved medieval castles, traditional villages and monumental Roman remains. In 1948 it was granted semi-autonomous status in recognition of its French culture and language. The region encompasses the towering peaks of the French and Swiss Alps, Mont Blanc, Monte Rosa, the Matterhorn and Gran Paradiso, whose snow-covered slopes are ideal for winter sports. The most popular resort is Courmayeur, both for winter sports and as a summer base for excursions by car, foot or cable car. The valley is famous for its castles in the southeast, built in the Middle Ages by ruling families both as military outposts and palatial residences. The finest are Fenis, Issogne and Verres.

Aosta, capital of the Valle d'Aosta, is an industrial town and popular with visitors. The town, enhanced by its mountain setting, makes a good base for trips to the Parco Nazionale del Gran Paradiso (p. 76) and Valle del Gran San Bernardo. It is often called the Rome of the Alps, and its long stretches of city walls, Porta Pretoria (gateway), Roman theatre, Arch of Augustus and Roman forum all impressively illustrate its ancient past.

VENICE

Arguably Italy's most compellingly beautiful city, Venice is unique, a city built on water in the midst of a lagoon, with a plethora of churches and museums to experience. Its heart is Piazza San Marco and the great Basilica di San Marco, while elsewhere stately palaces line the canals and tantalizing streets and squares invite exploration.

MAJOR SIGHTS

Basilica di San Marco

**The great Byzantine-Venetian basilica—a reflection of Venice's historic role as a bridge between East and West.
The spiritual heart of Venice and the focal point of the Piazza di San Marco.
One of the world's finest medieval buildings, filled with
mosaics and precious objects.**

Crowded benches in front of the massive portals and bronze doors

The main cupola with a detailed mosaic depicting the Ascension

A view of the five domes from the Campanile

RATINGS	
Historic interest	●●●●●
Cultural interest	●●●●○
Photo stops	●●●●○
Value for money	●●●●○

TIPS

● Cover your arms and shoulders when visiting the basilica.

● Queues start to build up by about 9.30am and the wait can be more than an hour, so get there early. It tends to get quieter just before closing time.

● You can get access to the basilica for prayers from 8am via the side door (off Piazzetta dei Leoncini).

SEEING THE BASILICA DI SAN MARCO

The best approach is by foot from the west end of the Piazza (*vaporetto* stop Vallaresso). Aim to arrive early before the queues build up, and be prepared to wait. There's a fixed route round the interior. Allow your eyes to accustom to the low light levels, and take your time; this is an overwhelming building.

HIGHLIGHTS

THE LOGGIA
For a superb overview of the basilica, climb the steep stairs from the atrium to the gallery, where you'll find yourself at eye level with the mosaics (see below). From here you can gain access out onto the Loggia, a splendid vantage point from which to view the piazza.

THE BRONZE HORSES
Also here are replicas of the famous bronze horses (the originals are inside). These powerfully evocative creatures were looted from Constantinople in 1204 and are the only surviving four-horse chariot group from antiquity. They were thought to have been made for the Hippodrome in the third century, but they could be as much as 500 years older. Apart from a brief spell in Paris in the Napoleonic years, they have stood at San Marco for 800 years.

THE MOSAICS
The Sant'Alipio doorway, one of five leading to the atrium, is the only door with an original 13th-century mosaic. In the glittering darkness, shafts of light and slanting sunbeams illuminate more than 4,000sq m (43,000sq ft) of mosaics illustrating stories from the Bible. The early Byzantine-Venetian examples are the finest and include the Pentecost dome, nearest the entrance, the Ascension in the central dome, and Christ Emmanuel in the eastern dome. Old as it looks, the great Christ Pantocrator above the apse is actually a faithful 16th-century copy of the 11th-century original.

The throngs in Piazza San Marco admiring the fabulous façade

A glittering mosaic on the arch surmounting one of the portals

BASICS

✚ 422 C3 • Piazza San Marco, San Marco, 30124 Venezia

☎ Pala d'Oro and Tesoro: 041 522 5697. Loggia: 041 522 5205

🕐 Basilica, Tesoro and Pala d'Oro Mon–Sat 10–6, Sun 2–5. Loggia daily 9–5.30

💶 Basilica, Tesoro and Pala d'Oro €1.50. Loggia €1.20 (no reductions). Tickets can be booked at www.alata.it

🚤 *Vaporetto*: Vallaresso/San Zaccaria

📖 Wide range at various prices. *Electa* is the best of those published in Italy; it covers various specific sights in Venice (available at the Palazzo Ducale)

🎫 Stalls in atrium and Loggia selling postcards, religious souvenirs and tourist guides to Venice

THE PALA D'ORO

The focal point at ground level is the iconostasis, a marble Byzantine screen that hides the chancel and high altar. The remains of St. Mark lie beneath the altar, which is backed by the Pala d'Oro, an opulent gold and silver altarpiece. Made by a Sienese master in 1342, it is covered with more than 3,000 precious stones and 80 enamel plaques, many of which date from the 10th to 12th centuries.

CHAPEL OF THE MADONNA NICOPEIA AND THE TREASURY

To the left of the Pala d'Oro is the Chapel of the Madonna Nicopeia, a tiny, much-revered 12th-century Byzantine icon, and there is more Byzantine work in the Treasury. Look out for the 12th-century incense censer in the shape of a domed church.

BACKGROUND

The present basilica, built between 1063 and 1094, is the third to occupy this site. The original was built in 832 to house the remains of St. Mark the Evangelist, brought by merchants from Alexandria to become the city's patron saint. During the 11th century, Venice was influenced culturally by Byzantium, hence the centralized Greek cross plan and multiple domes of the newer church. The interior also owes much to the East, while the façade was altered between the 11th and 15th centuries with the addition of Gothic-style marble columns and carved stonework.

The upper portion of the red-brick Campanile, 99m (325ft) high, viewed from Piazza San Marco (far left). Begun in 912, it also doubled as a lighthouse. It had to be totally rebuilt after collapsing in 1902, and was reopened to the public in 1912

Canal Grande
•

**Take a boat ride along one of the world's most mesmerizing waterways.
A host of magnificent *palazzi* and churches line its famous banks.
Sit back and watch the water traffic that keeps Venice alive and on the move.**

The Canal Grande—a waterway for traditional and modern boats

The Ponte di Rialto is illuminated at night

Gondolas on the Canal Grande near San Marco

THE SIGHTS

RATINGS	
Good for kids	●●●●●
Historic interest	●●●●●
Cultural interest	●●●●●
Photo stops	●●●●●

TIPS

● The *vaporetto* is the cheapest and probably most entertaining way of seeing the Canal Grande. Gondolas; a water taxi is a more expensive options.

● It is best to begin at the station end and keep San Marco for the end of the trip.

● For the best chance of getting a good vantage point (and a seat) get on at Piazzale Roma.

● *Vaporetti* can be very crowded, particularly during the morning and evening rush hours. The best time is between 12.30 and 3 (siesta), along with very early or late in the day.

● Few palazzi along the Canal Grande are floodlit, but a night ride is still a great experience.

SEEING THE CANAL GRANDE

Bisecting the city, the Canal Grande is Venice's main thoroughfare, a sinuous waterway lined with a procession of glorious buildings spanned by three bridges. It is 4km (2.5 miles) long and varies in width from 30m to 70m (100ft to 230ft), with an average depth of around 5m (16ft). Three *sestiere* (city districts)—Cannaregio, San Marco and Castello—lie to the east of the canal, with three more—San Polo, Santa Croce and Dorsoduro—to the west. Along its length are *traghetti* stations, from where gondolas ply back and forth across its width. There are few places where you can walk or sit beside the canal; the best places are at the railway station, at San Marcuola and Santa Sofia, by the Ponte di Rialto, on Campo San Vio, in front of Santa Maria della Salute and at San Marco. The best way to appreciate it is to board the No. 1 *vaporetto* at Piazzale Roma or Ferrovia and relax as far as Vallaresso or San Zaccaria. The whole trip takes 45 minutes.

HIGHLIGHTS

FERROVIA TO RIALTO

The present 1950s railway station *(ferrovia)* replaced the original 1846 construction, built when the causeway to the mainland was created; the stone-built Ponte dei Scalzi went up in 1934. On the right is the domed church of San Simeone Piccolo (1738) and on the left is the ornate façade of the Scalzi (1656), followed shortly by the entrance to the wide Canale di Cannaregio, the gateway to Venice in its pre-causeway days. The brick church soon after this is San Marcuola, unfinished since the money ran out in the 18th century; the two impressive buildings opposite are the Fondaco dei Turchi, trading headquarters for the Turks in Republican days, and the Deposito dei Megio, once a granary. In winter, the Casino moves to the Renaissance Palazzo Vendramin Calergi, where Richard Wagner died in 1883. Opposite, to the left, is the white baroque façade of San Stae. Two highlights are Longhena's Ca' Pesaro on the right (1652), now housing the Museo d'Arte Moderna *(Tue–Sun 10–6, Mar–Oct; Tue–Sun 10–5, rest of year; tel 041 5240695)*, and the Gothic Ca' d'Oro (p. 86). Across the water lie the *pescheria* (fish market) and Rialto market stalls; the long building beside them is the

A water taxi (left) and two gondolas (right) moored on the Canal Grande

Tribunale Nuove (1555), now the Assize Court. Opposite, on the left, is the Fondaco dei Tedeschi, once home to German merchants, and overhead is the graceful sweep of the Ponte di Rialto.

RIALTO TO ACCADEMIA
Highlights on the next stretch are the Gothic 13th-century Palazzo Barzizza (right), and the Palazzo Mocenigo (left), where Byron lived in 1818. The sweeping bend is called La Volta, after which the huge Palazzo Giustinian and Ca' Rezzonico (p. 86) are on the right, along with the 18th-century Palazzo Grassi, one of Venice's prime exhibition venues. More Gothic façades follow before the Accademia and its bridge (1932) come into view (p. 88–89).

ACCADEMIA TO SAN MARCO
Below the bridge, Campo San Vio fronts the water on the right, followed by Palazzo Barbarigo, decorated with 19th-century mosaics, and the Palazzo Venier dei Leoni, home to the Guggenheim Collection. Opposite is the Ca' Grande, designed by Sansovino in 1545, followed by some of Venice's grandest hotels. Look for the tiny Gothic Palazzo Dario on the right as the great plague church of Santa Maria della Salute approaches. The canal ends at the Dogana di Mare (customs), opposite which are the Giardini Reali, laid out by Napoleon, and the glories of San Marco.

BACKGROUND
Running northwest to southeast, the Canal Grande was originally the main thoroughfare for merchants approaching the Rialto. An uninterrupted sequence of palazzi and churches lines the canal, their façades lapped by water. Built across four centuries, these superlative buildings cover the whole span of Venetian styles of architecture.

BASICS

✠ 422 C3

🚤 *Vaporetti*: Piazzale Roma, Ferrovia, Riva de Biasio, San Marcuola, San Stae, Ca' d'Oro, Rialto, San Silvestro, Sant' Angelo, San Tomà, San Samuele, Ca' Rezzonico, Accademia, Giglio, Salute

A statue from the Guggenheim collection housed in the 18th-century Palazzo Venier dei Leoni on the Canal Grande

Bright houses reflected in the waters of Burano's canal

Gothic arches under the staircase leading up from the courtyard at the Ca' d'Oro palace

THE SIGHTS

BURANO

✚ 423 off F1 ℹ Piazza San Marco 71f, San Marco, 30120 Venezia, tel 041 529 8740 ◷ Daily 9.30–3.30 ⛴ *Vaporetto*: Burano
www.provincia.venezia.it

For a change of pace, Burano is an island tucked away in the northern lagoon, whose brilliantly painted houses and miniature canals provide some of Venice's best photographic opportunities. Burano, and Mazzorbo next door, were among the first settlements in the lagoon. As Venice proper boomed, Mazzorbo declined, but Burano thrived as a fishing community, where the men went to sea and the women stayed home to make gossamer-fine lace, once famous all over Europe. The *rii* (canals) are still busy with boats and all the paraphernalia of fishing, and the *fondamente* (streets along the canals) are lined with houses of varying shades. Lace is still on offer everywhere, although few women make the real thing now; you can see it at the Scuola di Merletti, established in the 1870s in an attempt to preserve the skills for generations.
Don't miss The morning fish market; the fish restaurants along Via Galuppi, the main street.

CA' D'ORO

✚ 422 C2 • Calle della Ca' d'Oro, Cannaregio, 3939 Venezia ☎ 041 523 8790 ◷ Mon 8.15–1.30, Tue–Sun 8.15–7.15 🎟 Adult €3, child (under 12) free ◻ Overlooking the sculpture garden ⊞ ⛴ *Vaporetto*: Line 1 Ca' d'Oro
www.cadoro.org

One of the city's finest and most flamboyant examples of a Gothic palazzo, the Ca' d'Oro (Gold House) stands over the Canal Grande just above the Rialto. It was built for the Contarini family in the early 15th century, but changed hands repeatedly until it

was heavily (and badly) restored in the 1850s by the Russian Prince Troubetskoy. Forty years later, Baron Franchetti bought and restored it, filling it with his painting, sculpture and coin collections. As a result, the ground floor regained its medieval layout, with a courtyard, tiny pleasure garden and main door opening on to the water. An exterior staircase leads to the upper floors, where the family lived. These floors, imaginatively converted into light and airy galleries, now house the collections, and have beautiful Gothic loggias overlooking the canal. Artistic highlights include Andrea Mantegna's powerful *St. Sebastian* and the ghostly fragments of frescoes by Giorgione that once decorated the nearby Fondaco dei Tedeschi.
Don't miss Views of the water traffic on the Canal Grande from the upper loggias; the 15th- and 16th-century Flemish tapestries.

CA' REZZONICO

✚ 422 B4 ℹ Fondamenta Rezzonico, Dorsoduro, 3136 Venezia ☎ 041 241 0100 ◷ Wed–Mon 10–6, Apr–Oct; Tue–Sun 10–5, rest of year 🎟 €6.50 ⛴ *Vaporetto*: Ca' Rezzonico
www.comune.venezia.it/museicivici

This grandiose palazzo on the Canal Grande is now a museum devoted to the hedonistic, dying days of the Republic. Emerging from a lengthy restoration in 2001, the Ca' Rezzonico, with its huge rooms, gilded stuccowork, frescoed ceilings and opulent textiles, is a fabulous expression of patrician wealth.

As you glimpse the façade from the canal or walk through the courtyard you can see why the building costs of the palazzo virtually bankrupted the Bons, who commissioned Baldassare Longhena to design the building in 1667. Seventy years later, the unfinished palazzo was acquired

by the Rezzonicos, who poured money into the building and decor. Its most original architectural feature is the ballroom. Two floors high, this immense space was the scene for some of the 18th century's most prestigious events. From here, a series of ornately decorated, interconnecting rooms fans out, each furnished with fine contemporary pieces. Highlights include the Tiepolo ceiling panels in the Throne Room and Nuptial Room, the flower-decorated Murano glass chandeliers, and furniture designed by Andrea Brustolon. In the gallery look for the quirky genre paintings by Pietro Longhi and the superb Tiepolo panels from Villa Zianigo, the painter's home. The Pulcinella (Carnival Clown) scenes will charm, but it is the surreal Mondo Novo (New World) panels that will linger in the memory.

CAMPO SANTA MARGHERITA

✚ 422 B3–4 ℹ Campo Santa Margherita, Dorsoduro, 2618 Venezia ⛴ *Vaporetto*: Ca' Rezzonico

At the heart of the *sestiere* (district) of Dorsoduro, Campo Santa Margherita is one of Venice's liveliest squares. Browse the morning market stalls, sit in the cafés, eat one of the best ice-creams in the city (at Causin), eavesdrop on raucous local housewives and mingle with the university crowd—all in all, a slice of Venetian life.

The square is surrounded by old Gothic houses, many dating from the 14th century. The central expanse is broken by market stalls, trees and benches, while in the middle there is an oddly shaped small building, the Scuola dei Varoteri, once the headquarters of the tanners' guild. At the north end stands the church of Santa Margherita, which has been

The palace of Ca' Rezzonico from the Canal Grande

Market stalls in the Campo Santa Margherita, the heart of the Dorsoduro district

beautifully restored and now forms part of the university. Look for the St. Margaret's dragon on the campanile and, on the façade of a house at the same end of the square, the saint standing on the beast. At the opposite end, past the vegetable and fish stalls and the interesting shops, you will find the entrance to the Scuola dei Carmini (p. 102).

CANAL GRANDE

p. 84–85.

COLLEZIONE PEGGY GUGGENHEIM

✚ 422 B4 • Palazzo Venier dei Leoni (entrance on Fondamenta Venier), Dorsoduro, 701 Venezia ☎ 041 240 5411 🕐 Wed–Mon 10–6 🎫 Adult €8, child (under 12) free 🚤 Vaporetto: 82 direction Lido to Accademia 🍴 Snacks and lunches overlooking the sculpture garden 🏛
www.guggenheim-venice.it

The Palazzo Venier is one of the Canal Grande's most eccentric buildings, an oddity whose construction began in 1759 but had progressed only as far as the first storey before the Venier money ran out. Its bizarre appearance appealed to the rich American millionairess Peggy Guggenheim (1898–1979), who realized its potential as a showcase for her collection. She began collecting contemporary art in the 1920s, buying from and dealing in the works of a whole generation of innovative abstract and surrealist artists. She married one of the great exponents, Max Ernst in 1941, but divorced him in 1946 and moved to Venice. Now administered by the Guggenheim Foundation, the collection is one of Venice's top attractions, its sculpture, paintings and furniture the perfect antidote to an excess of Byzantine, Gothic and Renaissance art.

The light-filled rooms are approached through a garden court, scattered with sculptures by such artists as Alberto Giacometti (1901–66) and Henry Moore (1898–1986), all shaded by trees and greenery. Examples of work by all the big names of the early and mid-20th-century movements of cubism, surrealism, abstract expressionism and constructivism adorn the walls. Look for works by Marc Chagall, Jackson Pollock, Paul Klee, Max Ernst, Alexander Calder, Joseph Cornell and Marino Marini, whose startling Angel of the Citadel is on the terrace overlooking the canal.

GALLERIA DELL'ACCADEMIA

p. 88–89.

GESUITI

✚ 422 C2 • Campo dei Gesuiti, Cannaregio, 30121Venezia ☎ 041 528 6579 🕐 Mon–Sat 10–noon, Sun 4–6 🚤 Vaporetto: Fondamenta Nove

Fans of baroque architecture must not miss the Jesuit Church of Santa Maria Assunta, known as the Gesuiti. The Jesuits, with their close ties to the papacy, were never popular in Venice and it was not until 1715 that they commissioned Domenico Rossi to build a church. He made up for the delay by going for maximum impact—a church with a vast façade and a mind-bogglingly ornate interior.

Inside you are struck by the baldachin over the altar, modelled on Bernini's version in St. Peter's in Rome, and festoons of drapery that billow from every corner and decorate every inch of wall space. What appear to be swags and drapes of figured damask and brocaded velvet are actually intricately carved and polished pieces of green and white marble. With scarcely a corner unadorned, it all adds up to a visual feast that is far more memorable than the comparatively pedestrian paintings by Palma il Giovane in the sacristy. The best painting, though badly lit and hard to see, is a night scene by Titian, the Martyrdom of St. Lawrence, over the first altar on the left.

GIUDECCA

✚ 422 B5 🚤 Vaporetto: Santa Eufemia, Palanc, Redentore, Zitelle

Take a boat across the Giudecca canal to escape the crowds, explore a unique part of the city and visit one of Palladio's finest churches. During the ninth century the island of the Giudecca began to develop as a location for the richly decorated summer palazzi of the aristocracy. By the 19th century it had become the city's industrial area, filled with boatyards and factories. Over the past 50 years, industry has declined and the Giudecca is today largely a residential area, with a diverse population and its own distinctive way of life.

A broad fondamenta runs along the canal on the north side of the island, which is where you will find the main sights: the churches of the Redentore (Mon–Sat 10–5, Sun 3–5), built by Palladio in 1577 in thanks for Venice's deliverance from the bubonic plague, and the Zittelle and Santa Eufemia. You will also find rows of local food shops, bars and restaurants, modest houses and grand 14th-century palazzi.

At the west end is the vast red-brick bulk of the Molino Stucky, a former flour mill built in the 1890s. The mill closed in 1954 and there have been endless discussions concerning its future; some of the building has already been converted into luxury apartments and there are plans for a cultural forum. At the other end is the Cipriani, Venice's most expensive hotel.

Galleria dell'Accademia

**One of the world's great specialist collections.
Comprehensive overview of the very best of Venetian painting.
Well displayed in three historic buildings.**

A painter at the bottom of Ponte Accademia *Part of the* St. Ursula Cycle *by Vittore Carpaccio*

RATINGS	
Historic interest	● ● ●
Cultural interest	● ● ● ● ●
Specialist shopping	● ● ● ●
Value for money	● ● ● ●

TIPS

● Staffing shortages mean that sometimes certain rooms are closed, so if there is something specific that you want to see, ask before you buy your ticket.

● The €11 combined ticket for the Gallerie Academia, Ca' d'Oro (p. 86) and Museo Orientale is a good bargain.

● You can book timed tickets if you don't want to stand in line *(Mon–Fri 9–6, Sat 9–2, tel 041 520 0345)*.

SEEING THE GALLERIA DELL'ACCADEMIA

The Accademia's 24 rooms take a couple of hours to see properly. Pick up a plan from the entrance desk, and if you're interested in art, an audioguide. Visit early or late to avoid the crowds—it is particularly busy on Sundays.

HIGHLIGHTS

THE SAN GIOBBE ALTARPIECE BY GIOVANNI BELLINI—ROOM 3
By the mid-15th century, the Bellini family had developed the concept of the *sacra conversazione*, a unified composition of the Madonna and saints. This superb altarpiece, all architectural detail, balance and warmth, is a prime example, painted at the time of the 1478 plague.

LA TEMPESTA BY GIORGIONE—ROOM 5
Giorgione's contribution to the development of Venetian painting was huge. In this, his most enigmatic work, its iconography still unsolved, we see the growing importance of realistic landscape and light—a far cry from the rigid gold used just over a century before.

CHRIST IN THE HOUSE OF LEVI BY VERONESE—ROOM 10
Figures stand out against a background of classical architecture in this stupendous set piece. The painting was originally titled *The Last Supper*, but was judged so secular by its patrons that Veronese faced heresy charges if he failed to change it; cleverly, he simply changed the name.

MIRACLE OF ST. MARK FREEING THE SLAVE BY TINTORETTO
Tintoretto's technical wizardry still shocks in this picture of the hurtling figure of St. Mark swooping down to help a persecuted slave, painted for the Scuola Grande di San Marco in 1547.

A further part of the St. Ursula Cycle *by Vittore Carpaccio*

The San Giobbe altarpiece (1487) by Giovanni Bellini

GALLERY GUIDE

The rooms are arranged chronologically except for 19–24, which are specific collections.

Room 1: The Primitives—Byzantine and international Gothic gold-ground paintings, typified by Paolo Veneziano.
Rooms 2–3: 15th-century altarpieces and works by the Bellini family, Sebastiano del Piombo, Cima de Conegliano and Carpaccio.
Rooms 4–5: Giovanni Bellini, Mantegna, Piero della Francesca, Cosmè Tura and Giorgione.
Rooms 6 and 10: Titian, Jacopo Tintoretto and Paolo Veronese—the Venetian superstars.
Rooms 7–8: Lorenzo Lotto, Romanino and Jacopo Palma il Vecchio.
Room 11: Veronese and Tiepolo.
Rooms 14–18: The 17th and 18th centuries: pictures and genre paintings by Tiepolo, Canaletto, Bellotto, Guardi, Pietro Longhi and Rosalba Carriera.
Rooms 19–20: Stories of the Relic of the Cross by Vittore Carpaccio, Gentile Bellini and others.
Rooms 21–22: *St. Ursula Cycle* by Vittore Carpaccio.
Room 23: Former church of Santa Maria della Carità with 15th-century paintings by the Bellini and Vivarini families.
Room 24: Former Albergo Room of Santa Maria della Carità.

DISCOVERY OF THE TRUE CROSS BY GIAMBATTISTA TIEPOLO—ROOM 11

Painted for a church in Castello, now destroyed, this ceiling panel perfectly embodies Tiepolo's style—dizzying perspective, startling light and sugary, light-hearted hues.

PROCESSION IN THE PIAZZA DI SAN MARCO BY GENTILE BELLINI—ROOM 20

Created in 1496, this work shows the Piazza di San Marco as it was more than 500 years ago, with St. Mark's and the Doge's Palace much as they appear today. Carpaccio's painting of the Rialto nearby makes a good contrast, as there is little that's recognizable in the 21st century.

ST. URSULA CYCLE BY VITTORE CARPACCIO—ROOM 22

Crammed with charming anecdotes and details, the *St. Ursula Cycle* was painted in around 1498. It's the complicated tale, mixing reality and imagination, of a princess who, accompanied by her fiancé and 11,000 virgins, attempted to cross Europe to Rome, only to be massacred in Cologne.

PRESENTATION OF THE VIRGIN BY TITIAN—ROOM 24

This beautiful picture, painted between 1534 and 1539 for the Scuola della Carità, still hangs in its original position. The composition balances landscape, architecture and figures, with the small figure of the Virgin ascending the stairway.

BACKGROUND

The Accademia di Belle Arte, which houses the Galleria dell'Accademia, was founded in 1807 under Napoleon, who had suppressed dozens of churches and monasteries and needed somewhere to house their artworks. The art school still exists, but today the Accademia is primarily known as one of Europe's finest specialized art collections. It takes over three connected former religious buildings, the Scuola Grande della Carità, its adjacent church of Santa Maria, and the monastery of the Lateran Canons.

BASICS

🗺 422 B4 • Campo Carità, Dorsoduro, 1050 Venezia ☎ 041 522 2247
🕐 Mon 8.15–2, Tue–Sun 8.15–7.15
💶 Adult €6.50, child (under 18) free
🚤 *Vaporetto*: Line 1 and 82 to Accademia
🎧 Tours in English and Italian, Mon–Sat 11–1, 3.30–5, Sun 10–2, tel 041 522 2247. Audiotours in English, Italian, French and German, €4
📖 Full and short illustrated guides in Italian, English, French, Spanish, German and Japanese, €15.50 and €8.20
🏪 One shop and a stall selling good postcards, prints, good-quality gifts and art books (mainly on Renaissance art and artists)
🚻 ♿

www.artive.arti.beniculturali.it
www.gallerieaccademia.org

THE SIGHTS

The roof and dome of the church of Madonna dell'Orto (above) and a close up view of the statues lining the roof of the church (left)

MADONNA DELL'ORTO

One of Venice's most unspoiled churches.
Contains some of Tintoretto's most compelling work.

The original church was founded at the end of the 14th century. It was dedicated to St. Christopher, the patron saint of voyagers, in the hope that he would keep an eye on the ferry service to the northern islands and the gondolas that ran from the jetty. He was demoted in 1377 when a statue of the Madonna and Child, which was said to be miraculous and which had been attracting a following in a nearby vegetable garden, was moved here. This Madonna still stands in the Chapel of San Mauro, while St. Christopher presides over the main door. The church was rebuilt between 1399 and 1473. Tintoretto's 16th-century paintings on the choir, apse and side walls represent 30 years of his working life. After the 1966 floods, this church was the first major restoration project funded by the British Venice in Peril Fund, and its first chairman, Sir Ashley Clarke, is commemorated by a plaque in the chapel near the main altar.

THE FAÇADE
Overlooking its own square and a canal, the beautiful Gothic façade has similarities to those of the Frari and Santi Giovanni e Paolo (p. 99), but the false gallery at the top is unique. The figure of St. Christopher is by Nicolò di Giovanni and the portal by Bartolomeo Bon. Rising behind is a splendid onion-shaped cupola, balanced by a slender campanile, one of the prominent landmarks of the northern lagoon.

THE PAINTINGS
The three naves draw the eye towards the chancel, site of two huge canvases by Tintoretto, the *Making of the Golden Calf* and the *Last Judgement*, fine examples of movement, light and drama. In the apse are the *Beheading of St. Christopher* and *St. Peter's Vision of the Cross*, both full of swooping angels, while the right aisle's mystical *Presentation of the Virgin in the Temple* provides a peaceful contrast. Radiant blues shine in *St. Agnes* in the Contarini Chapel, and there is a superb Cima da Conegliano over the first altar on the right. Be sure to find *Saints John the Baptist, Mark, Jerome and Paul* by Cima da Conegliano (1494) and Tintoretto's tomb in the chapel to the right of the chancel. **Don't miss** *Last Judgement; Presentation of the Virgin in the Temple*.

Detail of mosaic floor, Basilica di Santa Maria e Donato, Murano

A traditional gondola on display in the Museo Storico Navale

MURANO

🔲 423 E1 · 🔲 Piazza San Marco 71f, San Marco, 30120 Venezia, tel 041 5298740 🕐 Daily 9–3.30

🚤 Vaporetto: Murano
www.comune.venezia.it
www.provincia.venezia.it

Murano, 10 minutes by boat from Fondamenta Nuove, is a self-contained community of around 5,000 people, with a miniature Canal Grande, an excellent museum, old *palazzi* and fine churches. It has been the focus of the famous Venetian glass industry since the 13th century. There are many glass showrooms in the city proper, but if you want to buy glass or see it being made, Murano is the place to go.

Five or six main canals thread their way through the island, lined with shops and houses and crossed by bridges—a miniature version of Venice. You can leave the boat at the Colonna or Faro, explore the island and re-embark at Venier at the other end of the main canal.

The main attraction is the glass, and there are workshops all over the island where you can see master craftsmen demonstrate the skills of flamework, twisting and blowing. Learn more in the Museo di Vetro (Glass Museum), in the splendid 17th-century Palazzo Giustinian, where the history and production of Murano's glass are explained *(Thu–Tue 10–5)*. Don't overlook the 12th-century Basilica di Santa Maria e Donato, Murano's main church, with a colonnaded portico, a lively mosaic floor from

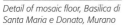

A pair of Venetian glass parrots made on the island of Murano

1140 and a grave Byzantine *Madonna* above the altar.
Don't miss The master craftsmen at work; the Museo di Vetro; the Basilica di Santa Maria e Donato.

MUSEO CIVICO CORRER

🔲 422 C4 · Ala Napoleonica, Piazza San Marco 52, San Marco, 30124 Venezia ☎ 041 522 6525 🕐 Daily 9–7, Apr–Oct; daily 9–5, rest of year 💷 €4 🚤 Vaporetto: Vallaresso
www.comune.venezia.it/museicivici

The Museo Correr bills itself as the Museum of Venetian Civilization, focusing on city life during the great days of the Republic. Set in a series of grand and elaborate rooms, many overlooking the piazza, it is now directly linked with the Museo Archeologico and the Biblioteca Marciana, so you can easily explore the whole complex (it occupies the upper floors of the Ala Napoleonica, the Procuratie Nuove and Sansovino's library).

At the museum's core are the 16th-, 17th- and 18th-century collections of Teodoro Correr, given to the city in 1830. Tours take you through halls devoted to the accomplished sculpture of Antonio Canova (1757–1822). Next is a series of princely rooms, overlooking the piazza, that provide an insight into the ducal elections, the workings of the Arsenale and everyday life and entertainment. Upstairs the Quadreria contains some fine works, notably *Two Venetian Noblewomen* by Vittore Carpaccio (1472–1526) erroneously known for years as *The Courtesans*. The route then leads through the Museo Archeologico (Greek and Roman art strictly for

enthusiasts) before reaching the opulent state rooms of the Biblioteca Marciana. Here there is a huge variety of manuscripts and early books displayed beneath an impressive ceiling covered in allegorical painting.
Don't miss The Museo Archeologico; the sculptures by Antonio Canova; Carpaccio's *Two Venetian Noblewomen.*

MUSEO STORICO NAVALE

🔲 423 E4 · Campo San Biagio, Castello, 2148 Venezia ☎ 041 520 0276 🕐 Mon–Fri 8.45–1.30, Sat 8.45–1 💷 €2.50 🚤 Vaporetto: Arsenale
www.regione.veneto.it/cultura/musei

Venice's power and wealth came from the sea, and few places better demonstrate this than the Museo Storico Navale, a child-friendly museum devoted to the history of sailing. Four floors are crammed with model ships, uniforms, weaponry, navigational instruments and more.

The museum occupies an old granary building on the water's edge, beside the Rio dell'Arsenale, a stone's throw from the entrance to the Arsenale. Highlights are the richly gilded Bucintoro, a model of the Doge's state barge, the huge 16th-century galleass (a large galley) and the last surviving private gondola, which once belonged to Peggy Guggenheim. There are vessels from all over the world, cannons and torpedoes, dress uniforms, sextants and astrolabes—more than 25,000 exhibits in total. Keep an eye out for the superb scale model of the *cammello,* a device used to lift ships from low water in the lagoon, and the idiosyncratic collection of naïve votive paintings, giving thanks for salvation from storm and shipwreck.
Don't miss The Bucintoro; the *cammello.*

THE SIGHTS

Palazzo Ducale

**The political and judicial hub of the Venetian government.
The biggest, grandest and most opulent civic building in Venice.
A dream-like Gothic palace—one of the architectural highlights of the city.**

A close-up of the Palazzo Ducale's balcony;
Sala del Senato (left)

The delicate tracery and elegantly regular
columns of the façade viewed from the water

SEEING THE PALAZZO DUCALE

The Palazzo Ducale (Doge's Palace), seat of Venice's temporal power, is connected to the Basilica di San Marco at the east end of the Piazza di San Marco, a 45-minute walk or half-an-hour ride by *vaporetto* from the railway station. The meeting place of the councils that ruled Venice, the home to the Doge, the law courts, the civil service and the prisons, the palazzo overlooks both the piazzetta and the waters of the Bacino di San Marco. Founded as a castle in the ninth century, its present appearance as a masterpiece of Venetian Gothic architecture dates from the 14th century, a magnificent reminder of the city's past glories. Whether you approach it via the water or by strolling through the piazza, the first impressions of this fairy-tale palace are unforgettable.

HIGHLIGHTS

THE EXTERIOR, THE PORTA DELLA CARTA AND THE COURTYARD

One of the world's finest examples of Gothic architecture, the exterior of the Palazzo Ducale runs along the water's edge and the piazzetta. The waterfront façade was finished in 1419 and the side on the Piazzetta was built in the 15th century. The beautiful pink-and-white frontage has an airy arcade topped by a gallery supporting the mass of the upper storeys; the play of light and shade over the masonry enhances the impression of harmony. The columns and pillars at ground level are mainly copies of the 14th- to 15th-century originals, now housed in the Museo dell'Opera, off the interior courtyard.

The main entrance into the palazzo is the Porta della Carta, a grand piece of florid Gothic architecture, built by Bartolomeo and Giovanni Bon between 1438 and 1442. This provides access through a portico to the courtyard, an enclosed space with a first-floor loggia. The most imposing approach to the loggia is undoubtedly via Sansovino's 1485 Scala dei Giganti (Giant's Staircase), used by the Doge at his inauguration. There is another flamboyant Sansovino stairway, the stucco-and-gilt Scala d'Oro (Golden Stairs), leading from the loggia to the upper floors.

RATINGS	
Historic interest	●●●●●
Cultural interest	●●●●
Photo stops	●●●●
Value for money	●●●

TIPS

● Expect parts of the Palazzo Ducale to be closed; a building of this age requires constant restoration.

● The Museum Card for the Musei di Piazza San Marco (€11) provides entrance to all the museums in Piazza San Marco (Palazzo Ducale, Museo Correr, Museo Archeologico Nazionale, Biblioteca Nazionale Marciana).

● A Museum Pass (€15.50) is available for all Venice's civic museums in the Musei di Piazza San Marco (Palazzo Ducale, Museo Correr, Museo Archeologico Nazionale, Biblioteca Nazionale Marciana), the Musei di Settecento (Ca' Rezzonico, Palazzo Mocenigo, Casa di Carlo Goldini, Ca' Pesara) and the Musei delle Isole (Museo del Vetro and Museo del Merletto).

The Sala della Bussola

THE DOGE'S APARTMENTS

The Doge, elected from Venice's patrician families, was the one politician to sit on all the major councils and the only one elected for life—a position of such potential power that it was hedged about with endless restrictions to prevent abuse of power. After his election, the Doge gave his entire life over to the service of the State, and his apartments reflect this lack of privacy. They comprise a series of surprisingly intimate rooms, magnificently if austerely decorated, with splendid ceilings and superb fireplaces. Here, the Doge received deputations and ambassadors and oversaw council deliberations. The finest and biggest chamber is the Sala delle Mappe (Map Room), painted with maps of the whole of the 16th-century known world, with Venice firmly as the central focus.

THE ANTICOLLEGIO, THE COLLEGIO AND THE SALA DEL SENATO

The extraordinarily rich decoration of the state rooms in the Palazzo Ducale is intended to illustrate the history of Venice and was painted by some of the greatest 16th-century Venetian artists. The aim was to impress visiting emissaries, many of whom passed through the palace on official business. The Anticollegio served as a waiting room for ambassadors hoping to see the Doge; four mythological paintings, created in 1577–78 by Tintoretto (1518–94), hang on the walls, while facing the window is Veronese's *Rape of Europa*. From here, the ambassadors moved to the adjoining Collegio to be received. This was also the room where the inner cabinet met. The ceiling panels are by Veronese (1528–88), pure propaganda showing Justice and Peace as mere sidekicks to Venice herself. Venice triumphs yet again in Tintoretto's painting in the middle of the ceiling in the next door Sala del Senato, where the 300-strong senate met to receive reports from returning ambassadors and debate questions of commerce, war and foreign policy.

THE SALA DEL MAGGIOR CONSIGLIO

The first-floor Sala del Maggior Consiglio is the largest room in the palazzo, stretching almost the entire length of the waterfront side of the building. This lavishly decorated room was the great council chamber where the 2,600 patricians met. The paintings in this room were commissioned to replace those lost in a fire in 1577. *Paradiso* on the far wall was begun by Tintoretto, then aged 70, who was responsible for its complex iconography. It was completed after his death by his son, Domenico (1562–1637). The *Apotheosis of Venice* on the ceiling is by Veronese. Devoted to the concept of Venice the superpower, their meaning is more straightforward. Around the walls are portraits of the first 76 Doges. Look for the gap, where there is a black veil instead of a Doge; this space should have commemorated Doge Marin Falier, but he was executed for conspiring against the State in 1355. If the windows are open on the left side of the hall, step out onto the balcony for lovely views across St. Mark's Basin.

Displays of weaponry, armour and a cannon in the Palazzo Ducale

Gilded, painted ceilings in the largest room in the palazzo, the Sala del Maggior Consiglio

THE PONTE DEI SOSPIRI AND THE PRIGIONI NUOVE

Until the 16th century, all Venetian criminals served their sentences in either the attics or the waterlogged basement of the Palazzo Ducale. This changed after the construction of the Prigioni Nuove (New Prisons) in 1598; from then on petty villains enjoyed the comforts of what was considered to be Europe's most sophisticated prison accommodation. The prisons are separated from the main palace by a canal, which is crossed by the world-famous Ponte dei Sospiri (Bridge of Sighs). Designed by the aptly named Antonio da Ponte, it is probably Venice's (if not the world's) most photographed bridge. By the 19th century the romantic legend was firmly established that once prisoners crossed this enclosed first-floor bridge they would never return. In the prison block, steep stairs lead down to the warren of cells, some of which have their number and capacity painted over the door. At the bottom there is a small courtyard for exercise, once home to an unofficial tavern.

BACKGROUND

The Palazzo Ducale was designed not only to provide a home for the Doge, but also to house the machinery of the State—the councils, committees and officials who administered the government of the city. From the 14th century only those noble families listed in the so-called *Libro d'Oro* (*Golden Book*) sat on the councils, and the building reflects their power, wealth and prestige as well as that of Venice itself. The Palazzo Ducale began to assume its present shape in 1340 when a new hall for the Maggior Consiglio (Great Council) was built. Much of the rest of what we see today dates from the mid-15th century. There were devastating fires in 1574 and again in 1577, but it was decided to restore the damage rather than replace it with something new, leaving the magical Gothic exterior unaltered. The block across the Canale della Paglia, which is approached via the Ponte dei Sospiri (Bridge of Sighs), went up in the late 16th century. Since the fall of the Republic in 1797, the Palazzo Ducale has had many different functions; today, as well as being open to the public, it houses various city offices.

GALLERY GUIDE

Itinerari Segreti: A guided tour behind the scenes, taking in the warren of offices and small chambers that link the public rooms of the palazzo, as well as the old prisons in the basement (must be booked in advance).

Museo dell'Opera: A ground-floor museum displaying, among other exhibits, the best of the palazzo's exterior arcade capitals.

Arco dei Foscari: A late Gothic arch in the courtyard, commissioned by Doge Francesco Foscari in 1438, designed and built by Antonio Bregno and Antonio Rizzo.

Sala del Magistrato: A small room housing some outstandingly bizarre paintings by the Flemish artist Hieronymus Bosch (c1450–1516), collected by the Grimani family.

Armoury: A huge and somewhat daunting collection of armour, weapons and instruments of war, mostly captured from Venice's enemies.

Bocche di Leone: 'Postboxes' adorned with lion's heads—in various parts of the palazzo, notably the loggia, the Sala della Bussola and the Sala della Quarantia Criminal—which served as delivery boxes for anonymous accusations made by Venetian citizens against each other.

PIAZZA SAN MARCO AND THE CAMPANILE

The historic heart of Venice.
Some of the city's finest Byzantine, Gothic and Renaissance architecture.
Bordered by compelling museums, chic shops and cafés.

As you emerge from the narrow surrounding streets into the piazza, its sheer scale is breathtaking—not for nothing did Napoleon describe it as 'the biggest drawing room in Europe'. Within the arcades that line three sides of the piazza are Florian's and Quadri's, two historic cafés with plush interiors, impeccable service and tables outside on the piazza. They are very expensive, but a drink here is quite an experience, often accompanied by an orchestra.

THE PIAZZETTA AND THE CLOCK TOWER

At the east end of the piazza's wide expanse stands the Basilica di San Marco. The open space runs down to the water's edge, St. Mark's Basin, and is flanked on the right by the Biblioteca Marciana and the Zecca, designed by Sansovino between 1527 and 1537, and the Palazzo Ducale (p.92–95) on the left. A winged lion, the symbol of Venice, and St. Theodore, the city's first patron saint, top its two columns. On the other side of the basilica, the tiny space fronted by ancient marble lions, known as the Piazzetta dei Leoncini, is overlooked by the Torre dell'Orologio. This zodiacal clock, with mechanical figures and crowned with a golden lion, was designed by Mauro Coducci and built between 1406 and 1506.

THE ARCADES AND THE CAMPANILE

The arcaded buildings that run down the long sides of the piazza are the offices of the Procurators of San Marco; the 16th-century Procuratie Vecchie, to the north, and the Procuratie Nuove, built a century later, to the south. After the fall of Venice in 1797, the two were linked by another arcaded building, now home to the Museo Civico Correr (p. 91), the Ala Napoleonica. In front of San Marco, the campanile (bell tower), a great place for city and lagoon views, was designed in 1514. What you see is a copy, as in 1902 the entire tower collapsed. No other buildings were damaged but the custodian's cat was killed. It was rebuilt *'Com'era, dov'era'* ('Like it was, where it was') and Sansovino's Loggetta at the foot of the tower was pieced together from the fragments.
Don't miss The Piazzetta; the Torre dell'Orologio.

RATINGS

Historic interest	●●●●○
Cultural interest	●●●●○
Photo stops	●●●●○
Walkability	●●●●○

TIPS

● In peak season, come early or late to avoid the crowds.

● Choose a clear day to go to the top of the campanile as heat haze or mist significantly reduces visibility.

BASICS

✛ 422 C3/4 • Piazza San Marco, San Marco, 30170 Venezia ☎ Campanile: 041 522 4064
◉ Campanile: daily 9–9, summer; daily 9–5, winter
✋ Campanile lift €6
🚤 *Vaporetto*: Vallaresso

Bustling Piazza San Marco (above) and the clockface of the Campanile (inset)

RIALTO

**The traditional setting of one of Italy's most vibrant markets.
A place to jostle with the natives and experience
a slice of Venetian life.**

The Rialto was one of the earliest parts of the lagoon to be settled: the word *Rialto* is a corruption of *Rivoaltus*, the upper bank, the highest area and thus less likely to be flooded. By the 10th and 11th centuries, the Rialto was Venice's commercial heart and one of Europe's most important trading areas. In 1097 the market became a permanent fixture. A pontoon of boats linked the two banks, but in the 12th and 13th centuries the first of five wooden bridges was built across the canal. Venetian merchants controlled trade between Europe and the Far East, while Europe's major banks and international trading companies set up offices here. The name Rialto was as familiar to medieval moneymen as that of Wall Street or the City of London is today.

PONTE DI RIALTO
The idea of a stone bridge at the Rialto was first mooted in 1557 and a competition was held to choose the best design, with big names such as Michelangelo, Palladio and Sansovino all submitting their plans. The prize went to the aptly named Venetian, Antonio da Ponte, for his revolutionary single-span suggestion. Two *fondamente* (canalside streets) stretch along either side of the water, one of the few places in Venice where you can actually stroll along the edge of the Canal Grande (p. 84–85). The San Marco side is the Riva del Ferro, named after the iron that was once unloaded here, while opposite, the Riva del Vin is a reminder that this was originally the discharge point for wine barrels.

THE MARKET
Behind the Riva del Vin is a labyrinthine maze of narrow streets, many named after the goods sold during the great days of the Republic: Ruga de'Orefici (Goldsmiths' Row), Ruga Speziali (Spicemakers' Street), Riva dell'Olio (Oil Quay) and Campo della Pescheria (Fish Square). Nearby is the Rialto market and its surrounding specialist shops, the city's main place for food shopping, where people bargain for meat, fruit, vegetables and, above all, fresh fish and seafood.

The little church of San Giacomo, on the San Polo side of the bridge, is said to be Venice's oldest, founded, according to legend, on the same day as the city itself, 26 March 421. The clock above the church is famous for its inaccuracy; it has been incorrect since its installation in the 15th century.

RATINGS	
Good for kids	● ● ● ○
Specialist shopping	● ● ● ●
Photo stops	● ● ● ●
Good for food	● ● ● ●

TIP

● The fish market is closed on Mondays.

BASICS

✚ 422 C3 🚤 *Vaporetto:* Rialto

Traffic criss-crossing the Canal Grande in front of Ponte di Rialto (above) and the Campo della Pescheri, where you can buy fresh fish and seafood, the staples of Venetian cuisine (above right)

The view over Venice from the top of San Giorgio Maggiore

A silhouette of the Santa Maria della Salute seen from San Marco

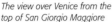

SAN GIORGIO DEI GRECI

⊞ 423 D3 • Fondamenta dei Greci, Castello, 30122 Venezia ☎ 041 523 9569 ◉ Mon–Sat 9–12.30, 2–4.30 ⛴ *Vaporetto*: San Zaccaria

San Giorgio dei Greci is a tangible reminder of the foreign communities that lived and settled in Venice. Renaissance Venice had a large Greek population, particularly after Constantinople fell to the Turks in 1453, and the Greek community received permission to build their own church in 1539. The church was designed by Sante Lombardo, with an interior that is completely Orthodox in layout and design. Look for the *matroneo* (women's gallery) above the main door and the iconostasis (screen) that separates the high altar from the body of the church. The icons on the screen are a mixture of dates and styles, the oldest dating back as far as the 12th century. The campanile, drunkenly leaning towards the canal, is one of the landmarks in this part of the city.

SAN GIORGIO MAGGIORE

⊞ 423 D4 • Isola di San Giorgio Maggiore, 30123 Venezia ☎ 041 522 7827 ◉ Mon–Sat 9–12.30, 2.30–6.30, Sun 2.30–6.30, Apr–Sep; Mon–Sat 10–12.30, 2.30–5, Sun 9.30–10.30, 2.30–4.30, rest of year ⛴ *Vaporetto*: San Giorgio

The open waters of St. Mark's Basin frame the great Palladian church of San Giorgio Maggiore. The island of San Giorgio was home to a Benedictine monastery from the 10th century to 1806, and in 1565 Andrea Palladio was commissioned to design a church for the monks. He united two temple fronts in the façade: Four central columns that rise to the full height of the nave are flanked by shorter, Corinthian columns, which match the height of the

aisles—an arrangement echoed in the luminous interior and emphasized by the use of white marble and stucco. This is a triumphantly light and airy building, full of soaring space decorated with fine pictures by Tintoretto and his school. Stop to admire the works on either side of the chancel, *The Fall of Manna* and the *The Last Supper*, both of which emphasize the importance of the Eucharist, before taking the lift up the campanile for views over the city and lagoon. **Don't miss** Tintoretto's paintings; the campanile.

SANTA MARIA DEGLI MIRACOLI

⊞ 422 C3 • Campo Santa Maria Nuova, Cannaregio, 30121 Venezia ☎ 041 275 0462 ◉ Mon–Sat 10–5, Sun 1–5; closed Sun, Jul–Aug 🎟 €2. Santa Maria degli Miracoli is one of the CHORUS group of 15 artistically important churches; a pass covering entry to all 15 costs €8 ⛴ *Vaporetto*: Rialto www.chorus-ve.org

The exquisite Church of Santa Maria degli Miracoli is tucked away in Cannaregio. It was built between 1481 and 1489 to house a miraculous image of the Madonna by Nicolò di Pietro, which still hangs over the altar. The church is entirely covered inside and out with polychrome marbles, creating a jewel-casket effect, with one side of this perfect Renaissance church running along a quiet canal.

Begin by looking closely at the exterior, designed and created, as was the inside, by the Lombardo brothers, Renaissance stoneworkers who uniquely fused architecture, decoration and sculpture. Marble in subtly different shades covers every surface, while graceful pilasters make the church appear longer. The interior has some of the most intricate carving in Venice,

seen at its best when the sun streams in, illuminating the rose, white and silver-grey marble. The altar steps and balustrade leading to the raised choir are beautifully carved with figures, while fine filigree stonework covers the columns below the nuns' choir and a carved frieze runs right around the church.

SANTA MARIA DELLA SALUTE

⊞ 422 C4 • Dorsoduro, Campo della Salute, 30123 Venezia ☎ 041 522 5558 ◉ Church: daily 9–12, 3–6.30, Apr–Sep, Sacristy: daily 3–5.30, Apr–Sep 🎟 Sacristy €1.50 ⛴ *Vaporetto*: Salute

An unmistakable feature of the Venetian cityscape, the gleaming white bulk of the great baroque 17th-century Church of Santa Maria della Salute looms over the San Marco entrance to the Canal Grande. Built in thanksgiving for the end of the disastrous plague of 1630, which wiped out a third of the city's population, the church has outstanding paintings by Titian (c1490–1576). Baldassare Longhena designed the huge, domed, octagonal construction, his first commission.

From the canal-side, a flight of steps leads up to the Palladian façade, with huge half-columns. The main dome is buttressed by circular volutes, affectionately known to Venetians as *orecchioni* (little ears), surrounded by more than 120 exuberant statues and ornate decoration. By contrast, the interior is austere, with six chapels clustered around the central space. On the high altar, the marble Virgin and Child are shown rescuing Venice from the plague. **Don't miss** There are eight Titians in the sacristy, including *The Sacrifice of Abraham* and *David and Goliath*, and Tintoretto's *Marriage Feast of Cana*; the church at night is illuminated.

SANTI GIOVANNI E PAOLO

Dubbed the 'Pantheon of Venice', this is the final resting place of Venice's Doges and heroes.

Northern Castello is home to the huge Gothic Church of Santi Giovanni e Paolo, or, in Venetian dialect, San Zanipolo. The L-shaped *campo* (square) that fronts the church is a good vantage point from which to appreciate the impressively large exterior: the church is 100m (330ft) long, 38m (125ft) wide and 33m (108ft) high. Constructed between 1246 and 1430, of red brick with stone ornamentation, Santi Giovanni e Paolo is among the most ambitious expressions of Gothic architecture in Venice, complete with a soaring façade and five apses at the east end.

The main portal has Byzantine reliefs and marble columns from an abandoned church on the island of Torcello (p. 102). The most ornate of four tombs built into the façade is that of Doge Giacomo Tiepolo, who in 1234 reputedly dreamed that he should found a church here, on what was then a swamp.

THE INTERIOR

The vast, shadowy interior is a single spatial unit punctuated by simple columns. The walls are lined with tombs and monuments by some of Venice's most famous Renaissance artists and sculptors. They include some of the best pieces by the Lombardo family of sculptors. No fewer than 25 Doges are buried here. Particularly striking are the Morosini, Vendramin, Nicolò Marcello and Corner monuments, and the Lombardo Mocenigo monuments on the rear entrance wall. Paintings to look for are the superb polyptych *St. Vincent Ferrer* by Giovanni Bellini, *St. Antonius Pierozzi Giving Alms to the Poor* by Lorenzo Lotto, in the right transept, and the ceiling paintings by Veronese in the Cappella del Rosario. There is some good Murano stained glass in the transept, designed by Bartolomeo Vivarini and made at Murano (p. 91).

THE COLLEONI STATUE AND SCUOLA GRANDE DI SAN MARCO

The Lombardo family were also responsible for the elaborate façade of the Scuola Grande di San Marco, which stands at right angles to the front of the church. Completed in 1495 with stunning marble *trompe l'oeil* panels, it was one of the major Venetian *scuole* and today houses Venice's main civic hospital. Opposite the entrance, and the focal point of the small *campo*, is Andrea Verrocchio's taut and powerful equestrian statue of the mercenary *condottier* Bartolomeo Colleoni.

RATINGS	
Historic interest	●●●●●
Cultural interest	●●●
Value for money	●●●●●

BASICS
✚ 423 D3 • Campo Santo Giovanni e Paolo, Castello, 30122 Venezia
☎ 041 523 7510
⏰ Mon–Sat 7.30–12.30, 3.30–7, Sun 3.30–6
🎟 Free
📖 In Italian, English, French, German, €3.60
📷 🚤 *Vaporetto*: Ospedale

The statue of condottier Bartolomeo Colleoni (above) and a close-up of the heavily armoured figure on top of the tomb of Doge Michele Steno, one of the many important monuments inside the church (above right)

The flower-filled cemetery on the island of San Michele

Inside the Church of San Polo

The altarpiece inside the Church of San Zaccaria

SANTA MARIA FORMOSA

✚ 423 D3 • Campo Santa Maria Formosa, Castello, 30122 Venezia ☎ 041 523 4645 🕐 Mon–Sat 10–5, Sun 1–5; closed Sun, Jul–Aug 💶 €2 🚤 Vaporetto: San Zaccaria, Rialto www.chorus-ve.org

The church of Santa Maria Formosa gives its name to the surrounding *campo*, a typically Venetian square that is constantly busy with the comings and goings of both Venetians and visitors, a great place to experience life in Castello. This irregular space is bordered by a fine range of palazzi. The ancient church got its name from a seventh-century vision that appeared to St. Magnus, where he saw the Virgin as a buxom and shapely matron—*formosa*.

The present church was designed by Mauro Coducci in 1492; he retained the original 11th-century Greek cross plan, threading a Renaissance design around a typically Byzantine layout. The campanile is baroque. The church has two façades, one on the canal (1542) and one on the *campo* (1604), both added after Coducci's death. The harmonious grey-and-white interior has three naves and barrel-vaulted side chapels. Look for the triptych in the first chapel on the right, showing the Virgin in her role as Our Lady of Mercy by Bartolomeo Vivarini, with scenes from her life on either side.

SAN MICHELE

✚ 423 D2 • Isola di San Michele, 30122 Venezia 🕐 Cemetery: daily 7.30–4. Church: daily 7.30–12.15, 3–4 💶 Free 🚤 Vaporetto: San Michele (from Fondamenta Nuove)

The island of San Michele, a few minutes' journey across the lagoon from the Fondamenta Nuove, is the final resting place for Venetians. But the cemetery is by no means a morbid place. Infused with a gentle and romantic melancholy, it is busy with Venetians bringing flowers for their loved ones. Today it is only a temporary resting place as it became full years ago. Bones are now removed after 10 years or so and taken to an ossuary.

Begin by pausing at Venice's first Renaissance church, the beautiful San Michele in Isola, designed by Mauro Coducci in the 1460s. From here a walkway leads through the cloisters of the monastery; the brothers look after the church and cemetery. It is covered in an array of stacked tombs, dramatic sculpture, photographs and flowers. Most tourists head for the Protestant section to visit the tomb of American poet Ezra Pound (1885–1972), before tracking down the graves of Russian composer Igor Stravinsky (1882–1971) and Russian ballet impresario Sergei Diaghelev (1872–1929) in the Greek and Orthodox section. The children's area is poignant, and there is a corner dedicated to gondoliers, whose graves are decorated with stone gondolas.

SAN POLO

✚ 422 B3 • Campo San Polo, San Polo, 30125 Venezia ☎ 041 275 0462 🕐 Mon–Sat 10–5, Sun 1–5; closed Sun, Jul–Aug 💶 €2 🚤 Vaporetto: San Tomà, San Silvestro www.chorus-ve.org

The district of San Polo, the Venetian version of San Paolo (St. Paul), gets its name from this church, an old ninth-century foundation. Tucked into a corner of the square of the same name, the church faces the canal, though it has lost its waterfront façade and entrance. The original building was Byzantine, but Gothic elements such as the side portal, the rose window and the wooden ceiling were added in the 14th

and 15th centuries. In 1804 there were more alterations in an attempt to impose a neoclassical look; some were removed in the 1930s. The campanile, detached from the church, has suffered less since its construction in 1362; look for the pair of stone lions at the base. Inside, the main draw is Tiepolo's cycle of the Crucifix in the oratory behind the main church. These dazzling paintings show scenes from *The Stations of the Cross*.

SAN ZACCARIA

✚ 423 D3 • Campo San Zaccaria, Castello, 30122 Venezia ☎ 041 522 1257 🕐 Mon–Sat 10–noon, 4–6, Sun 4–6 💶 Church: free; chapels of St. Athanasius and Tarasius, sacristy and crypt: €1 🚤 Vaporetto: San Zaccaria

San Zaccaria, dedicated to the father of John the Baptist (said to be buried here), is the only Venetian church with an ambulatory and crypt. On a square off the Riva degli Schiavone, it is a Venetian mix of Gothic and Renaissance styles.

The ambulatory is instantly striking, an elegant ring of elliptical cupolas lit by long windows. The church is stuffed with 17th- and 18th-century paintings, of distinctly variable quality. Standing artistically apart from this mass is Giovanni Bellini's luminously stunning and serene *Madonna and Four Saints,* in the second chapel on the left. St. Tarasius's Chapel was once part of the original church and houses three ornate *ancone* (volutes supporting a cornice) by Antonio Vivarini and Giovanni d'Alemagna, wonderfully hieratic pictures in sumptuous gold Gothic frames. This chapel also gives access to the permanently waterlogged crypt, the burial place of eight of the early Doges. It is confirmation that the water continues to rise in Venice.

SANTA MARIA GLORIOSA DEI FRARI

The Franciscans' Venetian power base and the city's second-largest church.
The perfect setting for some of Venice's famous works of art and monumental tombs.

The Franciscans, *frari* in Venetian dialect, came to Venice around 1222 and built their first church on the site in the 1270s. As the order developed, they outgrew it, and work started on a new church and bell tower in 1340. The latter was finished in 1396, but it was not until the 1430s that the church was completed. The adjoining cloisters, chapter house and convent (now housing the Archivio di Stato) were built at the same time. The convent was suppressed under Napoleon, but today the Frari is a parish church still in the care of the Franciscans.

GREAT PAINTINGS

Built of terracotta brick with a typical Gothic stone exterior and architectural details, the Frari is huge—102m (335ft) long, 48m (158ft) wide and 28m (92ft) high—and has one of the tallest bell towers in Venice. Enter the vast nave (the 12 pillars represent the Apostles) and you will be immediately drawn to Titian's famously radiant and dynamic *Assumption* (1518) over the high altar, one of the most important and innovative paintings of the Venetian High Renaissance. To the left of the main altar is Titian's *Madonna di Ca' Pesaro* (1526), commissioned by Bishop Pesaro and showing members of his family. In the sacristy, the inspiring and tranquil triptych *Madonna and Child* (1488) by Giovanni Bellini is noted for its skilful use of perspective; it is still in its original frame. Immediately to the right of the high altar is Donatello's sculpture of *St. John the Baptist,* the only work by the Florentine master in Venice. In the Monks' Choir (*Coro dei Frati*), the 124 wooden choir stalls were carved by Marco Cozzi in 1468.

MONUMENTAL TOMBS

Less immediately appealing and memorable than the paintings but of equal interest are the monumental tombs. The rear section of the nave has a 19th-century monument to Titian and opposite there is a large neoclassical marble pyramid containing the heart of the sculptor, Antonio Canova (1757–1822). Look for the late Gothic monument to Doge Foscari (1457) near the high altar, and the Renaissance monument to Doge Tron (1476) nearby. The composer Claudio Monteverdi (1567–1643) is buried in a chapel to the left of the high altar.

TIPS

● Enter via the left transept but once inside start your visit from the back of the church.

● If you are visiting between Christmas and the end of January, don't miss the *presepio* (crib), one of the city's best, with sound and light effects and moving figures.

BASICS

✚ 422 B3 • Campo dei Frari, San Polo, 30125 Venezia ☎ 041 272 8611
🕐 Mon–Sat 9–6, Sun 1–5
💶 €2. The Frari is one of CHORUS group of 15 artistically important churches; a pass covering entry to all 15 costs €8
📖 Several versions, with differing levels of information, in English, Italian, French, German, Spanish, €4–€9
🎧 Audioguides
🚤 *Vaporetto*: San Tomà

www.basilicadeifrari.it

The wooden cross beams accentuate the height of the Frari's fine Gothic ceiling

The façade of the Scuola Grande di San Rocco

A quiet, tree-lined canal on the island of Torcello

SCUOLA GRANDE DI SAN ROCCO

✚ 422 B3 • Campo San Rocco, San Polo, 30125 Venezia ☎ 041 523 4864
🕐 Daily 9–5.30, Apr–Oct; daily 10–4, Nov, Mar; Mon–Fri 10–1, Sat–Sun 10–4, Dec–Feb 💶 €5.50 🌐 In Italian, English, French, German and Spanish, €4.50–€15 🎧 Audiotours in Italian, French, English included in ticket
🚤 Vaporetto: San Tomà

There is little in Venice so powerful as the colossal picture cycle by Tintoretto in the Scuola Grande di San Rocco. These 54 compelling and moving paintings, produced by the artist in three bursts of creativity over a period of 23 years, cover the walls and ceilings of the headquarters of the richest of the 15th-century *scuole* (confraternities).

The building was designed by Bartolomeo Bon in the early 16th century and was decorated between 1564 and 1587. Chronologically, the panels begin upstairs, in the Sala dell'Albergo, where there is the ceiling portrayal of *St. Roch in Glory,* the painting that won Tintoretto the commission. One wall is dominated by the *Crucifixion,* a powerful synthesis of narrative and passionate devotion. The Main Hall has Old Testament scenes on the ceiling and a Life of Christ cycle on the walls, all set off by sumptuous woodcarving and gilding. At the peak of his stylistic development Tintoretto's use of light and form lends an almost impressionistic feel to his works *Annunciation, Flight to Egypt* and *Massacre of the Innocents.*

SCUOLA DI SAN GIORGIO DEGLI SCHIAVONI

✚ 423 D3 • Calle dei Furlani, Castello, 30122 Venezia ☎ 041 522 8828
🕐 Tue–Sat 9.30–12.30, 3.30–6.30, Sun 9.30–12.30, Apr–Oct; Tue–Sat 10–12.30, 3–6, Sun 10–12.30, Nov–Mar 💶 €3
🚤 Vaporetto: San Zaccaria

This intimate little building on a side canal houses one of the most appealing of all Venetian Renaissance picture cycles. After the splendours of the great set-pieces, the low-key charm of Vittore Carpaccio's paintings is a great contrast. By the 15th century, the Slavs had established an important community in Venice, and obtained permission to found their own *scuola* here. In 1502 they commissioned Carpaccio (c1460–c1525) to decorate the interior with scenes from the lives of three special saints revered by the Slavs, St. George, St. Tryphon and St. Jerome.

The Carpaccio cycles occupy a dimly lit, wood-panelled chamber entered directly from the street. Much of their appeal stems from their wealth of meticulous detail. The iconography is confusing, but it is easy to spot St. George despatching the dragon, while the princess, surrounded by half-dismembered corpses, looks on in rapture.

SCUOLA GRANDE DEI CARMINI

✚ 422 A4 • Campo dei Carmini, Dorsoduro, 2617 Venezia ☎ 041 528 9420 🕐 Mon–Sat 9–6, Sun 9–7, Apr–Sep; Mon–Sat 9–4, Sun 9–1, Oct–Mar 💶 Adult €5, child (under 10) €2 🚤 Vaporetto: Ca' Rezzonico, San Basilio

The Scuola Grande dei Carmini was the only one to escape the maraudings of Napoleon's troops, and is thus the only surviving *scuola* with an 18th-century appearance. Tucked away just off the atmospheric Campo Santa Margherita, this Carmelite confraternity base has some flamboyant interior decoration.

Pause before you go in to admire the formal symmetry of the façade, designed by Longhena between 1668 and 1670. This was the Venetian headquarters of the Carmelites, a religious order devoted to the Virgin Mary. From here they practised their charitable works. In 1739 they employed the artist Giambattista Tiepolo (1696–1770) to decorate the upper hall, a task that occupied him for 10 years. Access upstairs is via an ornate staircase, and the hall itself is dominated by Tiepolo's nine audacious panels. Incomprehensible iconography aside, they can be appreciated for their swirling figures off-beat composition and the extraordinary accomplishment of trompe-l'oeil perspective.

TORCELLO

✚ 423 off F1 ℹ Piazza San Marco 71f, San Marco 30124 ☎ 041 529 8740
🕐 Mon–Sat 9.30–3.30 🚤 Vaporetto: Torcello
www.comune.venezia.it

On the marshy, neglected island of Torcello, 9km (5 miles) north-east of Venice in the northern lagoon, you will find a handful of working Venetians, a single muddy canal and the oldest building in the lagoon, the superb ninth-century Basilica di Santa Maria Assunta.

In the fifth century, this was Venice's earliest settlement; by the 1300s the population numbered over 20,000. But the rise of the Rialto and the mosquito-fed fevers took their toll in the 14th century, forcing the inhabitants to flee. All that remains is a few houses, an 11th-century church and the basilica.

The interior of Santa Maria Assunta, first built in 638, is serene and cool, with a superb marble pavement and a series of outstanding mosaics, dating from the ninth to the 12th century, including a melancholy *Madonna* in the apse and a magnificently detailed *Last Judgement* on the back wall.

THE NORTHEAST AND EMILIA-ROMAGNA

Prosperous and thriving since ancient times, this area includes some of the country's loveliest cities—Bologna, Parma, Padova and Vicenza. Europe's finest Byzantine mosaics are found at Ravenna, while the soaring and dramatic peaks of the Dolomites are perfect for summer walking and winter sports.

MAJOR SIGHTS

The Romanesque basilica in Aquileia

Karneid Castle at the end of the Eggental, a spectacular valley road through Trento Alto-Adige, with Bolzano in the distance

THE SIGHTS

AQUILEIA

✚ 435 J3 🛈 Piazza Capitolo 4, 33051 Aquileia, tel 0431 91087
www.turismo.fvg.it

Most great Roman cities were transformed into settlements that survive as modern cities, but Aquileia (33km/20 miles south of Udine), once the fourth most important centre in Italy, is little more than a tangle of ruins, a few houses and a superb Romanesque basilica. Founded in 181BC as a defensive and trading hub, it is now a peaceful hamlet.

In AD314, a Christian Patriarchate was founded here and Theodore, the first patriarch, built a basilica. Sacked by Attila and then by the Lombards, it was rebuilt in the early 11th century by Poppo, the patriarch at the time. The basilica's chief treasure is the mosaic floor, its Christian and pagan scenes as fresh as when they were laid by Theodore in 320. The basilica and bell tower, visible for miles around, are the focus today, while around them lie the grassy ruins of the Roman city, much of whose stone was stolen by the Venetians for their buildings. Climb the bell tower, see Roman finds in the Museo Archeologico and the Museo Paleocristiano, and maybe visit Grado, one of the Adriatic's least-known resorts, slumbering among the dunes and lagoons 12km (7 miles) away.
Don't miss the mosaics in the basilica.

BOLZANO (BOZEN)

✚ 434 G2 🛈 Waltherplatz/ Piazza Walther 8, 39100 Bolzano, tel 0471 307000 🚉 Bolzano
www.bolzano-bozen.it

Bolzano enjoys one of the highest standards of living in Italy, and is a good starting point for a trip into the Dolomites. The town is strongly Tyrolean—it was only

after World War I that it became part of Italy. It lies at the heart of an excellent wine-producing region, and is low-key and relaxed, with a handful of sights, plenty of cafés and one of the foremost museums in the Alto-Adige (Südtirol).

The town stands at the confluence of the rivers Talfer (Talvera) and Eisack (Isarco), 86km (53 miles) northeast of Trento and surrounded by mountains whose lower slopes are planted with vines and apple trees. West of the Talfer sprawls the 'Italian' town, laid out by Mussolini in the late 1920s. Most visitors concentrate on the old town to the east, where arcaded streets spread out from the central Waltherplatz (Piazza Walther). The duomo stands on one side, a distinctive tiled building whose elaborate tower is a local landmark.
Don't miss Ötzi, the 5,000-year-old mummy in the Museo Archeologico.

BRESSANONE (BRIXEN)

✚ 434 G2 🛈 Viale Stazione 9, 39042 Bressanone, tel 0472 836401
🚉 Bressanone/Brixen
www.brixen.org

Bressanone makes a good stopping-off point en route to or from the Brenner Pass. It is a popular year-round resort, with easy access in winter to miles of pistes and excellent summer walking in the surrounding mountains.

Founded in 901 as the seat of an important bishopric, the town stands on the River Eisack, 47km (29 miles) northeast of Bolzano. The heart of the town is focused on the duomo, with porticoed streets and frescoed medieval buildings. The duomo was ruthlessly modernized in the 18th century, but the Romanesque cloisters are intact. Local artists created the frescoes in the 1390s and there are more

examples in the 11th-century baptistery. The duomo's treasure is kept in the Museo Diocesano, in the sumptuous 13th-century Bishop's Palace.

You can sample a local wine at the Abbazia di Novacella, just north of town.
Don't miss The collection of crib figures in the crypt.

CIVIDALE DEL FRIULI

✚ 435 J3 🛈 Corso Paolina d'Aquileia 4, 33043 Cividale del Friuli ☎ 0432 731461 🕐 Mon–Fri 9–1, 3–6
🚉 Cividale del Friuli

A few miles from the Slovenian border, delightful Cividale (7km/ 10 miles east of Udine), founded by Julius Caesar in 50BC, is little known to visitors. Its tangle of medieval streets and squares line the banks of the River Natisone, and it is one of the few places in Italy with tangible reminders of the Lombards. This Teutonic warrior race invaded in the sixth century, embraced Christianity and left behind some of the finest Lombard carvings in Italy.

Simply walking around Cividale is a pleasure; it is small enough to get your bearings but big enough to have some great architecture. The river, spanned by the Ponte del Diavolo (Devil's Bridge), is particularly pretty. Cividale's sights lie west of the river; the pearl is the Tempietto Longobardo (Lombard Temple), whose eighth-century stucco arch with gentle smiling saints, a peerless example of Lombard art. There is more Lombard carving in the Museo Cristiano (in the precincts of the 15th-century duomo), notably the *Baptistery of Callisto* and the *Altar of Ratchis*, a haunting masterpiece. The main museum is the Museo Archeologico Nazionale, where finds from Lombard tombs include stunning examples of carving and intricate jewellery.

The illuminated Fontana del Nettuno in Piazza Maggiore

BOLOGNA

Capital of Emilia-Romagna, known for its beauty, wealth, left-wing politics and cuisine. An ancient settlement full of history.

Bologna is endowed with beautiful streetscapes—arcades of mellow brick and stone, juxtaposed with the stark shapes characteristic of the high-tech industry that generates the money that sustains the expensive restaurants and elegant shops. Bologna is a classic Roman city that, after the Dark Ages, became a free *comune* and subsequently, in the 15th century, gave way to rule by an individual family, the Bentivoglio, until annexed by the Papal States. Its university is one of Europe's oldest and is of great importance.

THE MEDIEVAL CORE

The compact historic core is medieval in plan, scattered with churches, monuments, civic buildings and museums. Elegant porticoed streets radiate from two main squares, Piazza Maggiore and Piazza del Nettuno, with most of interest to visitors on the eastern side of the city. Around Piazza del Nettuno, named after Giambologna's Fontana del Nettuno, rise medieval civic palaces. Behind it, Piazza Maggiore is dominated by the late Gothic Church of San Petronio, Palazzo dei Notai, home to 14th-century lawyers, and the Museo Civico Archeologico *(Tue–Sat 9–6.30, Sun 10–6.30)*. Farther east are some of the loveliest streets and buildings—a series of porticoes punctuated by attractive squares. Head for Via Clavatura, with its tempting food stalls, before exploring the Archiginnasio complex, the oldest part of the university. More arcades lead south to the Church of San Domenico, built in 1251 to house the relics of the saint, enclosed in the superb Arca di San Domenico, sculpted by Pisano and the young Michelangelo. Only two of the dozens of towers from the Middle Ages survive; climb Torre degli Asinelli *(daily 9–6, Apr–Oct; daily 9–5, rest of year)* for great views. From here the university quarter is within striking distance.

THE UNIVERSITY

Via Zamboni leads to the heart of the university, in the medieval palaces. Palazzo Poggi has two quirky museums *(Tue–Fri 9.30–2.30, Sat, Sun and holidays 10.30–3.30, tel 051 209 9360)*: an idiosyncratic assemblage of anatomical waxworks, and the Specola, an early celestial observatory.

RATINGS

Historic interest	●●●●●
Cultural interest	●●●●
Photo stops	●●●
Walkability	●●●

TIPS

- Bologna makes few concessions to tourists, so don't expect cheap accommodation or restaurants, other than in the university area. It is vital to book a hotel in advance as rooms are in constant demand for trade fairs.
- Two organizations provide 2-hour guided walks (in English) from the tourist office in Piazza Maggiore. No booking required.
- There are 40-minute tours of the Museo della Specola at the university. For information about tours in English, tel 051 209 9398 or 051 209 9398.

BASICS

436 G5

Piazza Maggiore 1, 40124 Bologna
tel 051 246541
Daily 9–8
Bologna

Bicycles are a common sight in the medieval town of Ferrara

Castel Tirolo (Schloss Tirol) in Merano was built in the 12th century for the Counts of Tyrol and is now the museum of Tyrolean history

THE SIGHTS

CONEGLIANO

✚ 435 H3 ℹ Via XX Settembre 61, 31015 Conegliano, tel 0438 21230
🚉 Conegliano
www.comune.conegliano.tv.it
www.trevisotour.org

Low-key but prosperous, Conegliano is a beguiling mix of simple buildings and expensive antique shops. It's an excellent stop en route north through the Veneto. The town perches on the edge of the hilly area, 33km (20 miles) north of Treviso, surrounded by vineyards that produce the best *prosecco,* a light, dry, sparkling wine. You can follow the Strada del Prosecco west to Valdobbiadene, tasting as you go.

Conegliano neatly splits into the medieval and Renaissance old town and a grander, neoclassical quarter. In the old section, the Contrada Grande/Via XX Settembre, is an arcaded street lined with palazzi, restaurants and shops. The duomo, with a 14th-century frescoed portico, lies west of the main square, Piazza Cima. Farther uphill is the birthplace of Conegliano's most famous resident, the High Renaissance painter Giambattista Cima (c1459–1517). Look for his *Sacra Conversazione* in the duomo. Above town looms the *castello* (castle), now the town's museum. The collection is unexciting, but the views enjoyed while strolling uphill are superb.

FERRARA

✚ 434 G5 ℹ Castello Estense, 44100 Ferrara, tel 0532 209370/299303
🚉 Ferrara
www.ferrarainfo.com

A major player on the Renaissance political scene, Ferrara was ruled by the dynamic d'Este family. Their court was one of Europe's most prosperous, and their money paid for the palaces and artistic treasures that are scattered around. Beautiful Romanesque façades, excellent museums, a warren of medieval streets and gracious piazzas make up the city.

Ferrara stands on the banks of the Po di Volano, an offshoot of the River Po, 55km (35 miles) northeast of Bologna. Within the walls, which can be explored on foot or bicycle, the city is divided by the Viale Cavour/Corso Giovacca. Most sights of interest lie in the *centro storico* to the south. Start at Castello Estense, a bulky, moated 14th-century fortification with sumptuous state apartments and spooky dungeons. Nearby, the cathedral has a beautiful Romanesque-Gothic façade and an interior of 18th-century ornate gold. Follow the vaulted Via delle Volte south to Palazzo Schifanoia, a former Este summer palace, or cross the Viale Cavour to Palazzo dei Diamanti, where there are four museums, including the Pinacoteca Nazionale, tracing the history of painting in Ferrara.

MERANO (MERAN)

✚ 434 G2 ℹ Corso Libertà 45, 39012 Merano, tel 0473 272000 🚉 Merano
www.meraninfo.it

If you plan to explore the Alto-Adige (Südtirol) and want a base with a touch of sophistication, Merano is a good choice. It has chic shops (with an Austrian accent), restaurants and hotels, a lively cultural scene, gracious architecture and pretty gardens. This mountain-ringed town, with an unexpected Mediterranean-type micro-climate, found a new role for itself in the 1800s as a major spa resort. Elegant thermal buildings, solid villas and civic buildings were built around its medieval heart, and parks and promenades were laid out.

The town lies on the banks of the Passirio River, 30km (19 miles) northwest of Bolzano. The buildings of the medieval core cluster around the 14th-century duomo, while 13th- and 14th-century arcaded streets, lined with tempting shops, run parallel to the river. Passeggiata d'Estate and Passeggiata d'Inverno are two beautiful garden walks laid out in the 1860s and the 1870s, while the 4km (2.5-mile) Tappeiner promenade runs north above the town. The terraced Trautmansdorff Botanical Gardens are planted with shrubs and trees from all over the world.

MODENA

✚ 436 F5 ℹ Via Scudari 12, 41100 Modena, tel 059 206660 🚉 Modena
www.comune.modena.it
www.sosvacanze.it

Modena, a quietly prosperous town along the Via Emilia, makes a good outing from Bologna, 55km (35 miles) southeast, or a pleasant stopping point en route to Lombardy. Historically Modena is a rival to Bologna, but it has an entirely different atmosphere. It has a splendid Romanesque cathedral, tranquil arcaded squares, baroque palaces and an excellent museum complex. Today's money comes from the knitwear, ceramics and Ferrari factories on its outskirts. Modena's most famous modern citizen, the opera singer Luciano Pavarotti, gives the occasional summer concert here. It is good for shopping and there are some excellent restaurants and bars.

The town's historic core is split by the Via Emilia. Just south of the Emilia is Piazza Grande, lined with shady arcades and elegant cafés. Along one side is one wall of the magnificent 12th-century Romanesque duomo, with a leaning tower and fine carving. The web of medieval streets and pleasant squares makes Modena a serendipitous place to explore.

Cortina d'Ampezzo is surrounded by splendid peaks. It is well served by cable cars and is great for skiing, but it comes at a price

DOLOMITI

**Europe's most dramatic and beautiful mountains.
Jagged pinnacles and needle-sharp rock formations.
Skiing in winter, high-altitude hiking and rock-climbing in summer.**

Fertile green valleys, villages of wooden houses with window boxes dripping with geraniums, swathes of mountain flowers and air like champagne make Dolomiti an outdoor feast. Geologically different from the rest of the Alps, the Dolomites are composed of ancient coral reefs, formed beneath the seabed 250 million years ago and uplifted 190 million years later. Wind, ice and storms acted on the relatively soft, pinky-orange limestone, creating the astounding shapes that are so distinctive. The lower slopes are wooded or covered in alpine pasture, and vines and apples are cultivated in the fertile valley.

YEAR-ROUND ACTIVITIES
In the 20th century the massifs have developed into a year-round recreational area. There are ski resorts and a good network of cable cars and lifts. There are pistes to suit all levels and there is cross-country skiing, sledging and tobogganing in the valleys. The walking is some of the best in Europe, with a network of scenic trails. Accessed by cable cars and lifts, they are linked by *rifugi alpini* (mountain refuges, *end Jun–Sep*). By using the refuges, you can walk the *alte vie*, eight long-distance trails.

THE DIFFERENT REGIONS
The Italian-speaking Cadore Dolomites lie north of Belluno in the Veneto. The main resort is the glitzy Cortina d'Ampezzo, venue for the 1956 Winter Olympics.

In the western Dolomites, Trento and Bolzano are two beautiful main towns. The Val di Fassa is the heart of the old Ladino region. An exhibition at the Castel de Tor Museum is dedicated to this unique culture; the Ladino language is still alive, and each valley has its own dialect. To the west rises the Catinaccio/Rosengarten Massif, one of the most dramatic ranges. The main areas of the Brenta group are Madonna di Campiglio and Molveno. Dramatic rock formations, great summer walking and winter sports make the area very popular. The most important valleys are the Val di Sole, with meadows and pretty villages, and the wooded Val di Non.

RATINGS				
Good for kids	●	●	●	●
Outdoor pursuits	●	●	●	● ●
Photo stops	●	●	●	● ●

TIPS

● If you plan some serious walking, invest in good maps (available in most villages—Kompass maps are excellent) and take proper equipment and provisions.

● Remember that even over short distances driving can take time as the roads are twisty.

● It is worth learning a few basic German phrases.

BASICS

🔢 434 G2

ℹ Piazzetta San Francesco 8, 32043 Cortina d'Ampezzo, tel 0436 3231
🕐 Daily 9–12.30, 3.30–6.30
🚉 Trento, Bolzano, Merano

www.infodolomiti.it
A multi-lingual site helping you to pick an area in the dolomites that best suits you. They have photos of all the different areas and provide good information on the ski resorts, road, air and rail links and visitor itineraries.

www.fassa.it
www.sunrise.it/dolomiti
www.dolomitimolveno.it
www.vinschgau.suedtirol.com

TIPS

● Driving in Padova is confusing and parking a problem, so come by train if you can. The station is about 10 minutes' walk and there are buses.

● The main tourist office is in the station, so pick up a map as soon as you arrive.

● Access to the Cappella degli Scrovegni is limited to 25 people at a time; advance booking is vital during high season and advisable all year round *(tel 049 820 4550).*

MAKE A DAY OF IT

Venice: p. 81–102
Vicenza: p. 114

BASICS

✚ 434 G4

ℹ Stazione Ferroviaria, 35100 Padova, tel 049 875 2077
◷ Mon–Sat 9–7, 3–6, Sun 9–noon
▣ Padova

www.padova.it/apt

The Basilica di Sant'Antonio (top) was dedicated to St. Anthony, a preacher who modelled himself on Francis of Assisi

PADOVA (PADUA)

**Famous for Giotto's frescoes in the Scrovegni Chapel and its Byzantine basilica, a historic pilgrimage site.
A university city with the most vibrant nightlife in the area and some of the best markets in Italy.**

Historic Padova (Padua), the Veneto's most important economic hub and an ancient university city, combines lively, spacious squares and narrow, medieval streets with important works of art and monuments, elegant shops, buzzing markets and green spaces. With its efficient transport connections, it is also a good base for exploring the region.

WHERE TO GO

Padova's overlords were the Da Carrara family from 1337 until the capture of the city by the Venetian Republic in 1405. Great cultural patrons, they attracted stars such as Giotto, Dante and Petrarch, and Padova remained a cultural focus even after the fall of the city. Many people come only to see Giotto's frescoes in the Cappella degli Scrovegni and the Venetian art collections in the Musei Civici; others head straight for the attractive squares, Piazza della Frutta and Piazza dell'Erbe. The two are divided by the bulk of the 13th-century Palazzo della Ragione or Il Salone *(daily 9–7, Feb–Oct; daily 9–6, rest of year)*, ringed with cafés, bars and shops. The eclectic Caffè Pedrocchi on Via VIII Febbraio was once Padova's main intellectual salon *(Tue–Fri 9.30–12.30, 3.30–6, Sat–Sun 9.30–12.30, 3.30–7; bar: daily 8am–11pm).*

BASILICA DI SANT'ANTONIO

The Basilica di Sant'Antonio (or Il Santo) is one of Italy's main pilgrim shrines *(daily 6.30am–7.45pm, Apr–Oct; daily 6.30am–7pm, rest of year)*, begun after the death in 1232 of St. Anthony of Padua. In the square is Donatello's majestic equestrian bronze of the mercenary Erasmo de Narni, known as *Gattamelata (honey cat).*

GIOTTO AND THE VENETIAN SCHOOL

Padova's most precious jewels are in Cappella degli Scrovegni *(daily 9–7, tel 049 200020)* and the adjoining Museo Civico on Piazza Eremitani *(daily 9am–10pm)*. Between 1303 and 1309 Giotto painted a series of scenes in the chapel from the life of Christ and the Virgin. Like his Assisi cycle, this marked a turning point in Western art, introducing a naturalism not seen in the stylized art of the Middle Ages. The museum's excellent collection of works by Paduan and Venetian artists includes a Giotto crucifix and two exquisite Giorgione paintings.

Detail of the Byzantine frescoes in the baptistery in Parma

Sun worship on one of Rimini's many beaches

PARCO NAZIONALE DELLO STELVIO

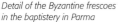 434 F2 ℹ Comitato di Gestione per la Provincia Autonoma di Bolzano, Piazza Municipio 1, 39020 Glorenza, tel 0473 830430
www.stelviopark.it

The Parco Nazionale dello Stelvio embraces the entire Ortles range, sprawling across Lombardy, Trentino and the Alto-Adige (Südtirol). It is one of Italy's most important and largest national parks, ideal for winter sports and spectacular summer walking. The landscape includes high peaks, fertile valleys, woodland, more than 50 lakes and 100 glaciers. There is a great deal of diversity in the animal and plantlife here. The park is criss-crossed with superb hiking trails, and many visitors head away from the roads, spending nights in *rifugi* (mountain refuges).

The Ortles (3,950m/12,960ft) are south of the Val Venosta (Vinschgau), a broad valley east of Merano. Three roads thread through the foothills from the valley into the massif: Val Martello, Val d'Ultimo and Val di Solda. These are jumping-off points for the park. In summer drivers can cross the park via Passo dello Stelvio (2,758m/ 9,050ft), the second-highest pass in the Alps *(early Jul to mid-Sep)*. Begin your explorations at the park's main information office in Glorenza, a miniature walled city. The whole area is very Austrian and, away from the tourist areas, you will need to speak some German.

PARMA

🚩 434 F5 ℹ Via Melloni 1, 43100 Parma, tel 0521 218889 🚉 Parma
www.turismo.comune.parma.it/turismo

Parma's name is synonymous with *prosciutto* (Parma ham) and *parmigiano* (Parmesan cheese).

But this rich, cultured provincial city also has artistic treasures and a strong musical tradition. The old city has a beautiful cathedral, Renaissance palaces, and a famous opera house. It also has good designer shops.

Parma's three most famous residents are the artists Correggio (c1490–1534) and Parmigianino (1503–40) and the musician Artur Toscanini (1867–1957).

The elegant, pedestrianized streets at the heart of the city are on the east of the River Parma. The three main piazzas—della Pace, Duomo and Garibaldi—are as different in themselves as Parma's most important monuments. Most notable are the 11th-century duomo *(daily 9–12.30, 3–7)*, a lovely Lombard-Romanesque church with interior frescoes by Corregio, and the beautiful octagonal 12th-century baptistery, built of pink Verona marble with sculpted friezes. This simple ensemble contrasts with the Renaissance magnificence of Santa Maria della Steccata and its frescoes by Parmigianino *(daily 9–noon, 3–6)*. Also important are the well-displayed artistic pieces in the Palazzo della Pilotta, the perfectly restored Renaissance Teatro Farnese and, across the river, in verdant parkland, the Palazzo Ducale *(Mon–Sat 9–noon)*. The Casa Natale e Musei di Arturo Toscanini, the birthplace of Tocanini, is not far from here on Via Rodolfo Tanzi.

PIACENZA

🚩 433 E4 ℹ Piazza Cavalli, 29100 Piacenza, tel 0523 329324 🚉 Piacenza
www.comune.piacenza.it
www.provincia.piacenza.it

Piacenza is a perfect example of Emilia-Romagna's unostentatious, prosperous provincial towns. It is off the main tourist trail, near the Lombardy border. The Roman

town marked the end of the Via Emilia, a major military road. In the Middle Ages it flourished as a free city, then came under control of the Farnese and the Bourbons, and was the first town to join the embryonic Italian state in 1848. With fine medieval buildings and churches, a couple of museums and good shops, it is a great place to stop and sample the local cooking.

Piacenza, in the flat Po Valley, is misty and raw in winter and baking hot in summer. The Lombard-Gothic, redbrick Palazzo de Comune dates from 1280, as does the San Francesco church. From the piazza, Via XX Settembre leads to Piazza del Duomo, scene of a weekly market.

RAVENNA

p. 110.

RIMINI

🚩 437 H6 ℹ Piazza Federico Fellini 3, 47900 Rimini, tel 0541 56902 🚉 Rimini
www.riminiturismo.it

Rimini's beaches, 51km (32 miles) south of Ravenna, stretch for more than 16km (10 miles), a strip of hotels, arcades, shops, restaurants and clubs. In peak season it heaves with noisy crowds day and night; off-season, it is dead. The beach has many privately owned *stabilimenti*, fenced-off areas that you pay to use, and there are very few free areas on the beach. The hotels are good, but there is virtually no accommodation in August, as Italian families pour in. Some parts of town have a bad reputation after dark.

If hedonism doesn't appeal, explore the amphitheatre, palazzi and the Renaissance Tempio Malatestiano, an unusual building that served as a chapel and a monument to Sigismondo Malatesta, a 15th-century mercenary of the worst kind.

THE SIGHTS

A mosaic dating from AD450 in the mausoleum of Galla Placidia

RATINGS

Historic interest	●●●●
Cultural interest	●●●●
Walkability	●●●

TIPS

● Book tickets in advance if you want to visit the Mausoleum of Galla Placidia between 1 March and 15 June *(tel 0544 219938)*. At busy times you will only have a few minutes inside.

● The Ravenna Visitcard is a combined ticket for all the main sights. Buy it at any of the sights in low season or book in advance.

● To see the mosaics at Sant' Apollinare in Classe, take bus 4 or 44 (hourly) from outside the railway station.

● The main sights are floodlit and open on Friday evenings throughout July and August.

BASICS

✚ 437 H6

ℹ Via Salara 8–12, tel 0544 35404
🕐 Mon–Sat 8.30–7, Sun 10–4
🚉 Ravenna

www.turismo.ravenna.it
A bright website in Italian and English with all you need to know about Ravenna; the city and mosaics, the coast, the flora and fauna, the latest events, accommodation and tourist information services.

RAVENNA

Capital of the Roman Empire, later ruled by Byzantine Constantinople.
The world's most accomplished Byzantine mosaics, decorating fifth- and sixth-century churches and monuments.

In AD402, with the imperial court installed at Milan and the Roman Empire threatened by invaders from the north, Emperor Honorius decided to move his capital to Ravenna, an easily defensible marshland town near the important naval base of Classis, on the Adriatic coast. After the fall of Rome in AD410, Ravenna became the imperial capital, fittingly ornamented with lavish monuments. The city fell to the Goths in AD476, but they, too, were Christian and pursued the building design, a process continued by the Byzantines after their annexation of Ravenna in the sixth century. The city later came under Venetian control, but was sacked in the 16th century and absorbed into the Papal States, becoming part of Italy after 1870. Ravenna was heavily bombed in World War II and it has been extensively rebuilt, but it still has an important port, 12km (8 miles) from the old city.

THE MOSAICS

The most important sites date from fifth- and sixth-century Roman, Ostrogoth and Byzantine eras, and are Unesco World Heritage Sites. They are scattered around the Piazza del Popolo, where shoppers on bicycles weave in front of outdoor cafés. A few minutes' walk south is the complex of the Basilica of San Vitale, the mausoleum of Galla Placidia (p. 30) and the Museo Nazionale.

San Vitale *(daily 9–7)* was begun in 525 under the Roman emperor Theodoric and completed by the Byzantine ruler Justinian in 548. It is typically Byzantine, with a central dome supported by eight columns. The apse is covered with glowing mosaics showing Christ, the Apostles, and biblical scenes in the choir, while the side walls are covered in processional scenes. Across the grass is the mausoleum of Galla Placidia, half-sister of Honorius. Tiny and jewel-like, it is richly ornamented with blue and gold mosaics. Also important is the Basilica of Sant'Apollinare Nuovo *(daily 9–7)*, built in the sixth century by Theodoric; mosaics high above either side of the nave show martyrs bearing gifts for Christ and the Virgin. There are more mosaics in the Neonian and Arian baptisteries, and a short bus ride away, at Classe, in the sparce but evocative Basilica di Sant'Apollinare *(Mon–Sat 8.30–7.30, Sun 1–7)*.

The copper cupolas of Treviso's duomo, originally built in the Middle Ages and rebuilt between the 15th and 18th centuries

Modern architecture and funky stained glass in Trieste Airport

TRENTO

🔲 434 G3 🔲 Via Alfieri 4, 38100 Trento, tel 0461 983880 🔲 Trento www.apt.trento.it

Capital of Trentino, and 150km (93 miles) north of Verona, Trento stands on the River Adige, surrounded by green hills. Ruled for centuries by prince-bishops, the town rose to prominence when Bishop Bernardo Cles made it the meeting place for the 16th-century Council of Trent, the Counter-Reformation movement. He opened up the old medieval town with the construction of Via Belenzani, which cuts a straight line through to Piazza Duomo, site of the Romanesque duomo.

At the foot of the hills is Castello del Buonconsiglio, the prince-bishops' residence and one of the first castle-palaces in Italy. Its courtyards, loggias and sumptuous state apartments form the perfect setting for Trento's greatest artistic work, the ravishing fresco cycle *The Months of the Year* (c1400), full of flirting nobility and labouring peasants.

For a change of pace, take the cable-car up Monte Bordone to see the alpine plants in the botanical garden at Viotte.

TREVISO

🔲 435 H4 🔲 Piazza Monte di Pietà 8, tel 0422 547632 🔲 Treviso www.provincia.treviso.it

With frescoed façades, porticoed streets and shimmering waterways, historic Treviso is quite different from its neighbours. Modern money comes from knitwear—Treviso is home to Benetton—while past glories are reflected in fine early Gothic buildings and Renaissance churches. The city was painstakingly rebuilt after bombing in World War II, and there is a great sense of the new Italy here, with relics of the past co-existing hap-

pily with casual, stylish wealth. The excellent shops include tempting delicatessens, and the nightlife buzzes.

Treviso is ringed by Venetian-built walls, bordered by the River Sile. Willow-fringed branches of the river weave through the old town, at the heart of which is the Piazza dei Signori. Here is the Palazzo dei Trecento, first built in 1217, and behind are the churches of San Vito and Santa Lucia, with superb frescoes by the 14th-century Tommaso da Modena, considered the finest artist of his age after Giotto. To the east is a maze of streets and waterways around the bustling market (don't miss the *pescheria*, fish market). Calmaggiore is an attractive arcaded street with fine shops. At the far end, the duomo has a Titian *Annunciation*, but more interesting artistically is the Dominican Church of San Nicolò, rich with frescoes.

TRIESTE

🔲 435 K4 🔲 Via Rossini 6, 34100 Trieste, tel 040 365248 🔲 Trieste ✈ Trieste R Dei Legionari (TRS) www.triestetourism.it

Trieste's slightly battered neoclassical streets and buildings, built by the Austrians as a port, contrast with a clutch of Roman remains and a dramatic medieval castle and cathedral. With its café culture, literary associations (writer James Joyce lived here) and contrasting socialist and right-wing politics, Trieste is border territory—a mix of cultures, languages and allegiances that straddles the bridge between the Mediterranean world and that of Teutonic and Slavic central Europe. With exceptionally friendly people and great food, it is an ideal base for exploring the Carso, a plateau that stretches into Slovenia.

Trieste's position is stunning, with a grid of 18th-century streets,

the Borgo Teresiano, nestling between the sea and a limestone plateau. Piazza d'Unità d'Italia is a splendid square, open on one side to the sea. Behind rises the hill of San Giusto, where you find the city's oldest buildings with the best sea views. Highlights are the Romanesque Cattedrale di San Giusto, Venetian mosaics and a 13th-century fresco cycle in the Capella di San Giusto, and the Risiera di San Sabba, a thought-provoking museum in a World War II concentration camp.

UDINE

🔲 435 J3 🔲 Piazza I Maggio 7, 33100 Udine, tel 0432 295972 🔲 Udine www.regione.fvg.it

More Italian in spirit than Trieste, Udine is the second city of Friuli-Venezia Giulia. It is a comfortable provincial town with more than a touch of Venetian style—arcaded streets, canals, restaurants and a relaxed pace of life make it worth exploring. It is also a stronghold of Friulian nationalism—listen for the Slovenian influences in the dialect. Surprisingly few people visit Udine and it deserves to be better known.

The sprawling outskirts might put you off, but the *centro storico* is unspoiled, with a distinct personality. It is overshadowed by the *castello*, said to have been built with soil carried in the helmets of Attila's invading Huns. Reach it from Piazza Libertà, described as the most beautiful Venetian square on *terra firma*: The striped Loggia del Lionello echoes the Doge's Palace; there is a lion of St. Mark, and a fine Palladio gateway leading past a Venetian Gothic gallery to the castle.

Don't miss Tiepolo's *Abraham and the Sacrifice of Isaac*, a ceiling panel in the Palazzo Arcivescovile, one of his first major commissions.

Verona

**Impressive Roman remains, medieval castles, Romanesque and Renaissance churches and palaces.
A beautiful city, the setting for Shakespeare's *Romeo and Juliet*.
Streets lined with expensive shops and fashionable restaurants.**

Verona's Roman amphitheatre has capacity for 22,000 people

SEEING VERONA

Beautiful Verona—Roman ruins, rose-red medieval buildings and romantic dreams of young love—is the largest city in mainland Veneto, a quietly prosperous, cultured place where tourism plays second fiddle to the rest of the economy. Most of the historic heart of Verona is enclosed by a loop of the River Adige, with a few other important sights on the north bank. Wonderful churches and buildings are scattered throughout the pleasant streets, which are themselves punctuated by lovely squares.

RATINGS				
Historic interest	●	●	●	○
Specialist shopping	●	●	●	●
Walkability	●	●	●	○
Good for food	●	●	●	●

TIPS

● The historic heart is closed to traffic for most of the day, so come by train or use the car park near the station.

● You can rent a bicycle in Piazza Brà *(tel 333 536 7770)*.

● The Verona Card, valid for a day or a week, includes unlimited travel and museum admissions and is available from the tourist office. Pick up a free copy of *Passport Verona* for up-to-date listings.

● Verona is the venue for plays and musical events all year round, including great jazz and rock concerts, often in historic monuments and in open spaces outdoors.

● Verona has a great café scene and is much livelier in the evenings than Venice. It is also a better bet for buying clothes.

HGHLIGHTS

THE ARENA

Piazza Brà, 37121 Verona ☎ 045 800 3204 ⏰ Mon 1.45–6.30, Tue–Sun 8.30–6.30, Sep–Jun; daily 9–3.30, Jul–Aug (opera season); closed to visitors during performances 🎫 €3.10

Piazza Brà should be your first stop, an irregular open space dominated by one of the city's best-known monuments, the great Roman amphitheatre. Built in the first century AD, it is the third-largest of the surviving Roman amphitheatres in Italy. A 13th-century earthquake destroyed most of the exterior arcade, but the interior is intact, with steeply pitched tiers of pink marble seats and dizzying views from the top. Since 1913 people have flocked to Verona to catch a performance during its summer opera season.

BASILICA DI SAN ZENO MAGGIORE

Piazza San Zeno, 37121 Verona ⏰ Mon–Sat 8.30–6, Sun 1–6 🎫 €2.10

Farther west from Castelvecchio stands San Zeno Maggiore, a Romanesque church founded in the fourth century that attained its present form around 1398; a set of superb 11th-century bronze doors open into a lofty interior with Roman columns and an altarpiece by Andrea Mantegna (c1431–1506). The church is the burial place of Pepin the Short, king of the Franks. Father of Charlemagne and founder of the Frankish dynasty of the Carolingians, he led his army into Italy to defeat the Lombards in AD754.

PIAZZA DELLE ERBE

From Piazza Brà, Via Mazzini, an elegant and tempting pedestrian-only shopping street, leads north to the Piazza delle Erbe, the setting for a lively daily market, and the Piazza dei Signori, the heart of medieval Verona. Piazza delle Erbe is surrounded by exquisite buildings: The Torre de Lamberti soars above the brightly frescoed Casa Mazzanti, and there is a loggia, a 14th-century fountain and a fine Lion of St. Mark.

PIAZZA DEI SIGNORI

From Piazza delle Erbe an arch leads to the old civic area, the Piazza dei Signori, the focus of which is a statue of the Renaissance poet

Dante Alighieri (1265–1321). The candy-striped Palazzo della Ragione has a fine Romanesque-Gothic courtyard. The building behind Dante is the Renaissance Loggia del Consiglio dating from 1493, with the Tribunale next to it. Don't overlook the Scaligeri tombs, next to the Tribunale, covered with statuary and Scaligeri emblems, dogs and ladders.

Cangrande II's Ponte Scaligero on the River Adige near Castelvecchio (left)

CASA DI GIULIETTA
Via Capello 23, 37121 Verona ⏰ Daily 9–6.30 🎟 €3.10

The ivy-clad walls and balcony of the Casa di Giulietta (below)

From Piazza delle Erbe, Via Cappello leads southeast to the so-called Casa di Giulietta (House of Juliet), a graffiti-adorned Mecca for love-sick teenagers and bus tours; the balcony was added in 1935.

LA CATTEDRALE
⏰ Mon–Sat 10–5.30, Sun 1.30–5.30 🎟 €2.10
On the northern point of the promontory is the Romanesque cathedral, which has a beautiful apse and a fine *Assumption* by Titian in the first chapel of the left aisle.

BACKGROUND

Verona is on the River Adige, 50km (30 miles) west of Vicenza, at the bottom of an Alpine pass, and was first colonized by the Romans in 89BC. It became a regional capital and survived the Ostrogoth and Frankish invasions of AD489 and AD754, becoming a free *comune* in 1107. Feuds and vendettas between the city's noble families dominated the next century or so and provided the basis for William Shakespeare's tale of doomed love, *Romeo and Juliet,* set in Verona. By the late 1200s one family had emerged as top dogs, the Scaligeris, a terrifyingly successful mercenary clan who named themselves after dogs. They were ousted in their turn by the Milanese Viscontis in 1387. In 1402, having had their fill of lords, Verona turned to republican Venice, and remained part of *La Serenissima* (the Venetian Republic) until 1797, after which the city passed to the Austrians, who retained control until 1866, when Verona and Venice became part of the new Kingdom of Italy. The city was badly bombed during World War II, but quickly recovered to become one of Italy's outstanding economic success stories.

BASICS
✛ 434 F4

ℹ Via degli Alpini 9 (Piazza Brà), 37121 Verona, tel 045 806 8680
⏰ Daily 9–5
🚉 Verona

www.tourism.verona.it
You can send e-cards, get the latest weather forecast or get the latest view over Piazza Bra via the webcam at this website dedicated to Verona and Lake Garda. They also have a guide for visitors and information on accommodation, regional food and wine, events and sport. Italian, English and German versions.

THE SIGHTS

RATINGS

Historic interest	●●●
Cultural interest	●●●●●
Photo stops	●●●●
Walkability	●●●

TIPS

● If you plan to stay, be sure to book ahead—Vicenza has surprisingly few hotels and it is a big conference city.

● A Vicenza Card, a combined ticket, costs €7 and gives entrance to all the main attractions at big reductions.

● There are car parking areas at the east and west ends of town—follow the signs, and catch the shuttle bus into town.

● You can rent a bike at the station.

MAKE A DAY OF IT

Padova: p. 108

BASICS

✚ 434 G4

🛈 Piazza Duomo 5, 36100 Vicenza, tel 0444 544122 ◉ Daily 9–1, 2–6

🚆 Vicenza

www.vicenzae.org

Relief work on the pediment of a building topped with statues, with a copper spire behind, in the Piazza dei Signori

VICENZA

A Unesco World Heritage Site, home to some of the finest examples of Palladio's neoclassical architecture.

In 1404, under threat from stronger forces in Padua, Verona and Milan, the free *comune* of Vicenza offered itself to Venice and became a satellite city. As a Venetian possession, the city was given Gothic palaces, but its big architectural makeover came in the 16th century, when Andrea Palladio (1508–80) started to develop his own neoclassical style. Palladio was born in Padua, but found his major patron, the humanist nobleman Trissino, in Vicenza. Between 1549 and his death in 1580 he transformed the face of the city.

PALLADIO'S CLASSICAL MASTERPIECES

Corso Andrea Palladio, lined with superb *palazzi*, ends at Piazza Matteoti. The Palazzo Chiericati, designed by Palladio in 1550, now contains the Museo Civico, with paintings by Tintoretto, Tiepolo and Veronese *(Tue–Sun 10–6, Jun–Aug; Tue–Sun 9–5, rest of year)*. Across the piazza is the Teatro Olimpico, Europe's oldest indoor theatre, opened in 1585 *(Tue–Sun 9–5, Sep–May; Tue–Sun 9–7, rest of year)*. Palladio died before it was complete, but his designs inspired the astonishing *trompe l'oeil* backdrop—it appears to be hundreds of metres deep, but it only stretches back 15m (50ft).

PALLADIO'S BASILICA

At the heart of the *centro storico* is Piazza dei Signori, site of Palladio's dazzling basilica, his first major project and the one that made his reputation, and the stunning double-tiered Loggia del Capitaniato.

PALAZZI

Fruit and vegetables have been sold in the Piazza dell'Erbe since medieval times. Near here on Contrà Porti and Contrà Riale are several palaces, the highlights are the Palazzo Thiene, Palazzo Barbaran (Museo Palladiano, *Tue–Sun 10–6*) and Palazzo Colleoni Porto. The fine baroque Palazzo Montanari contains the other main museum exhibiting Longhi genre paintings *(Fri–Sun 10–6)*. Notable churches include the reconstructed duomo (the original was destroyed in World War II), 13th-century Santa Corona, notable for its paintings by Bellini and Veronese, and Santo Stefano. The hill to the south is Monte Bérico, an important plague shrine topped by a 17th-century basilica. Nearby, is Andrea Palladio's famous Villa Capra (1567), also known as the Villa Rotonda because of its symmetrical plan with a central circular hall.

FLORENCE

Florence was the birthplace of the Renaissance and the focal point of creative activity for some of the world's greatest artistic talents. The city's churches and museums contain familiar masterpieces, while the narrow streets are lined with splendid palaces and elegant shops. Highlights are the Duomo, the Piazza della Signoria and the Galleria degli Uffizi.

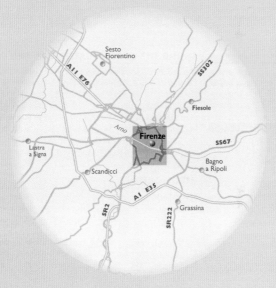

MAJOR SIGHTS

Duomo e Museo dell' Opera del Duomo

One of the most important early-Renaissance architectural complexes in Italy. The first free-standing dome to be constructed in the post-Roman period.

RATINGS	
Good for kids	●●●●●
Historic interest	●●●●●
Cultural interest	●●●●●
Value for money	●●●●●

TIP

● Skimpy shorts and sleeve-less tops are frowned upon.

Detail of The Pietà *by Michelangelo in the Museo dell'Opera del Duomo (top)*

A souvenir umbrella in the style of the Duomo (above left)

The octagonal Battistero di San Giovanni decorated with geometric marble motifs (above middle)

Detail of the bronze reliefs on the south doors of the baptistery illustrating the life of St. John the Baptist, designed by Andrea Pisano (above right)

View over the Duomo (right)

SEEING THE DUOMO, BATTISTERO AND CAMPANILE

The sublime, if somewhat grimy, complex of the Duomo, Campanile and Battistero lies a few blocks north of the Piazza della Signoria and the River Arno and less than 20 minutes' walk east from the railway station. The three buildings stand in their own piazza, a clear space that is constantly busy with visitors. The best way to tackle the Duomo is to start early in the day to beat the tour groups. Many of the best artworks are displayed in the Museo dell'Opera del Duomo, behind the east end of the Duomo.

HIGHLIGHTS

THE DUOMO

The Duomo of Santa Maria del Fiore is huge—there is room inside for 20,000 people. It is worth walking right around its green-and-white striped marble exterior to appreciate the vast proportions. Several doors punctuate the walls, the most elaborate being the Porta della Mandoria with its relief of the *Assumption* sculpted by Nanni di Banco in 1420. By contrast, the ornate Gothic façade dates from the 19th century; the original was destroyed in the late 1500s.

Compared with the outside, the interior is remarkably austere. Over the years many of the finest artworks have been moved to the Museo dell'Opera del Duomo, leaving the Duomo relatively bare. This enables you to appreciate the soaring space beneath the Gothic arches, the patterned marble pavements, the scale of the dome itself, and the superb mid-15th-century stained-glass windows, some of Italy's best.

There are two equestrian memorials dedicated to two of Florence's most famous *condottieri*: A monument to Niccolò da Tolentino (1456) by Andrea del Castagno, and a far sharper-edged portrait (1436) of Sir John Hawkwood, an English mercenary, by Paolo Uccello. Terracotta reliefs by Luca della Robbia decorate both north and south sacristy doors, and a superb bronze reliquary urn by Ghiberti stands in the central apse.

Steps to the ancient Church of Santa Reparata lead down from the south aisle; excavated in the 1960s, this ancient and confusing space has archaeological finds and, more inspiring, the tomb of Brunelleschi.

Climbing the rather claustrophobic 463 steps of the dome is a must; it is the high point of this great building, rewarded with sweeping views.

Duomo

✠ 425 D2 • Piazza del Duomo, 50122
Firenze ☎ 055 230 2885

🕐 Mon–Wed, Fri 10–5, Thu 10–3.30,
Sat 10–4.45, Sun and holidays
1.30–4.45; closed 1 Jan, Easter Day, 15
Aug and 25 Dec 🎟 Free ❓ Free
guided tours. Fixed audioguide points in
the Duomo, €1 📖 Guidebooks cover
the whole complex, in Italian, English,
French, German and Spanish, €10
📖 Duomo bookshop sells guidebooks,
art books, postcards, gifts and posters

Museo dell'Opera del Duomo

🚻 🅿 Underground parking at
Santa Maria Novella (10-minute walk);
parking for visitors with disabilities in
Piazza del Duomo

KEY

A Portale Maggiore with relief
   Maria in Gloria by A. Passaglia
B Porta dell Mandoria
C Cripta di Santa Reparata,
   remains of old cathedral

1. L'Assunta window by Ghiberti
   Incoronazione di Maria
2. Equestrian painting of Niccoló da
   Tolentino, by A. del Castagno
3. Equestrian figure of Giovanni
   Acuto (John Hawkwood)
   painted by P. Uccello
4. 14th-century window, and
   below, *Dante and the Divine
   Comedy* by D. di Michelino
5. Marble altar (Buggiano)
6. In the door, lunette, *Risurrezione*, by Luca della Robbia
7. Sagrestia nuova o della Messe
8. Above the altar, two angels
   (Luca della Robbia), below the
   altar reliquary of St. Zenobius
   by Ghiberti
9. Lunette, *Risurrezione*,
   terracotta by della Robbia
10. Sagrestia vecchia o dei canonici
11. Altar by Michelozzo
12. Entrance to the dome
13. Bust of Brunelleschi, by A.
    Cavalcanti
14. Stairs to the Cripta di Santa
    Reparata

MUSEO DELL'OPERA DEL DUOMO

The Museo dell'Opera del Duomo contains the sculptures and paintings of the Duomo complex, too precious to be left to the mercy of modern pollution. Ghiberti's *Gates of Paradise* (see below) probably steals the show, but there is a *Pietà* by Michelangelo that many see as equally exquisite. The sculptor was 80 when he created it, his last work, and intended it to be for his own tomb, but never finished it; the figure of Nicodemus is said to be a self-portrait. Donatello, the greatest of Michelangelo's precursors, is represented by two works: A gaunt and bedraggled *Mary Magdalene* and the powerful figure of the prophet *Habbakuk*. Donatello carved this for the campanile and it is so realistic he is said to have seized it, crying 'Speak, speak'. His lighter side emerges in the choir loft from the Duomo, carved with capering *putti* (children), the perfect contrast to Luca della Robbia's version, ornamented with earnest angels.

GHIBERTI'S BAPTISTERY DOORS IN THE MUSEO DELL'OPERA

Having finished the north doors in the baptistery in 1425, Ghiberti set to work on the doors for the east side, a work of such beauty that Michelangelo named them the 'Gates of Paradise'. Completed in 1452, they are made up of 10 relief panels of biblical subjects, exquisitely carved in low relief. Their artistic importance is in their use of perspective, extending the scenes far into the background—a totally new concept at the time that became typical of the Renaissance. The composition is far more naturalistic than the earlier baptistery doors, with figures grouped off-centre to intensify the drama of each scene. The baptistery doors are Ghiberti's finest achievement. On the frame of the left-hand door is his self-portrait–the smug-looking gentleman with a bald head.

THE BATTISTERO

The octagonal baptistery, entirely encased in green and white marble, is one of Florence's oldest buildings, probably dating from around the sixth to seventh century, and remodelled in the 11th century. It is most famous for its three sets of bronze doors, the south set dating from the 1330s by Andrea Pisano, and the north and east by Lorenzo Ghiberti. Ghiberti, aged 20, won the commission for the north doors in a competition and worked on them from 1403 to 1424, embarking on his finest achievement, the east set (see above), immediately afterwards. The panels in the doors you see are reproductions; the

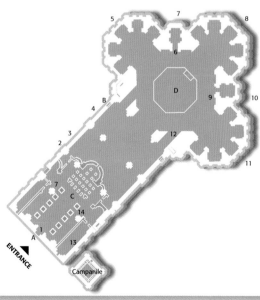

originals are kept away from 21st-century pollution in the Museo dell'Opera del Duomo.

INSIDE THE DOME
The interior of the dome glitters with Florence's only mosaic cycle, the earliest dating from 1225. Begin by looking above the entrance door and follow the history of the world from the Creation to John the Baptist, before taking in the main image of Christ and the Last Judgement, together with the Apostles and the Virgin.

THE CAMPANILE
Giotto designed the campanile in 1334, but he died before it was completed. Both Andrea Pisano, who took over after Giotto's death in 1337, and Talenti altered the original design considerably, strengthening the walls and adding large windows. The building is covered with bands of green, white and pink marble and is decorated with copies of sculptures and reliefs showing prophets, patriarchs and scenes from the Old Testament; the originals are in the Museo dell'Opera del Duomo. There are 414 steps to the top of the campanile, well worth it for the 360-degree views of Florence and the surrounding hills.

BACKGROUND
The sixth- to seventh-century baptistery was originally Florence's cathedral, later replaced by the Church of Santa Reparata, whose remains lie beneath the present building. In the 13th century, the city fathers decided to replace it, largely to flaunt the city's political clout and growing wealth and size. In 1294 the project was entrusted to Arnolfo di Cambio, and work continued throughout the 14th century, with various architects realizing his plan. The campanile was finished by 1334 and by 1418 the nave and tribunes were complete. The building awaited the massive dome planned for the crossing—the only drawback being that nobody had yet worked out how it would be built. The architect Filippo Brunelleschi offered his services, refusing to explain his solution, but exuding confidence. The building committee finally gave him the job, insisting that he work with his rival Lorenzo Ghiberti, who was responsible for the baptistery doors. In 1436 the dome was completed, and the cathedral consecrated. The lantern was finally completed in the 1460s.

The mosaic ceiling inside the Battistero

Battistero
424 C2 • Piazza del Duomo, 50122 Firenze ☎ 055 230 2885 ⏰ Mon–Sat noon–6.30, Sun and holidays 8.30–1.30; closed 1 Jan, Easter Day, 8 Sep, 24 and 25 Dec 🎧 Audioguide

Museo dell'Opera del Duomo
425 D2 • Piazza del Duomo 9, 50122 Firenze ☎ 055 230 2885 ⏰ Mon–Sat 9–7.30, Sun and hols 8.30–1.30; closed 1 Jan, Easter Day, 25 Dec 💶 Adult €6, under 6s free

Campanile
425 D2 • Piazza del Duomo 9, 50122 Firenze ☎ 055 230 2885 ⏰ Daily 9–7; closed 1 Jan, Easter Day, 8 Sep, 25 Dec 💶 Adult €6, under 6s free

www.operaduomo.firenze.it
Covers every aspect of the Duomo complex, including the Battistero, Campanile and Museo dell'Opera del Duomo. Good plans, photographs and a useful introduction that will steer you towards the highlights.

Detail of frescoes on the ceiling of the Badia Fiorentina

The Crucifixion before the Proconsul in the Cappella Brancacci

Funerary figures by Michelangelo in San Lorenzo

BADIA FIORENTINA

✚ 425 D3 ℹ️ Via del Proconsolo, 50122 Firenze, tel 055 264402 🕐 Mon 5–6

The Benedictine abbey of Badia Fiorentina was founded by Willa, the widow of the Margrave of Tuscany, at the end of the 10th century to commemorate her husband. The church bell, mentioned by Dante in the *Paradiso*, sits inside the beautiful tower. The church opens for limited periods and it is undergoing restoration, but the art makes it worth a visit.

On the left of the entrance is Filippino Lippi's enchanting *Madonna Appearing to St. Bernard*. On the opposite wall is a sculpted marble altarpiece by Mino da Fiesole, the artist also responsible for the marble monument to Ugo, Willa's son and the benefactor of the church, in the left transept. A door to the right of the choir leads to the upper loggia of the Chiostro degli Aranci (Cloister of Oranges), a reminder that monks once grew orange trees in this peaceful setting. Designed by Bernardo Rossellino between 1432 and 1438, it has a well-preserved series of frescoes illustrating scenes from the life of St. Benedict.

CAPPELLA BRANCACCI

✚ 424 A3 ℹ️ Piazza del Carmine, 50125 Firenze, tel 055 238 2195 🕐 Wed–Sat, Mon 10–5, Sun and public holidays 1–5; last entrance 4.30 🎫 Adult €4, under 18s €1.50 www.museoragazzi.it

This small chapel at the end of the right transept of the Church of Santa Maria del Carmine has some of the most significant works of Florentine Renaissance painting—the Cappella Brancacci frescoes. Although the church's exterior is dull—a rough stone façade rebuilt after a fire in

1771—the chapel and frescoes survived and, thanks to restoration carried out in the 1980s, are now vibrant once again.

The chapel, so small that only 30 people can enter at one time, is covered with paintings by Masolino, Masaccio and Filippino Lippi. Certain sections date back to 1425. In particular, look for Masolino's *Temptation of Adam* and *Healing of the Cripple,* and Masaccio's *Expulsion of Adam and Eve*. In contrast to the two-dimensional portrayals characteristic of Masaccio's predecessors, the depiction of Adam and Eve being expelled from the Garden of Eden, and their consequent anguish, is particularly emotive.

CAPPELLE MEDICEE

✚ 424 C2 ℹ️ Piazza Madonna degli Aldobrandini 2, 50123 Firenze, tel 055 238 8602 🕐 Daily 8.15–5; closed 2nd and 4th Sun and 1st, 3rd and 5th Mon of each month, 1 Jan, 1 May 🎫 Adult €6, under 18s free 🎫 🅿️ Under Santa Maria Novella Station (5-minute walk) www.firenzemusei.it

The Medici's main monument, the Cappella dei Principi, is awesome in its dimensions and kitsch opulence, proof of their wealthy egotism. This gloomy monstrosity can be appreciated for its sheer size. The other chapel, Sagrestia Nuova, is modest in comparison and has statues by Michelangelo.

The chapels are at the eastern end of the Church of San Lorenzo, where most of the Medici family are buried. Glass cases display gold and silver objects from the church treasury, including beautifully crafted reliquaries and a 16th-century pearl-encrusted mitre. Stone steps lead to the Cappella di Principi; the Grand Duke's octagonal mausoleum was begun in 1604, and is lined with marble and gems.

The Sagrestia Nuova has some superb examples of tombs and

statues by Michelangelo. The tomb of Lorenzo, Duke of Urbino, is decorated with the famous reclining figures of *Dawn* and *Dusk*. The corresponding statues on the tomb opposite, that of Giuliano, Duke of Nemours, represent *Day* and *Night* and are considered Michelangelo's finest. The beautiful statue of the *Madonna and Child* is also by Michelangelo, along with the two carved candelabra on the altar.

CASA BUONAROTTI

✚ 425 E3 ℹ️ Via Ghibellina 70, 50122 Firenze, tel 055 241752 🕐 Wed–Mon 9.30–2 🎫 €6.50 🎫

The Casa Buonarotti is a typical Renaissance town house. Now the Michelangelo museum, it provides an interesting insight into the life and times of one of the world's most famous artists.

Michelangelo Buonarotti (1475–1564) bought the house in 1508. On his death he left the property and several works of art to his nephew Leonardo, who in turn left it to his son, also named Michelangelo. He was an art collector and in 1612 he turned part of the house into a gallery dedicated to his great-uncle. The last direct descendant of the family founded the present museum in 1858. Three of Michelangelo's sculptures and a few of his drawings are on display, along with works of art collected and created by his descendants.

There are several portraits of Michelangelo and the marble bas-relief of *The Madonna of the Steps,* his earliest known work. Particularly charming are the Camera degli Angeli, a chapel, and the library with a frieze illustrating famous Florentines.

DUOMO AND MUSEO DELL'OPERA DEL DUOMO

p. 116–119.

THE SIGHTS

GALLERIA DELL'ACCADEMIA

Michelangelo's *David*—the most famous sculpture in the world. Painting and sculpture from the 14th to the 16th centuries— when Florence reigned supreme in artistic output.

The Galleria dell'Accademia, in the Accademia di Belle Arti, was established in 1784 as part of the art school, allowing students to study alongside great Florentine painting and sculpture. The entrance is dominated by the plaster model of Giambologna's 1582 statue of the *Rape of the Sabines,* under the Loggia dei Lanzi in Piazza della Signoria.

MICHELANGELO'S DAVID AND NONFINITI

A wide gallery leads to the statue of *David,* transferred to the specially built apse from Piazza della Signoria. Michelangelo was commissioned to make the statue by the city of Florence, and began work on the massive block of marble—5m (16ft) tall— in 1501. He was only 29 when he finished the piece in 1504, immediately establishing himself as the leading sculptor of the time. The statue shows the young David in meditative pose as he prepares for his fight with Goliath, aware that the salvation of his people depends upon him. Once finished, *David* became a symbol of republican liberty.

In the corridor that leads to the apse are five other remarkable sculptures by Michelangelo. The four celebrated *Slaves*, made between 1519 and 1536, were originally intended for the tomb of Pope Julius II in St. Peter's, Rome. They appear to be incomplete, hence the alternative name of *Nonfiniti*. There is also a statue of St. Matthew, one of 12 Apostles commissioned but never completed.

EARLY FLORENTINE WORK

Florentine paintings from the 13th and 14th centuries are displayed across three rooms. Four other rooms showcase 15th- and 16th-century Florentine paintings. A painted panel from a marriage chest, known as the *Cassone Adimari,* shows a lively and much-reproduced mid-15th-century wedding scene in front of the baptistery. There is also an early *Annunciation* by Filippino Lippi and an early Botticelli *Madonna and Child with the Young St. John and Two Angels.*

MUSICAL INSTRUMENTS

The fine collection of musical instruments, begun by the last of the Medicis, is in a series of rooms off the Sala del Colosso and belongs to the Conservatory. It includes the famous Medici Viola, made in 1690 by Antonio Stradivari.

RATINGS

Historic interest	●●●●●
Cultural interest	●●●●●
Specialist shopping	●●●
Value for money	●●●

BASICS

🗺 425 D1 • Via Ricasoli 60, 50122 Firenze ☎ 055 238 8612
🕐 Tue–Sun 8.15–6.50 (hours often extended in summer); Easter Sun and Mon 8.15am–10pm, 1 May 8.15–8; closed 1 Jan, 25 Dec
💶 Adult €6.50, under 18s free
📖 €8, €14
🎧 English, French, Spanish, German, Japanese, Italian from €6.50. Guided tours, tel 055 294883
🅿 Ample parking at the Parterre, Piazza della Libertà (10-minute walk); parking for visitors with disabilities outside

www.sbas.firenze.it/accademia
www.firenzemusei.it

Michelangelo's David (top) and a marble copy of the statue at the Palazzo Vecchio in Piazza della Signoria, where the original once stood (above right)

Galleria degli Uffizi

**Priceless paintings and sculptures from the world's most important collection of Renaissance art.
Giotto's *Maestà*, Botticelli's *The Birth of Venus* and Titian's *Venus of Urbino*.
Superb collection of Roman and Hellenistic sculpture.**

RATINGS	
Good for kids	● ● ● ●
Cultural interest	● ● ● ● ●
Specialist shopping	● ● ●
Value for money	● ● ● ●

GALLERY GUIDE

Rooms 2–6: Giotto, 14th-century Florentine, International Gothic
Rooms 7–9: Early Renaissance
Rooms 10–14: Botticelli
Room 15: Leonardo da Vinci
Rooms 16–24: Perugino, Signorelli, Giorgione, Corregio
Rooms 25–26: Michelangelo, Raphael and Andrea del Sarto
Rooms 27–29: Mannerism
Room 30: Emilian painting
Room 31: Veronese
Room 32: Tintoretto
Rooms 33–45: 16th- to 18th-century—Rubens, Caravaggio and Rembrandt

The Holy Family *by Michelangelo*

SEEING THE GALLERIA DEGLI UFFIZI

Set aside plenty of time to see the Uffizi—there is so much art of such importance that a flying visit is out of the question. Do not attempt to see the entire collection in one day, though. In a first visit concentrate on Rooms 1 through 15, which present major Florentine works, Tuscan Gothic and Early Renaissance in the East Corridor, and 16th-century artists in the West Corridor. You can avoid a wait by booking tickets in advance.

HIGHLIGHTS

MAESTA: GIOTTO—ROOM 2
A painting of the Madonna enthroned, combining Byzantine tradition with the first crucial steps towards the realism of Renaissance painting.

ADORATION OF THE MAGI: GENTILE DA FABRIANO—ROOM 6
This intricate picture (1423), with its sumptuously-portrayed fabrics, epitomizes the zenith of the International Gothic movement.

PORTRAIT OF THE DUKE AND DUCHESS OF URBINO: PIERO DELLA FRANCESCA—ROOM 7
A double portrait showing the sitters' profiles; the Duke lost his right eye in battle and was always portrayed from the left.

MADONNA AND CHILD WITH ANGELS: FILIPPO LIPPI—ROOM 8
Painted in 1465; the beautiful model for the Virgin was Lucrezia Buti, a nun, with whom the painter eloped.

THE BOTTICELLI WORKS—ROOMS 10–14
The Uffizi's most famous paintings are *Primavera* and *The Birth of Venus*. *Primavera* symbolizes spring, with a Zephyr chasing Flora, transforming her into spring and covering her with flowers. *The Birth of Venus* is inspired by Politia's poem and illustrates Zephyr and Chloris blowing the nude, classical figure of Venus ashore on the edge of a scallop shell.

LEONARDO DA VINCI—ROOM 15
Early works painted by da Vinci when he was living in Florence. See his large *Annunciation* (1475), along with the *Adoration of the Magi*

(1481), noted for its busy composition, remarkable character studies and curious symbolism. Left unfinished when Leonardo moved to Milan, it is in its preparatory state, sketched out in red-earth pigment.

THE HOLY FAMILY: MICHELANGELO—ROOM 25

Also known as the *Doni Tondo*, this painting was created between 1504 and 1505 for the marriage of Agnolo Doni and Maddalena Strozzi. It's Michelangelo's only completed tempura, a precursor to the Sistine Chapel frescoes.

THE RAPHAEL PAINTINGS—ROOM 26

Several important works hang here, including the luminous *Madonna del Cardellino*, a self-portrait, and the portrait group *Leo X with Giulio de' Medici*, painted shortly before the artist's death.

SALA DI PONTORMO E DEL ROSSO FIORENTINO—ROOM 27

Mannerism at its most startling, with attenuated forms and vivid shades.

VENUS OF URBINO: TITIAN—ROOM 28

This sensuous nude with a wistful and chaste gaze was painted in 1538 and described by Lord Byron as 'the definitive Venus'.

BACKGROUND

The gallery in the vast Palazzo degli Uffizi extends from Piazza della Signoria to the River Arno. Originally intended to be government offices (*uffizi*), the U-shaped building was constructed between 1560 and 1574 by Giorgio Vasari, under the orders of Cosimo I de' Medici. Succeeding Medici dukes added to the collections, which were bequeathed to the people of Florence by the last member of the family, Anna Maria Lodovica, in 1737, on the condition that the works never leave the city. The museum continues to acquire paintings and drawings. In 1993 a terrorist bomb caused great damage, and the gallery has undergone major reorganization. A huge development project is scheduled to take place over the next few years.

Prints for sale outside the gallery (top); Raphael's Madonna of the Goldfinch

BASICS

🕂 424 C3 • Piazzale degli Uffizi, 50122 Firenze ☎ 055 238 8651

🕐 Tue–Sun 8.15–6.50 (hours usually extended in summer); booking in advance Mon–Fri 8.30–6.30, Sat 8.30–12.30, tel 055 294883, www.firenzemusei.it

💷 Adult €6.50, under 18s free

📖 Official guidebook from €4.50

🎧 Audio tours in English, French, Spanish, German, Japanese, Italian from €6.50

☕ Café overlooking Piazza della Signoria

🚻 🅿 Limited parking on Lungarno Serristori (10-minute walk); underground parking at Santa Maria Novella station (15-minute walk); parking for visitors with disabilities in Piazza della Signoria

www.sbas.firenze.it

One of several fountains in the Giardino di Boboli

A painted mummy case in the Museo Archeologico

Medieval furnishings in the Museo della Casa Fiorentina

THE SIGHTS

GIARDINO DI BOBOLI

✚ 424 B5 • Palazzo Pitti, Piazza Pitti, 50125 Firenze ☎ 055 265 1838 ◷ Daily 8.15–7.30, Jun–Aug;; daily 8.15–6.30, Apr, May; daily 8.15–5.30, Mar; Sep, Oct; daily 8.15–4.30, Nov–Feb; closed 1st and last Mon of each month 🚻 Adult €4, under 18s free. Tickets are also valid for 3 days for the Museo delle Porcellane and the Museo degli Argenti in the Pitti Palace 🖳 🏛

This green space in the middle of Florence, a cool oasis on a hot summer's day, is the perfect fresh-air antidote to the many indoor sights in the city. Even at the height of summer, the warren of small lanes and pathways provides a welcome refuge from the tourist trail. Elaborate fountains, grottoes, elegant buildings and formal gardens sit happily alongside lichen-covered statues and secluded glades, a playground for local cats.

The gardens are laid out on a hillside behind Palazzo Pitti (p.128–29) and stretch from the palace up to Forte Belvedere. They were designed by Niccolò Tribolo (1500–50) for Cosimo I de' Medici and were opened to the public in 1766. Near the main courtyard of Palazzo Pitti is the magnificent Grotta Grande. In each of the four corners are copies of Michelangelo's unfinished *Slaves* (the originals are in the Galleria dell'Accademia, p.121). Walk up the terraces to the Neptune fountain (1571), where you can either take a detour to the elegant, frescoed Kaffeehaus for wonderful views and refreshments, or continue up to the top of the garden to the large statue, *Abundance*.

Off the beaten track, follow the magnificent Viottolone, a wide, steep path lined by cypress trees and statues leading to the lower part of the garden. At the bottom is the magical Isolotto, an island surrounded by an oval-shaped moat, adorned with statues, lemon trees and the huge Oceanus Fountain.

Don't miss Before you leave, pass by the Bacchus Fountain, a comic sculpture of Cosimo I's pot-bellied dwarf riding a turtle, a bizarre highlight.

MUSEO ARCHEOLOGICO NAZIONALE

✚ 425 E2 • Via della Colonna 38, 50121 Firenze ☎ 055 23575 ◷ Mon 2–7, Tue, Thu 8.30–7, Wed, Sat–Sun 8.30–2 🚻 €4, 18–26 years (EU nationals) €2, under 18s, over 65s (EU nationals) free 🏛
www.comune.firenze.it

The Museo Archeologico Nazionale has an excellent collection of art and ancient artefacts, including the most important Etruscan and Egyptian collections in Italy—a welcome relief from the potential overload of Renaissance art in the city.

The museum is in the elegant, 17th-century Palazzo della Crocetta on a busy street east of Piazza della Santissima Annunziata. One of the most important pieces in the museum, the restored bronze *Idolino,* is exhibited in a room on the ground floor. The torso of this statue of a young man, probably once used as a lampstand, is thought to date from the first century BC.

The Etruscan collection includes the famous bronze *Chimera,* part lion, part goat and part snake, dating from the late fifth to the early fourth century BC. Here also is the monumental *Arringatore,* or *Orator,* dating from the Hellenistic period, and a statue of Minerva.

The Egyptian collection includes mummies, statuettes, sarcophagi and vases, along with a 14th-century Hittite chariot made of bone and wood. On the second floor is a collection of Attic vases dating from the sixth and fifth centuries BC. Outstanding among these is the famous François Vase. Made in Athens around 570BC, this huge, highly decorative piece is one of the earliest examples of its kind.

MUSEO DELLA CASA FIORENTINA ANTICA

✚ 424 C3 • Via Porta Rossa 13, 50122 Firenze ☎ 055 238 8610 ◷ Daily 8.15–1.50; closed 1st and 2nd Sun and 1st, 3rd and 5th Mon of the month 🚻 €2 🏛
www.sbas.firenze.it

This stately, 14th-century palace (also known as the Museo del Palazzo Davanzati) has been closed since 1995 for renovation work and is not due to open until late 2004. It is not worth visiting until the museum fully re-opens.

The former home of the wealthy Davizzi family, the palace has been restored to its original condition and converted into the Museo della Casa Fiorentina Antica, providing a rare and vivid insight into the life of city merchants, artists and noblemen during the Middle Ages.

The façade is typical of a 14th-century house of its period, with three floors rising above arches. The large loggia at the top was added in the 16th century. The interior, including the wall paintings, furnishings, tapestries, ceramics, paintings and domestic objects, are all typical of a Florentine house built between the 15th and 17th centuries.

The only part of the palazzo presently on view to the public is the spacious entrance hall, temporarily housing items of furniture and other objects. Once the museum reopens, additional rooms on the third floor will be on view for the first time and there are plans for the loggia to be opened to the public.

The Annunciation *by Fra Angelico*

MUSEO DI SAN MARCO

**A shrine to Fra Angelico, little changed since the 1400s.
See his paintings in their original context, the Dominican
Convent of San Marco.
Ethereal images full of endlessly fascinating detail.**

The Convent of San Marco, within which the museum resides, is next to the church of the same name. The original convent on the site was of the Silvestrine Order, but it was given to the Dominicans by Cosimo il Vecchio, who commissioned the architect Michelozzo to enlarge the existing buildings. Fra Angelico (c1400–55), also known as Beato Angelico, lived here from 1436 to 1447. The museum was founded in 1869 and in 1921 most of Fra Angelico's panel paintings were transferred here from other museums in Florence.

THE CLOISTERS AND THE PILGRIMS' HOSPICE
A visit starts in Michelozzo's peaceful Cloister of Sant'Antonio. In the middle is an ancient cedar of Lebanon and at each corner is a small lunette fresco by Fra Angelico. Off this cloister is the Pilgrims' Hospice, a long room full of beautiful paintings by Fra Angelico, glowing in bright jewel shades and gold leaf. At one end of the room is the superb *Deposition from the Cross* (c1435–40), while at the other is the famous *Linaiouli Tabernacle* (1433) with its *Madonna Enthroned and Saints*. The border consists of musical angels, often reproduced on Christmas cards. In this room is also the great *Last Judgement* altarpiece (1431) and a series of charming reliquary tabernacles in gold frames featuring 35 tiny scenes from the life of Christ.

Other paintings here are by Fra Bartolomeo, Giovanni Sogliani, Lorenzo Lippi and others. Before climbing the stairs to the monks' quarters, visit two more frescoes: Fra Angelico's large *Crucifixion and Saints* (1441–42) in the Chapter House and Domenico Ghirlandaio's *Last Supper* in the small refectory.

THE MONKS' CELLS
At the top of the stairs to the dormitory is one of Angelico's most famous frescoes, the *Annunciation* (1442). The 44 tiny cells where the monks lived each has a shuttered window and a small fresco by Fra Angelico or his assistants. Those by the master himself are in cells 1 to 9. Note the beautiful angel in Cell 3 and the nativity scene in Cell 5. Girolamo Savonarola, the rebel priest who was prior in 1491, occupied the Prior's Cell. Other famous inhabitants include Fra Bartolomeo, the painter who was a friar.

TIPS

● The museum can be busy; a visit out of peak season allows you to experience the spirituality of the place, which may be compromised by the crowds.

● Only 120 people are allowed up to the dormitories at one time, so book your visit in advance *(tel 055 294 883)*, arrive early in the morning or be prepared to wait.

BASICS

✚ 425 D1 • Piazza San Marco 1, 50121 Firenze ☎ 055 238 8608
🅒 Mon–Fri 8.15–1.50, Sat–Sun 8.15–7; closed 1st, 3rd and 5th Sun and 2nd and 4th Mon of each month 🎫 Adults €4, 18–26 years (EU nationals) €2, under 18s, over 65s (EU nationals) free
📖 Official guidebook €7.50
🚻 ♿ Includes lavatories for visitors with disabilities
🅿 Parking at the Parterre (10-minute walk); parking for visitors with disabilities in Piazza San Marco

www.sbas.firenze.it
An Italian site bringing together the major museums and galleries in Florence. Site plans of the major collections and pictures of the highlights.

Detail of the stone carvings of patron saints on the walls of the Church of Orsanmichele

The stylish courtyard at Palazzo Medici-Riccardi

THE SIGHTS

MUSEO DI STORIA DELLA SCIENZA

➕ 425 D3 • Piazza dei Giudici 1, 50122 Firenze ☎ 055 265311 🕐 Mon, Wed–Fri 9.30–5, Tue, Sat 9.30–1, Jun–Sep; Mon, Wed–Sat 9.30–5, Tue 9.30–1, Oct–May 💶 Adult €6.50, 7–14 €3, under 7s free
www.imss.fi.it

This fascinating and informative museum explores the history of physics, chemistry, astronomy and medicine through several examples of mathematical and scientific instruments, many of which, besides being practical, are beautifully decorated.

As you look at the exhibits, the significant contribution Florence and Tuscany have made to the history of science becomes clear. Room IV is dedicated to Galileo Galilei (1564–1642), one of Tuscany's famous sons, who was born in Pisa and died in Florence, having spent years in the service of the Medici family. One of his many achievements was the perfection of the telescope, and here you can see the one through which he observed Jupiter's four satellites for the first time. Another room charts the progressive improvement of the telescope from Galileo's first examples, perfected in 1610.

There's a room dedicated to the development of the mechanical clock, with beautiful examples of pocket watches. Room XVIII has some gruesome 18th-century anatomical waxworks and terracotta models that demonstrate possible complications of childbirth, along with sets of 18th-century surgical instruments, including one for amputation.

ORSANMICHELE

➕ 424 C3 • Via Arte della Lana, 50122 Firenze ☎ 055 284944 🕐 Mon–Fri 9–noon, 4–6, Sat–Sun and holidays 9–1, 4–6; closed 1st and last Mon of each month

The unique Orsanmichele (currently closed for restoration) was built as a market in 1337, and the original building had a granary on the upper floor. When the market was moved in 1380, the ground floor became a church. The city's guilds commissioned some of the best artists of the day to make statues of patron saints to sit in the canopied niches, and so created a permanent outdoor exhibition of 15th-century Florentine sculpture. Some of the original statues are still here, including Ghiberti's bronzes of St. Matthew (1419–22) and St. Stephen (1427–28).

Inside, faded frescoes of patron saints decorate the walls. The jewel here is Andrea Orcagna's Gothic tabernacle, a large decorative work commissioned by the survivors of the Black Death in 1349.

OSPEDALE DEGLI INNOCENTI

➕ 425 E2 • Piazza SS Annunziata, 50122 Firenze ☎ 055 249 1708 🕐 Thu–Tue 8.30–2; last entrance 1.30 💶 Adult €2.60, 6–18 €1. 50

The Ospedale degli Innocenti opened as a foundling hospital in 1445. It was the first of its kind in Europe and remained open as an orphanage until 2000. It was home to the first school of obstetrics in Italy, and groundbreaking studies into nutrition and vaccinations were carried out here. The building is an important architectural landmark —its beautiful loggia by Filippo Brunelleschi is an early Renaissance masterpiece.

A portico with nine arches borders Piazza Santissima Annunziata, one of the loveliest squares in Florence. The spandrels are adorned with the familiar blue and white *tondi* (glazed terracotta medallions) of babes in swaddling clothes by Andrea della Robbia, while at one end of the loggia is the window-wheel where babies were left by their mothers. In the Museo dello Spedale are fine paintings, including Domenico Ghirlandaio's vivid *Adoration of the Magi* (1488). At one end of the room is a poignant collection of identification tags left by mothers in the hope that one day they might see their children again.

PALAZZO MEDICI-RICCARDI

➕ 425 D2 • Via Cavour 3, 50129 Florence ☎ 055 276 0340 🕐 Thu–Tue 9–7; last entrance 6.30 💶 Adult €4, 6–12s €2.50, under 6s free 🎫

The massive Palazzo Medici-Riccardi was built by Michelozzo some time after 1444 as a town mansion for Cosimo il Vecchio, and was the residence of the Medicis until 1540. The Riccardi family bought the palace in 1659 and enlarged it. It is now the headquarters of the provincial government. The surprise after the slightly rugged and imposing exterior is one of the most delightful little places in Florence, the Capella dei Magi.

The main, columned courtyard is suitably impressive, and the adjacent gardens are filled with lemon trees in huge terracotta pots. The main staircase off the courtyard leads to the chapel, which is covered by Benozzo Gozzoli's beautifully restored frescoes of the *Procession of the Magi to Bethlehem* (1459–63). Gozzoli also dotted the scene with members of the Medici family and other celebrities of the day. The gallery is a large and elaborate baroque room decorated with mirrors, plasterwork and ceiling frescoes by Luca Giordano (1683). Look out for the restored *Madonna and Child* by Filippo Lippi in the smaller adjoining room.

MUSEO NAZIONALE DEL BARGELLO

A superb collection of sculpture by stars such as Michelangelo and Donatello—and yet rarely crowded. Wonderful terracotta pieces by the della Robbia family and an unusual collection of miniature mannerist bronzes.

The forbidding, crenellated Palazzo del Bargello, home to the Bargello Museum, was built in 1255 as the Palazzo del Popolo, the seat of the city's government. In the 16th century the police headquarters was here, along with a prison, which was in use until 1858. The museum was first opened to the public in 1865.

GROUND FLOOR

Begin in the Gothic courtyard with its fine statues and sculptures. Until 1786, executions were carried out here, and condemned prisoners would spend their last night in the chapel on the first floor.

Off the courtyard, the spacious hall has the most celebrated sculptures, by Michelangelo and his contemporaries. Michelangelo's works include an early *Bacchus Drunk* (c1497), a humorous portrayal of the god of wine, and the marble tondo of the Madonna and Child with the infant St. John, known as the *Pitti Tondo* (c1503). Important works by Benvenuto Cellini include *Narcissus*, carved from a block of Greek marble, and *Apollo and Hyacinth,* once in the Boboli Gardens. There is also a life-size preliminary bronze cast of his famous *Perseus*.

FIRST FLOOR

The loggia has a group of bronze birds by Giambologna, made for the Villa di Castello. The Gothic Salone del Consiglio Generale contains works by Donatello and his contemporaries. His *Marzocco Lion*, the symbol of Florence carved in *pietra serena*, is the focus of the room. On the walls hang two of the trial bronze panels made by Ghiberti and Brunelleschi for the baptistery doors, a marble relief of the *Madonna and Child with Angels* by Agostino di Duccio and a number of delightful glazed enamel Madonnas by Luca della Robbia.

DECORATIVE ARTS

There are several rooms dedicated to European and Middle Eastern decorative art, including fabrics, carpets, ceramics, jewellery and clocks, and a large room filled with characteristically lively enamelled terracottas by Giovanni della Robbia. Also worth seeing are the Renaissance bronzes, the most important collection of its kind in Italy.

BASICS

✚ 425 D3 • Via del Proconsolo 4, 50122 Firenze ☎ 055 238 8606
🕐 Daily 8.15–1.50; closed 1st, 3rd and 5th Sun, and 2nd and 4th Mon of every month, 1 Jan, 1 May and 25 Dec
💶 Adults €4, 18–26 (EU nationals) €2, under 18s, over 65s (EU nationals) and art history students free
📘 Official guide €7.50
🅿 Limited parking on Lungarno della Zecca Vecchia (10-minute walk); ample parking under the station (15- to 20-minute walk). Parking for visitors with disabilities in Piazza San Firenze 🚻

www.sbas.firenze.it/bargello/index.html

The courtyard of the Museo Nazionale del Bargello (above) and Andrea della Robbia's Ritratto d'Ignota *(above right)*

Palazzo Pitti

A building of immense proportions with extensive grounds.
Florence's largest and most opulent *palazzo*, once the main seat of the Medicis.
Home to the Galleria Palatina, Florence's most important picture collection
after the Uffizi, and seven other collections.

The vast 205m (673ft) façade of the Palazzo Pitti

RATINGS

Good for kids	●●●
Historic interest	●●●●
Cultural interest	●●●
Photo stops	●●●

BASICS

✚ 424 B5 • Piazza Pitti, 50125 Firenze
☎ 055 238 8614
⊙ Palatina, Appartamenti and Carrozze: Tue–Sun 8.15–6.50. Argenti: Daily 8.15–2; closed 1st and last Mon of the month. Arte Moderna: Daily 8.15–1.50; closed 2nd and 4th Sun, and 1st, 3rd and 5th Mon of the month. Porcellane: Daily 8.15–1 hour before sunset; closed 1st and last Mon of the month. Costume: Daily 8.15–1.50; closed 2nd and 4th Sun, and the 1st, 3rd and 5th Mon of the month
💺 Palatina and Appartamenti: Adult €6.50, under 18s (EU nationals) free. Boboli, Porcellane and Argenti: Adult €4, under 18s (EU nationals) free. Arte Moderna and Costume: Adult €5, under 18s (EU nationals) free
🎧 Palatina audiotours €3.50
☕ Café with a terrace on the main courtyard
🏪 In Palatina and main courtyard
👫 🅿 Underground parking at Santa Maria Novella station; limited parking on Lungarno Serristori; parking for visitors with disabilities Piazza Pitti

www.firenzemusei.it

SEEING THE PALAZZO PITTI

The Pitti collections are huge, so it makes sense to concentrate on the Galleria Palatina, a suite of 26 rooms covered with paintings. The works are displayed much as they were in the 17th century, adorning the walls from floor to ceiling in no discernible chronological order. Allow 2–3 hours to fully appreciate the paintings before moving on to another gallery that takes your fancy. Be prepared for crowds, and also for sections or collections that are closed; you can book ahead to avoid disappointment *(tel 055 294883)*. There is much to see, but make sure you leave time to relax afterwards in the Giardino di Boboli (p. 124).

HIGHLIGHTS

THE COURTYARD
The main entrance to the palace leads you through to Ammanati's splendid courtyard (1560–70), an excellent example of Florentine mannerist architecture. It was used as a stage for lavish spectacles between the 16th and 18th centuries, and is still the venue for concerts and ballet in the summer.

GALLERIA PALATINA
MADONNA AND CHILD: FILIPPO LIPPI–SALA DI PROMOTEO
Painted in 1452 and known as the *Pitti Tondo*, Lippi's famous work perfectly combines exquisite painting and intense spirituality. The eye is drawn to the pure face of the Virgin, the central point, surrounded by scenes from the life of her mother, St. Anne, and the Christ Child lying on her knee.

MADONNA DELLA SEGGIOLA: RAPHAEL–SALA DI SATURNO
Raphael painted this tondo in 1514, and it has been at the Pitti since the 18th century. Although heavily influenced by Venetian painting, evident in its use of light and shade, the painting follows a strictly Florentine form, its shape emphasizing the tender curves of the Virgin and Child.

PIETRO ARETINO: TITIAN–SALA DI APOLLO
Portraiture gained importance during the High Renaissance, as the Church lost its total control on subject matter, and new money brought self-made men to prominence. Titian painted this portrait of the satirical poet Pietro Aretino in 1545, after Aretino had moved from Mantua to Venice, Titian's native city.

SLEEPING CUPID: CARAVAGGIO–SALA DELL'EDUCAZIONE DI GIOVE
This plump little sleeping Cupid is full of allegorical references to passion and lost love. Caravaggio painted it when he was in Malta in 1608. By this time he had already lived in Rome, where he had studied and grasped the fine details of human anatomy and was beginning to concentrate on the development of *chiaroscuro*, the contrast of light and dark, a technique expertly employed in his work later on in his life.

Inside the Grotto del Buontalenti (1583–88) in the Giardino di Boboli, the formal gardens of the Palazzo Pitti

APPARTAMENTI REALI

These royal apartments have been expertly and sensitively restored to their 19th-century condition. From the 17th century onwards they were the residence of the Medicis, the Lorraine dukes, and the Savoy family, including Italy's first monarch, King Umberto I. They are hard to beat in terms of extravagance; gilding and stucco work, rich damask hangings, vast chandeliers, enormous gilt mirrors, period furnishings, paintings and sculptures are frequent and impressive.

MUSEO DEGLI ARGENTI

In a series of sumptuous state rooms, this museum concentrates on luxury *objets d'art* amassed by the Medici dukes. There is a huge range of items, from antique vases collected by Lorenzo Il Magnifico to stunningly worked, but aesthetically banal, figurines, and a vast array of inlaid pieces.

BACKGROUND

Construction began on the Palazzo Pitti in 1457, supposedly to a design by Brunelleschi. It was originally the private residence of the banker Luca Pitti, a rival of the Medici family, and his descendants, but in 1549 the family funds dried up and it was purchased by Cosimo I's wife, the Grand Duchess Eleonora. It became the official residence of the Grand Dukes and was occupied by ruling families until 1919, when it was presented to the state by Vittorio Emanuele III. Under Medici ownership it was repeatedly enlarged, notably in the 16th century, when Bartolomeo Ammanati (1511–92) lengthened the façade and built the courtyard, while the side wings were added in the 18th and 19th centuries. The Medici family began decorating and amassing the collections in the 17th century. The main galleries opened to the public in 1833 and the Galleria d'Arte Moderna, Florence's modern art museum, joined the gallery complex in 1924.

GALLERY GUIDE

Galleria Palatina: The main collection, strong on 16th-century works, particularly Raphael, Titian and Andrea del Sarto. In a wing of the main palace.

Galleria d'Arte Moderna: Works spanning the mid-18th to mid-20th centuries. In the main building on the floor above the Galleria Palatina.

Museo degli Argenti: *Objets d'art*, gold and jewellery from the Medici collections. Accessed from the main courtyard.

Museo del Costume: Rotating exhibitions of historic clothes from the early 18th to mid-20th centuries. In Palazzina Meridiana in the south wing.

Museo delle Porcellane: French, Italian, German and Viennese porcelain and ceramics. In a pavilion at the top of the Boboli Gardens.

Appartamenti Reali: Lavishly decorated state apartments following on from the Palatina.

Collezione Contini Bonacossi: A picture collection on long-term loan, strong on Spanish painting. Next to the Museo del Costume in the Palazzina Meridiana.

Museo delle Carozze: Carriage collection—currently closed.

Statue in the Sala di Venere (Room 4) in the Galleria Palatina

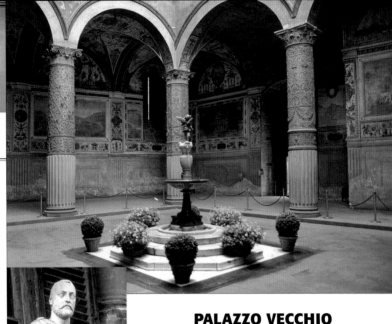

PALAZZO VECCHIO

**Florence's town hall, an outstanding example of Florentine civic purpose, with superb rooftop views from the loggia. Vast, elaborately decorated public rooms and intimate private apartments.
Fine sculptures, including *Victory* by Michelangelo.**

The palace stands on the site of the medieval Palazzo dei Priori, rebuilt to Arnolfo di Cambio's design. Designers of *palazzi comunali* throughout Tuscany based their designs on its battlemented structure. Cosimo il Vecchio was imprisoned in the asymmetrically placed tower before his exile in 1433. Savonarola was also imprisoned here in 1498, but went on to be burned at the stake in Piazza della Signoria.

RATINGS

Historic interest	●●●●
Cultural interest	●●●●
Value for money	●●●

BASICS

✚ 425 D3 • Piazza della Signoria, 50122 Firenze ☎ 055 276 8465
🕐 Fri–Wed 9–7, Thu 9–2
🎟 Adult €5.70, under 12s free
🎧 Audiotours in Italian, English, French, German, Japanese, €4.10
📖 From €4.65
♿ ♀♂
🅿 Nearest parking under Santa Maria Novella Station (15-minute walk). Parking for visitors with disabilities in Piazza Signoria

www.comune.fi.it
www.museoragazzi.it

A copy of Verrochio's Pluttino Fountain in the courtyard (top); a marble bust on the façade (above left)

THE COURTYARD

Past the main entrance is the courtyard, reconstructed by Michelozzo in 1453. It was elaborately decorated by Giorgio Vasari in 1565 to celebrate the marriage of the son of Cosimo I to Joanna of Austria.

FIRST FLOOR

The largest room is the Salone dei Cinquecento, a meeting room for the 500-member Consiglio Maggiore. Vasari painted the frescoes to celebrate Cosimo I's triumphs over Pisa and Siena. The most notable sculpture is Michelangelo's *Victory*.

Next door, the tiny, windowless Studiolo di Francesco I has allegorical paintings by Vasari and small bronze statues by Giambologna and Ammanati. It was here that the melancholic son of Cosimo I pursued his interest in alchemy. On the same floor, Vasari and Cosimo I's assistants decorated the Quartiere di Leone X with ornate illustrations of the history of the Medici family.

SECOND FLOOR

Access to the Quartiere di Eleonora di Toledo, the private apartments of Cosimo I's wife, is via a balcony across the end of the Salone del Cinquecento, providing a close-up view of the ceiling. The chapel, decorated with frescoes of various saints, is one of Bronzino's most important works. The Sala dei Gigli owes its name to the lily (*gigli*) motif, a symbol of the city. Here also is Donatello's bronze statue, *Judith and Holofernes* (1455). Niccolò Machiavelli used the Cancellaria next door as an office from 1498 to 1512, when he was a government secretary. The *guardaroba*, or wardrobe, contains a fascinating collection of 57 detailed maps of the world as it was then known.

PIAZZA DELLA SIGNORIA

**Florence's most noble and famous piazza—the place to get a real feel for the city.
A vast open-air, traffic-free sculpture gallery with elegant cafés and restaurants.**

This wide, open square marks the heart of the *centro storico*, and next to the Galleria degli Uffizi (p. 122–123). The Piazza della Signoria has been the political focus of Florence since the Middle Ages. Surrounded by tall buildings, notably the vast, sombre Palazzo Vecchio (see opposite), this is where the ruling city elders called open-air public assemblies in times of crisis. The crowd was often provoked by speeches on the *arringhiera* (oration terrace), a raised platform, and the gatherings frequently degenerated into violence. The area in front of the Palazzo Vecchio was named Piazza del Popolo in 1307.

The Calcio Storico, a football match each year in medieval costume in the piazza (top); Ammanati's statue of Neptune

THE SCULPTURES

The enormous Loggia dei Lanzi (also known as the Loggia della Signoria) was designed to be used by dignitaries for formal meetings and ceremonies. It was completed in 1382 and has been used as an open-air sculpture museum since the late 18th century. Dominating the front is Cellini's mannerist bronze *Perseus* (1545). Considered his greatest work, it shows Perseus triumphantly holding aloft the severed head of Medusa. Near it is Giambologna's last work, the *Rape of the Sabine Women*, completed in 1583. Donatello's *Judith and Holofernes* was the first of the statues to be placed in the piazza (this is a copy—the original is in the Palazzo Vecchio).

In front of the main entrance to the Palazzo Vecchio stands a copy of Michelangelo's *David* (the original is in the Accademia, p. 121). The other large statue nearby is Bandinelli's *Hercules and Cacus* (1534), described by his rival Cellini as an 'old sack full of melons'. At the corner of the Palazzo Vecchio is Ammanati's massive fountain (1575), with the undignified figure of Neptune. The large equestrian bronze, Giambologna's monument to Cosimo (1595), shows detailed scenes of Cosimo's coronation and victory over the Sienese. The plaque in the pavement in front of the fountain marks the spot where Girolamo Savonarola was burned at the stake as a heretic and traitor on 23 May 1498. A ceremony to mark his death is held in the square annually on this day.

RATINGS	
Good for kids	● ● ●
Historic interest	● ● ● ● ●
Cultural interest	● ● ● ●
Walkability	● ● ● ●

TIPS

● An elegant, expensive, table at the Café Rivoire is a good place to people watch. Or perch on a stone bench under the Loggia dei Lanzi.

● Free open-air concerts are held here in summer.

BASICS

🗺 424 C3 • Piazza delle Signoria, 50122 Firenze
🅿 Parking at Lungarno Torrigiani (10-minute walk)
🏛 In Palazzo Vecchio

Rape of the Sabine Women

Two of the Four Seasons *statues on Ponte Santa Trinità*

Ponte Vecchio—one of the most famous bridges in the world—has survived against the odds

PIAZZALE MICHELANGELO

➕ 425 E5 • Piazzale Michelangelo, 50125 Firenze

It is worth making the climb, or taking a bus, to Piazzale Michelangelo, for the unrivalled views over Florence. Here you can marvel at the life-size replica of Michelangelo's *David* in the middle of the square or enjoy the panoramic view and a drink at one of the terraced bars. On a clear day, views extend way beyond the city to the surrounding hills, and the sunsets are fantastic. On Sunday afternoons the place is heaving with everyone taking advantage of the city's best photo opportunity.

Up on a hillside south of the Arno, Piazzale Michelangelo's wide, open space is bordered by a stone balustrade on the northern side overlooking the city. It is about halfway along the broad, leafy *viale* that winds through this part of the city, so traffic can be heavy at peak times.

PONTE SANTA TRINITÀ

➕ 424 C3 • Piazza Santa Trinità, 50123 Firenze
www.firenzeturismo.it

The Santa Trinità bridge has the best view of the Ponte Vecchio and is a fine monument in itself. It is also remarkable, for in 1944 it was destroyed—along with all the other bridges in Florence except the Ponte Vecchio—by bombing, and was carefully reconstructed using stone from the original quarries. What you see today is a faithful replica of Ammanati's 1567 bridge.

Three wide, graceful arches make up the bridge, which links elegant Via Tornabuoni to the north and the characterful Oltrarno to the south. In each of the four corners stands a statue, the original *Four Seasons*. They

fell into the river during the World War II bombing, but were salvaged and reassembled (the last piece, the head of *Spring,* was fished out in 1961).

PONTE VECCHIO

➕ 424 C3 • Ponte Vecchio 50123, Firenze 🅿 Limited meter parking on Lungarno Serristori (5-minute walk); underground parking at Santa Maria Novella station (15-minute walk); parking for visitors with disabilities on Via Guicciardini (100m/110 yd)

If you can ignore the crowds and the modern gold shops, the Ponte Vecchio gives you a taste of what the medieval city was like—as well as a good view of the River Arno, its palaces and the adjacent Ponte Santa Trinità.

The present bridge was built in 1345, a reconstruction of an earlier structure washed away by a flood. Until 1218 this had been the only access across the river. At the end of the 16th century, Grand Duke Ferdinand I replaced the evil-smelling hog-butchers' shops that lined the bridge with gold- and silversmiths, and they have remained here ever since. The bridge has survived two major traumas in recent history: In 1945, while all the other bridges in Florence were destroyed by bombing, the Ponte Vecchio was saved on Hitler's orders; then in 1966 the waters of the Arno rose so high that a fortune in gold was washed away in the floods.

Small shops and houses line the bridge on both sides, supported on brackets that overhang the river. They are painted in mellow shades of ochre, and with their wooden shutters, ancient wrought-ironwork and awnings they have retained their medieval appearance. Vasari's 1565 corridor is clearly visible running over the top of the eastern shops. Originally designed to be a secret passageway for

Cosimo I, it joins the Galleria degli Uffizi (p. 122–123) and the Palazzo Pitti (see p. 128–129).

SANTISSIMA ANNUNZIATA

➕ 425 E1 • Piazza Santissima Annunziata, 26618I Firenze ☎ 055 239 8034 🕐 Daily 7–12.45, 4–6.30 🎟 Free

This unexpectedly large and grand building is well worth a visit. In the mid-15th century it was one of the most important churches in Florence. It was founded in 1250 to protect a miraculous picture of the Virgin, it was expanded between 1444 and 1481 by Michelozzo, who also designed the Chiostrino dei Voti in front of the church, an unusual glass-roofed atrium decorated with frescoes by Andrea del Sarto (1486–1531) and some of his contemporaries.

The church stands on the north side of Piazza Santissima Annunziata, its façade made up of a graceful portico that leads into the Chiostro dei Voti. On the right are frescoes by Rosso Fiorentino of the *Assumption* and to the left is Jacopo Pontormo's *Visitation*. The interior is dark, yet lavishly decorated with marble and gold leaf. The tabernacle commissioned by the Medici family in the 15th century contains the miraculous painting of the Madonna, said to have been painted by a monk with help from an angel. Unusually, the large apse behind the main altar is entered by way of a triumphal arch—clearly influenced by Roman architecture.

More notable works of art in the main body of the church include, in the left aisle, an *Assumption* by Perugino (c1450–1523) and *The Holy Trinity with St. Jerome* by Andrea del Castagno (c1421–57). The splendid organ in the nave, built between 1509 and 1521, is the oldest in the city and the second oldest in Italy.

SANTA CROCE

The largest Franciscan church in Italy, reputedly founded by St. Francis.
Cappella dei Pazzi—one of Brunelleschi's most important works and a masterpiece of the early Renaissance.
Several important Florentines are buried here.

In the heart of one of Florence's most attractive areas, the present Santa Croce was begun in 1294 and completed in the 1450s. The original plain front was replaced in the 19th century with an elaborate neo-Gothic one. The interior is vast, with a wide nave and superb stained-glass windows by Agnolo Gaddi. Although some frescoes are in a disappointing condition, there are some exceptional works.

THE LEFT (NORTH) AISLE
Lorenzo Ghiberti (1378–1455) is buried under the tomb-slab with the eagle on it. There is also a monument to Galileo Galilei (1564–1642), the great scientist who spent his latter years in Florence.

THE EASTERN END
The polygonal sanctuary in the eastern end is covered with vivid frescoes by Gaddi. On either side are small chapels, each dedicated to an eminent Florentine family of the day, with frescoes by Giotto. The Bardi di Libertà Chapel has frescoes by Bernardo Daddi and an altarpiece by Giovanni della Robbia. The Bardi di Vernio Chapel has frescoes by Masi di Banco, while Donatello's wooden crucifix hangs in the Bardi Chapel in the north transept. The frescoes in the Castellani Chapel are by Gaddi, whose father Taddeo was responsible for the beautiful paintings in the Baroncelli Chapel. Next to the Baroncelli Chapel a corridor leads to the Medici Chapel by Brunelleschi.

THE RIGHT (SOUTH) AISLE
In the right aisle are the tombs of Michelangelo (designed by Vasari), the poet Dante, and Niccolò Machiavelli.

CAPPELLA DEI PAZZI, THE CLOISTERS AND MUSEUM
From the right aisle there is access to Brunelleschi's Cappella dei Pazzi. He was still working on this masterpiece of tranquillity when he died in 1446. Inside, in contrast to the elaborate Gothic tendencies of the age, grey *pietra serena* stone, simply carved in classical lines, is set against a white background. At the base of the elegant dome, 12 terracotta roundels by Della Robbia depict the Apostles.

BASICS

✚ 425 E3 • Piazza Santa Croce, 50122 Firenze
☎ 055 244619
🕐 Mon–Sat 9.30–5.30, Sun 1–5.30
🎫 Adult €3 (also covers museum); child (11–18) €2; child (under 11) free
📷 €8
🎧 Free tours in English, French, German, Spanish, Italian Mon–Sat 10–12.30, 3–5, Sun 3–5 (tours given by volunteers, so times and availability of languages may vary). Audioguides at fixed points: English, French, Spanish, Italian €1
🚇 🅿 Lungarno della Zecca Vecchia (10-minute walk); parking for visitors with disabilities in Piazza Santa Croce

www.firenzeturismo.it

TIP

● Calcio Storico, an established football (soccer) match, is played in medieval costume in Piazza Santa Croce or Piazza della Signoria on 24 June (St. John's Day–patron saint of Florence). Other dates are picked from a hat on Easter Sunday (p. 251).

The decorative floor tombs of illustrious Italians in the Basilica di Santa Croce

Neat hedges and lawns within the cloisters of San Lorenzo

A bronze turtle in Piazza Santa Maria Novella

The column-framed window of San Miniato al Monte

THE SIGHTS

SAN LORENZO

⊞ 424 C2 • Piazza San Lorenzo, 50123 Firenze ☎ 055 216634 ⊙ Church: Mon–Sat 10–5.30. Cloister: Mon–Sat 10–6, Sun 9–1 🖼 Adult €2.50; child (6s and under) free

The principal members of the Medici dynasty from Cosimo Il to Cosimo il Vechio III are buried in this church. The basilica that once stood on the site was consecrated in 393 and is thought to have been the oldest church in Florence. The Medici commissioned Brunelleschi to rebuild it in 1425, enlisting Michelangelo's expertise for certain projects. There are fewer important works of art here than elsewhere in Florence, but the church is a shining example of archetypal Renaissance architecture.

The basilica dominates the bustling market area of San Lorenzo, rising above the lively and sometimes tawdry stalls that attract bargain-hunters. The interior is dominated by the grey shades of *pietra serena* stone columns and the grey-white marble floor designed by Brunelleschi. Donatello's massive rectangular pulpits in the nave were his last work. Off the left transept is the Sagrestia Vecchia by Brunelleschi, featuring a vault with terracotta tondi by Donatello, who also made the bronze doors. The small dome above the altar is decorated with frescoes of the zodiac in midnight blue and gold. You can wander out of the main door on the left into the graceful two-tiered cloisters that frame the garden planted with orange trees.

SANTA MARIA NOVELLA

⊞ 424 B2 • Piazza Santa Maria Novella, 50123 Firenze ☎ Church: 055 215918; museum: 055 282187 ⊙ Church: Mon–Thu, Sat 9.30–4.30, Fri, Sun 1–4.30. Museum: Mon–Sat 9–4.30, Sun 9–1.30 🖼 Church: adult €2.50, under 18s free. Museum: adult €2.60, under 12s free 🖼 www.smn.it

This Gothic church has numerous works of art but it attracts significantly fewer visitors than San Lorenzo and Santa Croce. It is a beautiful building, with outstanding stained-glass windows, chapels with important frescoes and calm cloisters.

The church stands on Piazza Santa Maria Novella, and has a striking black-and-white marble façade. Its lofty interior, with high stone vaulting decorated with stripes, is calm and uncluttered. The church's most famous fresco, Masaccio's *Trinità* (c1425), is remarkable for its use of perspective. The sanctuary is decorated with delightful frescoes by Domenico Ghirlandaio (1485–90), showing the lives of the Virgin Mary, John the Baptist and the Dominican saints. Next to it is the Filippo Strozzi Chapel in which there are some frescoes by Filippino Lippi illustrating the lives of St. Philip and St. John.

There are more important frescoes in the Museo di Santa Maria Novella, in the church's convent.

SAN MINIATO AL MONTE

⊞ 425 E5 • Via Monte alle Croci, 50125 Firenze ☎ 055 234 2731 ⊙ Daily 8–7.30, summer; daily 8–12.30, 2.30–7.30, rest of year 🖼 Free

The Church of San Miniato al Monte, on a hill to the south of the city, is the finest example of a Romanesque church in Tuscany. Apart from being a beautiful church in itself, the site provides wonderful views across the Arno and the *centro storico* as far as Fiesole and the hills. A visit requires an uphill walk from town or a bus ride.

Built in 1013, the famous façade can be seen from all over the city. White-and-green-geometrical marble designs surround a glittering 13th-century mosaic of Christ between the Virgin and St. Minias. Little has changed inside the church since the 11th century. In the middle of the nave the 1207 marble floor is made up of intarsia panels decorated with animals and constellations of the zodiac. The Cappella del Crocifisso has a freestanding tabernacle carved by Michelozzo (1396–1472) and terracotta pieces by Luca della Robbia (1400–82). At 5.30pm (4.30pm in winter) you can hear the Benedictine monks, who inhabit the convent next door, singing Gregorian chants.

SANTO SPIRITO

⊞ 424 B4 • Piazza Santo Spirito, 50125 Firenze ☎ 055 210030 ⊙ Church: Mon–Tue, Thu–Sat 10–noon, 4–5.30, Wed 10–noon, Sun 4–5.30. Cenacolo: Tue–Sun 9–1.30 🖼 Church: free. Cenacolo: adult €2.10; child (under 20s) €1.60 www.firenzeturismo.it

The massive Santo Spirito was the last church designed by Filippo Brunelleschi (1377–1446). Its most notable feature is the simple 18th-century façade, now an emblem for the Oltrarno district of Florence. This is a great place to escape the crowds and discover artistic gems.

Brunelleschi began designing the church in 1444 and the work was finally finished in 1481. The huge structure, with its strange, blank façade, dominates pretty Piazza Santo Spirito. In spite of its grandeur, it is still a parish church and its broad steps provide a convenient outdoor sitting room for the local residents.

Inside, grey *pietra serena* stone dominates, with massive columns, arches and vaults creating a harmonious space. The walls are lined with 38 chapels.

TUSCANY AND UMBRIA

With its rolling hills, villas, vines, olives and cypresses, the landscape of Tuscany and Umbria is synonymous with the idyllic Italian dream. Settled and cultivated for 5,000 years, the regions are home to hilltop villages and serene towns and cities such as medieval Siena, fortified Lucca, Pisa, Perugia and Orvieto. If you still have any energy left after sightseeing you can escape to the Apennine peaks in the east.

MAJOR SIGHTS

Basilica di Santa Chiara (above) and the fountain in Piazza del Comune

ASSISI

Medieval treasures associated with the lives of San Francesco (St. Francis) and Santa Chiara (St. Clare).

Assisi, the birthplace of St. Francis (1182–1226), stands on the beautiful terraced slopes of Monte Subasio, above the Valle Umbra. A powerful city in the Middle Ages, Assisi fell into obscurity in the early 16th century, but it again became a popular destination for visitors and pilgrims after the discovery of the bodies of St. Francis in 1818 and St. Clare in 1850 generated a renewed interest in Assisi's medieval art.

BASILICA DI SAN FRANCESCO

The construction of the Basilica di San Francesco began in 1228. Combining Umbrian Romanesque with French-inspired Gothic architecture, the complex consists of two churches, one above the other. The cool and dimly lit lower church (1228–30), was decorated with frescoes by some of the greatest painters of the 13th and 14th centuries, including Cimabue and Giotto. The four frescoes over the main altar depict St. Francis in glory and the virtues of the Franciscan order—poverty, chastity and obedience. Don't miss Cimabue's simple portrait of St. Francis in the right transept. St. Francis is buried in the crypt.

By contrast, the painstakingly restored upper church (1230–53) has high vaulted arches and is bright and airy. A series of 28 frescoes by Giotto illustrates the life of St. Francis.

BASILICA DI SANTA CHIARA

St Francis' contemporary St. Clare (1193–1253), founder of the Order of the Poor Clares, dedicated her life to the Franciscan movement. Her Romanesque basilica, with its pink and white striped stonework and huge flying buttresses, was built between 1257 and 1265. Some Giotto-school frescoes survive, but the highlight is the iconic painting of *St. Clare and Eight Scenes from Her Life* behind the altar, painted in 1283 by an unknown Umbrian artist. St. Clare's remains are in the crypt.

PIAZZA DEL COMUNE

At the heart of Assisi is the Piazza del Comune, the site of the Roman Forum. Here the imposing Torre del Popolo stands next to the Temple of Minerva, intact with its elegant Corinthian columns. Erected in the first century BC, it has been a church since 1539. Overlooking the town is Rocca Maggiore, a fearsome 14th-century fortress *(daily 9–8)*.

RATINGS	
Historic interest	●●●●
Cultural interest	●●●●●
Photo stops	●●●
Walkability	●●●●

TIPS

● Shorts, miniskirts, sleeveless tops, mobile phones and flash photography are not permitted in the churches.

● *Calendimaggio*, a medieval costume festival with street parades and music, takes place on the first Thursday, Friday and Saturday in May. The Festa di San Francesco is on 3 or 4 October.

BASICS

🗺 437 H8

ℹ Piazza del Comune 22, 06082 Assisi, tel 075 812534 🕐 Mon–Sat 8–6.30, Sun 10–1, 2–5, summer; Mon–Sat 8–2, 3–6, Sun 9–1, rest of year

❓ Tickets for Rocca Maggiore, Pinacoteca and Foro Romano from €1.70, www.sistemamuseo.it 🎫 Official guides can be hired in English, French Spanish, German, Russian and Swedish (tel 075 815228, www.umbria.org/tour-guides) 🚆 Santa Maria degli Angeli

St Francis' wooded retreat, the Eremo delle Carceri, to the east of Assisi; the convent there now dates from 1426 (left)

The Abbazia di Monte Oliveto Maggiore

The hilltop town of Amelia became a Roman municipality in AD90, but the town's origins date from the 12th century

THE SIGHTS

ABBAZIA DI MONTE OLIVETO MAGGIORE

436 G8 ☎ 0577 707611 🕐 Daily 9.15–noon, 3.15–5, May–Sep; daily 9.15–noon, 3.15–6, rest of year 🅿 Free

Come here to soak up the beauty of this isolated medieval abbey, still home to a monastic community. Many of its ancient buildings are closed to visitors, but you can go into the Grand Cloister.

Near Chiusure, 9km (6 miles) northeast of Buonconvento, the abbey is set on a hillside surrounded by olive, oak and cypress trees. Founded by Bernardo Tolomei, a member of a wealthy Sienese family, the delightful old buildings date from 1272. The Chiostro Grande (Grand Cloister) has a fresco cycle on the life of the founder of the Benedictine order, St. Benedict. It was created by Luca Signorelli, who began the work in 1498, and by the Milanese artist, Sodoma, who completed the majority of the work between 1505 and 1508. The church has a 15th-century layout, with wooden choir stalls carved by Fra Giovanni da Verona. The monks have a library of 40,000 books and other documents, along with a workshop where they restore old books.

ABBAZIA DI SAN PIETRO IN VALLE

438 H–J9 ☎ 0744 780316 🕐 Daily 10–5; closed occasionally 1–2 🅿 Free 📖 ❓ Custodian in the village will show you around (her family has been providing the service free for 100 years)–in Italian only, but she speaks very slowly

Set in idyllic surroundings, with its tall campanile rising above woods, San Pietro in Valle is steeped in history. Founded by Faroaldo II, the Longobard Duke of Spoleto, in 720, this abbey has some exceptional frescoes and beautiful cloisters. The restored fresco cycle in the nave depicts scenes from the Old and New Testaments, and is considered to be one of Italy's most important examples of Romanesque art for the variety of scenes depicted and the complexity of the work (late 12th to early 13th century). Look for the lively images of Noah being called to Eternity and Adam naming the animals. More frescoes cover the apses—those in the right-hand apse are by followers of Giotto. A small fresco in the left aisle illustrates the *Dream of Faroaldo*; it shows Faroaldo being visited by St. Peter, who is instructing him to build a monastery on this holy spot in his honour.

Also to be found in the open nave are a a rare seventh-century Longobard altar showing the signature of the original craftsman (Ursus), and five Roman sarcophagi carved with mythological scenes and reused as tombs for Faroaldo and his family.

AMELIA

438 H9 ❗ Via Orvieto 1, 05022 Amelia (before Porta Romana on the first floor), tel 0744 981453 ❓ Guided tours by arrangement. Information plaques at important landmarks **www.**umbria2000.it

Amelia (Roman Ameria), in the beautiful Amerino district, is surrounded by hilly Umbrian countryside. The imposing polygonal walls, built of huge local stones between the sixth and fourth centuries BC, can be seen on either side of the Porta Romana. The famous bronze statue of the Roman captain Germanicus, nephew of Tiberius and father of Caligula, unearthed in 1963, is housed in the Museo Archeologico (Tue–Sun 10.30–1, 4.30–7.30, Jul–Aug; Tue–Sun 10.30–1, 4–7, Apr–Jun and Sep; Fri–Sun 10.30–1, 3.30–6, rest of year).

An amazing example of ancient plumbing and engineering can be seen in the Cisterne Romane, under Piazza Matteotti (Sat, Sun and public holidays 10.30–12.30, 4.30–7.30). Its 10 chambers have a capacity of 4,400cu m (155,400cu ft) of water.

The charming Piazza Matteotti, reached via steep cobbled streets, has some interesting buildings, including the Renaissance-style Petrignani Palazzo, now the civic offices.

Don't miss The duomo in Piazza Lojali has an 11th-century campanile.

AREZZO

437 G7 ❗ Piazza della Repubblica 28, 52100 Arezzo, tel 0575 377678 ❗ Arezzo

Arezzo thrived during the Middle Ages as a major hub of gold and jewellery and its historic old town still survives. About 80km (50 miles) southeast of Florence, it sits on a hilltop overlooking a fertile plain near the Arno, dominated by its cathedral and fortress. Many people come simply to enjoy Piero della Francesca's famous fresco cycles, *The Legend of the True Cross*, in the Church of San Francesco (daily 8.30–noon, 2–7, summer; daily 8.30–noon, 2.30–6.30, rest of year, tel 0575 24001).

One of Italy's most famous paintings, painted on the walls around the high altar in the Cappella Bacci (Mon–Fri 9–7, Sat 9–6, Sun 1–6; closed 1 Jan, 1 May, 13 June, 4 Oct) between 1453 and 1466, illustrates the legend of the cross on which Christ was crucified. There is another fresco by Piero della Francesca in the duomo (daily 6.30–12.30, 3–7). A short stroll away is the Passeggio del Prato, an attractive park overlooked by the Fortezzo Medicea (1538–60), a castle built by the

The Piazza Grande in Arezzo, the venue for the Giostra del Saracino (medieval jousting) in late August and a monthly antiques fair

Statue of a monk at the Abbazia di Monte Oliveto, Buonconvento

THE SIGHTS

town's Medici rulers. The Museo Archeologico *(daily 8.30–7.30)*, the Roman amphitheatre, has some priceless collections of locally produced pottery.

The alleys around the main square, Piazza Grande, are full of dark workshops smelling of wood, where artisans restore antique furniture. On the first Sunday of the month the town is taken over by an excellent antiques fair.

BAGNO VIGNONI

➕ 436 G8 ℹ️ Strada di Bagno Vignoni, 53027 S. Quirico d'Orcia, tel 0577 888975

Bagno Vignoni is one of Tuscany's most fascinating sights, a village whose old stone buildings cluster around a large, open-air pool filled with water from a natural hot spring. When the air is cool, a mist rises from the warm water and drifts over the village square. The spring was known in Etruscan times, and the waters were enjoyed over the years by the Romans, along with popes and saints, including Catherine of Siena. In medieval times the baths became a resting place for pilgrims going along the Via Francigena, the pilgrims' route over St. Bernard's Pass and through Italy to Rome. Today this is still a great place to stop and rest, with plenty of restaurants. There's a children's playground near the parking area.

BARGA

➕ 436 F6 ℹ️ Via di Mezzo, 4555051 Barga, tel 0583 724743 (freephone in Italy 800 028497) 🚂 Fornacci di Barga or Barga Gallicano (nearer to town); long uphill climb from both www.barganews.com www.commune.barga.lu.it

Off the beaten track, yet easily accessible, Barga makes an ideal trip into the country for anyone staying in Lucca or Pisa. Stroll

through its attractive, winding streets, shop for local produce, or simply enjoy a drink in one of its historic cafés.

Barga sits on a hill above the Serchio Valley, 28km (17 miles) north of Lucca, with lovely views of the Alpi Apuane. The town has strong links with Scotland, as many of its residents emigrated to Glasgow. Many people speak English and the town even has its own fish-and-chip fair in August.

It has kept much of its medieval appearance and layout, with remnants of the old walls and narrow, steep streets stretching down from the imposing duomo. It is a fairly steep climb to the duomo, but well worth it simply for the views.

Don't miss Caffé Capretz, a historic and atmospheric café established in 1870; for local produce, visit Mazzolini Andrea, a delectable shop on Via di Mezzo that sells a wide range of foods, from chestnut flour to mountain pecorino cheese.

BUONCONVENTO

➕ 436 G8 ℹ️ Museo di Arte Sacra della Val d'Arbia, Via Soccini 18, 53020 Buonconvento, tel 0577 807181 🚂 Buonconvento

Buonconvento is a small historic town, an important trading post in the mid-13th century and a prominent stopping-off point for pilgrims along the Via Francigena.

About 27km (17 miles) south of Siena, the town is at the confluence of the Arbia and Ombrone rivers, between Siena and Montalcino. Its outskirts are unattractive but well-preserved medieval parts are surrounded by walls built between 1371 and 1381.

The Museo d'Arte Sacra *(Tue–Sun 10.30–1, summer; Sat–Sun 10–1, 2–5, winter))* is a museum of religious art displaying Sienese paintings from the 14th to the

17th century, including an *Annunciation* by Andrea di Bartolo and the *Madonna del Latte (Madonna of the Milk)* a breastfeeding Madonna by Luca di Tomme. It also has displays of jewellery, wood and marble sculptures.

Don't miss The 14th-century Church of Santi Pietro e Paulo has an early 15th-century fresco by an unknown Sienese artist and a *Madonna and Child* (1450) by Matteo di Giovanni.

CHIANTI

➕ 436 G7 ℹ️ Comune, Via Ferruccio 40, 53011 C in C (Si), tel 0577 742311 www.chiantinet.it

The Chianti region, between Florence and Siena, is generally explored by driving down the Chiantigiana (SS222), a designated scenic wine road that runs through the heart of the district. This seductive area of rolling hills, liberally sprinkled with vineyards, has produced wine since Etruscan times. The landscape is often wild, characterized by rich farmland, heavily wooded slopes, isolated villas and numerous vineyards. Taste the produce, then visit some of the region's pretty towns such as Castellina in Chianti, Greve in Chianti (the unofficial capital) and Radda in Chianti.

Castellina in Chianti was once of great strategic importance as it sits on the border between the territories of Siena and Florence. You can still see its ancient fortress and walk along the Via delle Volte, a tunnel-like road that runs around the walls and was formerly used by soldiers.

Radda in Chianti *(tel 0577 738494)* is a hilltop town offering great views over the region, with fine buildings dating from the 15th and 16th centuries.

The lovely town of Greve in Chianti *(tel 055 854 6287)* has plenty of wine shops, cobbled streets and alleyways to explore.

The Renaissance church of Madonna del Calcinaio on the hillside a few miles from the Tuscan town of Cortona

A woman decorating ceramics, a common sight in Deruta

CITTÀ DI CASTELLO

✚ 437 H7 ℹ️ Off Piazza Matteotti, 06012 Perugia, tel 075 855 4922
❓ CartaMusei (€5), valid for one week, gives reduced entry to certain museums (including Pinacoteca Comunale, Collezione Burri, Museo del Duomo and Centro Documentazione Tradizioni Popolari)
www.umbria2000.it
www.guideinumbria.com

Città di Castello has an interesting range of ancient and modern art housed in its elegant palazzi and former tobacco-drying sheds, where traditional crafts continue to thrive. Surrounded by medieval walls, the town occupies a central position in the Upper Tiber Valley. The Pinacoteca Comunale, in Palazzo Vitelli alla Cannoniera, is an important gallery in Umbria. The oldest painting here is a large altarpiece by Maestro di Città de Castello, *Madonna in Trono col Bambino*, surrounded by six angels (13th century). In Room 6 is the only painting by Raphael to remain in the Pinacoteca, the *Gonfalon of the Holy Trinity*, one of his first works. It has been used for hundreds of years as a *gonfalone* (banner) during religious festivals and has suffered wear and tear. In Piazza Gabriotti, the newly restored ecclesiastical museum, the Museo del Duomo (*Tue–Sun 10–1, 2.30–6.30, Oct–Mar; Tue–Sun 9.30–1, 2.30–7, Apr–Sep*), houses the Treasure of Canoscio from the palaeo-Christian period (sixth century), a rare collection of embossed silver ceremonial objects used during Mass.

CORTONA

✚ 437 H7 ℹ️ Via Nazionale 42, 52044 Cortona, tel 0575 630352

Cortona is the highest town in Italy. It is a steep climb up to the Fortezza Medicea, but worth it for the breathtaking views of Lake

Trasimeno (p. 141). Substantial parts of the town's Etruscan walls are incorporated into the medieval structure, and churches and fine museums grace the precipitous cobbled streets.

From the focal point, Piazza della Repubblica, it is a short stroll to Piazza del Duomo, the setting for the Museo Diocesano (*daily 10–5, tel 0575 62830*). The highlights include two masterpieces by Fra Angelico, an *Annunciation* and a *Madonna and Child with Saints*, along with works by Sassetta, Bartolomeo della Gatta and Luca Signorelli. The archaeological star is a second-century Roman sarcophagus carved with scenes depicting Dionysus's battle with the Amazons, a work much admired by the Renaissance sculptors Donatello and Filippo Brunelleschi. The town's Etruscan past is recalled in the Museo dell'Accademia Etrusca (*daily 10–5*), which has a huge fifth-century bronze lamp, some exquisite jewellery, urns and vases, and an impressive, if incongruous, ancient Egyptian collection.

DERUTA

✚ 437 H8 ℹ️ Piazza dei Consoli 4, 0653 Deruta, tel 075 971 1559; Mar–end Jun only

Deruta has been famous for its ceramics and majolica since the 14th century. Shops selling pottery abound, and in the old town you can visit the Museo Regionale della Ceramica (*daily 10.30–1, 3.30–7, Jul–Aug; Tue–Sun 10.30–1, 3–6, rest of year, tel 075 971 1000*). This restored museum building traces the history of ceramics from the earliest examples of terracotta to lavish Renaissance majolica. Among the fascinating exhibits is a display of plates presented as wedding gifts, devotional plaques, spouted drug jars and even a shoe-shaped handwarmer. The museum also

contains fragments of floor from Perugia's Rocca Paolina and Priors Chapel. The old town has a fountain by its main street, and many of the façades of the shops and buildings are covered in ceramic tiles. Next to the museum is the 14th-century Church of San Francesco, which has Umbrian frescoes.

ISOLA D'ELBA

✚ 436 E8 ℹ️ Calata Italia 43, 193 Portoferraio, tel 0565 914671 🚢 From Piombino

Most people visit the mountainous island of Elba to explore the place where Napoleon lived in exile from May 1814 to February 1815, but others come to enjoy the delightful scenery, unspoiled beaches and bustling resort towns. There are plenty of historic sites to visit, including Napoleon's former villa and ancient, abandoned mines. The island is also an excellent place for walking.

About 10km (6 miles) west of the mainland and an hour's ferry ride from Piombino, Elba is a natural mosaic made up of gulfs, headlands, a precipitous coastline, peaceful bays, maquis scrub, wooded mountains and terraced vineyards. It is the largest island in the Tuscan archipelago, a group of islands once described as the 'necklace that slid from the neck of Venus'. There are several walking trails as well as a cable-car to the top of Mount Capanne, from where you can enjoy excellent views of the archipelago.

In Portoferraio, the Palazzina dei Mulini, Napoleon's home while he was exiled, is now a museum (*Wed–Mon 9–7, Sun and holidays 9–1*) housing period furniture and Napoleon's library.

Porto Azzurro, the island's Spanish capital, is a busy resort dominated by a huge fortress that was once used as a prison.

Bridge crossing the River Serchio in Castelnuovo di Garfagnana

The waterfront at Passignano on Lago di Trasimeno, from where you can get to Isola Maggiore

FIESOLE

436 G7 Piazza Mino da Fiesole 36, 50014 Fiesole, tel 055 598720
www.commune.fiesole.fi.it

On a hilltop 7km (4 miles) northeast of Florence, Fiesole offers sweeping views. Lovers of ancient ruins will enjoy its archaeological park, while art enthusiasts can head for the Museo Bandini.

Originally an Etruscan settlement, Fiesole grew in importance under the Romans; evidence of both can be seen in the Area Archeologica east of the main square, Piazza Mino da Fiesole. Here is a well-preserved Roman amphitheatre, Roman baths, a Roman temple and some sixth-century Etruscan ruins.

Piazza Mino da Fiesole is where you'll find the duomo, shops and restaurants. From here you can climb Via San Francesco for views of Florence. The Museo Bandini *(daily 9.30–7)* has ivories, ceramics and paintings on display, while the Church of San Domenica has a delicate *Madonna with Saints and Angels* by Fra Angelico.

GARFAGNANA

436 F6 Centro Visite Parco Alpi Apuane, Piazza delle Erbe 1, 55032 Castelnuovo di Garfagnana, tel 0583 65169 Castelnuovo di Garfagnana
www.garfagnanavacanze.it
www.pacapuane.toscana.it

This delightful and largely undiscovered area north of Lucca is dotted with historic little towns and laced with a range of trails for excellent walking for all abilities. If you have a car, you can visit the spa town of Bagni di Lucca, visited by Lord Byron, the area's main hub of Castelnuovo di Garfagnana, and the remote hamlet of San Pellegrino in Alpe. Even without a car, you can reach towns such as Barga (p. 139). The area is perfect for wildlife lovers, as the surrounding Alps are home to many species of bird, including the golden eagle.

The Garfagnana is on the eastern side of the River Serchio, which forges a path between the rugged Alpi Apuane and the gentler, more rounded slopes of the Garfagnana on the other. The most rugged part of the Garfagnana is the natural park of Orecchiella, near Castelnuovo.

Castelnuovo di Garfagnana is a pleasant, bustling town at the heart of the Garfagnana. It has an open-air market every Thursday.

San Pellegrino in Alpe is an ancient pilgrimage area, and has a good folk museum. The winding roads mean that the area cannot be explored quickly, but it is off the main tourist trail and is easily accessible from Lucca and Pisa.

GUBBIO

437 H7 Piazza Oderisi 6 (off Corso Garibaldi), 06024 Gubbio, tel 075 922 0693
www.umbria2000.it

Gubbio's limestone grey medieval buildings are built on a series of dramatic terraces against the backdrop of Mount Ingino, 40km (25 miles) from Perugia.

The spectacular Palazzo dei Consoli (town hall) is home to the Museo Civico *(daily 10–1, 3–6, tel 075 927 4298)* and its unique treasure, the *Tavole Iguvine* (Eugubine Tablets).The seven bronze plaques (second- to first-century BC) are written in the ancient Umbrian language, using the Etruscan and Latin alphabets. Discovered in 1444, they are the most important sacred texts in the whole of Italian classical antiquity, comparable in importance to the Rosetta Stone. They provide information about worship, legal systems, the city-state structure and the religious ceremonies of the ancient Gubbian community.

A centuries-old ritual, *Corsa dei Ceri,* takes place here annually on 15 May, the eve of St. Ubaldo's Day (Gubbio's patron saint). The *ceri* are three 4m (13ft) wooden structures, each weighing about 200kg (440lb), made of two octagonal prisms joined by a central mast and crowned with statues of St. Ubaldo, St. George and St. Anthony. The *ceri* bearers race up through the streets to Basilica di Sant'Ubaldo on Mount Ingino.

Within these walls, near the Roman theatre, is the 13th-century Church of San Francesco, where the Spadalonga family gave St. Francis refuge after he was rejected by his family.

LAGO TRASIMENO

437 H8 Piazza Giuseppe Mazzini, 06061 Castiglione del Lago, tel 075 965 2484 Castiglione del Lago
www.umbria2000.it

Lake Trasimeno is the largest inland lake in the Italian peninsula, but it is also one of the shallowest, with an average depth of 6m (20ft). Its bays, capes and islands are surrounded by fertile hillsides dotted with castles and olive groves. There are beaches, a wild nature reserve, jetties for boating, fishing and daytrips by ferry to its two main islands, Isola Polvese and Isola Maggiore. Isola Maggiore is tiny, with a pretty 14th- to 15th-century village. It is inhabited by fishermen, and the women still make traditional 'Irish stitch' lace. Footpaths around the island pass olive groves, holm oaks and cypress trees. St. Francis spent Lent here in 1211, and Castello Guglielmi (Villa Isabella), on the southern tip is built over a former Franciscan convent. On the eastern shore of the lake, San Feliciano is a pretty fishing village where traditional mats, baskets and wicker chairs are still made. From here take a summer ferry to Isola Polvese, the lake's largest island, which is being made into a nature reserve.

RATINGS

Value for money	● ● ●
Good for kids	● ●
Historic interest	● ● ● ● ●
Photo stops	● ● ● ● ●

TIPS

● Lucca is easily explored on foot. The station is only 10 minutes' walk away and parking is not easy, so it is worth visiting by train.

● Do as the locals and get around by bicycle; they can be rented from the tourist office or numerous places around town (look for *noleggio*).

● Walk along the famous encircling walls (4km/2.5 miles).

● For great views over the city, climb the Torre Guinigi, easily recognized by the tree sprouting improbably out of the top.

BASICS

✚ 436 F6

🛈 Piazzale Verdi, 55100 Lucca, tel 0583 583150
🕐 Daily 9–7, summer; 9–5, rest of year
🚉 Lucca

www.commune.lucca.it

Mature trees line sections of the broad town wall (above); a Virgin and Child by Civitali in San Michele church (above left)

LUCCA

A well-preserved medieval town—the birthplace of Puccini. Completely encircled by 17th-century walls.

Lucca lies in the heart of a fertile plain in northwest Tuscany, an hour's drive from Florence and 22km (14 miles) northeast of Pisa. The Piazza San Michele is the site of the old Roman forum, hence the name of the Romanesque church here, San Michele in Foro. The church *(daily 7.30–noon, 3–6)* dates from 1070 and has a dazzling exterior of striped marble walls and an intricate medley of tiny loggias, decorated columns and lavish carvings. A few minutes' walk away is the Casa di Puccini *(daily 10–6)*, the birthplace of Giacomo Puccini, composer of operas such as *Tosca* and *Madame Butterfly*. His former home is now a museum where you can see letters, posters and illustrations of his operas, and the piano at which he composed his last work.

THE CATHEDRAL

Lucca's cathedral, the Duomo di San Martino *(daily 7–7, mid-Mar to 31 Oct; daily 7–5, rest of year)*, has 13th-century reliefs on and around the three principal doors, including some by Nicola Pisano, a noted 13th-century Pisan sculptor. Inside is Lucca's most important artwork, the *Volto Santo (Holy Face)*. A cedarwood crucifix, it is said to be an exact likeness of Christ, carved by Nicodemus. In the sacristy *(Mon 9.30–5.45, Sat 9–6.45, Sun 11.20–11.50, 1–4.45, mid-Mar to 31 Oct; Mon 9.30–4.45, Sat 9.30– 6.45, Sun 11.20–11.50, 1–4.45, rest of year)* is the tomb of Ilaria del Carretto, a sublime funerary monument by the Sienese sculptor Jacopo della Quercia, depicting the wife of Paolo Guinigi, a medieval ruler of the city.

Next to the cathedral is the Museo della Cattedrale *(daily 10–6, mid-Mar to 31 Oct; Sat–Sun 10–2, rest of year)*, which displays paintings and various religious objects.

ARTISTIC TREASURES

The Museo Nazionale di Villa Guinigi *(Tue–Sat 8.30–7.30, Sun 8.30–1.30, tel 0583 496033)* has an eclectic collection of paintings, sculpture, textiles, Roman and Etruscan archaeological finds, silverware and important works by the painter Fra Bartolommeo and the sculptor Matteo Civitali. The Museo Nazionale di Palazzo Mansi *(Tue–Sat 8.30–7.30, Sun 8.30–1.30)*, also in a former palace, is worth visiting to see the sumptuous apartments, tapestries, precious *objets d'art* and fine furniture. Particularly impressive is the 18th-century bridal chamber, richly decked with gold.

Montalcino's timeless streets are a pleasure to wander around

Fishing boats in Porto Santo Stefano near Monte Argentario

MAREMMA

⊞ 438 G8 🛈 Parco Regionale della Maremma, Via Besagliari 7–9, 58010 Alberese, tel 0564 407098; summer only
www.parcomaremma.it

Cowboys on horseback herd long-horned bulls in this area of empty, often melancholy countryside, often referred to as the Wild West of Tuscany. The Maremma is the name given to the coastal plain that stretches from Cecina (south of Pisa) to Civitavecchia in Lazio. It includes the Monte Amiata range. Unspoiled coastal areas with wide, sandy beaches dominate the western part, while the landscape inland has been covered for centuries in wild, marshy tracts of maquis—fragrant scrub containing a variety of herbs (such as thyme), wildflowers and low bushes. The Etruscans started draining the region, but it reverted to malarial swamp until it was finally drained by Mussolini.

The area between Principina a Mare and Talamone on the Tyrrhenian coast is a nature reserve, where you might spot porcupines, wild boar and deer, as well as migratory birds. The park visitor centre is in Alberese, about 14km (9 miles) south of Grosseto, capital of the Maremma.
Don't miss Grosseto, a walled town with a 13th-century red and white cathedral and an archaeological museum.

MASSA MARITTIMA

⊞ 438 F8 🛈 Via Todini 3, 58024 Massa Marittima, tel 0566 902756

A former mining town might not have much to offer the visitor in most countries, but this ancient city has some fascinating artworks, a fine 12th-century cathedral, an archaeological museum and a museum commemorating the town's mining history.

South of Volterra, 66km (41 miles) east of Centro Carapax, Massa Marittima overlooks the valley of the Pecora River. The town is divided in two: the lower, Città Vecchia (Old Town), and the upper, Città Nuova (New Town), the sense of which is debatable, as it dates from 1228.

There is a fortress between the two, built after the area was conquered by Siena in 1335. The old town has a striking, sloping medieval square, dominated by the cathedral, while the new town has a 13th-century tower with far-reaching views over the surrounding metal-rich hills.

The duomo was initially built in Romanesque style and later enlarged in the Gothic style. Dedicated to St. Cerbone, it has a baptismal font dating from 1267 and a sculpture carved in 1324 by Giraldo da Como. The Palazzo Podesta *(Tue–Sun 10–1, 4–7)*, a 13th-century *palazzo* housing the museum of archaeology, has many not very interesting Etruscan finds and a small collection of medieval works of art, including a superb *Maestà (Majesty)* by Ambrogio Lorenzetti.

MONTALCINO

⊞ 436 G8 🛈 Via Costa del Municipio 8, 53024 Montalcino, tel 0577 849331
www.prolocomontalcino.it

Montalcino is one of Tuscany's most important wine-producing towns, the home of the excellent rich red Brunello, the lighter Rosso di Montalcino and the fragrant Moscadello di Montalcino. The streets are liberally scattered with wine shops *(enoteca)*, where you can often taste before purchasing.

High on a hilltop 40km (25 miles) south of Siena, the town is dominated by its *rocca* (fortress), a picture-perfect 14th-century castle *(daily 9–8)*. From the battlements you can look out over the Crete, with the bare hills on one side and the wooded slopes of the Val d'Orcia on the other. The Palazzo Comunale, a fine civic palace built in 1292, dominates Piazza del Popolo, the main square. The Fiaschetteria Italiana *(daily 7.30–midnight)* here is a bustling café established in 1888 with an ornate mirrored interior.

The Museo Civico *(Tue–Sun 10–1, 2–5.50)*, the town's principal museum, is in the former convent of Sant'Agostino; with medieval and late Gothic artworks, wood sculptures from the 14th and 15th centuries and a collection of majolica jugs.

Montalcino is a good place from where to explore the Abbey of Sant'Antimo and the villages of the Val d'Orcia.

MONTE ARGENTARIO

⊞ 438 F9 🛈 Corso Umberto 55, Archetto del Paliol, 58019 Porto Santo Stefano, tel 0564 814208
🚇 Orbetello

If you would like to see where the Italian jet set hides out, this is one place worth visiting. Southwest of Grosseto, Monte Argentario was once an island, but the shallow waters silted up and it is now a promontory linked to the mainland by causeways. It was on one of the beaches here that the painter Caravaggio died in 1609.

At one time owned by the Spanish, it became part of Tuscany in the 19th century. Its Spanish heritage can be seen in Porto Santo Stefano, where a Spanish fortress still stands, and in Porto Ercole, where there are three Spanish forts.

The harbours of the nearby villages are filled with expensive yachts, while the southern tip of the promontory is less developed and sophisticated. The highest point is Monte Telegrafo, from where there are good views over the Maremma.

THE SIGHTS

Montefalco's Piazza del Comune is the highest point in town

The classical church of San Biagio outside Montepulciano

The medieval town of Narni with its rustic ochre buildings

MONTEFALCO

▦ 438 H8 ⓘ Museo Civico de San Francesco, Via Ringhiera Umbra 6, 06037 Montefalco, tel 0742 379598 www.montefalcodoc.it

High up in rolling countryside, Montefalco is known as *La Ringhiere dell''Umbria* (Balcony of Umbria). Extensive views of the green Valle Umbra unfold from its majestic circular piazza. The medieval walls form a solid circle around the town, punctuated by towers and gates.

Enter via the second-century gate of Sant'Agostino and climb the Corso to Piazza del Comune. Streets branch off downwards from this irregular-shaped square. The Museo Pinacoteca di San Francesco in the former 14th-century church, has paintings dating from the 13th to the 17th century, including works by Perugino. The highlights are the world-famous 15th-century frescoes by Benozzo Gozzoli in the central apse, illustrating scenes from the life of St. Francis.

Montefalco is famous for traditional linen crafts, red wine (particularly the Sagrantino) and gastronomy. The excellent wine shop Enoteca di Benozzo, in the main square, specializes in wine, truffles and oil.

MONTEPULCIANO

▦ 437 G8 ⓘ Via di Gracciano nel Corso 59a, 53045 Montepulciano ☎ 0578 757341 ◷ Daily 9–12.30, 2.30–7, summer; 9.30–12.30, 3–6, rest of year ☒ Chiusi-Chianciano Terme (24km/15 miles away) www.prolocomontepulciano.it

On a narrow ridge, with medieval streets, Montepulciano attracts lovers of art and culture, who come to admire the cathedral, palaces and Renaissance architecture. Wine buffs also enjoy the local Vino Nobile, judged so fine by a 16th-century pope that he

'ennobled' it. When the town sided with Florence in 1511, it underwent a Renaissance overhaul, a vast building project that involved some of the era's leading architects, including Antonio Sangallo and the mannerist master Vignola. Today Montepulciano plays host to various cultural events, including an International Arts Workshop every summer.

The Museo Civico *(Tue–Sun 10–7, Aug; Tue–Sun 10–1, 3–6, rest of year, tel 0579 717 300)* has an impressive collection of ancient pottery, medieval sculpture, Etruscan tombs and cinerary urns, along with paintings by Sienese artists. The main square, Piazza Grande, is dominated by the duomo *(daily 9–noon, 3–6)*, whose altarpiece is an *Assumption* by Taddeo di Bartolo. In the baptistery are numerous reliefs, terracottas and other sculptures by an array of medieval and Renaissance artists, including Andrea della Robbia. There are plenty of wine shops and restaurants in town, including the elegant Caffé Poliziano, with its art nouveau interior.

On the outskirts is the Church of San Biagio, built by Sangallo in the mid-16th century.

MONTERIGGIONI

▦ 436 G7 ⓘ Largo Fontebranda 5, 53035 Castello di Monteriggioni, tel 0577 304810 www.monteriggionicastello.it

It is impossible to miss Monteriggioni. Set on a hill with grey walls punctuated with towers, it has the appearance of a granite crown. This perfectly preserved Tuscan village is in better condition than popular San Gimignano (p. 151) and, although there is not much to visit inside the walls—just a little church and a shop—the defensive walls are remarkable.

The town was founded by the Sienese in 1203 to defend the

northern approach to Siena from the Florentines. The enclosing walls were built between 1213 and 1219, destroyed in 1244 by invading Florentines and rebuilt between 1260 and 1270. Its 14 grim towers were described in Dante's *Inferno* as resembling giants.

NARNI

▦ 438 H9 ⓘ Piazza dei Priori, 05035 Narni, tel 0744 715362 ☒ Narni www.comune.narni.tr.it

The ancient hill town of Narni is built on a rocky spur overlooking the Nera gorge. From the grid of ancient Roman streets, a road climbs up to two labyrinthine medieval districts and the spectacular *rocca* (fortress), a papal stronghold built in 1370 by Albornoz.

From Piazza Garibaldi, past the bronze fountain and the medieval tower, is the cathedral of San Giovenale (1145), entered through an arch to Piazza Cavour. The main doorway has a graceful Renaissance portico with a frieze of garlands above the arcade, and the interior is a fusion of Romanesque and baroque styles. From here on, Via Garibaldi, which has been the main street since Roman times, becomes Piazza dei Priori, once the Roman forum. The square was narrowed in medieval times with the construction of two tower-houses, the Palazzo del Podesta and Palazzo dei Priori. The latter has a fine 14th-century loggia attributed to Gattapone.

NORCIA

▦ 439 J8 ⓘ Via Solferino 22, 06047 Norcia, tel 0743 816090 www.norcia.net

Norcia, in a fertile valley at the foot of the Sibillini Mountains on the Marche border, is a town of wide streets and low stucco-

An elegant arcade and a stone carving of a lion at the bottom of the steps in Piazza San Benedetto, Norcia

Looking out over the Tuscan countryside from Pienza's walls

fronted buildings—all built after the 1859 tremors, when a maximum height of 12.5m (41ft) was set. In Corso Sertorio, the main square, you can see a statue of St. Benedict, the father of Western monasticism, who was born here in 480. The Basilica di San Benedetto, the Palazzo Comunale and the Castellina are all on the piazza.

The Castellina houses Norcia's Civic Museum (daily 10–1, 5–7.30, summer; daily 10–1, 3–5, rest of year), and was built in 1554 as a cross between a fortress and a government palace. There are archaeological displays and a diocesan collection with a fine 13th-century Deposition from the Cross, a Risen Christ by Nicola da Siena, a Madonna and Child by Antonio da Faenza and a glazed terracotta Annunciation by Luca della Robbia.

Well known for the expert knifework, Norcia's butchers were often empoyled as surgeons in the Middle Ages. Today, Norcia is still famous for its norcinerie (pork butchers' shops). Around the square there are food shops bursting with local delicacies like wild boar sausages, black truffles, cheese and wild lentils gathered in the Sibillini Mountains.

ORVIETO

p. 146.

PARCO NAZIONALE DEI MONTI SIBILLINI

p. 147.

PARCO REGIONALE MONTE SUBASIO

437 H8 ☎ 0742 301144 ⓒ Closed to traffic 8pm–6am 🚌 Spello or Assisi

Monte Subasio rises behind Assisi, overlooking the Valle Umbra, and has played a part in the town's history and culture. It was from here that the timber and rose-pink Subasio stone, so characteristic of

the area, was taken to construct the city. St. Francis, who had a passion for nature, is said to have walked here.

The Subasio mountain range is a protected area, reaching heights of 1,290m (4,232ft), and extending over 7,500ha (18,532 acres). Monte Subasio was once entirely covered by a forest of tall holm oaks. Today a splendid group of these oaks remains around the Franciscan hermitage, the Eremo delle Carceri.

These woods are considered to be among the most important of their kind in Italy, and are protected by the Monte Subasio Regional Park. Reforestation efforts have introduced black hornbeams, young oaks, ash, spruce and black pines.

From the Porta Cappuccini on the edge of Assisi you can drive over the broad, flat mountain beyond Spello to Collepino, with its thick olive terraces. The unsurfaced road over the top has potholes; it is not recommended in winter, but in spring crocuses and cornflowers are in abundance.

PIANO GRANDE

439 J8 🛈 Via Solferino 22, 06047 Norcia, tel 0743 816090

Known as the rooftop of Umbria, the vast plateau of the Piano Grande is surrounded by uninterrupted views. This karst limestone region is the largest in Italy and has many underground cavities and passages caused by the dissolution of the rock, which aid drainage.

In Castelluccio, the Mergani hole plunges to such a depth that its bottom has yet to be discovered. Aquatic and migratory birds inhabit the marshes in the karst basins of Colfiorito. In spring and early summer the Piano Grande is covered in a thick carpet of wildflowers; red and yellow poppies, cornflowers, saxifrage, lily of the

valley, and violets are just some of the many species here. Among them are the yellow flowers of the famous Castelluccio wild lentils. People come from miles around to admire the Fioritura dei Piani (Blossoming of the Plains). It is very popular with hang-gliders.

At the far end of the plain is the weather-beaten village of Castelluccio. At about 1,450m (4,757ft) above sea level, it is the highest village in Umbria and the last outpost of the region. Castelluccio is a good base from which to explore the national park. There is a hang-gliding and para-sailing school here.

PIENZA

✚ 437 G8 🛈 Corso Rossellino 59, 53026 Pienza, tel 0578 749071 www.infinito.it/utenti/ufficio.turistico

Pienza lies in ravishing, rolling countryside in the southeast corner of Tuscany, close to the hilltop town of Montepulciano and 55km (34 miles) southeast of Siena. A compact town, it consists of a maze of small lanes that radiate from the main square. Once within its ancient walls, you will be enchanted by its timeless atmosphere and crisp beauty, qualities recognized by Unesco, which has ensured that Pienza will be preserved for future generations.

The cathedral (daily 8–1, 2.30–7) has paintings by five prominent Sienese painters, commissioned by Pope Pius II. Behind it, from the lanes and alleyways that run along the top of the walls, there are beautiful views towards Monte Amiata. The Museo Diocesano (Wed–Mon 10–1, 3–6), in Cosso Rossellino, brings together paintings, sculptures, tapestries and other medieval and Renaissance pieces of art from various churches in the area, including a 14th-century cope (priest's cloak-like vestment) embroidered by English monks.

TIPS

● The Orvieto Underground takes you on a guided journey through the tunnels and caves under the city *(www.orvieto underground.it)*.

● The centuries-old *Festa La Palombella* (Festival of Doves) takes place at Pentecost each year in and around the cathedral square.

BASICS

➕ 438 H8

ℹ Piazza Duomo 24, 05018 Orvieto, tel 0763 341772

◉ Mon–Fri 8.15–1.50, 4–7, Sat 10–1, 4–7, Sun and holidays 10–noon, 4–6

❓ Carta Orvieto Unica, €12.50/€10.50, includes entrance to Cappella di San Brizio in the duomo, Museo Claudio Faina, Orvieto Underground and the Torre del Moro; it also covers up to 5 hours' free parking and free city transport. Available from above sites and the tourist information office

🚂 Orvieto

A view across the rich volcanic vineyards to Orvieto

ORVIETO

Surrounded by vineyards that produce the renowned wine. One of the Italy's great art cities, with a cathedral that's the best of its period in Italy and exciting archaeological sites.

Orvieto is one of the oldest settlements in Umbria, already in existence when the Etruscans arrived in the eighth century BC. The Corso Cavour winds up from Piazza Cahen to Piazza della Repubblica, where it runs over the Roman *decumanus* (the main east–west thoroughfare) and the site of the Etruscan, and later Roman, forum. The Museo Claudio Faina *(daily 9.30–6, Apr–Sep; Tue–Sun 10–5, rest of year)*, in the Palazzo Faina, has an impressive collection of Etruscan finds.

THE DUOMO

The duomo *(daily 7.30–12.45, 2.30–6.15, Mar–Oct; daily 7.30–12.45, 2.30–5.15, rest of year)* was built to commemorate the miracle of Bolsena. In 1264 a priest from Prague visiting Bolsena on a pilgrimage to Rome witnessed blood dripping from the communion host on to the altar cloth. Pope Urban IV was so impressed that he ordered the blood-stained linen to be brought to a shrine built to house the holy cloth, the Cappella del Corporale. The cathedral's striking façade was begun by Lorenzo Maitani in 1304 but not completed for 300 years. At the top of the steps, bas-reliefs depict biblical scenes. In the right transept is the Cappella di San Brizio (separate ticket required); its cycle of frescoes, unique in Renaissance Italy, was worked on first by Fra Angelico, with assistance from Benozzo Gozzoli, and then by Luca Signorelli.

CURIOSITIES

Near the funicular station and the Rocca dell'Albornoz, in Piazza Cahen, is the Pozzo di San Patrizio *(daily 10–6.45)*, a vast well with a shaft dropping 62m (203ft) constructed to guarantee a supply of water during a siege. Spendthrifts in Italy are said to have 'pockets as limitless as the Pozzo di San Patrizio'. The Necropoli Etrusca del Crocifisso del Tufo (City of the Dead) *(daily 8.30–7)* dates back to the sixth century BC. The alleys are lined with chamber tombs made from blocks of tufa.

ORVIETO WINE

Well known since Etruscan times, Orvieto is one of the most ancient wines of Italy. The vines benefit from the mild climate and the mixture of clay and sandy soil full of volcanic minerals. The Enoteca Regionale *(Mon–Fri 11–1, 5–7, Sat–Sun by appointment)* in Piazza San Giovanni run guided tours and wine tastings.

PARCO NAZIONALE DEI MONTI SIBILLINI

**An area of outstanding natural beauty, perfect for driving, walking, mountain-biking and skiing.
A haven for some very rare species of birds and wildflowers.**

The Sibillini Mountains Park extends across 70,000ha (173,000 acres) of protected land in Umbria and the Marche, with more than 20 summits higher than 2,000m (6,562ft). The highest, Monte Vettore, measures 2,476m (8,123ft). As can be seen in the massive limestone outcrops, sheer slopes, steep cliffs and deep escarpments scored by springs and waterfalls, the area is of karst origin—limestone with cavities, passages and underground drainage, caused by the dissolution of the rock.

ANIMAL AND PLANTLIFE

The wild, open spaces make the park a winner with wild flowers. To date around 1,800 botanical species have been recorded. Above the tree line extremely rare species of plants, such as the Apennine edelweiss *(Leontopodium nivale)* and gentians live in the grazing areas. Wildcats, wolves, deer and porcupine are just some of the wildlife that roam the park, but you are more likely to see flocks of grazing sheep, known as the white gold of the Sibillini Mountains, or shaggy white cattle. Eagles, peregrine falcons, goshawks and Alpine chough all nest in the park.

FACT OR FICTION

The Saracens came up from Sicily and raided the Valnerina region around the end of the ninth century. In the Upper Nera Valley there are many castles and watch-towers from where the inhabitants of the valley defended themselves against the raids. In the 15th and 16th centuries, the Sibillini Mountains were known all over Europe as a land of myth and legend. The rugged, magical landscape has inspired many popular romance tales, including the story of Sibyl, a divine nymph who lived in the caves in the mountain of the same name near Montemonaco and was thought to be able to foresee the future.

Another popular local legend concerns Pilate: Buffaloes are said to have pulled the lifeless body of the Roman procurator Pontius Pilate into the waters of a demoniac lake, which turned red. In reality, the reddish waters of the circular Lago di Pilato come from the indigenous species of shellfish that live in the lake, a tiny crustacean called *Chircephalus marchesonii*.

RATINGS				
Good for kids	●	●	●	●
Outdoor pursuits	●	●	●	●	●
Photo stops	●	●	●	●	●
Walkability	●	●	●	●	●

TIPS

● Pick up a map of the area at any of the park's offices or tourist information points.

● The park's noticeboards and literature carry a characteristic blue and green emblem.

● There are many refuge points, ideal for picnic stops.

BASICS

⊞ 439 J8

ℹ Via Madonna della Peschiera 1, Preci, tel 0743 937000
🕐 Daily 9.30–12.30, 5–7, Aug; Mon–Fri 9.30–12.30, 5–6, Sat–Sun 9.30–12.30, 3.30–6.30, rest of the year
❓ Mountain refuges at Forca Canapine and at ski resorts, tel 0743 823012; (Rifugio Perugia), tel 0743 8323015; (Monti del Sole), tel 0743 823002

www.sibillini.net
The official website of the Parco Nazionale dei Monti Sibillini has more information on the geography, plant and animal life in the park and the projects that are protecting them. There is also information on the best way to visit the park with practical information on hiking and mountain-biking.

Castelluccio Piano Grande in the Parco Nazionale

The Piazza IV Novembre in front of Perugia's duomo

THE SIGHTS

RATINGS

Historic interest	●●●○
Cultural interest	●●●○
Walkability	●●●○

TIPS

● The legendary Bar Pasticceria Sandri (Corso Vannucci 32) serves mouth-watering pastries, recently voted one of the top 10 *pasticcerias* in Italy.

● An antiques market is held in Giardini Carducci on the last Sunday of the month.

BASICS

✚ 437 H8

ℹ Palazzo dei Priori, Piazza IV Novembre 3, Perugia, tel 075 573 6458
◷ Daily 8.30–1.30, 3.30–6.30 (holidays 9–1)
🚇 Perugia

A detail of one of the duomo's statues (above)

PERUGIA

**The cosmopolitan capital of Umbria, a city of immense cultural vitality and diversity.
Home to two universities, a world-famous jazz festival and a rich heritage.**

The city, which was a settlement as far back as the ninth century BC, became part of the Roman state under Emperor Augustus in the first century BC. A series of monastic complexes developed within the walls in the 13th and 14th centuries. The city landscape changed again during the Renaissance and baroque period, when the new landed nobility built showy palaces. Today you can take an archaeological journey into the bowels of medieval Perugia by escalator: It takes you from Piazza Partigiani to Piazza Italia via a network of underground streets. Or take respite in the Orto Botanico Medievale, the old monastic garden behind San Pietro Convent, laid out with medicinal plants and herbs.

HEART OF THE CITY

The hub of the city is Piazza IV Novembre, an embodiment of the city at the height of its political and cultural power. The duomo, on the square, was begun in 1300 by Fra Bevignate and has an exterior pulpit from where San Bernardino preached. Inside, the chapel of St. Bernardino contains Federico Barocci's *Deposition* (1567), and the Cappella del Santo Annello has the Virgin Mary's prized wedding ring.

GALLERIA NAZIONALE DELL'UMBRIA

The top floors of the handsome Gothic Palazzo dei Priori are home to the Galleria Nazionale dell'Umbria and its excellent collection of Umbrian painting and sculpture. There are works here by the Maestro di San Francesco, Arnolfo di Cambio, Fra Angelico and Piero della Francesca—all artists of enormous importance during medieval and Renaissance periods. There are also paintings by Pietro Vannucci, known as Perugino. If you do not have time to explore the whole gallery, head for the Sala dell'Udienza, where there is some of Perugino's best work, a complex fresco cycle celebrating the harmony between classical mythology and Christian belief. Cappella de San Severo *(daily 10–1.30, 2.30– 6.30, Apr–Oct; Wed–Mon 10–1.30, 2.30–5, rest of year)*, in Piazzetta Raffaello, has the only fresco in Perugia by Raphael. He painted part of the fresco on the upper wall, *The Trinity Surrounded by Saints,* before leaving to work on the Vatican in Rome.

Pisa's duomo, crowned by an elliptical dome, stands beside the famous Leaning Tower

PISA

Campo dei Miracoli—home of the famous leaning tower, a striking cathedral and Italy's largest baptistery.
A lively university city with attractive old churches, excellent museums and bustling streets lined with shops.

Pisa reached the peak of its power in the 11th and 12th centuries, but this golden age was followed by naval defeats, the collapse of its commercial empire and the silting up of the harbour. In 1406 it was taken over by Florence, and the Medicis embarked on major rebuilding while turning Pisa into a focus for science and learning. Little of the city's former glory remains, as much of it was destroyed during World War II.

THE LEANING TOWER OF PISA

Pisa's most important treasures stand on the Campo dei Miracoli and include the Torre Pendente (Leaning Tower) *(daily 8–8, Apr–Sep; daily 9–5.30, Mar and Oct; daily 9–5, Nov–Feb)*, the duomo, the baptistery and the Camposanto, a medieval cemetery. Begun in 1173, the Leaning Tower was intended as the cathedral's bell tower. As it was built on sandy soil, it began to lean before it had been completed. By 1284 the lean was 90cm (35in) from the vertical, and medieval engineers were attempting to correct it. By 1350, when the tower was completed, the lean was 1.45m (4.75ft). In 1990 the tower was closed to allow scientists to stabilize it—it was now 4.5m (14.75ft) from the vertical, and getting worse. Tons of lead were attached to the northern side, steel cables were attached to hold it in place, and a wedge of soil was removed. Gradually the structure began to settle into the cavity and within five months had returned to the position it held in 1890.

OTHER HIGHLIGHTS

The duomo (1064) *(Mon–Sat 10–7.30, Sun 1–7.30, Apr–Sep; Mon–Sat 10–5.30, Sun 1–5.30, Mar and Oct; Mon–Sat 10–12.30, 3–4.30, Sun 3–4, Nov–Feb)* has an ornate marble-striped exterior and carvings depicting New Testament stories. Inside, note the carved pulpit by Giovanni Pisano. Begun in 1152, the baptistery is the work of Giovanni and Nicola Pisano, with a pulpit carved with scenes from the life of Christ. The Camposanto *(daily 8–7.30, Apr–Sep; daily 9–5.30, Mar and Oct; daily 9–4.30, Nov–Feb)*, a medieval cemetery within a Gothic cloister, was decorated with some of Tuscany's most important frescoes, but only a few survived a World War II bomb.

RATINGS	
Good for kids	●●●●●
Historic interest	●●●
Cultural interest	●●●●
Photo stops	●●●●●

TIPS

● It is much cheaper to buy a combined ticket to all the sights in the Campo dei Miracoli.

● There are excellent bus and train connections to the city, so leave the car behind.

● When visiting the leaning tower, leave handbags at the cloakroom; no children under 8 are allowed up.

MAKE A DAY OF IT

Florence: p. 115–134.
Lucca: p. 142.

BASICS

✚ 436 F7

🛈 Piazza Duomo 1, 56100 Pisa, tel 050 560464 🕐 Daily 9–7, Jun–Sep; Mon–Sat 9–6, Sun 10.30–4.30, rest of year (gets busy after 10am) 🎫 Combined ticket for all attractions (excluding the tower) at the ticket office or Museo dell'Opera: 2 attractions €6; all attractions €8.50 🚆 Pisa Centrale 🎧 Leaning Tower guided tour (35 minutes). Timed tickets should be booked in advance at the ticket office or online at **www.opapisa.it** (€15)

www.pisa.turismo.toscana.it
www.duomo.pisa.it

The Church of the Baptistery of San Giovanni, Pistoia

Pitigliano's medieval skyline, on a volcanic ridge

A detail of the Bacchus Fountain in the central square at Prato

PISTOIA

➕ 436 F6 🛈 Palazzo dei Vescovi, Piazza Duomo 4, 51100 Pistoia, tel 0573 21622 🚉 Pistoia
www.tourismo.toscana.it

The heart of Pistoia is Piazza del Duomo, with its 14th-century baptistery and sumptuous cathedral. The town has several other churches worth visiting, a museum and the historic Caffé Valiani. Every Wednesday and Saturday morning one of Italy's largest markets is held on Piazza del Duomo.

Pistoia's surroundings are uninspiring, but the town has a Renaissance heart. It sits at the foot of the Apennine Mountains, 47km (29 miles) east of Lucca, and its name probably derives from the Latin *pistores,* meaning 'bakers'—it was a town that supplied provisions to the Roman troops. The opulent cathedral has a striking silver altarpiece, the *Dossale di San Jacopo,* made between 1287 and 1456 with figures by Filippo Brunelleschi. The 14th-century Church of the Baptistery of San Giovanni has a font made in 1226 and a 16th-century, gold-painted wooden altar. The Church of San Giovanni Fuorcivitas is proud of its *Visitation* by Luca della Robbia. The Museo Civico's collection includes paintings that chronicle Pistoia's art, ranging from Romanesque to 19th-century works.

PITIGLIANO

➕ 438 G9 🛈 Piazza Garibaldi 51, 58017 Pitigliano, tel 0564 617111
www.grosseto.turismo.toscana.it

Pitigliano, 8km (5 miles) south of Sovana, is a medieval town that was once an Etruscan settlement. Its main attraction is the 16th-century Palazzo Orsini, which accommodates an impressive collection of Etruscan finds in its beautifully decorated rooms. Elsewhere you can see the remains of a large 14th-century aqueduct.

Pitigliano's jumble of mellow buildings is delightfully set on a volcanic ridge that rises dramatically from the countryside. The village was once owned by the powerful Orsini family and was home to a thriving Jewish community until World War II. The synagogue is a poignant reminder of the town's Jewish heritage. Explore the many cobbled streets and interesting alleyways that surround the Palazzo Orsini on the main square inside the fortress, and enjoy the views of Monte Amiata. The cathedral has a lovely 18th-century baroque façade and a medieval belfry.

PRATO

➕ 436 G6 🛈 Via Luigi Muzzi 38, 59100 Prato, tel 0574 24112 🚉 Prato
www.prato.turismo.toscana.it

Prato, nestling between Pistoia and Florence, has several good museums and galleries and some interesting churches, despite now being a largely industrial town. Romantics might also be attracted by the news that Prato is where the monk and artist Filippo Lippi met and fell in love with a nun, Lacrezia Buti, whom he married.

Prato means meadow, but today the town is surrounded by industry. It has long association with textile manufacturing and has been famous for its fabrics since the 13th century. Most of the sights are within the medieval walls that enclose the old part of town. The mighty turreted walls of the Castello dell'Imperatore, built by Frederick II between 1217 and 1248, are reminiscent of castles of the Swabian period, when Frederick II, King of Sicily, controlled Puglia and Sicily, at which time there were huge developments in literature, the science and poetry.

The duomo, at the heart of the city, was built in the 12th century. The *Pulpit of the Sacred Girdle* by Michelozzo and Donatello graces its exterior, while the interior contains frescoes by Filippo Lippi, including a famous depiction of Salome dancing at Herod's feast. You can see more works from the duomo in the Museo dell'Opera del Duomo.

The Church of Santa Maria delle Carceri, built in the form of a Greek cross, is regarded as a masterpiece of Renaissance architecture and contains terracotta works by Andrea della Robbia.

SAN QUIRICO D'ORCIA

➕ 436 G8 🛈 Via Dante Alighieri 33, 53027 San Quirico d'Orcia, tel 0577 897211 🕒 Apr–Oct, 19 Dec–6 Jan only

San Quirico, 15km (9 miles) east of Montalcino and 10km (6 miles) west of Pienza, is a strange mixture of the enchanting and the banal, with bland, post-World War II housing next to exquisite medieval churches and 16th-century gardens. It stood on the Via Francigena, the pilgrim route to Rome, and fine medieval houses line the Via Poliziano.

The main attraction is the Collegiata, a 12th-century church off Piazza Chigi, built on the ruins of an eighth-century church. Of note are the Lombard-influenced carvings around the doors. Highlights inside include inlaid Renaissance choir stalls and a *Virgin and Child Enthroned with Four Saints* by Sano di Pietro. The Church of Santa Maria di Vitaleta features a terracotta *Madonna* by Bartolomeo della Robbia. The Horti Leoni were laid out in 1580 and are made up of a flower garden and a natural woodland area. If you have time to wander around this partly walled village, you can also take a look at the Palazzo Chigi, decorated with Roman frescoes.

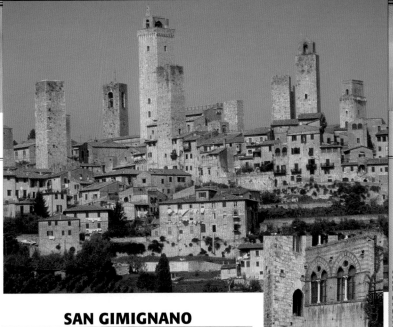

SAN GIMIGNANO

A visual spectacle that cannot fail to delight.
Nicknamed 'the medieval Manhattan', for its ancient towers
that spear the skyline.
A popular daytrip from Florence and Siena.

San Gimignano flourished throughout the Middle Ages, largely due to its position on the Via Francigena pilgrim route. The town split into factions over allegiance to the papacy and the empire—those supporting the pope were known as Guelphs, those supporting the emperor, Ghibellines—and during these years of conflict, the wealthy families in the town built 72 protective towers, 14 of which still dominate the area.

THE COLLEGIATA

The main street, Via San Giovanni, links the squares Piazza della Cisterna and Piazza del Duomo. Here is the Collegiata, a cathedral until it lost its status as a bishopric. Little on its façade prepares you for the interior, covered with dazzling frescoes *(Mon–Fri 9.30–7.30, Sat 9.30–5, Sun 1–5, Mar–Oct; Mon–Sat 9.30–5, Sun 1–5, Nov–20 Jan; open for Mass only 21 Jan–28 Feb)*. On the rear wall is a *Last Judgement* by Sienese painter Taddeo di Bartolo, alongside an *Inferno*, a *Paradiso* and a *St. Sebastian*. The second cycle on the right wall is by Barna di Siena and the Old Testament cycle opposite is by Bartolo di Fredi.

PALAZZO DEL POPOLO

To the left of the Collegiata stands the Palazzo del Popolo, the main museum *(daily 9.30–7.20, Mar–Oct; daily 10–5.50, rest of year)*. Within are paintings by Florentine, Umbrian and Sienese artists such as Filippino Lippi. The Sala del Consiglio (or Sala di Dante, because it was here that Dante, as a Florentine diplomat, met members of San Gimignano's council) is dominated by Lippo Memmi's *Madonna Enthroned*.

MUSEO D'ARTE SACRA AND THE MUSEO ARCHEOLOGICO

The Museo d'Arte Sacra *(daily 9.30–7.30, Apr–Oct; 9.30–5, Nov–Dec and Mar; closed Jan–Feb)* is a museum of religious art in Piazza Pecori, while the Museo Archeologico *(daily 11–6, Mar–Oct; Sat–Thu 11–6, Nov–Dec; Fri–Mon 11–6, Jan–Feb)* houses a small collection of Etruscan objects in a former convent.

Don't miss Gelateria di Piazza, a famous ice-cream shop; Fonti Medievali—Lombard, Romanesque and Gothic fountains—by Porta delle Fonti. the 54m (175ft) Torre Grossa, the tallest tower, with the best views.

RATINGS

Historic interest	●●●●
Cultural interest	●●●
Photo stops	●●●●●
Walkability	●●●●

TIP

● Do not try to park in town.

BASICS

✚ 436 F7

ℹ Piazza Duomo 1, 53037 San Gimignano, tel 0577 940008 🕐 Daily 9–1, 3–7, Mar–end Oct; 9–1, 2–6, rest of year 🎫 Combined tickets for the Museo Civico, Museo Archeologico and Torre Grossa, Spezeria di Santa Fina, Museo Ornitologico and Galleria d'Arte Moderna: adult €7.50; child (6–18) and over 65s €5.50

www.sangimignano.com

MAKE A DAY OF IT

Siena (p. 152–153)
Florence (p. 115–134)
Volterra (p. 156)

Just some of San Gimignano's 15 medieval towers (top)

Siena

**One of the most beautiful medieval cities in Italy, second only to Florence in its artistic and architectural treasures.
The Campo, a piazza surrounded by medieval palaces, is the venue for Siena's world-famous horse-race, the Palio.**

The shell-shaped Campo, first laid out in the 12th century

A typical Sienese street scene

Inside the Museo dell'Opera del Duomo

TIPS

● Buy one of the combined tickets to save money.

● For a great view of the Campo and excellent ice cream, head for Gelateria La Costerella on Via di Città (corner of Costa dei Barbieri and Via di Fontebranda).

● Tickets for seats for the Palio are hard to come by and expensive, but you can, like most Sienese, watch free from the Campo. It can be very hot and crowded. The event is televised live on RAI 1.

Romulus, Remus and 'mother' atop a marble plinth in a courtyard of the duomo

SEEING SIENA

Siena ranges over three hills, and its extremely steep streets are tiring to explore. However, no-one will want to rush a visit, for Siena is a glorious Gothic concoction, and its soft yellow and reddish brown buildings—the 'raw sienna' and 'burnt sienna' of an artist's palette—are a visual feast. The heart of the city, the semicircular Campo, acts like a magnet; just come and sit at the café tables and soak up the beauty of the scene. While practically any one of the churches are worth a visit, there are also plenty of good shops and some surprising sights, such as the ornately decorated 18th-century pharmacy, Quattro Cantoni on Via S. Pietro.

HIGHLIGHTS

THE CAMPO

Every year, on 2 July and 16 August, the Campo fills up for the Palio, a vital part of Siena life since the Middle Ages. The three-lap horse-race is ridden by 10 jockeys in medieval costume, representing 10 of the city's 17 *contrade* (wards). The race is preceded by spectacular parades and flag-throwing.

Whatever the time of year, it is hard to tear yourself away from the scene in the Campo, but the Museo Civico *(daily 10–7)* in the Palazzo Pubblico, on the Campo, demands attention. Many of its rooms are richly decorated with frescoes by some of Siena's finest artists, including one of the best examples of an early medieval secular fresco cycle in Europe, Ambrogio Lorenzetti's *Allegories of Good and Bad Government* (1338). Entrance to the museum also allows access to the Torre del Mangia, the imposing tower over the Campo. Climb the 503 steps for rewarding views.

THE DUOMO

Piazza del Duomo ☎ 0577 283048 🕐 Daily 7.30–7.30, Mar–Oct; daily 7.30–5, rest of year 🎫 Free

Piazza del Duomo cannot rival the Campo for scale or spectacle, but it is here you'll find the city's most interesting buildings, and many artistic treasures. The duomo alone could easily occupy at least an hour. Its magnificent, black-and-white and richly decorated

façade was overseen by the sculptor Giovanni Pisano, who also carved the lavish pulpit. Some 40 Sienese artists worked on the marble floor, a series of 57 inlaid pictures. The Umbrian artist Pinturicchio painted the vivid frescoes (1509) in the entrancing Libreria Piccolomini, a tiny room on the left of the nave.

The Romanesque-Gothic façade of the duomo

MUSEO DELL'OPERA DEL DUOMO

Piazza del Duomo 8 ☎ 0577 283048 ⊙ Daily 9–7.30, Mar–Oct; daily 9–1.30, rest of year 🖽 €5

Treasures in the Museo dell'Opera del Duomo (or Museo dell'Opera Metropolitana) include a relief of the *Madonna and Child* by Donatello and Duccio's vast *Maestà*. In the Battistero di San Giovanni the font has bronze panels by Sienese sculptor Jacopo della Quercia, and Florentines Donatello and Lorenzo Ghiberti.

PINACOTECA NAZIONALE

Via San Pietro 29, 53100 Siena ☎ 0577 281161 ⊙ Mon 8.30–1.30, Tue–Sat 8.15–7.15, Sun 8.15–1.15 🖽 €4.15

Siena produced some of the greatest Italian painters of the 13th and 14th centuries, and the Pinacoteca Nazionale has the city's best collection of paintings by this influential school. Artists represented include Duccio di Buoninsegna, the first to move painting on from the austere traditions of Byzantine art, Simone Martini, and brothers Pietro and Ambrogio Lorenzetti.

BACKGROUND

Siena was reputedly founded by Senius, son of Remus, one of the two founders of Rome. By 1125 Siena was a free commune, despite the rivalry with Florence that was to dominate its medieval history. The old enemy was defeated in 1260 at the Battle of Montaperti, the high point of a century during which Siena was one of Europe's wealthiest cities. The Black Death of 1348 scarred the city, but two charismatic saints emerged and dominated the ensuing period of spiritual uncertainty: St. Catherine of Siena and St. Bernardino. Siena struggled against a succession of papal, imperial and autocratic rulers; she owed allegiance to Charles V, suffered a devastating siege at the hands of Florence and eventually, in 1559, succumbed to the military might of the Grand Duchy of Tuscany. Today Siena is a bustling provincial city grown rich on banking, agriculture and tourism.

BASICS

➕ 436 G7

ℹ Piazza del Campo 56, tel 0577 280551
⊙ Mon–Sat 9.30–7.30, Mar–Nov; Mon–Fri 8.30–1, 3–7, Sat 8.30–1, rest of year
🖽 Combined tickets for: Museo Civico and Torre del Mangia (€9.50); Ospedale di Santa Maria della Scala, Centro di Arte Contemporanea (€9); Museo dell'Opera del Duomo (Metropolitana), Libreria Piccolomini, Battistero di San Giovanni (€7.50), Museo dell'Opera del Duomo (Metropolitana), Libreria Piccolomini, Battistero di San Giovanni, Oratorio di San Bernardino, Museo Diocesano (€9.50)
🚉 Siena

www.terresiena.it
This sleek and informative website run by Siena's tourist authority won the Interactive Key Award in 2003. They have information in Italian, English and Japanese about Siena's accommodation, food and museums and they have an execellent selection of e-postcards with scenes of Siena that you can send to friends for free while you are away.

The bright interior of the Basilica di San Salvatore

RATINGS

Historic interest	● ● ● ●
Cultural interest	● ● ●
Photo stops	● ● ●
Walkability	● ● ● ●

TIPS

● The Basilica di San Salvatore has no lights, so try to visit before sundown.

● Have an ice-cream or coffee at Bar La Portella, on a little promontory with views down the valley.

● The annual Festival dei due Mondi, founded in 1958, usually takes place at the end of June *(www.spoletofestival.it)*.

● There is an antiques fair in Piazza della Libertà on the second Sunday morning each month.

BASICS

🔲 439 H8

ℹ Piazza della Libertà 7, 06049 Spoleto, tel 0743 238920 🕐 Mon–Fri 9–1, 4–7, Sat–Sun 10–1, 4–7, summer; Mon–Fri 9–1, 3.30–6.30, Sat 10–1, 3.30–6.30, Sun 10–1, rest of year 🚆 Terni, Perugia, Roma. Buses run from station to city. Tickets can be bought at newsstands and *tabacchi*

www.conspoleto.co
An Italian/English website promoting tourism in Spoleto with information on accommodation in the area.

SPOLETO

**Famous as the venue of composer Gian Carlo Menotti's summer Festival of the Two Worlds.
The fortress and cathedral form the backdrop for the open-air performances.**

This city has some impressive examples of Romanesque architecture and art. The archaeological museum, in the Monastery of Sant' Agata, tracks the early stages of the city's development with Roman portraits and furniture dating from the invasion in 241BC. A visit to the Roman theatre, built in the first century BC, is included in the price of the museum ticket. The site was excavated and restored in the 1950s, and two marble portraits of Augustus and Caesar found here are now in the museum. The theatre is used every summer for dance performances during the Festival dei due Mondi.

BASILICA DI SAN SALVATORE

The Romanesque façade of the cathedral and the wooded hills behind form the ideal backdrop for the festival's open-air opera and concerts. The exterior is striking—an elegant Renaissance portico, with two external pulpits, added to the original Romanesque façade with Byzantine-style mosaics. Filippo Lippi is buried here, and as you enter the building the eye is drawn towards his final masterpiece, frescoes depicting the *Crowning of the Virgin*, the *Annunciation* and the *Nativity*.

PAPAL FORTRESS

In the 14th century, Cardinal Albornoz built the imposing *rocca* (fortress) *(Mon–Fri 10–8, Sat–Sun 10–9)* as a symbol of papal power. The various levels are connected by stone stairways that intersect with Spoleto's winding streets. On a fine day you can see as far as Assisi (p. 137). The fortress was transformed into a residential palace in the mid-15th century by Rossellino, who added the delightful two-tiered loggia in the central courtyard. A series of popes and governors lived here, including Lucrezia Borgia, and it was used as a prison from the 18th century until 1982. Restoration work is underway and there are plans for a museum.

Don't miss The Pinacoteca *(daily 10.30–1, 3.30–7, summer; daily 10.30–1, 3–5, rest of year)* has a *Madonna and Child with Saints* by Lo Spagna, *Maddalena Penitente* by Guernico, and Paolo Barbieri's *Spezieria;* Sant'Eufemia is a tiny Romanesque gem near the cathedral.

Looking up towards Spello from the surrounding vineyards

Piazza del Popolo during a rally in Todi

SANSEPOLCRO

437 H7 Piazza Garibaldi 2, 52037 San Sepolcro, tel 0575 740536

This small and delightful town is filled with Renaissance buildings and churches. Along with its artistic heritage, the town is noted for its lace-making and jewellery. It is also the setting for the Palio of the Crossbow, a famous crossbow shooting event.

At the foot of the Apennines in the Tiber Valley, 8km (5 miles) northeast of Anghiari, Sansepolcro is said to have been founded by two 10th-century monks returning from the Holy Land with relics of Christ's sepulchre. It is packed with medieval palazzi and stone-built towers surrounded by ancient walls. The town's major claim to fame is as the birthplace and home of the Renaissanace artist Piero della Francesca (1416–92). The Museo Civico (*daily 9–1.30, 2.30–7.30, Jun–Sep; daily 9.30– 1, 2.30–6, rest of year*) has a collection of works by him, including *The Resurrection*, *The Madonna della Misericordia* and *San Giuliano*. It also has works by Raffaellino del Colle and Santi di Tito, who were also local artists. The Church of San Lorenzo has a *Deposition* by Rosso Fiorentino.

SIENA

p. 152–153.

SOVANA

438 G8 Nearest tourist information is at Pitigliano, (see page 150)

Sleepy Sovana might be small but it has several striking reminders of its illustrious past. On the border with Lazio, 80km (50 miles) southeast of Grosseto, the village consists of little more than a single street, Via di Mezzo, with the ruins of a fortress at one end. There are Etruscan, Roman and medieval relics scatterd about, and the limestone cliffs are dotted with ancient tombs.

The birthplace of Hildebrand, who became Pope Gregory VII in 1073, Sovana has a fine cathedral. A highlight is the Church of Santa Maria, a 13th-century church with a Romanesque exterior, frescoes by the Sienese school, and a carved ciborium (altar canopy)—a rare palaeo-Christian work dating from the eighth or ninth century. There is an Etruscan graveyard on the outskirts of the village dating from the seventh century BC.

SPELLO

437 H8 Piazza Matteotti 3, 06038 Spello, tel 0742 301009
Spello
www.comune.spello.pg.it

The enchanting town of Spello (Roman Hispellum) lies under the slopes of Monte Subasio. It is a smaller version of Assisi (p.137), and its cobbled streets and medieval houses of pinkish stone offer superb photographic opportunities from just about every angle.

The town's Roman origins are immediately visible as you approach the Porta Consolare, one of five remaining gates. The town was founded at the beginning of the first century BC and enjoyed prosperity right through the imperial period.

Climb up to Via San Angelo and you pass the tiny Cappella Tega, which houses, behind glass, a crucifixion fresco by Nicolo Alunno. From Via Consolare the street becomes Via Cavour, and in a small square to the right is the town's main church, Santa Maria Maggiore (13th to 17th century). It was built over the ruins of a Roman temple and is decorated with a sequence of three delightful frescoes by Pinturicchio, telling the story of the early life of Jesus.

The Pinacoteca Comunale (town art gallery) is in the Palazzo dei Canonici, next to Santa Maria Maggiore (*Tue–Sat 10.30–1, 3–6.30, summer; Tue–Sat 10.30–12.30, 3–5, rest of year*). Among the works on display is a mid-13th-century Umbrian sculpture of the *Madonna and Child Enthroned*, an enamelled silver processional cross by Paolo Vanni and a portable diptych by Cola Petruccioli, both late 14th century.

TODI

437 H8 Piazza Umberto 1, 5–6, 06059 Todi, tel 075 894 5416
www.apmperugia.it
www.umbria2000.it,
www.comune.todi.pg.it

Todi's museum, churches and palaces make it a popular hilltop town, but it has managed to remain unspoiled.

The main square, the Piazza del Popolo, is bordered by magnificent buildings. On the south side is the battlemented Palazzo dei Priori, opposite the sweeping steps of the cathedral, whose Gothic façade features an early 14th-century rose window above carved wooden doors. The interior is fairly simple, with a 14th-century altarpiece and choir stalls of inlaid wood. In the crypt are three sculptures by Pisano, originally part of the façade.

On the east side of the piazza, the Palazzo del Popolo, built in 1213, stands next to the Palazzo del Capitano, built in 1293. The two are connected by a broad external stairway and the top floors house the Museo Pinacoteca (*Tue–Sun 10.30–1, 2.30– 6*). Exhibits trace the history of Todi; in the grand hall is an outstanding altarpiece by Lo Spagna, *The Coronation of Mary with Choir of Angels and Saints*, painted in 1511.

The Tempio di San Fortunato (*Tue–Sun 10.30–1, 3–6.30,*

One of the narrow cobbled lanes in Trevi

Umbria's famous truffles

Prancing horses carved out of alabaster displayed in Volterra

Mon 3–6.30) sits grandly on Piazza Umberto. Frescoes by Umbrian painters from the 13th and 14th centuries decorate its chapels, and the crypt houses the tomb of the poet St. Jacopone, who died in Todi in 1306. There is a bronze sculpture of him at the foot of the steps of San Fortunato. You can climb the 153 steps of the Campanile di San Fortunato, accessed from the interior of the church, for views over the city and the surrounding countryside.

TREVI

438 H8 Piazza Mazzini 5, 06039 Trevi, tel 0742 781150 Trevi
www.protrevi.com

Halfway between Assisi (p. 137) and Spoleto (p.154), Trevi is known as the City of the Olive. This warm-stoned hilltop town is surrounded by olive groves—there are about 200,000 trees on the slopes. The town celebrates the new season's oil with a festival every autumn.

Trevi has Roman origins and its heart is enclosed by medieval walls and gates. The former convent adjoining the Church of San Francesco makes an interesting museum space, comprising the Museo della Civiltà dell'Ulivo di Trevi (Museum of Olive Oil Cultivation) and the Raccolta d'Arte di San Francesco di Trevi (San Francesco Collection) (Tue–Sun 10.30–1, 2.30–6, summer; 10.30–1, 2.30–5, rest of year). The vaulted area downstairs has olive presses and huge antique storage jars. The museum also runs a cookery school. Upstairs, the San Francesco art collection includes an altarpiece by Lo Spagna, *The Coronation of the Virgin*, which was formerly in the 14th-century Church of San Martino.

Facing Sant'Emiliano in Palazzo Lucarini is the Trevi Flash Art

Museum (Tue–Fri 3–7, Sat–Sun 10–1, 3–7), which has an internationally renowned contemporary art collection.

Also worth visiting is the Church of the Madonna delle Lacrime, which has an *Adoration of the Magi* by Perugino and a painted altarpiece by Lo Spagna.

VALNERINA

439 J8 Via Cesave Battista 7, 05100 Terni, tel 0744 423047
 Weekdays only
www.comune.terni.it

The Valnerina, the Valley of the River Nera, begins in Visso, in the north of the Marche, and winds its way down to Terni, in the southern reaches of the region. Against a backdrop of rugged mountains, the river has carved deep ravines through the countryside, providing views around every bend. Fortress villages, towers and churches perch either side of the river, underlining the importance of this ancient route that has for centuries connected the Tyrrhenian Sea with the Adriatic.

Syrian monks fleeing persecution during the early period of Christianity hid in the caves and woods. The monks set up hermitages in the Valnerina and Castoriana valleys, and these became the nucleus of the abbeys and monasteries that were founded later, including Sant' Eustizio and San Pietro in Valle.

The Nera River Park protects the area around the river's lower reaches, along with its tributary, the Velino. The region is famous for its black truffles, herbs, wild asparagus, river trout and crayfish. At various points along the valley, there are opportunities for river sports such as canoeing and rafting, rock-climbing and even bungee-jumping, and as you travel along the SS209, the road that follows the river, you can easily visit any of a string of his-

toric villages and hamlets.

The clear, cold waters of the river feed the 165m (540ft) Cascata delle Marmore waterfalls. The highest waterfalls in Europe, they are, surprisingly, a man-made phenomenon: They were created in 271BC by a Roman consul, Manius Curius Dentatus, who diverted the River Velino into the Nera.

VOLTERRA

436 F7 Piazza dei Priori 20, 56048 Volterra, tel 0588 87257
www.volterratur.it

Volterra lies high in the volcanic hills, 50km (31 miles) west of Siena, in the triangle formed by Siena, Pisa and Florence. On a clear day you can see the islands of Corsica and Elba (p. 140) off the Tuscan coast.

The town was founded by the Etruscans as an important stronghold and its medieval heart is Piazza dei Priori, with its 12th-century duomo and 13th-century octagonal baptistery. Volterra also has a good art gallery housing a *Deposition* by Rosso Fiorentino and a very well-preserved Roman theatre. This was built in the first century BC and unearthed only in the 1950s, having been covered by a rubbish dump.

The Parco Archeologico is the site of an Etruscan and Roman acropolis, while the Museo Guarnacci (daily 9–7, summer; daily 9–2, rest of year) exhibits one of the most important collections of Etruscan works in the world.

Other highlights in the town include the Porta all'Arco, a rare Etruscan arch dating from the fourth century BC, and the Palazzo dei Priori. Complete with battlemented tower, this was the first town hall built in Italy (1208–54) and was the model for the Palazzo Vecchio in Florence (p. 130).

ROME

Capital of modern Italy and home to the Vatican, the historic city of Rome has reminders of its past at every turn. Its history can be traced through its superb Roman monuments, great medieval churches, Renaissance palaces and rich museums, all set against a backdrop of bustling streets and bubbling fountains.

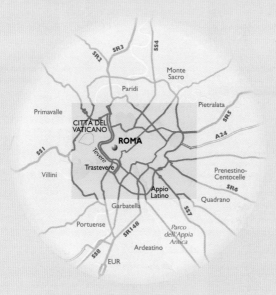

MAJOR SIGHTS

Basilica di San Pietro

**The most famous church in Christendom.
The spiritual capital of the Roman Catholic faith and the focus of the
Papal Vatican State.
Testament to the genius of Michelangelo, architect and sculptor.**

A bird's-eye view of Piazza San Pietro and Bernini's colonnade

Looking towards the basilica from Piazza San Pietro (below) and the South Wind depicted on a plaque in the square (bottom)

SEEING SAN PIETRO

It is the monumental scale of the Basilica di San Pietro (St. Peter's), the largest Roman Catholic building in the world, that is mesmerizing. The proportions are huge—it is 218m (715ft) long, 137m (450ft) high, and covers a total of 22,067sq m (237,535sq ft). It can accommodate 60,000 people. With 778 columns, 44 altars, 135 mosaics and 395 statues, the interior is overwhelming. Concentrate on the highlights: the view of and from Michelangelo's soaring dome, one of his earliest and most moving sculptures, and Bernini's contributions to the interior.

HIGHLIGHTS

THE PORTICO

The approach to the basilica is impressively grand, through the embrace of Bernini's colonnade (284 columns and 140 statues). The obelisk in the middle of the square was brought here by Caligula from Alexandria in Egypt. As you reach Bernini's broad staircase, note the central balcony above the portico, the Loggia delle Benedizioni, where the Pope stands to bless the people gathered in the square below. Inside the portico, the last bronze door on the right is the Holy Door, opened only every 25 years, in a Holy Year (the last was 2000). Over the central door is what remains of Giotto's *Navicella* mosaic (1298).

MICHELANGELO'S LA PIETÀ

The most famous of all the statues in San Pietro, now protected by bulletproof glass, is in the first chapel in the right aisle as you enter. Michelangelo's masterpiece *La Pietà* was begun in 1498, when he was a tender 24 years old. It is his only signed work; he engraved his name on a band across the Virgin's breast, and an M inside her right hand. Look up to see his other contribution to the building, the vast dome, covered in mosaics.

BERNINI'S SCULPTURES

Directly under Michelangelo's dome is Bernini's *baldacchino*, an amazing bronze canopy 29m (50ft) high. Its twisted bronze columns are decorated with golden olive and laurel branches and bees, the emblem of Urban VIII's Barberini family. It stands over the Altar of the Confession, where only the Pope may celebrate Mass.

Beneath this is St. Peter's tomb, lit by 99 lamps, and to the right sits a statue of St. Peter (attributed to Arnolfo di Cambio from the late 1220s), his right foot worn by the touch of pilgrims. Behind the *baldacchino*, in the end apse, are Bernini's baroque monument to Urban VIII and his extraordinary *cattedra*, which encases a chair that was supposedly used by St. Peter.

The rooftop statues and the dome (far left); the bronze canopy over the altar inside (left); Michelangelo's La Pietà (1498–99) in the Cappella della Pietà (bottom)

Nuns ascend the wide flight of steps up to the basilica (above)

At the top of the left aisle, past the Cappella della Colonna—dedicated to St. Leo, who persuaded Attila the Hun to spare Rome—is a chapel containing the monument to Alexander VII, by Bernini, portraying Death as a skeleton. Past many more papal monuments, and almost back at the portico, is the baptistery. The basin is made from an ancient porphyry sarcophagus taken from the tomb of Hadrian.

THE GROTTOES AND THE DOME

Under one of the dome's great supporting pillars is the entrance to the Vatican grottoes, which are lined with tombs of emperors and popes. To climb the dome, take the elevator to the cupola and terrace, then climb the 330 steps for a closer look at the mosaics. The final, more challenging ascent, via a narrow, spiral staircase, takes you to the top of the lantern, from where you can marvel at the panoramic views of Rome.

BACKGROUND

It was here, in about AD67, that Nero had the Apostle Peter crucified, and it was over his tomb that Constantine built the first basilica, in 324. By 1452 it had started to crumble and Nicholas V began restoring it. Decades of architectural debate followed until 1547, when Pope Paul III appointed Michelangelo to control the project. Michelangelo refused all payment, insisting that he work for the glory of God. He began rebuilding the church in the form of a Greek cross, with a central dome and four cupolas. Then, in 1606, Pope Paul V decided to make some alterations. He chose a Latin cruciform, and employed Carlo Maderno to extend the complex, making a nave and a new portico, while Bernini transformed the interior with baroque touches. San Pietro was finally consecrated by Pope Urban VIII in 1626.

BASICS

✚ 426 B3 • Piazza San Pietro, 00120 Roma ☎ 06 6988 2019/1662

🕐 Basilica: daily 7–7, Apr–Sep; daily 7–6, rest of year. Cupola: daily 8–6, Apr–Sep; daily 8–5, rest of year (1 hour before closing, access by elevator only). Museo del Tesoro: daily 9–6.30, Apr–Sep; daily 9–5.30, rest of year. Grottoes: daily 9–5, Apr–Sep; daily 8–5, rest of year. Necropoli: Mon–Sat 9–3.30. Visits must be requested 2 weeks in advance in writing to Officio Scavi di San Pietro, tel 06 6988 5318, fax 06 6987 3017. Basilica closed during papal celebrations

💶 Basilica: free. Dome: from €4. Museo del Tesoro: €5. Grottoes: free. Necropoli: €9. Free tickets for papal ceremony at main entrance.

🚇 Ottaviano–San Pietro

🎫 Tours: Groups with reservation. No private tours before 10.30am (tel 06 6988 4466)

📖 €5

🍽 Via Della Conciliazione, Borgo Pio

♿ With disabled access

www.vatican.va

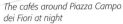
The cafés around Piazza Campo dei Fiori at night

Castel Sant'Angelo viewed from Ponte Sant'Angelo

The Fontana di Trevi is even more charismatic at night

ARCO DI COSTANTINO

✚ 427 F5 • Piazza del Colosseo, Roma
🚇 Colosseo 🚋 Tram 3, 117

Rome's best-preserved and largest Roman arch, the Arco di Costantino stands proudly alongside the old Roman triumphal way. Highly decorated and nearly 25m (82ft) high, it was built by the Senate and people of Rome in AD315 to commemorate Emperor Constantine's victory over the tyrant Maxentius, after which he granted freedom of worship to the Christians. An inscription on each side celebrates his coming to power, and scenes show combat against the Dacians and the triumphs of Constantine and his son. When first carved, the bas-reliefs between the statues of the four Dacian prisoners showed episodes in the life of Marcus Aurelius, but his features were later altered to resemble those of Constantine. The four medallions showing hunting and sacrifices came from a monument to Hadrian (AD117–138).

BASILICA DI SAN PIETRO

p. 158–159.

PIAZZA CAMPO DEI FIORI

✚ 427 D4 • Piazza Campo dei Fiori, 00186 Roma 🚋 Tram 8

Piazza Campo dei Fiori bustles with *trattorie*, bookshops and a famous market. Relax with a drink at one of the famous *vinerie* and delight in one of the most attractive and lively squares in Rome. In ancient times it was used as grazing land for cattle—hence the name, which means field of flowers. Many of the nearby streets and squares are named after the various artisan workshops in the area. It was also the venue for capital executions. In 1600 the philosopher Giordano Bruno, who advocated the separation of political and religious power, was burned alive on the spot where his statue stands. The statue, by Ettore Ferrari (1887) and the Cinema Farnesen are traditional meeting places for intellectuals and anti-establishment thinkers. **Don't miss** The Il Forno bakery sells some of the best pizzas in Rome.

CASTEL SANT'ANGELO

✚ 426 C3 • Lungotevere del Castello 50, 00120 Roma ☎ 06 681 9111
🕐 Tue–Sun 9–7. Prison: Sun by guided tour 💰 Adult €5, under 18s free
🚇 Ottaviano–San Pietro 🚻 🍴

Mausoleum, fortress and papal stronghold, this imposing ancient monument is now home to the Museo Nazionale's collection of ceramics, weapons, furnishings and Renaissance paintings. As you approach over the Ponte Sant' Angelo, pause to share with the ten stone angels their view of the Tiber and San Pietro. Commissioned in AD135 by Hadrian to be the resting place for himself and his family, the castle remained a mausoleum until Caracalla's death in AD217. Aurelian later converted it into a fortress.

Legend has it that when Rome was struck by the plague in 590 Pope Gregory the Great organized a procession to pray for the city. As the people approached the mausoleum, the statue of Archangel Michael rose into the air holding aloft a flaming sword, signalling the end of the plague. From then on it was called Castel Sant'Angelo. In the ninth century, Leo IV linked it to the Vatican with a high defensive wall topped by the Passetto, a covered walkway.

Castel Sant'Angelo has also served as a prison, whose guests included sculptor and metalworker Benvenuto Cellini and the adventurer Giuseppe Balsamo. **Don't miss** The frescoes in the papal apartments.

COLOSSEO

p. 162–163.

FONTANA DI TREVI

✚ 427 E3 • Piazza Trevi, 00187 Roma
🚇 Barberini

Immortalized in Federico Fellini's 1960 film *La Dolce Vita*, the Fontana di Trevi (Trevi Fountain) is the most photographed fountain in Rome. Nicola Salvi won a competition to design a fountain to replace one that stood here, at the junction of three roads (*tre vie*), but it was not completed until 1762, after his death.

In the middle, Neptune rides a shell-shaped chariot drawn by seahorses steered by giant tritons. Behind is a baroque façade with statues of Plenty, Health and the Four Seasons. In 19BC, General Agrippa built a 19km (12-mile) aqueduct to bring water to the baths near the Pantheon. The story is told in bas-reliefs: On the right a young girl leads Agrippa's soldiers to a spring; on the left he approves plans for the aqueduct. Today the water, called Acqua Virgo, runs underground in one of the few Roman canals still in use, supplying central fountains.

Toss two coins over your shoulder into the fountain, make a wish and, it is said, you will return to Rome and your wish come true.

GESÙ

✚ 427 E4 • Piazza del Gesù/Via degli Astalli 16, 00186 Roma ☎ 06 697001
🕐 Daily 6–12.30, 4–6.15 🚋 Tram 8

For fans of the baroque the highlight of this church, dedicated to the Holy Name of Jesus and completed in 1584, is the chapel of St. Ignatius of Loyola. He lived, died and founded his Jesuit order here, and this chapel is the work of the famous Jesuit architect Andrea Pozzo. It is heavy with stucco, bronzes, sculptures, marbles and precious stones.

PIAZZA DEL CAMPIDOGLIO

A grand piazza on the Capitolino, the most famous of Rome's seven hills and the hub of the Roman Empire. A showplace for Michelangelo's majestic work.

Michelangelo was called upon to redesign this piazza as part of Pope Paul III's plan to restore the city to its ancient splendour after the Sack of Rome in 1527. The magnificent buildings that stand on three sides of the square—the Palazzo Senatorio, the Palazzo Nuovo and the Palazzo dei Conservatori, built on the site of the great temple of Jupiter Capitolinus—were part of his scheme.

THE CORDONATA
The new piazza was designed for Emperor Charles V's triumphal entry into Rome in 1536, and the best approach is the Cordonata, Michelangelo's elegant ramp intended for the emperor. The top of the Cordonata is flanked by two large statues of Castor and Pollux, the mythical sons of Jupiter, standing by their horses. To their left and right is a display of captured enemy arms from the reign of Domitian. The balustrade is embellished with columns from the Via Appia and statues of Constantine the Great and his son Constantine II in full military dress.

THE PIAZZA
The floor of the piazza is inlaid with a star-shaped pattern, in the middle of which Michelangelo placed a plinth for the equestrian statue of Marcus Aurelius. This escaped the fate of the many statues of pagan emperors that were melted down and reused during the Middle Ages. The original is in the Musei Capitolini (p.167); this is a copy.

PALAZZO SENATORIO
The Palazzo Senatorio (Senate House) was built during a period when the people of Rome demanded an end to the power of the papacy and re-established a republic. Michelangelo designed a new façade, subsequently built by Giacomo della Porta, and the *palazzo* became the hub of political activity in the 16th and 17th centuries. A fountain near the steps is flanked by two huge bearded statues representing the Nile, and the Sphinx, the Tiber, Romulus and Remus and the she-wolf.

MUSEI CAPITOLINI
Note the twin balconies of the Palazzo dei Conservatori and Palazzo Nuovo, designed by Michelangelo, with statues looking across at each other. These buildings house the Musei Capitolini (p. 167).

RATINGS	
Historical interest	●●●●
Cultural interest	●●●●
Photo stops	●●●
Walkability	●●●●

BASICS

✚ 427 E4 • Piazza del Campidoglio, 00186 Roma

🚇 Colosseo

🚋 Tram 8 to Argentina

📖 In the museum shops (Libreria Capitolina)

🚻 First floor of Palazzo Caffarelli

🏛 In the museums

www.museicapitolini.org

A silhouette of the statues of Castor and Pollux guarding the Cordonata by the Palazzo Senatorio (top); a reclining statue at the Palazzo Nuovo (above)

Colosseo

**The largest monument of imperial Rome in existence, an amphitheatre where gladiators fought to the death with wild beasts.
Rome's number one landmark and symbol of classical times.
Superbly designed sports arena that is the model for modern stadia.**

Archways inside the Colosseo | *The Colosseo, illuminated, viewed from Via dei Fori Imperiali* | *The four levels of the Colosseo*

RATINGS	
Good for kids	●●●○
Historic interest	●●●●●
Cultural interest	●●●○
Photo stops	●●●●●

TIPS

● Buy your entrance ticket at the Palatine, as there is often a very long wait at the Colosseo.

● If you want a clearer idea of what the interior of the stadium was like, take a guided tour. The service provided by the Italian *Sovrintendenza dei Beni Culturali* is very good.

SEEING THE COLOSSEO

The Colosseo (Colosseum) stands just to the east of the Foro Romano, encircled by the Caelian, Palatine and Esquiline hills. The best approach is from the Via dei Fori Imperiali, where you'll get a good sense of its scale and size. Walk around the outside before tackling the damaged and confusing interior. Take a guided tour or an audioguide to help you visualize the arena's past glory.

HIGHLIGHTS

THE EXTERIOR

The elliptical structure covers about 2.4ha (6 acres), and enough survives of the exterior to give a good idea of its original appearance, though the marble facings, painted stucco and statues have all gone. Externally, the Colosseo measures 188m by 156m (617ft by 512ft) and rises to 48m (159ft), with a façade of three tiers of arches and an attic. The tiers are faced with three-quarter Doric, Ionic and Corinthian columns, and the attic has square window openings. At the top were 240 brackets and sockets that anchored the *velarium*, a shade and bad-weather canopy that could be pulled across the interior. The holes you see on the walls once held the metal clamps that pinned the massive blocks together; they were pillaged, together with tons of stone, for later building.

THE ARCADES AND SEATING

Inside, arcades run right around the outer edge of the building on each level, linking the stairways that connect the different floors. Passages from the arcades accessed, via 80 doorways, the tiers of marble benches, some still complete. The spectators were arranged by rank, with humble citizens and women at the top, a special box, closest to

The Colosseo is the largest surviving structure of the Roman Empire

the action, naturally, for the emperor, and ringside seats for the senators and Vestal Virgins. The tickets, which were wooden plaques, carved with the entrance numbers, are still visible above the exterior arches. The system was very efficient, and the organizers could move up to 70,000 people in or out in a matter of minutes.

THE ARENA

The middle of the Colosseo is a jumble of ruins, all that's left of the labyrinthine passages beneath the arena itself. In Roman times, this area had wooden flooring covered with canvas and sand—the word 'arena' comes from the Latin word for sand. The four principal entrances were used by the gladiators, stagehands and corpse removers. Far more dramatic entrances were made through trapdoors in the floor—you can still see their outlines. These opened into the passages and lifts from where men and wild animals emerged—tens of thousands of animals, sent to Rome from all over the Empire, were slaughtered at the Colosseo. Other passages were water conduits, and the arena was regularly flooded for water battles.

Gladiatorial games began in the morning with an elaborate procession, the prelude to staged hunts when wild animals were pitted against each other or pursued by *bestiarii*, gladiators specializing in animal slaughter. The lunch break was accompanied by executions, a taster for the day's climax—the individual gladiatorial combats.

BACKGROUND

Known since the eighth century as the Colosseo, the arena was built by the three Flavian emperors, Vespasian, Titus and Domitian. Construction started in AD72, and the inaugural games were held in AD80. It was the first permanent amphitheatre built in Rome, brilliantly combining grandiose design with practicality. Games and fights were held here right up to the end of the Empire in the sixth century. During the Middle Ages the Colosseo was used as a fortress, and from the 15th century as a source of building materials for some of Rome's finest *palazzi*. By the late 1700s the crumbling structure was a romantic and overgrown ruin, and since 1750 it has been dedicated to the Christian martyrs killed in its arena. Conservation began in the 19th century and is ongoing.

BASICS

➕ 428 F4–5 • Piazza del Colosseo, 00184 Roma ☎ 06 700 5469

🕐 Mon 9–2, Tue–Sun 9–7.15, Apr–Sep; daily 9–sunset, rest of year

💳 Adult €10, under 18s free. Timed tickets: Palatine and Colosseum valid 24 hours. Roma Archaeologia Card valid 7 days for Colosseum, Palatine, Baths of Caracalla, Palazzo Altemps, Palazzo Massimo, Baths of Diocletian, Crypta Balbi, Tomb of Cecilia Metella and Villa dei Quintili, €20

Ⓜ Colosseo

🚋 Tram 3, 8

🎧 Tours €3, daily on the hour 9–5, Apr Oct; daily on the hour 9–3, rest of year. Audiotours, €4

📖 Official guide published by the Sovrintendenza dei Beni Culturali

🏛

🚻 Outside on south side (open to 6pm), inside and in the Metro station

www.archeorm.arti.beniculturali.it
An Italian site bringing together the key archeological sites in Rome, with photos, site maps and information on the Collosseo, the Domus Aurea, the Museo Nazionale Romano, the Terme di Caracalla, the Mausoleo di Cecilia, Metella and the Villa dei Quintili.

Foro Romano

The political, commercial, economic and religious focal point of
Republican Rome.
One of the city's most important archaeological sites, with many famous
monuments spanning more than 900 years.

The broad Via Sacra links two triumphal arches

A section of the right aisle of the ruins of the formerly lavish Basilica di Massenzio (AD308)

RATINGS	
Historic interest	● ● ● ●
Cultural interest	● ● ● ●
Photo stops	● ● ●
Walkability	● ● ● ●

TIP

● The Forum can be confusing, so before you enter, get an overview of the general layout from the Via del Campidoglio, the northern side of the Piazza del Campidoglio (p. 161) or the Orti Farnesiani (p. 167) gardens.

● Take something to drink, as there are no bars or cafés in the immediate area.

Detail of the Arco di Settimio Severo

SEEING THE FORO ROMANO

The Roman Forum was the hub of daily life in the days of ancient Rome, and its ruins lie in what is still the heart of the city, between the Colosseum and Piazza Campidoglio and the great Victor Emmanuel monument. There are several points of entry, but the main entrance, and the best one, is from the Via dei Fori Imperiali. This leads immediately onto the Via Sacra, the most ancient road, which runs through the heart of the Roman Forum, linking two triumphal arches, the Arco di Settimio Severo and the Arco di Tito. The most important sights lie between these arches. At first the Forum seems nothing more than a jumbled collection of ruins with one or two intact buildings—you'll need a plan to get your bearings.

HIGHLIGHTS

VIA SACRA, TEMPIO DI ANTONINO E FAUSTINA, BASILICA AEMILIA

The Via Sacra, which bisects the Forum, linked the Palatine to the Capitoline hills. Holy sanctuaries lined the way, and victorious generals led processions along the route to give thanks to Jupiter in the temple of Jupiter Capitolinus. Near the main entrance are the remains of temple of Antoninus and Faustina, the best-preserved temple in the Forum, chiefly because it was converted to a Christian church in the seventh century. To the right is a large area of broken columns, the Basilica Aemilia, built in the second century AD to house the law courts.

TEMPIO DI VESTA AND TEMPIO DEI CASTORI

Back near the main entrance, by the Via Sacra, is the circular white Temple of Vesta, where the six Vestal Virgins, priestesses to the goddess of fire, kept the sacred fire alight. The women lived in the House of the Vestal Virgins next door (the central courtyard with its three pools survives), dedicating most of their lives to the service of the goddess and receiving social privileges in return.

Nearby are the three Corinthian columns that remain of the Tempio dei Castori (Temple of Castor and Pollux), built to commemorate the Battle of Lacus Regillus, during which the two divine figures helped the Romans defeat the Latins.

BASILICA JULIA, CURIA, ARCO DI SETTIMIO SEVERO

The Via Sacra runs westwards beside the steps of the ruined Basilica Julia, built by Julius Caesar after he returned from the Gallic Wars. Across the Forum proper from here is the remarkably intact, red-coloured Curia (senate house), politically the Roman Republic's most important building. It was here that famous orators and statesmen made their speeches.

At the western end of the complex, the triumphal Arch of Septimius Severus was built in AD203 by his sons, Caracalla and Galba, to

commemorate the 10th anniversary of the emperor's reign and his victory over the Parthians between AD197 and 202. Statues of Septimius Severus and Caracalla stand on top of the arch.

BASILICA DI MASSENZIO AND ARCO DI TITO

East of the main entrance to the Foro Romano, the Via Sacra passes the Basilica di Massenzio (Basilica of Maxentius), the largest and most impressive of all the ruins, built by Consantine and Maxentius in the fourth century. Note its arches, constructed of poured cement.

At the far end of the Foro the Via Sacra is spanned by the Arco di Tito, built on the Palatine after Titus's death in AD70 to commemorate his victory over the Jews and the capture of Jerusalem.

BACKGROUND

In the eighth century BC the site of the Foro Romano was a marshy area between the Capitoline and Palatine hills, used as a burial ground and a meeting place for the leaders of the nearby agricultural settlements. The area then came under the rule of the Etruscans, who drained the land. In 497BC one of the first temples to be built here was dedicated to the Etruscan god of crops. The area developed as the hub of social, civic and political life. As Rome grew in wealth and power, triumphal arches and monuments were erected to celebrate the victories of the Roman Republic, and the area became the city's financial focus. With its *comitium*, a square in front of the Curia, and the *rostra*, where the tribunes met, the Forum became the focal point for the men who planned the future of the empire.

By 44BC, however, the Forum had become over-crowded, and Julius Caesar moved the Curia and *rostra* to the Fori Imperiali. Mercati Traianei (Trajan's Market) became the city's commercial hub, and in AD391, with Christianity spreading, Theodosius closed the pagan temples. From then the Foro gradually fell into ruin, its buildings became a quarry for building stone, and what had been the power behind a mighty empire reverted to cattlefields.

The Forum began life as a market

BASICS

🗺 427 F4 • Via dei Fori Imperiali, Via Sacra, Via di San Teodoro, Via di San Gregorio (entrance to the Palatine), 00186 Roma ☎ 06 3996 7700
🕐 Foro: daily 9–7.30 (ticket office closes at 6.30). Groups with reservations may enter at any time. Palatine: daily 9–6.30, Apr–Sep; daily 9–3.30, rest of year.
💶 Foro: free. Palatine: €8; 18–24 years (EU nationals) €4; under 18s (EU nationals) free. Timed tickets: Palatine and Colosseum valid 24 hours
🚇 Colosseo
🚋 Tram 3 📷 Tours: Foro: €3.50; daily at 10.30 in English

Detail of the remains of an architrave surmounting a solitary Corinthian column in the Foro Romano

RATINGS

Historic interest	● ● ●
Cultural interest	● ● ● ●
Specialist shopping	● ● ●

TIPS

● If possible, book in advance as only 360 people are allowed in every 2 hours.

● There is a free guided tour of the Secret Garden on Saturday at 10.30 and Sunday at 9.30 and 10.30. Get there early, as there are only 20 places *(tel 06 8207 7304)*.

BASICS

✚ 428 F1 • Piazzale Scipione Borghese 5, 00197 Roma (entrance in Via Pinciana) ☎ 06 854 8577
🕐 Daily 9–7 (last entry 6.30)
💶 Adult €8.50, under 18s €2. Advance booking required
🎧 2-hour tour with an art historian in English (9.10am, 11.10am) and Italian (11.10am, 1.10pm, 5.10pm), €5. Booking in advance required (through website or fax 063 265 1329). Audiotours in Italian, English, Spanish, French and German, €2
📖 💻 ♿ 👥 🅿 On Via Pinciana
Ⓜ Spagna

www.ticketeria.it
You can make advance bookings for the Galleria Borghese via this website, along with many other famous museums and galleries in Italy that require reservation.
www.galleriaborghese.it
This site has pictures of some of the highlights in the collection.

Canova's reclining statue of Paolina Borghese, sister of Napoleon

GALLERIA BORGHESE

A remarkable and much-loved collection of art in the peaceful setting of the Villa Borghese. Masterpieces include some of the most famous sculptures by Bernini and Canova, and paintings by Caravaggio, Titian and Raphael.

Cardinal Scipione, Ortensia Borghese's son, was passionate about art and founded this outstanding collection of sculpture and painting. He was also a man without scruples, however. For example, he arranged for Raphael's *Deposition* to be stolen from a church in Perugia and put the painter Domenichino in jail for refusing to give him his *Diana*. In 1620 his collection was moved to the Villa Pinciana. At the end of the 19th century the villa was sold to the Italian State to settle debts, and in 1903 the once-secret gardens were given to the municipality of Rome.

ROOM I

The main draw is Canova's sensuous sculpture of Paulina Borghese, Napoleon Bonaparte's sister, controversial in its day for its naked depiction of a wealthy subject.

ROOMS II, III AND IV

These rooms display sculptures by Bernini. First is *David*, preparing to fight the giant Goliath. The piece is thought to be a self-portrait. In homage to Bernini's patron, Scipione Borghese, his harp features an eagle's head, a Borghese family emblem. Note how the facial expression changes as you move around the statue. Next is *Apollo and Daphne*, showing Daphne changing into a laurel tree as she escapes Apollo's advances. Bernini's energetic statue *The Rape of Proserpina*, shows Pluto, god of the underworld, attempting to rape Demeter's daughter.

ROOM VIII

The six Caravaggio paintings here are noted for their use of *chiaroscuro*. This technique of highlighting figures with a shaft of light from the surrounding darkness is used beautifully in the *Madonna dei Palafreni*.

OTHER HIGHLIGHTS

Paintings by Raphael, Pinturicchio and Perugino are exhibited in Room IX. Correggio's *Danaë* illustrates Jupiter's love for her. In Room XVIII is the stolen *Deposition* by Raphael (1507).

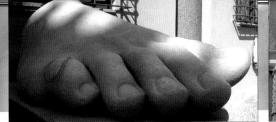

A giant foot in the Palazzo dei Conservatori at the Musei Capitolini

Exterior of the Palazzo Barberini by Borromini and Bernini

MUSEI CAPITOLINI

🔲 427 E4 • Piazza del Campidoglio, 00186 Roma ☎ 06 6710 2071
🕐 Tue–Sun 9–8 🎟 Adult €6, under 18s free 🚇 Colosseo 🎫
www.museicapitolini.org

The Palazzo dei Conservatori and the Palazzo Nuovo make up the Musei Capitolini, home to one of Rome's richest collection of sculptures, mosaics, frescoes and paintings. Once the headquarters of the city's magistrates, in 1450 the Palazzo dei Conservatori became the world's first public museum when it began to show bronze statues given to the Romans by Pope Sixtus IV. In the courtyard are fragments of a colossal statue of Constantine. Inside, highlights include the delightful *Spinario,* a first-century Greek bronze of a boy extracting a thorn from his foot, and the famous sixth-century Etruscan bronze of the Capitoline she-wolf. The art gallery has a collection of 16th- and 18th-century paintings. The Palazzo Nuovo has more excellent pieces, including energetically carved sarcophagi, the headless *Capitoline Venus* and a bronze of Marcus Aurelius. **Don't miss** The reliefs from the triumphal arch of Marcus Aurelius are superb.

MUSEI VATICANI

p. 168–171.

ORTI FARNESIANI

🔲 427 E–F5 • Via dei Fori Imperiali/Via Sacra/Via di San Teodoro/Via di San Gregorio, 00186 Roma ☎ 06 3996 7700 🕐 Daily 9–7, Apr–Sep; daily 9–3.30, rest of year 🎟 Adult €8; 18–24 years €4; under 18s free. Ticket valid for Palatino and Colosseo 🚇 Colosseo

A cool retreat, the Orti Farnesiani (Farnese Gardens) are worth climbing the Palatino for. The gardens were laid out in the 16th century by Vignola at the behest of Cardinal Farnese. Shady paths meander through scented orange groves and cypresses.

PALATINO

🔲 427 E5 • Via dei Fori Imperiali/Via Sacra/Via di San Teodoro/Via di San Gregorio, 00186 Roma ☎ 06 3996 7700 🕐 Daily 9–7, Apr–Sep; daily 9–3.30, rest of year 🎟 Adults €8, under 18s free. Tickets valid for Palatino and Colosseo 🚇 Colosseo

One of Rome's seven hills, the Palatino is considered the cradle of the city. Legend has it that Romulus ploughed a deep furrow around the foot of the hill to define the original city boundary. Take a walk through the shady Orti Farnesiani (see above) or sit and enjoy the views of the Forum. In Republican times the hill was an élite residential area. Augustus lived here, and it became the preferred site for imperial palaces. There are temples dedicated to Apollo and Cybele, goddess of fertility, the frescoed Casa di Livia (Augustus' wife), Domitian's Domus Flavia, Domus Augustana and stadium, and the baths of Septimius Severus. Look for the House of the Griffons, where frescoes depict winged mythological animals, and the Loggia Mattei, a noble 15th-century palace. The museum has archaeological finds from excavations on the hill.

PALAZZO ALTEMPS

🔲 427 D3 • Piazza Sant'Apollinare 44, 00186 Roma ☎ 06 683 3759
🕐 Tue–Sun 9–7.45 🎟 Adult €5, under 18s free 🎫 Audiotours, €4
www.pierreci.it

Part of the Museo Nazionale Romano complex and home to a remarkable collection of classical sculpture, Palazzo Altemps is one of Rome's finest Renaissance buildings. Girolamo Riario, nephew of Pope Sixtus IV, commissioned the palace in 1477 and it was completed by the Altemps family

a century later. The Italian state acquired the building in 1982 to accommodate classical masterpieces that had belonged to the Mattei, Altemps and Ludovisi families. The courtyard is the handsomest feature, with marble and frescoes. Subjects in the Hall of Portraits include Julius Caesar and Marcus Aurelius. The highlight is The Room of Moses, which houses one of the most important sculptures in the Ludovisi collection, the *Ludovisi Throne.* The fifth-century, bas-relief sculpture depicts Aphrodite rising from the waves with her two handmaidens.

PALAZZO BARBERINI

🔲 427 F3 • Via Barberini 18, 00184 Roma ☎ 06 3263 2810 🕐 Gallery: Tue–Sun 9–7. Apartments: Tue–Sun 9.30–1.15, 2.15–6.45 🎟 Gallery: free. Apartments: Adults €6.30, under 18s €1.30 🚇 Barberini 🅿 🎫
www.ticketeria.it

This imposing palace is the work of three great baroque artists. Commissioned in 1623 by Pope Urban VIII, it was completed in 1633 by Bernini and Borromini. The palace houses the national collection of 12th- to 18th-century works once owned by Rome's aristocratic families, but the interior is also a sumptuous expression of high baroque style. In the entrance hall are two remarkable staircases, the wide monumental one on the left by Bernini, and the smaller, spiral one on the right by Borromini. Pietro da Cortona's *The Triumph of Divine Providence,* on the ceiling of the Gran Salone, is considered one of the masterpieces of baroque painting. Other highlights are Caravaggio's *Narcissus,* Titian's *Venus and Adonis* and Raphael's *La Fornarina.* Other highlights include a Holbein portrait of Henry VIII and *Judith and Holofernes* by Caravaggio. You may also tour the 18th-century private apartments.

THE SIGHTS

Musei Vaticani

•

The largest and richest museum complex in the world—at least 1,400 rooms. Sculpture, paintings and *objets d'art* spanning more than 3,000 years, from every corner of the Classical and modern world. The Sistine Chapel and Michelangelo's famous frescoes.

SEEING THE MUSEI VATICANI

The vast complex includes the museum, galleries and parts of the papal palace, richly decorated by the world's greatest artists. The galleries, themselves of great architectural interest, have a diverse collection of art, with a particular emphasis on Western art and sculpture.

HIGHLIGHTS

The entire complex fills a large space in the city

RATINGS				
Good for kids	◐ ◐			
Historic interest	◐ ◐ ◐ ◐ ◐			
Value for money	◐ ◐ ◐ ◐			
Walkability	◐ ◐ ◐			

TIPS

● Shorts and bare upper arms are unacceptable attire.

● To avoid crowds, arrive as the museum opens or late in the morning. Wednesday morning can be peaceful as people are in the Piazza di San Pietro for the papal blessing.

The Vatican Gardens (above middle); ancient sculpture (below); the clever and elegant spiral staircase has two separate spirals for ascending and descending (right)

CAPPELLA SISTINA

The Cappella Sistina (Sistine Chapel) was built by Pope Sixtus IV between 1473 and 1481, both as the pontiff's private chapel and as a venue for the conclave of cardinals who gather to elect each new pope. It is a huge, cavernous structure, with an intricate Cosmatesque mosaic floor and a marble screen by Mino da Fiesole. But, above all, it is the frescoes, entirely covering the walls and ceiling, that attract up to 20,000 visitors a day.

Even during the construction of the chapel, Sixtus was planning the interior decoration, settling on scenes from the Old and New Testaments as the subject matter, with an emphasis on the parallels between the lives of Moses and Christ. From Florence, he summoned Sandro Botticelli, together with Domenico Ghirlandaio, Cosimo Rosselli and Perugino. These artists, joined by Pinturicchio, Luca Signorelli and Piero di Cosimo, worked for 11 months, producing a series of glowing works. The two most important scenes are Perugino's *Christ Gives the Keys to Peter* and Botticelli's *The Punishment of Korah*, each showing the Arco di Costantino in the background.

Though undoubtedly masterpieces, they tend to be overshadowed by Michelangelo's frescoes on the ceiling and altar wall, arguably Western art's finest achievement and certainly the largest work ever planned and carried out by one man. Julius II commissioned the ceiling in 1508, and Michelangelo completed it in 1512, an artistic *tour-de-force* combining narrative scenes, architectural *trompe l'oeil* effects and statuesque figures of immense beauty. The central panels illustrate the Creation and tell the story of Noah, surrounded by a decorative scheme dominated by the figures of the Prophets and Sibyls containing wonderful details, including the famous *ignudi* (nude youths).

Years later, in 1535, Michelangelo was again summoned to the chapel, this time by Paul III, to decorate the altar wall with scenes of the Last Judgement, a task that occupied him until 1541. Even before it was finished, the amount of nudity offended many, not least the pope's master of ceremonies. Furious, Michelangelo depicted him in the bottom right-hand corner of Hell as Minos, the doorkeeper, complete with ass's ears. Later, Pius IV objected to the nudity to such an extent

One of several massive sculpted heads on the terrace

BASICS

✚ 426 B3 • Viale Vaticano, 00165 Rome ☎ 06 6988 4676

◎ Mon–Fri 8.45–4.45 (last entrance 3.20), Sat 8.45–1.45 (last entrance 12.20), Mar–Nov; Mon–Sat 8.45–1.45, rest of year. Open last Sun of month; closed for public holidays

💶 Adult €10, child (under 6) free

🎫 2-hour guided tour, €4; book at information point or tel 06 6988 5100. Audiotours in Italian, English, French, German, Spanish, Japanese, €5.50

🎧 €7.50 💳 🏛 🚻

P Gianicolo underground parking

Ⓜ Cipro Musei Vaticani, Ottaviano-Vaticano

www.vatican.va
This website dedicated to the Vatican City is very stylish and informative. Under the section on the Vatican Museums you can view the collection online, read about the artworks and zoom in on individual paintings for a closer look. There are also online tours and up to date practical information, such as opening times and prices that you will need.

One of the Pope's Swiss Guards

he commissioned Daniele da Volterra to paint over the genitals—an exercise that earned him the name Braghettone, the trouser-maker. The censorship was removed during the restoration of the chapel frescoes of the 1980s and '90s, a project said to have cost more than $3 million.

STANZE DI RAFFAELLO

Not content with the painting of the Cappella Sistina, in 1508 Julius II embarked on a major project to decorate his private apartments, today known as the Stanze di Raffaello (Raphael Rooms). The Stanza della Segnatura, the pope's study, is deservedly the most famous room and was Raphael's first major Roman commission, painted between 1508 and 1511.

The four frescoes, compositions imbued with balance and harmony, are allegories representing the humanist ideals of theology, philosophy, poetry and justice. The *School of Athens* emphasizes truth acquired through reason, with all the great classical thinkers represented and the central figures of Plato—probably a portrait of Leonardo da Vinci —and Aristotle dominating the scene. The figure on the left is said to be Michelangelo, added after Raphael had a sneak preview of his work in the Cappella Sistina. Opposite is the *Disputation of the Holy Sacrament*, while the side walls show *Parnassus*, home to the Muses, and the *Cardinal Virtues*.

Chronologically, the next room to be painted was the Stanza di Eliodoro, with its energy-charged *Expulsion of Heliodorus* and serene *Miracle of Bolsena*. The latter tells the story of the medieval miracle that occurred in that town, when a priest who doubted the doctrine of tran-substantiation saw the wafer bleed during Mass. The window wall has a superb night scene, showing the *Deliverance of St. Peter from Prison*.

The Stanza di Costantino depicts the life of Constantine, the first Christian emperor, while the main focus in the Stanza dell'Incendio, commissioned by Leo X, is the miraculous quenching of a *Fire in the Borgo*, which occurred when Leo IV made the sign of the cross.

THE SIGHTS

PINACOTECA VATICANA

The Pinacoteca, founded in 1816 by Pius VI, occupies a separate building (1932) within the museum complex. It is widely considered to be Rome's best picture gallery, with works from the early and High Renaissance to the 19th century. Among these are some of the most remarkable early paintings in Rome, with Giotto's *Stefaneschi Triptych* stealing the show (Room II). Painted in the early 1300s it shows the *Martyrdom of St. Peter and Paul.* St. Peter is shown being crucified, at his own request, upside down, as he felt unworthy to die the same way as Christ. The next rooms are devoted to 15th-century Italian art; look for Fra Angelico's lovely *Madonna and Child with Saints* in Room III and the serene Umbrian pictures in Room VII, particularly Perugino's luminous *Madonna and Child.* Room VIII is the Pinacoteca's finest, with a collection of Raphael's work, including tapestries, woven in Brussels

Maps of the papal lands in the Galleria delle Carte Geographiche

from his cartoons, that once hung in the Cappella Sistina. Dominating the room, however, is the *Transfiguration,* a sublime work that was hung above the artist's coffin and completed by his pupils later. The triumphant figure of the ascending Christ pulses with energy amidst piercing light and lowering cloud formations, a superb contrast to the artist's first major composition, the *Coronation of the Virgin,* painted when he was only 20. The gentle *Madonna of Foligno* was commissioned in 1512 as a votive offering.

In Room IX is Leonardo da Vinci's unfinished and curiously monochrome *St. Jerome,* one of only a few of da Vinci's works whose authorship has never been disputed. Here, too, is the exquisite *Pietà* by the Venetian painter Bellini. Venetian painting is featured heavily in Room X in two canvases by Titian, a glowing *Madonna with Saints* and the subtle *Portrait of Doge Nicolò Marcello.* There are further psychological insights in Caravaggio's despairing *Deposition* in Room XII, all muted tones and intense *chiaroscuro* light.

BACKGROUND

Pope Innocent III (1179–81) began building a palace near the Basilica San Pietro, the permanent seat of the papacy, and his successors enlarged and embellished it. Major work was carried out under Nicolò V in the mid-15th century, and in the 1470s Sixtus IV added the Cappella Sistina. Both Julius II (1503–13) and Leo X (1513–22) built and decorated further buildings—Julius commissioned Michelangelo to paint the Cappella Sistina and Raphael to decorate his private rooms. In the 18th century the collections were arranged into a museum, with galleries built to display sculpture, paintings, and *objets d'art*—a huge project that continued into the 20th century.

LOWER FLOOR

Museo Pio Clementino: The cream of the classical sculpture collection is in this museum's octagonal courtyard. Two statues here influenced Renaissance sculptors more than any others, the *Laocöon* and the *Apollo Belvedere.* Highlights within include a beautiful Hellenistic *Sleeping Ariadne,* candelabra from the Villa Adriana at Tivoli, and Roman portrait busts, including a splendid Julius Caesar.

Museo Gregoriano Egizio: Founded in the 19th century by Gregory XVI, this museum displays a reconstruction of the Temple of Serapis from the Villa Adriana at Tivoli, mummy cases, mummies and tomb treasures.

Museo Gregoriano Profano: Built in 1963 and opened in 1970, a museum with a collection of antique and Christian art moved here from the Lateran Palace.

Museo Pio Cristiano: A collection of documents and objects illustrating religions of the world.

Museo Storico Vaticano: A unusual collection of papal transportation, including carriages.

Museo Chiaramonti: Another collection of Roman sculpture, in particular portrait busts.

Braccio Nuovo: A beautiful collection in a superb architectural setting.

Biblioteca Vaticana: A huge, brilliantly frescoed hall with letters from Petrarch, Michelangelo and Martin Luther, and King Henry VIII's love letters to Anne Boleyn.

UPPER FLOOR

Museo Gregoriano Etrusco: Founded in 1837, this is a major Etruscan collection of sculpture and funerary art.

Galleria delle Carte Geographiche: This upper-floor gallery links the museums with the papal palace. It was painted in 1580 by Ignazio Danti with maps of Italy, Mediterranean islands, papal possessions in France, the Siege of Malta and Venice.

Cappella di Nicolò V: Serene and delicate frescoes (1446–49) by Fra Angelico in the pope's private chapel.

A map of Sardinia in the Galleria delle Carte Geographiche, painted by Ignazio Danti, a Dominican monk

Painted ceilings and elegant statues in the Palazzo Doria

The Piazza Navona is a good place to come at night

The Spanish Steps, a popular meeting place for centuries

PALAZZO DORIA PAMPHILJ

427 E4 • Piazza del Collegio Romano 2, 00186 Rome ☎ 06 679 7323
🕐 Daily 10–5 💶 €8, under 18s €5.70. Book concert tickets 10 days in advance Fri–Wed 10–4 and on concert days from 7.30pm (tel 800 907080) ℹ Informative audiotours 🎧 🚻 ▣ www.doriapamphilj.it

Overlooking the Via del Corso, this is one of the largest palaces in Rome, with a good collection of paintings displayed in four resplendent galleries.

Gallery 1 has several important paintings by Titian, Coreggio, Raphael, Caravaggio and Paolo Veronese. Caravaggio's *Flight into Egypt* is controversial as he used the same model for the Virgin Mary in this painting and for Magdalena in another painting in this gallery. Gallery 2 is dedicated to the Flemish artists, including Rubens and Breughel the Elder. In Gallery 3 a portrait of Pope Innocent X by Velazquez, the highlight of the collection, hangs next to a bust of the same pope by Bernini. Gallery 4 has 17th-century landscapes by Claude Lorrain. There are guided tours of some of the private apartments, including the Andrea Doria Room, adorned with Gobelin tapestries, and the ballroom.

PALAZZO MASSIMO

428 G3 • Largo di Villa Peretti 1, 00185 Rome ☎ 06 481 5576
🕐 Tue–Sun 9–7.45 💶 Adult €6, child (under 18) free 🚇 Repubblica, Termini 🎧 www.pierreci.it (online reservations)

Palazzo Massimo alle Terme, an imposing building, houses the Museo Nazionale Romano and its collection of sculptures, mosaics, frescoes and coins from the end of the Republican Age (second century BC) to the late Imperial Age (fourth century AD).

The ground floor displays portraits from the Republican period and an interesting collection of coins. In Room V are a statue of Augustus and a marble altar from Ostia showing the wedding of Mars and Venus, along with a sculpture of Apollo and the sleeping Aphrodite from the Villa Adriana in Tivoli. In Room VII is the magnificent statue of Niobe's daughter trying to extract an arrow from her back.

Other rooms display portraits, bas-reliefs and sarcophagi, and remarkable mosaic floors and beautiful frescoes discovered in Villa Farnesina in Trastevere and the Villa Livia on the Palatino. The second floor can be visited only as part of a group or with a guide so book in advance or wait for a group or a guide to come along.

PIAZZA NAVONA

427 D3 • Piazza Navona, 00186 Rome ☎ 06 329 2326 🕐 Tue–Sat 9–noon, 4–7, Sun 10–1, 4–7 💶 Free

Piazza Navona is a lively, crowded place at the heart of the city, a popular meeting place for both Romans and visitors. You can go to an exhibition at Palazzo Braschi, watch street performers, have your portrait painted, or take part in a political demonstration. Alternatively, sit and enjoy a drink at one of the outdoor cafés.

The piazza was laid out in the late 15th century on the ruins of a stadium. From 1650 to the late 19th century the square was flooded in summer and used for aquatic games. Brightly painted carriages floated on the water like boats while people freshened up in the temporary 'lake'.

Today the real attraction is the famous Fontana dei Fiumi (Fountain of the Four Rivers), created by Bernini in about 1651, in the middle of the square. It represents the Danube, the Ganges, the Nile and the Rio de la Plata.

At the southern end of the piazza the Fontana del Moro, commissioned by Pope Gregory XIII and designed by Giacomo della Porta in 1576, features dragons and dolphins. The central figure of the so-called Moor—actually a marine divinity—was added in the mid-17th century. The Fontana del Nettuno, at the northern end of the piazza, dates from the 19th century.

PIAZZA DI SPAGNA E SCALINATA DI TRINITÀ DEI MONTI

427 E2 • Piazza di Spagna, 00187 Rome 🚇 Spagna

Piazza di Spagna and the Scalinata di Trinità dei Monti (the Spanish Steps) are famous as a meeting place for visitors from all over the world. The steps are a popular place to pose, people-watch or just sit and enjoy life carrying on all around you. The view of Rome from the top is unequalled.

The square was called Platea Trinitatis, in honour of its church, until the 17th century, when the Spanish ambassador took up residence here and changed the name to Piazza di Spagna. Francesco de Sanctis built the elegant flight of 138 steps in the 1720s. With the 16th-century Franciscan Church of Trinità dei Monti at the top, they form the perfect backdrop for the annual international fashion show *Donne sotto le Stelle* (Women in Starlight).

At the top of the steps is an obelisk found in the Horti Sallustiani, while at the bottom is the Barcaccia, a boat-shaped fountain created by the Berninis, father and son. Built in 1629 to commemorate the Great Flood of 1598, it shows a boat sinking under the floodwaters. Low water pressure means the fountain is sluggish and the boat is often full of water.

PANTHEON

**Simple, solid and austere, an architectural *tour de force* by the engineers of ancient Rome.
Pagan temple turned Christian church—now Italy's best-preserved building from antiquity.**

The original Pantheon was built by Agrippa, according to the inscription on the façade. It was erected in 27BC in honour of the heavenly gods and was also dedicated to the Julia family, thought to be direct descendants of gods. Agrippa's building was destroyed in the great fire of AD80 and the Pantheon was rebuilt in the early second century by Emperor Hadrian. In the sixth century, Emperor Phocas gave the Pantheon to Pope Boniface IV, who turned it into a Christian church. The building was then covered in bronze and lead, and despite being pillaged over the years, the covering helped to preserve the dome and other surfaces. The portico of Egyptian granite columns was once a fishmarket. Pope Urban VIII had the bronze on the ceiling removed in the 17th century for use on Bernini's *baldacchino* in San Pietro (p.158), but the bronze doors survive from ancient Rome.

THE DOME

The design is superbly simple: a dome on a circular base attached to a rectangular portico. With a diameter wider than the dome of San Pietro, this is the largest dome ever built before the introduction of reinforced concrete, testimony to the amazing ingenuity of the Roman engineers. The height of the dome from the floor is identical to its diameter, 43.3m (142ft). The walls supporting the dome are 7m (23ft) across, and the thickness of the dome itself diminishes from base to apex. The unglazed oculus, the circular hole in the middle of the dome (9m/29.5ft across), is the only source of natural light. A statue of Jove Ultōr, the Avenger, who punished the murderers of Caesar, once stood directly under the oculus, and shrines and niches once held statues of the 12 Olympian gods, along with emperors Hadrian and Augustus. The tombs of Italy's first two kings and the artist Raphael are the only tombs you can see today.

PIAZZA DELLA ROTONDA

The Pantheon faces Piazza della Rotonda, a pretty square with cafés, a fountain, and a13th-century BC Egyptian obelisk built by Ramses II, brought to Rome and used in the Temple of Isis and Serapis in Campo Marzio, then moved here by Pope Clement XI. In the evening this is a lively place with people dining or enjoying coffee and ice-cream.

RATINGS

Historic interest	● ● ● ●
Cultural interest	● ● ●
Walkability	● ● ●

TIPS

● There is not much information to help visitors on site, so have your guidebook handy.

● Have a drink in one of the cafés or sit around the central fountain of the piazza to enjoy the view of the Pantheon.

BASICS

✚ 427 D3 • Piazza della Rotonda, 00186 Rome ☎ 06 6830 0230
🕐 Mon–Sat 8.30–7.30, Sun 9–6.30, public holidays 9–1. No visits during celebration of the Sun 10.30am Mass
🎟 Free
🚊 Tram 8 to Argentina
🅿 In the Square
🍴 On Piazza della Rotonda

Shafts of sunlight shine through the oculus, illuminating the porphyry, granite and yellow marble walls and floors

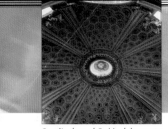
Sant'Andrea al Quirinale's ornate ceiling

The statue of Santa Cecilia in Santa Cecilia in Trastevere

A bridal couple at the Church of Santi Cosma e Damiano

THE SIGHTS

SANT'ANDREA AL QUIRINALE

✚ 427 F3 • Via del Quirinale 29, 00187 Roma ☎ 06 4890 3187 🕓 Wed–Mon 8–12, 4–7 🚇 Barberini

Known as 'the Baroque Pearl', this elegant little oval church, designed by Bernini, has a very peaceful atmosphere. Bernini himself often came and sat here. It was commissioned by Cardinal Camillo Pamphili in 1658 as the church of the Jesuit novitiate in Rome, and employed the most talented workers, decorators and sculptors of the time. An elegant flight of steps leads to the semi-elliptical portico. Inside is another oval space, with eight deep rectangular chapels ranged around it, linked by the elliptical cornice. The pillars are made of red Sicilian marble. The dome above the altar is richly decorated with gold and stucco cherubs by Antonio Raggi. In the first chapel on the right paintings by Gianbattista Gaulli depict the death of St. Francis Xavier, while the relics of St. Stanislaus, a young Jesuit novice who died here, are in the third chapel on the left. Look for the coats of arms of the Pallavicini, Spinola and Melzi families in the marble floor.
Don't miss The beautiful frescoed vault in the sacristy.

SAN CARLO ALLE QUATTRO FONTANE

✚ 427 F3 • Via del Quirinale 23, 00187 Roma ☎ 06 488 3261 🕓 Daily 10–1, 3–6 🎟 Free 🚇 Barberini www.sancarlino-borromini.it

This extremely small church is said to be no larger than one of the columns supporting the dome of San Pietro. Known as San Carlino, it was designed in 1638 by the great baroque artist Francesco Borromini and is opposite his rival Bernini's Sant' Andrea al Quirinale. This was

Borromini's first work, but also his last—he committed suicide after adding the façade in 1667. The architecture reflects the tormented and contradictory state of mind of its creator.

Overall, the interior is simple—an elliptical plan with stuccoed niches—but every concave section is mirrored by its convex opposite, forming strange shapes and visual effects. The intricately designed coffered ceiling, with sunken ornamental panels, exemplifies the bizarre yet elegant effect that Borromini managed to create in such a small space.
Don't miss Borromini's beautifully proportioned cloister, with two rows of Doric columns and convex corners.

SAN GIOVANNI IN LATERANO

p. 176.

SANTA CECILIA IN TRASTEVERE

✚ 427 D5 • Piazza di Santa Cecilia 22, 00153 Roma ☎ 06 589 9289 🕓 Daily 9.30–12.30, 5–6.30. Cavallini fresco: Tue, Thu 10–noon, Sun 11.15–12.15 🎟 Free 🚊 Tram 8

The approach to this basilica, dedicated to Cecilia, the patron saint of musicians, is through a courtyard garden where fragrant flowers surround a fountain. Ahead are the ancient columns of the 12th-century portico and the Romanesque campanile. Pope Paschal I built the church in the ninth century, on the site of the home in which Cecilia was killed by Emperor Marcus Aurelius. In the much restored baroque interior is Stefano Maderno's beautiful sculpture of St. Cecilia, modelled on the body that, miraculously, was found intact inside her tomb when it was opened in 1599.

Other treasures include the Gothic altar canopy by Arnolfo di

Cambio and early ninth-century apse mosaics depicting Jesus with Saints Paul, Agatha, Peter, Paschal, Valeriano and Cecilia. Of interest, too, are the remains of the 13th-century fresco the *Last Judgement* by Pietro Cavallini that once covered the walls of the central nave.

The Chapel of the Bath, at the end of the right-hand nave, is said to contain the bath in which St. Cecilia was martyred, and a painting by Guido Reni depicts her beheading.

SANTI COSMA E DAMIANO

✚ 427 F4 • Via dei Fori Imperiali 1, 00186 Roma ☎ 06 699 1540 🕓 Daily 8–1, 3–6. Nativity: Tue–Sun 9.30–12.30, 3–6 🎟 Free; Nativity: €1 🚇 Colosseo

Consecrated in 526 by Pope Felix IV in honour of twin Arab physicians, this was the first Christian church to reuse a building in the Roman Forum. It was formed by joining the library of the Foro della Pace to part of the round temple dedicated to Romulus, the remains of which are still visible inside. In the 16th century, Pope Urban VIII Barberini, a Franciscan commissioned the architect Arrigucci to restore the building. The present-day façade of the church and the cloister were built at this time, and the original Roman church was hidden underground in a crypt. The highlight is the sixth-century mosaics in the apse showing the Apostles Peter and Paul presenting the Saints Cosmas and Damian to Christ. The baroque high altar partially hides the detail of Christ as the Lamb surrounded by the 12 apostles. The 17th-century ceiling is decorated with sunken panels, with paintings depicting the triumph of the saintly brothers along with the Barberini family emblem, bees.

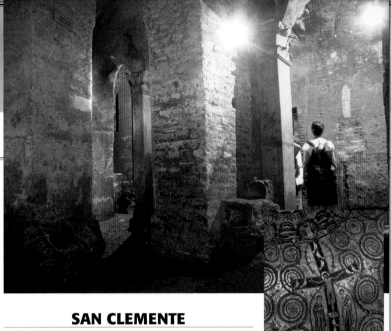

SAN CLEMENTE

**Over 2,000 years of history can be pieced together in a
cross-section over three levels.
A 12th-century church, a fourth-century church, and a
first-century temple—one above the other.
Magnificent mosaics and a temple to Mithras.**

The present church was built in the 12th century after its predecessor
was damaged in a Norman attack in 1084. The lower church has a
similar layout, but was wider, and very little of the original walls of this
fourth-century building survive. According to legend, St. Cyril, evange-
lizer to the Slavs, brought St. Clement's relics to Rome and laid them
here in 869. On the lowest level are buildings from imperial Rome,
including a well-preserved Mithraic temple.

THE MITHRAIC TEMPLE

Head straight for the underground level by taking the steps in the
sacristy down through the first church (second level). Here are two
buildings dating from Roman days. One is thought to have been
Rome's mint; the second was the house of a rich family, built of brick
with an underground courtyard and later converted into a temple for
the Persian god, Mithras. Mithraism was a pre-Christian, all-male cult,
popular with soldiers, and this is the best preserved of a dozen
Mithraic temples found in the city. The temple was used until the
fourth century, when Christians probably destroyed it. From the temple, walk along a narrow passage, at the end of which you can hear
the sound of water running in an underground watercourse.

THE LOWER CHURCH—THE FIRST SAN CLEMENTE

Go back up the steps to the lower San Clemente basilica, built in 375,
consisting of a nave and two aisles. Pillars and walls added in the 11th
and 12th centuries support the church above. Frescoes date from the
eighth to 11th centuries; the one depicting St. Sisinius is remarkable
for the inscriptions below, perhaps the oldest in the Italian language.

THE UPPER CHURCH—THE SECOND SAN CLEMENTE

Little altered since it was built, San Clemente is dominated by a choir
screen and the golden 12th-century mosaic of the Crucifixion in the
apse. Birds and animals are entwined in foliage, the Virgin and St.
John stand alongside the cross represented as the Tree of Life, and
the four rivers of Paradise spring from the foot of the cross. The cosmatesque inlaid floor is one of the best preserved in Rome.

RATINGS	
Good for kids	●●
Historic interest	●●●●●
Specialist shopping	●●
Value for money	●●●●

TIPS

● Buy a plan before you start,
as in the underground and
second level basilicas there is
no defined route and you may
miss points of interest.

● Start with the underground
church.

BASICS

✚ 428 G5 • Piazza San Clemente/Via
San Giovanni in Laterano, 00184 Roma
☎ 06 7045 1018
🕐 2nd and 3rd level: Mon–Sat
9–12.30, 3–6, Sun 10–12.30, 3–6. Upper
Basilica: all day
✋ 2nd and 3rd level, €3. Upper
Basilica, free
🚇 Colosseo, San Giovanni 🚌 👫

*The underground Mithraic
Temple below the Church of San
Clemente (above left); one of
the mosaics in the apse (above)*

The nave of San Giovanni in Laterano

SAN GIOVANNI IN LATERANO

The cathedral church of Rome, the papal residence for hundreds of years, up to the 14th century.

RATINGS

Value for money	● ● ●
Good for kids	● ●
Historic interest	● ● ● ● ●
Photo stops	● ● ● ● ●

TIP

● If you go in the morning and have time, walk around Via Sagno, the famous flea market.

BASICS

✚ 428 H5 • Piazza di Porta San Giovanni in Laterano 4, 00184 Roma
☎ 06 6988 6433
🕐 Basilica: daily 7–6.45. Cloister: daily 9–6. Baptistery: daily 7–12.30, 3.30–7.30. Scala Santa: daily 6.15–noon, 3–6.15. Museo Storico del Vaticano: Sat 9.30–12.15, first Sun of the month 8.45–1
💶 Basilica, Scala Santa, baptistery: free. Cloister: €2. Cappella Sancta Sanctorum: €2.50. Museo Storico del Vaticano: €4
🚇 San Giovanni
🚌 Tours: basilica, cloister, baptistery, Scala Santa (book in advance; tel as above, Mon–Fri 9–1, or email), in all languages, €5. Guided tour to Museo Storico del Vatticano. Audiotours: basilica and cloister, in all languages, €2. *Mater et caput* guided tour: tel 06 6988 6392 or email mater.caput@org.va
📖 🏛 🎭

The first basilica, named after the family that owned the property on which it was founded, was built by Constantine between AD313 and 318. At the time, it represented the victory of Christianity over paganism. In 314 Pope Sylvester I took up residence in the Lateran buildings and it was the official papal residence until the papacy moved to Avignon in the 14th century, though popes were crowned here until the 19th century. San Giovanni has been rebuilt many times—damaged by vandals, an earthquake and two fires, it was finally restored by Borromini in the 17th century in the baroque style.

The basilica's 1735 baroque façade by Alessandro Galilei (modelled on San Pietro) is crowned with 15 gigantic statues of Christ, the Apostles and the Church Fathers. The portico has bronze doors taken from the Foro Romano's *curia*, and a huge statue of the first Christian emperor, Constantine. The last door on the right, the Holy Door, is opened only during the Jubilee or Holy Year, every 25 years.

Inside, the central nave is flanked with niches containing statues of the 12 Apostles. The dove from the coat of arms of Innocent X, who commissioned Borromini, is set over each recess, with bas-reliefs depicting stories from the Old and New Testaments. To the right of the entrance a restored fragment of a fresco by Giotto shows Boniface VIII declaring the first Holy Year, in 1300. In contrast to the unadorned nave, the transept is a fine example of mannerist ornamentation. A 14th-century tabernacle above the altar (at which only the pope may celebrate Mass) contains relics of St. Peter and St. Paul. Several frescoes depict the Good Shepherd, the Crucifixion, the Virgin Mary and various saints. In the apse is a mosaic of the figure of Christ, a 19th-century restoration of a 13th-century copy of a fourth-century original by Jacopo da Camerino and Jacopo Torriti. Notice the small figure of St. Francis on the left, included because da Camerino and Torriti were Franciscan monks.

The most beautiful part of the cathedral is the cloister—a peaceful refuge, with slim columns, and inlaid marble and gold mosaics.

THE BAPTISTERY AND SCALA SANTA

In Piazza San Giovanni, the octagonal baptistery, the first in Christendom, survives from Constantine's era. The Scala Santa (Holy Staircase), a flight of 28 steps with glass sheets covering what is thought to be a trail of Christ's blood, leads to the Sancta Sanctorum, a chapel with frescoes by the great 13th-century painters, Cimabue and Pietro Cavallini.

The Bocca della Verità in Santa Maria in Cosmedin

The sixth-century BC obelisk on the back of Bernini's marble elephant in the square outside the Church of Santa Maria Sopra Minerva

THE SIGHTS

SANTA MARIA ARACOELI

✝ 427 E4 • Via dell'Aracoeli, 00186 Roma ☎ 06 679 8155 ◷ Daily 9–12.30, 2.30–4.30 🖐 Free 🚇 Colosseo

The Church of Santa Maria in Aracoeli stands on the Capitoline Hill at the top of a wide, steep flight of steps. Today's church dates largely from the end of the 13th century, when Franciscan monks took over a Benedictine monastery church that stood on the site of the Ara Coeli (Altar of Heaven), built by Emperor Augustus. The steps, traditionally climbed by newly married couples, offer a splendid view of the city, and lead to an austere brick frontage lightened only by doors and tiny rose windows. Inside, a gilded ceiling commemorates the Battle of Lepanto in 1571. Other highlights are the marble floor and the pulpit, good examples of cosmatesque inlay work, and Pinturicchio's frescoes in the first chapel on the right, depicting the life and death of St. Bernardino of Siena. The left transept leads to a little chapel dedicated to the Holy Child; its wooden statue is celebrated for its miraculous healing powers.

SANTA MARIA IMMACOLATA DELLA CONCEZIONE

✝ 427 F3 • Via Vittorio Veneto 27, 00187 Roma ☎ 06 487 1185 ◷ Daily 7–noon, 3–7. Capuchin cemetery: Fri–Tue 9–noon, 3–6 🖐 Free/contribution to the cemetery 🚇 Barberini www.cappucciniviaveneto.it

Also known as the Church of the Capuchins, this austere Counter-Reformation church is famous for its ghoulish ossuary. It contains the bones of about 4,000 Capuchin monks who lived and died in the once-adjacent convent between 1528 and 1870. The macabre display in the crypt includes chandeliers made from human bones. There are separate chapels for femurs and tibias, pelvises, skulls and skeletons (some still dressed). The floor is scattered with soil from Palestine. The church was built in 1624 by Cardinal Antonio Barberini, a Capuchin monk whose tombstone in front of the main altar is inscribed *Hic jacet pulvis, cinis et nihil* (Here lies dust, ashes, nothing). This brother of Pope Urban VIII clearly did not share the Barberini love of grandeur. Look also for Guido Reni's painting *St. Michael Trampling the Devil.*

SANTA MARIA IN COSMEDIN

✝ 427 E5 • Via Bocca della Verità, 00186 Roma (Piazza Venezia/Circo Massimo) ☎ 06 678 1419 ◷ Daily 9–7.30 🖐 Free 🚇 Circo Massimo

By 772 the church built here in the sixth century on the site of a pagan temple had become the church of the local Greek community, and it was they who called it Cosmedin (lovely) because of its décor. It is also known as Santa Maria in Scuola Greca because people still come to Greek Orthodox Mass here.

It is most famous for the Bocca della Verità (Mouth of Truth), a large stone inside the porch that was used as a drain cover by the ancient Romans. It's said that if a person places their hand inside its gaping mouth and tells a lie, the mouth clamps shut, severing the liar's fingers.

Between 1118 and 1123 the church was rebuilt and the elegant Romanesque bell tower was added. Inside, the nave and two aisles are divided by ancient Roman columns. There is fine cosmatesque marble-inlaid work in the floor, pulpits, screen and paschal candlestick. There is also a fragment of an eighth-century mosaic in the sacristy.

SANTA MARIA MAGGIORE

p. 178.

SANTA MARIA SOPRA MINERVA

✝ 427 E3 • Piazza della Minerva 42, 00186 Roma ☎ 06 673926 ◷ Daily 8–6; no visits during Mass 🖐 Free 🚋 Tram 8 www.basilicaminerva.it

In 1280 two Dominican friars, Sisto and Ristoro, who designed Santa Maria Novella in Florence, began building a church here on the site of a pagan temple to Minerva. The baroque-style refurbishment of the interior in the 16th and 17th centuries masked the church's medieval Gothic structure, a rarity in Rome, and the church was further embellished in the 19th century when the Dominican architect Girolamo Bianchedi added frescoes to its walls and vaults. Kept by Dominican friars, the Minerva offers a peaceful escape from the crowds in the Piazza della Rotonda.

St. Catherine of Siena, a tertiary of the Dominicans, is buried beneath the high altar. Frescoes in the Capranica chapel illustrate her life. More famous are the frescoes by Filippino Lippi in the Carafa Chapel, depicting the life of the Dominican St. Thomas Aquinas and the Assumption. Other works of art include the statue of *Christ Risen* by Michelangelo. To the left of the altar is the tomb of the great Florentine artist and Dominican monk Fra Angelico, who died here in 1455.

Other noteworthy funerary monuments include tombs of the Medici popes, Leo X and Clement VII, sculpted by Antonio da Sangallo, and that of Maria Raggi, by Bernini. To the rear are the cloisters and the Dominican convent. It was here that Galileo was condemned for insisting that the earth moves around the sun.

The interior of the church, the finest example of an early Christian basilica in Rome

RATINGS

Good for kids	● ●
Historic interest	● ● ●
Cultural interest	● ● ● ● ●
Value for money	● ● ●

TIPS

● Start in the Loggia delle Benedizioni, where a mosaic tells the story of the basilica.

● There is little information on site and parts of the basilica are closed to the public or can be seen only with a guide.

● The basilica is badly lit, so bring a flashlight to get a closer look.

BASICS

✚ 428 G4 • Piazza Santa Maria Maggiore, 00184 Roma ☎ 06 483195

◷ Basilica: daily 7–7. Cappella Sforza: Mon–Fri 9–5. Museum: daily 9.30–6.30. Sacristy: daily 7–12.30, 3–6.30

💶 Basilica and Cappella Sforza: free. Museum: adult €4, child (under 18) €2

Ⓜ Cavour or Termini, Vittorio Emanuele

🚌 Guided tours, tel 06 483058. Loggia delle Benedizioni: daily 4–6, €2.60; Presepe di Arnolfo di Cambio: Mon–Sat 9.30–1, €1.50. Audiotours: €1

🈺 🏛

👥 Access for visitors with disabilities

🅿 On the square, €1 per hour

www.prtour.it

SANTA MARIA MAGGIORE

Shares with San Pietro, San Giovanni in Laterano and San Paolo fuori le Mura the privilege of papal sovereignty. Sumptuously decorated with bright mosaics, the only one of the four to have kept its early Christian structure.

In the fourth century, the story goes, Pope Liberius had a dream in which the Virgin Mary told him it would snow that night and that he was to build a church in her honour where the snow settled. That night, 5 August 356, it snowed on the Esquiline Hill, and Santa Maria Maggiore was constructed on top of it. It was probably commissioned by Sixtus III in AD432—the first basilica to be built by a pope rather than an emperor.

THE BASILICAN NAVE

The interior of this immense church has kept its original medieval structure. Above the Roman columns in the nave, 36 fifth-century mosaic panels illustrate Old Testament stories. Easier to see are the mosaics depicting scenes of Christ's life on the arch at the entrance to the Cappella Paolina. The nave's 16th-century coffered ceiling by Giuliano da Sangallo is said to be decorated with some of the first gold brought from America. The floor is 12th-century cosmatesque inlay work.

THE BALDACCHINO AND MOSAICS

The *baldacchino* (altar canopy) by Ferdinando Fuga is made of porphyry columns with bronze foliage. It stands over the Confession (crypt), where a silver urn is believed to contain fragments of Christ's wooden cradle. The chancel arch is decorated with a fifth-century, Byzantine-style mosaic showing the cities of Jerusalem and Bethlehem, and Jesus as a child at the Feast of the Epiphany. The apse has a fine mosaic depicting the *Coronation of the Virgin Mary* (1295) by Jacopo Torriti. To the right of the apse is the humble tomb of the sculptor Gian Lorenzo Bernini.

THE CHAPELS

The Cappella Paolina is also known as the Cappella Borghese after the family of Pope Paul V, who commissioned the bejewelled surround to the altar and whose elaborate tomb is here. Next to this is the Cappella Sforza, designed by Michelangelo. Across the nave, the Cappella Sistina, commissioned by Pope Sixtus V and built by Domenico Fontana in 1585, is almost a church in its own right, with a dome, frescoes and papal tombs. The highlight is the *Presepe* (Nativity crib) by Anolfo di Cambio, which stood outside from the sixth century but was moved on Sixtus' orders, during the process of which much of it was broken.

Inside the Church of Santa Maria del Popolo

Statues outside the Basilica di Santa Maria in Trastevere

Detail of one of the beautiful mosaics in Santa Prassede

SANTA MARIA DEL POPOLO

🔲 427 D2 • Piazza del Popolo 12, 00187 Roma ☎ 06 361 0836 ⏰ Mon–Sat 7–noon, 4–7, Sun 8–1.30, 4.30–7.30 💷 Free Ⓜ Flaminio, Spagna

Tucked into a corner of the Piazza del Popolo, Santa Maria del Popolo is famed for its collection of Renaissance art. Replacing an 11th-century chapel on the traditional site of Nero's grave, St. Mary of the People was built by Andrea Bregno, and paid for by the people of Rome, in 1472, in simple Renaissance style. The baroque embellishments to the interior were added later. In the della Rovere chapel the altar painting *The Adoration of the Child* is by Pinturicchio, and frescoes on the life of San Girolamo are the work of his pupil Tiberio d'Assisi. In the choir are masterpieces by Andrea Sansovino, monuments to Cardinal Ascanio Sforza (1505) and Cardinal Girolamo Basso della Rovere (1507). The early stained glass is by the French artist Guillaume de Marcillat. In the little Cappella Cerasi are Caravaggio's two magnificent works of 1601, *The Conversion of St. Paul* and *The Crucifixion of St. Peter*. The Cappella Chigi was built in 1516 as a mausoleum for the Chigi family, with sculpture, paintings and mosaics all designed by Raphael.

SANTA MARIA IN TRASTEVERE

🔲 427 D5 • Piazza di Santa Maria in Trastevere, 00153 Roma ☎ 06 589 7332 ⏰ Daily 7.30–1, 4–7 💷 Free 🚃 Tram 8 ⬛ ♿

The picturesque quarter of Trastevere, in which the medieval gem of Santa Maria stands, lies on the right bank of the Tiber. The atmosphere of the church and its setting are unique, and part of its charm is that it remains a community church. Legend has it that in 38BC a fountain of oil suddenly started flowing here, heralding the birth of Jesus Christ, and Pope Callixtus (217–22) built a sanctuary to commemorate the miracle. The present-day basilica was built in the 12th century, using materials from the Terme di Caracalla. The mosaics on the façade, probably 12th century, have survived as Rome's only example of what all the city's medieval church façades once looked like. Inside, the mosaics in the apse are beautiful above all else. In the half-dome, 12th-century mosaics show Mary embraced by her son and flanked by popes and saints. Below this, Pietro Cavallini's masterpiece depicts scenes from the life of the Virgin (1290). More 12th-century mosaics on the chancel arch depict the prophets Isaiah and Jeremiah. The central panel of the 17th-century coffered ceiling has an *Assumption* by Domenichino. Try to visit after dark, when the basilica's golden façade is floodlit and you can sit at one of the outdoor cafés in the piazza.

SAN PIETRO IN VINCOLI

🔲 428 F4 • Piazza San Pietro in Vincoli, 00184 Roma ☎ 06 488 2865 ⏰ Daily 7–12.30, 3–7; no visits during Mass Sun 11am 💷 Free Ⓜ Colosseo

The main tourist attraction in San Pietro in Vincoli is the chains that bound St. Peter. The church is in a charming square of the same name, and is always crowded. Initially erected in the third century and consecrated in 439 by Sixtus III, this early church was largely rebuilt, with the addition of a Renaissance portico, in the 15th century. Tradition holds that two sets of chains were used to bind St. Peter—one in Jerusalem, the other in the Mamertine prison—and when placed side by side they miraculously fused together. The ceiling fresco illustrates the event. The chains are in an urn under the high altar. The church's other attraction is Michelangelo's *Moses*, one of 40 statues commissioned to adorn a mausoleum for Julius II intended for San Pietro, but never completed. The huge seated figure of Moses, sculpted from Carrara marble, is shown with the Ten Commandments tablets under his arm.

SANTA PRASSEDE

🔲 428 G4 • Via di Santa Prassede 9/A, 00184 Roma ☎ 06 488 2456 ⏰ Daily 7–noon, 4–6.30; closed 7–noon, Aug 💷 Free Ⓜ Cavour, Termini, Vittorio Emanuele

Santa Prassede is home to one of Rome's most important Byzantine treasures, the San Zeno chapel, built by Paschal I as a mausoleum for his mother, Theodora, and known as the Garden of Paradise because of the unique beauty and richness of its gold mosaics. A house of worship has stood on this spot since AD489, rebuilt and restored many times before it was enlarged in 822 by Paschal I to house relics of martyrs taken from the catacombs. The jewel in Santa Prassede's crown are the ninth-century mosaics by artists brought from Byzantium in the San Zeno chapel, depicting Christ Pantocrator, the saints and Virgin Mary, but the apse and the triumphal arch are also covered with beautiful mosaics. These show St. Peter and St. Paul introducing St. Prassede and her sister, St. Pudenziana to Christ and, in the arch, New Jerusalem, Christ and the saints. The Chapel of San Zeno also has an excellent example of ornamental *opus sectile* paving in multihued marble. In a corner stands the Column of the Flagellation, brought from Jerusalem in 1223.

Outside the chapel is Bernini's first work, a memorial to Bishop Giovan Battista Santoni.

The remains of Terme di Caracalla

The Via Appia Antica, still partly paved with Roman cobbles

The fake Greek temple in the Villa Borghese gardens

TERME DI CARACALLA

🔶 off 428 F5 • Viale delle Terme di Caracalla 52, 00153 Roma ☎ 06 575 8626 🕐 Tue–Sun 9–6, Mon 9–2, Apr–Sep; Tue–Sun 9–3, Mon 9–1, rest of year 🎫 €5; 18–24 years €2.50; under 18s free 🚇 Circo Massimo 📷 www.archeorm.arti.beniculturali.it

The Terme di Caracall (Baths of Caracalla) in Celio are one of the most impressive ancient Roman complexes. Designed primarily to care for the body, the baths were also a cultural meeting place. Begun by Septimius Severus in AD206 and opened by emperor Caracalla in AD217, they were functional until AD537 when the Goths destroyed the aqueducts that supplied the water. There was an immense pool for cooling the body called a *frigidarium*, a large, hot, circular room known as a *caldarium*, rooms for hot and warm baths, porticos, halls, gymnasia, statues, libraries, gardens and a stadium. Up to 600 people were able to bathe at one time. All the rooms were decorated with alabaster, granite and mosaics, most of which are intact. Recent excavations have uncovered an underground Mithraic temple. Open-air opera is staged here in summer.

VIA APPIA ANTICA

🔶 off 428 F5 • Via Appia Antica, 00178 Roma 🚇 Circo Massimo

The Via Appia (Appian Way), known as Regina Viarum (Queen of the Roads), was the first road built by the Romans. The magistrate Appius Claudius began building it in 312BC, and by the second century BC it reached Brindisi, a distance of 589km (366 miles). Now 213km (132 miles) long, running between Rome and Capua, it is closed to cars, and a green park lines the route—a popular spot with Romans at weekends. It is paved with *basoli*,

basalt rock stones of polygonal shape, many of which are intact. You can walk on these ancient stones, passing venerable busts and statues, churches, catacombs and ancient villas.

In Rome, the road begins at Porta San Sebastiano. Look for the ancient column inserted in a modern wall marking the first mile. At the corner with Via Ardeatina is the Church of Domine Quo Vadis, Latin for 'Lord, where are you going?' It was here that St Peter, escaping Nero's persecutions, was stopped by Jesus, who asked him to return to Rome and face his destiny. On the other side of the Via Appia are the ruins of Maxentius's circus and imperial residence. The tomb of Cecilia Metella, wife of Marcus Crassus, son of the Republican Roman ruler, stands at a crossing with a road of the same name. From here pine and cypress trees, statues and funerary monuments flank the way. Farther along are the remains of a nymphaeum, the pleasure house of Villa dei Quintili, the largest villa in ancient Rome's suburbs. Along the way, look for the catacombs of St. Priscilla, St. Callisto and St. Sebastian.

VILLA BORGHESE

🔶 427 F1–2 • Villa Borghese, 00187 Roma 🚇 Flaminio, Spagna

The Villa Borghese's beautiful avenues and paths, embellished with ancient statues and fountains, make it one of the grandest parks in Rome. Cardinal Borghese created both it and the imposing Villa Pinciana, or Casino Borghese, in the early 17th century to house his rich art collection. Highlights of the gardens are the Casino della Meridiana, the aviary and the artificial lake with its little island, in the middle of which stands an 18th-century Ionian-style temple to Aesculapius, the Greek god of

medicine. At the heart of the park is Piazza di Siena, a popular venue for international horse-races. There is also a zoo.

VILLA GIULIA AND THE MUSEO NAZIONALE ETRUSCO

🔶 427 E1 • Piazzale Villa Giulia 9, 00196 Roma ☎ 06 320 0562 🕐 Daily 8.30–7.30 🎫 Adult €4, child (under 18) free 🚇 Flaminio 📷 🏛 www.ticketeria.it www.beniculturali.it

The national museum of Etruscan art and relics is in the splendid 16th-century Villa Giulia, near Piazza del Popolo. The way of life, and death, of this mysterious civilization is displayed in this quiet corner of Rome, once Julius III's country villa. Surrounded by a series of courtyards, the villa has a loggia by Ammanati, sumptuous interiors and a nymphaeum with caryatids, rockeries, false grottoes and a Vasari fountain.

The Etruscan museum was founded here in 1889 to house the pre-Roman heritage of Latium, Umbria and southern Etruria, found in the necropolises of Cerveteri and Veio. It contains treasures and objects from the Etruscan, Faliscan and Greek civilizations. Hall 7 houses statues from Veio made of polychrome terracotta, including one depicting Heracles in combat with Apollo for the doe, a masterpiece. These statues all come from one temple in Veio and are thought to be the work of Vulca, who carved the statues for the Temple of Jupiter on the Capitol in 509BC. The most celebrated piece of Etruscan art is the *Sarcophagus of the Spouses*, found in the Cerveteri halls. It dates from the end of the sixth century BC and indicates that the Etruscans believed in an afterlife. A vase decorated with the Etruscan alphabet is displayed in Hall 15.

LAZIO AND THE MARCHE

Low-key Lazio and the remote Marche have some of Italy's best-kept secrets, with undiscovered cities such as Urbino, great gardens and villas like those of Tivoli, and 4,000-year-old Etruscan treasures at Tarquinia. There is also a great deal of variety—the inland lakes and the mountain town of Ascoli Piceno contrasting with the summer resorts on the east and west coasts.

MAJOR SIGHTS

The 13th-century Palazzo di Capitani del Popolo

A violin-maker measures the thickness of a fiddle front

RATINGS	
Good for kids	●●●
Historic interest	●●●●
Cultural interest	●●●
Specialist shopping	●●●

BASICS

➕ 439 J8

ℹ️ Piazza del Popolo, 63100 Ascoli Piceno ☎ 0736 253045

🕐 Mon–Fri 8–1.30, 3–7, Sat 8–1.30, Sun 9–1.30, Easter–Sep; Mon–Fri 8–1.30, 3–7, Sat 8–1.30, rest of year

🚉 Ascoli Piceno

www.turismo.regione.marche.it

MAKE A DAY OF IT

Urbino: p. 190
Offida: p. 185

ASCOLI PICENO

**Romanesque churches, medieval towers, baroque palaces, and busy cafés.
An ancient town of white travertine marble, with narrow streets and porticoed piazzas.**

Some 65km (40 miles) southwest of Fermo, Ascoli is today a prosperous town relatively untouched by tourism. It began as a strategic Roman settlement founded after the defeat of the local Piceni tribe. During medieval times rich families living in the town, like those in San Gimignano (p. 151), built defensive towers as a symbol of their wealth and dominance. At one time there were around 200 spearing the skyline; many were destroyed on the orders of Frederic II, but about 50 remain.

THE WHITE CITY

Architecturally, Ascoli is striking, built largely from white travertine stone. At its heart is Piazza del Popolo, lined with an elegant Renaissance porticoe, reminiscent of those in Bolgona (p. 105). It is dominated by the 13th-century Palazzo dei Capitani, once the seat of the *comune* (town council), and the Church of San Francesco. Visitors and locals are also drawn to this square by the delightful Caffè Meletti, an art deco café decorated with huge mirrors, wooden floors and marble tables. Various famous people have sought refreshment here over the years since it opened in 1903, including novelist Ernest Hemingway; try the local liqueur, the aniseed-tasting Anisetta Meletti. Piazza Arringo, built over the Roman forum, is home to the 15th-century duomo, dedicated to St. Emidius, whose relics are kept in the crypt. In a chapel on the right of the nave is a polyptych considered to be one of Carlo Crivelli's finest works.

MUSEUMS

The Diocesan Museum *(Tue–Sun 8.30–7.30)*, in the Palazzo Panichi, displays a collection of prehistoric and Roman archaeological finds, while the Pinacoteca Civica *(daily 9–1, 3–7)* art gallery is in the Palazzo Comunale, also on the square, which is worth visiting just to see the palace's rich red drapes, marble floors and chandeliers. Among the pieces on show are an *Annunciation* by Guido Reni and Titian's *St. Francis Receiving the Stigmata*, along with works by Carlo Crivelli and Pietro Alemanno.

The restored Abazzia di Montecassino

An Etruscan tomb in the necropolis near Cerveteri

Crenellations crown the Augustan walls of Fano

THE SIGHTS

ABAZZIA DI MONTECASSINO

✠ 440 K10 • Via G. di Biasco 54, 03043 Cassino ☎ 0776 21296
🕐 Mon–Sat 8–8. Abbey: daily 8.30–12.30, 3.30–6 🚆 Cassino, then bus to the abbey·

St. Benedict, supposedly guided by three ravens, chose this dramatic site to found a monastery in 529. High on a mountaintop, 200km (125 miles) south of Rome, the huge white bulwarks of the abbey of Montecassino can be seen for miles around. This strategic position has meant that the abbey has frequently been involved in conflict, and it has been destroyed and rebuilt many times. During World War II the Nazis made the abbey their regional headquarters, and on 15 February 1944 it was destroyed by Allied bombing. The rest of the abbey was faithfully reconstructed in a medieval style. It has a slightly sterile appearance, but the views from here are superb (much of the abbey is closed to the public).

Large parts of the town of Cassino were also destroyed during World War II. The ruins of the Roman town of Casinum, however, can still be seen.
Don't miss The crypt is the only original part of the abbey building that remains.

CASTEL GANDOLFO AND LAGO ALBANO

✠ 438 H10 🛈 Piazza Libertà 5, Castel Gandolfo, tel 06 932 4081

Castel Gandolfo, 24km (15 miles) south of Rome, is named after the powerful Genoese Gandolfi family, who originally built a castle here in the 12th century. The palace, built over the ruined castle in 1624 and later remodelled by Pope Pius XI, comes into its own in July, August and September when the papal court transfers here from the Vatican. The palace can be seen only from the outside, but large numbers of visitors flock here just for a sight of it. The Pope generally appears in the palace's courtyard at noon to address the public.

The palace is the dominant feature of the town, but don't overlook the Church of San Tommaso di Villanova, designed by Bernini, with frescoes by Pietro da Cortona.

Castel Gandolfo looks out over the waters of Lake Albano, the largest of the lakes in this region. Along the Via Appia, which runs down the length of the lake's west shore, are ancient towns such Albano Laziale, founded as a Roman camp, as well as a number of restaurants and cafés.

CERVETERI

✠ 438 H10 • Necropi della Banditaccia, Piazza Libertà 5, 00052 Cerveteri ☎ 06 994 0001 🕐 Tue–Sun 9–7, May–Sep; Tue–Sun 9–4, rest of year

Cerveteri was one of the wealthiest Etruscan towns in Italy and dates back to the 7th century BC. Known as Kysry (Roman *Caere*) in ancient times, it accumulated its wealth by trading the rich mineral deposits found in the Tolfa hills nearby.

Today the heart of the town is largely medieval in appearance and the Etruscan remains for which it is famous are found 3km (2 miles) to the west.

The Necropoli della Banditaccia were laid out to create a 'city of the dead', providing space for 5,000 tombs dating from the seventh to first century BC. With streets and houses like a town, this extraordinary burial site and the archaeological finds here give a fascinating insight into Etruscan culture. The tombs are carved into the rock or covered by earth, and several are elaborately constructed, including the Tomba degli Scudi e delle Sedie, in the form of an Etruscan house. Slaves were cremated and their ashes put in with their masters.
Don't miss The Museo Nazionale di Cerveteri *(Tue–Sun 9–7)* displays just some of the many Etruscan objects, such as vases, that were buried with the dead. Other finds from these tombs are on display in the Villa Giulia in Rome (p. 180).

FANO

✠ 437 J7 🛈 Via Battisti 10, 61032 Fano, tel 0721 803534 🚆 Fano

Fano's beaches make it a popular, but not overcrowded, resort, with a good choice of either sandy beaches sprinkled with sun umbrellas, or pebbly stretches with promenades.

Fano is 11km (7 miles) south of Pesaro on the Adriatic coast, and was once a Roman port on the Via Flaminia, but little of its Roman heritage remains visible. Today it is split by the railway, with the modern resort on one side and the old town on the other. In addition to some imposing palaces, Fano has a museum and art gallery, the Museo Civico and Pinacoteca, in the 15th-century Pazzo Malatesta. It has a collection of Roman mosaics, medieval coins and paintings by artists such as Michele Giambono, Giovanni Santi and Guido Reni, along with some 19th- and 20th-century works.

The impressive Biblioteca Federiciana has on display more than 200,000 volumes and two 17th-century globes, one of the earth and one of the skies.
Don't miss The highlight of the historic heart is the Arco di Augusto, a Roman triumphal arch built by Emperor Augustus in AD2 to celebrate the foundation of the city.

One of the huge statues at the Villa Aldobrandini in Frascati

The distant promontory of Capodimonte, viewed from across Lago di Bolsena

FRASCATI AND COLLI ALBANI

438 H10 | Piazza G. Marconi, 00044 Frascati, tel 06 942 0331 | Frascati

A popular destination with both Romans and tourists, Frascati has been a retreat for the rich for centuries and is still dominated by one of their villas, Villa Aldobrandini, begun by Giacomo della Porta in 1598 but not completed until 100 years later. You can't go inside the villa as it is still lived in by the family, but the grounds are worth a visit. They are adorned with large water features and sculptures; you can visit them free with a permit obtained at the visitor centre at Piazza G. Marconi (*grounds: Mon–Fri 9–1, 3–6, Apr–Sep; Mon–Fri 9–1, 3–5, rest of year; visitor centre: closed Sat afternoon and all Sun*).

The Colli Albani, the hills to the south of Frascati, 21km (13 miles) southeast of Rome, form a backbone to the Castelli Romani towns, so called because they grew up around the feudal castles of Rome's wealthy families. The soil of this 60-km (37-mile) chain of volcanic hills is very fertile and produces many good wines, the best-known being, naturally, Frascati. Give it a try in one of the local bars, where it is often available from huge wooden barrels.

There are a number of little towns to visit in the area besides Frascati, including Nemi and Rocca di Papa—a jumble of medieval streets and the most dramatically positioned town in the Collini Albani.

GROTTE DI FRASASSI

437 J7 • Genga ☎ 0732 90080 or 90090 ⏰ Guided tours 9.30, 11, 12.30, 3, 4.30, 6, Mar–Jul, Sep–Oct; continuous tours 8–6.30, Aug; Mon–Fri 11.15, Sat 11, 12.30, 3, 4.30, Sun 9.30, 11,

12.30, 3, 4.30, 6, Nov–Feb ♿ Adult €11, child (6–14) €9, under 6 free ⏰ Genga, then shuttle bus in summer **www.frasassi.com**

This is one of the most interesting cave complexes in Italy, situated next to the Church of San Vittore delle Chiuse, near Genga. The intriguing underground world of silent lakes and countless stalactites and stalagmites, 61km (38 miles) from Ancona, provides an arresting contrast to the surrounding countryside.

Discovered in 1971, the caves opened to the public in 1974. So far, 13km (8 miles) of limestone caves have been explored, and the complex is thought to extend a further 35km (22 miles). Less than 2km (1.25 miles) is open to the public, but it is sure to impress.

The Grotta Grande del Vento (Great Cave of the Wind) is possibly the largest cave of its kind in Europe, so huge that Milan Cathedral could fit inside. The warrens of other caves bear such evocative names as the Hall of the Candles, the Hall of the Bear and the Hall of Infinity. Theatrically lit walkways lead through them all.

LAGO DI BOLSENA AND BOLSENA

438 G9 | Piazza Matteotti 12, 01223 Bolsena, tel 0761 799923

Lago di Bolsena, 112km (70 miles) north of Rome, is the largest volcanic lake in Italy and the fifth largest in the country. It is lined with busy towns such as Capodimonte, where the waters lap the edge of the town, Gradoli, which lies at the heart of a large wine region, Etruscan Montefiascone and medieval Bolsena. Boat trips run from Capodimonte and Bolsena to Isola Bisentina (*daily 9.30–12.30, 5–8*), an island in

the middle of the lake where you can visit Etruscan tombs and the Farnese family gardens.

On the hillside overlooking the lake, Bolsena's medieval castle dates back to the 13th century and today contains a museum displaying archaeological finds from the lake and objects from the Roman city of Volsinii (Roman Bolsena). On Piazza Santa Cristina stands the collegiate Romanesque Church of Santa Cristina. The oldest part of this church is the grotto, where the miracle of Corpus Christi is said to have taken place in 1236; blood supposedly dropped from the Host on to the altar cloth, and the priest who witnessed it felt it proved the real presence of Christ. The grotto contains a 15th-century polyptych attributed to Sano di Pietro and Benvenuto di Giovanni, along with frescoes by painters from the Umbrian-Sienese school.

LORETO

439 J7 | Via Solari 3, 60025 Loreto, tel 071 977139 | Loreto **www.loreto.it**

Loreto, 22km (14 miles) southwest of Portonovo, is second only to Lourdes in importance as a place of pilgrimage—thousands make the journey every year to see the Virgin Mary's house. It was transported here from Nazareth by the Angeli family during the 13th century. In the 16th century an enormous church, the Santuario della Santa Casa, was built over the house to protect it.

The Santuario della Santa Casa is in Piazza della Madonna, in the heart of town. The Santa Casa (Holy House) is inside, directly beneath the dome of the church and protected by an ornate marble screen by the Italian Renaissance architect Bramante. Around the Santa Casa are the

The remains of the Capitolium at Ostia Antica

Take time to sunbathe or shelter under the parasols on one of the white, sandy beaches near Portonovo

sacristies of San Marco, San Giovanni and San Luca, which contain works by Melozzo da Forlì and Luca Signorelli. Outside in the square is the Fontana della Madonna, a fountain designed by Giovanni Fontana and Carlo Maderno, one of the architects who worked on San Pietro in Rome.

Opposite the church is the Palazzo Apostolico, begun by Bramante in 1509 and now occupied by the town's museum and art gallery. The collection includes notable paintings by Lorenzo Lotto.

OFFIDA

🕂 439 K8 🛈 Borgo Giacom Leopardi, 63035 Offida, tel 0736 88871; summer only

Easily reached from Ascoli Piceno and the coastal towns of the region, Offida is famous in the Marche for its fine lace, which has been produced by the women of the town for generations. There are plenty of places to purchase their craftwork, and the Lace Museum has examples of local lace, including a 19th-century tablecloth, dainty bridal shoes and an exquisite dress modelled by Naomi Campbell in 1997 for Antonio Beraddi.

Offida is surrounded by vineyards and the gently rolling hills to the west of San Benedetto del Tronto. It has a pleasant, unhurried atmosphere, with streets that invite exploration. The town's main focus is the square, which is flanked by the 14th-century Palazzo Comunale, home to the archaeological museum, a small art gallery and the Teatro Serpente Aureo.

From here it is about five minutes' walk to the Church of Santa Maria della Rocca, up on an exposed hillside overlooking the surrounding countryside. The monks used its crypt as a

hospital from the 12th century during restoration in the 1980s, it was discovered that wide cavities in the walls had been used to bury the dead.

OSTIA ANTICA

🕂 438 H10 • Via Romanogli 717, 000125 Ostia ☎ Mon–Fri 06 5635 2830; Sat–Sun 06 5635 2830 🕐 Tue–Sun 8.30–6, Apr to mid-Oct; Tue–Sun 8.30–5, Mar; Tue–Sun 8.30–4, Nov–Feb 🎟 Adults €4, under 18s free 🍴 Ostia Antica 🖨 💻 www.itnw.roma.it/ostia/scavi

Ostia Antica is Italy's best-preserved Roman settlement after Pompei (p. 204). The sprawling remnants of this once-bustling town include shops and workshops, Mithraic shrines, barracks, tombs, grain warehouses *(horrea)*, baths, inns and domestic dwellings.

In about 335BC a small fishing community settled on this site 23km (14 miles) west of Rome. The settlement grew to become Rome's principal port, trading commodities from all over the empire. With the outbreak of the First Punic War, the port also became an important naval base and by the second century it had a population of nearly 500,000. Excavations of the site began in the 19th century and have so far revealed about one half of the town.

The Terme di Nettuno (Baths of Neptune), the first main building on the right after the Porta Romana, was built by Hadrian and preserves a series of elaborate mosaics depicting Neptune and Amphitrite. The mill is equally well preserved, with millstones, basins and kneading machines on view. The amphitheatre was built in the age of Augustus, with capacity for 3,000 people. At the end of the second century its capacity was extended to 4,000, and later it was adapted for the

staging of aquatic shows. The Thermopolium in the Via di Diana was once a bar; you can still see the marble counter, washbasins, stove, benches for the customers and wall paintings illustrating the menu.

PARCO DEL CONERO

🕂 439 J7 🛈 Centro Visite Parco del Conero, Via Peschiera 30/a, 60020 Sirolo, tel 0719 331879; Daily 9–1, 4–7, Jun–Sep; Mon–Sat 9–1, rest of year 🖨 www.en.conero.it

This is one of the most beautiful areas on the Adriatic and a good destination for those wanting to enjoy the outdoors. There are numerous coastal resorts where you can swim, sail, scuba-dive and windsurf, and for walkers there are 18 waymarked tracks around Monte Conero. There are many rare plants and excellent birdwatching opportunities, as well as some sites of cultural and geological interest to explore.

The park covers 5,800 hectares (14,300 acres) and is dominated by Monte Conero (572m/ 1,877ft). At the top of the mountain are the remains of a Palaeolithic settlement dating back 100,000 years.

To its north is Portonovo, a pretty bay that is home to the 11th-century church of Santa Maria di Portonovo, mentioned by Dante in *La Divina Commedia*. To the south is Sirolo, the area's main resort, with good beaches that are safe for children. Close by is Numana, where you can visit the Santuario della Croce, a shrine containing a wooden crucifix dating from the 12th to 13th century that is said to have miraculous powers.

On the road to Numana, Sirolo is home to the Villa Vetta Marina, the site of a convent founded by St. Francis in 1215.

THE SIGHTS

The quiet main square of the small hillside town of San Severino Marche, founded by refugees who were fleeing raiding barbarians in the sixth century

PESARO

✚ 437 J6 ℹ Viale Trieste 164, 61100 Pesaro, tel 0721 69341 🚊 Pesaro www.commune.pesaro.ps.it

Founded by the Romans in 184BC, Pesaro is a busy provincial town characterized by a pleasant old town, elegant, broad streets and a waterfront lined with white-stucco hotels overlooking soft, sandy beaches. The hub is Piazza del Popolo, where you'll find the most impressive building, the 15th-century Palazzo Ducale.

Pesaro's beaches make it a great place for anyone simply wanting to relax in the sun. It also attracts opera lovers, as it was the birthplace of the composer Rossini (1792–1868), and is the venue for a festival celebrating his works every August. His birthplace, Casa di Rossini, is a small museum, which preserves the original furnishings and memorabilia of the composer. Heavy bombing in World War II destroyed much of the city, so it lacks the charm of other Italian cities, but it still has its art treasures.

Paintings in the Museo Civico include Giovanni Bellini's masterpiece, *The Coronation of the Virgin.* The ceramic collection includes a terracotta work by Andrea della Robbia.

SAN LEO

✚ 437 H6 ℹ Piazza Dante 10, 91018 San Leo, tel 0541 916231

Some 12.5km (8 miles) east of Novafeltria, San Leo sits precariously on top of a tall cliff and is reached by a single-track road cut into the rock. Named after a Dalmatian saint, who was said to have converted the area to Christianity in the fourth century, the town was originally a defensive fortress.

The dramatic beauty of the landscape was the inspiration for Dante's *Purgatorio,* and it still attracts visitors.

San Leo is dominated by its castle, which Machiavelli considered to be the greatest fortress in Italy. It also served as a prison, notably to Count Alessandro di Cagliostro, a leading freemason, alchemist and medium who was sentenced to death during the Inquisition. The little village sits in the shadow of the fortress, on the remarkably preserved cobbled square, Piazza Dante. Here—in addition to several good restaurants and cafés—is the 12th-century Romanesque duomo, erected in honour of St. Leo, and La Pieve, the town's oldest church, founded in the eighth century.

SAN MARINO

✚ 437 H6 ℹ Palazzo del Turismo, Contrada Omagnano 20, 47031 San Marino, tel 0549 882410 www.omniway.sm

Marino, a stonemason fleeing religious persecution, supposedly founded this autonomous town in AD301. Between Romagna and the Marche, 14km (9 miles) southwest of Rimini, the town has a commanding position on a hilltop, with impressive battlements on the highest ridges. It covers an area of just 61sq km (24sq miles) and still declares itself an independent republic, with its own mint, postage stamps and international soccer team. This makes it the longest-surviving republic in Europe.

San Marino is something of a tourist trap, so you have to fight your way past numerous souvenir shops to enjoy its main attraction—the views from the fortress on Mount Titan. This mountain is said to have been used by the Titans, mythological gods of ancient Greece, to help them reach the sky and defeat Jupiter.

SAN SEVERINO MARCHE

✚ 439 J8 ℹ Pro Loco, Piazza del Popolo 43, 62027 San Severino, tel 0733 638414 🚊 San Severino

A town with a rich artistic heritage, San Severino Marche was the birthplace of the Salimbeni brothers, whose works adorn the local churches and art gallery. The town's past is revealed further in the archaeological museum, which also has remains from the Roman town of Septempeda.

There are two parts to the town: The Borgo, which focuses on the medieval Piazza del Popolo, and the ancient *castello* (castle) on the Montenero Hill, the heart of the old town. The Pinacoteca Civica (art gallery), just above the piazza in the lower part of town, has works by Lorenzo and Jacopo Salimbeni, paintings by Alunno, and the great Mannerist artist Pinturicchio's painted wood masterpiece, the *Madonna della Pace.* In the sixth-century Church of San Lorenzo in Doliolo, at the top of Via Salimbini, are the remains of a pagan temple and frescoes by the Salimbeni brothers. The 10th-century Duomo Vecchio is also decorated with frescoes by the brothers. The Duomo Nuovo, with a *Madonna* by Pinturicchio, is also worth visiting.

SPERLONGA

✚ 439 J11 ℹ Via Emanuele Filiberto 5, 04024 Gaeta, tel 0771 461165; summer only 🚊 Fondi Sperlonga

Sperlonga is Lazio's most fashionable resort, 98km (61 miles) southeast of Castel Gandolfo. Like the town of Gaetà, Sperlonga juts into the Tyrrhenian Sea, on the region's prettiest stretch of coastline, shaped by little coves and promontories and several attractive beaches. The houses are whitewashed, and the narrow streets make the town an

The Convento di San Benedetto clings to the rockface in the small medieval town of Subiaco

A section of the Roman aqueduct at Tarquinia

appealing place to explore, although it can get very busy in summer. Combine time on the beach and a leisurely meal in a restaurant with a visit to nearby historical sites—perhaps the Grotta di Tiberio (Cave of Tiberius) and its museum, with works of art and several classical sculptures.

At Gaeta you can also visit the tomb of Cicero, the great Roman orator and writer, killed in 43BC.

SUBIACO

🏠 439 J10 🚶 Via Cadorna 59, 00028 Subiaco, tel 0774 822013

Subiaco is an isolated town on the edge of the Simbruini Mountains, 28km (17 miles) south of Anticoli Corrado. There were once 12 monasteries around the town, but now only two remain, both a short distance from the town. It was here in the fifth century that St. Benedict wrote the famous *Benedictine Rule*, the cornerstone of Western monasticism. He lived in a nearby cave, the Sacro Speco, now part of the Convento di San Benedetto. The cave is in a lower part of the monastery; steps lead down to an early 13th-century fresco of St. Francis. It is this monastery and the Monastery of Santa Scolastica that attract most visitors to the town. Reached by a 25-minute walk from town, the Convento di Santa Scholastica has three painstakingly restored cloisters. The first, from 1580, is decorated with columns from Nero's villa, the second (1052) is one of the oldest in Italy, and the third dates from the 13th century.

TARQUINIA

🏠 438 G9 🚶 Piazza Cavour 1, 01016 Tarquinia 🚉 Tarquinia, then bus

The cultural and political capital of Etruscan Italy, Tarquinia is famous for its necropolis, 6,000 original Etruscan tombs that honeycomb the Monterozzi plateau to the east of the town. There are a handful that can be visited within the ancient town. The Hellenistic-style wall paintings inside span about 500 years, depicting mythical scenes, banquets, games and horse-races. The tombs with the most fascinating paintings are *The Augurs* (530BC), *The Lionesses* (late sixth century BC) and *The Leopards* (470BC).

The modern town overlooks the Tyrrhenian Sea, and here are more reminders of the past in a museum that has a wide variety of Etruscan objects. On display are tomb paintings, jewellery, coins and vases, but the highlight is a pair of Etruscan terracotta winged horses from the fourth century BC. There are also some medieval sites worth visiting here, including the 12th-century Church of Santa Maria in Castello.

TIVOLI

p. 189.

TOLENTINO

🏠 439 J8 🚶 Piazza della Libertà, 62029, Tolentino 0733 972937 🚉 Tolentino

Tolentino is one of Italy's lesser-known towns but it has plenty to attract history lovers, including frescoes in the Basilica of San Nicola, several Romanesque churches, and a fine 18th-century theatre.

Its position in the Chienti River valley, 100km (62 miles) north of Ascoli Piceno, made it an important industrial focus in the Middle Ages, the river water being used to drive mills. Today Tolentino has kept its industrial tradition, and the historic heart is surrounded by a sprawl of uninspiring modern buildings.

An ancient bridge, the Ponte di Diavolo (Devil's Bridge), leads to the 13th-century Basilica di San Nicola da Tolentino, the home of St. Nicholas until he died in 1305. Inside is a fresco cycle by Pietro da Rimini, painted early in the 14th century in the style of Giotto.

Tolentino also has some interesting museums: the Museo dell' Opera del Santuario has paintings, frescoes and rich religious objects, while the slightly more unusual Museo della Caricatura e dell'Umorismo nell'Arte displays a collection of caricatures by Italian and foreign artists.

URBINO

p. 190.

VITERBO

🏠 438 H9 🚶 Piazza San Carluccio 5, 01030 Viterbo, tel 0761 304795 🚉 Viterbo Porta Romana

Viterbo is the largest town in northern Lazio, 81km (51 miles) north of Rome. Originally an Etruscan town, it was colonized by the Romans in 310BC. The outskirts are uninspiring, but the walled centre is lively, with plenty of good bars and restaurants, as well as a number of cultural sites.

It is worth visiting simply to soak up the atmosphere of the ancient medieval quarter, San Pellegrino—an intriguing maze of narrow streets lined with romantic-looking houses, enticing archways, balconies and external staircases. The town was home to artists such as Lorenzo da Viterbo (1440–76), and it was the official papal residence for many years.

The heart of town is Piazza del Plebiscito, from where you can walk along the Via San Lorenzo to Piazza San Lorenzo, an airy square built on the site of an Etruscan acropolis. The 13th-century Palazzo Papale and the striking Romanesque duomo are both found here. At the Villa Lante at nearby Bagnaia, you can walk in the Renaissance garden and enjoy its open-air thermal pools.

THE SIGHTS

TIVOLI

Fountains and aquatic displays in the beautiful gardens at Villa d'Este.
Romantic remains of Emperor Hadrian's luxurious Villa Adria, the largest ever built in the Roman Empire.

Tivoli's scenery and cool hilltop location 40km (25 miles) east of Rome made it a popular spot for wealthy Romans to build their country villas.

VILLA ADRIANA

Via della Via Adriana, 00010 Tivoli ☎ 0774 382733 ⊙ Daily 9–6, summer; daily 9–5, rest of year 🎟 Adult €6.50, under 18s free 🏛 🚻 🛍

Villa Adriana's ruins sprawl lazily away from Tivoli through peaceful olive groves. Begun in AD125 and completed 10 years later, the Villa Adriana was so vast that it covered an area as great as the heart of imperial Rome. It was the largest and most costly palace ever built in the empire, with two bathhouses, libraries, temples, and a Greek theatre, as well as apartments. The villa even had a beach heated by steam pipes buried under the sand, and a series of underground service passages big enough to accommodate horses and carts. The parkland is dotted with soothing pools and buildings connected by covered walkways. The Teatro Marittimo is a small palace built on a private island in an artificial lagoon; it is thought to have been Hadrian's private retreat, where he indulged in his love of music, poetry and painting.

VILLA D'ESTE

Piazza Trento, 00010 Tivoli ☎ 0774 333404 ⊙ Tue–Sun 8.30–6.45, May–Aug; Tue–Sun 8.30–6.15, Sep; Tue–Sun 8.30–5.30, Oct; Tue–Sun 8.30–4, Nov–Jan; Tue–Sun 8.30–4.30, Feb; Tue–Sun 8.30–5.15, Mar; Tue–Sun 8.30–6.30, Apr. Closes one hour after last entry 🎟 Adult €6.50, under 18s €3.25 🏛 🚻 🛍

The Villa d'Este is in Tivoli itself, next to the main square, Largo Garibaldi. Its gardens are famous for their fountains. Pirro Ligorio adapted the former convent into a country retreat for Cardinal Ippolito d'Este, son of Lucrezia Borgia and the Duke of Ferrara, in 1550. The gardens are both theatrical and elegant, with water spouting from all corners and cascading down every surface. Particularly impressive are the Viale delle Cento Fontane (Avenue of a Hundred Fountains) and the Fontana dei Draghi (Fountain of the Dragons), built in honour of Pope Gregory XIII, whose emblem was a short-tailed dragon. But the most visually striking aquatic display has to be the main fountain in the gardens, the Fontana di Biccierone (Fountain of Glass) by Bernini. A curious addition is the Rometta, with scale models of Rome's major buildings.

RATINGS	
Good for kids	●●●●
Historic interest	●●●
Photo stops	●●●●●
Walkability	●●●●

TIP

● Spring and autumn are the best times to visit to avoid the biggest crowds.

BASICS

✚ 438 H–J10

ℹ Near Piazza Garibaldi, 00010 Tivoli, tel 0774 311249

⊙ Wed–Fri 9–1, 3–6, Mon–Tue, Sat 9–1

🚇 Tivoli

❓ Both villas are so popular that many companies run bus tours from Rome.

The Fontana dei Draghi at the Villa d'Este (top); one of the more unusual water features (above); statues among the ruins of the Villa Adriana (left)

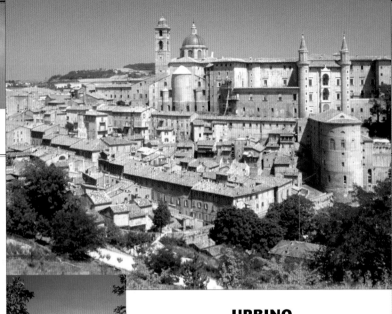

URBINO

**One of Italy's best-preserved Renaissance cities.
The home town of Raphael and Bramante, a city with an
unmistakable artistic legacy.**

In the 15th century the court of Duke Federico da Montefeltro was
one of the most civilized in Europe, and the city of Urbino is still an
elegant and urbane place to explore. The town was important during
the Romans' time, but there is little visible evidence of this period
except for the Teatro Romano. Urbino was extensively redesigned in
the 15th century by Federico da Montefeltro, and this medieval layout
is the one you see today. The artist and architect Raphael (1483–
1520) was born in the city and Bramante (1444–1514) was born in
nearby Fermignano. A number of other great artists worked here,
including the Salimbeni brothers, Luca della Robbia, Pisanello and
Piero della Francesca. The Casa di Raffaello, Raphael's birthplace, is
now a small museum displaying reproductions of his paintings and
works by his father.

RATINGS

Good for kids	●●
Historic interest	●●●●
Cultural interest	●●●
Photo stops	●●●●

BASICS

✚ 437 H7

ℹ Via Puccinotti 35, 61029 Urbino, tel
0722 2613

🕐 Mon–Sat 9–1, 3–7, Sun 9–1

*The 15th-century Palazzo
Ducale, housing the major
museum and galleries of Urbino
(top); a typically quiet road
meanders through the rolling,
cultivated countryside around
Urbino (above)*

PALAZZO DUCALE

The great Palazzo Ducale *(Tue–Sun 8.30–7.45, Mon 8.30–2)* is
Urbino's largest edifice, almost a city within a city. Described as 'won-
drous' by Giorgio Vasari, the Italian painter and art historian, the palace
was designed by Luciano Laurana in the 15th century, exemplifying
elegant, geometric discipline. The heart of the palace is the Cortile
d'Onore (Courtyard of Honour), said to be one of the most beautifully
proportioned Renaissance courtyards ever built. Inside you can explore
the Duke's study, noted for its inlaid wood, his audience room, in
which hang two masterpieces by Piero della Francesca—a *Flagellation*
and *The Madonna of Senigallia*—and the Duchess's apartments *(open
by prior arrangement)*, where you will find Raphael's *The Mute* and a
Last Supper by Titian. From Piazza del Mercatale, an unusual spiral
staircase leads to Corso Garibaldi and the main square.

THE DUOMO

The duomo dates from the 15th century and was rebuilt by Giuseppe
Valadier after it collapsed in an earthquake in 1789. The Museo
Diocesano Gianfrancesco Albani, within the cathedral, contains 14th-
century frescoes from a local church and paintings by Andrea da
Bologna and Iacopo Barocci. The late 14th-century Oratorio di San
Giovanni Battista is decorated with a dazzling fresco cycle by Lorenzo
and Jacopo Salimbeni.

THE SOUTH

There are some major highlights in this area—noisy Naples, the preserved ancient Roman city of Pompei and volcanic Vesuvio are the stars. From here the coastline leads to the laid-back deep south, with dramatic mountains, sun-baked inland plains and historic towns. East lies more prosperous Puglia, worth exploring for towns like Lecce and the untouched coastline.

MAJOR SIGHTS

A mythical beast on the façade of the Basilica di San Nicola in Bari

Inside the Reggia di Caserta

An entrance portico at Castel del Monte in Puglia

ALBEROBELLO

✚ 443 P12 🛈 Piazza Sacramento 19, 70011 Alberobello, tel 080 432 6030
🚉 Alberobello
www.alberobellonline.it

Trulli are strange-looking white-washed limestone houses of a style that may date back to prehistoric times. They have a few tiny windows and cone-shaped roofs formed from spirals of grey limestone slabs. With more than 1,000 of them, Alberobello is the *trullo* capital and looks quite unlike any other town. Built mainly in the 18th century, this unique community is a UNESCO World Heritage Site. Enjoy the other worldly atmosphere of the streets—ignoring the souvenir shops. Some of these bizarre dwellings have been converted into art galleries, craft shops and cafés with rooftop panoramas. The oldest *trulli* are in the Aia Piccola area, north of Via Indipendenza. Other highlights include Trullo Sovrano, a rare two-storey *trullo* built in the 18th century and now a museum-house *(daily 10–8, summer; 10–5, winter)*, and Rione Monti, where hundreds of *trulli* are home to the best of the galleries and craft shops. Visit too the *trullo*-style parish church, Chiesa di Sant'Antonio (1926).

L'AQUILA

✚ 439 J9 🛈 Piazza Santa Maria di Paganica 5, 67100 L'Aquila, tel 0862 410808 🚉 L'Aquila
www.abruzzoturismo.it

This cultured university city is uninviting at first glance and is sedate and insular. However, once inside the old town, art lovers will find plenty to appreciate in its churches, squares and fountains.
Frederick II of Hohenstaufen founded L'Aquila ('the eagle') in about 1245. The 15th-century moated fortress that dominates the old town houses the Museo Nazionale d'Abruzzo *(Tue–Sun 8am–9pm)*. Icons, sculptures and works of art from the 16th to 18th centuries are displayed, along with archaeological finds.
Walk along the steep cobbled path into Piazza San Vito to the extraordinary Fontana delle 99 Cannelle, a fountain with 99 gargoyle heads. The Tre Marie Restaurant, one of the best in the Abruzzo, dates from the 18th century. Kings and statesmen may have dined here, but the excellent food is still affordable.

BARI

✚ 443 P11 🛈 Piazza Aldo Moro 33a, 70122 Bari, tel 080 524 2361 🚉 Bari
www.pugliaturismo.com/aptbari

Puglia's rival to Naples is the biggest town on the long heel of Italy's boot, and most visitors use it as a ferry port for Greece, Croatia and Turkey, or as a gateway to the southeast coast. The modern city is brash and smart, but the old town is a delightfully confusing warren of narrow streets, courtyards and archways—deliberately designed to confuse invading pirates and armies. Fine Romanesque churches can be found before emerging in front of the reassuring fortifications of the massive *castello*. The Basilica di San Nicola *(daily 7–1, 4–7)* is a beautiful example of 11th-century Romanesque architecture, with relics of the original Santa Claus, Bishop Nicholas. The modern town south of Corso Vittorio Emanuele II has gleaming luxury boutiques that rival any in Milan, Florence or Rome.

CASERTA

✚ 440 K11 🛈 Via Nazionale Appia Caserta, tel 082 327 7111 🚉 Caserta
www.caserta.it

The magnificent Reggia di Caserta, in the middle of this little-known southern corner, is a compulsory stop for lovers of formal gardens and royal palaces. Built at the foot of Mount Tifitani, this impressive white palace was commissioned by the Bourbon king Carlos II in 1752, and took almost 100 years to complete.
There are 1,000 elaborately decorated rooms within the royal apartments, but they are now almost empty. It is the external grandeur that is so striking, and the extensive gardens, both formal Italian and English in style, are on a par with those of the Palace of Versailles in France. A cascading waterfall flows through one part of the gardens, flanked by manicured lawns and trees. Stroll and discover other water features in the 18th-century English garden, a paradise in spring and early summer. The guided tours through the English garden are recommended.

CASTEL DEL MONTE

✚ 442 N11 • SS 170, 70031 Andria
☎ 0883 569997 🕐 Daily 10–7.30, Mar–Sep; daily 9–6, rest of year
🎟 Adult €3, under 18s free
www.proloco.andria.ba.it

Of Emperor Frederick II's many south Italian fortresses, Castel del Monte is by far the most impressive and handsome. Cresting a peak with views of the low hills of the surrounding Murge, 18km (11 miles) south of Andria, this octagonal, crown-like fortress has an austere Gothic exterior. A slim octagonal tower stands at each of the eight corners, and the eight rooms on each of the castle's two floors are set around an octagonal courtyard. Frederick's refined tastes are reflected in their finely sculpted columns and arches of pink, green and white cipollin marble—inspiration for the monks' monumental library in the 1986 film *The Name of the Rose*, based on Umberto Eco's book and starring Sean Connery.

CAPRI

**A miniature kingdom, an island with an enchanting quality, untarnished by the influx of mass tourism.
Take in bird's-eye views, nose around imperial gardens and villas and marvel at the famous blue grotto.**

Capri is at the mouth of the Gulf of Naples, where the Faraglioni, two great jagged rocks, rise sentry-like out of the sea. Capri town's heart is the Piazzetta, where the baroque cathedral watches over the café scene. An infinite list of royals, stars, politicians and other VIPs, including Graham Greene and D.H. Lawrence, have lost their hearts to Capri, either acquiring homes here or anchoring their yachts in the bay.

Caesar Augustus fell under Capri's spell in about 29BC, when he traded the bigger and richer island of Ischia to Naples in exchange for Capri. The Villa Jovis, built for Emperor Tiberius in AD1, is an imposing example of the Roman love affair with the island. Tiberius moved his court here and lived here until his death in AD37. A 45-minute walk from Capri town, the villa overlooks the Gulf of Naples. Stand and admire the views on the spot where unfortunate enemies of the emperor were flung to their death, so creating the saying 'See Naples and die'.

MONTE SOLARO
Mount Solaro, the highest peak on the island at 589m (1,932ft), surveys the streets of terraced houses winding their way uphill, brushing past olive groves and fragrant rosemary bushes. A trip to Capri is worth it just for the chairlift ride to the top of Monte Solaro; it skims the tops of the pine trees and provides fantastic views over the Bay of Naples and the Amalfi coast. At the top is Anacapri, a charming village where you can visit the Villa San Michele, built by the Swedish author Axel Munthe (1857–1949), in a superb panoramic setting. Here small terraced houses sit alongside immaculate white villas immersed in Mediterranean and subtropical vegetation.

GROTTA AZZURRA
If you are staying longer than a day or so, consider a boat trip to the Grotta Azzurra (Blue Grotto). Experience the unique blue glow of the cave, caused by the reflection of natural sunlight passing through its underwater cavity. Little rowing boats carry passengers through the opening of the grotto, so small that you have to lie flat on the bottom of the boat. Boats leave regularly from the Marina Grande, the main harbour.

RATINGS
Good for kids	●●●●
Historic interest	●●●
Outdoor pursuits	●●●
Photo stops	●●●●

BASICS
🔳 440 K12

🛈 Piazza Umberto 1, 80070 Capri, tel 081 8370634

🕐 Daily 8.30–8.30, Easter–Oct, 9–1, 3.30–6.30, Nov–Easter

🛈 Via G. Orlando 59, 80071 Anacapri, tel 081 8371524

🕐 Mon–Sat 9–3

⛴ Regular ferry or hydrofoil services from Sorrento and Naples on the mainland

www.capri.it
Caprionline have extensive hotel and restaurant listings with contact details, descriptions, photos and prices. There is also basic information available on what you can see and do on the island and the boat trip operators. Italian and English versions.

The Faraglioni Rocks characterize Capri's coastline

At the lively town of Ischia Ponte, on the island of Ischia, a causeway stretches across to the mid 15th-century Castello Aragonese (right of photo)

ERCOLANO (HERCULANEUM)

✚ 440 K12 • Ercolano Scavi, 80056 Ercolano ☎ 081 777 7008 🕐 Daily 8.30–6, summer; 8.30–3.15, rest of year 🚃 Circumvesuviana railway connects Ercolano to Sorrento and Naples 💶 Adults €10, under 14s €5; 3-day combined ticket valid for Pompei €18 www.pompeiisites.org

This interesting archaeological site is often bypassed for the more glamorous Pompei, but the eruption of Vesuvio in AD79 that buried Pompei also submerged Ercolano, preserving both settlements.

Probably the most famous of the well-preserved houses is Villa dei Papiri, the home of a rich and powerful Roman statesman, thought to be either Lucio Pisone, Julius Caesar's father-in-law, or his son. More than 50 marble and 20 bronze sculptures were found in the villa, together with an amazing collection of 1,700 Greek and Roman papyri. The villa and Roman theatre can only be visited by advance booking *(fax 081 861 3183)*.

Other highlights include the Casa del Atrio Mosaico, with its beautifully preserved mosaic flooring. Most of the objects found in excavations are in the Archaeological Museum in Naples (pp. 198–200).

FORESTA UMBRA

✚ 441 N10 ℹ️ Ufficio Amministrazione Foreste Demaniali del Gargano, 71030 Foresta Umbra, tel 0881 560967; irregular opening times in winter 🚃 Gargano railway runs along forest periphery between San Severo and Péschici www.parks.it/parco.nazionale.gargano/garganoparco/foresta.umbra

Take a break from the summer heat in the cool of this rich and varied forest at the heart of the Gargano Peninsula (see opposite). Signposted trails lead through a protected nature reserve, with picnic areas along the way.

The Foresta Umbra's 5,500 hectares (13,600 acres) account for half of the Gargano promontory's woodlands. After the aleppo pines of the coast, the dominant trees are maple, hornbeam, birch and beech. The Valle del Tesoro is where you will find the forest's biggest beech tree *(faggio)*, a giant 40m (131ft) specimen with a 5-m (16.5ft) circumference (signposted *Colosso del foresto*). The forest also has 65 species of orchid. Animals to look for include deer, curly-horned mouflon sheep, boar and Italy's largest colony of badgers, while birdwatchers can spot the Dalmatian woodpecker, sparrowhawk, buzzard and royal or tawny owl. With only a couple of hills rising above 1,000m (3,300ft), the forest is a mixture of dense vegetation and clearings created by the karst limestone formation of caves and sinkholes that provide waterholes for the wildlife.

GALLIPOLI

✚ 443 Q13 ℹ️ Piazza Imbriani 9, 73014 Gallipoli, tel 0833 262529; summer only, plus Tue and Thu, Oct and Mar 🚃 Gallipoli

Gallipoli is built on an extended headland, 37km (23 miles) south of Lecce, with the old town standing on an island linked to the modern town by a seven-span bridge. While the new town may seem unprepossessing, the old town has the mysterious charm of a labyrinthine Arab city.

Not to be confused with the World War I battlefield in Turkey, Gallipoli is Greek in origin (the ancient Greek name, *Kalé polis*, means beautiful city). The old town is full of white-painted houses along narrow, winding streets and alleys and has a fine 17th-century baroque cathedral.

The handsome carved friezes of the honey-coloured façade are influenced by the cathedral of its sister city, Lecce (p.196), where Gallipoli-born painter Giovanni Andrea Coppola went on to make his name.

From the waterfront Riviera road, which encircles the old town, there are views of the fishing port and the nearby beaches.

ISCHIA

✚ 440 K12 ℹ️ Via Iasolino, 80077 Ischia, tel 081 507 4231 ⛴️ Hourly ferries from Naples; 55-minute journey on the fast service www.ischia.it

About 10km (6 miles) long and 7km (4 miles) wide, the island of Ischia is surrounded by soft golden sands and enjoys a temperate climate almost all year round. It is famous for its spa facilities, ranging from mud-bath treatments to natural hot springs. Safe family beaches and summer nightlife make this a popular holiday destination.

The gardens of the beautiful villa of La Mortella *(Tue, Thu, Sat–Sun 9–7, Apr–Oct)*, created by British composer William Walton and his widow Susana, have more than 1,000 different species of plants. Forio is an attractive town with a sunny beach, backed by the magnificent Poseidon Gardens. The village of Sant'Angelo can be reached only on foot and is connected by a causeway to the Rocca di Sant' Angelo, a green lava rock rising out of the sea.

Villa Arbusto *(daily 9.30–1, 3–7, May–Sep; daily 9.30–1, Oct–Apr)*, at Lacco Ameno, documents the history of the island from prehistoric to Roman times with ceramics, vases and underwater finds. The fragrant gardens, planted with magnolias, hibiscus, pomegranates and fig trees, are also open to the public.

Limestone arches and promontories along the Gargano Peninsula

GARGANO PENINSULA

**Rugged rocks, caves and cliffs, broad sandy beaches, neat whitewashed villages.
A great coastline for camping, watersports, picnics and hiking.**

Cave paintings on the peninsula's southeast coast are evidence that there were Stone Age settlements in the Gargano some 20,000 years ago. In the 13th century, Emperor Frederick II and his son Manfred built castles and watch-towers along the coast to fend off pirates and Saracens. The following centuries saw invasions by the Normans, Angevins and Spanish, and in the 17th century the Turks. The area remained relatively neglected until the 20th century. In 1979 a campaign to save the peninsula from the threat of real estate development began, leading to the creation of the Gargano National Park in 1995.

WHAT TO SEE AND DO

Known as the *sperone d'Italia*, the 'spur' of the Italian boot is about 45km (28 miles) wide in the middle and juts out 65km (40 miles) into the Adriatic Sea. Citrus groves and umbrella pines on the coast give way to the national park's densely wooded hills of the cooler interior.

Manfredonia is a good starting point, with a visit to Emperor Manfred's Castello (1256), now an archaeological museum. Southwest of the town is Siponto and the lovely 11th-century Romanesque Church of Santa Maria. The eastern coast, beyond the Baia di Vignanotica, is rugged and lined with rocky coves and grottoes, notably the Grotta Smeralda and Grotta dei Marmi.

At the eastern tip of the peninsula, Vieste (p. 210) is a popular resort with a castle, cathedral and sandy beaches at Pizzomunno and Castello. On the northern coast the fishing village of Péschici has preserved its picturesque medieval heart (p. 203). At the green heart of the peninsula you will find the beech and hornbeam woodlands of the Foresta Umbra (see opposite) and the little town of San Giovanni Rotondo. Its monastery, which was home to the 20th-century miracle-worker Padre Pio da Petralcino, is one of the most revered sites in Italy.

East from here is the pilgrimage town of Monte Sant'Angelo, where a church was built in 1273 over the Santuario di San Michele, a cave where the archangel Michael had appeared in a vision some 800 years earlier. Steps inside the church lead down to the sanctuary past a pair of 11th-century sculpted bronze doors.

RATINGS	
Good for kids	●●●●
Outdoor pursuits	●●●●
Walkability	●●●●
Photo stops	●●●

TIPS

● To swim in high summer, avoid the beaches and rent a boat to get to a secluded cove.

● Cool off in the inland forests.

MAKE A DAY OF IT

Foresta Umbra: See page 194
Isole Tremiti: See page 197
Péschici: See page 203
Vieste: See page 210

BASICS

✚ 441 M–N10

ℹ Via S. Antonio Abate 121, 71037 Monte Sant'Angelo, tel 084 568911
🕐 Tue and Thu 9.30–12.30, 4–6
🚉 Peschici

www.parks.it/parco.nazionale.gargano/
Weather forecasts, itineraries and information on points of interest and events in the park. Italian and English versions.

Small fishing boats at Péschici harbour (above)

RATINGS

Good for kids	◐ ◐
Historic interest	◐ ◐ ◐ ◐
Cultural interest	◐ ◐ ◐
Photo stops	◐ ◐ ◐ ◐

TIP

● Don't even think of driving in Lecce's chaotic traffic; park outside the *centro storico*.

MAKE A DAY OF IT

Gallipoli: See page 194
Otranto: See page 202
Táranto: See page 210

BASICS

✚ 443 Q12

🛈 Corso Vittorio Emanuele 24, 73100 Lecce, tel 08324 8092
🕐 Mon–Sat 9–1, 4–8, May–Sep; Mon–Sat 9–1, rest of the year
🚉 Lecce

www.pugliaturismo.com/aptlecce/
The official site of the Azienda di Promozione Turistica in Lecce. They have some interesting articles with pictures outlining the history, handicrafts and architecture of Lecce. There is also information on the holy sights and the Uragano villages, part of the former Greek settlements. Italian, English, French and German versions.

The detailed and ornate stonework on the façade of the baroque Basilica di Santa Croce

LECCE

**The most beautiful town in southern Italy, fancifully ornamented in its own style of baroque.
An oasis of bright and airy refinement, with extravagant churches, elegant 18th-century *palazzi* and sandstone houses.**

There are vestiges of early Hellenistic settlements (fifth and fourth century BC) in Lecce, the principal town in the Salentine Peninsula, but the town really entered history under Emperor Augustus as a Roman city named Lupiae (later Licea). An amphitheatre built during Hadrian's rule (first century AD) has been excavated in the main square, and Lecce's first bishop and patron, Sant'Oronzo, now honoured with a statue set on a Roman pillar, was one of Nero's Christian martyrs.

In the 11th century the Normans put Lecce back on the map, and the city expanded under the German emperors. Under Spanish rule in the 16th and 17th centuries the *centro storico* acquired its golden Renaissance and baroque glow (Emperor Charles V is celebrated by a triumphal arch). Prosperity attracted bankers and merchants from Florence, Venice, Milan and Genoa, who built grand palaces along the Via Palmieri and Via Libertini.

BAROQUE LECCE

The city's characteristic baroque ornamentation is made from the area's fine-grained golden sandstone, known as *pietra di Lecce*. Typical of this is Giuseppe Zimbalo's intricately sculpted rose window for the Church of Santa Croce (1646). Gabriele Riccardi created the more subdued interior. Architectural ornament makes an elegant theatrical set of Piazza del Duomo, comprising the seminary, Bishop's Palace and cathedral. The five tapering levels of the campanile were completed in 1682. Other baroque buildings—both churches and, even more ornate, private *palazzi*—are on Via Palmieri (Palazzo Guarini, Teatro Paisiello, Palazzo Palmieri) and Via Libertini. In particular look for the exuberantly decorated Chiesa del Rosario (Rosary Church). Completed in 1691, it was the last and most elaborate of Zimbalo's architectural achievements.

Outside the old city walls, the Norman Church of Santi Niccolò e Cataldo (1180) is a rare combination of Romanesque austerity and baroque ornament added in 1716. The adjoining 12th-century monastery has an elegant Renaissance fountain in its first cloister.

A major attraction of Lecce is the local cuisine: It is renowned for its lamb and baby goat (*capretto*) dishes, oven-baked aubergine (eggplant), *puccia* black olive bread, and fine regional wines—Alezio, Copertino and Leverano.

A tiny bay overlooked by medieval Maratea

The Sasso Caveoso in Matera, with ancient dwellings carved out of the rock and the Church of San Pietro Caveoso in the distance

ISOLE TREMITI

🚩 441 M9 🛈 Via E. Perrone 17, 71100 Foggia, tel 0881 723141/723650
🚢 Adriatica hydrofoil (tel 08131 72999) operates Jun–Sep from Manfredonia (2-hour journey, €42 round trip) or Vieste (1-hour journey, €27 round trip)
www.pugliaturismo.com/aptfoggia/

The three tiny islands known as Isole Tremiti lie in the Adriatic 22km (14 miles) north of the Gargano Peninsula. Consisting of limestone rocks and cliffs, with pine-wooded hills in the interior, they have a combined surface of 3sq km (1.2sq miles).

They are the perfect place for a daytrip from the mainland: You can swim in the clear waters of secluded coves, explore grottoes and walk along the rugged cliffs or through the interior's shady pine woods.

San Nicola is the smaller of the two inhabited islands, with a 15th-century monastic fortress and the small, 11th-century Church of Santa Maria a Mare. The island has no beaches, but there are some delightful rocky coves to swim in; there is nude bathing on the east coast.

The larger and more spectacular island of San Domino is 10 minutes by shuttle-boat (€1.25 each way). Its beaches are lovely—some accessible only by a climb down steep cliffs, and the grottoes—Grotta del Bue Marino, Grotta di Sale and Grotta delle Viole—are deservedly a major attraction.

MARATEA

🚩 442 M13 🛈 Piazza del Gesù 32, 85040 Maratea, tel 0973 876908/876455 🚉 Marina di Maratea, then bus

Here verdant mountains sweep down to a craggy coast characterized by numerous coves and small, secluded beaches. The little town of Maratea lies in the folds of the hills, connected to the sea by its pretty port. Confusingly Maratea has also given its name both to the port, which has very good fish restaurants, and to the main beach, Marina di Maratea, 5km (3 miles) away. The town itself is divided into Superiore and Inferiore. Superiore, the higher part, is largely in ruins after being deserted during the Middle Ages in favour of Inferiore, site of the present town of steps and narrow alleys. The Church of San Vito is the oldest church, built in the 11th and 12th centuries. At the summit, a sanctuary, Santuario di San Biagio, was built on the site of a Greek temple. There are fine views from the top of Mount Biagio, where you can also get a closer look at the enormous 22-m (72ft) marble statue of Christ that overlooks the town, port and beach.

MATERA

🚩 442 N12 🛈 Via de Viti De Marco 9, 75100 Matera, tel 0835 331983
🚉 Matera

This is a startling troglodyte town of dwellings cut into the limestone *sassi* (rockfaces) of a deep ravine, 80km (50 miles) south of Bari. Some were inhabited up to 7,000 years ago. There are many *chiesi rupestri* (cave churches) in the area, carved out by monks and often decorated with Byzantine murals. The poverty and disease that held the town in the early half of the 20th century were eventually cleaned up and the town became a UNESCO World Heritage Site in 1993. Now a few of the houses have been converted into apartments and art galleries.

A *strada panoramica* (scenic route) on the east side of the ravine has views over the two *sassi* districts, Sasso Caveoso to the southeast, and Sasso Barisano to the northwest. Walks into the heart of the *sassi* begin from Via Duomo and lead down to Via Fiorentini, which runs along the bottom of the ravine.

Leave time to visit San Pietro Caveoso and the nearby Santa Maria de Idris churches, both of which have 14th-century Byzantine rock paintings.

METAPONTO

🚩 442 P12 🛈 Via de Viti de Marco 9, 75100 Matera, tel 0835 331983

Archaeology buffs can combine a visit to the region's most important ancient Greek settlement with some pleasant sunbathing or swimming at the nearby beach resort, Lido di Metaponto. Metaponta is 50km (31 miles) south of Matera; the sandy beaches of Lido di Metaponto are 2.5km (1.5 miles) southeast of the archaeological museum.

The ancient site that was home to mystic scholar and mathematician Pythagoras in the seventh century BC is best seen in conjunction with a visit to the town's excellent Archaeological Museum *(Mon 2–7, Tue–Sun 9–7)*. It has a first-rate collection of ancient Greek jewellery and gold ornaments, ceramics and sculpture displayed in a handsome modern museum. At the archaeological site, signed 'Zona Archeologica', you can see the remains of a theatre, the marketplace (*agora*) and four temples, notably the Temple of Apollo Licius (sixth century BC).

Better preserved, 3km (2 miles) north of the main site, is the Temple of Hera (or Tempio delle Tavole Palatine), with 15 of its outer columns still standing *(daily 8am–half an hour before sunset)*.

NAPOLI (NAPLES)

See pp. 198–201.

Napoli (Naples)

**A beautiful coastal setting for one of Italy's most vibrant cities.
The best place to experience southern Italian urban life.
A seemingly dilapidated city, packed with historical and artistic treasures.**

A view over Naples from Castel San Elmo

A cart full of vegetables in the Porta Nolona market

Artichokes for sale

RATINGS			
Good for kids	●	●	●
Historic interest	●	●	● ●
Shopping	●	●	●
Walkability	●	●	●

TIPS

● Most areas are safe if you remain alert to petty crime—do not wear expensive jewels or carry much cash, and avoid back streets during the siesta or late at night.

● Traffic is chaotic and moves at a snail's pace, so use public transport and then walk.

● Opening times in general can be erratic, so be prepared to make more than one visit.

BASICS

✚ 440 K12

ℹ Piazza Gesù Nuovo, 80134 Naples, tel 081 5523328 ◐ Mon–Sat 9–7.30, Sun 9–2.30, summer
🚃 Napoli Centrale

www.inaples.it
A multi-lingual, comprehensive tourist authority site listing what's on in Naples.

Easter celebrations in the Spanish Quarter (right)

SEEING NAPLES

Naples is southern Italy's great city, pulsing with life, full of wonderful buildings and museums and flanked by an idyllic bay. Capital of the region of Campania, on Italy's west coast, it is 2.5 hours by fast train from Rome. It is as much famed for its citizens as its monuments, and there is nowhere else in Italy where you can find such a level of life lived on the streets, or such a stark demonstration of the north–south divide. With more than a million inhabitants, Naples is a big, sprawling city, so be prepared to walk; the upshot will be some fascinating discoveries and fabulous views.

HIGHLIGHTS

SPACCANAPOLI

✚ 200 B1 • Via Capitelli, Piazza del Gesù Nuovo, Via Benedetto Croce, Via San Biagio del Librai

The grid plan of streets that makes up the *centro storico* was the core of ancient Neapolis, and its three main streets—the ancient *decumani*—still slice relentlessly through the oldest part of the city. Spaccanapoli is one of these *decumani*; its name means 'split Naples' and it crosses the heart of the old city, a thoroughfare teeming with people and lined with churches, *palazzi* and idiosyncratic shops selling everything from books and musical instruments to religious objects and woodcarvings.

Spaccanapoli is made up of a string of streets, now mainly pedestrianized, from Piazza del Gesù to Via Viccaria Vecchia. The heart of the university district, it has plenty of bars and restaurants, including Scaturchio, one of Naples' oldest and best *pasticcerie*. Along its length, highlights include the rococo obelisk, the Guglia dell'Immacolata in Piazza del Gesù, the Church and Convent of Santa Chiara (see p. 201), Piazza San Domenico with its obelisk and castellated 13th-century church, and some fine Renaissance palaces.

MUSEO ARCHEOLOGICO NAZIONALE

✚ 200 B1 • Piazza Museo 19, 80135 Napoli ☎ 081 440166 ◐ Wed–Mon 9–7
🎫 €6.20

The Museo Archeologico Nazionale houses one of the world's most important collections of classical Roman sculpture, mosaics, gems,

THE SIGHTS

Duomo

✚ 200 B1 • Via Duomo 147, 80138
Naples ☎ 081 449097 🕐 Duomo:
daily 7.30–12.30, 4.30–7.30. Cappella di
San Gennaro: Sun–Fri 7.30–12.30,
4.30–7.30, Sat 7.30–12.30
A 13th-century Gothic cathedral
dedicated to San Gennaro, patron
saint of Naples; the first chapel
on the right contains two phials of
his blood, said to liquefy three
times a year. Also part of the
complex are the fourth-century
Basilica Santa Restituta (the oldest church in Naples), a baptistery
and a Renaissance crypt.

Palazzo Reale

✚ 200 B3 • Piazza del Plebiscito 1
☎ 081 580811 🕐 Thu–Tue 9–9
💳 €4.15
The 17th-century palace of the
Spanish viceroys of Naples,
extended in the 18th century by
the Bourbons and altered in the
19th century by the French.
Houses the historic Biblioteca
Nazionale (National Library), and
a series of grandiose state rooms.

wall-paintings, glass and silver, much of it plundered from the excavations around and to the south of Naples. The museum, founded in
1777, is badly labelled and confusingly laid out, with whole sections
often closed, but it is nevertheless outstanding, and the exhibits do
much to enhance visits to Pompei (p. 204) and Ercolano (p. 194).

The ground floor is devoted to sculpture, much from the 17th-
century Farnese collections, which were largely discovered in Rome.
Highlights are the muscular *Farnese Hercules* and the *Farnese Bull*
(200BC), the largest surviving classical sculptural group. Visit the
wonderfully vivid mosaic collection and the *Gabinetto Segreto*
(Secret Chamber), a collection of Roman erotica from Pompei, which
ranges from sensual wall paintings to phallic charms. Upstairs, rooms
are filled with more finds from Pompei and Ercolano, including a
naturalistic wall-painting of a graceful *Flora* scattering spring flowers,
and a *cave canem* (Beware of the Dog) mosaic from the entrance
to a house in Pompei.

CERTOSA DI SAN MARTINO

✚ 200 A2 • Largo San Martino 5, 80129 Napoli ☎ 081 578 1769 🕐 Tue–Fri
8.30–7.30, Sat 9–2, Sun 9–1 💳 €5
The huge hilltop Carthusian complex of the Certosa di San Martino was
founded in 1325, but what you see today dates mainly from the 16th
to18th centuries. The baroque church is crammed with the best of
Neapolitan painting and sculpture, and there are more riches in the
choir, sacristy and treasury. Explore the expertly restored, arcaded 16th-
century Chiostro Grande, the lavishly decorated Quarto del Priore and
the Pinacoteca in rooms set around the cloister with views over the city
and the bay. Don't miss the exhibition of *presepe*, crib figures—people
and animals fashioned for 18th-century Christmas cribs. The Certosa
is surrounded by terraced gardens, with sweeping views.

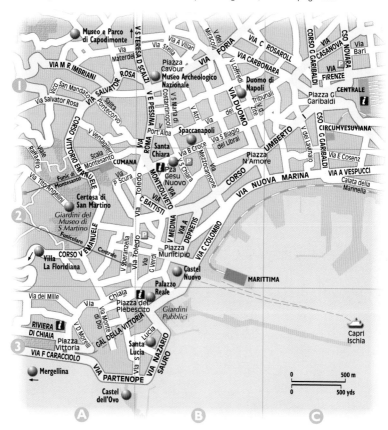

SANTA CHIARA

⊞ 200 B2 • Via Benedetto Croce/Via Santa Chiara 49, 80134 Napoli ☎ 081 552 6209 ⊙ Mon–Sat 9.30–1, 3.30–5.30, Sun and holidays 9.30–1

Santa Chiara is Naples' great Franciscan church, a simple and austere 14th-century Gothic conventual complex. Founded by King Robert of Anjou for his wife, Sancia, in 1310, it became a focal point for the Angevin rulers, several of whom are buried here. The original church, greatly altered over the centuries, was catastrophically bombed in 1943. Rebuilding started almost at once, using whatever could be salvaged, and the church, restored to its original Gothic appearance, re-opened in 1953. Three Angevin royal tombs survive: that of Robert himself and those of his son, Carlo and daughter-in-law, Mary of Valois.

Behind the church is the 14th-century cloister, remodelled by Domenico Vaccaro in 1742. He decorated the central garden with

72 octagonal pillars, interspersed with benches, each of which is covered with hand-painted majolica tiles. The church's Museo dell'Opera *(Thu–Tue 9–1, 4–6)* lies off the cloister, also providing access to a fascinating crib-scene, complete with street life, flying angels and a variety of people and animals.

MUSEO E PARCO DI CAPODIMONTE

⊞ 200 A1 • Via Miano 1, 80132 Napoli ☎ 081 749 9111 ⊙ Tue–Sun 8.30–7.30 ⊙ €7.25

Built in 1738 as King Charles III's hunting lodge, and surrounded by a wooded park, the Palace of Capodimonte houses one of Italy's richest museums. The bulk of the collection is made up of works acquired by Charles from his mother, Elizabeth Farnese. You can wander freely through the opulent royal apartments on your way to the majolica and porcelain collection, much of it made by the Neapolitan Capodimonte factory and painted with local scenes. Upstairs is a picture gallery, a collection amassed by the Farnese and Bourbon rulers and spanning the 15th to 17th centuries, with the emphasis on Renaissance painting. Botticelli, Perugino and Pinturicchio are all represented, but it is the High Renaissance works that shine, particularly the portraits by Titian, Raphael and Sebastiano del Piombo. Leave time to wander through the shady avenues of the surrounding park.

BACKGROUND

Greek settlers founded Neapolis in 750BC, and the city prospered under both Greek and Roman rule before declaring itself independent in 763. The Normans took the city in 1139, and were soon followed by the German Hohenstaufens, who held on until the Angevins took over in 1269. The Spanish moved in next in 1422 and remained in control for over 300 years. Bourbon and French rule followed before Naples became part of united Italy.

The city has a long history of foreign rule and neglect by government. Despite money pouring into the south under the Mezzogiorno scheme in the late 20th century, it is believed that a proportion of the Neapolitan economy remains under the control of the Camorra, the local Mafia equivalent. Unemployment and social deprivation remain common, but the late 1990s, when Antonio Bassolino was mayor, saw a burgeoning civic pride and a burst of creative activity.

Castel Nuovo

⊞ 200 B2 • Piazza Municipio, 80133 Napoli ☎ 081 795 5877 ⊙ Mon–Sat 9–7

A huge castle erected in 1282 by the Angevin rulers, converted into a royal residence by Aragonese; now accommodates the council offices and the Museo Civico.

Mergellina

⊞ 200 off A3

The waterfront area and ferry port, with its attractive harbour and spread of chalets, ramshackle bars and ice-cream parlours; a popular place for a seafood meal.

Castel dell'Ovo and Santa Lucia

⊞ 200 A3 • Borgo Marinari, 80132 Napoli ☎ 081 764 0590 ⊙ Mon–Sat 9–6, Sun 9–2

The oldest castle in Naples (ninth century) attained its present form in 1503. Restored in the 1970s after centuries of decline, it is now used for exhibitions and concerts. There are some excellent fish restaurants around the harbour.

Villa La Floridiana

⊞ 200 A2 • Via Cimarosa 77, Napoli ☎ 081 459188 ⊙ Mon–Sat 9–1 hour before sunset

A beautiful villa and park in the Vomero district, once the home of the Duchess of Floridia, morganatic wife of Ferdinand I. It now houses the Museo Nazionale della Ceramica, the porcelain museum *(Tue–Sun 9.30–11)*, with a superb Limoges and Meissen collection.

Vespas are a common sight, zipping around the streets of Naples (above left); the Capodimonte Gardens (above right)

The Doric Temple of Neptune (450BC) at Paestum

A river flows through the sparsely wooded lowlands of the Parco Nazionale d'Abruzzo

THE SIGHTS

OTRANTO

✚ 443 R12 ℹ Piazza Castello, 73028 Otranto, tel 0836 801436 🚗 Otranto

About 45km (30 miles) south-east of Lecce, this charming little fishing village has some splendid monuments to its Greek, Byzantine and Norman past—in the 11th century it was an important Crusader and pilgrim port. In the areas just outside the town people still speak a Greek patois rather than Italian, and in summer a car ferry runs from the port to Greece.

Many visitors come to Otranto for its convenient sandy beaches, which have good watersports facilities and fishing coves. The Normans' 11th-century Roman-esque Cattedrale di Santa Maria Annunziata *(daily 8.30–noon, 4–7)* has some spectacular Byzantine floor mosaics depicting Adam and Eve, Noah and the Flood, the Queen of Sheba, Alexander the Great and King Arthur. In grim contrast, the Martyrs Chapel contains the bones of 800 Christians massacred by the Turks in 1480. A hill covered with cypress trees on the southern edge of town marks the spot where the martyrs were beheaded. The massive *castello* (castle) *(exhibitions Mon–Sat 9.30–noon, Sun 10.30–12.30, 3.30–6.30, Oct–Mar)* dominates the south side of the port, built after the Turkish attack. The best beaches, notably Torre dell'Orso, are north of town.

PAESTUM

✚ 441 L12 ℹ Azienda Autonomo del Soggiorno e di Turismo di Paestum, Via Magna Grecia 887, 84063 Paestum, tel 0828 722322 🌐 Ancient site of Paestum: daily 9–1 hour before sunset 🚗 Paestum (1km from site)

Paestum, about 35km (22 miles) south of Salerno and about 3km (2 miles) from Capaccia Scalo,

has some of the best-preserved Greek temples outside Greece, standing in a memorable setting with mountains on one side and a marine vista on the other.

The area includes a temple dedicated to Poseidon (the site was known as Poseidonia), the god of the sea, known to the Romans as Neptune (450BC), a temple to Athena, and the basilica, which historians believe to have been built for Heres or Zeus. Stand in the fields, which in spring are filled with wildflowers, and contemplate the majesty of Neptune's temple. The site was created by the Greeks in the sixth century BC and was taken over by the Romans 200 years later, who changed the name. The structures are all built of a golden stone that glows richly in the afternoon sun. The site was deserted from the ninth century and rediscovered in the 18th.

The Museo Archeologico *(daily except 1st and 3rd Mon of month, 9– 7)* illustrates the fascinating history of this exceptional site. Of particular interest is the *Tomba del Tuffatore* (Diver's Tomb), one of the few remaining and best-preserved Greek mural paintings from the fifth century BC.

The area a few kilometres south of Paestum is worth exploring for its emerald green sea and deserted beaches.

PARCO NAZIONALE D'ABRUZZO

✚ 440 K10 ℹ Abruzzo Promozione Turismo Regional: well-signposted information points in all areas and villages, tel 800 502520; summer only 🚗 Avezzano, then bus to Pescasseroli www.abruzzoturismo.it

The Parco Nazionale d'Abruzzo was set up in 1923 by conservationists to protect native species of animals and plantlife threatened with extinction—a small revolution for a predominantly

agricultural region with a strong hunting tradition.

Particularly rare animals were the brown *marsicano* bear, the golden eagle and the chamois deer, all of which are now thriving again in their natural habitats. With more than 300 species of birds and 12,000 different species of wildflower, it is reputedly the oldest park of its kind in Europe.

This fertile wilderness covers an area of 44,000 hectares (108,720 acres) in the south of the Abruzzo region. The park's Visitor Centre in Pescasseroli has a small museum and rehabilitation centre for injured animals.

Steeped in tradition, Pescasseroli has managed to maintain its traditional sheep farming, woodcarving and stonework customs. The village is also the birthplace of Benedetto Croce (1866–1952), the Italian writer, philosopher and politician. Stay to sample the local way of life and benefit from the range of park facilities, including horse-riding, mountain-biking and guided tours along some 150 marked walks and trails.

Within driving distance of Pescasseroli, in the terraced white-stone village of Civitella Alfedena, is the Centro Lupo (Wolf Museum), where you can learn all about the wolf packs who live in the park (p. 13).

PARCO NAZIONALE DEL GRAN SASSO

✚ 439 J9 ℹ Via XX Settembre, 67100 L'Aquila, tel 0862 22306 www.abruzzoturismo.it www.parconazionalegransasso.it

The Parco Nazionale del Gran Sasso, nicknamed Little Tibet because of its 2,912m (9,551ft) Gran Sasso mountain peaks, was set up in 1991 to preserve the animals and plants unique to the area.

Tossica, in the hills of the Parco Nazionale del Gran Sasso, with the Gran Sasso ridge in the background

Three mountain ranges, a fertile, cultivated valley and the nearby Adriatic coastline are all visible. Well-signposted footpaths and trails throughout the park make this an ideal destination for walkers, while winter sports enthusiasts can choose from the many ski resorts in the area.

The Cima Alta, a rocky vista about 1km (0.5 mile) from Prati di Tivo, is easily accessible and a good place to begin any walk or trek.

The soft rock characteristic of this section of the Apennines forms caves, gorges and impressive waterfalls, including those at Cento Fonti, Morricana and Volpara. In spring the flowers in the meadows and plains are a riot of different shades and at higher altitudes you can find edelweiss and wild orchids.

The Abruzzo chamois, an agile goat/ antelope once threatened with extinction in this region, has recently been reintroduced and about 50 now live in the park. There are also small packs of the Apennine wolf, as well as polecats, beech-martens, badgers and wildcats.

PARCO NAZIONALE DEL POLLINO

🚩 442 N13 **🛈** Park Centre (Sede Ente Parco), Via Mordini 20, 85048 Rotonda (Potenza), tel 0973 661692
www.parcopollino.it

The Parco Nazionale del Pollino is the largest national park in Italy and one of the richest in terms of wildlife. Famous for the loricate pines *(Pinus leucodermis)*, found only here and in the Balkans, the park is also home to eagles, ravens, pine martens, wildcats, roe deer, and the very rare Italian wolf *(Canis lupus italicus)*. Here, too, are over 1,700 species of wildflowers, including periwinkle, asphodels, gentians and peonies *(Paeonia peregrina)*.

This vast national park covers about 196,000 hectares (484,000 acres) of mountainous terrain, equally divided between Basilicata and Calabria, with areas of woodland, rocky outcrops, alpine meadows and unpolluted streams. The highest peaks are Monte Pollino (2,248m/7,344ft) and Serra Dolcedorme (2,267m/ 7,436ft), in the middle of the park.

Along the park's eastern borders, towns such as San Costantino Albanese and San Paolo Albanese are home to Albanian (Arbresh) communities which have largely preserved their own language, traditions and religious festivals since their arrival in the 16th century.

Southwest, the wildest area of the park, the Monti di Orsomarso, is named after the brown bears *(orso)* that once roamed here. There are many interesting towns scattered through the park, including Rotonda, the park's capital, whose visitor centre organizes excellent excursions into the park.

PÉSCHICI

🚩 441 M10 **🛈** Via E. Perrone, 71100 Foggia, tel 0881 723141 **🚊** Calenella, then bus
www.pugliaturismo.com/aptfoggia/

At the northern tip of the Gargano Peninsula (p. 195) and 80km (50 miles) north of Manfredonia, this tiny, walled medieval fishing village makes an ideal base for exploring the Gargano National Park—in particular the nearby grottoes just east along the coast at San Nicola and the Foresta Umbra in the interior (p. 194).

Dependent on an abbey on the Isole Tremiti (p. 197), built in the 10th century to fend off Saracen raids, its grey-domed houses and the maze of narrow winding streets are reminiscent

of an Arab village. The sandy bay at the foot of Péschici's promontory is where some of the Gargano's most attractive and popular beaches are to be found.

POMPEI AND VESUVIO

See pp. 204–207.

REGGIO DI CALABRIA

🚩 444 M16 **🛈** Via Roma 3, 89100 Reggio di Calabria, tel 0965 21171 **🚉** Reggio di Calabria Centrale or Lido (fewer trains) **🛳** Napoli and Catania (Sicily)

Reggio di Calabria is noteworthy mainly for being the gateway to Sicily, but it is also worth visiting if only for the Museo Nazionale, which has some priceless treasures from Calabria and Basilicata. In particular, seek out the *Bronzi di Riace (*460–430BC), two magnificent bronze warriors, and two rare painted panels by Antonello da Messina (c1460).

A busy modern city and seaport, Reggio was largely rebuilt in an organized grid fashion after the devastating earthquake of 1908. This is the toe of Italy's boot, and the coast of Sicily can clearly be seen from here—by night, the lights on her shore twinkle invitingly.

The city may not be the brightest star in Calabria's firmament, but the gardens of the Villa Comunale and the tree-lined coastal promenade along Viale Matteotti, with a diversity of palms, trees and shrubs akin to a botanical garden, leaven the traffic pollution and noise. At the northern end of the promenade, almost hidden by a grove of pines, is a small museum of musical instruments.

Nearby are the unprepossessing remains of a Greek defensive wall, and some ruins of baths and mosaics from the later Roman period.

Pompei and Vesuvio

A virtually intact first-century AD Roman town, complete with houses,
shops, temples and public buildings, a time capsule
sealed on 26 August AD79.
Walk around the summit of one of the world's most famous volcanoes.

Ruins at Pompei (above) and the bronze statue in the House of the Faun at Pompei (below)

RATINGS	
Good for kids	● ● ●
Historic interest	● ● ● ● ●
Photo stops	● ● ● ●
Walkability	● ● ●

TIPS

● Signposts in Pompei are few
and far between, so make sure
you have a good map and
guidebook before you start.

● Remember that most of
the important artistic finds
are now in the Museo
Nazionale
Archeologico in
Naples (p. 198).
Visit it either
before or after your
Pompei trip.

● Wear comfortable,
flat shoes and be prepared for
rough walking at both Pompei
and Vesuvio.

● Tackle Vesuvio in the early
morning and avoid windy days,
when conditions near the
crater can be bad.

● Pompei is exposed and it
can be very hot, so take plenty
of drinking water.

SEEING POMPEI AND VESUVIO

Mount Vesuvio, half-an-hour by train and bus from Naples, rises
to the south of the city, a peak of 1,281m (4,203ft) that forms
the backdrop to the beautiful bay. On the lower slopes, 13 communities house over 750,000 inhabitants, all of whom choose to
ignore the threat that looms over them. The Roman town of
Pompei, on the volcano's southern slopes, was caught unawares
by a massive eruption in AD79, which smothered the
town, its people and their goods and chattels.
Preserved for centuries, the site has been, and
continues to be, excavated, so as you walk up
and down the streets you can peer into
shops and private homes, read advertise-
ments and graffiti—and generally get a
unique picture of daily life in Roman times.

HIGHLIGHTS

VIA DELL'ABBONDANZA

Via dell'Abbondanza was Pompei's most important
thoroughfare, running through the middle of
the town from the Porta Marina in the west
(the main harbour gate) to the Anfiteatro
(amphitheatre) in the east. The Foro, the civic
heart of the town, lies off the west end of
Abbondanza, an elongated open space with a
colonnade running along three sides and the
remains of the Temple of Jupiter on the north side.
To the left is the porticoed entrance to the *macellum*,
the covered meat and fish market, while across the
road from the entrance to the Foro stands the basilica,
site of Pompei's law court and stock exchange. Farther
along the street are the Termae Stabiane, a large public
bath complex with an exercise court in the middle and
some well-preserved wall paintings.
Via dell'Abbondanza carries on past shops
and houses; look for the shop counters and

Detail of a fresco at Pompei

BASICS

POMPEI

440 L12 • Scavi di Pompei, Via dei Misteri 2, 80045 Pompei ☎ 081 857 5347

Daily 8.30–7.30 (last entrance 6), Apr–Oct; 8.30–5 (last entrance 3.30), rest of year

€10

Circumvesuviana to Pompei Scavi Villa dei Misteri

2-hour guided tours in Italian, English, French, German and Spanish, €90; audioguides in English, French, German, €5

€8–€15

Bar/restaurant with self service—expensive and usually very crowded; numerous restaurants just outside the site

300m (330 yd) from site entrance

www.pompei.biz
A very basic site outlining the history of Pompei and what you can see today. Italian and English versions.

VESUVIO

440 L12 • EPT, Via IV Novembre 82, 80056 Ercolano ☎ 081 788 1243

Daily 9–6

€6, covers a brief explanatory talk

Circumvesuviano to Ercolano, then bus

http://volcano.und.nodak.edu/vwdocs/volc_images/img_vesuvius.html
An excellent English-language site about the volcano, tracing the history of its eruptions through the centuries. Satellite photos and background information on the effects of the eruption that destroyed Pompei.

the symbols outside many of the commercial premises, which were aimed at drawing in the illiterate country people shopping in town.

VILLA DEI MISTERI

The Villa dei Misteri lies outside the main walls of Pompei, and was a working farm for much of its existence. It is probably the best-preserved of all Pompei's grand villas, a series of chambers and courtyards first built in the third century BC. Its name comes from the superb series of wall paintings in the *triclinium* (dining room)—a cycle of vibrant scenes showing a young woman's initiation rites into the Dionysiac mysteries, a popular cult in the early imperial era. The paintings, in vivid reds and ochres, are intensely clear and show sacrifice, dancing and flagellation. They are thought to have been copied by a local artist from third-century BC Hellenistic originals. Here you can also see a reconstruction of a winepress, with a decorative ram's head used for crushing grapes.

HOUSE OF THE VETTII

The House of the Vettii is named after its owners, the wealthy merchants Aulus Vetius Conviva and Aulus Vetius Restitutus, who spent their profits decorating their house with mythological paintings. It is one of Pompei's most beautiful houses, and gives an excellent picture of the domestic life of the town's upper middle-class citizens. The house was altered in the first century AD and the atrium, complete with strongboxes, leads straight through into the peristyle. There are frescoed chambers all around, illustrating such scenes as Hercules struggling with serpents, Ixion tied to a wheel and tortured for daring to set eyes on Zeus's wife, and Dirce being dragged to her death. Even the servants' quarters are decorated with erotic wall paintings, including a more than potent Priapus (phallic symbols were believed to ward off the evil eye).

Terme del Foro

Via di Mercurio ⏱ Daily 8.30–7.30 (last entrance 6), Apr–Oct; 8.30–5 (last entrance 3.30), rest of year

These public baths, north of the Forum, still have much of their original stucco decoration. There is a fine fountain in the hot room with a bronze inscription that records the cost of the fountain and the names of those who donated money towards its construction.

THE HOUSE OF THE FAUN

A block away from the House of the Vettii, the House of the Faun is one of the largest and most sophisticated houses in Pompei. It gets its name from the copy of the charming second-century BC bronze statue in the middle of the *impluvium* (an opening in the roof of the atrium); the original is now in the Museo Nazionale in Naples (see p. 198). The house, sprawling over almost 3,000sq m (32,300sq ft), probably belonged to a local dignitary. The floor mosaic at the entrance welcomes visitors with its inscription 'Ave' (Hail). The front of the house is arranged around two atria (halls); behind is a peristyle and graceful portico, which led to a discussion hall for public meetings. This was decorated with a million-piece mosaic floor depicting the 300BC Battle of Issus (now in the museum in Naples). As in many of Pompei's grander houses, the gardens have been lovingly restored.

The remains of the Anfiteatro in Pompei   *Detail of the ruins at Pompei*

House of the Tragic Poet

Via di Mercurio ⏱ Daily 8.30–7.30 (last entrance 6), Apr–Oct; 8.30–5 (last entrance 3.30), rest of year

One of the upmarket houses on Via di Mercurio, named after its theatrical mosaics. The entrance mosaic of a fierce but welcoming dog bears the inscription *cave canem* (Beware of the Dog).

MOUNT VESUVIO

Mount Vesuvio's fertile volcanic soil has made it attractive to farmers for centuries, and even today the lower slopes are heavily planted with olives, vines and vegetable crops, while wild plants cover the scars of the lava flows left after the last eruption, in 1944, which caused widespread damage to the surrounding towns.

Vesuvio is now a designated national park and a UNESCO Biosphere Reserve, seen at its best in early summer, when the slopes are covered in wildflowers and bird life is at its liveliest and most interesting. It is only when you climb the slopes above the official

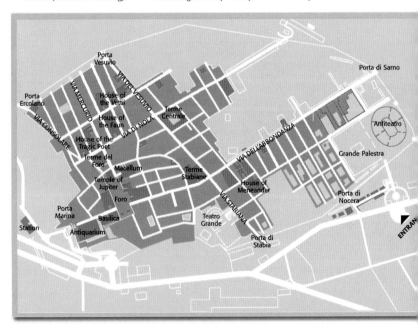

THE SIGHTS

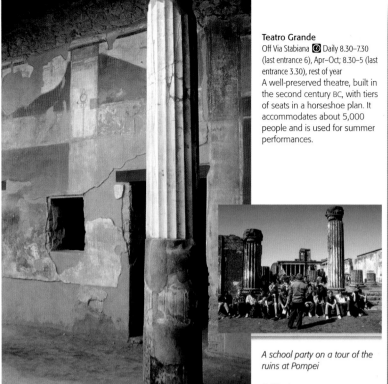

Teatro Grande
Off Via Stabiana 🔘 Daily 8.30–7.30 (last entrance 6), Apr–Oct; 8.30–5 (last entrance 3.30), rest of year
A well-preserved theatre, built in the second century BC, with tiers of seats in a horseshoe plan. It accommodates about 5,000 people and is used for summer performances.

A school party on a tour of the ruins at Pompei

Anfiteatro
Off Via dell'Abbondanza 🔘 Daily 8.30–7.30 (last entrance 6), Apr–Oct; 8.30–5 (last entrance 3.30), Nov–Mar
This is one of Italy's oldest amphitheatres. Built in 80BC, it had capacity for between 12,000 and 14,000 people and was used for gladiatorial combats. It could hold about half of Pompei's population; much of the seating area is intact. It is used during summer for concerts and classical plays.

House of Meneander
Off Via dell'Abbondanza
🔘 Sat–Sun 2–4
One of the largest houses in Pompei, this probably belonged to the family of Nero's wife, Poppaea. It dates from the third century BC and has a central garden and peristyle with an intricate floor mosaic, a domestic shrine *(lararium)* in the atrium and a room painted with scenes from the Trojan War.

parking area that you first appreciate its rocky aridity. The stony zigzag path up to the rim of the crater winds through lava, gravel and cindery rock. At the top, you can peer down into the crater 200m (650ft) below and enjoy good views of steaming fumaroles and stratified pyroclastic deposits across the void.

The Museo dell'Osservatorio Vesuviano has interesting exhibits that outline the volcano's geology and the threat that future eruptions pose.

BACKGROUND

Pompei is the world's best-preserved surviving Roman town, frozen in time by the catastrophic eruption of Vesuvio on 24 August AD79. Founded as a Greek colony, the town became part of Rome in about 200BC, thriving as a chic holiday resort for rich Romans and as a trading place exporting wine and fish products. It was severely damaged by an earthquake in AD63, and the volcanic eruption 16 years later was the final nail in the coffin. Of the 20,000 inhabitants it is thought that about 2,000 people died, including Pliny, the Roman naturalist, at Stabiae (Castellammare) nearby. His nephew, Pliny the Younger, recorded the events of the days in a letter to the historian Tacitus.

Excavations began in earnest in 1748, and continue today. Pompei has yielded more information about everyday Roman life than any other site, as well as artistic treasures.

Vesuvio, the cause of the disaster, is the only active volcano in mainland Europe. It last blew in 1944 and it is generally thought to be well overdue for another eruption—the longer the period of quiescence, the greater the risk. The mountain is constantly monitored. Scientists believe that the danger lies not in ash deposits and lava flows, but in a surge of super-heated, poisonous gas that could roll down the slopes at more than 80km (50 miles) per hour—much like the cloud that was responsible for so many deaths in AD79.

Fishing on the shores below the town of Scilla

Hills bordering a moutain lake in the Sila Grande, Calabria

RIVIERA CALABRESE

✚ 442 N14 ℹ Corso Mazzini 92, 87100 Cosenza, tel 0984 27271 🚉 Rail line runs right along the coastline

The Calabrian Riviera is a term used to describe a succession of beaches and resorts along the Tyrrhenian coast. The more popular resorts, such as Tropea (p. 210), are busy in the summer, but away from these areas and out of season it should be possible to find a quiet spot to swim and relax.

For most of its length, the Tyrrhenian coast is a comparatively narrow strip of land flanked by the Appennino Lucano and Appennino Calabro mountains, where rocky, tree-lined shores give way to coves and long, sandy beaches. Worth visiting are the beaches of Praia Mare, close to the Basilicata border, and the nearby Isola di Dino. Diamante, an attractive town with narrow streets and good restaurants, also merits a visit. Amantea, another coastal resort, has a recently discovered sixth-century BC Greek sanctuary, while Pizzo is famous for its beach and curious little church, Chiesa di Piedigrotta, decorated with rock carvings of religious icons and famous people.

SCILLA

✚ 444 M16 ℹ Co/Pro Loco, Piazza San Rocco, 89058 Scilla, tel 0965 754003 🚉 Scilla

This pretty fishing town lies 20km (12 miles) north of Reggio di Calabria (p. 203), with fine views across the Straits of Messina to the hills of Sicily. It has an interesting fishermen's quarter, an beautiful bay that is perfect for swimming and sunbathing, and plenty of cafés and restaurants.

The town of Scilla occupies a rocky crag and the shore on either side. To the east is the port and fishermen's quarter and to the west is a suburb built around the beach. The old houses of Chianalea (fishermen's area), reach right down to the water's edge, with front doors opening directly on to the port.

The crag supporting the castle is allegedly the Scylla of Greek legend, and the swirling waters of the straits are its counterpart, Charybdis—the mythical sea monsters that were the personification of these hazards. There have been fortifications on the rock since the fourth century BC, but the present castle dates mainly from the 17th century and is now used for cultural events. During the Napoleonic Wars the castle was occupied by the French, then the English, and later by Garibaldi, who came here during his reunification campaign.

SIBARI

✚ 442 N13 ℹ Via Amendola 1, Cassanoionio, tel 0981 76352

The Sibari region is blessed with long stretches of beach, especially in Villapiana, 9km (6 miles) to the north, but it is most famous for the ancient site of Sybaris-Copia, founded on the banks of the River Crati almost 3,000 years ago. It grew to become an immensely rich city (the word *sybarite*, someone who enjoys luxury, comes from its name), but it was destroyed in the fourth century BC when Croton (modern Crotone) obliterated the city by diverting the River Crati over the remains. Today nothing is visible above ground, but the excavations can be viewed, and the nearby museum, the Museo Nazionale Archeologico della Sibaritide in Casa Bianca, has finds excavated from here and other sites.

Sibari is on the Ionian coast 70km (44 miles) southwest of Taranto. Ancient Sybaris gave its name to this fertile coastal plain between Cape Spulico and Cape Trionfo. The mouth of the River Crati is home to one of the few colonies of Mediterranean seals.

SILA

✚ 444 N14 ℹ Corso Mazzini 92, 87100 Cosenza, tel 0984 27271

This extensive, mountainous plateau lies at the heart of Calabria, east of Cosenza and north of Catanzaro, and supports some of southern Italy's most unusual plantlife and animals. It is wonderful walking territory, particularly in spring, and the winter snows provide ample opportunities for downhill and cross-country skiing, mostly around the towns of Camigliatello Silano and Lorica.

Since controls in tree felling and hunting have been introduced, forests of beech, oak and pine clothe much of the mountainsides, and are inhabited by foxes, badgers, black squirrels, otters and a few specimens of the rare Italian wolf.

A wild and unspoiled region, the plateau, which includes the small Parco Nazionale della Sila, is composed of three separate massifs: La Sila Grande to the north, Sila Greca, and Sila Piccola to the south. The average height is 1,000m (3,280ft).

The visitor centre at Cupone, close to Lago Cecita, has a display of the natural history of the park, a botanical garden and an arboretum. Head for Lago Arvo and Cecita for walking, good scenery and a chance to fish for trout in Lago Arvo.

Camigliatello Silano, the capital of the area, is a great place to enjoy the local crafts and food. It is also the best place seek out hotels, restaurants and tourist information.

SORRENTO PENINSULA AND THE AMALFI COAST

**The Sorrento Peninsula—a heady mix of cobalt blue sea,
plunging cliffs, orange and lemon groves.
The perfect place to relax and soak up the sun and an ideal
base for exploring Pompei, Capri, Naples and the Amalfi Coast.**

THE SIGHTS

SORRENTO

Piazza Tasso, the main square in Sorrento, is a quintessential Italian square. Sit at one of the outdoor cafés and drink in the atmosphere around the maze of narrow streets and shops selling bottles of *limoncello,* the local liqueur. Decadent, grand hotels perch on the cliffs with splendid views over the sea on one side and lush gardens on the other.

Take time out from the beaches and cafés to visit Palazzo Correale and its museum. This 15th-century villa has an impressive collection of porcelain, glass, china and paintings dating from the 17th to 19th centuries. The grand cathedral dates from the 14th century and has paintings by artists from the Neapolitan school, a marble archbishop's throne and wooden choirstalls handcarved by Sorrentine craftsmen.

Take the public ferry or one of the many well-publicized private boat trips from Sorrento along the coast and around the bay to Capri (hourly in summer and at least six times a day in low season).

AMALFI COAST

From the southern side of the Sorrento Peninsula, the beautiful Amalfi Coast runs east to Salerno, with steeply terraced villages of stuccoed houses and seafood restaurants clinging to jagged cliffs. It is best known for its thrilling coastal drive, the 80km (50-mile) stretch of winding hairpin bends that leads from Positano to Salerno with vistas over the shimmering Gulf of Salerno at every turn.

Amalfi itself, so the legend tells, was created by Hercules, who fell in love with a nymph called Amalfi. Their love was short-lived as she died young, but Hercules promised to bury her in the most beautiful spot in the world, and built the city of Amalfi in her honour. History books, on the other hand, tell us that it was founded after the death of Emperor Constantine, in AD447. Drive or take the blue SITA bus to the pretty villages of Praiano, Positano and Cetara. Praiano is 10km (6 miles) west of Amalfi. A further 6km (4 miles) from Praiano is Positano, popular with artists, stars and sophisticates, with an excellent if expensive array of restaurants and hotels. In spite of this, it has kept its fishing-village charm. East from Amalfi, Cetara, known as 'the tuna town', because of its tuna and anchovy festivals in May and June, has two lovely beaches.

RATINGS	
Good for kids	● ● ● ●
Specialist shopping	● ● ●
Outdoor pursuits	● ● ● ●
Photo stops	● ● ● ● ●

TIP

● Petty theft is rife, particularly in crowded areas, so avoid carrying large amounts of money or valuables and keep a close eye on bags.

BASICS

✚ 440 K–L12

🛈 Amalfi Tourist Office • Corso Roma 19, 84011 Amalfi, tel 089 871107
🕐 Mon–Sat 8.30–1.30, 3.30–7.30, Jul–Oct; Mon–Sat 3.30–5, rest of year
🚉 Sorrento; Circumvesuviana–light railway from Naples to Sorrento

www.sorrentoweb.it
An Italian site mainly providing hotel and restaurant lisitngs for the Sorrento area. Also provides some basic information on the main attractions, lists of museums, cinemas and shops and links to the ferry operator's websites.

Positano (above) and a shop selling lemons in Amalfi (right)

An example of Greek statuary in the Museo Nazionale in Táranto

White houses in the old town of Vieste, perched on the rocks overlooking the Adriatic Sea

TARANTO

✚ 443 P12 🛈 Corso Umberto I, 74100 Taranto, tel 0994 532392 🚉 Taranto www.comune.taranto.it

An ancient Greek colony, founded by the Spartans in 706BC, Táranto, 88km (55 miles) southeast of Bari, has fine Greek sculpture, gold jewellery and Roman mosaics in its celebrated Museo Nazionale.

Vestiges of the Temple of Poseidon can be seen in the medieval quarter (*città vecchia*). The commercial and industrial districts of the modern town (*borgo nuovo*), on the mainland, and joined to the old town by bridges, may put off casual visitors, but it is worth staying to see the Museo Nazionale di Táranto (*daily 8.30–7.30*), which is temporarily housed in the Palazzo Pantaleo. It has a collection of masterpieces, including a sixth-century BC bronze of Poseidon, two marble sculptures of Eros and Aphrodite (fourth century BC) and a beautiful collection of gold jewellery in the Sala degli Ori (*being restored at time of writing*).

Táranto is also famous as the ancient home of the hairy tarantula spider that caused a disease traditionally cured by dancing the *tarantella*. The latter is not to be confused with *tarentello*, a local culinary delicacy (tuna fish pie) that is a good enough reason in itself for many gourmets to make the trip here.

TRANI

✚ 442 N11 🛈 Piazza Trieste 10, Palazzo Palmieri, 70059 Trani, tel 0883 588830 🚉 Trani

The region's finest Romanesque cathedral, a charming harbour, some first-rate art galleries and good seafood restaurants make Trani, 42km (26 miles) northwest of Bari, one of the most appealing towns on the coast of Puglia.

The town and its people enjoy an uncommon reputation for sophisticated elegance. The beauty of the 12th-century cathedral is enhanced by its isolated position on a promontory overlooking the Adriatic. The handsomely weathered limestone of this three-tiered church, at once graceful and massive, changes from pink to white to gold through the day. Grand bronze doors lead into the Norman interior, built over a crypt in which is housed the Ipogea di San Leucio, a sixth-century Palaeo-Christian tomb.

Set around the sheltered harbour, beside the 15th-century Gothic Palazzo Caccetta, several good restaurants serve seafood brought in from the early morning fish market.

Street names in the medieval *centro storico* behind the harbour are evidence of the town's mercantile heyday and Jewish heritage, notably Via Cambio (Street of the Moneychangers) and Via Sinagoga. Today the narrow streets conceal attractive art galleries and antique shops. The view from the Spanish fort, Fortino di San Antonio, is superb.

TROPEA

✚ 444 M15 🛈 Pro Loco, Piazza Ercole, 89861 Tropea, tel 0963 61475 🚉 Tropea

Tropea's charms are self-evident. Built on a sandy cliff, the little town of narrow streets and pleasant squares overlooks the sea and its two sandy beaches, from where you can make out the island of Stromboli and the coast of Sicily. There are plenty of cafés, restaurants, and pizzerias, as well as two small museums displaying Roman and medieval pottery and a collection of early Christian tombstones.

A short climb takes you to the most eye-catching feature of the town, the Benedictine Monastery of Santa Maria dell'Isola, up on a rock near the sea. Nearby is the town's port, recently enlarged to accommodate visiting yachts as well fishing vessels.

Each year on 3 May, the Sagra del Cammello (Festival of the Camel) commemorates the defeat of the Saracens, when the vanquished Saracen commander was paraded on a camel before being summarily burned at the stake. Today a symbolic bursting of the camel and fireworks suffice.

VIESTE

✚ 441 N10 🛈 Piazza Kennedy, 71019 Vieste, tel 0884 708806 🚢 Ferries to Isole Tremiti

Quite simply Puglia's best beach resort, Vieste, 57km (35 miles) northeast of Manfredonia, has convenient sandy beaches, popular with families, secluded rocky coves and picturesque grottoes that can be explored from boat cruises.

The peninsula's easternmost town is also an ideal starting point for day-trips by ferry to Isole Tremiti (p. 197) and a great base from which to explore the Gargano Peninsula (p. 195).

The town's whitewashed houses sprawl over two promontories jutting into the Adriatic. At the edge of the *centro storico*, the cathedral is 11th-century Romanesque with 18th-century baroque embellishments. The *castello*, built by Emperor Frederick II in 1240, is closed to the public, but you can enjoy a great view of the Gargano coast from the outside.

South of town are the long sandy beaches of Pizzomunno and Castello, along with Grotta Smeralda (Emerald Cave) and Grotta dei Marmi (Marble Cave).

SICILY AND SARDINIA

Sicily's history spans 5,000 years and this beautiful island, home over the centuries to Greeks, Romans, Arabs and Normans, has everything from classical sites and cities, such as Palermo and Siracusa, to high inland mountains and dramatic coastline. Sardinia has its own charms—the internationally renowned resorts of the Costa Smeralda and the evocative town of Cagliari.

MAJOR SIGHTS

The Castello di Lombardia in Enna, Sicily

THE SIGHTS

CEFALÙ

➕ 445 K16 ℹ️ Corso Ruggiero 77, 90015 Cefalù, tel 0921 421050
🚉 Cefalù
www.cefalu-tour.pa.it

As you approach Cefalù the view is unforgettable—the cathedral rising above the medieval streets, all squeezed onto a promontory between the sea and a towering crag, La Rocca. This lively, popular seaside town, 75km (46 miles) east of Palermo, just about has it all, from scenery and sandy beaches to museums and historical monuments, plus shops, cafés and restaurants. Cefalù's most important treasure is the cathedral, founded in 1131 by Sicily's first king, Ruggiero II. Particularly precious is the Byzantine-style mosaic of Christ Pantocrator in the apse. For a view of the town and the second-century BC Temple of Diana, climb to the top of 278-m (912-ft) La Rocca.

ENNA

➕ 445 K17 ℹ️ Via Roma 413, 94100 Enna, tel 0935 528228 🚉 Enna

At 1,000m (3,280ft), Enna is Sicily's highest provincial capital and notable for its awe-inspiring views of the mountains, including, on a clear day, Mount Etna. The fortress town, inhabited before the arrival of colonists from Gela in 664BC, has an imposing ruined, 13th-century castle, Castello di Lombardia. Don't miss the view from the Torre Pisana (480BC), at the Rocca Cerere, site of the temple to Ceres, Greek goddess of agriculture. The Museo Alessi (daily 8–8) in Via Roma has treasures from the duomo. The Chiesa San Salvatore (1261) is an exquisite little baroque church; get the keys from Signore Armenio, owner of the barbershop in Via Salvatore.

AGRIGENTO

**A spectacular complex of ancient Greek temples.
The medieval town, often overshadowed by the temples,
is a delight to explore.**

Even if ancient Greek ruins are not usually part of your itinerary, make this group an exception. Most of the temples in Akragas, to use the name given to the site by the sixth-century BC Greek colonizers, were built in the fifth century BC, a period of prosperity that ended with the Carthaginian invasion of 406BC. The city was successively reconquered —and its name changed—by Corinthians, Romans, Saracens and Normans. It was only in 1927, under Mussolini, that the name Agrigento came into use.

RATINGS		
Good for kids	●●	
Historic interest	●●●●	
Cultural interest	●●●●	
Walkability	●●●	

BASICS

➕ 445 J17

ℹ️ Viale della Vittoria 522, 92100, tel 0922 401352
🕐 Thu–Tue 9–1, Wed 9–1, 3–6
🚉 Agrigento

www.provincia.agrigento.it

Agrigento lies along a ridge on the southwest coast of Sicily. The medieval heart is west of the ridge, where Arab and Norman influences can still be seen and the steep streets are dominated by the cathedral. East of the medieval quarter, north of Via Atenea, is the beautiful 13th-century Cistercian Monastero di Santo Spirito and its museum (daily 10–1, 4–6).

Along the SS115 towards Porto Empedocle, the birthplace of Nobel Prize-winning dramatist Luigi Pirandello (1867–1936) is now a museum dedicated to his life.

THE VALLEY OF THE TEMPLES

The famous archaeological zone, Il Valle dei Templi (daily 8.30–1, 3–7), south of the city, is where the ruined temples rise from a plain dotted with almond, eucalyptus and pine trees. Three huge temples lie east of the entrance, the most spectacular being the Doric Il Tempio della Concordia (daily 8.30–10), built about 450BC and amazingly intact. Next are the vast Il Tempio di Giove Olimpico and a group of small buildings dedicated to Demeter and Persephone (daily 8.30–7). The Museo Archeologico (Wed and Sat 9–6, Sun and Mon 9–1) has finds from local sites, notably a giant stone telamon (male figure) and a fifth-century BC krater (bowl) depicting Perseus and Andromeda.

The Valle dei Templi (left); the cliff-top town of Erice (above)

The crater of famous Mount Etna in Sicily

A fountain splashes merrily in the sweet wine capital, Marsala

ERICE

⊕ 445 H16 🛈 Via Guarrasi 1, 91016 Erice, tel 0923 869388

This medieval town, atop a 755-m (2476ft) mountain, is one of the most beautiful in Sicily, with impressive views of Trapani and the Egadi Islands. It has aged gracefully and from the time of the Elymian settlers, who came here around 1500–1250BC, through to the Roman era, Erice was venerated as a place where deities were honoured. The Museo Civico Antonio Cordici displays a fourth-century BC head of Aphrodite and an *Annunciation* by Antonello Gagini. Be sure to try some of Erice's famous pastries.

ETNA

⊕ 445 L17 🛈 Via Garibaldi 63, 95030 Nicolosi, tel 095 911505 🚌 Nicolosi www.aast-nicolosi.it

Of all the sights in Sicily, Etna is the most extraordinary. Frequent eruptions may make a visit to the crater impossible, but if you have the chance, take it.

Etna stands at 3,350m (11,000ft). It is Europe's largest live volcano, and one of the world's most active. Believed by the ancient Greeks to be the forge of Hephaestus, god of fire, it usually trails a plume of smoke, visible from at least half the island. The wooded lower slopes provide scope for walking and wonderful scenery and views. Here you will find chestnut, oak and pine, while higher up, the crumbling lava fields (*sciara*), support the perfumed Etna broom.

ISOLE EGADI

⊕ 445 H16 🛈 Piazza Saturno, 91100 Trapani, tel 0923 545522 🚢 Ferry from Trapani

These islands provide what many visitors seek: a slower pace of life, idyllic scenery, country walks, the occasional sandy beach, rocky coves and crystal-clear water for diving and snorkelling. All this is only minutes by hydrofoil, or a bit longer by ferry, from Trapani. The islands can get busy, especially during May and June, when the brutal spectacle of La Mattanza (slaughter of tuna) takes place in Favignana.

The largest of the three islands is Favignana. The Grotta del Genovese, on Levanzo, has some of the oldest-known wall paintings in Sicily, dating from 10,000 to 6000BC. These can be visited overland via a footpath or, more easily, by sea. Marettimo has the highest peak of the three, Pizzo Falcone, at 884m (2,900ft).

ISOLE EOLIE

⊕ 445 L15 🛈 Via Vittorio Emanuele 202, 98155 Lipari, tel 0909 880095 🚢 Ferry from Milazzo or Naples

Each island in this fascinating archipelago has its attraction: Alicudi and Filicudi—remoteness and tranquillity; Panarea—beauty and sophistication; Salina (the movie *Il Postino* was filmed here)—Malvasia wine; Stromboli and Vulcano—the excitement of volcanic islands; and Lipari—encounters with the islands' ancient past. Most of the islands have beaches; all have rocky coves and inlets perfect for sun-bathing, swimming, and diving.

The islands were originally volcanic but now only Stromboli and, to a lesser extent, Vulcano show signs of activity. Lipari's Museo Archeologico Eoliano, near the duomo, houses an important collection of Greek theatrical masks, some beautiful fourth-century BC *kraters* (bowls) and carved obsidian, a type of volcanic glass that in the Neolithic period was traded for its sharp cutting edges and was the source of Lipari's wealth.

The islands become very busy in July and August. Lipari is the largest and most developed, while the more remote and less accessible Alicudi and Filicudi are comparatively untouched by the tourist trade.

MARSALA

⊕ 445 H17 🛈 Via IX Maggio 100, 91025 Marsala, tel 0923 714097 🛈 Marsala www.prolocomarsala.org

For wine lovers, a visit to the heart of Sicily's famous wine-producing region is a must. The town has another claim to fame: It was here, in May 1860, that Garibaldi and the One Thousand landed at the start of the campaign to unify Italy. It is also a good place from which to visit the island of Mozia, site of an important Phoenician colony.

Marsala is surrounded by vineyards, on Cape Lilibeo, Sicily's westernmost promontory. Site of the ancient Carthaginian colony of Lilybaeum, the historic quarter is in the northwest of town, next to the Roman archaeological site. The Museo Archeologico (daily 9–1.30, Wed and Sun 9–1.30, 4–7) has finds from the site as well as the only Punic battleship ever found, dredged from the sea bed north of Marsala and dating from third century BC.

Museo Garibaldi (Tue–Sun 9–1.30, 4–8) displays items relating to the Risorgimento, including an important painting by Renato Guttuso, La Battaglia di Ponte dell'Ammiraglio. The Museo degli Arazzi Fiamminghi (Tue–Sun 9–1, 4–7) has 16th-century Flemish tapestries.

Marsala's reputation has been damaged by overproduction of inferior sweet wines, but the authentic Marsala wine can still be sampled in enoteche (cellars).

If you have time, visit the Convento del Carmine, a 12th-century Carmelite monastery (daily 10–1, 4–7).

Elaborate balconies on the Via Corrado Nicolaci in Noto

Detail of a mosaic in the Villa Imperiale at Piazza Armerina

Ruins of an ancient temple at Selinunte

THE SIGHTS

MONREALE

✚ 445 J16   ℹ Salita Belmonte 43, Villa Igea, 90142 Palermo, tel 0916 398011

The hillside town of Monreale, 8km (5 miles) southwest of Palermo, has treasures to equal those of the capital. The Norman cathedral is the greatest monument to the Normans in Sicily, an inspiring sight, with stunning mosaics.

Monreale is set on the lower slopes of the hills that surround Palermo, with views to the sea beyond. There are some attractive piazzas and cafés and a massive central 12th-century cathedral. Designed to impress, it was commissioned by William II in an attempt to undermine the influence of his rival, the Archbishop of Palermo, whose power base was the less impressive cathedral of Palermo. Glittering mosaics cover almost every surface of the interior, culminating in the main apse with Christ Pantocrator with angels and saints. Climb the stairs near the right aisle for a view of the Gulf of Palermo, Monreale and the beautiful, mesmerizing cloisters of the former 12th-century Benedictine abbey.

NOTO

✚ 445 L18   ℹ Piazza le XVI Maggio, 96117 Noto, tel 0931 573779   ▣ Noto

The golden façades of Noto's handsome buildings are masterpieces of Sicilian baroque architecture. The town is also known for its almond pastries and its wine, notably Moscato di Noto. In May, Via Corrado Nicolaci is carpeted with flowers for the Primavera Barocca (Baroque Spring) flower festival.

The town lies on the slope of Colle delle Meti, 32km (20 miles) south of Siracusa, and was designed and built from scratch by Giuseppe Lanza after the original town was destroyed by an earthquake in 1693. His careful planning produced a neat and ordered town, with many magnificent buildings. The local stone, although attractive, is not durable; the collapse of the cathedral dome in 1996 was a wake-up call and now many buildings are shrouded in scaffolding while repairs are carried out. The baroque Palazzo Ducezio is wonderfully proportioned and has a beautiful portico; ask to see the Sala degli Specchi (Hall of Mirrors), which displays the text of a telegram from Garibaldi to the patriots of Noto, and a fresco by Antonio Mazza. Other highlights include the balconies of the Palazzo Villadorata, with carved angels, lions, horses and mythical creatures, the duomo, and the Church of San Domenico, by Rosario Gagliardi.

PIAZZA ARMERINA (VILLA DEL CASALE)

✚ 445 L17   ℹ Via Cavour 15, 94015, tel 0935 680201

Piazza Armerina, a small town in the Erei Mountains, is famous for the Roman mosaics in the third-century AD Villa del Casale, at the foot of Monte Mangone, 5km (3 miles) southwest of Piazza Armerina. In recognition of the importance of these mosaics, the villa has been made a World Heritage Site. Abandoned in about the year 1000 and engulfed by a landslide in the 12th century, it was not excavated until the early 1900s. Buildings discovered include a central courtyard, baths and a gymnasium. The mosaics depict animals and birds, and in the renowned Sala delle Dieci Ragazze (Room of the Ten Girls), lithe young gymnasts. The quantity and quality of the mosaics indicates that the villa belonged to someone of importance, perhaps Emperor Maximianus Herculius (AD286–305).

SEGESTA

✚ 445 H16 • Parco Archeologico, 91013 Segesta ☎ 0924 952356   🕐 Daily 9–7; closed 1 hour before sunset 🎫 €4.50, under 18s free   ▣ Segesta Tempio

For the sheer beauty of their setting, the ruins of Segesta are hard to beat. The jewel is the beautiful fifth-century BC Doric temple, one of the finest remaining examples of classical architecture. Segesta was founded in the 12th century BC by the Elymians, but subsequent alliances with the Carthaginians brought the city into conflict with the Greeks. In the third century BC Segesta capitulated to the Romans and the city began to decline. The ruins are spread across a low hill overlooking a wide fertile valley and surrounded by rolling hills. Built into the hillside, the theatre could seat some 4,000 spectators.

SELINUNTE

✚ 445 H17   ℹ Parco Archeologico, 91022 Selinunte ☎ 0924 46251   ☎ Mon–Sat 8–8, Sun 9–noon, 3–6 🎫 €4.50, under 18s free   ▣ Castelvetrano
www.apt.trapani.it

Selinunte, 45km (28 miles) east of Marsala, was founded in about 650BC. For a long while the city maintained an alliance with the Carthaginians, and during this period, between about 550 and 480BC, most of its temples were built. The death knell sounded in 250BC, when its citizens razed it to the ground before fleeing ahead of the invading Romans.

This vast archaeological park occupies about 270 hectares (667 acres). Highlights include Temple E, built in the fifth century BC and reconstructed in the 1950s, and the Temples of the Acropolis—particularly the mid-sixth-century BC Temple C, the oldest on the site.

The cathedral; fish at the Piazza Ballaro market (right)

PALERMO

A lively, vibrant city, encompassing some of Sicily's most beautiful and interesting historical monuments. A reflection of the island's chequered history. Peerless examples of the mosaics of Norman Sicily.

Palermo lies on a coastal plain in northwest Sicily. Chaotic and noisy, it can be exhausting, but there are some incredible sights: Arabo-Norman and Byzantine architecture jostles with Spanish and baroque. There is excellent shopping on the elegant Viale della Libertà and Via Maqueda, while Via Roma has lively bars, cafés and markets. At the hub of the old city are the Quattro Canti, four 17th-century Spanish baroque façades forming gateways to the ancient quarters of the city.

Founded by the Phoenicians in the eighth century BC and subsequently occupied by the Romans and Byzantines, Palermo reached its zenith under the Saracens, becoming a major focus of Arab civilization. The Normans, too, left an extraordinary architectural legacy. There followed the Holy Roman Emperor Frederick II (Frederick I of Sicily), the French Angevins and, until the 18th century, the Spanish. Despite this being the period that introduced much of Palermo's best baroque architecture, the city began to slide into disrepair and only recently has a programme of restoration improved the situation.

NORMAN HERITAGE

Visit the Arabo-Norman Church of San Cataldo, with its red domes, and the Byzantine-Norman La Martorana *(Mon–Sat 8–1, 3.30–7)* with fine mosaics. Along Corso Vittorio Emanuele is Il Capo, the cathedral *(Mon–Sat 7–7)*; the exterior is a masterpiece of Sicilian-Norman carving, while the baroque interior houses tombs of kings. Another red-domed gem is San Giovanni degli Eremiti, unsurpassed in its peaceful cloisters. A visit to the Capella Palatina *(Mon–Fri 9–12, 3–5, Sat 9–10, 11–1)* is compulsory for the sheer beauty of its mosaics—perhaps the most accomplished example of Arabo-Norman art.

OTHER HIGHLIGHTS

In Via Roma, the Museo Archeologico Regionale *(Tue–Fri 8.30–7, Sat, Sun 8.30–10pm)* has a rich collection of Greek sculptures, including the fifth-century BC bronze *Youth of Selinunte* and carved friezes from Selinunte. On the outskirts, La Zisa and La Cuba are the bizarre and grisly Cappuccin catacombs *(daily 9–noon, 3–5)*.

RATINGS				
Good for kids	●	●	●	
Historic interest	●	●	●	●
Specialist shopping	●	●	●	●
Walkability	●	●	●	

TIP

● Driving in Palermo is not fun, and parking is worse. If you can, come by train. The station is 15 minutes' walk and buses run regularly. If you have to drive, Sunday is best, when many Sicilians leave the city or lunch with their families.

MAKE A DAY OF IT

Monreale: See page 214
Cefalù: See page 212

BASICS

⊞ 445 J16

🛈 Piazza Castelnuovo 35, 90141 Palermo, tel 091 583847
🕐 Mon–Fri 8.30–2, 3–7, Sat, Sun and public holidays 9–1
🚆 Palermo Centrale

www.palermotourism.com

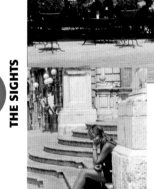

SIRACUSA

The most formidable Greek power base in Sicily for 500 years. World-renowned classical ruins and a great Greek theatre. Fabulous finds from sites all over Sicily displayed in an impressive archaeological museum.

Siracusa lies on Sicily's southeast coast, 60km (37 miles) south of Catania, divided between the mainland and the island of Ortygia. The city's historic heart, Ortygia is a maze of small streets, shabby in parts but with much baroque charm, with shops, cafés and restaurants. The sixth-century BC Tempio di Apollo, in Piazza Pancali, is one of the oldest in Sicily, but more impressive is the fifth-century temple of Athena, incorporated into the cathedral in Piazza del Duomo. Some of its Doric columns can be seen embedded in the walls. The façade was rebuilt in baroque style after a massive earthquake in 1693, along with many of the surrounding buildings, transforming the piazza into a beautiful square. In Via Capodieci, the Museo Regionale d'Arte Medioevale e Moderna *Tue–Sat 9–1, 3–7, Sun 9–1)* exhibits Sicilian and Arabic ceramics, sculpture and paintings.

In 734BC the Corinthians colonized the island of Ortygia, swiftly expanding onto the mainland. The colony continued to flourish under the first of Siracusa's 'tyrants', Gelon (540–478BC), and eventually grew to rival the power of Athens. In 415BC Athens invaded, but her fleet was annihilated and prisoners were confined in the quarries that are now the archaeological park. After falling to the Romans in 213BC, the city began to decline, a process unrelieved by Byzantine and Saracen occupations. Things improved under Norman, then Spanish rule. Extensive rebuilding followed the 1693 earthquake, and Ortygia has many fine examples of the period's baroque style. The industrial buildings of modern Siracusa may not appeal to everyone, but are evidence of ongoing prosperity.

CLASSICAL REMAINS

The Parco Archeologico Neapolis *(9am to 2 hours before sunset)* lies northwest of Siracusa's high-rise developments. Classical ruins stand in a pleasant, open setting dotted with pines. The great third-century BC Teatro Greco is cut into the white rock of the hillside. Not far away is the second-century AD Roman amphitheatre, while in the southern area is the Ara di Ierone II, an altar on which, at one feast, no fewer than 450 oxen were sacrificed. Other important sites include the Orecchio di Dionisio (Ear of Dionysius), a man-made grotto probably used as a sounding board for theatrical performances.

RATINGS

Good for kids	● ● ●
Historic interest	● ● ●
Specialist shopping	● ● ● ●
Good for food	● ● ● ●

MAKE A DAY OF IT

Noto: See page 214

BASICS

✚ 445 M18

🚹 Via Sebastiano 45, Siracusa, tel 0931 67710

🕐 Daily 8.30–1.30

🚉 Siracusa

www.apt/siracusa.it

The charming Piazza del Duomo with the cathedral and fifth-century Temple of Athena

Cloisters in Trapani (above);
Taormina's Greek theatre (right)

TRAPANI

🔲 445 H16 ℹ️ Piazza Saturno, 91100 Trapani, tel 0923 545522 🚋 Trapani
www.apt.trapani.it

The city of Trapani occupies a sickle-shaped peninsula on the northwest coast of Sicily. At its tip are the historic heart, with a tangle of alleyways, and the port and ferry terminal, while the modern city lies at its base, at the foot of Mount Erice.

Trapani is a perfect base from which to visit Erice, Segesta, Marsala, the Isole Egadi—which can be reached from the ferry terminal of La Stazione Marittima di Trapani—and the salt pans and salt museum at Nubia, 5km (3 miles) south. Trapani itself has some unusual works of art in its churches and museums

In the western part of the old town, the Chiesa del Purgatorio houses the *Gruppi dei Misteri*, 20 tableaux of life-size figures that tell the story of Christ's final days. Each is owned by a specific city guild, and on Good Friday they are carried in procession through the town during one of the island's most important festivals. In Via San Pietro, the 16th-century Gothic-Renaissance Church of Santa Maria del Gesù has a beautiful Andrea della Robbia *Madonna degli Angeli*.

The 14th-century convent of Santuario dell'Annunziata, in the eastern part of the city in Via Conte Agostino Pepoli, has a delicate rose window in the façade and, inside, the venerated sculpture of *Madonna di Trapani*, possibly by Nino Pisano. The adjacent Museo Nazionale Pepoli *(Tue–Sun 9–1.30, Sun and public holidays 9–12.30)* houses antiquities, including a wooden 18th-century guillotine, works of art dating from the 17th century and other objects, including the flag of the steamship that brought Garibaldi to Sicily.

TAORMINA

Sicily's most select and attractive holiday resort, not least because of its stunning Greek theatre.
Exclusive shops that attract a chic clientele.

The town's prominent position on the slopes of Monte Tauro, 48km (30 miles) south of Messina, provides views of the coast and Mount Etna. Narrow alleyways lead from the main thoroughfare, Corso Umberto I, on which are most places of interest. In Piazza Vittorio Emanuele, Palazzo Corvaja houses the Museo Siciliano d'Arte e Tradizione Popolari *(Tue–Sun 9–1, 4–8)*, with fascinating collections from religious paintings to domestic utensils. Farther south are Piazza IX Aprile and La Porta di Mezzo, gateway to the oldest part of town. Badia Vecchia has an archaeological museum *(Tue–Sun 9–1, 4–8)* whose collection includes a Roman child's sarcophagus that was being used as a pig trough.

Taormina became a city of high status after the Roman conquest of 241BC. However, prosperity ended when the city allied itself with Pompey rather than his rival Octavian, who wreaked his revenge by deporting the entire population. When he became emperor, Octavian repopulated the city, but the golden days were over and under Saracen, Norman and Spanish occupations the city sank into obscurity. Civil unrest after the death of Frederick II in 1250 all but destroyed the town, and it was not until the 18th century and the advent of the Grand Tour, when the fashionable toured the Mediterranean visiting ancient ruins, that Taormina's fortunes improved.

THE GREEK THEATRE

Via Teatro Greco leads to Taormina's most famous monument, the third-century Greek theatre *(daily 9–7, Apr–Oct; daily 9–5.30, rest of year)*. Commanding excellent views of Etna, it is thought to have held up to 5,400 spectators. It was rebuilt in the second century BC by the Romans to present gladiatorial shows rather than drama.

RATINGS				
Good for kids	●	●	●	
Historic interest	●	●		
Cultural interest	●	●	●	●	●
Specialist shopping	●	●	●	●	●

TIP

● During July and August Taormina is packed, crowded and expensive. Don't drive—parking places will be scarce.

MAKE A DAY OF IT

Siracusa: See opposite
Etna: See page 213

BASICS

🔲 445 M16
ℹ️ Palazzo Corvaja, Corso Umberto 1, 98039 Taormina (Me), tel 0942 23243
🕐 Mon–Sat 8.30–2, 4–7
🚋 Taormina-Giardini, then steep climb up to town or bus

Marshland close to the coast at the resort town of Alghero

The sweeping sandy beaches and tree-lined shores of spectacular Cala Gonone

THE SIGHTS

ALGHERO

✚ 445 C12 🛈 Piazza Porta Terra 9, 07041 Alghero, tel 079 979054 🚋 An open tourist train, the Trenino Catalano, tours Jun to early Sep. Departs from the port daily 10, 1, 3.30, 9, Apr, Jun, Sep; 10, 1, 4.30, 11, Ju–Aug. Adults €5, children €3 🏛 Alghero www.infoalghero.it

The coast around Alghero is known as the Coral Riviera for its production of beautiful coral jewellery in shades from pink to blood red. The province of Sassari is popular with the rich and famous, who moor their yachts or land their private jets here to enjoy the lovely beaches and emerald green water. Most of them flock to Porto Cervo and the Spiaggia Rosa, an amazingly pink beach of protected status. Alghero's aquarium, the Mare Nostrum Aquarium (*www.aquariumalghero.com*), is the only exhibition of marine and still-water wildlife in Sardinia, including sea-horses, piranhas and sharks.

Once under Aragon rule, Alghero has a distinctly Spanish feel to it, and the local dialect is a mixture of Catalan and Sardinian. The highlight is the Necropolis of Anghelu Ruju (*daily 9–7, Apr–Oct, 9.30–4, rest of year*). This funeral complex, about 10km (6 miles) out of Alghero on the road to Porto Torres, has about 40 *ipogei* (funeral monuments), including sepulchres known as the *domus de Janas* (fairy or witch houses).

BARBAGIA

✚ 445 D13 🛈 Mandrolisai Via IV Novembre 23, 08038 Sorgono (Nu), tel 078 460099

The Barbagia area is on the west side of the Gennargentu Mountains. This isolated region was once a land of bandits, infamous throughout the ages for feuds and vendettas. The largest town has little more than 3,200 inhabitants, and often the only living things encountered on the harsh trails of this wild landscape are sheep and a shepherd or two. The hamlets and towns are not geared up for tourists, so don't expect to find facilities everywhere. However, the people have a strong sense of hospitality and it is worth trying to overcome the language barrier to get an insight into local life, folklore, ancient traditions and crafts such as cheesemaking, wood-carving and the fashioning of copper and brass. Several roads wind through the region, and those who brave the tortuous bends are rewarded with views over the steep, harsh slopes and the beech and chestnut forests.

Aritzo has several hotels and restaurants and is famous for its delicious handmade *torrone* (nougat). On the last Sunday of October is the chestnut festival, when sweet and savoury chestnut concoctions are the attraction. Look for the *tacchi*, stone relics from the Mesozoic era found in several areas, including Belvì and Desulo. The most famous is the mushroom-shaped 'Texile', near Aritzo and visible from miles away.

CALA GONONE

✚ 445 D12 🛈 Piazza Italia 19, 08100 Nuoro, tel 078 432307

Cala Gonone is one of the most spectacular coastal areas on Sardinia. The rocky, barren cliffs that tower over the transparent Tyrrhenian Sea on this scenic east coast reach almost 1,000m (3,280ft). The coast of Orosei, in which Cala Gonone is located, is now a natural marine reserve, protecting seals and other species. Swim in the clear, emerald waters, sunbathe on the soft white sand or take a boat trip to the Grotta del Blu Marino, a natural limestone formation with wide arches, to see monk seals.

Set in the province of Nuoro, Cala Gonone began life as a port for ships transporting wood, coal, wine and cheese, but as early as the 18th century it developed its present role as a tourist port. In the peak season it hums with chic yachts, boats and ferries going back and forth to the bays and coves. One of the most secluded but most popular coves, Cala Luna, can be reached only from the sea or by a long walk through the scenic mainland.

Dorgali, in the hills 9km (6 miles) above Cala Gonone and overlooking Lake Cedrino, is a large agricultural town with a flourishing and varied craft industry. It also produces excellent sheep and goats' cheese, as well as some of the island's best wines.

CASTELSARDO

✚ 445 C11 🛈 Viale Caprera 36, 07100 Sassari, tel 079 299544

Ancient walls encircle the historic area of this little medieval town, clinging to a spear of rock on a promontory overlooking Asinara Bay. Every year the historic hub is taken over by the Feast of Luni Santi, which begins at dawn on the Monday before Easter. Members of the Confraternità dell'Oratorio di Santa Croce are chosen to represent the 12 *apostoli* (apostles) and carry sacred objects—a chalice, chains, a crown of thorns, a cross, a hammer and other symbolic articles. Twelve other people are chosen to be members of the *cantori* (choir) and sing polyphonic chants, the ancient form of the spiritual Sardinian music. The songs and processions go on for 24 hours and are rounded off with a Pantagruelian dinner.

In the Church of Santa Maria, seek out the 13th-century crucifix and, in the cathedral of Sant' Antonio Abate, the gilt-inlaid altar and pulpit.

The late 19th-century Bastione di San Remy built into the bastions

CAGLIARI

An ancient town with an interesting legacy of monuments, including a Roman amphitheatre.
Capital of Sardinia's southern province, a region of beautiful hills, hamlets, beaches—and some fiery liquors.

Cagliari is thought to date back to Phoenician days and has been invaded countless times over the centuries by the Carthaginians, the Romans, the Barbarians, the Pisans, the Spanish and, in 1718, the English, before surrendering to the Italian royals, the Savoia. Inevitably, all these civilizations and cultures have left their mark on the city.

The city is at the heart of the Gulf of Cagliari, also known as the Bay of Angels. Its medieval quarter sits on the hill of Colle di Castello. The most scenic of the access roads is Viale Regina Elena, from where you can admire the view of the cathedral and the Palazzo Reale. The Belvedere del Bastione di Santa Croce is a tranquil area that looks out over the city towards the Sulcis Mountains.

Cagliari is a large modern city, the biggest in Sardinia, but its *centro storico* (historic centre), overlooked by the remains of the *rocca* (fortress), is compact, and so many hours can fruitfully be spent wandering around. The Castello, the attractive medieval quarter and home to many of the more interesting monuments, is isolated from the rest of the city by the walls and towers built by the Pisans. The Roman amphitheatre *(Tue–Sun 10–1, 3–6, Apr–Oct; Tue–Sun 10–4, rest of year; occasionally closed for musical events)*, carved into the rock on the slopes of the Buon Cammino Hill, dates from the second century AD. It is thought to have had a capacity for around 10,000 spectators, and the pits for the lions and other wild beasts are still visible. In the summer, concerts and operatic performances take place here. If you can obtain a ticket, the atmosphere is magical.

OTHER ATTRACTIONS

To get a feel for the wildlife and plants of the area, go to Monte Arcosu, an oasis of wildlife where the Sardinian deer and other local animals and plants are actively preserved.

Typical liquors of the province include Mirto, distilled from a type of blackcurrant, and Gennargentu and Filu di Ferro (iron wire) grappa, so called because when the farmers produced it in secret during World War II they buried the bottles under the ground and left a wire protruding a few inches to mark the spot.

RATINGS	
Good for kids	● ● ●
Historic interest	● ● ●
Cultural interest	● ● ● ●
Good for food	● ● ● ●

TIP

● In August the area is particularly hot and humid, and the city loses some of its local shine as residents go on holiday.

BASICS

✚ 445 D14

ℹ️ Piazza Matteotti 9, 09124 Cagliari
☎ 070 664923/669255
🕐 Daily 8–2, 4–8, summer; daily 8–8, rest of year
🚈 Cagliari

www.regione.sardegna.it
This is the official sight of the Regione Autonoma della Sardegna. Here you can find out more about Sardinia's history, geography, economy, traditions, culture, crafts and food. There are Italian, English, French, German and Spanish versions.

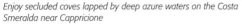

Enjoy secluded coves lapped by deep azure waters on the Costa Smeralda near Cappricione

Cork oaks in the northern Gallura area

COSTA SMERALDA

✚ 445 E11 👤 Arzachena, 07020 Cannigione, tel 078 982624

The Costa Smeralda is widely known as a playground for the rich and famous. Celebrity spotting is best in July and August. No stay would be complete without a boat trip to nearby islands such as Soffi, Bisce or Mortorio, part of the Parco Nazionale della Maddalena. The 55km (34-mile) Costa Smeralda has some of the loveliest beaches in Europe, including the Poltu di Li Cogghji and the Spiaggia del Principe.

Karim Agha Khan, an Islamic prince, fell in love with the Costa Smeralda when he came here in 1962. He settled in the little fishing village of Porto Cervo and transformed it into a sophisticated resort. This part of Sardinia is undeniably beautiful, with pure white beaches and transparent turquoise and emerald waters, but for those whose budget will not stretch to this, there are other areas that are just as lovely, with hotels a fraction of the price.

Some of the bends along the coastal roads are hair-raising, but a drive in any direction is rewarded with panoramic vistas.
Don't miss The natural spectacle of Capo d'Orso, a granite sculpture above Palau with views as far as Punta Sardegna.

GIARA DI GESTURI

✚ 445 D13 👤 Via G. B. Tuveri, 09029 Tuili (Ca), tel 070 936 4277
www.ctmcagliari.it
www.regione.sardegna.it

This plateau lies above Gesturi, an attractive village with an interesting history, ancient stone houses and a 15th-century Gothic church. Volcanic in origin, the plateau is about 500m (1,640ft) above sea level, approximately 4km (2.5 miles) wide and 12km (7.5 miles) long.

The Giara di Gesturi is the last place in Europe where wild horses—numbering 600 or 700—truly roam free. Alongside the horses live many other wild animals, including wild boar, woodpeckers, and foxes.

Not far away, on the main Giara road, the village of Bruncu Màdugui is famous for its prehistoric *nuraghi*. These towers, made from rough blocks of stone, were used as dwellings, fortresses or devotion sites and are thought to date from about 6000BC. They connected up with other *nuraghi* settlements, forming a defensive network that covered 45sq km (17sq miles).

NORA

✚ 445 D14 • Nora Sito Archeologico, 09010 Capo di Pula (CA) ☎ 070 920 9138 🕐 9am–dusk 🎫 Adult €5.50, under 14s €2.50 📷 Guided visits every hour

This is Sardinia's most fascinating and best known archaeological site. The Phoenicians settled here as early as the eighth century BC, but the ruins that survive are mainly Roman. These include a theatre, burial sites, baths, a temple and some beautiful mosaics. It is also known as the sunken city, because part of the sloping site is submerged under the sea.

Nora is on a narrow strip of land about 35km (22 miles) south of Cagliari. The *nuraghi* towers found in the area suggest that the site dates from the eighth century BC. During the third and fifth century AD the Sardi people rebelled against the Romans and Nora went into a decline. Malaria epidemics and attacks by pirates followed, and Nora succumbed to Vandal occupation from 456 to 466AD. People moved away to safer parts, and the city, which depended on marine trading for survival, declined further still. In the seventh century the city was

turned into a defensive fortress, but bands of Arabs attacked it from the sea and the few inhabitants left could no longer resist.

Be sure to see the Roman mosaics in the Terme di Levante, dating from the fourth century AD, and the foundations of the Punic Temple of Tanit.

PARCO NAZIONALE DEL GENNARGENTU

✚ 445 D13 👤 Piazza Italia 19, 08100 Nuoro, tel 0784 30083; summer only 🚆 Ferrovie Sardegna railway calls at several stations (timetables for the Trenino Verde at FS rail offices or travel agents, tel 800 460220, www.trenino verde.com)
www.parcogennargentu.it

This park is one of the last great Mediterranean wildernesses, characterized by cropped, bare valleys and grazing animals. Explore cork, walnut, hazelnut and chestnut woods in the valleys. Wild boar are prolific, along with hares, foxes, moufflons (wild mountain sheep) and wild cats, while majestic golden eagles soar through the intense blue skies over the highest peak, Punta la Marmona (1,834m/6,017ft).

The locals in the villages and hamlets work hard to maintain ancient crafts, such as fine embroidery and the making of *launeddas* (traditional bamboo instruments), and culinary traditions, such as unusual cheeses, aniseed, hazelnuts, honey and biscuits made with alcohol.

The Trenino Verde, a tourist train, links Mandax and Arbatax. The journey of 159km (99 miles) takes almost five hours and can be broken up with overnight stops.

For a delightful trek within the park, take the 3- to 4-hour walk to the Cala Luna, one of the most beautiful beaches on the island, passing through woods and by caves and waterfalls.

This chapter gives information on things to do in Italy other than sightseeing. Italy's best shops, arts venues, nightlife, activities and events are listed region by region.

What to Do

SHOPPING

Shopping, an essential part of the *bella figura*, is taken seriously by both men and women in Italy, where quality is the focus and personal service reigns supreme. It's seen at its best in the rich north of the country, particularly in Milan, Florence, Turin, Rome and Bologna, but every provincial capital has its fair share of stylish shops, and you'll find some nice surprises in even the smallest towns. In design and fashion, the big names have conquered the world, but there's more to retail therapy than haute couture and designer labels. Craftsmanship is highly valued and everything from furniture to underwear can still be made to order. You will certainly find a greater selection of the goods that Italy exports world-wide at better prices, but the back streets are the place to go to find the tiny stores and workshops selling souvenirs and self-indulgent purchases.

Out-of-town shopping arcades, outlet stores and factory shops are slowly making an appearance, while towns traditionally associated with a particular product—ceramics, silk, jewellery—have a huge choice at excellent prices. Wine, food and olive oil is sold direct and you'll be able to taste and buy other local food products at one of the many summertime *sagre*, food festivals (p. 234).

MARKETS

There are daily food markets in provincial and regional capitals and other large towns. They generally take place in a purpose-built market hall or in a specific piazza or street, selling meat, groceries, fish, dairy products, fruit and vegetables. Where there's a daily food market, the weekly market will be devoted to clothes, shoes, household goods, plants, flowers, toys, toiletries and fabrics. Rome's major markets are around Piazza Vittorio, Piazza Testaccio, Porta Portese and Via Sannio. In Florence the most prominent are Mercato Centrale, Mercato di Sant'Ambrogio and Mercato Nuovo. In Venice, head for Rialto, a famous focal point for trade since the 10th century.

CHAIN STORES

NAME	Menswear	Womenswear	For children	Shoes	Cosmetics and toiletries	Sports equipment and clothes	Accessories	Household	Books, music and DVDs	Perfume	HEAD OFFICE
Beauty Point					✓					✓	06 904 0631
Benetton	✓	✓	✓								0422 519111
BluNauta	✓	✓					✓				06 696421
Cisalfa						✓					035 455 6111
Coin	✓	✓	✓	✓	✓	✓	✓	✓		✓	041 239 8000
Etam	✓	✓	✓				✓				33 1 5590 7575
Ethic		✓									06 41200621
Felrinelli									✓		02 725721
Foot Locker				✓		✓					02 4528 1314
Frette			✓					✓			039 60461
Furla				✓			✓				051 620 2711
Geox				✓							0423 282529
Intimissimi	✓	✓									06 6830 1784
Mandarina Duck							✓				51 764411
Mariella Burani		✓									0522 373131
Oviesse			✓								039 651638
Prénatal	✓	✓	✓								0423 9251
Replay	✓	✓	✓	✓	✓	✓	✓	✓		✓	041 239 8000
Stefanel		✓									0422 8191
Upim	✓	✓	✓	✓	✓	✓	✓	✓		✓	06 446 5579

DEPARTMENT STORES

Department stores have been slow to catch on in Italy, even though the main chains have been around for a number of years. Standa and Upim cover the lower end of the scale, and are found in provincial capitals as well as major cities, while COIN and Rinascente, found only in larger towns and cities, are classier.

SUPERSTORES

Superstores are becoming more widespread and concentrate on food, household items and white goods. They are found on the outskirts of middle- to large-sized towns and cities, along with factory outlets.

OPENING HOURS

These are fairly standard and apply for most of the year, but be prepared for erratic changes.

● Supermarkets, larger stores and tourist-oriented shops generally stay open all day (orario continuato).

● Shops are open from 8.30–1 and 5.30–7 Monday–Saturday.

● Clothes shops may not open until 10.

● Only food shops are open on Monday mornings and they often close on Wednesday afternoons.

● Hours may change from mid-June till the end of August; some shops close completely when their owners go on holiday, while others stay open later for visitors.

● Small shops may close for anything from a week to a month during July and August when Italians are on holiday.

● A chemist (farmacia) somewhere around the area you are staying in will be open for prescriptions 24 hours a day; this is done on a rota system and chemists post addresses and opening times in their windows.

WHAT TO BUY

Handicrafts

Italy has a strong artisan tradition that continues to flourish. There is a huge range of regional handicrafts to seek out, such as olive-wood bowls and plates in Tuscany and Murano glass in Venice, with many products only available

WHAT TO DO

As well as individual designer boutiques and small specialist shops, Italy, like most other Western European countries, has its fair share of chain stores. The most renowned Italian export is Benetton, who have more than 300 stores in their home country. You will encounter branches of chain stores listed in the chart below in shopping districts and malls throughout Italy.

NUMBER OF SHOPS	DESCRIPTION	SHOP WEBSITE
70	Glossy cosmetics store, selling all the best-known brands at bargain prices.	www.beautypoint.it
300	Some of the best and most affordable casualwear in Italy.	www.benetton.com
80	Simple designs, good-quality fabrics and good all-round value.	www.blunauta.it
200	All the well-known brands of sportswear, sports equipment and trainers.	www.cisalfa.com
79	A department store selling mid-range to elegant stock.	www.coin.it
24	French version of H&M; less hip, but affordable and imaginative.	www.etam.com
29	Cool, cheap and original, with a focus on vintage looks and ethnic fabrics.	www.ethic.it
54	One of the best bookshops in Italy, with regular book launches by writers.	www.lafeltrinelli.it
99	All the trainers you could ever want under one roof.	www.footlocker-europe.com
41	Beautifully crafted linens for the home, and enticing nightwear.	www.frette.it
83	Handcrafted leather bags and footwear with an ultra modern twist.	www.furla.it
105	Modern styles with soles that keep water out, but let your feet breathe.	www.geox.com
447	Cute and indulgent underwear at affordable prices.	www.intimissimi.it
61	Functional, high-tech leather bags and leisurewear.	www.mandarinaduck.com
22	Well-tailored womenswear–from romantic and retro to sexy and revealing.	www.mariellaburani.it
188	Everything your baby or toddler needs in one store.	www.prenatal.it
54	The place to go for jeans and funky accessories.	www.replay.it
222	Low-end to medium-priced clothes (including swimwear) and homeware.	www.oviesse.it
336	Affordable, but up-to-date fashion for women.	www.stefanel.it
140	Department store selling cheap but sturdy fashions and household items.	www.upim.it

in the area they are made. Florence has an abundance of artisan workshops specializing in picture frames, soft-furnishings, accessories and restored antique furniture.

Paper
Beautiful handmade paper, often marbled or block-printed, are top buys in Florence, Tuscany and Venice.

Ceramics
Ceramics and pottery are produced all over Italy with designs and glazes varying from region to region. The little town of Deruta in Umbria is overflowing with workshops. You can buy ceramics all over the country, but there's more choice and items are cheaper to buy in their hometown. Other top places for ceramics are Santo Stefano di Camastra on the north coast of Sicily, the northern lakes and Puglia.

Fashion
Fashion is the shopping focus in Italy, and you will find big names and chain stores in every major city and large town. Stores selling popular Italian exports generally carry a larger range than you'd find at home at more competitive prices. Smaller stores sell individual items with a distinct Italian twist.

Jewellery
Italy is one of the world's biggest jewellery manufacturers. Production is most prolific in Arezzo in Tuscany. Naples is famous for its coral and cameos, but there's a well-established tradition of in-house design across the country, and many jewellers will make pieces to order.

Shoes and Leather
You'll find shoes, belts, bags and accessories in Italy at both ends of the price range—don't neglect the markets, great trawling grounds for bargains.

Linens and Underwear
Italian women see luxurious underwear as their birthright,

and you'll find plenty to choose from among the wisps of silk, satin and lace. Como is a major silk-producing town—a lot goes to Milan designers, but there's a huge amount on sale at source, too.

Food and Wine
Every region has its own unique brands of local food and wine, available in food shops, markets or deli-catessens. Buy such items when you see them—move on 20km (32 miles) and you may be out of the production area.

WHAT TO DO

DESIGNER LABELS			
DESIGNER	**LINES**	**MAJOR STORES**	**WEBSITE**
Armani	Fashion, shoes, leather goods	Rome, Venice, Florence, Milan	www.emporioarmani.it
Benetton	Fashion	Venice, Florence, Milan	www.benetton.com
Bottega Veneta	Shoes, leather goods	Rome, Venice, Milan	www.bottegaveneta.com
Bulgari	Jewellery	Rome, Florence, Milan	www.bulgari.com
Dolce and Gabbana	Women's fashion	Rome, Milan	www.dolcegabbana.it
Emporio Armani	Fashion, shoes, leather goods	Rome, Venice, Florence, Milan	www.emporioarmani.com
Fendi	Shoes, leather goods	Rome, Venice, Florence, Milan	www.fendi.it
Ferrè	Women's fashion	Milan	www.gianfrancoferre.com
Frette	Linens, tableware	Rome, Florence, Milan	www.frette.com
Gucci	Fashion, shoes, leather goods, jewellery	Rome, Venice, Florence, Milan.	www.gucci.com
Krizia	Women's fashion	Rome, Milan	www.krizia.net
Laura Biagiotti	Women's fashion	Rome, Venice, Florence, Milan	www.laurabiagiotti.it
La Perla	Fashion, children's fashion, shoes	Rome, Venice, Florence, Milan	www.laperla.com
Max Mara	Women's fashion	Rome, Venice, Florence, Milan	No website
Missoni	Women's fashion	Rome, Venice, Florence, Milan	www.missoni.com
Prada	Fashion, shoes, leather goods	Rome, Venice, Florence, Milan	www.prada.com
Pucci	Women's fashion	Florence, Milan	www.emiliopucci.com
Roberto Cavalli	Women's fashion	Rome, Milan	www.robertocavalli.net
Salvatore Ferragamo	Men's fashion, shoes, leather goods	Rome, Florence, Venice, Milan	www.salvatoreferragamo.it
Trussardi	Fashion, shoes, leather goods	Rome, Florence, Milan	www.trussardi.it
Valentino	Women's fashion	Rome, Florence, Milan	www.valentino.it
Versace	Fashion, shoes, leather goods, jewellery, linens, tableware	Rome, Milan	www.versace.com

PERFORMANCE

There is plenty to keep you entertained in Italy, from cinema and theatre to classical music and opera. This is the home of opera, and you should be able to catch something from the year-long schedule in a romantic or historic venue. The main concert and theatre seasons run throughout the winter, while festivals and outdoor spectacles take over in the summer.

CINEMA

Italy makes around 100 films a year, and the Cinecittà cinematic powerhouse near Rome is constantly busy producing foreign and Hollywood films and nurturing native talent. Given this, it's not surprising that cinema is thriving in Italy, and you can catch anything from the latest blockbuster to the most obscure art-house movie.

The main problem will be the language. It's acknowledged that Italian dubbing is the best in the world, so films are automatically dubbed rather than subtitled. In Rome, Milan, Florence and Naples, you should be able to find a cinema showing VO (*versione originale*) movies; elsewhere, outside film festivals, films are likely to be in Italian. In summer films may be screened outdoors, in piazzas and parks.

● City cinemas generally have four showings; 4.30, 6.30, 8.30 and 10.30. Smaller cinemas show films at 8.30 and 10.30.

● Box offices usually open half an hour before the first showing.

● Arrive early on Fridays and Saturdays, when cinemas can be very busy.

● Tickets normally cost around €7, with reductions for the early shows on Monday, Tuesday, Thursday and Friday and all day Wednesday.

● Very few cinemas accept payment by credit card.

● At busy times, some cinemas sell *posto in piedi* (standing only) tickets; there is no discount for these.

CLASSICAL MUSIC, BALLET AND DANCE

The huge number of summer classical music festivals testifies to the Italian passion for the great composers. During the winter months, most cities and towns of any size will have a regular schedule of classical and orchestral music, though you're unlikely to hear anything avant-garde or contemporary.

As in so much else, when it comes to musical taste, Italians are staunchly conservative, happy with a diet of popular classics. Conscious of their funding, organizers, with the odd exception, stick to the tried and tested. Ballet and dance are in much the same position. Unlike theatre, ballet gets no official subsidies and little corporate sponsorship, and consequently standards, even in Rome, are low. Most major opera houses have a ballet season, but the best time to see ballet is during the summer festivals, the most famous being the International Ballet Festival held in Nevi, near Genoa, in July. Contemporary dance has little support and even less funding; the best time to see something memorable is during the summer festivals.

MUSIC IN CHURCHES

Concerts are often staged in some of Italy's most beautiful churches, providing a chance to hear organ, orchestral and choral recitals in superb surroundings, often with acoustics to match. Look out for posters or ask at local tourist offices.

OPERA

There are hundreds of opera houses in Italy, mainly dating from the late 18th and 19th centuries. Many are still home to their own opera companies, or at the very least, in regular use throughout the season.

Permanent companies pay their way by putting on classical music concerts and ballet for at least part of the season.

If you are an opera fan, don't miss the opportunity to see Italian opera performed on home soil—popular entertainment with a great deal of audience participation. Shows can be held up after arias for minutes at a time while the audience show their

appreciation (or disapproval), and many houses still have unofficial cliques that attend every performance and control the crowd. It makes a refreshing change from the reverent hush that accompanies opera in other countries.

Saschall, Florence's major music venue (above)

- The season runs from October to March, with minor differences from city to city.
- Top names tend to sing for the first few nights of a production only, so keep an eye on cast-lists.
- Italian opera houses generally have stalls, three to four tiers of boxes round the house, and a gallery. Stall seats and middle- and lower-tier boxes are the most expensive. Prices range from €20 to €70 depending on the venue and company.
- Top places for summer opera outdoors are the Roman sites of the Terme di Caracalla in Rome (www.opera.roma.it) and the Arena in Verona (www.arena.it).

FOLK AND REGIONAL MUSIC
If you're looking for the sounds of traditional Italy, head for the *festas* when local bands and groups will be out in force. In more remote areas, you may catch a glimpse of some national costumes and dances. Sardinia, Sicily, the Abruzzo, Puglia and the German-speaking northern regions are good places to hear folk music.

The festivals organized by the political parties are also good for folk music, often accompanied by dancing. The *Festa dell'Unità*, child of the *Democratici di sinistra*, is the biggest of these, taking place in towns and villages all over the country. There's more

The Teatro Communale in Florence (above)

regional and folk music at some of the city summer festivals, where lively Latin-American and Cuban music sets the tone.

ROCK AND JAZZ
International bands and stars tend to concentrate on Milan, Rome and other major cities, performing in the larger stadiums. Concerts are well advertised with posters. Local rock is performed all over the country—it's at its best and most innovative in central and northern Italy and in the university towns.

Jazz takes centre stage at a number of summer festivals, notably Umbria Jazz in July and August, but you'll hear it in bars and clubs in the larger towns. Visit www.allaboutjazz.com/italy for the latest listings and jazz news.

THEATRE
Unless you're an Italian-speaker, it's unlikely you'll want to go to the theatre in Italy. Many of the most beautiful and historic provincial theatres are primarily opera houses, doubling up as venues for drama, music and dance, so it's worth checking the press to see what's on.

Apart from Rome and Milan, other cities with a thriving theatre scene include Turin, Bologna, Venice, Florence, Naples and Palermo. Most provincial capitals have a theatre, busiest during the winter season from September to April.

In summer, there are open-air festivals throughout the country celebrating theatre, music and dance. These often take place in classical theatres and arenas, or the courtyards and gardens of historic buildings—check with the tourist office for upcoming events.

LISTINGS

ROME
Trovaroma—free on Thursdays with La Repubblica.
Roma C'è—Fridays from newsstands.
Zero6—free in shops and bars.

VENICE
Leo Bussola—free from tourist offices.
Venezia News—from newsstands.

FLORENCE
Firenze Oggi (Florence Today)—free in hotels and bars.
Firenze Spettacolo—Fridays from newsstands.

TICKETS

ROME
Available direct from venues or agencies, who will charge a *diritti di pervendita* (booking supplement):
Orbis
Piazza Esquilino, Roma
Tel 06 482 7403
Ricordi
Via Cesare Battista, Roma
Tel 06 679 8022

FLORENCE
Available direct from venues or:

Box Office
Via Alamanni 39, Firenze
Tel 055 210804

VENICE
Available direct from venues or from ticket booths:
Vela
Piazzale Roma, Venezia
Tel 041 2424
www.hellovenezia.it

WHAT TO DO

NIGHTLIFE

Rome and Milan are the big party cities, closely followed by university towns like Bologna, Florence and Perugia, and major provincial centres such as Turin, Genoa and Naples. Night-time activity moves to the coastal resorts during the summer, when the open-air bars and clubs attract huge crowds.

OPENING HOURS
Things start to hot up around midnight, but many bars have a prolonged happy hour from 7 to 9. In smaller towns and rural areas, the opposite's the case, and you may struggle to find a bar open after 11.

BARS
Bars are open from early till late and serve everything from breakfast, coffee and snacks to beer, wine and aperitifs, with no licensing hours to curtail your drinking. Evening-only bars often have live music nights and guest DJs. The main objective for most Italians is to be seen, so there's plenty of posing and little hard-core drinking going on.

CLUBS
● There is not much difference between music bars and small clubs in Italy.

● Many charge an entrance fee, which usually includes a free drink.
● Some clubs make you take out membership (*tessera*). Prices vary and it may be free.
● If there is no entrance fee, you may receive a card, which

The Matilda Club in Sorrento (above)

is stamped when you buy drinks or go to the lavatory and totalled up when you leave.

ROME
The *centri sociali* have catapulted Rome's night scene into the 21st century. Emerging 20 years ago, the *centri* were originally squats, where young people occupied disused public buildings, turning them into art spaces and music venues. Non-profit-making, today they run day-time educational courses and services as well as great night-time entertainment. Importing vibrant musicians from all over Europe, the *centri* have raised the standard of Rome's night scene in general. Entrance is cheap: Expect to pay €3.50–€6. Find out more from listings magazines, *La Repubblica's* Rome section and *Trovaroma*. Rome's main clubs and bars are in Testaccio, the *centro storico* (around Piazza Navona and Campo dei Fiori), Trastevere and San Lorenzo.

FLORENCE
Many central bars and clubs are underground and have no air-conditioning. Some shut in summer, when the action moves to the coast. As in Rome, there's a clutch of *centri sociali*, organizing live music and dance nights. Opening times are erratic and, as with everywhere, things can change without warning.

VENICE
There's not much nightlife in Venice at first glance. For the pick of the live venues and

clubs head for Mestre and Marghera, or take a boat to Jesolo or Cavallino in summer. The liveliest areas are Campo Santa Margherita in Dorsoduro and Fondamenta della Misericordia in Cannaregio.

RIMINI
Italy's answer to Ibiza, Rimini has a frenetic summer club scene that stretches along the coast from Bellariva to Cattolica. The whole area is served by night-long public transport. There are more than 1,600 hotels, amusement parks, and a plethora of bars and restaurants: find current listings in *Chiamami Città* or *Guida d'Estate*, or visit www.riminifiera.it or www.riminiturismo.it.

GAY AND LESBIAN NIGHTLIFE
Over the last 10 years Italians have become far more tolerant towards gay and lesbian relationships, but there's still a long way to go in rural areas, and the gay scene remains low profile in the south. If you're looking for gay bars and clubs, head for the larger cities; Florence is particularly gay-friendly, and there's plenty going on in Rome and Milan.
● *Babilonia* is a monthly publication which has gay listings for the whole of Italy (€5.20 at newsstands).
● Log on to www.arcigay.it, the official site of Italy's foremost gay and lesbian network, or www.mariomieli.org, a prominent Rome-based gay and lesbian group.

LISTINGS
Major cities have local listings, on sale at news-stands. Newspapers also have the latest information, particularly for late-night music and the club scene. Tourist offices will be able to help, and bars are a good place to pick up flyers.

SPORTS AND ACTIVITIES

Italy's best-loved spectator sport is football, passionately followed by millions of fans. Hot on its heels is basketball, introduced after World War II and now hugely popular, with the national team ranked among the best in the world. Baseball and American football have also crept in from across the Atlantic, while the Italian passion for cycling is totally home grown. If you're a sports fan, try to join the crowds somewhere for a truly Italian sporting experience.

San Siro stadium, home of AC and Inter Milan (below)

FOOTBALL

● The season runs from the end of August until June, with a two-week break from the end of December into January.
● The Italian League is divided into four main divisions; Serie A, Serie B, Serie C1 and C2. There are 18 teams in Serie A.
● Matches take place on Sunday afternoons. Home games are played virtually every Sunday from September till June in cities with two major teams, such as Milan and Rome.
● Ticket prices range from €15 to €85. The cheapest seats are in the *curva* at each end of the pitch, and the most expensive are along the side of the pitch, in the *tribuna*.
● Tickets can be purchased from venues, merchandise outlets or agencies.
● General information: **www.lega-calcio.it**
● Team sites: **www.asromacalcio.it** **www.sslazio.it** **www.juventus.it**

www.inter.it
www.acmilan.it
www.acfiorentina.it
www.veneziacalcio.it

CYCLING

Hundreds of local clubs take to the roads each weekend, and cyclists out en masse and spectators lining the streets are a common sight all over the country. The main event is an annual-round Italy race, the *Giro d'Italia*, which takes place in the second half of May, attracting competitors from all over the world.

OTHER SPORTS

● Find more information on Italy's seven major basketball leagues at www.basketball.it.
● Rugby is beginning to make its mark, and interest has grown since Italy's inclusion in the Six Nations Championship in

2000. Home games are played at the Flaminio Stadium in Rome (www.sixnationsrugby.com).
● International athletics meetings are held in both Rome and Milan.
● Italy hosts two Formula 1 Grand Prix motor races annually; the San Marino Grand Prix at Imola in April (www.formula1.sm) and the Italian Grand Prix at Monza near Milan in September (www.monzanet.it).
● The Concorso Ippico Internazionale di Piazza di Siena, a prestigious show-jumping event, takes place in Rome from the end of April to the first week in May (www.fise.it).
● The Campionato Internazionale di Tennis (Italian Open) runs for 10 days in May in Rome (www.masters-series.com).

LISTINGS

Events are advertised in listings magazines, Italy's two daily sports newspapers, *La Gazzetta dello Sport* (the pink paper) and the *Corriere dello Sport*, and in Friday newspapers. Local tourist offices may be able to help you find out where you can buy tickets.

Horseracing at the Ippodromo di Firenze—Bet on Le Mulina (trotting races) or La Cascine (flat racing) at this complex 4km (2.5 miles) from the city

Activities

A bit of exercise is often just the antidote to sightseeing or lazy days on the beach, and you'll find sports facilities all over Italy. Even the smallest towns have a *palestra* (gym), where you can work out, and in resorts and holiday areas there is an excellent range of activities and sports to keep you busy. During the long, hot summers, swimming and watersports are popular, and there are plenty of pools and beaches. Classy resort hotels have pools and tennis courts, and some will fix you up with a round of golf. Many *agriturismi* organize activities such as horse riding, mountain biking and walking—all great ways to explore the countryside.

GYMS

Italian gyms are mainly private, so you'll need to take out a temporary membership. Larger city gyms charge a daily rate ranging from €10 to €25.

Expect to find weights and machine rooms and a good choice of classes; the entrance fee sometimes includes a class—Tai chi, yoga or Pilates.

Bigger gyms may have a sauna, Turkish bath and solarium, and you can book a massage or some hydrotherapy; big city gyms may have squash or tennis courts.

JOGGING

Italians are gradually coming round to the idea of running, though it's still largely a middle-class occupation and only popular in the more prosperous parts of the country. Rome, Milan, Florence and Venice all organize annual marathons, and running clubs are beginning to make their mark. If you just want to get out early and jog, avoiding ankle-twisting cobbled streets, try the suggestions below.

ROME

Villa Borghese: Rome's most prestigious park is home to the Galleria Borghese and is only a few minutes from the Spanish Steps. It has wide paths lined with cool pines, but it can be crowded at weekends.

Villa Pamphilj: A lovely park on the slopes of the Gianicolo behind Trastevere; the park serves one of Rome's better-heeled suburbs and has good paths and some workout stations.

Circo Massimo: Run around the pine fringed expanse of the city's biggest chariot-racing venue near the Forum and Colosseum for a workout and a taste of ancient Rome.

Villa Ada: Out in the suburbs, this leafy park is near the Catacombe di Priscilla. Its lakes are lined with running paths, a green retreat at the heart of the modern Salaria residential area.

FLORENCE

Giardino dei Semplici: Once a Medici physic garden, this oasis of greenery near San Lorenzo has some good shady paths.

Giardino di Boboli: On a hill across the Arno, central Florence's only park has some testing wide paths.

Forte Belvedere: This area at the top of the Boboli Gardens is a great place to get away from the busy, crowded streets and run while enjoying the superb views over the city.

VENICE

Zattere: Avoid the maze of bridges and canals and head for this wide waterfront area in Dorsoduro with views across Giudecca.

Giardini: Head east along the Fondamenta to Venice's public gardens, with great views over the lagoon, towards the residential area of Sant'Elena.

SWIMMING

During the searing heat of summer it's a relief to take to the water. Most holiday villas will have a shared pool at least, and hotels are usually equipped with a pool. Many small towns, especially those along the coast, offer a public swimming pool. In the main cities, where swimming pools, like gyms, are usually privately run, you may need to take out a temporary membership to enjoy the facilities. Some pools offer day-tickets as well as weekly and monthly subscriptions.

Italian resort beaches are divided into sections, each run as a *stabilimento balneare* (bathing establishment). These are private, and you'll have to pay a hefty fee. Your fee should cover the use of a changing cabin, sun lounger and umbrella. Each *stabilimento* normally has showers, loos and eating and drinking facilities, some of which are quite grand.

Beach standards are high, with sand cleaned and raked overnight, but water cleanliness can vary. Expect high international standards at major resorts, in remote areas and where the coast is rocky. Avoid swimming near major cities, ports or industrial coastal areas.

All Italian resorts have a legal obligation to allow free access to a section of the beach, so it is possible to avoid payment if you want a quick dip. However, these free access areas are often small and the beaches unkempt.

If you're swimming off rocks, bear in mind that the water can be very deep.

Lakes and rivers, particularly in the mountain regions, are cool and refreshing choices for a swim on a hot day. Alternatively, splash out and sample the mineral-rich waters of one of Italy's many natural hot springs (p. 232).

of rounds to get your money's worth. Expect to pay upwards of €65 and extra for club, trolley and electric cart rental. If you want to play a lot of golf while you are in Italy you could opt for an all inclusive golf holiday such as those organized by The Holiday Group (www.golfingtrips.co.uk) in Britain, or USA Golf Holidays (www.usagolfing holidays. com) or Jerry Quinlan's Celtic Golf (jqcelticgolf.com) in the US.

CYCLING

Cycling is a way of life in Italy, and a hugely popular spectator sport. You can easily rent a bicycle to get around cities or venture out of town onto marked cycle routes—tourist offices provide maps of the trails. Join the locals and rent a bike to get around the prosperous towns of Italy's flatlands. There are excellent cycle routes throughout the Po valley, with well thought out itineraries and general information provided by the local tourist boards. If you're in hilly country, think twice before embarking on what could be a tough day in high temperatures. Renting a bicycle is straightforward; ask at local tourist offices for further information, or consider an organized cycling holiday.

GOLF

Golf is still a prestigious game in Italy and fairly exclusive. The main Italian cities all have smart clubs on their outskirts and you'll find courses attached to some resort hotels in the northern regions.

Most clubs will want to see proof of membership for your home club and may also ask for handicap details before allowing you to play. Green fees normally cover the whole day, so there's always the chance to squeeze in a couple

TENNIS

There are plenty of opportunities all over Italy to enjoy a game of tennis on a summer evening. Most towns and cities have clubs where you can hire a court throughout the day, and many hotels inland and on the coast have their own facilities—book in advance during the summer.

WALKING AND HIKING

Italy's mountainous north is the obvious place to go if you're looking for the best hiking and walking. From Val d'Aosta in the west across to Trentino-Alto Adige in the eastern Dolomites, there's superb walking to cater for all abilities.

Serious hikers and climbers can make for the hills and enjoy long-distance, high-altitude routes, sleeping at refuges overnight and not seeing a valley floor for days on end.

If you fancy something gentler, gondola cable-cars provide easy access to

HIKING TIPS

● You'll find detailed maps of the more popular areas in bookshops and tourist shops; Kompass is a good series.
● If you are planning to go into the mountains or off the beaten track, take a map with a scale of no less than 1:50,000.
● Bear in mind that, away from the national parks, there are few marked paths and you will need a good map or local knowledge to find your way.
● Always wear suitable clothes and footwear, take plenty of water, something to eat, and leave word of where you're going and what time you expect to be back.

well-marked paths and trails, or you could simply stroll through the quiet lanes that link the villages. The mountain regions are all keen to promote their walking, and tourist offices provide a variety of brochures and itineraries.

TOP NATIONAL PARKS

ABRUZZO, LAZIO E MOLISE
www.parks.it
Straddling three regions, this is Italy's third-largest national park. The wild Apennine country and mountains are an ideal habitat for brown bears, wolves and chamois. Information offices in Pescasséroli (*tel 0863 910097*), Opi (*tel 0863 910622*), and Villetta Barrea (*tel 0864 89333*).

CINQUE TERRE
Tel 0187 920633
www.parks.it/parco.nazionale.cinque.terre
A coastal park in Liguria that preserves agricultural and natural landscapes.

GARGANO PENINSULA
Tel 0884 568911
www.parcogargano.it

An extensive limestone promontory—the spur of the boot of Italy.

GRAN PARADISO
www.parks.it
Italy's oldest national park covers three valleys, Cogne, Valsavarenche and Val de Rhêmes, in Val d'Aosta around the Gran Paradiso mountain range. Noted for chamois, ibex and moutain flora. Information offices at Noasca *(tel 0124 901070)* and Ceresole Reale *(tel 0124 953186)*.

GRAN SASSO E MONTI DELLA LAGA
www.parks.it
www.gransassolagapark.it
In the Abruzzo this park has the highest Apennine peaks flanking the Campo Imperatore. Information office at Amatrice *(tel 0746 826344/9336609)*.

MONTI SIBILLINI
www.parks.it
www.sibillini.net
Spread over eastern Umbria and the Marche, this park is famous for its wolves, excellent birdwatching and superb alpine flora. Information office at Norcia *(tel 0743 817090)*.

STELVIO
www.parks.it
www.stelviopark.it
A spectacular Dolomite park stretching from Lombardy to Trentino-Alto Adige. Superb summer high-level walking, flora and fauna. Information offices at Bormio *(tel 0342 910100)*, Fraches *(tel 0473 830510)*, Cogolo di Peio *(tel 0463 754186)* and Rabbi Fonti *(tel 0463 985190)*.

HORSEBACK RIDING
This is becoming an increasingly popular holiday activity in Italy, and you'll find horse riding establishments all over the country, with specialized tour operators running guided riding holidays through some

of the most beautiful areas.
Things are better organized in central and northern Italy and information is available at APT offices. Many *agriturismo* enterprises offer riding as an activity.
If you intend to ride on holiday, bring your own riding hat and any safety equipment with you as it may be of a low standard or not provided.

WINTER SPORTS
The Italian Alps are a major European skiing destination, with many specialized tour operators offering all-in skiing packages to the main resorts. The Alps are accessible from Milan, Turin, Bologna and Venice, while the Abruzzi Mountains are easily reached from Rome and Naples.
There are weekend, low-key resorts with a handful of lifts and a few runs virtually all over the country. Good options for a couple of days on the slopes include the Tuscan and Umbrian Apennines, the Abruzzo, the Sila in Calabria and inland Sicily. Italian skiers' top priority is often to cut a fine figure in designer skiwear, making for a more relaxed atmosphere than in other parts of the Alps.
If you want to arrange your own ski package, *Settimane Bianche* (White Weeks) are excellent value. They offer an all-inclusive accommodation package and hefty reductions on ski hire and lift passes—all you have to arrange is your transport to the resort. The regional tourist boards in Val d'Aosta or Trentino-Alto Adige have brochures, which give details of participating hotels, prices and contact details.

A.I.A.T AOSTA
Piazza Chanoux 42, 11100 Aosta (AO)
Tel 0165 236627
Fax 0165 40532
www.regione.vda.it/turismo

Riding out with the National Equestrian bureau (right)

APT ALTO-ADIGE
Piazza Walther (Waltherplatz) 8, 39100 Bolzano (BZ)
Tel 0471 307000
Fax 0471 980128
www.bolzano-bozen.it

WATERSPORTS
With their country's long Mediterranean coastline, it's hardly surprising that Italians have embraced watersports. There's the choice of lake or sea if you're planning on joining in.
You can sail, water ski and windsurf on the northern lakes and all around the coastline, while river canoeing and kayaking are extremely popular, particularly in Val d'Aosta, Piedmont, Lombardy and Trentino-Alto Adige.
Italians are keen scuba divers and Campania, Calabria and Sicily have the best underwater gardens to explore, but the less experienced can enjoy snorkelling along the rocky parts of the west coast. At many resorts you can sign up for a day's introductory course, or hire equipment if you're already experienced. Unfortunately few instructors

for beginners speak fluent English. Local tourist offices have details of schools and there are plenty of adverts around in seaside resorts.

If you just want to soak up the sun on the water, pedaloes are popular in every coastal holiday town, particularly along the sandy stretches of the Adriatic.

Health and Beauty

SPAS

With those fanatical bathers, the Romans, as their ancestors it's not surprising that Italians enjoy their spa waters. Italy is blessed with mineral-rich, naturally heated springs, and there are *terme* (spas) all over the country. There is a long , well-established tradition of using mineral waters to encourage better health, and to treat everything from allergies and skin problems to liver complaints, arthritis and rheumatism.

Many spas still function purely as therapeutic clinics, where doctors will work out a regime for different medical conditions, but an increasing number of *centri benessere* (health and beauty centres) are catering for those who want to be pampered in style.

Spa hotels now provide much more than the odd massage or dip in a pool, and you can book in for a few days of total relaxation and self-indulgence in a resort hotel.

Some spas are self-contained and fairly isolated, while others are in towns, where you'll find plenty to do when you're not taking the waters. To find out more visit www.hotelbenessere.it, with links to spas all over Italy.

Rafting Umbria lead guided rafting excursions on the River Corno in the Parco Nazionale dei Monti Sibillini (above right)

TOP SPA RESORTS

ABANO TERME AND MONTEGROTTO TERME, VENETO

Consorzio Terme Euganee
Abano–Montegrotto
Largo Marconi 8, Abano Terme,
35031 Padova
Tel 049 866 6609
Numero Verde 800 255161 (free number from inside Italy)
Fax 049 866 6613
www.abanoterme.net
www.abanomontegrotto.it

Two spas in the Euganean hills of the Veneto in northeast Italy. Both specialize in water and mud treatments, which are considered to be beneficial in the treatment of rheumatic and arthritic conditions and skin disorders.

CHIANCIANO TERME, TUSCANY

Terme di Chianciano SpA
Via delle Rose 12, Chianciano Terme,
53042 Siena
Tel 0578 68292/3
Fax 0578 60622
www.chiancianoterme.com
www.termechianciano.it

This southern Tuscan spa specializes in treating liver and bladder complaints. There are

MERANO, TRENTINO-ALTO ADIGE

Terme di Merano
Via Piave 9, Merano, 39012 Bolzano
Tel 0473 24724

Fax 0473 237724
www.emmeti.it/Salute/TAA/Merano
A large spa resort in the eastern Dolomites, surrounded by mountains. The radioactive waters are used to treat rheumatism, digestive disorders, gynaecological diseases, kidney conditions and vascular disease.

SATURNIA, TUSCANY

Hotel Terme di Saturnia
Saturnia, 5805 Grosseto
Tel 0564 600800
Fax 0564 600111
www.termedisaturnia.com
Saturnia is popular with those seeking rest and relaxation. This long-established luxury spa resort hotel is more dedicated to pampering and beauty than medical treatments, though the highly sulphurous waters have many beneficial qualities.

MONTECATINI TERME, TUSCANY

Viale Verdi 41, Montecatini Terme,
51506 Pistoia
Tel 0572 7781/0572 778487
Fax 0572 778444
www.montecatini-terme.com
www.termemontecatini.it

three springs, and the emphasis is on medical treatments rather than beauty.

A huge spa, with nine springs and beautiful fin-de-siècle buildings. The emphasis is on health and rehabilitation rather than relaxation and pampering. They focus on the treatment of gastric disorders, heart conditions, and circulatory and respiratory problems.

WHAT TO DO

FOR CHILDREN

Children are considered part of mainstream society in Italy and so you'll find few child-specific facilities and amusements. There is still plenty to do though, with the bonus that children are respected and integrated into whatever's going on.

FAMILY FRIENDLY AREAS
The northern lakes are great for watersports and boat trips, as well as walking and horse riding. Tuscany and Umbria have plenty to keep most outdoor families occupied from exploring tiny towns to cycling, hiking and horseback riding. The mountain regions of the Veneto, Lombardy and the Alto Adige have hotels specializing in family activities.

BEACHES
The seaside holiday is a major part of Italian family life. Resorts all over the country are busy during the holiday period from July to August. Small children will be happier at resorts along the Adriatic coast and in the flatter areas of the west coast (Tuscany, Lazio and Calabria), where there are plenty of sandy beaches with shallow bathing, beach games and playgrounds. Older children will probably prefer the more scenic areas such as the Cinque Terre or the Amalfi coast—underwater gardens that are great for snorkelling and spotting fish. Bear in mind that few *stabilimenti* (see p. 229) have lifeguards, so children should not be left unattended.

Take a virtual ride through time in Rome's Time Elevator

PARKS
Although all the major cities have parks, only the biggest have grassy areas large enough for children to play games and run around in. However, many have playgrounds, with a selection of swings, slides and roundabouts, and they are good places for a picnic. Ask at tourist offices if there is a travelling funfair coming to town; fairs tend to visit on or around the community's major feast day.

CITIES
Tourist information offices will be able to recommend attractions that are likely to appeal to children. In Rome, Florence and Venice you can buy guidebooks aimed at children. Cities that older children may enjoy include Rome (lots of ruins and bloodthirsty tales), Milan (some excellent child-oriented museums) and Florence (the Children's Museum of Florence, Museo Stibbert and the Museo di Storia della Scienza).

DISCOUNTS
In Italy, admission prices for museums, galleries and other attractions are nearly always reduced for children and some are free to those under five. Prices are normally displayed, but it's always worth asking if they are not advertised.

THEME PARKS
There are a number of theme parks scattered throughout Italy, so you should be able to find some amusements near your base. Some are very large, with exciting rides and roller-coasters for all ages and new attractions added every year.

Gardaland is Italy's biggest theme park, a Disney-style complex with an Italian twist. The park's mascot is Prezzemolo (Parsley), a kindly green dinosaur. It has everything from stomach-churning rollercoasters to scary space rides and water rapids.

Italians flock to *The Flying Island*, an orbiting space station, and *The World of Barbie*, dedicated to Italy's most popular doll. Most parks are open throughout the year and have long summer opening hours—many are open until midnight.

CONTACT DETAILS
FANTASY WORLD
Capriate San Gervasio (BG)
Tel 02 909 0169
www.fantasyworld.it

LUNEUR
Via delle Tre Fontane, Roma
Tel 06 592 5933
www.luneur.it

EDENLANDIA
Viale Kennedy 76, Napoli
Tel 081 239 4090
www.edenlandia.it

GARDALAND
Castelnuovo del Garda, 37014 Verona
Tel 0456 449777
www.gardaland.it

WHAT TO DO

FESTIVALS AND EVENTS

There's no shortage of festivals in Italy celebrating religious holidays, the arts and gastronomic specialities—a great excuse for a local community to party. Celebrations are organized by Italians for Italians, but they are open to anyone who's willing to participate in the right spirit. That spirit differs enormously according to each festival's focus, so be prepared for everything from intense religious feeling to exuberant high sprits. Major festivals, such as Carnevale in Venice and Siena's Palio, attract visitors from all over the world, and if you're planning on attending book your accommodation well in advance. You'll find low-key local events throughout the country during the summer. Keep an eye open for posters and ask at tourist offices for up-to-the-minute information. For an enthusiastic overview of Italian festivals, from the grandest to the quirkiest, visit www.hostetler.net.

arenas, churches and piazzas are transformed into venues for many of the cultural events. These festivals cover everything from Greek theatre to opera, dance, rock and jazz, and many run for well over a month. Some, such as Spoleto's Festival dei Due Mondi, Venice's Biennale and the Verona Opera Festival are world-class events, which need to be booked in advance.

Central Italy is particularly prolific, and if you're in Tuscany or Umbria during the summer an evening dose of culture is easy to find. The main ones to look out for are Florence's Maggio Musicale Fiorentino, Umbria's Sagra Musicale Umbra and Umbria Jazz, all ranking high on the international circuit.

FOOD FESTIVALS
For a true taste of Italy seek out the *sagre* (food festivals), where you can sample many local products. Everything from truffles to trout is celebrated, with stalls and long tables laid out with the local fare and handicrafts in all their guises. These are truly small-town festivities, providing a unique insight into rural Italian life. The eating and drinking is often accompanied by a brass bands and dancing, all rounded off with a noisy fireworks display.

RELIGIOUS FESTIVALS
These festivals are closely linked to the church calendar. Holy Week, Christmas, which is celebrated by elaborate *presepi* (cribs) set up in churches, Corpus Domini, commemorating the cult of the Blessed Sacrament, and the August feast of the Assumption of the Virgin are celebrated across the country. The Day of the Dead (November 1) is when Italians return to their native towns and villages to tend their relatives' graves and reunite with their whole family.

At local levels, every town and village has its own patron saint, whose feast day is celebrated with processions and solemn church services, culminating in late-night partying. You'll find religious

festivals everywhere, but the farther south you travel, the more fervent they become.

TRADITIONAL FESTIVALS
The Venetian festivals, celebrating the city's past grandeur, are superb, but for an adrenaline rush head for Siena and the passion and spectacle of the Palio, a hair-raising bareback horse race. Inhabitants of many small towns celebrate their history by dressing up in traditional costumes and processing through the streets, drumming and waving flags.

ARTS FESTIVALS
Italy has a lively arts festival scene, most active during the summer, when amphitheatres,

The RomaEuropa Festival

THE NORTHWEST

As you would expect in this high-earning, high-spending region, there's plenty to spend your money on. Turin and Milan are the big consumer hotspots, with some of the country's chicest and most diverse shopping, but there is plenty on offer throughout the area—the wealth is apparent on the well-heeled streets of even in the small towns. The strong northern work ethic has given birth to an equally strong let-your-hair-down-and-party philosophy, and the area has plenty of cultural entertainment, clubs and bars and some outstanding sporting opportunities. *Bambini* are well-served too, with fun parks, child-friendly museums and summer-time attractions. Head for Milan, Turin and Genoa for serious shopping and the best of entertainment, the lakes and mountains for clear air and exercise and the Ligurian coast for glitzy and luxurious beach life. If you like watching sport as the Italians do, you will be spoilt for choice. This region is famous for being home to the country's top soccer teams and a world class Formula 1 motorracing circuit. If you want to play, you will find some of the best summer-time golf and tennis facilities in the country here, while winter is the time for posing on the pistes.

Shopping

MILANO (MILAN)

ARMANI
Via Manzoni 31, 20121 Milano
Tel 02 6231 2605
www.emporioarmani.it
This flagship Armani shop is a veritable fashion megastore. Children's clothes, lingerie, accessories, and the latest fashions are spread accross eight floors.
🕐 Mon–Sat 10.30–7.30 🚇 Monte Napoleone

DISCOVERY
Piazza del Mercanti, 20123 Milano
As with many Milanese goods, the records on this stall, within striking distance of the duomo, are exceptional. Browse through rare LPs by the Beatles, Lou Reed and Jimi Hendrix, all priced around €8. Picture discs cost slightly more. You will find the stall on Passaggio Santa Margherita, just off Piazza del Mercanti
🕐 Mon–Sat 9–6 🚇 Duomo

LE SAC OUTLET FACTORY
Via Carnevale 13, 20121 Milano
Tel 02 376 0399
You can find bargain bags, belts and purses (leather and snakeskin predominate) here. Many items come with chic labels, and prices range from €50 to €500—reasonable compared to some of the other big stores nearby.
🕐 Tue–Fri 9.30–2, 3.30–7.30, Mon 3.30–7.30, Sat 9.30–1, 2.30–7.30
🚇 San Babila

LOUIS VUITTON
Via Monte Napoleone 14, 20121 Milano
Tel 02 777 1711
www.louisvuitton.com
Get your hands on the world's most distinctive luggage. Branded bags, purses and cases for the international jet set. The nearby branches of Bruno Magli and Samsonite are also useful if you need extra luggage space to take home your shopping.
🕐 Mon–Sat 9.30–7.30, Sun 11–7.30
🚇 San Babila

MANDARINA DUCK
Via Orefici 10, 20123 Milano
Tel 02 8646 2198
www.mandarinaduck.com
Mandarina Duck has two floors of funky, functional handbags and purses. The shop is close to Milan's central Piazza del Duomo, next door to the British Abbey National bank. Full sets of non-leather

PRADA
Corso San Andrea 21, 20121 Milano
Tel 02 7600 1426
www.prada.it
The windows of this flagship store, near Via Monte Napoleone, are jam-packed—purses, bags and shoes beckon those with style and money. Immaculately

turned out staff are there to help you choose from Prada's reassuringly expensive range.
🕐 Daily 10–7.30 🚇 San Babila

luggage start at around €350.
🕐 Tue–Sat 10–7.30, Mon 3–7
🚇 Duomo

SISLEY
Via Dogana 4, 20123 Milano
Tel 02 8050 9415
www.sisley.com
This is very much a flagship fashion store for this smart-casual Italian label. In sight of the duomo, Sisley's huge window displays and moderately priced clothes draw the shoppers in in droves. Quality Italian shirts for men are around €40. T-shirts for women start from around €12. This branch also stocks Sisley's latest lingerie collection.
🕐 Mon–Sat 10–7.30, Sun 11–7
🚇 Duomo

GERLA
Corse Vittorio Emanuele II 88, 10123 Torino
Tel 011 545422
Thousands of tiny, tasty chocolates lined up in antique glass cabinets vie for customers' attention. The ornate chocolate cakes cost around €15. Each purchase comes gift-wrapped—a great present if you don't eat it on the way home. Piedmontese savoury specials—as well as fruit tarts, sweet breads and pastries—complete the spread.
Mon–Fri 9–7.30, Sat 8.30–1, 3.30–7.30, Sun 8.30–1 ⊟ 15

STICKY FINGERS
Via delle Orfane 24, 10122 Torino
Tel 011 521 7320
www.sticky-fingers.it
In the heart of the Roman Quarter, Sticky Fingers brings the 1960s and '70s back into fashion. Beautiful faux-vintage trousers, shirts and dresses from €50 fill this tasteful and well-stocked shop. Check out the classy Simon Kneen boutique next door, too.
Tue–Sat 11–2, 5–10 ⊟ Buses to Piazza della Repubblica

Performance

BERGAMO
TEATRO DONIZETTI
Piazza Cavour 15, 24121 Bergamo
Tel 035 416 0611
A wide range of music is played at this old theatre, from productions of Grease to hard-hitting Verdi. Also home to three big international music festivals: jazz in February, piano in May and an opera festival every autumn.
8.30pm; some Sun shows from 3.30pm €35

COMO
TEATRO SOCIALE
Via Bellini 3, 22100 Como
Tel 031 270171
www.teatrosociale.como.it
This 1,000-seat auditorium sits majestically in its own square, between the duomo and the Nord Lago rail station. The major theatre in town, the Sociale is the perfect venue for opera and classical music.
Weekly performances Oct–May
€11–€60

GARDONE
IL VITTORIALE THEATRE
Piazza Vittorialle, 25083 Gardone Riviera
Tel 0365 296519
www.vittoriale.it

An open-air theatre operating in summer in the grounds of the magnificent Il Vittoriale villa. Performances range from ballets to classical musicals. Tickets are available from the box office outside the grand manor.
Performances 7.30, Jun–Aug
€25

GENOVA (GENOA)
TEATRO CARLO FELICE
Piazza dei Ferrari, 16123 Genova
Tel 010 881504
www.carlofelice.it
Unmissable premises on the Piazza dei Ferrari. Opera domi-

nates, but there are plenty of other classical and show performances woven into the schedule. There are some good cafés and bars round the corner from the theatre. Reserve tickets on the website.
Performances 8pm €16
17, 18, 19, 20, 30, 32, 35, 37, 39, 40, 41 or 46 to Piazza dei Ferrari

MILANO (MILAN)
ODEON
Via Santa Radegonda 8, 20121 Milano
Tel 02 874547
Ten-screen multiplex cinema in the heart of town, showing all the latest blockbusters. Many are screened in their original language. Half of the theatres provide access for people with disabilities, and all have air-conditioning. Cheaper tickets available for daytime shows.
Most evenings (contact for details)
€6.50 Duomo

TEATRO ALLA SCALA
Piazza della Scala, 20121 Milano
Tel 02 7200 3744
www.lascala.milano.it

Milan's most famous playhouse is the venue for a huge variety of classical and operatic musical performances. As well as entertainment this stunningly beautiful theatre has an on-site bookshop, bar and history museum to explore. You can book tickets and find details of up-and-coming events on their flash website.
Most evenings from 8pm
€10–€150 Monte Napoleone

WHAT TO DO

TORINO (TURIN)

TEATRO REGIO TORINO
Piazza Castello 215, 10122 Torino
Tel 011 881 5241
www.teatroregio.torino.it
You will find this unmissable theatre on the corner of Piazza

Castello next to Via Guiseppe Verdi. It hosts musicals, plays and the occasional opera all year round. There are plenty of places to have a drink on the nearby Via Po, after the show.
🕐 7.30pm 💰 €43.50 🚊 11, 12

Nightlife

COMO

LUCA'S BAR
Via Ugo Foscolo 7, 22100 Como
Tel 031 310 8672
Happy-go-lucky 20- to 40-somethings live it up at this

intimate bar that provides a warm welcome. Tasty Warsteiner beer on tap and a bar stuffed full of free nibbles keep the clients satisfied. The bar is right next to Como's small train station.
🕐 Mon–Sat 8–1am 🚉 Nord Lago

MILANO (MILAN)

ALCATRAZ
Via Valtellina 25, 20121 Milano
Tel 02 6901 6352
www.alcatrazmilano.com
This live music and disco venue is rock-orientated. One of the city's largest venues, it attracts more than 1,000 happy dancers at the weekend. It is frequented by the occasional famous face and the well dressed, so its best to dress to impress, as with most Milanese clubs. It only really gets going after midnight.
🕐 Fri–Sat 11pm–4am 💰 €14
🚇 Garibaldi

ATM
15 Bastione di Volta, 20121 Milano
Tel 02 6552 2365
This wacky bar inside an old ATM Milano bus stop provides Milan's beautiful people with cocktails and dancing until late into the night. The Indian food served here is not of the best quality.
🕐 Mon–Sat 8pm–3am 🚇 Lanza

PLASTIC
120 Viale Umbria, 20123 Milano
Tel 02 733996
www.clubplastic.biz
This buzzing disco for gay and straight revellers has a drag night on Tuesday. Even after 30 years it remains a popular and busy venue, but it's only open three nights a week.
🕐 Thu–Sat 11pm–4 am 💰 €12
🚇 Duomo

POGUE MAHONE
1 Via Salmini, 20135 Milano
Tel 02 5830 9726
Lots of Brits, Irish and Australians hang out at this friendly Irish pub. Watch football matches on the big-screen TV while enjoying a €5 pint of Guinness and a bacon sandwich. They occasionally have Irish music and dancing.
🕐 Tue–Fri 11am–4pm, 6pm–11.30pm, Sat 6pm–2am, Sun 11am–1.30am
🚇 Porta Romana

ROLLING STONE
Corso XXII Marzo 32, 20135 Milano
Tel 02 733172
www.rollingstone.it
Listen to live rock, punk, indie and jazz at this hangout near the Porta Vittorio rail station. It is very realxed and there is no dress code. Listings are in Milan's free newspapers.
🕐 Thu–Sun 7am–1pm, 8.30pm–4am
💰 Free entry unless a live band is playing 🚉 Stazione Porta Vittorio

TOCQUEVILLE
Via de Tocqueville 13, 20121 Milano
Tel 02 2900 2973
www.tocqueville13.it
This posh club is popular with footballers and you might spot a few famous faces. Thursday and Sunday are the big nights. Entry is easier on other nights. Pricey nibbles available.
🕐 Daily 9pm–3am 💰 €15
🚇 Garibaldi

TORINO (TURIN)

LA DROGHERIA
Piazza Vittorio Veneto 18, 10121 Torino
Tel 011 812 2414
A frenetic bar with seven relaxed anterooms and a mix of antique furnishing and ultra-modern metal chairs. The loft-style chill-out zones upstairs have inviting sofas. Tapas snacks available from €4.
🕐 Daily 11am–2am 🚊 11 or 12 to Piazza Vittorio Veneto

Sports and Activities

SPECTATOR SPORTS

MILANO (MILAN)

ITALIAN GRAND PRIX
Parco di Monza, 20052 Monza
Tel 039 248 2212
www.monzanet.it
The Italian Grand Prix at Monza in mid-September is one of the highlights of the Formula 1 calendar. Call, or print a booking form from the Monza website.
🕐 Sep 💰 €35–€500 🚉 Monza is clearly signed 20km (12 miles) north-east of Milano

TORINO (TURIN)

JUVENTUS LIVE FOOTBALL
Piazza Crimea 7, 10131 Torino
Tel 011 65631
www.juventus.com
Italy's most decorated football club. Juve play alternate weeks at the Stadio delle Alpi. Tickets start from €15 but you can pay up to several hundred euros for the best seats.
🕐 Every other weekend, Sep–Jun 💶 €15 (cheapest ticket) 🚌 The Stadio delle Alpi is clearly signed 4km (2.5 miles) southwest of the city centre

ACTIVITIES

COLA DI LAZISE

PARCO TERMALE DEL GARDA
Villa Dei Cedri Spa, Piazza di Sopra 4, 37010 Cola di Lazise
Tel 045 759 0988
www.villadeicedri.com
This old-style manor house has indoor and outdoor thermal spas. Hydromassage and Jacuzzis inside—pools, caves, ponds and waterfalls in the elaborate grounds. Deluxe apartments are available for those wanting to stay. There's also water polo and some good restaurants.

🕐 Daily 9–1am, Apr–Sep 💶 €160 for 2 per night 🚗 On minor road between Castelnuovo, Peschiera and Lake Garda

MILANO (MILAN)

CENTRO SPORTIVO MARIO SAINI
Via Corelli 136, 20134 Milano
Tel 02 756 1280
Hit a few tennis balls on an open-air clay court or have a

SPECIAL IN MILANO

AC MILAN AND INTER MILAN LIVE FOOTBALL
Via Piccolomini 5, 20151 Milano
Tel 02 4009 2175
www.acmilan.com, www.inter.it
Catch one of Italy's most illustrious clubs, AC Milan or Inter Milan, at the San Siro stadium. Tickets for a match with either sell out fast, so buy your tickets in advance from their club shop in Via Turati, from FNAC in Via Torino, online on their website or through TicketOne.

🕐 Every other weekend, Sep–Jun 💶 €14 (cheapest ticket) 🚌 Free bus before matches from Metro Lotto

game on one of the 12 indoor synthetic courts. Quality equipment is available for hire at the club. Non-members are welcome, but tennis whites are appreciated.
🕐 Daily dawn–dusk 💶 €6.50 before 6, €10.50 after 6 🚌 38

STRESA

MOUNTAIN BIKE HIRE
Piazzale Lido, 28838 Stresa
You can rent mountain bikes from the cable-car station (next to Stresa's Carciano boat port) and ride up to Mount Mottarone (1,455m/4,772ft). The long, slow descent is magnificent.
🕐 Daily 8–8, Mar–Oct 💶 €20 for full day

TORINO (TURIN)

CIRCOLO GOLF
Via Agnelli 40, Fiano, 10070 Torino
Tel 011 923 5440
www.circologolftorino.it
This is a classy 19-hole, 72-par golf course with plenty of activities to choose from. The club has a practise field, swimming pool, bar, fine restaurant, and jewellery and fashion shops. The heat tends to be quite bearable up here too.
🕐 Tue–Sun 8–8, Mar–Dec 15 💶 A round of golf is €52 on a weekday, €78 at the weekend. Equipment hire extra 🚗 Take the Venaria Reale exit from the Tangenziale Nord from Milan

For Children

GENOVA (GENOA)

LA CITTÀ DEI BAMBINI
Porto Antico, 16124 Genova
Tel 010 247 5702
www.cittadeibambini.net
This is one of Genoa's few sights specifically aimed at kids of all ages. The focus is on learning about technology and the world in a fun-fuelled and fully interactive way. Adults can leave their children to entertain themselves under the

supervision of trained staff, and feel free to do some shopping and explore Genoa's premier tourist district.
🕐 Tue–Sun 10–6, Oct–Jun; 11.30–7.30, Jul–Sep 💶 €5 🚌 1, 2, 3, 4, 7, 8, 12 or 15 to the Porto Antico complex

WHAT TO DO

PESCHIERA

AQUAPARADISE

Via Fossalta 1, 37010 Peschiera
Tel 0457 590622
www.canevaworld.it

The biggest of all Lake Garda's aquaparks with water slides and a wave machines. Float down the rapids on blow-up tubes, or dive-bomb hundreds of feet down the Stuka slide. The restaurants are tacky but amusing—choose from the salad bar, the pizzeria or one of the fast-food outlets.

🕐 Daily 10–7, mid-May–Sep 👤 Adult €30, child (under 1m) free 🚌 Regular shuttle buses from train station 🚉 2km (1.25 miles) from Peschiera

MEDIEVAL TIMES

Via Fossalta 1, 37010 Peschiera
Tel 0457 590622
www.canevaworld.it

A whole evening of medieval fun and entertainment for all the family awaits you here. Walk around a Ruritanian castle, watch the jousters, then eat and drink all you can at the king's feast. Crazy court jesters and some serious sword fighting make this unsuitable for the very young.

🕐 Daily shows 7pm and 9.30pm, Jul–Aug; 7pm only, rest of year 👤 €30 (discounts for additional entry into other Canevaworld entertainment sites, such as the adjoining Aquapark) 🚌 Regular shuttle buses from train station 🚉 2km (1.25 miles) from Peschiera

Festivals and Events

FIERA DI SANT'ORSO

30–31 January
Aosta

Traditional street fair in honour of Sant Orso, a sixth-century Irish monk who lived in Aosta and was an expert wood-worker, carving sandals for the poor. Today, more than 700 woodcarvers exhibit and sell their work, mostly traditional bowls and utensils, while artisan lace and fabrics are

also on available. Local restaurants serve regional specialities throughout the two-day fair.

BATTLE OF THE ORANGES

21–24 February
Ivrea
www.carnevale.ivrea.it

Dating from the 12th century, this festival commemorates the assassination of the tyrannical Count Ranieri by a miller's daughter. Today, a girl is chosen annually to lead the festivities, which include historical processions and pageants. The high point is a series of 'battles' fought between rival factions, with more than 400 tons of oranges used as ammunition and thrown from wonderfully decorated horse-drawn carts.

WORLD FIREWORKS CHAMPIONSHIP

1st week in July
San Remo
www.sanremo.it/fuochi

Italians are world-famous for their firework displays and the major companies operate world-wide. There's no better place to see what they can do than at San Remo, when incredible fireworks burst noisily and spectacularly over the port for a whole week. Look out for the pyrotechnics on the water.

FESTIVAL DEL MARE

15 August
Diano Marina

The feast of the Assumption is celebrated all over Italy with processions and general jollity, but pyrotechnic-lovers should head for Diano Marina on the Piedmont coast to see the superb firework displays over the sea.

SETTEMBRE MUSICA

September
Torino
www.comune.torino.it

Most of September is devoted to this music festival, which combines classical, modern,

jazz and world music at various venues around the city. As befits the home of the RAI National Symphony Orchestra, standards are high; great venues include the Lingotto centre and the Teatro Regio opera house.

GIOSTRA DELLE CENTI TORRI AND PALIO

1st Sunday in October–1st weekend in November
Alba
www.langhe.com/

A donkey race that dates from the 12th century when troops from Asti chased the Albese inside their walls and ran a palio outside. The Albese promptly organized their own race inside the walls—but used donkeys. This is re-enacted to mark the opening of the National Truffle Fair, which runs for three weeks—the most famous celebration of the delicacy in Italy.

MERCATO DI SANT'AMBROGIO

7 December
Milano

A festival in honour of Sant'Ambrogio, Milan's ninth-century patron saint and the city's first mayor. Stalls selling a bit of everything appear around the church of Sant' Ambrogio and thousands of people take the day off work to attend. Also called Oh Bej! Oh Bej! after the children's cries of delight in the 16th century.

ILLUMINAZIONE

21 November–9 January
Torino
www.comune.torino.it

For the six weeks around Christmas over 20km (12 miles) of Turin's streets are illuminated by lighting specialists from all over Europe. Areas on show include shopping streets, piazzas, and walkways beside the River Po— the perfect backdrop to Christmas shopping.

VENICE

As much a consumer's mecca as it was in its historic heyday, Venice, most seductive of cities, lays out its wares in glittery style. This is a city that still specializes—in glass, fabrics, jewellery, sumptuous papers and carnival masks. Get off the beaten track and wander the side streets crammed with tiny specialist shops selling one-off pieces, or stick to the main routes and snap up designer clothes, soft leather and gossamer-fine lingerie. Browsing around antiques shops and bookshops is a pleasure and shopping for souvenirs with a real Venetian twist is a delight.

Culture-seekers will find plenty of entertainment—Vivaldi's music played in his own church, opera in the beautiful Fenice (phoenix) opera house that, true to its name, has risen from the flames once more. If you're looking for more 21st-century entertainment, it's pretty low-key, but there's a clutch of lively clubs. You'll get plenty of exercise walking the streets, but if you need more, there's tennis and golf on the doorstep, or you could take to the water and learn to row Venetian style—standing up.

Shopping

ART, CRAFTS AND ANTIQUES
IL CANOVACCIO
Calle del Bande, 5369/70 Castello, 30122 Venezia
Tel 041 521 0393
There are many mask shops in Venice, but this one stands out from the crowd. As well as the elaborate, feathery Venetian classics so popular with visitors, it stocks dozens of quirky theatrical and mythical animal masks, which children and adults will love. All hand-made on the premises. Expect to pay from €20.
🕐 Daily 9–1, 5–7; closed Mon 9–1
🚤 Rialto or San Zaccaria

GILBERTO PENZO
San Polo 2681, Calle Seconda dei Saoneri, 30125 Venezia
Tel 041 719372
www.veniceboats.com
Gilberto's slavishly academic yet practical approach to recreating Venetian boats in miniature, including gondolas, is respected the world over. His crowded workshop is fascinating and you can buy boats of all sizes, including inexpensive kits to build yourself when you get home.
🕐 Mon–Sat 9.30–12.30, 3–7l
🚤 San Toma

VENINI
Murano 47–50, Fondamenta Vetrai, 30141 Venezia
Tel 041 273 7211
www.venini.com
If you're serious about buying some Murano glass, spend an afternoon on the island to browse and see how it's made. The great thing about this house of glass is that it's not too packed, so you can actually see and appreciate the craftsmanship and detail. A good balance of traditional designs, using gold threads *(aventurine),* and artier pieces.
🕐 Mon–Sat 9.30–7.30 🚤 Colonna, Murano

BOOKS
LIBRERIA LINEA D'ACQUA
San Marco 3717, Calle della Mandola (della Cortesia), 30124 Venezia
Tel 041 522 4030
www.librerialineadacqua.it
This welcoming bookshop has an interesting range of English-language guides to Venice, as well as some thoughtfully chosen coffee-table art books, popular fiction, poetry and plays. Sit down and take the weight off your feet as you leaf through whatever takes your fancy. Look out for the water lapping against the canal-side door

during *acqua alta* (high-water tides).
🕐 Mon–Sat 10.30–12.45, 3.30–7.15
🚤 Rialto

FASHION AND LINGERIE
EMPORIO ARMANI
San Marco 989, Calle dei Fabbri, 30124 Venezia
Tel 041 523 7808
www.emporioarmani.it
A typically sleek set-up by the world-renowned fashion house. Everything is immaculately folded, yet unlike most Italian shops you are encouraged to touch. Smooth contemporary music plays while customers casually flash their plastic and sanp up the latest Armani goods.
🕐 Mon–Sat 9.30–7.30, Sun 11–7
🚤 San Marco

MISTERO
Castello 4755, Ruga Giuffa, 30122 Venezia
Tel 041 522 7797
Mistero is three shops next to one another: one sells items for the home, another sells fashion for the young and the third sells ladies' clothes (including bigger sizes). The ladies' shop—Atelier—has tops, trousers, dresses and scarves imported from India, and there's a huge selection of vibrant styles to chose from.
🕐 Mon–Sat 9.30–12.30, 3.30–7.30
🚤 San Zaccaria

LA PERLA
San Marco 4828, Campo San Salvador, 30124 Venezia
Tel 041 522 6459
www.laperla.com
Venice is the most romantic city in the world, so you will want to make sure you are wearing the most romantic lingerie. You can get some exquisite pieces here, made from sumptuous materials. There is night- and swimwear on sale too. The staff are helpful and very discreet.
🕐 Mon–Sat 9.30–7.30 🚤 Rialto

FABRICS

JESURUM
San Marco 60–61, Procuratie Nuove, 30124 Venezia
Tel 041 522 9864
Considered the top name for lace in Venice. Even if you can't

afford the prices, this shop is worth a look before you go lace shopping, as it shows you what real Burano lace looks like—you'll be able to spot a poor (often Chinese) imitation afterwards.
🕐 Daily 10–7.30 🚤 San Marco or San Zaccaria

FOOD AND DRINK

CASA DEL PARMIGIANO
Erberia, 214 Rialto, 30125 Venezia
Tel 041 520 6525
www.aliani-casadelparmigiano.it
Right next to the fish market, this little family-run shop sells big cheeses and even bigger prosciutto. Locals shop here too—watch which cold cut they buy for inspiration. A number of cheeses and salamis are vacuum-packed, ideal for taking home.
🕐 Mon–Thu 8–1.30, Fri–Sat 8–1.30, 5–7.30; closed Sun
🚤 Rialto or San Silvestro

PANIFICIO VOLPE
Cannaregio 1143, Calle del Ghetto Vecchio, 30123 Venezia
Tel 041 715178
Panificio Volpe specializes in traditional Jewish bread and pastries, and is one of the finest patisseries on the island. Venice is not renowned for its bread, and this is one of the few decent bakeries—its

SPECIAL

RIALTO MARKET
Near the Rialto Bridge, on the San Polo side
Wander around Rialto for fruit and vegetables or head down to the *pescheria,* or fish mar-

ket, to see the strangest creatures in the lagoon, some still alive. A great experience that hasn't changed for centuries.
🕐 Mon–Sat 8am–noon 🚤 Rialto

reputation is such that you'll have to get here early to see the full range of products.
🕐 Mon–Sat 7.30–1, 5–7.30 🚤 Guglie

VINO E VINI
Castello 3301, Fondamenta di Furlani, 30122 Venezia
Tel 041 5210184
If you're unsure which kind of wines you should be taking home, ask the staff at Vino e Vini. You will get an enthusiastic response and leave the shop with enough knowledge to impress your friends back home. A Mionetto *prosecco* (considered the best) starts from €10. You can also fill up empty bottles here from €4.
🚤 San Zaccaria or Arsenale

MARKETS

SAN POLO MARKET
Via Guiseppe Garibaldi, Castello, 30122 Venezia
Via Garibaldi feels like the main street of a small town, and this smaller but lively market attracts all the local

characters. If you are visiting the Museo Storico Navale (p. 91) or the Biennale, it is worth browsing and enjoying a relatively tourist-free experience.
🕐 Mon–Sat 8am–1pm 🚤 Arsenale

SHOES AND ACCESSORIES

BOTTEGA VENETA
San Marco 1337, Calle Vallaresso, 30124 Venezia
Tel 041 522 8489
www.bottegaveneta.com
An elegant shop, famed for its superior leather goods. This is an opportunity to get your hands on the new lines while staying in the Veneto region. Kit yourself out with belts, bags and wallets. A great place to buy classic gifts that are practical and enduring.
🕐 Mon–Sat 10–7.30, Sun 11–7
🚤 San Marco

Performance

CLASSICAL MUSIC, DANCE, OPERA

FONDAZIONE QUERINI STAMPALIA
Santa Maria Formosa 4778, Calle Querini, Castello, 30100 Venezia
Tel 041 271 1411
www.querinistampalia.it
This cultural institution organizes a diverse array of artistic events. The Foundation was inaugurated in 1869 and has an unrivalled collection of old books and artworks. Each Friday and Saturday classical concerts are held in the opulent surroundings of the 15th-century *palazzo salone.*
🕐 Concerts Fri and Sat at 5 and 8.30pm 🎫 €6 (including museum and exhibition admission) 🚭 🚤 Rialto/ San Zaccaria

GRAN TEATRO LA FENICE
San Marco 1965, Calle del Fenice, 30124 Venezia
Tel 041 786511
www.teatrolafenice.it
The spiritual headquarters of 19th-century opera and classical ballet was ravaged by fire in

1996. After lengthy legal proceedings and building delays, the building is due to reopen for business in

2003/2004. Tickets are available from the Cassa di Risparmio in Campo San Luca.
🎟 €40 ◎ 🚊 Santa Maria del Giglio

SCUOLA GRANDE DI SAN ROCCO
Campo San Rocco, Santa Croce, 30135 Venezia
Tel 041 523 4864; 041 962999 for tickets
www.musicinvenice.com
This famous 16th-century guild

has a rich musical tradition. Its splendid interior contains famous Tintoretto paintings, including *The Annunciation* and *The Adoration of the Wise Men*—an ideal venue for the regular and popular baroque music concerts. You can book tickets on-line via their website or over the telephone.
🎟 €30 ◎ 🚊 San Toma

SCUOLA GRANDE DI SAN TEODORO
Campo San Salvador, San Marco, 30124 Venezia
Tel 041 521 0294
www.imusiciveneziani.com
This magnificent guild building hosts baroque and operatic concerts all year round. Vivaldi's *The Four Seasons* is often performed, as is music from Mozart, Donizetti and Verdi with the added bonus that the orchestra and singers dress in 18th-century costume.
◎ All year Tue–Sun. Contact for times
🎟 €21–€31 ◎ 🚊 Rialto

TEATRO FONDAMENTE NUOVE
Cannaregio 5013, Fondamente Nuove, 30121 Venezia
Tel 041 522 4498
Venice's premier avant-garde dance and ballet theatre is not far from the Chiesa di Gesuiti (p. 87) and the Misericordia bar scene. Check out a modern production here, then head for Paradiso Perduto and the other night spots. It also stages alternative rock gigs.
🎟 €10 ◎ 🚊 Fondamente Nuove

CONTEMPORARY LIVE MUSIC
900 JAZZ CLUB
San Polo 900, Campiello dei Sansoni, 30125 Venezia
Tel 041 522 6565
www.jazz900.com
This is one of northeast Italy's premier jazz clubs, with a pretty decent pizzeria to boot. It attracts plenty of Italian and international artists. Dark wood and jazz memorabilia surround the small tables and chairs at this intimate venue.
◎ Tue–Sun 12–2.30, 7–midnight
🎟 €10 🚊 San Silvestro

Nightlife

CASANOVA
Cannaregio 158A, Lista di Spagna, 30125 Venezia
Tel 041 275 0199
This internet café-cum-disco

attracts a diverse group: students, tourists and the gay-and-lesbian crowd. This is one of Venice's truly wild night spots. In the early evening it shows live football on the Tele+ network.
◎ Daily 9am–4 am 🎟 €10
🚊 Ferrovia

IGUANA
Cannaregio 2515, Fondamenta della Misericordia, 30125 Venezia
Tel 041 713561
Mexican bar/restaurant drawing a crowd seeking songs and sangria. Happy hour is 6 to 7.30pm, but it's best to come later when the staff have warmed up. Great for the young or young at heart. The burritos and fajitas are good, too.
◎ Tue–Sun 10am–3pm, 6pm–1am
🚊 Madonna dell'Orto

INISHARK
Castello 5787, Calle del Mondo Novo, 30122 Venezia
Tel 041 523 5300
Typical Irish pub which of course serves Guinness, but also shows football on a wide-screen TV. The owners Alberto and Maria extend a warm welcome and are consistently entertaining. As Irish a pub as you'll find in Italy.
◎ Tue–Sun 7pm–1am 🚊 Rialto

MAGIC BUS
Secondo Zona Industire 118, Via della Industrie, Marcon, 30175 Venezia
Tel 041 595 2151
www.magicbus.it
A brightly deocrated, pop-art school bus greets you as you enter. Expect nights of electro-pop, ambient, techno and jungle, or their traditional Saturday night when rock, pop, funk and nu-metal get the corwd bouncing. Keep an eye out for gigs by alternative Italian bands such as Articolo 31, famous DJs like Justin Robertson, and legends like The Stranglers.
◎ Fri–Sat 11.30pm–5am 🎟 €7
🚊 ACTV Bus from Piazzale Roma

PICCOLO MONDO (EL SUK)
Accademia, Dorsoduro 1056, 30123 Venezia
Tel 041 520 0371

This is a small, elegant and intimate club with a dash of

'70s-style. It attracts a wide spectrum of people: from well-dressed Italians to student types from the nearby Università di Cà Foscari.

🕐 Daily 9pm–4am 🎫 €10
🚤 Accademia

Sports and Activities

SPECTATOR SPORTS

BASKETBALL

REYER VENEZIA AND APG BEARS BASKETBALL GAMES
Via Vendramin 10, Mestre, 30173 Venezia
Tel 041 534 5250
www.reyervenezia.it and
www.bears.shineline.it

Basketball is very popular in Italy. The Reyer club is one of the leading female clubs and the APG Bears are the local men's team. If you're a sports fan or you want to get amongst the crowd and see some spectacular ball skills, games are played at the Palasport Taliercio on Sundays.

🕐 Sun 6pm 🎫 Free (usually)
🚆 Train to Mestre, then a 12 bus to Via Vendramin

FOOTBALL

AC VENEZIA FOOTBALL FIXTURES
Isola Sant'Elena, 30122 Venezia
Tel 041 238 0711
www.veneziacalcio.it

The open-air Stadio Penzo is on the island of Sant'Elena, to the east of San Marco. AC Venezia (nickname: *i fioi,* 'the penalties') are a Serie B outfit who have also played in the top-flight Serie A. Expect firecrackers, flag-waving, singing and a lot gesticulating and moaning in the nasal Venetian dialect. Tickets are available on the day.

🎫 *Curve* (behind the goal) €10, *distinti* (side of pitch) €20
🚤 Sant'Elena

ACTIVITIES

GOLF

CIRCOLA GOLF VENEZIA
Via del Forte, Alberoni, 30011 Lido di Venezia
Tel 041 731333

At the far end of the island, near the fortress, is the excellent, well-groomed 18-hole, par 72, Alberoni golf course. It was designed in 1928 and has practice greens, a club house and a restaurant. Equipment hire is available and there are lots of trees and challenging hazards to negotiate!

🕐 Tue–Sun 8–8, Nov–Mar; Tue–Sun 8–8, the rest of the year 🎫 €55 weekdays, €65 weekends 🚤 Santa Maria Elisabetta (Lido), then bus B

ROWING

REALE SOCIETÀ CANOTTIERI BUCINTORO
Fondamenta Dogana e Salute 15, Dorsoduro, 30123 Venezia
Tel 041 522 2055
www.bucintoro.org

Experienced rowers as well as novices are welcomed by the famous Reale Società Canottieri Bucintoro, based near La Punta della Dogana and the Salute church. Try your hand at *voga veneta* (Venetian rowing standing up), *canottaggio* (ordinary rowing) or sailing. Lessons are also available for children. Phone for details of the latest courses on offer.

🕐 Tue–Sun 10–7 🎫 From €50 for a series of rowing lessons 🚤 La Salute

SKYDIVING

Aeroclub di Venezia, Aeroporto G. Nicelli, San Nicolo, 30126 Venezia
Tel 041 526 0808
www.skydivevenice.com

Fancy flying over the lagoon and looking down on San Marco from above? This club has 20 years' experience and has carried out more than 25,000 jumps. One-off jumps are available after a short but thorough introduction course. All equipment and qualified tuition is included in the price.

🕐 By appointment only 🎫 Phone for details of the latest courses (Signor Michele Zanella, tel 041 961154)
🚤 Santa Maria Elisabetta (Lido), then bus A to San Nicolò

TENNIS

TENNIS CLUB CA DEL MORO
Lido 6, Via Ferruccio Parri, 30126 Lido |di Venezia
Tel 041 770801

Bring your tennis kit and a supple wrist to this fantastic club on the Lido. Phone in advance to reserve one of the dozen or so floodlit clay courts and to hire rackets, balls, line officials, umpire and ballboys. Gym and pool also available.

🕐 Daily 8.30am–11pm 🎫 €9 per hour 🚤 Santa Maria Elisabetta (Lido) and then bus B

SPECIAL

GONDOLA RIDE

Gondola jetties: Riva degli Schiavoni, San Marco, 30124 Venezia
Traghetto jetty: Campo del Traghetto, San Marco, 30124 Venezia

For those prepared to pay for romance, a gondola ride, particularly at night, allows you to see Venice at its most magical. To see the Canal Grande and the main tourist attractions, head for the gondola jetties near Ponte Rialto or the Palazzo Ducale. You'll note that gondoliers are rarely very busy; but, they are still difficult to bargain with.

Agree a price before you ride and make sure you get your full time. For a budget trip (50 cents!), try a *traghetto* ride across the Canal Grande. There are eight in all, including a route to La Salute from Santa Maria del Giglio, which is particularly interesting.

🎫 From €70 for 6 people for 50 minutes (double if you want to be serenaded); *traghetto* ride 50c

Festivals and Events

CARNEVALE

10 days preceding Shrove Tuesday, February
Tel 041 522 5150 (tourist office)
Tel 041 717065 (Carnival Committee)
www.carnevale.venezia.it
www.meetingeurope.com (The Ball)

Carnevale was Republican Venice's ultimate anything goes festival, famous all over Europe. It has been revived to become a hugely successful 10-day festival, with costumes, masks and fun and games all over the city. People flock to parade the streets in fancy dress and splendid masks. One of the hottest carnival tickets among tourists and the Venetian glitterati is for the official Baroque Ball (Il Ballo Tiepolo), which takes place at the splendid Palazzo Pisani-Moretta. If you can't afford this, there are four other balls to choose from and various other events.
🎫 Ballo Tiepolo €390

BIENNALE INTERNAZIONALE D'ARTE

June–November in odd-numbered years
Tel 041 521 8711
www.labiennale.org

Venice's Art Biennale began in 1895 as a showcase for the best in modern art, an aim it still pursues. It's based round a series of pavilions in Castello in the east of the city, each designed and maintained by an exhibiting country and only open during the festival. Artists compete for the Golden Lion award and there's a large themed exhibition, divided between the Italian pavilion and the Corderie dell'Arsenale.

IL REDENTORE

3rd weekend of July
www.comune.venezia.it/turismo/feste

A two-day festival celebrating Venice's deliverance from the plague of 1576, in honour of which the church of the Redentore was built on the Giudecca. A pontoon bridge spans the Giudecca canal so people can cross to the church, and there's a huge party on the Saturday evening, when hundreds of boats, crammed with families, take to the water to picnic and watch the spectacular firework display.

VENICE INTERNATIONAL FILM FESTIVAL

Late August–1 week
Lungomare Marconi, 30126 Lido di Venezia
Tel 041 272 6501
www.labiennale.org

A stylish film festival that attracts both big-budget movies, and uncommercial arthouse films all competing for coverted awards. Held on the Lido, where the big stars occupy the ornate fin-de-siècle hotels, there's plenty of associated razzmatazz. The Palazzo del Cinema is the venue for the main-screen auditorium (more than 1,000 capacity), but tickets get snapped up for the premieres. During the festival the Arena Estiva di Campo San Polo is transformed into an open-air cinema. Flickering images projected onto the crumbling Venetian buildings adds to the drama.
🎫 €8 before 6pm, €25 for premieres
🚇 Casino 61 and San Silvestro

REGATA STORICA

1st Sunday in September
www.comune.venezia.it/turismo/feste

Venice's biggest water festival, which kicks off with a superb costumed procession in ornate boats down the Canal Grande. This is followed by rowing races, which carry big prize money.

FESTA DELLA SALUTE

21 November
www.comune.venezia.it/turismo/feste

A truly Venetian festival that commemorates the deliverance of the city from the plague of 1631, which triggered the construction of the great church of the Madonna della Salute. A pontoon bridge crosses the Grand Canal opposite the church, and people cross to light candles and attend mass.

THE NORTHEAST AND EMILIA-ROMAGNA

Busy, prosperous northeast Italy has lots going for it—great shopping, beautiful scenery from mountains to beaches, and historic towns that have glided seamlessly into the 21st century. Visitors on the cultural trail will find plenty to take their minds off art and history in the rich provincial cities of Bologna, Parma, Verona, and Padua, where quality stores jostle for space. Designer wear, stylish home goods, antiques and jewellery are the focus, but the best finds, particularly in Emilia-Romagna, will indubitably involve food and wine from some of Italy's best, and most famous, delicatessens. Up in the mountains, shopping has a distinctly Austrian feel, as do the cultural offerings throughout the autonomous Trentino-Alto Adige. The whole region is summer-festival land, where you can hear opera in a Roman arena, folk music at local celebrations or dance the night away at some of Italy's biggest and brashest clubs. Work it all off by day in the Dolomites, where you can enjoy the crisp air and some of Italy's finest scenery, or head for the coast and bask on the beach.

Shopping

SPECIAL IN BOLOGNA

TAMBURINI
Via Caprarie 1, 40124 Bologna
Tel 051 234726
www.tamburini.com
This is the finest delicatessen in what is considered the

gastronomic capital of Italy. The large display of local produce includes fresh pasta (such as black pasta coloured with squid ink and tortelloni stuffed with pumpkin), cheeses, hams and salamis. Make sure you smaple the gourmet ingredients at the self-service café (open noon–2.30).
🕙 Mon–Wed, Fri–Sat 8–7, Thu 8–2

PADOVA (PADUA)
PRATO DELLA VALLE MARKET
Prato della Valle, 35100 Padova
Every Saturday the Prato della Valle—claimed to be the largest town square in Italy, and a marketplace since the 11th century—is turned into an open-air market selling

clothes, kitchenware, shoes, woven baskets and more. An antique fair takes place on the third Sunday of the month.
🕙 Sat dawn–dusk

ROBERTO CALLEGARI
Via Davila 8, 35100 Padova
Tel 049 876 3131
Padua's top jewellery shop—in a town with a large number of jewellers—is less than 10 minutes' walk north of the middle of town. It sells watches, jewellery and antique silver.
🕙 Tue–Sat 9.30–12.30, 3.30–7.30

VERONA
L'ENOTECA DELL'ISTITUTO ENOLOGICO ITALIANO
Via Sottoriva 7, 37100 Verona
Tel 045 590366
www.enotecaverona.com
Near the river on the east side of the old town, these old wine cellars lie beneath a 17th-century palace. Visitors have been tasting and buying top wines here for more than 40 years. There is an excellent selection, and afternoon wine tasting sessions take place daily, with a different wine to sample every week. Pasta and jams on sale too.
🕙 Tue–Sat 9–12.30, 3.30–7.30, Mon 9–12.30

SALUMERIA G. ALBERTINI
Corso Sant'Anastasia 41, 37121 Verona
Tel 045 803 1074
The central location of this jam-packed shop makes it ideal for buying picnic food to take to the opera in the Arena.

Sample the local prosciutto, wines and cheeses, or dive into the big barrel of olives.
🕙 Daily 8–8

Performance

BOLOGNA

CANTINA BENTIVOGLIO
Via Mascarella 4/b, 40100 Bologna
Tel 051 265416
www.cantinabentivoglio.it
Large, elegant bar in the university district. One of the top jazz venues in town, with

WHAT TO DO

music every night from 10. Good, cheap food. Music outdoors in July and August.
⏱ Daily 12.15–2.45, 8–2 💶 €4

NOSADELLA
Via Nosadella 19/21, 40123 Bologna
Tel 051 331506
www.nosadella.it
A two-screen cinema about 10 minutes' walk southwest of the city's hub. They show films in English on Mondays and in other languages on other days.
⏱ Four screenings daily, 4pm–midnight 💶 Adult €7, child €4.50 ◎

TEATRO COMMUNALE
Largo Respighi 1, 40126 Bologna
Tel 051 529999
www.comunalebologna.it
Wagner preferred to premiere his operas here in Bologna's leading venue, an auditorium in the heart of the university district that first opened its doors in 1763.
⏱ Sep–Jun 💶 €30–€100 ◎

PADOVA (PADUA)
AUDITORIUM POLLINI
Via C. Cassan 15, 35121 Padova
Tel 049 875 6763
www.amicimusicapadova.org
One of the main concert venues in Padua, hosting performances by, among others, the Orchestra di Padova e del Veneto. It has capacity for 600 people.
⏱ Oct–Mar 💶 €10–€22 ◎

VERONA
STIMMATE
Via Montanari 1, 37121 Verona
Tel 045 800 4843
The only cinema in the city

showing English-language films. It is walking distance from the piazza and the Arena.
⏱ English-language films Tue only
💶 €5.20 ◎

Nightlife

BOLOGNA
CLAURICAUNE
Via Zamboni 18, 40126 Bologna
Tel 051 263419
A bar on the edge of the university district, near the two towers. Its is regularly packed to bursting with students and young townspeople. On warmer evenings they spill out into the arcades in front.
⏱ Mon–Fri 12–2am, Sat 2pm–2am

ROSAROSE
Via Clavature 18, 40125 Bologna
Tel 051 225071
Lively, friendly bistro in the old market district in the heart of

town. Often packed with a youngish clientele. They serve drinks and good sandwiches—or you can graze on the food at the bar.
⏱ Wed–Mon 6–2

For Children

VERONA
ARENA
Piazza Bra, 37121 Verona
Tel 045 800 3204
This is one of the best-preserved Roman amphitheatres in Italy. When concerts are not taking place, kids can discover what it was like to be a gladiator in

this ancient playground, running around the high vaulted corridors and through the arches into the arena.
⏱ Mon 3.45–7.30, Tue–Sun 8.30–7, Sep–Jun; Tue–Sun 9–3, Jul–Aug
💶 Adult €3.10, child €1

GIARDINO GIUSTI
Via Giardino Giusti 2, 37129 Verona
Tel 045 803 4029
A magnificent garden in Veronetta, across the river from the heart of town. A peaceful spot for play and picnics. Get lost in the hedge maze or climb up to the grotto below a fearsome stone face and enjoy the view across to the city.
⏱ Daily 9–8, Apr–Sep; daily 9–dusk, Oct–Mar 💶 €5

Festivals and Events

CARNEVALE
Shrove Tuesday, February
www.comune.cento.fe.it/carnevale
One of Italy's oldest carnivals (1615), twinned with Rio de Janeiro's extravaganza. More than 500 floats throw out 15,000kg (33,000lb) of sweets into the crowd.

INTERNATIONAL OPERA FESTIVAL
June–August
Piazza Bra, 37121 Verona
Tel 045 800 5151
www.arena.it
Nothing tops the Roman Arena when it comes to setting. There is a great choice of popular operas, so book well in advance—and take a cushion.
💶 €16–€154

FLORENCE

After cultural overdose in Florence, a bit of retail therapy is high on the agenda, and you'll find something to suit all tastes. Shopping is taken seriously in Tuscany's restrained capital—nothing flashy, just style, elegance and discreet ostentation. Designer labels are prevalent, but there are home-grown temptations too—look out for beautiful paper goods, leather of all sorts, funky street fashion and jewellery. Souvenir shoppers do well here, with beautiful art reproductions, calendars and cookbooks; museums are good trawling grounds for these, and you shouldn't neglect kitchen and homeware stores or the city markets either.

Spent out, you'll find year-round entertainment, from winter opera to summer-time classical music, when outdoor concerts are performed all over the city as part of Florence's famous Maggio Musicale festival. To keep you busy in the evening, there are contemporary clubs and laid-back bars, with everything from a pint of Guinness to the latest house music or sounds from Brazil, plus the occasional big-name acts. If you want some exercise, you can work out, swim, boat on the Arno or play tennis, or simply head for the Stadio Artemio Franchi and join the fans watching Florentia Viola, Florence's football heroes.

Shopping

BOOKS

EDISON
Piazza della Repubblica 27r,
50123 Firenze
Tel 055 213110
Edison sells guides and books in English, but also maps, CDs, magazines and newspapers. The Internet café is a good place to sit, surf and watch the world news on huge screens.
🕐 Mon–Sat 9–midnight, Sun 10–midnight 🚌 A, 6

FASHION AND LINGERIE

ZINI
Borgo San Lorenzo, 50123 Firenze
Tel 055 289850
Stocks Italy's most up-and-coming designers—and the future is looking bright and captivating. The tailoring and cut of the clothes are impressive, but the originality comes in the interesting and innovative use of prints and fabrics.
🚌 A

FOOD AND DRINK

DOLCI E DOLCEZZE
Piazza Beccaria 8r, 50121 Firenze
Tel 055 234 5458
This old-style bakers is

internationally renowned and deservedly so. If you are only in Florence for a day, make sure you come here for a cake break.
🕐 Tue–Sun 8–8 🚌 A, 6, 31, 32

JEWELLERY

ARGENTERIA BRANDIMARTE
Via Lorenzo Bartolini 18r, 50124 Firenze
Tel 055 239381
www.brandimarte.it
The dedicated apprentices of the late Brandimarte Guscelli continue his unusual designs in silver, and you can see them at work here in the silver factory. Plates and goblets are decorated in relief with fruits, vines and leaves.
🕐 Mon–Fri 9–1, 2.30–6; closed Aug
🚌 D

FRATELLI PICCINI
Ponte Vecchio 23, 50123 Firenze
Tel 055 294768
If you want to go jewellery shopping on the Ponte Vecchio, make sure you take in Piccini's. Their lovely gold charms make a nice gift.
🕐 Daily 9.30–7.30, Apr–Oct; daily 9.30–1, 3.30–1, Nov–Mar 🚌 B, D

MARKETS

FLORENTINE MARKETS
Piazza San Lorenzo, Piazza Santo Spirito, Piazza dei Ciompi and Via dell'Ariento, Piazza Lorenzo Ghiberti, Piazza della Republica, Via Porta Rossa, Piazza del Mercato Centrale
Tel 055 234 0444 (tourist office)

Florence has a huge number of markets selling everything from food to antiques. There are also some superb flea markets. The most famous is in and around Piazza San Lorenzo, where you'll find leather and other assorted goods. There are stalls daily at Santo Spirito, selling bedding, shoes, clothing and haberdashery. On the second Sunday of the month there is an ethnic flea market, and on the third Sunday there are organic foods, Tuscan clothing and herbal remedies on sale. On the last Sunday of each month there's an antiques market in Piazza dei Ciompi (9–7). Head toward Via dell'Ariento and the Mercatone delle Cascine (Tue 7–2) for a morning of browsing and bartering. Even though you can't

WHAT TO DO

SPECIAL
SCUOLA DEL CUOIO (LEATHER SCHOOL)
Piazza Santa Croce 16, 50122 Firenze
Tel 055 244533
www.leatherschool.it
This workshop, at the back of the famous church, was once

run by Franciscan monks. If you intend to shop for leather goods, come here first to learn how to spot quality and craftsmanship. If you make a purchase at the on-site shop, they'll personalize the goods for you with a stamp.
🕐 Mon–Sat 9–6, Sun 10.30–4.30, Apr–Oct 🚌 B, C, 23

take plants back home, a walk round the plant market on Thursday mornings around the Piazza della Republica is a memorable experience. Mercato Nuovo (Porcellino) on Via Porta Rossa (daily 9–7) is full of inexpensive reproductions of Florentine classics, which makes it a great place for souvenir-hunters. The leather bags and shoes are often a good buy, too. The Mercato Centrale is full of mouth-watering Florentine delights— feast your eyes on the wonderful fruit and vegetable stalls, and the *salumeria* counters brimming with meats and cheeses.
🕐 Mon–Sat 8.30–7, 8.30–2pm in winter

SHOES AND ACCESSORIES
CELLERINI
Via del Sole 37r, 50123 Firenze
Tel 055 282533
Drop in to view some of the bags and purses that are wonderfully simple yet cleverly designed. Cellerini bags are

de rigueur among fashionistas and will elicit envious glances once you get back home.
🚌 A, 6, 11, 36, 37

STATIONERY
PINEIDER
Piazza della Signoria 13r, 50122 Firenze
Tel 055 284655
www.pineider.it
Pineider remains Italy's original and most prestigious stationer— the letters of Napoleon, Byron and Dietrich were scribed using Pineider's beautifully crafted tinted papers and inks. It also stocks exquisite leather-bound notebooks and accessories including seals.
🕐 Tue–Sat 10–7, Mon 3–7 🚌 23

Performance

CINEMA
CINEMA GOLDONI
Via Serragli 109, 50124 Firenze
Tel 055 222437
The Goldoni is one of only three Florentine cinemas to show films in their original language.
🕐 Contact for latest details 🎫 Adult €7, child €4.50 🚌 36, 37

CLASSICAL MUSIC, DANCE, OPERA
ESTATE FIESOLANA (OPEN-AIR SUMMER CONCERTS IN FIESOLE)
Piazza del Mercato 5, Fiesole, 50014 Firenze
Tel 800 414240
www.estatefiesolana.it
Sunset concerts and operatic productions are held at the 1st-century Teatro Romano during the summer months. Book in advance and then head for the verdant, tranquil Fiesole hills, above the city. Tickets also available at Via Alamanni 39 (*tel 055 210804*).
🕐 Jun–Sep 🎫 €52 🚌 7
Fiesole central

TEATRO COMMUNALE
Corso Italia 16, 50123 Firenze
Tel 055 211158
Tel 199 109910
www.maggiofiorentino.com
Florence's major venue for all things orchestral, balletic and operatic. The winter concert season runs from January to March, while opera and ballet is staged between September and March. Expect old

favourites like *Macbeth* and *Coppelia* as well as seminal composers' work from Bach to Wagner.
🎫 €22–€76 🚌 A, B

TEATRO GOLDONI
Via Santa Maria 12, 50125 Firenze
Tel 055 233 5518
Tel 199 109910
www.maggiofiorentino.com
This famous old theatre has a

capacity of 1,500. They stage opera and ballet productions such as *Carmen* and *Barbablù*, as well as various classical concerts.

€16.50 11, 36, 37

CONTEMPORARY LIVE MUSIC
PINOCCHIO LIVE JAZZ
Viale Giannotti 13, 50126 Firenze
Tel 055 683388
www.pinocchiojazz.it
Jazz musos will love this place as it attracts some of Italy's top artists, who can be heard during the club's annual two-season schedule. Members nod approvingly in this smoky venue while the musicians blow, brush and noodle their instruments into the night.

Membership fee plus €8 31, 32

SASCHALL
Lungarno Aldo Moro 3, 50136 Firenze
Tel 055 650 4112
www.saschall.it
Florence's leading music venue hosts big-name rock/pop acts and famous musicals. Expect to see international artists like Tori Amos and Italian stars such as Luca Carboni and PFM.

Recent musical productions have included *Grease* and *Irma la Dolce*.

€27, €19 3, 14, 31, 32, 34

THEATRE
TEATRO PERGOLA
Via della Pergola 12–32, 50121 Firenze
Tel 055 226 4335
www.pergola.firenze.it
Well-known theatre productions are regularly held in the sumptuous main *Sala* and the elegant *Saloncino*. In addition to staging Italian classics by the likes of d'Annunzio and De Filippo, many English- and French-language playwrights, including Wilde, Berkoff, Hugo and Feydeau, are also showcased.

Theatre productions Wed–Sat, concerts Sat afternoons, Sun evenings
€13–€27 C, 14, 23

Nightlife

CENTRAL PARK
Via del Fosso Macinate, 2, 50144 Firenze
Tel 055 353505
This is a true house music complex, complete with garden, eight bars, four dance

floors, restaurant and a VIP terrace. Italian house dominates but there's also plenty of room for chilling out with loungecore and smooth piano-bar music.

Tue–Sun 10.30–4.30 €17 1, 9, 12, 80

CRISCO
Via Sant'Egidio 43r, 50122 Firenze
Tel 055 248 0580
www.crisco.it
One of Florence's leading gay clubs, near the duomo in Santa Croce. In a city famed for its cross-dressing, expect to see the most glamorous transvestites you've ever seen.

Sun–Mon, Wed–Thu 10.30pm–3am, Fri–Sat 10.30pm–6am
€12 A, 14, 23

FIDDLER'S ELBOW
Piazza Santa Maria Novella 7a, 50123 Firenze
Tel 055 215056
The original Florentine Irish pub in Campo Santa Maria Novella, popular with students and tourists. Enjoy the best Guinness in town and catch up on the latest Premiership football action on the widescreen TVs.

Daily midday–1am A, 1, 14, 17, 36, 37

JARAGUA
Via Erta Canina 12/r, 50125 Firenze
Tel 055 234 3600
www.jaragua.it
Italy's first exclusively Latino music club is bags of fun and free to get into. The spicy South American food also appeals to the 30-something crowd. For those who don't know how to dance salsa or merengue, there are lessons available as well as many willing tutors on the dance floor.

Daily 9.30pm–3am C, D

LIDO
Lungarno Pecori Piraldi 1, 50122 Firenze
Tel 055 234 2726
This swanky bar along the River Arno has the feel of a colonial ship—you can even hire boats from here. Cocktails and innovative snacks are consumed to a sophisticated soundtrack of lounge, drum and bass and nu-jazz beats.

Tue–Sun 6pm–2am 8

MARACANA
Via Faenza 4, 50123 Firenze
Tel 055 210298
www.maracana.it
Six levels, a carnival stage and a party crowd make this club a winner with lovers of all things Brazilian. It's the place to watch carnival dancers, samba, sip *caipirinhas* (a cocktail made with lime juice and cachaça, Brazilian sugar cane liquor) and try some of the enormous *churrasco* (Brazilian barbequed meats).

The bar staff juggle bottles while some of the crowd attempt dance-floor soccer acrobatics.
🕐 Tue–Sun 8.30pm–4am 🖐 €12; free entry for women Tue, Thu and Sun 🚌 31, 32

TENAX
Via Pratese 46, 50127 Firenze
Tel 055 308160
www.tenax.org
Florence's premier house-music club, attracting big international names like Dimitri from Paris, Thievery Corporation, Grace Jones and Groove Armada. It has mind-blowing lighting and sound technology, as well as some very curious art installations. Also hosts live music acts.
🕐 Daily 11pm–4am 🖐 €15
🚌 5, 29, 30, 56

YAB
Via Sassetti 5, 50122 Firenze
Tel 055 215160
www.yab.it
Theatrical décor and renowned DJs make this one of Florence's hippest clubs. House music dominates the schedule, with hard house on Fridays and happy house on Saturdays. Monday's Smoove Night sees electric boogaloo acrobatics on the dance floor and hip-hop tunes aplenty.
🕐 Mon–Tue, Thu–Sat 11pm–4am
🖐 €14 🚌 A, 1, 6, 14

Sports and Activities

SPECTATOR SPORTS

FOOTBALL
FIORENTINA VIOLA
Sport - Santo Marte
Viale Manfredo Fanti 14,
50137 Firenze
Tel 055 262 5537
www.fiorentina.it
Watch the reborn Viola—complete with new name and owners—at the open-bowl,

47,000-capacity Stadio Communale Artemio Franchi. Expect fervent support for the club (formerly known as Fiorentina) who are fighting back after bankruptcy and demotion in 2002.
🕐 Alternate Sun, Sep–May 🖐 €5
🚌 3, 10, 11, 17, 20, 34

HORSERACING
LE CASCINE
Ippodromo delle Mulina, Viale dell'Aeronautica/Viale del Pegaso 1, 50144 Firenze
Tel 055 411107
The Ippodromo delle Mulina is the place to go and see

horseracing in Florence. If you fancy a flutter on a *galoppo* (flat race) or *trotto* (trotting race), many *tabbachi* (tobacco shops) have easy-to-use betting facilities.
🕐 Phone or check local press for upcoming meetings 🖐 €15 🚌 17c

MOTOR RACING
AUTODROMO DEL MUGELLO
Mugello
Tel 055 849 9111
www.mugellocircuit.it
Regular motor-sport events are held at this circuit owned by Ferrari. The biggest motorcycle races, including the Italian Grand Prix for 125cc and 250cc bikes, as well as the Superbike World Championship, draw large crowds who fill the banks alongside the track.
🖐 €5–€25 including parking
🚗 Take the 302 Faentina road passing Scarperia for Mugello or the A1 (Bologna–Firenze) motorway and exit at Barberino di Mugello

VENUES
PALASPORT
Palazzetto dello Sport, Viale Pasquale Paoli 3, 50137 Firenze
Tel 055 678841
Various sports events are staged at this sports arena near the home of football club Fiorentina Viola. Check the local press for upcoming roller- and figure-skating, skateboarding, archery, water polo, volleyball and six-a-side football tournaments.
🚌 17

ACTIVITIES

CANOEING
CANOTTIERI COMUNALI FIRENZE
Lungarno Ferrucci 4, 50126 Firenze
Tel 055 681 2151
www.canottiericomunalifirenze.it
Try your hand at canoeing at this club on the River Arno. In addition to kayaking sessions, there are a number of courses available for all ages. There's also the chance to try dragon boating, Polynesian canoeing or even a game of canoe polo.
🕐 Daily Mon–Sat 8.30–9, Sun 8.30–1
🖐 €95 joining fee (free for women)
🚌 8, 31, 32

CYCLING
FLORENCE BY BIKE
Via San Zanobi 120, Firenze
Tel 055 488992
www.florencebybike.it
Florence by Bike has a good selection of bicycles to choose

from should you wish to whizz around town or explore for the countryside. Prices start

WHAT TO DO

at €2.50 an hour for a classic model, or €18 for a day's use of a standard mountain bike. Reserve a place on the daily 32km (20-mile) bicycle tour in advance.
🅐 Daily 9–7.30 💰 €2.50 per hour
🚌 20, 25, 31, 32, 33

HOT-AIR BALLOONING

BALLOONING IN TUSCANY
Podere La Fratta, 53020 Montisi
Tel 0577 845211
www.ballooningintuscany.com
If you are feeling flush and have three companions, why not book a balloon ride over Tuscany? This small company, run by an English couple, organizes personalized balloon trips with a champagne breakfast. It is an hour's drive south of Florence, but the views are worth it.
🅐 Contact for details 💰 €200 (minimum 4 adults) 🚗 A1 towards Siena, Montisi exit

ICE SKATING

Piazza Santa Croce, 50122/ Fortezza da Basso, 50129 Firenze
Tel 055 2340444/226 4524 (tourist information)
In December and January each year, a temporary ice rink is constructed in Piazza Santa Croce or in the Fortezza da Basso. Glide around or just hold onto the edge and admire the surrounding architecture—either the magnificent Palazzi Cocchi-Serristori and dell'Antella or the imposing military structure.
🚌 C, 23/ 12, 14, 23, 28, 33, 80

TENNIS

CIRCOLO DEL TENNIS
Viale del Visarno 1 (entrance on Viale degli Olmi), 50144 Firenze
Tel 055 332651/2
www.ctfirenze.org
Florence's oldest tennis club (1898) has excellent facilities including 10 clay courts, swimming pool, football pitches, gym, sauna, restaurant/ bar and even a bridge room. Check the press for the latest details of

upcoming tournaments and events.
🅐 Daily 10–10 🚌 1, 9, 12, 16, 26, 27, 80

HEALTH AND BEAUTY

GENNY
Palazzo Pucci
Via de' Pucci 4, 50122 Firenze
Tel 055 214823
Where better to be pampered than at the Florentine home of decadence and glamour, the beautiful Palazzo Pucci. Relax and enjoy a massage, some hydro-therapy, reflexology and beauty treatments for face, body and nails.
🅐 Mon–Fri 9–7, Sat 9–1 💰 Back massage €35 🚌 14, 23

Festivals and Events

SCOPPIO DEL CARRO
Easter Sunday
Florence's Scoppio del Carro (Explosion of the Cart) dates back to the 11th century when a carousel of fireworks was lit to spread the good news of Easter. Today, a ceremonial cart, stuffed with incendiaries, arrives in the Piazza del Duomo, and a wire is run to the statue of the Virgin on top of the duomo and into the cathedral itself. At about 11pm, the wire is lit and a mechanical dove slides down to the cart causing a huge explosion and igniting all the fireworks.

MAGGIO MUSICALE FIORENTINO
May and June
Biglietteria Teatro Communale, Via Solferino 15, 50123 Firenze
Tel 055 211 1158
Tel 199 109910
www.maggiofiorentino.it
Florence's major music festival, held in venues both inside and outside across the city. Founded in 1933, it's Italy's longest-running music festival with a good mix of opera, ballet and classical music.
📅 🚌 B, D, 1, 9, 13

MUSICA DEI POPOLI FESTIVAL
October
Via Maestri del Lavorol 24b, 50134 Firenze
Tel 055 422 0300
www.flog.it/mus_pope.htm
In October each year, artists from around the globe descend on Florence for this International Folk Music festival. Italy's finest world music event has been running for more than 25 years and attracts a friendly crowd to its main venue, the Auditorium Flog.
🚌 4, 8, 14

SPECIAL

GIOCO DI CALCIO
Sundays in June
Ufficio Valorizzazione Tradizioni Popolari Fiorentine, Piazzetta di Parte Guelfa 1r, 50123 Firenze
Tel 055 261 6050/1/6
www.globeit.it/caf/storia.html
A no-holds-barred version of football that is played between the four city quarters, originally used to keep the city militia in fighting shape and to weld the

various factions into a united force. The final day is celebrated with a costumed processions and a flotilla of candle-lit boats and fireworks on the River Arno.
💰 €10–€25 🚌 C, 23

TUSCANY AND UMBRIA

Tuscany and Umbria, central Italy's main tourist areas, have got the lot—great shopping, traditional festivals and a plethora of sports. There's something to buy, or see, or do virtually 24 hours day. Throughout the region, you'll find all the usual Italian specials—leather, fashion, jewellery, lingerie—along with some great local products. Look out for antique stores, wonderful ceramics and pottery and food products of outstanding calibre. Wine and olive oil are sold direct from the growers, some of whom give vineyard and cellar tours and tastings.

If you're looking for entertainment, there is a huge variety of traditional *festas*. Siena's Palio tops the bill, but Arezzo, Pisa and Gubbio have their own unique celebrations, while towns like Lucca and Barga fill the air with some of the coolest sounds during their summer music festivals. There are theme parks and zoos for the kids, or spend a family day horseback riding through the rolling hills, canoeing down Umbria's swift rivers, or watching the hang-gliders in the Sibillini mountains. Evening events range from classical concerts to buzzing rock and club music, and there are plenty of cinemas showing original-language movies—some under the stars in summer.

Shopping

AREZZO

EMPORIO ARMANI
Corso Italia 306, 52100 Arezzo
Tel 0575 355262
www.emporioarmani.it
A branch of Emporio Armani offering 30 per cent discount off regular prices. Some of the fashion items are discounted by up to 70 per cent during the sales. Whatever time of year, you should find a bargain.
◉ Mon 4–8, Tue–Sun 9–1, 4–8, Apr–Sep; Mon 9–1, Tue–Sun 9–1, 3.30–7.30, Oct–Mar; Mon 9–1, Tue–Fri and Sun 9–1, 3.30–7.30, Sat 9–1, Jul–Aug

FIERA ANTIQUARIA
Piazza San Francesco, 52100 Arezzo
One of Italy's leading antiques fairs, Fiera Antiquaria floods Piazza San Francesco, Piazza Grande and the Logge Vasari. Filled with more than 600 dealers, with a range of items from 19th-century furniture to 17th-century glass and items dating back to the Renaissance. The fair lures both serious collectors and browsing visitors.
◉ 1st Sun of the month 7.30–7, Apr–Sep; 7.30–3, rest of year

PRADA FACTORY OUTLET
Località Levanella SS 69,
52025 Montevarchi
Tel 055 919 6528
Montevarchi, near Arezzo, is home to the Prada factory and its bargain outlet. You can get Prada bags, lingerie and shoes at up to 80 per cent discount. When you arrive, pull a ticket from the machine and wait your turn to enter. They also stock Miu Miu, Helmut Lang and Jil Sander.
◉ Mon–Sat 9.30–7.30, Sun 2–7.30
🚆 From Firenze to Montevarchi (about an hour), then taxi 🚗 Take the A1. Turn off at Valdarno junction and follow the signs

ASSISI

ENOTECA LOMBARDI
11 Via Borgo Aretino, 06081 Assisi
Tel 075 816697
A food store and *enoteca* (wine shop) selling more than 50 types of wine, with an emphasis on red Tuscan, Lombard and Piedmontese varieties priced €10 to €80. Truffle paste, roast peppers, artichoke pâté and dried porcini mushrooms also sold.
◉ Daily 9–7 🚌 Linea C every half hour from Assisi's rail station to piazza Unità d'Italia (3km/2 miles)

LUCCA

ANTIQUES MARKET
This large, traditional antiques market, near Corso Garibaldi and the southern walls, fills Piazza San Giusto, Piazza Antelminelli and the surrounding streets with a wide range of furnishings, rare coins and old jewellery on the third Sunday of every month. On the third Saturday and the fourth Sunday of the month, a crafts market sells local handicrafts.
◉ 3rd Sun of every month

CERAMISTI D'ARTE
Via Mordini 74–78, 56100 Lucca
Tel 0583 492700
Tuscan artists Stefano Seardo and Fabrizio Falchi sculpt and paint at this workshop. Pick up hand-painted decorative tiles, terracotta sculptures and marble mosaics made from

the prized Massa Carrara marble. Everything is produced according to traditional Italian ceramic techniques. Browsers are welcome.
◉ Mon–Sat 9.30–1, 3.30–8

LUCCA BOOK FAIR
Off Via Beccheria, 56100 Lucca
Just behind the Chiesa di San Giusto and running towards Piazza Napoleone and Piazza San Michele, Lucca's old bookstalls sell anything and everything that is printed. Shoppers will find old prints of Lucca and other Italian cities, modern

WHAT TO DO

BRANCALEONE DA NORCIA
Corso Sertorio 17, 06046 Norcia
Tel 0743 828311
The town is famous for its black truffles and wild boar, hence the abundance of these stores. Brancaleone excels in truffles with *salse al*

tartufo (truffle pastes) and loose truffles for sale. Local *pecorino di Norcia* (hard cheese) and Umbrian ricotta sit waiting to be popped into heavenly sandwiches.
🕐 Daily 8–8

postcards and comic books in various languages.
🕐 Daily 10–6

LUCCA MARKET
Via dei Bacchettoni, 56100 Lucca
Just inside the wall between San Jacopo and Elisa gates, Lucca's market, with stands selling clothing, flowers, food and household implements, is very good value, especially for clothes and shoes. The market is also good for silk flowers, table linen and old lace. Get here early for the best bargains.
🕐 Wed, Sat 9–1

PINKO UNDERGROUND
Via Oberdan 17, 06121 Perugia
Tel 075 572 3174
The sexy Italian label Pinko vies for space with the more practical US brand Converse at

this offbeat women's fashion shop, just one of the fascinating boutiques lining Via Oberdan. The staff model some of the more bizarre items like plastic shirts. Men's shop at Via Baglioni 52.
🕐 Mon 4–8, Tue–Sat 9–1, 4–8 🚌 6, 7, 9, 11 to Piazza Italia

VIA OBERDAN FABRICS MARKET
Via Oberdan, 06121 Perugia
In between the cool, inexpensive stores on the exciting Via Oberdan, more than 20 stalls sell a wide range of fabrics. Scarves, throws and ornamental pieces, in all shades, fabrics and sizes. Crystals and fairly cheap jewellery are also sold, as well as bags, incense and rugs.
🕐 Mon–Sat 4–8 🚌 6, 7, 9, 11 to Piazza Italia

LIBRERIA FOGOLA
Corso Italia 82, 56100 Pisa
Tel 050 502547
A tiny, tidy bookshop with very helpful staff and Internet access. Books covering every subject under the sun can be found on the shelves. You will find English-language books and tourist information here too and the staff speak English.
🕐 Mon–Sat 9–1, 4–8

PAOLO CAPRI SHOWROOM
Via Marino 2, 56100 Pisa
Tel 050 577111
Designer Paolo Capri's showroom is an outlet for jewellery, watches and frames. Florentine silversmiths create almost all of the items. There are also plenty of gifts taking inspiration from local traditions and culture.
🕐 Mon 4.30–7, Tue–Sat 9.30–12.30, 4.30–7

PAUL DE BONDT
Via Turati 22, Corte San Domenico, 56125 Pisa
Tel 050 501 896
A Dutch-born pastry chef, Paul de Bondt creates handmade

chocolates to order with meticulous attention to detail. De Bondt won the Euro-chocolate award in 1999 and the *tavoletta d'oro* (the golden bar) in 2003 for the best dark chocolate and the best milk chocolate bar in Italy. This Pisa outlet has everything from animal-shaped chocolates filled with almond paste to simple, rich truffles. But the *ganascia* chocolates, made with fresh cream and butter, are what De Bondt is most famous for.
🕐 Tue–Sat 10–1, 4–8; closed Jun–Sep

TENUTA TORCIANO
Via Crocetta 18, Ulignano, 53030 San Gimignano
Tel 0577 950055
www.torciano.com
In the hills just outside of San Gimignano, this shop is attached to a vineyard that has been run by the Giachi family since 1720. As well as selling their own olive oils they run wine-tasting sessions and courses.
🕐 Daily 8–8 🚌 5km (8 miles) from San Gimignano on the road to Certaldo–follow signs for Ulignano

CERAMICHE ARTISTICHE SANTA CATERINA
Via di Città 51, 74 and 76, 53100 Siena
Tel 0577 283098
www.ceramicart1.com
A family business run by the founder, Marcello Neri, his wife and son. The family works in the traditional Sienese style using only black, white, and *terra di Siena* (burnt sienna). Their art is inspired by the local architecture, particularly the duomo. Watch them at work in the studio or take a class.
🕐 Daily 10–8

CORTECCI ABBIGLIAMENTO
Via Banchi di Sopra 27, 53100 Siena
Tel 0577 280096
www.corteccisiena.it
The two branches of this shop stock a large collection of

men's and women's designer labels, including Gucci, Armani, Yves Saint Laurent, Christian Dior, Roberto Cavalli and Dolce & Gabbana. The Banchi di Sopra branch has the more classical collections, while the other branch, at Il Campo 30, stocks younger, trendier labels.

🕐 Mon 3.30–8, Tue–Sat 9.30–1, 3.30–8

DROGHERÍA MANGANELLI
Via di Città 61, 53100 Siena
Tel 0577 280002
A member of the Slow Food Movement (p. 24) and something of a local institution,

Drogheria Manganelli has been selling local produce since 1879. Today it continues to sell regional foods including cured meats, cheese, vinegar, wine, olive oil, homemade cakes, *ricciarelli* (almond biscuits) and pasta sauces. If you are interested in food and drink this is the place to go for some tasty purchases to take home.

🕐 Mon–Sat 9–8

SPELLO
ARTE LEGNO
Via Fonte del Mastro II 2, 06038 Spello
Tel 0742 302028
www.artelegnospello.com
At this fantastic shop, close to the Teatro Comunale Subasio in the highest lanes of Spello, most of the items are hand-carved from olive wood. Bowls, spoons, puppets, dolly pegs and breadboards are all on sale.

Look upwards at the wonderful old beams holding up the roof.

🕐 Mon–Sat 10–1, 4–7

SPOLETO
LA PATERA
Via del Palazzo dei Ducal 18, 06049 Spoleto
Tel 0743 223258
This glass-fronted shop with thick medieval doors, is just minutes from the Piazza della Libertà. The old domed brick roof in this visually stunning antiques store is from another century. Small works of art and pretty pen-and-ink drawings of Umbrian scenes are easy to carry home. Silver goblets, faded brooches and 1930s espresso cups are all displayed within an ancient glass cabinet.

🕐 Daily 10–1, 4–8

Performance

AREZZO
EDEN
Via Guadagnoli 2, 52100 Arezzo
Tel 0575 353364
A popular cinema in the town, famous for its role in Roberto Benigni's *Life Is Beautiful* (p. 415). Most films are screened in the original language with sub-titles. A bar sells drinks and snacks.

🕐 Wed–Mon 🎟 Adult €6.50, child €4 🅂

ASSISI
LYRICK THEATRE
Via Gabriele d'Annunzio, 06088 Assisi
Tel 075 812534 (tourist office)

A large, 1,000-capacity theatre within walking distance of Assisi's rail station. Productions of anything from *Grease* to dance festivals take place here, but only a handful of performances are in English.

🕐 All year 🎟 Contact for details 🅂

LUCCA
CINEMA ITALIA
Via Biscione 32, 55100 Lucca
Tel 0583 467264
One-screen cinema showing the latest Hollywood blockbusters, changing every two weeks (two shows a night on weekdays, four on Saturdays and holidays). Most films are shown in the original language.

🕐 Mon, Thu–Fri 8.30pm and 10.30pm, Sat and holidays 3.45pm, 6pm, 8.15pm and 10.30pm 🎟 Adult €7, child €5; all tickets €5 on Fri 🅂

NICOLAS
Viale S. Concordio 887, 55100 Lucca
Tel 0583 582378
Known for its live music concerts, Nicolas gives local musicians the chance to perform everything from jazz and blues to pop and reggae, as well as the odd traditional Italian song.

🕐 Tue–Sun 8pm–2am 🎟 Free

TEATRO DEL GIGLIO
Piazza del Giglio 13–15, 55100 Lucca
Tel 0583 467521
www.teatrodelgiglio.it
In September and October, this 19th-century opera house stages classical dramas. Dance, opera and classical music performances from November to March. Lucca's cultural forum also contains the Puccini Studies Centre.

🕐 Sep–Mar 🎟 Adult €25, child €12 🅂

NORCIA
TEATRO CIVICO NORCIA
Piazza Verdi, 06046 Norcia
Tel 0743 816022
A splendid old theatre, built in 1876, with an ornate red façade. The seats in the stalls

are so close to the stage that theatregoers can almost touch the performers. All of the shows are in Italian.

🎫 €10 🔲 📶 Unnumbered buses leave every 2 hours from Spoletto's Piazza della Vittoria, and twice daily from Roma Terminal bus station, for Norcia's Viale della Stazione

AMICI DELLA MUSICA DI PERUGIA
Palazzo dei Priori, 06123 Perugia
Tel 075 572 2271
www.amicimusicapg.it
Weekly classical recitals at this reasonably sized theatre in the heart of Perugia. Violin and piano soloists as well as artists playing in small groups.
🎫 Once a week, Oct–Jun 🎟 €7–€26 🔲 🚌 6, 7, 9, 11 to Piazza Italia

CINEMA DEL PAVONE
Corso Vannucci 61, 06123 Perugia
Tel 075 572 4911
Watch art-house films and blockbusters in their original language at this picture house in the middle of town. Choose between the latest Hollywood flick or a taste of avant-garde Spanish cinema.
🎫 Mon 🎟 €4 🚌 6, 7, 9, 11 to Piazza Italia 🔲

TEATRO MORLACCHI
Piazza Morlacchi, 06123 Perugia
Tel 075 575421
www.teatrostabile.umbria.it
Perugia's busiest theatre plays host to touring productions from some of Italy's most prestigious theatres. The magnificent 500-seat auditorium has fantastic views from almost every angle.
🎫 9pm, Oct–Apr 🎟 €7–€25 🔲 🚌 6, 7, 9, 11 to Piazza Italia

PISA

CINEMA TEATRO NUOVO
Piazza della Stazione 1, 56127 Pisa
Tel 050 41332
An art-house cinema popular with visitors and locals alike. The single screen shows films in their original language. and occasionally films are not sub-titled. Refreshments at the bar.
🎫 Daily 🎟 Adult €7, child €4.60 🔲

TEATRO VERDI
Via Palestro 40, 56127 Pisa
Tel 050 941111
www.teatrodipisa.pi.it/indexitalian.htm
Inaugurated in 1867, this is one of the most beautiful theatres in central Italy with a notable ceiling fresco. See opera, drama and dance in the 900-seat auditorium.
🎫 Sep–Jan 🎟 €13–€43 🔲

SAN GIMIGNANO

CINE ESTATE
Rocca di Montestaffoli, 53073 San Gimignano
Tel 0577 940008
Every weekend, as well as three nights during the week, San Gimignano's public park is transformed into an outdoor cinema. Hollywood blockbusters and European art-house films are shown in their original language.
🎫 Jun–Aug 🎟 Adult €6, child €5

Nightlife

AREZZO

GRACE
Via Madonna del Prato 125, 52100 Arezzo
Tel 0575 403669
www.grace.it
This trendy club, discotheque and sushi restaurant, run by three friends, verges on kitsch with its art deco seating and 1970s lighting.
🎫 Fri, Sat 12.30am–5am 🎟 €16

LUCCA

THE GOLDEN FOX
Viale Regina Margherita 207, 55100 Lucca
Tel 0583 491619
www.thegoldenfox.it
The Golden Fox prides itself on being a real English pub, even to the point of importing all its furnishings from England. English, Scottish and Irish draught beers are on tap.
🎫 Tue–Sun 8pm–1am

MOPLEN
Via San Leonardo 19, 55100 Lucca
Tel 0339 645 6012
Aperitifs start at 7pm in Lucca's premier gay/lesbian-friendly lounge bar. The clientele is young and mixed. The music is also varied—resident DJs play everything from 1960s tracks to drum and bass tunes.
🎫 Wed–Mon 7pm–1am

PERUGIA

ST. ANDREWS
Via della Cupa 2, 06123 Perugia
Tel 075 609522
St. Andrew should have been the patron saint of disco, because this place rocks. An international clientele, with a cave-like interior.
🎫 Daily 9pm–2am 🎟 €7

PISA

ÀBSOLUT
Via Mossotti 10, 56100 Pisa
Tel 050 220 1262
www.absolut.gay.it
By day an Internet café, by night a laid-back gay-and-lesbian pub with a young, friendly atmosphere. Entertainment is provided by live music and cabaret.
🎫 Tue–Sun 10pm–2am

OFFSIDE
Ospedaletto, Uscita Pisa Nord Est, Via Emilia, 56100 Pisa
Tel 340 496 4845
www.off-side.pisa.it
Themed evenings range from Friday's gay-and-lesbian night to live music gigs on Wednesday and Saturday nights and a cocktail and dance club on Sundays. Karaoke, the best night, is on Thursday.
🎫 Mon–Thu 8pm–2am, Fri–Sat 8pm–4am, Sun 6pm–4am

SAN GIMIGNANO

AVALON
Viale Roma 1, 53037 San Gimignano
Tel 0577 940023
www.avalon-pub.com
Avalon appeals to all tastes with its *birreria* (pub), *enoteca* (wine bar) and internet café

spread across three buildings in the old town. Occasional live music and karaoke nights. Minimum age 18.

🕐 Tue–Sun noon–2am, Jun–Aug; Tue–Sun 8pm–2am, rest of year

BIRRERIA IL BARONE ROSSO
Via dei Termini 9, 53100 Siena
Tel 0577 286686
www.barone-rosso.com
Food, drink and live music in the heart of Siena's medieval streets. Il Barone Rosso is a regular haunt for Sienese beer drinkers.

🕐 Daily 9pm–3am

Sports and Activities

SPECTATOR SPORTS

PERUGIA
AC PERUGIA
Stadio Renato Curi, Pian di Massiano, 06125 Perugia
Tel 075 500 6641
www.perugiacalcio.it
Founded in 1905, Perugia's football club has struggled to stay in Serie A. Games are worth watching if only to enjoy the enthusiastic fans and the indignant displays by manager Serse Cosmi.

🕐 Sun afternoon, Sep–Jun and other times 🎟 €18–€118

SIENA
STADIO COMUNALE
Via Mille 3, 53100 Siena
Tel 0577 281084
Crowded with passionate and vocal residents on match days, this football ground is home to AC Siena. The cheapest seating is in the 'red curve'.

🎟 €10

ACTIVITIES

AREZZO
LFI LIGHT-GAUGE RAILWAY
Arezzo Train Station, Piazza della Repubblica 1/A, 52100 Arezzo
Tel 0575 39881
www.trenitalia.com

The LFI (La Ferrovia Italiana) railway linking Arezzo with Stia, Bibbiena and Sinalunga is a rolling train museum. Its antique fleet of electric locomotives and steam engines take you through the surrounding countryside, past wonderful views. Book a seat on the steam train for a historic ride.

MARINA DI PIETRASANTA
TRENINO DELLE VACANZE
Fratelli Verona
Tel 0584 745737
With fantastic views of the Versilia coast, this *trenino delle vacanze* (little holiday train) runs from the middle of town along the coast of Marina di Pietrasanta during the summer season. The hour-long journey takes in the towns of Le Nocette, Motrone, Tonfano, Fiumetto, Pietrasanta.

🕐 Daily 5.30pm and 9pm, Jun–Sep
🎟 Adult €5, child €3 🚂 Pietrasanta or Viareggio 🚗 Versilia exit off the A12

NORCIA
RAFTING UMBRIA
Serravalle di Norcia, Strada Provinciale di Cascia, 06046 Norcia
Tel 0742 23146 or 348 351 1798
www.raftingumbria.it
Try the rivers in Sibillini National Park, east of Spoleto, for exhilarating rafting for all abilities. For those who'd

rather be a spectator, races are organized by local enthusiasts, with thrills and spills aplenty. By appointment only.

🕐 Daily 10, 1 and 4, Mar–Nov
🎟 Adult €30, child €20

PERUGIA
GOLF PERUGIA
Località S. Sabina, Ellera Umbra, 06074 Perugia
Tel 075 517 2204
Watching the morning mists roll over the lush green course is a great way to start the day at one of Perugia's most beautiful, and tricky, 18-hole golf courses.

🕐 Tue–Sun 8.30–6 🎟 €42 weekdays, €52 weekends

NESTLÉ PERUGINA
Via Pievaiola, San Sisto, 20143 Perugia
Tel 075 527 6796 or 075 527 6635
Chocoholics can gorge themselves at the Museo

Storico della Perugina. Antique chocolate-making equipment as well as packaging from the 20th century, including the first Baci Perugina products. Tours of the factory—a fascinating look at the company's history—can be booked in advance.

🕐 Mon–Fri 9–1, 2–5.30, Sat–Sun by appointment. Factory tours 11–5 by appointment 🎟 Free

PIEVE SAN STEFANO
NAZIONALE TURISMO EQUESTRE
ANTE - Associazione Nazionale per il Turismo Equestre e per l'Equitazione di Campagna
Via Ponte Castel Giubileo 27/A, 00100 Roma
Tel 06 382 8060
Umbria's mountainous environs provide some impressive terrain for horseback riding. The National

WHAT TO DO

Equestrian Tourism bureau can help you arrange a day's ride with a recommended establishment. There is also an extensive choice of horseback riding schools, stables and trails in Tuscany—a great way to explore Mount Amiata, Certaldo, Gambassi Terme and the surrounding landscape of vineyards, olive groves and terracotta farmhouses.

🕐 Contact individual establishments for details 💶 Approximately €25 for half a day/€45 per day

PISA

TENNIS CLUB PISA
Piazzale dello Sport 7, 56122 Pisa
Tel 050 530313
www.tennisclubpisa.it
Five outdoor clay courts (three with lighting for night games) and two indoor courts can be hired at this year-round tennis club. The clubhouse has a bar, changing facilities and a shop.
🕐 Daily 8am–10.30pm 💶 €11 per hour

RAPOLANO TERME

ANTICA QUERCIOLAIA THERMAL BATHS
Via Trieste 22, 53040 Rapolano Terme
Tel 0577 724091
www.termeaq.it
Antica Querciolaia has been a spa resort since Etruscan and Roman times. Its spring fills the thermal baths and there is an adjoining park with three open-air pools. Try a mud wrap or an inhalation treatment. Water erupts from the famous 'intermittent fountain' every 10 minutes.

🕐 Daily 10–6, Oct–Mar; Sun–Fri 9–7, Sat 9–midnight, May–Sep 💶 €49 for a 1-hour treatment. Swimming pool €11 (children €6) Mon–Thu, €13 Sat–Sun (children €8); children under 4 free 🚆 Rapolano Terme railway station is on the Siena–Chianciano Terme line 🚗 Valdichiana exit on the A1 or on the Firenza–Siena Valdichiana SS 326

SAN GUILIANO TERME

SAN GUILIANO TERME
Largo Shelley 18, 56017 San Guiliano Terme
Tel 050 818047
www.termesangiuliano.com

This 18th-century building, once used by the Grand Dukes of Tuscany, is in a beautiful park of olive trees in the Pisan foothills. The year-round spa specializes in facial and body treatments as well as sessions to revitalize the respiratory and immune systems. The hotel has a bar and restaurant.
🕐 Daily Mon–Sat 8.30–1, 2.30–6.30, Sun 8.30–1 💶 €28.50 for a 30 min massage. Weekend packages start at €128.50 🚆 The Pisa-to-Lucca line stops at San Giuliano 🚗 7km (4 miles) from Pisa on the Brennero Road (SS12) towards Lucca

SIENA

PISCINA COMUNALE
Via Coppi, Loc. Acquacalda,
53100 Siena
Tel 0577 47496
In the north of Siena, this outdoor public swimming pool has a number of diving boards and ample space for sunbathing.
🕐 Daily 9.30–7, 1 Jun–31 Aug; daily dawn–dusk, Oct–Jun 💶 Adult €5.20, child €3.10 🚌 10

For Children

COLLODI

PARCO DI PINOCCHIO
Via San Gennaro 3, 51014 Collodi
Tel 0572 429342
www.pinocchio.it
Open all year, the Pinocchio Park brings the story of the famous wooden puppet alive with mosaics, statues and fountains incorporating all the story's characters. Watch the energetic and entertaining

puppet shows or find amusement in the maze, playground, or exhibition centre. For refreshments, try the children's restaurant.
🕐 Daily 8.30–dusk 💶 Adult €8.50, under 16 €6.50, under 3 free 🚌 From Lucca to Collodi 🚗 15km (9 miles) from Lucca on the SS 435

POPPI

ZOO FAUNA EUROPA
Zoo Fauna Europa, 52015 Poppi
Tel 0575 504541/2
www.parcozoopoppi.it
Opened in 1972 by vet Dr. Roberto Mattoni, this zoo

preserves European species, including deer, wolves, bears, birds of prey, and species in danger of extinction, such as the Asinara donkey. There is also a botanical garden, pony rides and a children's play area. Restaurant, bar, picnic areas and free parking.

Daily 9–7 Adult €5, child (3–11) €4.50 Regular service from Firenze Trains to Poppi on the Arezzo–Stia line A 30-minute drive from Arezzo along the SS71. Follow signs for Bibbiena, then Parco Nazionale Casentinese or Parco Zoo Poppi

TIRRENIA
PARCO GIOCHI FANTASILANDIA
Viale Tirreno, 42, 56018 Tirrenia
Tel 050 30326

Fantasilandia is brimming with attractions for kids. Split into two sections, the park has one free area with an electric car track, miniature train and mechanical bull. The other area has waterslides and swings. There's also a park equipped for young children, with tricycles and pedal-cars. Bar and picnic tables.

Daily May–Sep; Sun and public holidays, rest of the year Pay section: Adult €10.50, under 16 €8.50, under 3 free Regular service between Pisa and Tirrenia Take the Pisa Centro exit on the A12 motorway, then follow signs to Tirrenia

WHAT TO DO

Festivals and Events

PALAZZO DEL POPOLO
27 December–1 January
05018 Orvieto
Tel 0763 341772
www.umbriajazz.com

The annual Umbria International Jazz Festival is Orvieto's most famous festival. It takes place in various locations throughout the city during the last week of December and the first week of January.

VIAREGGIO CARNEVALE
February/March
Piazza Mazzini, 22 c/o Palazzo delle Muse, 55049 Viareggio
Tel 0584 962568
www.viareggio.ilcarnevale.com

Viareggio's Carnevale is among Italy's biggest and best, with floats holding 200 people that wend their way along the waterfront four Sundays running. Gigantic moving puppets reflect current events and poke fun at famous people. It's all accompanied by music, dancing and food, and the National Lottery awards a huge prize to the best float.

Free Trains run from Pisa to Viareggio every hour Take the Versilia exit off the A12

HOLY WEEK CELEBRATIONS
March–April

Assisi, birthplace of St. Francis, celebrates the week before Easter with religious processions throughout the town commemorating the passion and death of Christ. This is a serious religious occasion, and the atmosphere of piety in this holiest of Umbrian towns is almost tangible.

FESTA DEI CERI
15 May
Gubbio
www.gubbio.com/ceri

A direct descendant of a pagan festival, Gubbio's Festa dei Ceri is unique. The *ceri* (candles) are three 66m (20ft high), immensely heavy wooden constructions, which are paraded through the town's streets before being raced up the steep slopes of Monte Ingino behind the town. It's all in honour of Gubbio's patron, Sant'Ubaldo, but there are plenty of authentic pagan phallic undertones surrounding this springtime celebration.

PALIO DELLA BALESTRA
Last Sunday in May
Piazza Grande, 06024 Gubbio

Watch the medieval custom of the Eugubian (from Gubbio)

and Sansepolcran (from Sansepolcro) battle it out to be crossbow champions. Don't miss the flag-throwing that precedes it.

THE CHIANTI WINE FESTIVAL
Last Sun in May–First Sun in June

Montespertoli sits on a hill in the center of the Chianti region and has spectacular views of Florence. One of the wine capitals of Tuscany, it is the perfect place to taste the best of the year's vintage. The Piazza San Pietro in the heart of the town is taken over by wine lovers and professional buyers alike who flock to this well established event.

ESTATE FIESOLANA
Mid-June to August
Fiesole
www.estatefiesolana.it

A summer festival of music, dance and theatre in the spectacular surroundings of Fiesole's Roman amphitheatre. There is a huge variety of music including classical, pop, contemporary jazz and gospel.

PALIO DI SAN RANIERI
17 June
Tel 050 560464 (Pisa tourist board)
www.comune.pisa.it

In celebration of Pisa's patron saint, this festival comprises eight oarsmen, a steersman and a climber who races to the top of a 10m (33ft) mast to grasp the winning banner at the finish. The race can be seen along the River Arno between the railway bridge and the Palazzo Medici. Try to get a spot at the Palazzo Medici to watch the mast-climbing finale.

Free

CORPUS CHRISTI
Mid-June
Orvieto
www.cittadiorvieto.com

The feast of Corpus Christi (known as Corpus Domini in Italy) is marked in Orvieto by superbly costumed proces-

sions through the town's streets, many of which are decorated with elaborate carpets of flower petals. A deeply moving experience.

LUMINARIA AND GIOCO DEL PONTE
Last Sunday in June
Pisa
Pisa's main festival focuses on tug-of-war games between 12 teams from the north and south banks of the River Arno, who attempt to push a 7-ton carriage over the Ponte di Mezzo—while dressed in Renaissance costumes. The highlight of the Luminaria are the blazing torches that light the houses and streets on either side of the river.

OPERA THEATRE OF LUCCA FESTIVAL
15 June–15 July
Vecchia Porta San Donato, 55100 Lucca
Tel 0583 583150
In summer Lucca's piazzas are filled with some of the world's best amateur and semi-professional singers and musicians. Sponsored by the Opera Theatre of Lucca and the Music College of the University of Cincinnati this is a great event and a showcase for new talent.
⚑ Free

ESTATE SAN GIMIGNANO
Mid-June to August
Piazza del Duomo 1, 53037 San Gimignano
Tel 0577 940008
A summer art festival with a strong musical element, including open-air opera recitals, classical concerts and film screenings in the ruins of the Rocca fortress.
⚑ €14–€40

FESTIVAL DEI DUE MONDI
End June–August
Spoleto
Tel 0743 44700
www.spoletofestival.it
A major performing arts

festival encompassing music, dance and theatre, founded in 1958 by the composer Carlo Menotti. It attracts world-class Italian and international companies who perform in settings both indoors and out. Also has a lively fringe, with some alternative performances.

UMBRIA JAZZ
July and August
Perugia
www.umbriajazz.com
Jazz is big in Italy and Perugia's been staging a major international festival since 1973, with a huge diversity of styles represented and some of the biggest names in the business. Events take place all over the city—a must for serious jazz lovers.

AREZZO WAVE
1st week in July
Corso Italia 236, 52100 Arezzo
Tel 0575 911005
www.arezzowave.com
Arezzo rocks for a week when

SPECIAL IN SIENA

IL PALIO
2 July and 16 August
Il Campo, 53100 Siena
Headquarters: Piazza Gramsci 7, 53100 Siena
Tel 0577 280551
www.comune.siena.it/contenuti/palio
www.ilpaliodisiena.com
The Palio—a bareback horse race around the Campo in Siena in honour of the Virgin Mary—is probably Italy's most famous festival. The high speed, confined space and lack of rules make it hazardous for horse and rider alike, if exhilarating for spectators. The race is over in a moment, but it takes weeks to prepare the accompanying pageantry, feasting and drama. This is a festival that the Sienese are immensely proud of, evoking passion on an extraordinary scale.
⚑ Free

Arezzo Wave comes to town. It's a huge rock festival that attracts nearly 250,000 people. Around 150 rock events take place over the week. Perhaps not up with Europe's biggest, but noisy and fun, with a good range of bands.
⚑ Free

VOLTERRA TEATRO
12–20 July
La Fortezza, 56048 Volterra
Tel 0588 80392
www.volterrateatro.it
Held in Volterra and the surrounding towns, this is Italy's leading avant-garde theatre festival. The schedule includes experimental drama, dance and film, with a good variety of international acts performing in English.
⚑ Adult €10, child €8

ESTATE MUSICAL LUCCHESE
July
Piazza Napoleone and Piazza Anfiteatro, 55100 Lucca
Tel 0584 46477
www.summer-festival.com
Previous acts at the Lucca Summer Music Festival, one of Tuscany's best-attended music festivals, have included Paul Simon, David Bowie, Oasis and Rod Stewart. Plenty of Italian bands, too.
⚑ Adult €5–€20, child €3–€15

SETTIMANE MUSICALE
July
Siena
Tel 0577 22091
www.chigiana.it
A prestigious classical music festival run by the Accademia Chigiana, Siena's renowned *conservatoire*. Concerts take place all over the city, and the festival usually includes a major opera production.

SIENA JAZZ FESTIVAL
24 July–7 August
Fortezza Medicea Anfiteatro, 53100 Siena
Tel 0577 271401
www.sienajazz.it

Since 1977, Siena Jazz has presented jazz performances and held seminars and masterclasses. Concerts are held in Piazza il Campo, Enoteca Italiana and Piazza Jacopo della Quercia.
🎵 Free

PUCCINI FESTIVAL
July–August
Teatro all'Aperto
55048 Torre del Lago Puccini
Tel 0584 359322
www.puccinifestival.it
Two paces from Villa Puccini (where Giacomo Puccini wrote his most famous works), Torre del Lago's opera festival draws 40,000 spectators every year to its four performances of Puccini classics.
🎵 €29–€96 🚗 A20—a minute drive from Lucca on the A11/SS1

FESTIVAL DELLE NAZIONE DELLA MUSICA DA CAMERA
August and September
Città di Castello
Tucked away in northeast Umbria, Città di Castello plays host each year to a splendid chamber music festival. The town's churches and palazzi are used to showcase Italian and international groups playing intimate music that spans the centuries.

BRAVIO DELLE BOTTE
Last Sunday in August
Montepulciano
www.valdichiana.it/montepulciano
This bizarre race, dating from 1372, sees a two-man team from each of Montepulciano's eight *contrade* (districts) rolling 80kg (176lb) wine barrels, mainly uphill, through the town's streets to the Piazza Grande. The is plenty of dancing and drinking going on in the crowd as well as plenty of encouragement for the rollers.

BARGA JAZZ FESTIVAL
Last week in August
Lucca and Barga
Tel 0583 711044

www.bargajazz.com
This international festival revolves around a jazz orchestra competition. Performances are held in the Teatro dei Differenti and on Piazza Angelio in Barga, as well as in Lucca's Palazzo Ducale and in Castelnuovo di Garfagnana's Piazza Umberto.
🎵 Adult €10, child €7.50 🚗 Barga 🚗 A40—a minute drive from Lucca (SS439 onto SS12, then onto SP2 and SP7)

GIOSTRA DEL SARACINO
Last Sunday in August and first Sunday in September
Piazza Grande, 52100 Arezzo
Tel 0575 377262
www.giostradelsaracino.arezzo.it
A vibrant medieval celebration of chivalry and jousting, which can be traced back to the Crusades combat training in the 14th century. The four opposing teams, from the four quarters of Arezzo (Crucifera, Foro, Sant'Andrea and Santo Spirito), compete for the Lancia d'Oro (The Golden Lance) trophy.
🎵 Free

RENAISSANCE DAY
First Sunday in September
In Scarperia in Mugello scenes from the 16th century come to life as music, archers, craftsmen, serfs, guards, and noblemen and women take over the streets for the day. Renaissance food can be sampled and paid for in florins, once the only currency accepted here.

LUMINARIA DI SANTA CROCE
13 September
Lucca
Lucca's treasured Volto Santo is carried in procession through the torch- and candle-lit streets of the town. The statue is adorned with silver slippers and a diamond-studded crown, and the whole town turns out in homage to the effigy.

SAGRA MUSICALE UMBRA
Middle 2 weeks of September
Perugia
www.sagramusicaleumbra.com
Umbria's summer season culminates in the Sagra Musicale, a prestigious music festival based in Perugia, with performances taking place in venues throughout the region. Orchestras and soloists come from all over Europe, and it's worth enquiring about what's on if you're anywhere in Umbria during the Sagra—you are bound to see something unique.

EUROCINEMA FESTIVAL
Third week in September
Via A. Pucci 138/A, 55049 Viareggio
Tel 0584 30750
www.europacinema.it
A film awards festival including film premieres, European TV and animated short films. Screenings are in a variety of languages with Italian subtitles.
🎵 Free 🚇 🚆 Trains run from Pisa to Viareggio every hour 🚗 Take the Versilia exit off the A12

SIENA INTERNATIONAL FILM FESTIVAL
26–29 September
Cinema Nuovo Pendola
Via San Quirico 13, 53016 Siena
Tel 0577 43012
www.sienafilmfestival.it
This film festival screens two films per night for three nights at the end of September. The schedule includes mostly art-house films, some of which are in English.
🎵 Adult €6.20, child €4.65 🚇 🚗 3

CHESTNUT FESTIVAL
During October
Every year in Marradi in Mugello they celebrate the chestnut harvest. Sample some delicacies made from the nut and you are sure to go home with bags full of fresh chestnuts and homemade treats.

ROME

Even if you don't go near a classical site or collection, there's enough in Rome to keep you busy for weeks. This is a consumer paradise, where shopaholics can spend with consummate success. Shops and markets are scattered all over the city, but head for the area around Piazza di Spagna for the big names and bespoke tailoring. The Via Nazionale has more cutting-edge temptations, but it is worth going across the river and into the *centro storico* for quirkier stuff and some great food shops. Rome's music scene is on the rise, with year-round opera, both in and out of doors, while the purpose-built Parco della Musica has at last given the city a world-class concert hall for music of all kinds. Palaeur, a huge stadium-turned-concert venue that hosts top international gigs, is its only rival. If you're in the mood for dancing, there are clubs and bars galore; Rome has great jazz and Latin music scenes. For the energetic there's swimming, tennis and golf, or sit back and watch a football or rugby match. Kids might enjoy this, but the child-friendly museums, fun parks and multimedia experiences are likely to be more appealing.

Shopping

ART, CRAFT AND ANTIQUES

COMIC'S BAZAR
Via dei Banchi Vecchi 127–128, 00186 Roma
Tel 06 6880 2923
The oddly misspelled name says it all—this is a topsy-turvy Aladdin's cave of furniture, lamps and objects. Their niche is Viennese Thonet lamps from the early 20th century (late art deco) and furniture from the 1800s to the 1920s. The owners have another, more contemporary and ethnic store, close by at Via Giulia 140/e.
🕐 Tue–Sat 9.30–7.30, Mon 3–7.30
🚌 46, 62, 64, 116, 492, 571 or any bus to Corso Vittorio Emanuele II

MATHERIA FARNESE
Via G. Garibaldi 53–55/a, 00153 Roma
Tel 06 581 7566
www.farnese.it
The owners of this shop create bright, handcrafted ceramic floor tiles inspired by Roman villas and 18th-century patrician houses. The group of architects and artisans also restore beautiful antique tiles, plates and jugs. This kind of craftsmanship comes at a price though.
🕐 Mon–Fri 10–7, Sat by appointment
🚌 23, 280: stop closest to Via Garibaldi

BOOKS

ANGLO AMERICAN BOOK CO.
Via della Vite 102, 00187 Roma
Tel 06 679 5222
www.aab.it
A short distance from the Scalinata di Triniti dei Monti, this is one of the better English bookshops in town, housed in a 19th-century building. The excellent selection includes music, cinema, philosophy, religion, science, fiction and children's books. They also stock visitors' guidebooks to Rome, Italy and most world destinations.
🕐 Tue–Sun 10–7.30, Mon 3.30–7.30
🚌 40, 62, 64, 116

FASHION AND LINGERIE

BRIONI
Via Barberini 79, 00187 Roma
Tel 06 484517
www.brioniroma.com
Brioni has dressed royalty and celebrities since 1945 earning a well-deserved reputation as one of Italy's top tailors. Leave your measurements here and you can call up for a suit anytime, anywhere. This, the oldest and largest of their

stores, which also stocks women's ready-to-wear items. Others can be found at Via Condotti 21a and Via Veneto 129.
🕐 Mon–Sat 10–7.30 (Condotti 21a); Mon–Sat 10–1.30, 3.30–7.30 (Via Veneto) 🚇 Barberini 🚌 63, 116, 175, 492, 590, 630

FIORUCCI
Via Nazionale 236, 00184 Roma
Tel 06 488 3175
Fiorucci's signature angels printed on T-shirts are everywhere in this store, to the delight of all teenagers and the young at heart. Downstairs are dresses, skirts and blouses by the likes of Fiorucci, Kenzo, Gaultier, Soleil, Kookai and Dolce & Gabbana, as well as jeans. Upstairs are kitsch shoes, Hello Kitty gadgets and more T-shirts.
🕐 Mon–Sat 9.30–8 🚇 Repubblica
🚌 H, 40, 60, 64, 70, 117, 170

LEAM
Via Appia Nuova 26, 00183 Roma
Tel 06 7720 7204
www.leam.com
Two stores within a few doors of each other, with top designer fashion and accessories for men and women. The best of Italian design under one roof. There are Armani, Gucci, Dolce & Gabbana, Prada and even Philippe Stark dresses. The shop assistants can be over-attentive (not uncommon in Rome). There is a roof terrace and bar in the women's store.
🕐 Mon 4–8, Tue–Sat 9.30–8 🚇 San Giovanni 🚌 87, 360

LEI
Via Nazionale 88, 00184 Roma
Tel 06 482 1700
Though the name on the shop window is understated in small letters, young Rome-based socialites and hip women in the know come here for their Dolce & Gabbana staples, Romeo Gigli

ready-to-wear, and a dazzling array of party dresses and delicate slip-on shoes by French designers like Stephane Kélian.

🔵 Mon–Sat 10–8, Sun 10–2, 4–7.30, Jul and Dec; Mon–Sat 10–8, the rest of the year 🚌 H, 40, 60, 64, 70, 117, 170

VALENTINO

Via Condotti 12, Roma
Tel 06 67391

One of the few Italian fashion designers to be based in Rome rather than Milan. Valentino

has been dressing the rich and famous since the late 1950s. Further branches are in Piazza Mignanelli (haute couture) and Via Bocca di Leone.

🔵 Mon 3–7, Tue–Sat 10–7 🅼 Spagna

FOOD AND DRINK

VOLPETTI

Via Marmorata 47, 00153 Roma
Tel 06 574 2352
www.volpetti.com

One of the best (though not the cheapest) delis in Rome. An astounding variety of breads, cheeses, hams, salamis, fresh pasta and ready-made dishes. Service is

SPECIAL

LA DOLCEROMA

Via del Portico d'Ottavia 20/b, 00186 Roma
Tel 06 689 2196

This Viennese *patisserie* is an unobtrusive little shop in the heart of the Jewish quarter. Once inside you'll understand why people make detours for it. Aside from the excellent *Sacher* cake (also available by the slice), you can buy cheesecakes of all sizes and with different fillings—from yoghurt to Austrian cream cheese—and various other mouth-watering Austrian specialities. There are also cookies and brownies to munch on to keep you going while you sightsee. Not the cheapest bakery in town, but the most memorable.

🔵 Tue–Sat 8–1.30, 4–8, Sun 10–1
🚌 H, 23, 63, 280, 630, 780 to Lungotevere dei Cenci, or walk from Largo di Torre Argentina or Piazza Venezia

professional and cheerful and you can sample the cheese to help you decide. Whatever happens, you won't come out empty-handed. Good for gifts. There's another, more expensive branch in Via della Scrofa in the city centre.

🔵 Wed–Mon 8–2, 5–8.15, Tue 5–8.15; closed Sun and in Jul and Aug
🅼 Piramide 🚌 23, 30, 60, 75, 280, 716 (or any to Piramide or Via Marmorata); tram 3

GIFTS AND SOUVENIRS

FABRIANO

Via del Babuino 173, 00187 Roma
Tel 06 32600361

Minimalist in design, this store sells stacks of paper goods and stationery such as notepads and address books, enticingly arranged by colour. Shades run the gamut from yellows, greens and blues to whites, browns and blacks. The paper is of the highest quality and

made by an 800-year-old firm; prices are predictably high. They sell briefcases, too.

🔵 Mon–Sat 10–7.30 🅼 Spagna or Flaminio 🚌 81, 117, 119, 590, 628

HEALTH AND BEAUTY

ROMA STORE

Via della Lungaretta 63, 00153 Roma
Tel 06 581 8789

Despite the unimpressive name, this shop stocks a tantalizing selection of hard-to-find and sophisticated British and French perfumes: L'Artisan Parfumeur, Creed, Etro, Penhaligon's, L'Occitane, Vetiver and Comptoir Sud Pacifique, to name but a few. Creams, imported US and UK brands of soap and toothpaste complete the range.

🔵 Daily 9.30–9 🚌 H, 780; tram 8

JEWELLERY

BULGARI

Via Condotti 10, Roma
Tel 06 679 3876
www.bulgari.com

The most splendid jewellery shop in Rome, but fantastically expensive. Andy Warhol called it the most important museum of art in the Western world. All glittering Renaissance-inspired pieces and a complete lack of refined taste.

🔵 Mon 3–7, Tue–Sat 10–7 🅼 Spagna

MARKETS

CAMPO DE' FIORI

Piazza Campo dei Fiori, 00186 Roma

Probably the most expensive, and without doubt the most liveliest market in Rome. Hawkers collect their wares

WHAT TO DO

from the nearby medieval storage vaults and set up shop in this charismatic location. There was a time when heretics were burned here, and traitors hanged. These days the only things hanging are the flowers and food.

⏱ Mon–Sat 8–2 🚌 46, 62, 64, 116

PORTA PORTESE
Porta Portese, 00153 Roma

Rome's most famous flea market styretches all the way

from the Porta Portese to Trastevere station. It also branches of down the side streets. From trendy clothes and antiques to junk, you can find all sorts here. Arrive early for the best buys, and beware of pickpockets.

⏱ Sun 6.30–1 🚋 Tram 3

UNDERGROUND
Via Francesco Crispi 96, 00187 Roma
Tel 06 3600 5345

Flea markets have sprung up all over Rome in the past few years. One of the best-established is this antiques and collector's market in the Ludovisi underground car park,

held once a month in the winter. More than 100 stalls sell prints, small antiques, frames, comics, lace and old vases. There are also children's stalls where toys are sold and exchanged.

⏱ 9–7 first Sun of the month, Oct–Apr (closed Feb) 🚇 Spagna 🚌 116, 119, 204, 630, 910 or any bus to Via Veneto

MUSIC

RICORDI MEDIA STORE
Via Cesari Battisti 120, 00187 Roma
Tel 06 6798022/3
www.lafeltrinelli.it

Rome's popular music store, in a nicely designed building that once housed the Verdi archives. It has the largest classical DVD/CD collection in Rome. There is a large Italian music section and sheet music and musical instruments are also sold. They have four other outlets: Termini, Viale Guilio Cesare, Piazza della Repubblica and Via del Corso.

⏱ Mon–Sat 9.30–8, Sun 3.30–8; closed Sun, Jul–Aug 🚌 40, 62, 64, 117 to Piazza Venezia

SHOES AND ACCESSORIES

FURLA
Piazza di Spagna 22, 00187 Roma
Tel 06 6920 0363
www.furla.it

Purveyors of chic bags and practical totes in bright shades, along with scarves, shoes and jewellery. Some wild style

combinations and original touches. Prices are moderate compared with other big-name accessory designers. The company has a fleet of

branches all over the world, and several more in Rome.

⏱ Daily 10–8 🚇 Spagna 🚌 116, 117, 119, 590

GIORGIO SERMONETA
Piazza di Spagna 61, 00187 Roma
Tel 06 6791960
www.sermonetagloves.com

The shop is fairly small and may feel cramped, but don't be fooled—just look up! Top-quality gloves—thousands of them—decorate this shop, and come in bright shades and styles to fit every hand. Prices range from €23 to €100.

⏱ Mon–Sat 9.30–8 🚇 Spagna 🚌 116,117

TOYS

LA CITTÀ DEL SOLE
Via della Scrofa 65, 00186 Roma
Tel 06 6880 3805
www.cittadelsole.it

A toy store for the progressive parent. Crammed with educational toys, puzzles, games and books divided up into sections for children aged 0 to 14, with a focus on creative playing and learning. All the best toys from big and small producers alike. Not a Playstation in sight!

⏱ Mon–Sat 10–7.30, Sun 11–7.30 🚌 116

Performance

CINEMA

PASQUINO
Piazza Sant'Egidio 10, 00158 Roma
Tel 06 581 5208

This is somewhat of a Roman

WHAT TO DO

institution. All films (about four per day on three screens) are shown in English, so many English-speakers in the audience. The crowded espresso bar is open before screenings.

🕐 Daily screenings at 5, 8 and 10.30 🎫 €7 🚇 🚌 Bus or tram to Viale Trastevere

CLASSICAL MUSIC, DANCE, OPERA

AUDITORIUM
Parco della Musica
Viale Pietro de Coubertin 30,
00197 Roma
Tel 06 808 2058
www.musicaperroma.it
Architect Renzo Piano has finally given Rome the concert hall it deserves. Opened in 2002, this year-round, three-auditorium complex is the

city's biggest music venue with a capacity of 4,600. Find it between Lungotevere Flaminio and Viale Tiziano.

🕐 Performances: Mon–Fri 7–9, 9–11; Box office: daily 11–6; Hello Ticket (credit card bookings): Mon–Fri 10–5 🎫 €8 🚇 🚉 Piazzale Flaminio, and then tram 🚌 Bus to Auditorio

TEATRO OLIMPICO
Piazza Gentile da Fabriano 17,
00196 Roma
Tel 06 326 5991, 0800 907 080 (toll-free)
www.teatroolimpico.it
This Accademia Filarmonica-owned venue is very comfortable, although it has been upstaged of late by the new Auditorium. The main season runs from September to May and the acoustics and range of productions are always excellent.

🕐 Daily 10–1, 3–5.30; after 8pm for same-day tickets 🎫 €20–€35 🚇 🚌 Bus or tram to Piazza Mancini or Stadio Olimpico

TEATRO DELL'OPERA DI ROMA
Via Firenze 72, 00186 Roma
Tel 06 481 7517
www.opera.roma.it
A hidden gem, too often overlooked by the locals. The interior is adorned with all the trimmings of a true opera house complete with velvet boxes. Not to be missed by those who love classical dance.

The theatre is beautiful and attracts first-rate dance troupes from all over the world. You are certain to see the cream of Roman society.

🕐 Performances: 9pm, Nov–May; Box office: Mon–Fri 9.30–2 🎫 €8–€120 🚇 🚌 Bus to Via Nazionale

CONTEMPORARY LIVE MUSIC

ALEXANDERPLATZ
Via Ostia 9, 00193 Roma
Tel 06 3974 2171
Rome's most famous jazz

venue holds jazz festivals all year round, and organizes outdoor concerts at Villa Celimontana in summer. American bands are often on the bill. Creole cuisine is served in their restaurant.

🕐 Mon–Sat 9pm–1.30am; closed first 2 weeks of Aug 🎫 €6.50 🚌 Bus to Piazza Risorgimento or Clodio

BIG MAMA
Vicolo San Francesco a Ripa 18,
00158 Roma
Tel 06 581 2551
www.bigmama.it
A storied jazz joint where local and international bands play in the cavernous, smoke-filled underground hideaway. The

audience sits close to the band, and it is not uncommon to see dancing on the tabletops.

🕐 Daily 9pm–1.30am; closed Jul–Oct 🎫 €6–€13 🚌 Bus to Viale Trastevere or Piazza Mastai

CARUSO
Via di Monte Testaccio 36, 00153 Roma
Tel 06 574 5019
The best bet for Latin beats, ranging from salsa to hip-hop. A mix of live bands and Rome's best DJs. It is always packed, especially on Sunday, which is disco night. There is an Arabic music nights, too.

🕐 Tue–Sun 10.30pm–3am 🎫 €8–€10 🚉 Piramide 🚌 Bus to Testaccio

PALALOTTOMATICA
Piazzale dello Sport
Viale dell'Umanesimo, 00144 Roma
Tel 06 540901
www.ticketweb.it

WHAT TO DO

www.palalottomatica.it
The biggest venue in the city, a huge sports stadium-turned-concert hall in EUR. It hosts all the top international acts—everyone from Sting to the Rolling Stones has played here at some time.

🕐 8pm (usually) 💶 Varies 🚇 Metro to EUR Palaeur and bus to Palazzo dello Sport

VILLAGGIO GLOBALE
Lungotevere Testaccio, 00153 Roma
Tel 06 5757 2333
This former slaughterhouse (the Mattatoio) is Rome's best-loved music venue. There's a huge outdoor courtyard for concerts and dancing. During larger events, food stands are set up inside.

🕐 6pm–3am (variable) 💶 €10 maximum 🚌 Bus to Testaccio or Lungotevere Testaccio

THEATRE

PALAZZO DELLE ESPOSIZIONI
Via Nazionale 194, 00184 Roma
Tel 06 482 8757
www.palazzoesposizioni.it
www.comune.roma.it
This is Rome's all-round cultural centre where theatre, film showings and art exhibitions take place under one roof. If all of the city's artistic juices could be captured in a single space, this would be it. It can be found near the huge tunnel that connects Via Nazionale to Via del Tritone. The complex is right at the mouth of the tunnel, on the left side of Via Nazionale.

🕐 9pm (usually). Box office: Wed–Mon 10–9 🚌 Bus to Via Nazionale

TEATRO DI ROMA
Largo Argentina 52, 00186 Roma
Tel 06 6880 4601
www.teatrodiroma.net
A leading year-round venue for beautifully staged productions in one of Rome's oldest theatres. A performance here is a night to remember. Dress to impress. There is a bar serving cocktails at the

intermission. The theatre is on the Campo de Fiori side of the extensive square, Largo Argentina.

🕐 9pm. Box office: Mon–Sat 10–2, 3–7 💶 €12–€27 🚌 Bus or tram to Largo Argentina

Nightlife

ANIMA
Via di Santa Maria dell'Anima 57, 00186 Roma
Tel 06 6889 2806
At the heart of Roman nightlife, west of piazza Navona this bar is a beloved hangout for foreigners and English speakers. Excellent fresh-fruit cocktails, ultra-modern decoration and highly respectable resident DJs.

🕐 Tue–Sun 9.30pm–2am 🚌 46, 62, 64, 116, 81, 87, 492

CUL DE SAC
Piazza Pasquino 73, 00186 Roma
Tel 06 6880 1094
In a little piazza off Piazza Navona, this is one of the

oldest wine bars in town and still one of the best. They have an excellent wine list, mouth-watering cheeses, meats and unusual dishes. Friendly service and frequent tastings.

🕐 Daily noon–4, 7–12.30 🚌 46, 62, 64, 492 to Corso Vittorio Emanuele II (get off near Sant'Andrea della Valle); 70, 81, 87 to Corso Rinascimento; 116 to Campo de' Fiori

THE GALLERY
Via della Maddalena 12, 00186 Roma
Tel 06 687 2316

www.thegallery.it
An enegetic, modern and elegant bar behind the Pantheon. Music from hip-hop to R&B to '70s and '80s revival draws a crowd that's young and ready to party.

🕐 Tue–Fri 8pm–3am, Sat–Sun 8pm–4am 💶 €10 🚌 116

MAX'S BAR
Via A. Grandi 7a, 00185 Roma
Tel 06 7030 1599
www.maxbar.net
Very busy gay bar for men of all ages. Being underground, it can become quite hot when it gets crowded. Consists of two bars, a dance floor, and large sitting/socializing area.

🕐 Thu–Tue 10.30am–3.30am 💶 €8–€11, Mon free 🚇 Manzoni

QUBE
Via di Portonaccio 212, 00159 Roma
Tel 06 438 5445
The young crowd dance till they drop in Rome's biggest underground disco. Friday night is 'Muccassassina' night, once gay and transgressive, now more straight and mainstream than alternative.

🕐 Thu–Sat 11pm–4am 💶 Variable cover charge 🚇 Tiburtina 🚌 71, 168, 204, 409, 492, 545, 649

SIDE MEETING POINT
Via Labicana 50, 00184 Roma
Tel 0348 692 9472
Gay, retro-kitsch bar. One of the few exclusively gay nightspots in Rome, partying spills out onto the pavement and road in the summer. This club has stood the test of time.

🕐 Daily 4pm–2am 🚇 Colosseo 🚌 Various buses

Sports and Activities

SPECTATOR SPORTS

FOOTBALLL

STADIO OLIMPICO
Viale dello Stadio Olimpico, 00194 Roma

WHAT TO DO

Tel 06 3237333
www.stadioolimpico.it
Football, football, football—
no spectator sport is more
important to Romans. The city
has two rival teams: Roma
fans sit on the south side of
the stadium and Lazio fans
on the north side.
🕐 Sun throughout season
✋ €15–€60 🚌 Bus to Lungotevere
Maresciallo Cadorna

RUGBY
STADIO FLAMINIO
Viale Tiziano, 00196 Roma
Tel 06 3685 7832
www.federugby.it
Don't be fooled into thinking
Italians only go mad for *calcio*
(football). The country is home
to 24 rugby clubs, and the best
games are in the capital when
club RDS Roma hits the field.
✋ €10–€30 🚌 Bus or tram to
Viale Tiziano

SPECTACLES
CINECITTÀ
Via Tuscolana, 00173 Roma
www.cinecitta.it
On warm summer nights,
Rome's celebrated film studio
opens to the public. Among
the attractions are chariot
races à la *Ben Hur*, when
gladiators and their horses are
dressed in the appropriate
Roman attire.
🕐 Sat pm, summer only ✋ €10
🚇 Cinecittà

ACTIVITIES

GOLF
CIRCOLO DEL GOLF DI ROMA
Via Appia Nuova 716/a,
00178 Roma
Tel 06 780 3407
www.golfroma.it
Excellent 18-hole golf course
surrounded by umbrella pines
and Roman ruins. There is a
great on-site restaurant. Non-
members may participate in
competitions on Sundays.
🕐 Tue–Sun 8–sunset ✋ €64 weekdays, €76 weekends 🚇 Colli Albani,
then a taxi ride

SWIMMING
PISCINA DELLE ROSE
Viale America 20, 00144 Roma
Tel 06 592 6717
Rome's largest open-air pool
and a great place to bring the
kids at weekends. It's at the
heart of the ultra-sleek
Palasport sports facility built
by Mussolini.
🕐 Daily 9–10pm ✋ €10
🚇 Palasport, EUR

TENNIS
CIRCOLO DELLA STAMPA
Piazza Mancini 19,
00196 Roma
Tel 06 323 2452
Owned by the Professional
Order of Italian Journalists,
this friendly tennis club has
both clay and synthetic-grass
courts at reasonable prices.
There are tennis lessons for
all levels.
🕐 Daily 8am–11pm ✋ €10–€30 per
hour 🚌 Bus to piazza Mancini

HEALTH AND BEAUTY
AVEDA SALON
Rampa Mignanelli 9, 00187 Roma
Tel 06 6992 4886
www.aveda.com
Pampering at its finest by
Aveda, Europe's leading
potions-and-lotions brand.

Energize yourself with plant
steam inhalation, skin hydra-
tion or mild aromatherapy.
Renew yourself with a manicure, pedicure or a quick wax.
A great place to stock up on
beauty products if you haven't
time for an Aveda Essential
Facial Treatment.
🕐 Mon 3.30–8, Tue–Sat 10–8

✋ €25 manicure, €31 plant steam
inhalation 🚇 Spagna

For Children

EXPLORA—IL MUSEO
DEI BAMBINI
Via Flaminia 82, 00192 Roma
Tel 06 361 3776
www.mdbr.it
Rome's first and only children's
museum, opened in 2001.
Four sections dedicated to
the human body, the environment, communications and
society. Plenty of signs and
material in English. Kids can
star in their own TV show,

work in a supermarket and
find out about living ecologi-
cally. Best for under eights.
Advance booking required at
the weekend.
🕐 Tue–Sun 9.30–7; closed Jul–Aug
✋ Adult €6, under 3 free 🚇 Flaminio
🚌 95, 117, 119, 204, 231, 490, 495, 618,
916; tram 2, 3, 19

LUNEUR PARK
Via delle Tre Fontane,
00144 Roma
Tel 06 592 5933
www.luneur.it
Built in 1953, the oldest fun
park in Italy has kept up with
the times. Activities and rides
ar both traditional and
adrenalin-pumping, with a
puppet theatre, several
haunted houses, bumper cars,
a lake with motor boats, and
rides called Flipper, Thriller
and Space Kickers. The park is
a lot bigger than it seems.
Suitable for kids and teenagers.

🕐 Mon, Wed–Thu 3–7, 5–2am, Fri 3–midnight, 5–2am, Sat 3–2, 5pm–3am, Sun and public holidays 10–1, 4–2am, 15 Jun–15 Sep; Mon, Wed–Thu 3–7, Fri 3–midnight, Sat 3–2, Sun 10–1, 3–10, the rest of the year 💶 Individual rides €1–€6; half-day visit €15–€25 🚇 Magliana, Palasport or EUR Fermi 🚌 706, 707, 714, 717, 765, 771

TIME ELEVATOR
Via S.S. Apostoli 20, 00186 Roma
Tel 06 699 0053
www.time-elevator.it
A multimedia experience illustrating the history of Rome from its founding in 8BC to the present day. With

headphones, a screen, a moving platform and other surprise special effects, this is a genuinely fun (if slightly cheesy and occasionally factually weak) introduction to the city. Watch Rome burn and see Caesar's assassination: worth the rather high entrance fee.
🕐 Daily screenings from 10am–10.30pm 💶 Adult €11, child under 12 €9.20 🚌 40, 62, 63, 64, 916 or any bus to Via del Corso or Piazza Venezia

Festivals and Events

BEFANA
December–6 January
According to legend, the Befana was an old woman who refused the Magi shelter on their journey to Bethlehem—she later regretted this, and still wanders the earth looking for the Christ Child. Befana is associated with the Christmas period, as is the wise old woman who flies from house to house delivering the good children's presents on 6 January—bad children get coal. A lively fair runs in the Piazza Navona during Christmas time. Toys and sweets are the main attraction: Look out for the sweet called *carbone*, which looks like lumps of coal.

ROMAEUROPA FESTIVAL
20 September–30 November
Tel 06 422 96300
www.romaeuroa.net

SPECIAL

OPERA FESTIVAL AT THE BATHS OF CARACALLA
Terme di Caracalla
Box office: Teatro dell'Opera via Firenze 72, 00184 Roma
Tel 06 481601
This is what grand opera and ballet are all about. Big productions such as Verdi's *Aida* are staged—complete with horses and elephants—inside the ruins of the

ancient Roman Baths of Caracalla. Shows are staged in the largest area of the baths, not the smaller indoor ones. Bring a cushion to sit on.
🕐 Performances 8pm , July; Booking office: Tue–Sat 9–5, Sun 9–1.30 💶 €20–€50 🚇 FAO 🚌 Bus to Terme di Caracalla

---

A major annual arts festival of classical and contemporary theatre, music and dance, held in different venues across the city.
💶 €5–€30, festival pass €135

ROME CITY MARATHON
3rd Sunday in March
Via dei Fori Imperiali, 00186 Roma
Tel 06 3018 3022, 06 3018 3016
www.maratonadiroma.it
Each spring runners flock to Rome and, like gladiators, they come down the avenue that cuts right through the Forum. This event is slowly gaining the equivalent status of the marathons held in London and New York.
🚌 Bus to Piazza Venezia

CONCORSO IPPICO INTERNAZIONALE DI PIAZZA DI SIENA
Late April–Early May
Villa Borghese, Piazza di Siena, 00186 Roma
Tel 06 327 9939
www.piazzadisiena.com
Few know it, but Rome plays host to an important annual equestrian event that has all the trimmings of the big horse shows around the world. Show jumping is the main event.
💶 Adult €10–€44, child €6–€7 🚌 Bus to via Veneto

CAMPIONATO INTERNAZIONALE DI TENNIS
1–15 May
Foro Italico, Viale dei Gladiatori, 00194 Roma
Tel 06 323 3807
Every May, Rome hosts the Italian Open tennis tournament. This is Europe's most competitive non-Grand Slam tennis event.
💶 €8–€55 🚌 Bus to Lungotevere Maresciallo Cadorna

LAZIO AND THE MARCHE

The tranquil provincial towns of the Marche and Lazio are a world away from the buzz of Italy's more frenetic regions. Despite its proximity to Rome, Lazio is a quiet area, with shops geared up to everday needs. Lovers of luxury will be more attracted to the wine towns around Rome, and you'll find good weekly markets in places like Viterbo.

The same is true in the Marche. Urbino's the best place for shopping, with the usual chain-store fashion names, and the bonus of a couple of splendid weekly markets. Don't neglect Ascoli Piceno, famed for its ceramics and antiques shopping. Both Urbino and Ascoli Piceno have a good cultural scene, with the emphasis on summer festivals, along with Lazio's larger towns, particularly Tivoli and Frascati. There's clubbing along the Marche coast, while children are catered for with waterparks and safe, sandy beaches.

Shopping

FIERA DELL'ANTIQUARIATO
Via del Trivio, Ascoli Piceno
Every Italian town has its flea market, but few could be

described as antiques fairs. However, at Ascoli Piceno's monthly antiques market—against the backdrop of the Chiesa di San Francesco—you can find real treasures. Look out for the glazed ceramics.
◉ 9–dusk, third weekend of every month

LAUDI SAVINA CERAMICS
Via Pisa 4, 63100 Ascoli Piceno
Tel 0736 44024
In past times Ascoli Piceno's local economy was fuelled by its ceramics industry. Take a walk up Via del Trivio to the oldest and prettiest district and see today's artisans working in dimly lit studios. One of the

most talented is Laudi Savina, whose floral and geometrical designs are reminiscent of Renaissance pieces.
◉ Mon–Sat 9–1, 3–8

FRASCATI

ENOTECA SAN MARCO
Piazza San Pietro 8, 00044 Frascati
Tel 06 941 9519
The bottles of wine are stacked right up to the ceiling, but the friendly assistants will help you choose the right one. Ample list of wines from Italy and abroad, including the celebrated local Frascati. Vintage and dated wines for the more demanding, plus grappa, champagne and calvados.
◉ Mon–Thu 10–1, 4.30–8, Fri–Sun 9.30–1, 4.30–8

GIOIE E COLORI
Via G. Matteotti 17, 00044 Frascati
Tel 06 941 7133
This cosy shop near the Piazza San Pietro has a wide choice of original silver, amber and other jewellery, along with scarves, bags and dolls.
◉ Mon–Sat 9.30–1, 4.30–8

URBINO

ENOTECA MAGIA CIARLA
Via Raffaello 54, 61029 Urbino
Tel 0722 328438
www.magiaciarla.com
This is where you should go to find the best wines. With 600 labels in stock—ranging from white verdicchio aged in oak to

ruby red reserves from the region—the store is also a wine museum. The elegant interior with the musty smell of a cantina makes it a great place for wine-tasting.
◉ Mon–Sat 9–1, 4–7.30

MERCATO SETTIMANALE DI URBINO
Viale B. Buozzi, 61029 Urbino
Tel 0722 2631 (tourist office)
Arrive early Sunday morning for the best finds: World War I helmets, 1950s chrome lamps and 16th-century dressers. Its worth hanging around until late morning when the prices go down.
◉ Sun 7–12.30

Performance

CINECLUB AT CINEMA PICENO
Cinema Piceno
Largo Alessandro Manzoni 6, 63100 Ascoli Piceno; outdoor screenings at Chiostro Sant'Agostino, Corso Mazzini 90, 63100 Ascoli Piceno
Tel 0736 254605
www.ascoli.info/cineclub/index.html
This movie club shows original, undubbed independent and international films throughout the year. They also organize an open-air cinema festival in August.
◉ Tue–Wed 9.15, Oct–Jun; open-air festival 3rd week in Aug 💳 €5 ◉

COTTON JAZZ CLUB
Largo Cattaneo 4, 63100 Ascoli Piceno
Tel 348 6056390 or 0861 80401
With so many good jazz festivals in the vicinity (Ancona, Urbino, Umbria), it's no surprise that a jazz scene has evolved in Ascoli Piceno. Big-name performers drop to jam in informal surroundings.
◉ Tue–Sun 8pm–1.30am

TEATRO VENTIDIO BASSO
Via del Trivio 44, 63100 Ascoli Piceno
Tel 0736 298305, 0736 298306 (infor-

mation), 0736 244970 (box office)
Named after a local military
hero, this mighty 1846 opera
house has wedding-cake layers
of balconies, glittering chandeliers and a neoclassical façade.
The playbill is eclectic, from
Puccini to *The Full Monty*. Box
office at Via del Trivio 50.
🕐 Thu–Sat 8.30, Sun 5.30, 8.30. Box
office daily 9–1, 3–8.30 💶 €8–€22

URBINO
CAPPELLA MUSICALE DEL
SS SACRAMENTO
Via Valerio 7, 61029 Urbino
Tel 0722 4120
Music students and visiting
ensembles perform at this
frescoed music venue (in the
Sala Vecchiotti), which has
existed for centuries.
Everything classical from string
quartets to church choirs.
🕐 Sat–Sun 9pm (usually) 💶 Free

SALA MANISCALCO, RAMPA
DI GIORGIO MARTINI
Corso Garibaldi, 61029 Urbino
Tel 0722 2613
Next to the Teatro Sanzio is a
curious music and theatre
venue built inside what looks
like a giant staircase. Events
include everything from jazz
performances to experimental
theatre.
🕐 8.30pm (usually) 💶 From €8

TEATRO SANZIO
Via Matteotti, 61029 Urbino
Tel 0722 2281
When this theatre was built in
1845, local citizens thought it
an eyesore that clashed with
Urbino's Renaissance harmony.
Today the Sanzio is considered
one of the city's most impor-
tant architectural sights.
🕐 Thu–Sun 8.30. Box office daily 9–1,
3–8.30 💶 €10–€70

Nightlife
GABICCE MARE
BAIA IMPERIALE
Via Panoramica, 61011 Gabicce Mare
Tel 0541 950312, 0541 952135
www.baiaimperiale.net

SPECIAL IN VITERBO
TERME DEI PAPI
12 Strada Bagni, 01100 Viterbo
Tel 0761 3501
www.termedeipapi.it
Beautiful grounds and a
sumptuous wooden-decked
swimming pool greet visitors
to the Terme dei Papi in the
northern Lazio province,
75km (47 miles) north of
Rome. Mud baths, herbal
inhalations, facials and
organic treatments are all
available.
🕐 Wed–Mon 9–9 💶 €60 mud bath
🚌 The Terme dei Papi is 5km
(3 miles) past the town

Must be seen to be believed.
Baia Imperiale claims to be
the biggest nightclub in the
world—and the most
photographed. Imperial
Roman decor, complete with a
column-lined amphitheatre
and Caesar statues for theme
park appeal. Dance to the live
bands, DJ's and Latin grooves
by the outdoor pool.
🕐 Daily 9pm–3.30am, Jul–Aug
💶 €15; free tickets can be requested at
www.out4fun.it 🚌 From Urbino, drive
15km (9 miles) to the Adriatic Sea at
Gabicce Mare, near Pesaro. Via
Panoramica is the coastal road. Look for
signs before the town

For Children
GUIDONIA MONTECELIO
AQUAPIPER
Via Maremmana Inferiore km 29300,
00012 Guidonia Montecelio
Tel 0774 3265 3839
www.aquapiper.it
Aquatic theme park with
children's pools, water slides,
wave machines and a
hydro-massage lagoon—
perfect for hot summer days.
There is an ice-cream kiosk, a
fast-food restaurant and a
picnic area.
🕐 Daily 9–7, Jun to mid-Sep 💶 Adult
€9–€14, under 10 €6, one child free

when accompanied by an adult
🚌 From Tivoli take S.S. Tiburtina
towards Rome, then turn left into Via
Maremmana Inferiore, following signs
for Guidonia Montecelio

Festivals and Events
FRASCATI SUMMER
FESTIVALS
June–September
Villa Torlonia, Frascati
Tel 06 941 7195 (Frascati Cultural
Office)
Throughout the summer, festi-
vals are organized in Frascati's
parks and villas, with open-air
shows, dance, cinema,
fireworks and night markets.

INCHINATA
14–15 August
Piazza Trento and nearby streets, Tivoli
Tel 0774 311249, 0774 319051
In this religious festival celebrating the Assumption of the
Blessed Virgin, images of Christ
and his mother bow
(inchinare) to each other in
Piazza Trento at the end of the
procession. Live music and
fireworks follow.

TORNEO DELLA QUINTANA
1st weekend in August
Ascoli Piceno
One of the Marche's loveliest
towns is the setting for this
summer festival of parades
and jousting. More than 1,200
people participate in the processions, with bands, drums
and flag-waving. A totally
authentic and passionate
spectacle.

SAGRA DELL'UVA
1st Sunday in October
Piazza dei Quattro Mori, 00047 Marino
Tel 06 938 5555
This famous festival celebrates
the new wine vintage with a
parade in the afternoon. Later,
the main fountain, dei Quattro
Mori, bubbles and overflows
with wine.
🚌 From Frascati take S.S. n.216
following signs for Marino

THE SOUTH

Good shopping in southern Italy, the country's poorest part, is something of a rarity, and if you're in the spending mood, do your purchasing in and around Naples or along the lovely coastline to the south of the city. The Sorrento peninsula and its tiny villages are among Italy's chicest holiday areas, a great hunting ground for beachwear and cool, elegant, evening resort clothes. In Naples itself, head for Santa Lucia for designer stores, while the area around Via Toledo will fit the bill at the lower end of the price range.

Other towns worth browsing around include Puglia's Bari and Lecce; towns in Calabria and Basilicata have chain-store fashion and weekly markets. For live entertainment, Naples is your best bet—there's classical music, opera and high-standard ballet, as well as cinema and some crazy clubs. The action spreads farther south in the summer, down the coast and out to the islands of Capri and Ischia, where you'll find great music venues and clubs in fabulous waterside venues.

The south is a great for outdoor activities, with sailing, windsurfing and swimming, plus some of the best scuba diving in the world. The walking in the southern hills is superb.

WHAT TO DO

Shopping

CAPRI

LIMONCELLO DI CAPRI
Via Roma 79, 80073 Capri
Tel 081 837 5561
www.limoncello.com
Limoncello liqueur may be abundant in these parts, but there's no denying this shop is one of the best of its kind on the island. The lemon-based spirit is great mixed with champagne or *prosecco,* and as an after-dinner *digestivo.*
🕐 Daily 9–7

NAPOLI (NAPLES)

BARTOLI
Via Cilea 67/71, 80129 Napoli
Tel 081 560 0808
This swanky jewellery shop has a huge choice of gems and watches. Beyond the glittering windows are exclusive brands including Cartier, Roman and Costantin e Vacheron.
🕐 Mon 4.30–8, Tue–Sat 10–1.30, 4.30–8 🚇 Piazza Vanvitelli

IL CANTUCCIO DELLA CERAMICA
Via Benedetto Croce 38, 80134 Napoli
Tel 081 5525857
You'll find this ceramics studio down a small street between Piazza del Gesù Nuovo and Piazza San Domenico Maggiore. Ceramics in a multitude of hues are for sale, but you can also take classes here and make your own.
🕐 Mon–Fri 10–6 🚇 Piazza Cavour

ENOTECA PARTENOPEA
Viale Augusto 2, 80100 Napoli
Tel 081 593 7982
Don't leave Naples without tasting some of the region's fine wines. The rich volcanic soil gives the wine a remarkable richness; ask the staff for an introduction to the region's offerings and grab a few bargain bottles to take home.
🕐 Fri–Wed 9–1.30, 4.30–7.30, Thu 9–1.30 🚇 Campi Flegrei

ERNESTO BOWINKEL
Piazza Martiri 24, 80121 Napoli
Tel 081 764 4344

A smartly coiffed Neapolitan gentleman will guide you through the fabulous antiques and artworks here. There are many smaller pieces that would make a worthy investment or great presents. Take time to ask about the history behind the paintings, historic prints, frames and elegant statues that fill this shop.
🕐 Mon–Sat 10–1.30, 4–7.30 🚇 Piazza Amedeo 🚌 102, 108, 122

MARINELLA
Riviera di Chiaia 287, 80122 Napoli
Tel 081 764 4214
www.marinellanapoli.it
If formal style is what you're after, then Marinella should be right up your street. This well-respected Neapolitan haunt has been patronized by the likes of Kennedy, Gorbachev and Caruso. The shop is famed for made-to-measure ties in silk, wool and other fabrics.
🕐 Mon–Sat 9.30–1.30, 3.30–8 🚇 Piazza Amedeo 🚌 102, 108, 122

MERCATO DI SANT'ANTONIO
Via Sant'Antonio Abate, 80139 Napoli
This market is always a feast for the senses and a little bewildering to the uninitiated. It's crammed with local produce, and transactions take place in the fast-paced local dialect. Don't miss out on the fantastic tomatoes grown in the foothills of Vesuvio. If you would like a small amount of something, ask for *un etto, per favore* (100g, please).
🕐 Daily 9–8 🚌 14, 135, 254

SORRENTO

ENOTECA BACCHUS
Piazza San Antonio 20, 80067 Sorrento
Tel 089 807 4610
www.enotecabacchus.com
Sommelier Paolo Schiattarella runs this shop and selects the vintages. There are more than 1,000 different labels to choose from, as well as prized bottles of grappa, cognac, whisky, brandy, calvados, rum and various liqueurs.

Ⓒ Daily 9–1, 4.30–10, Jun–Sep; 8.30–10pm, rest of year

Performance

LECCE

TEATRO PAIESELLO
Via Giuseppe Palmieri, 73100 Lecce
Tel 0832 245499
Expect Neo-Renaissance architecture, classical Greek motifs on a handsome 1872 façade and sumptuous interiors. Jazz, cabaret, classical and pop, plus Italian and international drama and dance productions.
Ⓒ Box office: Mon–Sat 10.30–1, 4.30–7 Ⓦ €8–€30 Ⓢ

NAPOLI (NAPLES)

FONDAZIONE NUOVA ORCHESTRA ALESSANDRO SCARLATTI
Piazza dei Martiri 58, 80121 Napoli (headquarters)
Tel 081 764 0590
The Orchestra Scarlatti stages concerts at San Severo al Pendino and other historical sites and theatres around Naples. Well-known classical works and Neapolitan music through the ages.
Ⓦ €5–€20 Ⓢ Ⓔ C4, 102, 128

MURAT LIVE CLUB
Via Bellini 8, 80135 Napoli
Tel 081 544 5919
www.muratliveclub.it
This club on Piazza Dante has an adventurous music policy—the eclectic schedule includes lots of jazz and funk, all imbued with a touch of Neapolitan style. They also

have the occasional world music night.
Ⓒ Daily 10pm–late Ⓜ Montesanto Ⓔ 137, 160, 161

TEATRO POLITEAMA
Via Monte di Dio 80, 80132 Napoli
Tel 081 764 5001
This theatre often has lavish productions by the Scuola di Ballo del Teatro di San Carlo in conjunction with illustrious international companies, including the Birmingham Royal Ballet and the Conservatorio di San Pietro a Majella.
Ⓒ Box office: Tue–Sat 10–1, 4.30–6.30 Ⓦ €12– €45 Ⓢ Ⓔ 102, 128

TEATRO SAN CARLO
Via San Carlo 98F, 80132 Napoli
Tel 081 797330
www.teatrosancarlo.it
The oldest opera house in Italy stages ballet as well as opera, classical concerts and short comic operas. It was here that some of the first ballet productions were performed, in the intermission between opera acts. Book tickets in advance.
Ⓒ Box office: Tue–Sun 10–1, 4.30–6.30 Ⓦ €23–€105 Ⓢ Ⓔ C4, 140, 149

RAVELLO

GIARDINI DI VILLA RUFOLO
Piazza Vescovado 1, 84010 Ravello
Tel 199 109910
www.ravellofestival.it
A Moorish-style villa and gardens that is a magnet for classical music fans. Wagner lived and composed at the nearby Palazzo Sasso. Ravello is a music captial, especially during the annual Festival

Musicale di Ravello held from early June to late August.
Ⓒ Mon–Fri 9–7.30, Sat 9–4, Apr–Sep; Mon–Fri 9–6, rest of year Ⓦ €4

SORRENTO

ARTIS DOMUS
Via San Nicolà, 80067 Sorrento
Tel 081 8772073
www.artisdomus.com
This elegant 19th-century villa is the Sorrentine haunt of poets and artists. Live pop/rock/jazz/folk music and club nights are held in an evocative and intimate setting. Excellent food and a fabulous cocktail bar/*birreria*.
Ⓒ Sat 8pm–late Ⓦ €5–€10

Nightlife

NAPOLI (NAPLES)

SOLO
Via Ferrigni 19, 80121 Napoli
Tel 081 764 7420
Two floors of modern, cool furnishings supply set the mood in this trendy club. They serves superb aperitifs and have a fine menu. Mainstream dance and house music.
Ⓒ Tue–Sun 10pm–3.30am Ⓦ €15 membership Ⓜ Piazza Amedeo Ⓔ 1, 140, 152

VELVET ZONE
Via Cisterna dell'Olio 11, 80134 Napoli
Tel 339 670 0234
www.velvetzone.it
This long-established club attracts a discerning crowd with its eclectic, alternative music policy. Live bands and respected international DJs often plat here.
Ⓒ Tue–Sun midnight–dawn Ⓦ €12 membership Ⓜ Montesanto

VIRGILIO
Via Tito Lucrezio Caro 6, 80123 Napoli
Tel 338 345 9007, 328 376 1518
Drag queens and a camp crowd flock to this open-air club to dance to classic hits and house on summer Saturday nights. It's a great place to people-watch.

◉ Sat 11.30pm–4am, Jun–Sep ▣ €13
🚇 Mergellina

YES BRASIL
Via Posillipo 405/c, 80123 Napoli
Tel 081 575 1118
Join the fun-loving crowd at this tropical club with Brazilian beats. Dancers in skimpy outfits shake their tassels to the accomplished percussionists and the bubbly staff will keep you topped up with Brazilian drinks and fare all night long.
◉ Daily 8pm–2am 🚇 Mergellina

POSITANO
MUSIC ON THE ROCKS
Via delle Grotte 52, 84017 Positano
Tel 089 875874
www.musicontherocks.it
Elegant club hewn out of the rocks serving fine cocktails. Italian-style piano bar most evenings and frequent appearances by well-known international DJs who spin house music.
◉ Daily 8pm–late, Apr–Sep ▣ €10

SORRENTO
CIRCOLO DEI FORESTIERI
Via Luigi de Maio 35, 80067 Sorrento
Tel 081 807 4033
An impressive villa with elegant salons and panoramic views of Vesuvio. Things hot up later with live music and karaoke.
◉ Daily 9pm–3am; closed Dec–Feb

MATILDA CLUB
Piazza Tasso 1, 80067 Sorrento
Tel 081 877 3236
www.matildaclub.net
A superb, six-level nightclub. Live acts and regular club

SPECIAL IN PRAIANO
L'AFRICANA
Vettica Maggiore, 84010 Praiano
Tel 089 874042
The most celebrated nightclub on this stretch of the Amalfi coast—a hangout of the 50s/60s set. A walkway hewn out of the rock leads to a network of caves that sit above the sea. Commercial dance and house music.
◉ Thu–Sun 10–5 ▣ €12

nights with house, Latin and dance music. Style and decor varies from elegant exposed walls to British pub to contemporary chic. Internet access is also available.
◉ Daily 7.30pm–4am ▣ €12

Sports and Activities
SPECTATOR SPORTS

NAPOLI (NAPLES)
AC NAPOLI
Stadio San Paolo, Piazzale Vincenzo Tecchio, 80125 Napoli
Tel 081 239 5623
www.calcionapoli.it
The San Paolo Stadium is seldom full to its 76,000 capacity these days. However, fans still provide fervent support, and there's a barrage of fireworks every other Sunday. Tickets available on the day.
◉ Alternate Sun (check local press for upcoming matches) ▣ €10–€30
🚇 Campi Flegrei 🚌 521, 522, 523

SS BASKET NAPOLI
PalaBlu
Via Miccoli 1, Monteruscello, Pozzuoli, 80072 Napoli
Tel 081 524 7900
Pompea Napoli's line-up usually includes a few Americans as well as Danes, Germans, Greeks, Slovakians and Irish. The PalaBlu arena has a capacity of 3,500. The

Lega Italiana Pallacanestro Serie A league runs between September and June.
◉ Sun ▣ €12–€40 🚇 Pozzuoli
🚆 Cumana train

ACTIVITIES

ARCO FELICE
Via Campiglione 118, 0078 Arco Felice
Tel 081 421479
This golf course is right next to Lago d'Averno, an eerie lake that is the entrance to Hell according to the ancient Greeks. The nine-hole Circolo Golf Napoli has equipment hire, putting greens, a bar and restaurant.
◉ Wed–Mon 8–dusk, Tue afternoon only ▣ €17 🚇 Pozzuoli 🚆 Cumana train 🚗 Take the Tangenziale (Naples Circular) and exit at Pozzuoli for Via Campana

BAIA
SEA POINT ITALY
Via Molo di Baia 14, 80070 Baia
Tel 081 868 8868
www.seapointitaly.it
A wonderful place to go diving, the Baia is rich in aquatic wildlife and submerged Greek and Roman sites. Sea Point Italy has a team of qualified instructors who can guide you through diving courses tailored for different levels.
◉ Tue–Sun 9–7, May–Sep; Tue–Sun 9–1, 3–7, the rest of the year ▣ Open-water diving course €250, snorkelling course €140 🚆 Cumana train to Baia

CETARA
WIND'S AMICI DI GUIDO
Spiaggia di Cetara, 84010 Cetara
Tel 089 339316
www.flysurfsalerno.it
This windy spot is the best place to windsurf and fly power kites on the Amalfi coast. Equipment hire and lessons are available from Wind's Amici di Guido.
◉ Daily 10–8 ▣ Lessons from €40 per day 🚗 A3 Napoli–Salerno, exit Vietri sul Mare

LECCE

SUN S.A.S.
Via Orsini del Balzo 70, 73100 Lecce
Tel 0832 349444
Relieve those weary limbs after sightseeing and strolling the Salento sand with a visit to this health and beauty parlour. Facial and body treatments are reasonably priced. They have a team of masseurs, and a great range of beauty products to take home.
Mon–Sat 9–9 Massage €30

NAPOLI (NAPLES)

CIRCOLO DEL REMO E DELLA VELA 'ITALIA'
Banchina Santa Lucia, 80132 Napoli
Tel 081 764 6393
www.crvitalia.it
For those interested in sailing, this club has something to suit all abilities. Lessons and courses are available.
Daily 8.30–midnight 102, 140, 150

CLUB ALPINO ITALIANO
Via Passaggio Castello dell'Ovo, 80132 Napoli
Tel 081 764 5343
If you fancy exploring the hills in the Campania region, the local branch of the Club Alpino should be your first port of call. They run trekking and climbing excursions to the summits of Vesuvius and Cervati.
Enquiries Tue, Fri 7pm–9pm
Adult €51, child €18 102, 140, 150

POSITANO

CENTRO SUB
Via Fornillo, 84011 Positano
Tel 089 812148, 089 812884
www.centrosub.it
Discover fauna and archaeological wonders with Centro Sub. Dives visit the Grotte dello Smeraldo and Isola Li Galli, where you can learn about underwater photography and marine biology. They welcome all, from beginners to pros.
Daily 10–6 Courses €40

SORRENTO

TENNIS SORRENTO
Viale Montariello 4, 80067 Sorrento
Tel 081 807 4181
Tennis Sport Sorrento
Via Califano, 80067 Sorrento
Tel 081 8071616
There are two tennis clubs in Sorrento, both very busy in the summer. Each has half a dozen clay and concrete courts. Equipment hire is available.
Daily 10–10 €10 per hour

For Children

NAPOLI (NAPLES)

EDENLANDIA
Viale Kennedy, Campi Flegrei, 80125 Napoli
Tel 081 239 4090
www.edenlandia.it
This theme park is just a short train ride away from the city. There are lots of attractions for all ages, including a fantasy castle, a 3-D cinema, variety shows, water rides and the exciting Star Wars ride.
Daily 10.30am–midnight, Jun–Aug; check hours for rest of year €2
152 Cumana train to Cumana Edenlandia

SOLFATARA
Via Solfatara 161, Pozzuoli, 80078 Napoli
Tel 081 526 2341
www.solfatara.it
Get closer to the volcanic rumblings of the earth's crust at Solfatara, a dormant volcano. Sulphurous fumes hang over the site, but the bubbling mud, fumaroles, and hot

waters are the real spectacle to see.
Daily 8.30am to 1 hour before sunset €5 Pozzuoli–Solfatara and then bus P9 or 152

Festivals and Events

SAGRA DI SAN NICOLA
1st weekend in May
Bari
Three festivities honour St. Nicholas, patron saint of Bari, aka Santa Claus. A parade processes to the basilica to symbolically deliver the saint's bones, which Bari sailors brought back to the city in 1807. The next day, the saint's statue is carried to a fishing boat, where it becomes the focus of another three days of celebrations. It's a festival untouched by tourism.

FESTA DI SAN GENNARO
Saturday before the 1st Sunday in May, 19 September, 16 December
Naples
The fourth-century martyr San Gennaro is Naples' patron saint, and his blood has been kept in a vessel in an opulent sidechapel of the duomo since1497. Three times a year, the blood is exhibited to a seething crowd and it liquefies. The time it takes to do so is said to portend the city's fortunes for the next year.

FESTA DI SAN DOMENICO
1st week in May
Cocullo
www.raiinternational.rai.it/festa/Serpari/Index.htm
This pre-Roman festival was adopted by the early Christian church. It's dedicated to San Domenico Abbate, who delivered the town from poisonous snakes. On his feast day, his statue is carried through the town, and draped en route with hundreds of live snakes.

SICILY AND SARDINIA

Sicily's buzzing markets are one of Italy's great sights, where you'll be spoilt for choice if you want to track down local food to take home. Palermo's are the best, but towns like Siracusa, Agrigento and Noto also warrant a visit. These are also the places to head for other shopping—high-street fashion, wonderful food, interesting wine and above all, the bright ceramics made at Caltagirone. The shopping is more fashionable at Taormina, Sicily's smartest resort, with hip fashion, beautiful linens and lingerie and souvenirs that range from the tasteful to the tacky.

For some unusual entertainment, catch a performance in the ancient Greek theatres at Taormina, Siracusa or Segesta, or hit Palermo for the island's funkiest nightlife.

Sardinia's capital, Cagliari, has the best of the island's shopping, though trendsetters might want to trawl the chic little shops tucked away in the Costa Smeralda developments. Sardinian cakes and pastries found all over the island are delicious and great presents to take home. Performance is strongest in Cagliari, but the clubs hot up in summer at resorts like Cala Gonone, and you shouldn't miss the traditional festivals in the island's interior.

WHAT TO DO

SICILY
Shopping

PALERMO

SICILY'S FOLK
Corso Vittorio Emanuele 450,
90133 Palermo
Tel 091 651 2787
Sicilian ceramics are among the most collectable in Italy. Caltagirone ceramics use blue, green and yellow glazes, depicting flowers, foliage and birds, and are Arab in style. There are some interesting, detailed figurines here, too.
◎ Mon–Sat 8.30–1, 3.30–7.30 ▣ 101, 122, 212

VUCCIRIA
Via Meli, 90213 Palermo
The Vucciria, near San Domenico, is still one of the world's great markets, with a host of fresh produce, including the shiny swordfish, plump San Marzano tomatoes and tasty figs. The sights and smells of the Vucciria are unforgettable and inspiring.
◎ Mon–Sat 8–1 ▣ 101, 212, 250

SIRACUSA

LA BOTTEGA DEL PUPARO
Via della Giudecca 19, 96100 Siracusa
Tel 0931 465540
Puppet shows are very much enjoyed in this part of Sicily, and not just by children. The puppets are full of character, some scowling, others laughing, and a few rather frightening. These traditional marionettes make great gifts or mementos.
◎ Mon–Sat 10–1, 5–8 ▣ 1

ISTITUTO DEL PAPIRO
Via XX Settembre 19, 96100 Siracusa
Tel 0931 483342
www.papiro.it
The Institute creates beautiful writing paper, bound books and lampshades out of papyrus. Many of the designs are heavily influenced by Greek and Egyptian art.
◎ Mon–Sat 9.30–1, 4.30–8 ▣ 1, 2

PESCHERIA
Molo Arezzo della Targia,
96100 Siracusa
The partially walled island of Ortigia is a fabulous setting for Siracusa's fish market. It draws big crowds who enjoy the spectacle of seafood, such as swordfish and giant clams. Ask for a tub of seafood salad, which you can eat on the *lungomare* (seafront).
◎ Mon–Sat 8–1 ▣ 1

Performance

PALERMO

TEATRO MASSIMO
Piazza Verdi, 90138 Palermo
Tel 091 605 3111
www.teatromassimo.it
Completed in 1897, this opera house heralded the beginning of Palermo's belle époque.

The house is certainly one of Europe's finest. The year-round entertainment includes opera, ballet and classical music.
▣ €60 ◎

SPECIAL IN TAORMINA

TEATRO GRECO
Via Teatro Greco, 98039 Taormina
Tel 0942 232220
Built by the Greeks around 250BC, this is arguably one of the greatest auditoriums in the world. Perched on the cliffs, it has stunning views of Mount Etna and the Bay of Axons. A variety of theatre, opera, cinema and music is shown here in the summer, but it's the views that steal the show.
◎ Jul–Aug ▣ €60

SIRACUSA

CINE TEATRO VASQUEZ
Via Filisto 5, 96100 Siracusa
Tel 0931 36823
This cinema shows mostly films dubbed into Italian. Perhaps the most entertainment comes from the audience, who tend to be over-exuberant and loud.
 €7

TEATRO DELL'OPERA DEI PUPPI
Via della Giudecca 17, 96100 Siracusa
Tel 0931 465540
The Sicilian nobility, despite being toppled in the 19th century, are still very well represented in these puppet shows. Although staged for children, the shows have enough political commentary and black humour to keep parents entertained.
Open all year for visits; performances Apr–Dec €8

TAORMINA

CINE TEATRO OLYMPIA
Via di Giovanni 8, 98039 Taormina
Tel 0942 628644
This small cinema draws many local people, and shows a selection of art-house and classic films as well as the latest blockbusters.
€8

Nightlife

PALERMO

AGRICANTUS
Via XX Septembre 82a, 90141 Palermo
Tel 091 309636
www.agricantus.org
More than just a bar, this place hosts world music bands, jazz groups, art exhibitions and dance productions. The multicultural crowd are always up for a good night out.
Daily 8pm–1.30am €6, free when there is no event

For Children

PALERMO

MUSEO INTERNAZIONALE DELLE MARIONETTE
Via Butera 1, 90133 Palermo
Tel 091 328060
www.museomarionettepalermo.it
Children will love this museum of puppetry. It has a wonderful collection of puppets from all over the world, such as Britain's Punch and Judy and some sinister local characters. Shows are put on each day.
Mon–Fri 9–1, 4–7 Adult €3, child €1.50

Festivals and Events

FESTIVAL SUL NOVECENTO
January
Palermo, Sicily
www.comune.palermo.it/Eventi
www.italiafestival.it/novecento
A performing arts festival with classical music, dance and opera to cheer the winter months. Initiated in 1995, it's been growing annually and takes place in venues all over the city.

CARNEVALE
February
All over Sicily and especially at Taormina and Acireale
www.festedisicilia.it/carnevale
Carnevale is enthusiastically celebrated with floats, parades, bands, dancing and fireworks all over Sicily, and particularly at Acireale and Taormina. Acireale festivities take place over 10 days and involve the entire town, with the big names in entertainment and spectacular pyrotechnics on the final Tuesday.

ALMOND BLOSSOM FESTIVAL
February
Agrigento, Sicily
www.festedisicilia.it/febbraio
Almond trees bloom early in Sicily and this festival, founded in 1937, celebrates both the coming of spring and

folklore and popular culture from all over the world. Events take place in the Greek temples, and the week culminates with parades and fireworks.

HOLY WEEK CELEBRATIONS
March–April
Sicily
Towns all over Sicily mark Holy Week with religious processions of great intensity. Statues are paraded through the streets and re-enactments of the Passion of Christ take place. Enna's parades are particulaly entertaining.

TEATRO GRECO
May–June
Siracusa, Sicily
www.siracusanet.it
The excellently preserved Greek theatre in the archaeological zone at Siracusa is the main venue for a festival of classical drama, when Greek plays are performed in their original setting. Far removed from modern theatre, the plays have a hypnotic quality, a superb way to appreciate the history of this ancient civilization.

FERRAGOSTO
15 August
Sicily
www.festedisicilia.it/agosto
The great feast of the Assumption is celebrated in towns and villages all over Sicily with processions, parades, music and fun. Expect to see sumptuously decorated statues carried shoulder high and the whole community letting its hair down late into the night.

SARDINIA
Shopping

CAGLIARI

IL FERRO BATTUTO
Via Oristano 18, 09127 Cagliari
Tel 070 502480

Ferro Battuto makes wrought-iron candlesticks, mirrors, lamps and furniture, all from original designs. Good reproductions of more classical designs are also produced.

 Mon–Sat 9–1, 5–7  7, 8

IL MERCATO DEL BASTIONE

Bastione di Saint Remy, 90127 Cagliari

Among the bric-à-brac at this antiques flea market are retro

clothing, stylish crockery, photographs, newspapers and personalized recipe books.

 Sun  7, 8

PASTICCERIA PIEMONTESE

Via Cocco Ortu 39, 09128 Cagliari
Tel 070 41365

Stop off at this shop for traditional Sardinian pastries such as *pistoccheddu prenu* (almond cream-filled pastry) and *candelaus prenus* (almond pastry fried in sugar and orange-blossom water). They also make beautifully wrapped sweets and pralines.

 Mon–Sat 9–1, 5–7  30, 31

Performance

CAGLIARI

CINEMA SOTTO LE STELLE

Marina Piccola, Viale Poetto, 09128 Cagliari

This 'cinema under the stars' shows general releases and cult films on a huge open-air screen at Marina Piccola—a magical way to watch a film on a warm summer's evening.

 Jul–Aug  €7

NOTTE DEI POETI

Nora, 09010 Cagliari
Tel 070 270577

Evenings of prose and poetry are held in the Roman amphitheatre in the town of Nora, just south of Cagliari. Events are organized by a local theatre company.

 Jul–Aug  €35  Cagliari–Nora A/R

TEATRO COMUNALE

Via Sant'Alenixedda, 09128 Cagliari
Tel 070 408 2230

A relatively new theatre, the Comunale has hosted a number of big names. Andrea Bocelli, a famous Italian tenor, made his debut here. Don't be put off by its ugly grey exterior; the productions are first rate.

 €60

Festivals and Events

S. ANTONIO ABATE FIRES

16/17 January
Mamoiada, Orisei, Torpè and other villages in the Nuoro province

This pagan festival, where villagers perform religious rites and blessings, culminates in the lighting of huge bonfires, which are left to burn throughout the night.

LA SARTIGLIA

February–last Sunday in Carnival and the following Thursday
Oristano

Riders test their skills to the limits at this horseback tournament in Oristano—watch and be entertained as mounted competitors try to pierce a star that hangs above the streets with a sword and a carved wooden stick.

SA DIE DE SA SARDIGNA (SARDINIA'S DAY)

28 April
Cagliari

This festival commemorates the Sardinian Vespers, who brought about a popular

SHIPWRECKS OFF SARDINIA
AIRSUB

Via Balilla 24–26, 09134 Cagliari–Pirri
Tel 070 506863
www.airsub.com

This company organizes year-round dives to the Roman and Spanish wrecks off the south coast of Sardinia. All equipment can be hired, and their shop sells a good range of snorkelling and diving gear.

 Mon–Sat 8.30–1, 4.15–8.15
 Dives €30–€250, equipment €8–€21

rebellion on 28 April 1794 that led to the expulsion of the Piedmontese and the Viceroy Balbiano from Cagliari and Sardinia.

SAGRA DI SANT EFISIO

1 May
Cagliari, Sardinia

Sardinia's most important religious festival commemorates Sant'Efisio, a fourth-century Roman martyr. The feast dates from 1657, when prayers to the saint delivered Cagliari from the plague. Decorated oxcarts and horsemen accompany the statue of the saint through the streets, and there is feasting, dancing and general jollity into the night.

SS. REDENTORE

29 August
Nuoro

This festival is a wonderful visual display of traditional costumes, horses, *traccas* (decorated carts), handicrafts and folk traditions. A singing competiton gives budding tenors the opportunity to showcase their talents and belt out a few traditional Sardinian songs.

WHAT TO DO

This chapter describes 17 driving tours and 9 walks that explore National Parks, historic towns and areas of natural beauty from the Cinque Terre in the north to Sicily in the south. The walks and tours are marked on the map on page 278. The tours are plotted on individual maps and the start points of the walks that are on the tours are marked with a star. Walks follow well-trodden paths, but it is advisable to buy a detailed map when walking in remote areas.

Out and About

TOUR AND WALK LOCATIONS

OUT AND ABOUT

A LOVERS' WALK IN THE CINQUE TERRE

This easy-to-follow walk is a great way to appreciate the beauty of some of the villages of the Cinque Terre as well as the stunning coastline.

THE WALK

Length: 4km (2.5 miles)

Allow: 1 hour

Start: Corniglia station

End: Riomaggiore station

Paths: Firm cliff paths. Despite being by the sea they are similar to mountain paths and lack protection in parts

Parking: Corniglia station

Lavatory: Manarola station

Maps: A free map is available on request from the Cinque Terre National Park visitor information office (near Manarola station)

Purchase a Cinque Terre card at the station that allows you to walk along the cliffs, which are protected. (One day costs €5.20, which also includes travel on buses and trains. A map of the paths is provided with your ticket along with a train and ferry timetable. Money raised goes towards the upkeep of the paths.)

From Corniglia station turn right. Go down the steep steps that run past the railway line, then walk under the railway. Keep to the right-hand side, walking between the green railings, and go left at the end. You soon pass a long line of green- and cream-painted beach huts, followed by a few bars. After about 500m (550 yards) there is a small wooden hut where you may have to show your walking pass.

Keep to the wide, stony path. Walk through a rather ugly metal gateway and immediately turn left and go up some steps. These bring you onto an enclosed path with a fence on the right-hand side. The village of Manarola is visible from here, perching on a rock. After about 100m (110 yards) you cross a metal bridge, after which you pass a small stone house on the left-hand side of the path.

From here the ground begins to drop away sharply on the right-hand side and then starts to go downhill. You come to an area where there are some picnic tables at a convenient look-out point, and you can walk down to reach a little beach. There is a plaque here to Giuseppe Arigliano, a local painter.

About 46m (50yd) after this the ground drops away steeply to the sea as you round a corner.

Manarola is now in front of you, a jumble of caramel-, rose- and cream-painted houses stacked on top of one another.

Walk down into the village. Follow the path past a restaurant called Marina Piccolo, climb uphill between several pizzerias and go over the railway. When you reach Ristorante Aristide on the left-hand side, you turn right and walk through a long white tunnel.

At the end you emerge in front of the office for the Cinque Terre National Park, by Manarola station.

Go to the left of the office and up a flight of stairs. You come onto a raised walkway, then walk past Bar del Amore with tables and chairs overlooking the sea. This is the start of the Via del Amore—the Lover's Way. Continue to walk through another roofed section of walkway, covered in graffiti.

Walk under a metal gateway and Riomaggiore station is in front of you. Murals painted by Silvio Benedetto cover the walls of Riomaggiore and Vernazza station, colourfully illustrating the cultivation of land and sea and the building of the dry-stone walls that shape this unique landscape.

Walk down the steps on the right to reach the station, from where you can get on a train back to Corniglia.

TIPS

● You can walk other sections of the Cinque Terre coastal path, but you will need to be fit as they are steep and there are many steps.

● You can book guided excursions, underwater trips and environmental education courses at the park offices.

WHEN TO GO

The best time to visit the area is in spring and autumn. It gets very busy in July and August and public holidays are best avoided.

WHERE TO EAT

There are cafés, pizzerias and picnic areas between Manarola and Riomaggiore.

PLACES TO VISIT

Parco Nazionale delle Cinque Terre

Stazione Ferrovari, Monterosso 19016

☎ 0187 817059 ◉ Daily 8–10

A boat speeding through the azure Ligurian Sea just off the coast of Manarola

OUT AND ABOUT

THE CINQUE TERRE

This scenic route winds around a dramatic part of the Ligurian coastline, past secluded villages that cling to the steep cliffs. This area, the Cinque Terre or Five Lands, is a National Park and a Unesco World Heritage Site. There are plenty of hairpin bends so this drive is not for the faint-hearted, but there are some superb views.

THE DRIVE

Distance: 103km (64 miles)
Allow: 3 hours
Start/end: Levanto

From Levanto, pick up the SP43 and drive through the industrial outskirts of the town. After 1km (0.5 mile) you reach a fork in the road where you turn left and begin to climb. Go through Busco, and then past Legnaro where there is a very sharp bend. There are good views from here of the pretty village of Chiesanovo on the right. When you come to a intersection, turn left, following signs to La Spezia. Continue, passing the little church of Santuario di Soviore, and after another 1km (0.5 mile) take a right turn signposted for Vernazza.

❶ The views over the sea from now on are spectacular with pink and toffee houses dotted over the hillsides below. The hills are terraced for the cultivation of vines, grown in small-layered patches held up by dry-stone walls (*muri a secco*).

After 3km (2 miles) you come to another intersection—keep going straight for La Spezia. The road dips, then after about 5km (3 miles) you come to another intersection where you turn left. (If you want to visit the village of Corniglia, turn right).

Vernazza on the Riviera Levante

❷ Corniglia is perched on the ridge of a rocky promontory at the foot of terraced vineyards. This fishing and farming community is similar architecturally to inland agricultural villages. The parish church of San Pietro, built in 1334 on the ruins of an old 11th-century chapel, has a baroque exterior and is one of the most beautiful Gothic-Ligurian buildings in the Cinque Terre.

After thick patches of conifer woodland, the landscape opens out again with good views of Manarola, which juts out precipitously into the sea.

❸ While you drive you may occasionally see the quaint monorail trucks used by the farmers to help harvest their grapes from the terraced fields. The rare wine Sciachetra is produced in this area. The proximity of the vines to the sea and their exposure to the sun creates the ideal conditions for maturing grapes with high sugar content. The sweet flavour and golden appearance of Cinque Terre wines make them an excellent complement to cheese, seafood and desserts.

Now head downhill to another intersection where you can turn right into the village of Manarola, or left to continue driving. This road, the SS370, climbs again for about 4km (2.5 miles), after

which you enter a tunnel. Continue straight ahead when you leave the tunnel and on your left-hand side you will see La Spezia, framed by mountains.

You soon come to an intersection, where you need to take a sharp right-hand turn at the traffic lights to join the SS530, which takes you to Portovenere. Follow this road as it climbs away from the harbour and after 8km (5 miles) you come to an intersection. Keep to the right, following signs for Portovenere.

After 3km (2 miles) you enter Portovenere (p. 77), a pretty wedge of coloured houses. After exploring follow the road back to La Spezia. There is a NATO base in the port, so be prepared for heavy traffic and large vehicles.

La Spezia **❹** is the biggest naval base in the country. The public gardens in the west of the town are just a short distance away from Piazza Chirodo and La Spezia's naval Arsenale, rebuilt after World War II. Just off the complex is the Museo Tecnico Navale, celebrating La Spezia's naval history with impressive displays of battle relics and models.

Follow the road going through the centre of La Spezia, then turn left at the next intersection and pick up the SS1 for Ricco del Golfo. You no longer overlook the coast now and the landscape has a quiet, rural feel to it. Drive through the village and on to Borghetto di Vara, where you follow signs for the SS1 and continue to Cornice.

After 1.5km (1 mile) you will reach another intersection; turn left, following signs to 'Levanto 14'. Drive on for another 3km (2 miles), then turn left at the intersection onto the SS566. In about 45m (50yd) you turn right again, go under a road bridge, through a tunnel and emerge at Ponte d'Osso. Continue downhill, enjoying views of Levanto as you descend into the village.

The coastline near Vernazza (left) and the brightly painted houses that line the waterfront of Portovenere (right)

E6

E6

WHEN TO GO
Late spring and early autumn are quieter than summer.

WHERE TO EAT
Taverna Garibaldi in Levanto is an excellent pizzeria (Via Garibaldi 57, tel 018 7808098, 12–2, 7.30–11).

PLACES TO VISIT
Museo Tecnico Navale
Viale Amendola, 19122 La Spezia
☎ 0187 783016
🕐 Mon–Sat 8.30–1, 4.15–9.45, Sun and holidays 8.30–1.15, Jul–Aug; Mon–Sat 8.30–6, Sun and holidays 10.15–3.45, rest of year

Small boats on the harbour side beneath the bright umbrellas of a café in Vernazza (above)

The dramatic coastline of the Cinque Terre attracts many artists (left)

A WINE TOUR FROM ALBA TO CUNEO

A vast array of wines is produced in Northwest Italy, and the best of them come from the Langhe hills in southern Piedmont. From the medieval town of Alba this tour takes you through a picturesque landscape of hilltop villages and castles, passing many *enoteche*, *cantine* and private cellars en route, where you can sample the local produce.

THE DRIVE

Distance:	92km (57 miles)
Allow:	1 day
Start:	Alba
End:	Cuneo

Capital of the Langhe district, Alba ❶ is famous for wine and white truffles. It was formerly known as the City of 100 Towers and although few of these survive, much of the town has kept its medieval appearance.

From Alba (p. 67) follow the signs for Diano d'Alba, a village about 8km (5 miles) to the south, set among rolling vineyards.

❷ The vineyards here produce the fruity and fresh Dolcetto DOC table wine. This easy-drinking, sociable wine is renowned for its purplish ruby-red colour, plum and cherry flavours and distinctive bitter-almond aftertaste.

Backtrack to the turning left for Grinzane Cavour in the Gallo d'Alba direction.

Castello di Cavour ❸, which belonged to Count Camillo Benso di Cavour between 1842 and 1849, offers guided tours. It is home to the Museo dell'Enoteca Regionale Piemontese (Museum of Piedmont Vintage Wines), with a collection of tools used in wine production and the finest

Annunziata Barcio wine in the private cellar of the former Abbey at Grinzane Cavour

enoteca (specialist wine shop) in the region. Established in 1967, it stocks an impressive range of Piedmont wines.

From the castle turn left for Gallo d'Alba, then left again, following signs for Serralunga d'Alba. Drive up the hillside to this medieval hilltop village, where the houses huddle around the foot of a 14th-century fortress. After exploring Serralunga, return in the direction of Gallo d'Alba. When you come to the main road turn left for Barolo.

Barolo, nestling in the rolling Piedmontese countryside

The medieval village of Barolo ❹, home of 'the king of wines, the wine of kings', perches on the hill, its castle visible for miles around. Its elaborately decorated rooms are open to visitors and include the famous Silvio Pellico Library. The antique wine cellar houses the prestigious Enoteca Regionale del Barolo (Regional Winestore of Barolo), which represents 11 boroughs in the Barolo area. Here you can stop and sample the wine and discover why they are so successful. On the upper floors is the Farming Museum, which illustrates the meticulous care and attention involved in producing Barolo's wines.

Leave Barolo following signs for La Morra, about 6km (4 miles) to the north.

La Morra ❺ is the capital of Barolo and produces a third of the wines; it also has superb views from the belvedere at the top of the town. Taste the local wines at the Enoteca Civica, which also has a wine exhibition, and at the Cantina Comunale (*Via Carl Alberto 2, tel 0173 509204, Wed–Mon 10–12.30, 2.30–6.30*).

Leave La Morra and take the road to Cherasco, crossing the River Tanaro.

❻ Cherasco has much to explore: a well-preserved 14th-century castle, historic palaces and churches. It is also the centre of the National Association of Snail Breeders and hosts gourmet gastropod events in September.

From Cherasco, take the Bra road and turn left onto the SS231, which leads to Cuneo ❼.

Cuneo is the main town of southern Piedmont and is renowned for its Tuesday market, which fills the huge, arcaded Piazza Galimberti. The deconsecrated 13th-century Church of San Francesco houses the local museum and is also worth exploring.

OUT AND ABOUT

New casks containing wine in a cellar of one of the many vineyards in the Piedmontese hillsides around La Morra

Right: Lines of young vines neatly staked out on the slopes of the Piedmontese hills, near the town of Barolo

WHEN TO GO

October is the best time to go for the grape harvest and the famous white truffles, though fog and rain may dampen your trip. Alternatively visit in late spring.

WHERE TO EAT

The Piedmont region takes its food very seriously. Truffles, cheese, hazelnuts and Barolo wine are just a few of the regional items often found on the menu. Try the Trattoria del Castello on the road up to Serralunga d'Alba (*closed Wed*) or the more expensive and elegant Locanda nel Borgo Antico in the centre of Barolo (*closed Thu lunch*). If you prefer a picnic there are some wonderful food shops in Alba.

PLACES TO VISIT

Enoteca Regionale and Museo dell'Enoteca Regionale Piemontese
Via Castello, 5, 12060 Grinzane Cavour

☎ 0173 262159
🕐 Wed–Mon 9.30–12.30, 2.30–6.30; closed Jan

Castello Falletti di Barolo
Piazza Falletti, 12060 Barolo
☎ 0173 334030. Enoteca 0173 56277
🕐 Fri–Wed 10–12.30, 3–6.30; closed Jan

LAGO DI COMO—LOWER LARIO

This drive follows the shores of the southern arms of Lake Como, past sumptuous villas and gardens, historic towns, resorts and fishing villages. High points are the village of Varenna, Villa Carlotta at Tremezzo and the ferry trip across the lake. The hills above the lake, easily accessed from many resorts, provide fine views and excellent opportunities for hiking.

THE DRIVE

Distance:	95km (59 miles)
Allow:	1 day
Start/end:	Lecco

From Lecco take the SS36 Sondrio road north, through a series of tunnels. Come off at the Mandello/Varenna exit (7km/4 miles). Drive along the shore to the village of Varenna ❶, lying at the foot of the Grigna Mountains.

Narrow alleys and stepped streets lead down to the lake, with its promenade.

Take the car ferry (every 30–45 minutes in peak season) across to Menaggio, a lively resort with a pleasant lakeside promenade. Drive south along the SS340 to Villa Carlotta, between the resorts of Cadenabbia and Tremezzo.

The famous Villa Carlotta ❷ was built by Marquis Clerici in the 18th century and was partially modified by Count Sommariva in the neoclassical style. Although it's now somewhat faded, you can still admire the original furniture and fine works of art inside. The villa has landscaped gardens, particularly lovely in spring, laid out by the subsequent owners, the Dukes of Sachsen Meiningen.

Continue south to Ossuccio, with its distinctive Romanesque tower topped by an unusual late-Gothic belfry. Just beyond Ossuccio take a boat from Sala Comacina to the Isola Comacina ❸.

The tiny Isola Comacina is Lake Como's only island, an influential political and military base in the Middle Ages. After siding with Milan in the 10-year war between Como and Milan, it was ravaged in 1169 by the people of Como. Ruins and a baroque oratory are all that remian of the strategic settlement.

Drive another 4km (2.5 miles) around to Argegno, at the south of the delightful Val d'Intelvi. A cableway here climbs to the

The bell tower of Ossuccio

village of Pigra, commanding a splendid view of the lake. A stretch of fairly wild coastline leads to the pretty village of Moltrasio, via Brienno. Perched on the rugged lakeshore, it was once famous for the grey stone in its quarries, which is used in the buildings all around the shores of the lake. The next resort is Cernobbio, renowned for the exclusive villas built here from the 16th to 18th century.

The most famous is the 16th-century Villa d'Este ❹, once the home of Princess Caroline, wife of King George IV of England. Since 1873 it has been a luxury hotel, and every one of the 161 sumptuously decorated rooms in this historic building are unique. Overlooking the lake and surrounded by 10 hectares (25 acres) of parkland, the hotel has an 18-hole golf course and a wide range of outdoor and indoor sports and leisure facilities including tennis courts, water-skiing, windsurfing, canoeing, squash courts, a gym and a spa.

The lakeside road leads south to Como.

❺ The fine walled city of Como is one of the most elegant places on the lake (p. 69 and town walk p. 287).

From Como follow the signs for Lecco, which bring you to the SS639. Fork left after 6km (4 miles), keeping to the SS639. The road bypasses Erba—a former resort, it is now a major industrial hub. Another 10km (6 miles) brings you to Civate, departure point for San Pietro al Monte, a major Lombard Romanesque complex with fine views and rare 11th- and 12th-century frescoes. Return to the main road, which passes through several tunnels before reaching Lecco (7km/4 miles).

OUT AND ABOUT

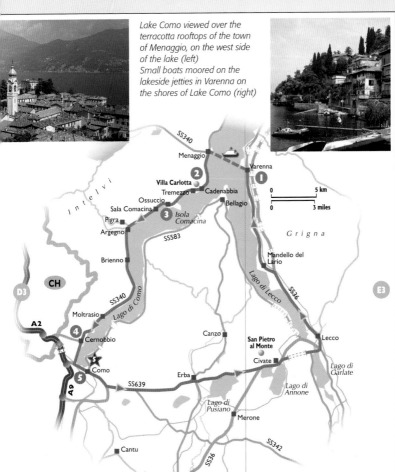

Lake Como viewed over the terracotta rooftops of the town of Menaggio, on the west side of the lake (left)
Small boats moored on the lakeside jetties in Varenna on the shores of Lake Como (right)

Lecco town on the shores of Lago di Lecco (above)

WHERE TO EAT

There are plenty of lakeside cafés and restaurants to choose from en route. In Sala Comacina the delightful La Tirlindana (*Piazza Matteotti 5, tel 0344 56637, daily 12.15–2.30, 7.30–11; closed Mon lunchtime, Mar–Sep; closed Mon–Thu, winter*) has wonderful homemade pasta.

PLACES TO VISIT

Villa Carlotta
Via Regina 2, 22019 Tremezzo
☎ 0344 40405
🕐 Daily 9–6, Apr–Sep; 9–11.30, 2–4.30, Mar and Oct
💶 Adult €6.50, child (under 6) free
www.villacarlotta.it

Villa d'Este
Via Regina 40, Como 22012 Cernobbio
☎ 031 3481
www.villadeste.it

A ferry boat docked in front of the fine buildings of the town of Bellagio, strategically positioned where the three basins of Lake Como intersect (above)

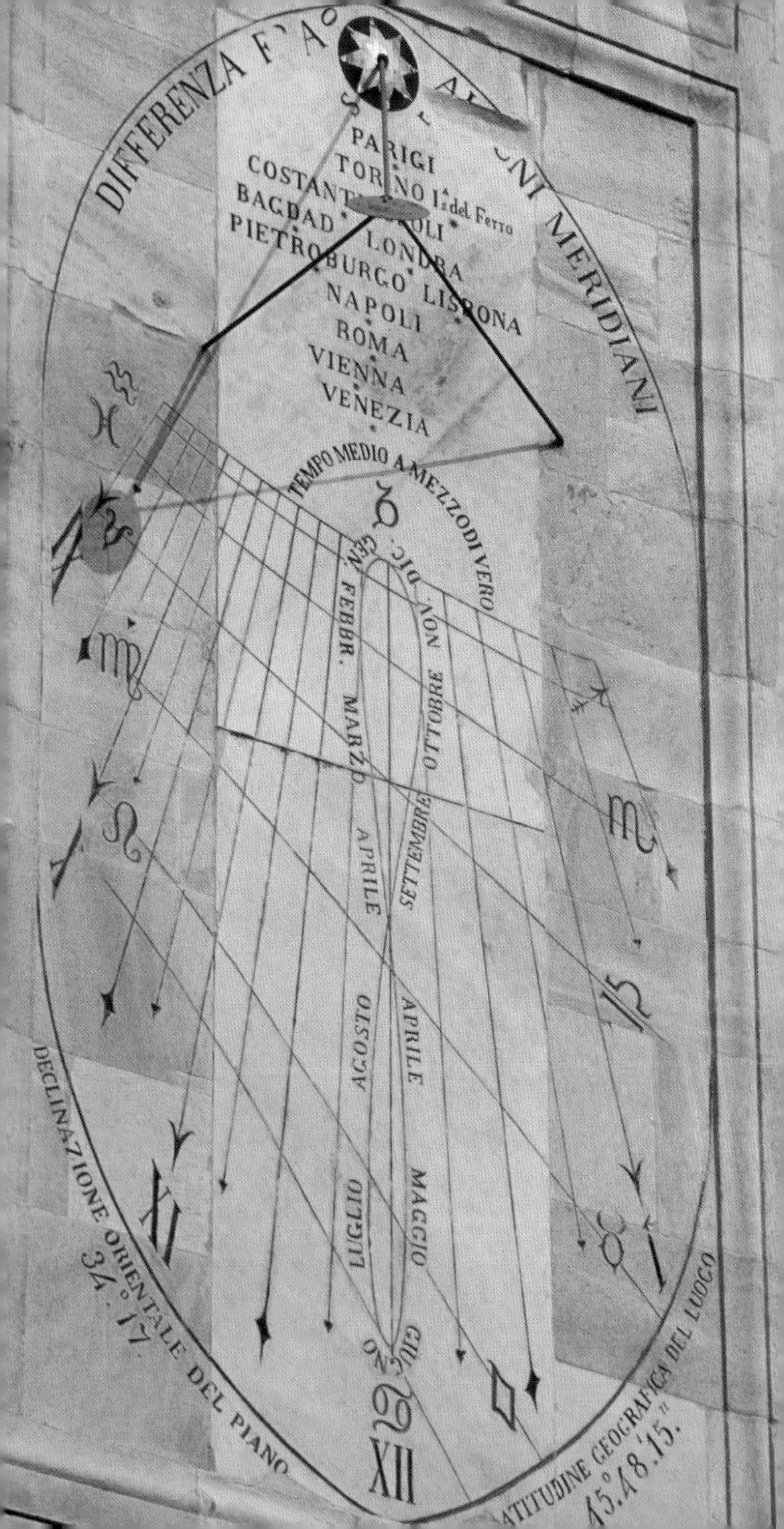

DIFFERENZA
MERIDIANI
PARIGI
TORINO
Is. del Ferro
BAGDAD
LONDRA
PIETROBURGO
LISBONA
NAPOLI
ROMA
VIENNA
VENEZIA
TEMPO MEDIO A MEZZODI VERO
GEN.
FEBBR.
MARZO
APRILE
AGOSTO
LUGLIO
GIUGNO
MAGGIO
APRILE
SETTEMBRE
OTTOBRE
NOV.
DIC.
XI
XII
I
DECLINAZIONE ORIENTALE DEL PIANO
34° 17'
LATITUDINE GEOGRAFICA DEL LUOGO
45° 48' 15"

COMO TOWN

Off the lakeside drive (p. 284–285), this walk meanders through the old centre of Como town (p. 69) past fine monuments, silk and leather shops and inviting *pasticcerie* and cafés, ending with a funicular ride up to the village of Brunate with fine views above and across the lake.

THE WALK

Length:	2.7km (1.7 miles)
Allow:	2 hours
Start:	Piazza Cavour
End:	Brunate

From the 19th-century Piazza Cavour, with its open-air cafés and views of the lake, take the Via Caio Plinio Secondo to the left of the Hotel Barchetta Excelsior. This leads into Piazza Duomo, the heart of the old centre and the finest square in the city.

Here you see the towering Torre del Comune dating from 1215, the Broletto (old Court of Justice), from the same period with stripes of pink, white and grey marble, and the magnificent Gothic/ Renaissance duomo, with its lavish marble exterior and 15th- to 16th-century sculpture.

From the duomo head down Via Vittorio Emanuele II.

Halfway down on the right is the five-sided apse of the Church of San Fedele and the carved 'door of the dragon'. The building opposite (16th–17th century) has been the town hall since 1853.

The street ends in Piazza Medaglie d'Oro, dominated by the archaeological and historical museums occupying the Palazzi Giovio and Olginati respectively. Pass under the arch

A sundial on the duomo (left). A statue of Alessandro Volta, the inventor of the battery (right)

on the left, along Via Serafino Balestra, formerly called Vicolo delle Orfanelli (Little Orphan Alley). Follow the medieval wall to the Torre di San Vitale, an imposing tower in the city walls. Turn right when you reach the busy Viale Battisti, keeping to the old city walls.

Continue south here and you come to the Basilica di Sant'Abbondio, a Romanesque construction that stands out in a rather dreary part of town.

From Viale Battisti turn right by the medieval tower, best viewed from the far side. Turn right at the end of the road, down Via Giuseppe Rovelli, take the first left and turn right for Piazza San Fedele.

This square was built on the site of the Roman

Como's duomo

forum, and until the 1800s the town market was held here. Today it is a small intimate space, with cafés, arcades and a couple of finely preserved medieval buildings, which contrast with the uninspiring façade of San Fedele, rebuilt in the early 20th century.

Exit the piazza on the side facing San Fedele, crossing Via Indipendenza, one of the main shopping streets. Continue straight ahead to return to Piazza Cavour. At the lakeside—a busy scene of boats and ferries—turn right, following the waterfront until you reach Piazza de Gasperi. The funicular here departs every 15 minutes and takes just over 6 minutes to reach Brunate, a village 720m (2,362ft) above the city, with magnificent views over Lake Como and the Alps.

WHEN TO GO
Avoid doing this walk between noon and 3 when the churches and museums are closed.

WHERE TO EAT
There are plenty of good cafés and restaurants to choose from en route.

OUT AND ABOUT

LIMONE–SIRMIONE

This drive skirts the northern and eastern shores of Lake Garda, stopping at historic towns along the way, dominated by Scaligeri castles, built by the della Scala family from Verona. In the north, dramatic peaks rise sheer from the deep waters; in the south, the lake broadens into a vast expanse of blue water.

THE DRIVE

Distance:	93km (58 miles)
Allow:	1 day
Start:	Limone
End:	Sirmione

❶ Limone sul Garda, which lies below white cliffs, is named after the lemon trees that once made it prosperous. A small resort, it has a centre of narrow alleys and a popular waterfront with lake-view cafés and restaurants.

From Limone sul Garda take the SS45 north through a series of tunnels for Riva del Garda.

At the northern tip of the lake, sitting spectacularly below the mountains, is Riva del Garda **❷**. Formerly a trading port, today it is a thriving resort with a prominent castle, home to the Museo Civico, and an attractive medieval core.

Follow the signs for Torbole (3.8km/2.4 miles to the east), a small resort that is a magnet for windsurfers as the northern winds guarantee action. Follow the main road (SS249) down the eastern shore of the lake, passing through tunnels, and continue as far as Malcesine.

❸ Dominated by the striking Castello Scaligero and set below the scenic Monte Baldo, Malcesine is the highlight of the lake's eastern shore. From the castle tower you can appreciate views of the surrounding walls and steep cliffs. Inside the castle there is a museum featuring a collection of weapons, archaeological finds and objects from the Italian Risorgimento (resurgence), the 50 year struggle for

liberation from foreign rule that culminated in the Unification of Italy in 1870. Malcesine's panoramic cable car will take you up to Monte Baldo, for excellent views and rare mountain flora, an ideal spot for a walk.

Continue south through a series of villages, the prettiest of which is Castelletto, where old houses group around the Piazza dell'Olivio. Travel along this road to reach Torri del Benaco.

❹ Despite being a ferry terminus, Torri del Benaco still retains its old character—a charming port with a castle on the lakeside. The della Scala family rebuilt the castle between 1383 and 1393 on Roman foundations and it now houses a museum. From Torri del Benaco to Peschiera del Garda most of the lakeside has been developed for tourism.

Stop at Punta di San Vigilio, occupied by the lovely Villa Guarienti, a church, park and beach. Beyond the resort of Garda is Bardolino **❺**.

This area is synonymous with light, fruity red wine.

Bardolino's wine museum, the Museo del Vino at the Cantina Zeni, has some interesting exhibits on the history of wine-making in the region, the highlight being the opportunity to taste (for free) the full range of wines made in the Gardesana area. Bardolino also has an olive-oil museum, with an exhibition illustrating the history of olive oil production in rural society that stretches back over a thousand years. Many different kinds of extra-virgin olive oil can be tasted and bought in the museum shop, which is also stocked with a wide variety of Italian delicacies including spiced oils, aromatic vinegar, pesto and a selection of wines from the Garda region.

Continue south towards Peschiera del Garda.

For many visitors the main attraction of Peschiera del Garda **❻** is the popular Gardaland (on the right before you reach the resort), northern Italy's answer to Disneyland. The town itself is a busy intersection, with a formidable fortress.

From Peschiera del Garda take the SS11, following the signs to Sirmione.

The loveliest of Garda's resorts and a Mecca for daytrippers, Sirmione **❼** stands on the tip of a thin, craggy peninsula extending 4km (2.5 miles) into the lake; the remains of a huge Roman villa (Grotte di Catullo) occupy a spectacular position there. A beautiful 13th-century castle, surrounded by the old quarter. Visitors' cars must be left outside the town.

A boat mooring at Sirmione on Lake Garda

OUT AND ABOUT

The hotel at Punta di San Vigilio, near Garda town (left)

A streetside stall selling lemons close to the central castle in Sirmione on Lake Garda (below)

WHEN TO GO

Avoid July and August when the roads are choked with traffic. Spring is the ideal time to go.

WHERE TO EAT

Lakeside resorts have no shortage of cafés, pizzerias and restaurants. There are plenty of places by the lake where you can picnic. One of the prettiest spots to stop for a drink or meal is the old port in Torri del Benaco.

PLACES TO VISIT

Gardaland
Castelnuovo del Garda, 37014 Verona
☎ 045 6449777
🕐 Daily 10–6, late mar to mid-Jun; 9am–midnight, mid-Jun to early Sep; 10–6, early Sep–end Sep; weekends only 10–6, Oct–early Nov. Closed in winter
💶 Adults€22; children (under 10) €18.50
www.gardaland.it

Museo del Vino
Cantina Zeni, Via Costabella 9, Bardolino
☎ 045 7210022
🕐 Daily 9–1, 2–6, Apr–Oct; Mon–Fri 9–1, 2–6, Nov–Feb; no wine-tasting in winter

Oleificio Cisano del Garda
Via Peschiera 54, 37011 Cisano di Bardolino VR-Lago di Garda
☎ 045 6229047
🕐 Mon–Sat 9–12.30, 2.30–7; Sun and holidays 9–12.30. Closed Sun Jan-Feb, Easter Sun, 15 Aug, 25–26 Dec, 1 and 6 Jan
🎫 Free
www.museodellolio.com
www.museum.it

Museo Civico
Piazza Battisti 3, Riva del Garda
☎ 046 4 573869
🕐 Daily 9.30–6, Jul–Aug; Tue–Sun 9.30–12.30, 2.30–6.30

Torri del Benaco
Via Costello, 370018 Malcesine
☎ 045 7400837
🕐 Daily 9.30–7.30; closed Oct–Mar
💶 €4

Museo del Castello Scaligero di Torri del Benaco
Informazione Turistica, Viale F.lli Lavanda 2, 37010 Torri del Benaco
☎ 0456296111
🕐 Mon–Sun 9.30–1, 4.30–7.30; Jun–Sep; Mon–Sun 9.30–12.30, 2.30–6, Oct–May
💶 €3

GRANDE STRADA DELLE DOLOMITI

This drive follows the Grande Strada delle Dolomiti (Great Dolomites Road), which was constructed in 1909 to link Bolzano and Cortina d'Ampezzo. It cuts through some of Europe's most breathtaking mountain scenery, navigating high passes and fertile alpine valleys. Pretty villages line the route, and cable cars and chair-lifts give access to the higher slopes.

THE DRIVE	
Distance: 90km (56 miles)	
Allow: 3 hours driving time	
Start: Bolzano	
End: Cortina d'Ampezzo	

Leave Bolzano/Bozen (p. 104) and head northeast in the direction of Bressanone/Brixen (p. 104). Take the SS241, which is signposted in brown for the Eggental, and head along the Valle d'Ega (Eggental) towards Lago di Carezza.

❶ As you hit the SS241 the road immediately twists and climbs as it cuts through a narrow gorge into the mountains. As it gradually opens up the high peaks of the Latemar and Catinaccio/Rosengarten massifs begin to appear, giving you the first taste of the area's scenic glories. Make your first stop at Lago di Carezza, beside a beautiful lake whose

Lago di Carezza

turquoise waters reflect the surrounding dark fir trees and mountain ridges. You can stretch your legs by following the well-made track around the lake, approximately a 30-minute stroll. From the lake the road continues to climb up to the Passo di Costalunga (1,745m/5,725ft), the first of the high passes along this route, which forms the boundary between the Alto Adige and Trentino regions.

Continue on the SS241 through the Passo di Costalungo, which drops down into the beautiful Val di Fassa.

Once over the pass, the road descends into the Val di Fassa ❷, a lovely alpine valley that attracts mountain sports enthusiasts in summer and winter. The River Avisio runs through the valley past a string of pretty villages, among them Vigo di Fassa, all catering to

holidaymakers. From Vigo di Fassa you can head up into the hills for a high-altitude walk through the Catinaccio mountains (p. 293).

About 1.5km (1 mile) past Vigo di Fassa turn left onto the SS48 towards Canazei. Drive up the valley past Canazei and stay on the SS48 towards the Passo Pordoi ❸ (2,239m/7,346ft).

For the next 12km (7.5 miles) you will wind around 27 hairpin bends and the road becomes increasingly dramatic and challenging, with views of soaring mountains all around and the green meadows of the Val di Fassa below. Passo Pordoi is the highest pass along the drive and you're likely to find yourself above the snowline at most times of year.

More hairpins snake down to Arabba ❹, a mountain village that is a popular resort with winter skiers. Stay on the SS48 through Arabba.

From Arabba the road threads its away along the sides of a heavily wooded valley, where houses are few and far between and there's a real sense of isolation amid the upland countryside. Another steep section of road snakes up to the Passo di Falzarego (2,105m/6,906ft). Look for the stark outline of the ancient Castello di Andraz on your left and the relatively rare stone pines that dot the slopes of the high meadows around here. At Falzarego the views open up across new mountain ranges and peaks before the road begins its descent.

Stay on the SS48 towards Cortina d'Ampezzo. The contrasts of landscape are stark on this last section of the drive, where rocky mountain slopes tower above deciduous forests and alpine pastures. The road passes

around the Olympic skating rink or ride on a horse-drawn sleigh or dog sled. Thrill-seekers can rent skidoos or experience an Olympic bob-sleigh run via the Taxi-bob-sleigh, which takes you to speeds of over 120kph/75mph *(tel 0436 860808)*.

TIPS

● The roads are good, but the route can be crowded with coaches.
● This route is twisty—best avoided by sufferers of vertigo and travel sickness.

A lonely mountain hut: Canazei in the Dolomites

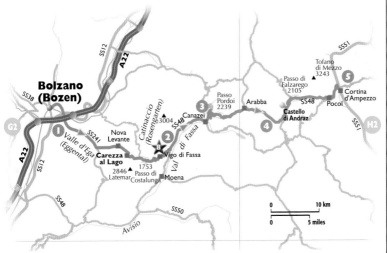

OUT AND ABOUT

through the village of Pocòl and emerges into the mountain bowl that encircles Cortina d'Ampezzo.

Affectionately known as the pearl of the Dolomites, Cortina d'Ampezzo ❺ is Italy's glitziest winter resort. It hosted the first televised Winter Olympics in 1956, and the awesome peaks formed the backdrop for some jaw-dropping scenes in the James Bond film *For Your Eyes Only* (1981) and *Cliffhanger* (1993), starring Sylvester Stallone. There are pistes for all skiing abilities, but if that doen't appeal, you can glide

Campitello, with the Sassolungo rock pillars behind

THE HEART OF THE CATINACCIO

This straightforward walk is one of the easiest and most spectacular of the high-altitude Dolomite trails, giving you a true taste of the power and beauty of the mountains. The route plunges deeper and deeper into the peaks of the Catinaccio (Rosengarten), lined with alpine flowers, trees and shrubs and all without struggling on foot from the valley bottom.

THE WALK

Length: 6km (3.7 miles)

Allow: 1.5–2 hours

Ascent: 100m/328ft

Start/end: Vigo di Fassa

Paths: Excellent, wide stony mountain trails. Can be slippery in icy/snowy conditions. Late spring and early autumn snow can hang around in patches, so shoes or walking boots with good grip are essential outside the peak summer season.

Parking: Funivia Ciampedie (Ciampedie cable-car) car park in Vigo di Fassa

Toilets: At rifugi (mountain refuge)

After parking the car, buy a return ticket for the *funivia (Daily, every 15 minutes, 8.30–1, 3.30–6; €9).* The cable car takes the strain, whisking you over 600m (1,970ft) up the mountain. As it ascends there are ever-widening views over the Val di Fassa and the Monzoni massif to the southeast. Leave the cable car at the top and walk out onto the Ciampedie plateau (1,998m/6,555ft).

Look for the waymark signpost (a little to the left) showing 540 and follow the trail down the hill with the *rifugio* (mountain refuge) building on your right. About 200m (655ft) after the path flattens, take trail 540 (waymarked) contouring to the right. This splendid path leads right into the heart of the Catinaccio (Rosengarten) range, some of the Dolomites' most impressive mountain scenery.

The German name for these peaks means 'Rose Garden', an apt reference to the blush pink of the stone, which looks its deepest at dawn and twilight. Legend has it that, betrayed by the colour and splendour of his roses, the king of the dwarves was dragged away from his mountain kingdom. He cursed the roses, binding them with a spell to make them invisible by day and

A snowy path in the Dolomites (left)

night. While he ranted, he forgot to mention dawn and dusk, which is when the mountains glow a vibrant pink.

Follow the trail through the woods, across two ski slopes, grassy in summer, and under the cables of two ski lifts.

The woods are pine, carpeted with alpine shrubs. The most common are juniper, alpenrose (*Rhododendron ferrugineum*), whose lovely pink azalea-like flower blooms from late June to August, and bilberry. Bilberries have small dark berries with a lustrous bloom and intense flavour; look for ripe fruit if you're walking in late August and September. The juniper berries that grow here have been used for centuries to flavour spirits and liqueurs and are still used today in many of the locally distilled *digestivi* and *aperitivi.*

Head deeper into the circle of peaks where the path undulates and the surrounding summits grow ever closer and more dramatic.

The highest peaks of the Catinaccio/Rosengarten group are the Cima Scalieret (2,887m/9,472ft) to your right and Punta Emma (2,919m/9,577ft) ahead and to your left. All these peaks are popular with rock climbers and many of them have *vie ferrate* (fixed iron ladders) to help mountaineers on the precipitous rock walls.

The path descends out of the woods and ahead of you stands the pink-washed building of the Rifugio Catinaccio (1,960m/6,430ft), where you can rest and admire the moutain peaks.

There are hundreds of *rifugi* throughout the Dolomites, some providing food and drinks, others offering

accommodation for hikers following the long-distance paths through the mountains.

Retrace your route back to the cable car. With the Catinaccio behind you, wide views open out to the mountains of the southeast.

The lumpy peak is the unmistakable silhouette of Marmolada, at 3,246m (10,650ft) the highest peak in the Dolomites, with its permanent glacier draped down one side.

If you are feeling fit you can tackle the other side of the range. Take the Paolina chair-lift from the Passo di Carrezza and follow trail 539 and 549 to Baita Pederiva. This is a 5km (3-mile) walk with more stupendous views.

A sign pointing the way through the pine woods in Catinaccio

WHERE TO EAT

Rifugi at Ciampedie (top of the cable car) or Rifugio Catinaccio at the far end of walk.

WHEN TO GO

The path is open all year round, but the less sure-footed should avoid the route during late autumn and winter, when the trail can get icy and slippery.

THE GARFAGNANA

This drive takes you through the cool mountains of the Garfagnana, the region north of Lucca that stretches between the rugged national parks encompassing Alpi Apuane in the west and the softer slopes of the Orecchiella in the east. Towns and villages are sprinkled about the hills, and there are plenty of paths if you wish to stop and explore on foot.

THE DRIVE	
Distance: 170km (106 miles)	
Allow: 8 hours	
Start/end: Lucca	

Leave Lucca (p. 142) through the Porta San Donato and pick up the SR12 signposted for Abetone. At the next turning follow the signs for Castelnuova Garfagnana. After 4km (2.5 miles) you will see the Lucchesi hills in front of you. Shortly afterwards, turn left at the brown signpost saying 'Garfagnana' (p. 141) and cross the bridge over the Serchio River onto the road that runs parrallel to the SR12 on the opposite bank of the river. Go through two tunnels and after about 4km (2.5 miles) turn left again. Stay on this road which passes through Diecimo, flanked by papermaking factories, an old local industry in this area. Drive on to the village of Borgo a Mozzano, where there is a bell tower on the left-hand side. Just after this is a sign saying 'Barga 18'; go over a bridge.

To the right of the road, spanning the river, is the distinctive 12th-century hump-back bridge known locally as Ponte del Diavolo ❶ (The Devil's Bridge). According to legend the builder sought help from the Devil to build it and in

The Ponte del Diavolo just outside Bargo a Mazzano

return the Devil demanded the soul of the first being who crossed the river. The builder is said to have outwitted the Devil by making sure that a dog went over the bridge first.

After about 8km (5 miles) take a right-hand turn signed 'Barga', cross the river, turn left into Calavorno, then drive on through Piano di Coreglia to reach Fornaci di Barga. Just at the entrance to this village take the right-hand fork to Barga, after which the road climbs uphill and the scenery becomes craggier and more alpine in appearance.

Barga ❷ is a hilltop town with a fine Romanesque cathedral that towers over the village (p. 138). Don't miss the

panoramic views of the mountains from the terrace by the cathedral entrance.

Drive on through Barga and follow the sign for Castelnuovo di Garfagnana. Cross another river and drive through Castelvecchio Pascoli, close to which is the house of Giovanni Pascoli, the celebrated 19th-century

The red-roofed houses of Castelnuovo de Garfagnana

Italian poet. Continue through Ponte di Campia and follow the SR445 for about 9km (6 miles) through the thickly wooded hills to reach Castelnuovo di Garfagnana. This is the largest town in the area, where the Regional Park Office provides maps, books and information on the region. When you reach the crossroads take the SP72 signposted for San Pellegrino in Alpe.

Drive through Campori ❸. As you leave, the road begins to wind steeply upwards, cutting through hills cloaked with chestnut trees. For many years the economy of the Garfagnana depended chestnuts, cheese and spelt (a type of wheat).

Continued on page 296.

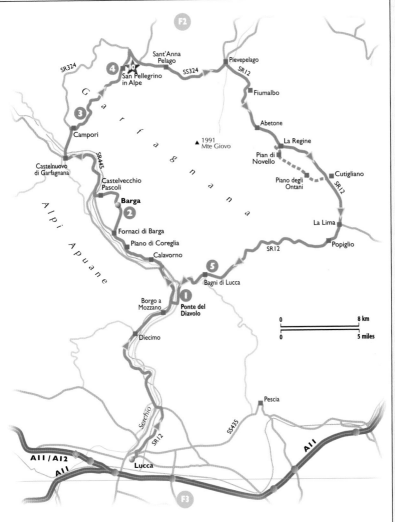

Spring and autumn are the best times to visit; August is the most crowded time and in winter snow and ice can make driving hazardous.

Barga's historic Caffe Capretz *(Piazza Salvo Salvi 1, tel 0583 723001, closed Tue)* is close to the Tourist Information Office. Here you can sit outside on a sunny day and enjoy a cappuccino and a pastry. Further along the route at San Pellegrino in Alpe is Albergo l'Appennino da Pacetta *(Piazza San Pellegrino 5, tel 0583 649069, daily 12–2, 7–9.30)*, a relaxed family restaurant and inn with a sister café on the other side of the road *(tel 0583 649069)*. All the food is homemade, from the cakes and pasta to the bread and

jam. There are also several places in Bagni di Lucca where you can grab a quick coffee.

Museo Etnografico Provinciale
Via del Voltone, San Pellegrino in Alpe
☎ 0583 649072
⏰ Tue–Sun 9–12, 2–5, 1 Apr–31 May; 9.30–1, 2.30–7, 1 Jun–30 Sep; Tue–Sat 9–1, Sun 9–12, 2–5, 1 Oct–31 Mar; Open Mon Jul–Aug

Thermal waters running from the mouth of a fountain in Bagni di Lucca, a resort founded by Elisa Baciocch, sister of Napoleon and princess of Lucca

After 13km (8 miles) you will reach San Pellegrino in Alpe **❹**.

San Pellegrino is a little mountain village that has attracted pilgrims and artists for centuries, including Michelangelo and the poet Shelley. This is a good spot for a walk (p. 297) and a bite to eat. It is also the home of the Museo Etnografico Provinciale, an excellent folk museum with exhibits on the agricultural of the Garfagnana.

Drive on from San Pellegrino and join the SR324, which winds

The spa resort of Bagni di Lucca

downhill. Follow the road as it passes through Sant'Anna Pelago and Pievepelago. At the crossroads, turn right taking the SR12 towards Abetone. Here you cross the river and start to climb again. Drive for 7km (4 miles) until you reach Abetone, a ski resort with a distinct alpine feel.

From Abetone the SR12 winds downhill to Le Regine. You can continue following the SR12 here, or take an alternative route through the mountain woods and villages by turning off to the right at the brown sign just

outside Abetone saying 'Piano degli Ontani'. Drive along this quiet little road for about 2km (1 mile), then take the left-hand fork and continue through the woods to reach Pian di Novello, a small skiing village. From here the road winds steeply downhill, through Piano degli Ontani, eventually rejoining the SR12 where you turn right and follow the road to La Lima. Bear right in La Lima on the SR12, then drive through Popiglio following the road for 17km (11 miles) until you reach Bagni di Lucca. Cross the small bridge on the right-hand side to reach the heart of the town.

❺ Bagni di Lucca gained a reputation as a spa town in the 19th century, attracting many illustrious visitors who came to take the waters including Lord Byron, Shelley, and Robert and Elizabeth Barrett Browning.

Cross back over the bridge and continue along the SR12, which passes the Ponte del Diavolo and takes you back to the city.

The River Lima, with Castelnuovo de Garfagnana reflected in the clear, still waters

THE PILGRIM TRAIL FROM SAN PELLEGRINO

This is an easy, but rewarding, circular walk high in the mountains of the Garfagnana. It starts and ends in the hamlet of San Pellegrino in Alpe, a settlement that grew up around the relics of St. Pellegrino and has attracted countless pilgrims since the 8th century. You can enjoy striking views over the mountains at several points along the trail.

THE WALK

Length: 4km (2.5 miles)

Allow: 1 hour

Start/end: Middle of San Pellegrino in Alpe, with the L'Appennino da Pacetto inn on your left and the museum on your right

Paths: Wide, firm tracks and one section of quiet road

Parking: Free parking in the centre of San Pellegrino in Alpe

Begin in the heart of the village, in the square between the museum and the inn. With the museum on your right, walk forward untill you find a red-and-white sign on the side of a building marked 'In giro monte spicio'. Go up the steps. Pass the

mobile phone mast on the right-hand side and follow the wide path flanked by trees. Follow this wooded path for just over 1km (0.5 mile).

The landscape now begins to open up, taking on the appearance of lonely moorland, with heather dotting the land on either side of the track. It can get foggy up here, but on clear days you should be able to enjoy some good views on the right-hand side.

Continue to follow the main track, ignoring any side routes, until the path intersects with a wide gravel track. You'll know

you've reached it as there is a green post marking the point where the paths cross.

If you turn to the right here you will come to a tiny stone building, known as Capella di San Pellegrino. Pellegrino, who was said to be the son of the king of Scotland, came to this area on a pilgrimage in the 7th century and stayed to provide refreshment and accommodation for other pilgrims.

To return to the main route, turn left and follow the wide track. Keep walking until you reach a bend in the path.

On the left-hand side of this bend is a rocky outcrop with an excellent viewpoint, a good photo opportunity. From here you can also appreciate just how high up you are.

Continue following the wide track, walking down until you reach a tarmac road. At this point you are on the border between Tuscany and Emilia-Romagna. Turn left and walk downhill, along the tarmac road. It's generally quiet, but still keep a sharp look-out for any passing cars. Follow this road until you return to San Pellegrino. There are some fantastic views of the mountains as you approach the village.

WHERE TO EAT

L'Appennino da Pacetto café in San Pellegrino, opposite the inn in Piazza San Pellegrino *(tel 0583 649069)*.

WHEN TO GO

This area can be covered with snow early in the winter so, despite the easy tracks, you should do this walk only in good weather.

An autumnal view of the hills around San Pellegrino in Alpe

OUT AND ABOUT

SIENA–VOLTERRA AND SAN GIMIGNANO

The delightful rolling countryside that characterises Tuscany features on this drive. You travel along quiet roads through gently undulating hills, past olive groves cypress trees and immaculately preserved hilltop towns and villages, many of which are generally overlooked by visitors.

THE DRIVE

Distance: 154km (96 miles)	
Allow: 8 hours	
Start/end: Siena	

From Siena, follow the road from the Porta Romana and turn right at the sign for the A1. Turn left shortly afterwards, signposted Firenze, and follow the road around the outskirts of Siena. After 6km (4 miles) go through a tunnel and follow the signs on the right for Monteriggioni.

You will soon see Monteriggioni's castle sitting high on the hill. Park at the bottom of the village ❶ and climb to the top. The climb is worth it to see this extraordinarily well-preserved medieval fortified town, encircled by tower-studded walls.

From Monteriggioni follow the signs saying 'Firenze 46'. Turn left at the sign for Colle di Val d'Elsa.

❷ The landscape now becomes flatter and is covered with vineyards–this area is known as Chianti Colle Senesi (Chianti of Siena). When you reach a roundabout (traffic circle) you will see a large sign on the left saying CALP—one of the biggest producers of rock crystal in the world.

Drive into Colle di Val d'Elsa ❸, going uphill to reach the Colle Altao, the old part of town, and parking in the car park on via della Porta Vecchia.

Defined by three levels—Borgo, Castello and Piano (the Borough, Castle and Plain)— Colle di Val d'Elsa is renowned for the production of fine, handcrafted crystal. The Borough is entered through the monumental Porta Nova that forms the gateway to a

string of fine 16th- and 17th-century noble houses: the town hall, Palazzo Usimbardi, Palazzo Buoninsegni and the magnificent, but unfinished, Palazzo Campana, which marks the entrance to the castle, the oldest part of Colle di Val d'Elsa. The Piazza del Duomo is overlooked by the Praetorial Court, the seat of the Museo Archeologico (Archaeological Museum), the 17th-century cathedral, the Bishop's Palace, housing the Museo Civico e d'Arte Sacra (Museum of Sacred Art), and the Via delle Volte, easily the most evocative corner of the town.

From Colle take the SS68, following signs for Volterra. After

A stall selling ceramic masks and local guidebooks in San Gimignano

6km (4 miles) the road starts to climb into the heart of the country. Go through Castel San Gimignano, after which there are glorious views of vine-dotted hills, olive groves, dark cypresses and fields of sunflowers. There is a thermal electric plant at Lardarello, 33km (21 miles) from Volterra. Look for steam

rising from the underground thermal springs that spurt from these hills. After about 8km (5 miles) you should begin to see Volterra on the horizon as you reach the top of the hill and shortly you will see a sign saying 'Casciana Terme/Pontedera 44', where it is possible to turn right and make a diversion for a short walk up Monte Voltraio.

After 1km (0.5 mile) you come to Volterra ❹, a delightful Etruscan town containing fine medieval buildings and a Roman theatre (p. 156).

Leave Volterra and follow signs for Pontedera. After 4km (2.5 miles) you will see a yellow sign on the left-hand side for San Cipriano, a little church that is an ideal spot for taking some photographs of the extensive views. Alternatively, keep going and follow the SP15 as it winds its way downhill, taking the right-hand fork and going over a modern bridge until you reach an intersection. Take the turning for Firenze and follow the SP4 for about 9km (6 miles). Turn right and follow the signs for San Gimignano. You will soon see the town perched on a hill in the distance; drive up and park outside the town walls.

San Gimignano ❺ (p. 151) is frequently referred to as the medieval Manhattan, due to its striking crown of ancient towers. It's worth stopping to walk around the unspoiled streets.

From San Gimignano, drive around the town walls to reach an intersection, where you turn right for Poggibonsi. Go straight over the next roundabout towards Poggibonsi. When you reach the uninspiring industrial town, go left at the next roundabout, and get on the

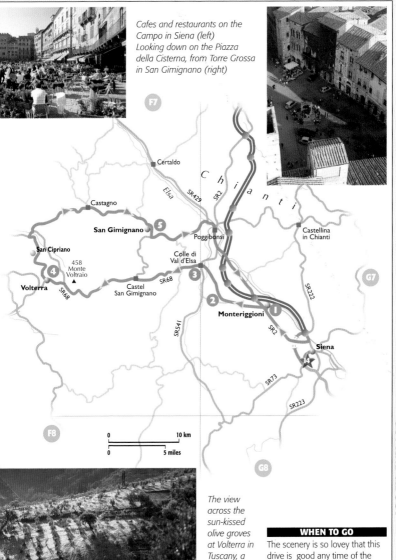

Cafes and restaurants on the Campo in Siena (left)
Looking down on the Piazza della Cisterna, from Torre Grossa in San Gimignano (right)

The view across the sun-kissed olive groves at Volterra in Tuscany, a steep tree-covered valley dropping down in the distance

WHERE TO EAT

There are several places to choose from in Volterra, including Trattoria da Bado (*Borgo San Lazzero 9, tel 0588 86477, 12–2, 7–9.30; closed Wed*) at the entrance to the town, which serves typical Tuscan dishes. Alternatively, if you just want a snack, there is an Internet Café on Via Porte Lago, which has a glass floor revealing the remains of a Roman grain silo. Just outside the town, off the SR439, is Villa Palagione, an elegant villa that is happy to cater for non-residents—a lovely rural spot for a snack or a meal. You have several choices of restaurants, cafés and pizzerias in San Gimignano. The Gelateria di Piazza in Piazza della Cisterna has a reputation for serving the best ice cream in town.

WHEN TO GO

The scenery is so lovey that this drive is good any time of the year, but to miss the crowds (particularly in San Gimignano) you should try to avoid summer and visit the area in early spring or late autumn.

PLACES TO VISIT

Museo Archeologico
Piazza del Duomo, Palazzo del Duomo, 53034 Colle di Val d'Elsa
🕐 Tue–Sun 11–12.30, 4.30–7.30
♿ €3

Museo Civico e d'Arte Sacra
Via del Castello 31, 53034 Colle di Val d'Elsa
☎ 0577 923888
🕐 11–12.30, 4.30–7.30
♿ €3

THE HEART OF FLORENCE

This walk starts and ends with two of Florence's great churches and is a good way to get a general feel for the city. Weaving in and out of the main tourist route, it takes in some of the *centro storico's* quieter lanes, lesser-known churches, palaces and small museums along the way.

THE WALK	
Length: 2km (1.2 miles)	
Allow: 1.5 hours driving time	
Start: Duomo	
End: Piazza Santa Maria Novella	

Begin at Piazza del Duomo, Florence's religious heart and one of the city's three main squares.

Florence's Duomo (p. 116) is one of Italy's most familiar landmarks, while the ancient Battistero (p. 118) holds a significant place in Florence's spiritual history. The views from the top of Giotto's campanile (see page 119) are stunning. At the top right-hand corner is the 14th-century Loggia del Bigallo, built for the Misericordia, a charitable institution whose members cared for plague victims in the 13th and 14th centuries. The beautifully carved porch served as a drop-off point for unwanted babies.

On the southwest side of the square is Via de' Calzaiuoli, 'street of the shoemakers', built on the site of a Roman road. Follow this pedestrianized, shop-lined street, the medieval city's main thoroughfare, to Piazza della Signoria, passing the unusual Church of Orsanmichele (p. 126) on your right along the way. Piazza della Signoria is the second of the big piazzas in the city and has been home to Florence's civic heart since medieval times. Leave the square on Via Vacchereccia, which emerges near the top of Via Por Santa Maria, once lined with medieval palaces that were destroyed by German bombing in 1944. A right turn brings you out to the Mercato Nuovo.

The Mercato Nuovo is also known as the Straw Market or 'Il Porcellino', after the famous bronze statue of a boar, a copy of the original by Pietro Tacca (1612)—its snout is worn shiny

by the daily affections of thousands of tourists. There has been a market on this site since the early 11th century. The elegant loggia was built by Cosimo I in 1547 and has been restored; it now shelters stalls selling souvenirs and leather goods.

Pass the market, turn left and walk down Via Porta Rossa.

On the left is the Palazzo Davanzati or the Museo della Casa Fiorentina Antica (p. 124), complete with top-floor loggia. At the end of the street lie Piazza Santa Trinità and its church, full of artistic treasures. In the middle of the square is the tall Column of Justice, a monolith brought from the Baths of Caracalla in Rome and given to Cosimo I in 1560 by Pope Pius IV. On the left stands the fine Palazzo Bartolini-Salimbeni, built between 1520 and 1523 by Baccio d'Agnolo, and beyond this the splendid Palazzo Spini-Feroni, one of the best-preserved private medieval palaces in Florence, now housing Ferragamo's flagship store and shoe museum. To its left, Borgo Santi Apostoli leads to the tiny sunken Piazza del Limbo, so-called because it stands on the site of a cemetery for unbaptized babies, and the Church of Santi Apostoli. Founded in the 11th century, it is one of the oldest churches in the city with a series of marble columns and capitals and a carved tomb by Benedetto da Rovezzano inside.

Once back in Piazza Santa Trinità, take the Via del Parione to the right of the church, then head down one of the two narrow alleys on the right. This emerges onto the intriguing Via del Purgatorio (road of purgatory). Turn left here into Via della Vigna Nuova.

The elegant façade of Palazzo Rucellai, designed by Leon Battista Alberti and built by Bernardo Rossellino between 1446 and 1451, faces you across a little square *(piazzetta)*. The lovely Loggia dei Rucellai, now home to a fashion store, is on your right.

Cross over Via della Vigna Nuova, turn right up Via dei Palchetti (at the corner of Palazzo Rucellai), then right again into Via dei Federighi. This leads into Piazza San Pancrazio.

Here you will find the ancient, deconsecrated Church of San Pancrazio, now home the Museo Marini dedicated to the work of the Florentine sculptor Marino Marini (1901–80). Just around the corner from here, on the right at Via della Spada 18, is the tiny Cappella di San Sepolcro. Built by Alberti in 1467 for the Rucellai family, it features a superbly carved marble inlay model of the Sanctuary of the Holy Sepulchre in Jerusalem.

From Cappella di San Sepolcro, walk back a little way along Via della Spada and turn left down Via del Moro, which is full of antiques shops. At Piazza Goldoni, turn right and continue along Borgo Ognissanti.

No. 60r is one of Florence's more unusual buildings, a well-preserved example of art deco architecture. A few doors down is the church and adjacent convent that give the street its name. It faces the river across the wide Piazza d'Ognissanti. To the right side is the 15th-century Palazzo Lenzi. Covered in elaborate graffiti work, it is now home to the French Consulate. Across the river you can see the Church of San Frediano in Cestello, one of the many churches in Florence whose façade was left unfinished.

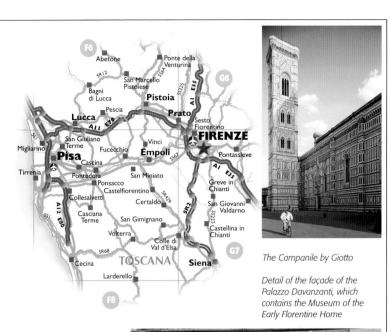

The Campanile by Giotto

Detail of the façade of the Palazzo Davanzanti, which contains the Museum of the Early Florentine Home

Backtrack a little and turn left up Via della Porcellana, lined with artisan workshops, then turn right at the top to emerge into the huge Piazza Santa Maria Novella. At the north end stands the magnificent Gothic church of the same name.

WHEN TO GO

Morning is the best time to explore Florence, when all the churches and museums are open. During the afternoon many of the smaller churches are closed and you will not be able to appreciate their remarkable interiors.

WHERE TO EAT

There are plenty of bars and cafés to choose from in this part of town. One of the nicest is Caffè Rivoire (Piazza della Signoria 5r, tel 055 214412, Tue–Sun 8am–midnight), which has a beautiful terrace. The Cantinetta dei Verazzano (Via dei Tavolini 18–20r, tel 055 268590, Mon–Sat 8am–9pm),

just off Via Calzaiuoli, serves coffee and cakes along with excellent wines and snacks.

PLACES TO VISIT

Museo della Casa Fiorentina Antica (p. 124)
Via Porta Rossa 13, Firenze
🕐 Tue–Sun 9–2; holidays 9–1

Santi Apostoli
Piazza del Limbo, Firenze
🕐 Mon–Sat 10–noon, 4–6, Sun 4–6

Museo Marini
Piazza San Pancrazio, Firenze
🕐 Wed–Mon 10–5; closed in Aug

Cappella di San Sepolcro
Via della Spada 18, Firenze
🕐 Mon–Fri 10–noon

The Fontana di Porcellino (Fountain of the Piglet) in the Mercato Nuovo. It is a bronze copy of a marble statue by Pitro Tacca (1612)

SIENA AND SOUTHERN TUSCANY

From Siena, this drive takes you south past the ancient abbeys of Sant'Antimo and Monte Oliveto Maggiore and the hilltop towns of Pienza, Montepulciano and Montalcino. Some of Italy's finest wines are produced in this region, so look for *enoteche* (specialist wine bars and shops) where any non-drivers can try a glass or two.

THE DRIVE	
Distance: 261km (162 miles)	
Allow: 11 hours (best spread over 2 days)	
Start/end: Siena	

From Siena take the SR2. In 3km (2 miles) you will see signs saying 'Buonconvento 25'. After another 8km (5 miles) turn left, staying on the SR2 for Buonconvento. When you come to a crossroads, keep driving along the SR2 to Buonconvento. Bear right after the bridge to enter the town.

2 As you climb uphill you will start to notice a large number of signs for *enoteche*, many of which offer free tasting.

After about 9km (6 miles), bear right at the top of the hill and join the SP14, following signs for Montalcino. Follow the city wall in an anticlockwise direction until you arrive at the roundabout at the top of the hill. There is free parking left of the roundabout. Alternatively there is pay parking on the right-hand side next to La Fortezza.

A Buonconvento blacksmith

Buonconvento **1**, unusual in this area in that it is not perched on a hill, has a medieval old town and a small museum, the Museo d'Arte Sacra. It was once an important stop on the Via Francigena, the historic pilgrims' route that stretched from Canterbury to Rome (p. 139).

Leave Buonconvento, following the SR2 through the town's bleak industrial outskirts. Turn right and join the SP45 for Montalcino. The scenery becomes prettier and you will soon see Montalcino on the hill ahead of you.

Montalcino **3** (p. 143) is particularly famous for its rich ruby red Brunello wine, characterized by an intense aroma and delicate, warm flavour with a hint of vanilla.

After exploring Montalcino, follow the brown signs from the roundabout at the top of the hill for Abbazia di Sant'Antimo, joining the SP55. The road now starts to wind downhill to the valley bottom and in about 2km (1 mile) you should spot the abbey, nestling below the hills on the right-hand side. Shortly turn right to reach the abbey, a good starting point for a walk.

From here, return to the road and drive up the hill to

Castelnuovo dell'Abate. Turn right at the top of the hill, following the sign saying 'Stazione Monte Amiata' on the SP22. You will now pass the Val d'Orcia, from where the road begins to wind downhill. Pass over a level crossing by Monte Amiata station and cross the River Orcia and you will come into the hamlet of Monte Amiata, after which the road begins to climb uphill again. When you reach the intersection, go to the left towards Castiglione d'Orcia. From here the road climbs even more steeply, with rewarding views. When you come to a junction, take a left turn and join the SR323. Continue driving towards Castiglione d'Orcia.

At the centre of Castiglione d'Orcia **4** is Piazza il Vecchietta (Square of the Old Women), dedicated to Lorenzo di Peter (1412–80). It is overlooked by the Palazzo Comunale, home to a fresco of the Madonna and Child with two saints (Sienese school) taken from the nearby Rocca d'Orcia. There are two churches worth seeing here: the Romanesque Church of Santa Maria Maddelena, and the Church of Santo Stefano with its 16th-century façade and two Madonnas by Simone Martini and Lorenzetti.

Drive through the village, then head downhill. After 5km (3 miles) turn left at the intersection to join the SR2. Continue until you reach Bagno Vignoni. **5** Park just outside town, on top of the hill.

This ancient spa has been used since Etruscan times and is dominated by an enormous outdoor pool of warm, sulphurous water (p. 138).

Go back downhill from the town, turn left at the end of the road

Continued on page 304.

OUT AND ABOUT

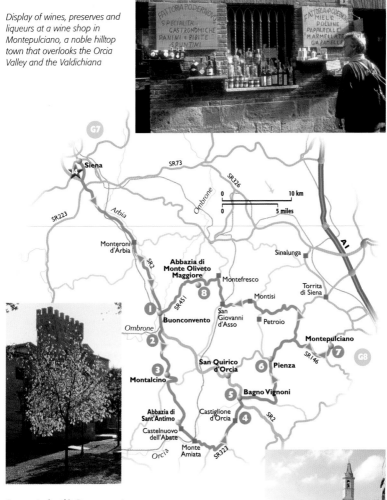

Display of wines, preserves and liqueurs at a wine shop in Montepulciano, a noble hilltop town that overlooks the Orcia Valley and the Valdichiana

Town gate (north), Buonconvento

City wall and duomo, Pienza

WHERE TO EAT

The Fiaschetteria Italiana, a lovely old café with an imposing interior in Montalcino, serves coffees, cakes, light meals and wine *(Piazza del Popolo 6, open 7.30am–midnight)*. There are plenty of cafés and restaurants to choose from in Bagno Vignoni, but particularly good is La Parata *(tel 0577 887508, Thu–Tue 10.30–2.45, 7.30–9.30)*. It serves a wide selection of *pannini* and cakes, along with local cheese, biscuits and olive oil, and you can sit outside on fine days. In Montepulciano you can enjoy cakes, snacks and a glass of wine at the art nouveau Caffè Poliziano *(Via di Voltaia nel Corso, open daily)*, which also serves meals in its restaurant.

WHEN TO GO

You can do this tour anytime of year, but July and August are the hottest and busiest months, while the countryside is at its best in spring and autumn.

PLACES TO VISIT

Museo d'Arte Sacra
Via Socini 18, Buonconvento
☎ 0577 807181
🕐 Tue–Sun 10.30–1. 3-7, Mar–Oct; Sat and Sun 10–1, 3–5, Nov–Feb
💶 €3.10
🚻

Abbazia di Sant'Antimo
Castelnuovo dell'Abate, Siena 53024
☎ 0577 835659
🕐 Daily 6–9.30
💶 Free

Abbazia di Monte Oliveto Maggiore
Near Asciano
☎ 0577 707611
🕐 Daily 9.15–noon, 3.15–5.45 (until 5 Oct–Apr)
💶 Free
🚻

The castle at Castiglione d'Orcia

and then take the next right to join the SP53 for Pienza. Turn left onto the SP18 and drive uphill. The striking red sandstone town of Pienza is in front of you. Park at the bottom of the hill.

The focul point of Pienza **6**, a UNESCO World Heritage Site, is its Piazza Pio II square, bordered by the Palazzo Piccolomini, the Palazzo Borgia and the cathedral. The cathedral's pure Renaissance exterior and late Gothic-style interior, similar to south German churches, contains several altarpieces by Sienese masters.

Leave Pienza and continue uphill

The landscape around Monte Oliveto Maggiore

until you come to an intersection. Turn right here for the SR146 and Montepulciano **7**. Follow the road until you reach Montepulciano, again parking outside the city walls.

The Tuscan town of Montepulciano has sweeping views and a maze of steep, winding streets and alleyways. Besides the Renaissance church of San Biagio, the town has many wine shops where you can purchase bottles of Vino Nobile, the famous local wine (p. 144). Aged in oak barrels for two years (three years for Reserva), this dry wine has a delicate bouquet with violet scents.

From Montepulciano, drive downhill. Turn right for Pienza on

the SS146 and after 7km (4 miles) turn right to join the SP15, a twisty road heading towards Torrita di Siena. Turn left just in front of a bar on the corner to join the SP57. Follow the road to an intersection where you take a sharp left past Petroio and then drive on for another 4km (2.5 miles), after which you turn right for Montisi.

The road now winds tightly downhill, passing through the woods until you reach an intersection. Turn left here and follow the SP14 through Montisi, on to the outskirts of San Giovanni d'Asso. When you come to the next intersection, turn right towards the remote Abbazia di Monte Oliveto Maggiore. Follow this road to Montefresco, then turn left at the intersection and drive on for another 3km (2 miles). At the next intersection go left, then shortly turn off to visit the late 13th-century Abbazia di Monte Oliveto Maggiore.

8 This Benedictine abbey (p. 138) stands in a wooded park on a scenic rise and is still inhabited by monks. Pause a while to admire the famous frescoes in the main cloister.

Leave the abbey and continue along the SR451 until you reach Buonconvento. From here, pick up the SR2 that leads back to Siena.

OLD SIENA

Wander through the heart of old Siena, beginning in the north of the city and winding south past medieval churches and palaces to the Campo. The route then takes you through the city's less-visited southern quarters, finishing in Piazza del Duomo, overlooked by the cathedral and the Spedale di Santa Maria della Scala.

THE WALK

Length: 2km (1.2 miles)
Allow: 2–3 hours
Start: Piazza San Domenico
End: Piazza del Duomo

Begin your walk in Piazza San Domenico, home to the church of the same name, containing frescoes by Sodoma (1477–1549). With your back to the church, walk down the Via della Sapienza opposite San Domenico, and after 100m (110yd) you will come to the Biblioteca Comunale degli Intronati.

This library was founded in 1759 in what was probably a 13th-century hospital. It contains more than 500,000 books and other documents, including letters by St. Catherine of Siena and many medieval Sienese painters and architects. At the next minor crossroads, is the Church of San Pellegrino alla Sapienza, built in 1767 over the site of a much older chapel.

Continue straight on at the church to emerge on Banchi di Sopra, a major street that follows the path of the Via Francigena, a centuries-old pilgrimage route between Rome and northern Europe. Ahead is Piazza Salimbeni, home to a trio of fine palaces: Palazzo Tantucci (1548) on the left, the 14th-century Palazzo Salimbeni to the rear, and Palazzo Spannocchi (1470) to the right (only open to the public during the Palio, p. 259). The Salimbeni family were prominent bankers and silk and grain traders, while Ambrogio Spannochi was the treasurer to the Sienese Pope Pius II.

A short diversion left on Banchi di Sopra brings you to the Church of Santa Maria delle Nevi (*rarely open*), reknowned for its high altarpiece, the *Madonna della Neve* (1477) by Stefano di Giovanni. Known

as Sassetta, he was considered to be the first person to paint a cloudy sky.

Retrace your steps on Banchi di Sopra and look for the church of San Cristoforo on the left.

Romanesque in origin, San Cristoforo was rebuilt in the late 18th century after earthquake damage. Opposite is the Palazzo Tolomei, part of the original fortress home of the Tolomei, one of Siena's most powerful medieval dynasties of bankers and merchants. It is the oldest surviving private residence in the city, dating from 1205. Pause to admire the statue of the she-wolf.

Continue south to the intersection with Banchi di Sotto and Via di Città, where you will find the Loggia della Mercanzia (1428–44), an attractive Gothic three-arched loggia. Little alleys either side take you into Piazza del Campo. Here you can admire the Campo from one of cafés or visit the Museo Civico. Leave the piazza by the Vicolo dei Pollaiuoli or the Via dei Rinaldini. Both bring you to Banchi di Sotto, where you turn right.

Immediately on your right stands the Palazzo Piccolomini, a majestic palace begun in 1469. Inside, on an upper floor, is the little-known Archivio di Stato (State Archive), full of fascinating works of art. Beyond the palace is Logge del Papa (Loggia of the Pope) built in 1462 on the orders of the Tuscan-born Pope Pius II (Enea Silvio Piccolomini).

Take the right-hand fork in front of the loggia and follow it around to the intersection with Via del Porrione, named after the Latin *emporium* or 'market place', referring to the Roman markets that stood close by. Cross Via dei

Porrione and walk through the arch down the Vicolo delle Scotte, passing Siena's Sinagoga (synagogue) on the right, the heart of the city's Jewish ghetto, created in 1571 by Cosimo I de Medici. Turn left on the Via di Salicotto, then take the first right to emerge on Piazza del Mercato. Cross the square and bear right to pick up the Via del Mercato, then turn left almost immediately to follow the Via Giovanni Dupre, with attractive alleys branching off either side. At the Chiesa di San Giuseppe on the left take the Via Sant'Agata straight onto a gravel area on your left towards the 13th-century Chiesa di Sant'Agostino, which contains paintings by Sodoma and Ambrogio Lorenzetti.

Head through the arch to the Via San Pietro and the Church of San Pietro (set back on your right) and the redbrick Pinacoteca Nazionale beyond. Just before the church take a sharp left onto the Via di Castelvecchio (an easily missed alley) and bear right for the Via di Stalloreggi. Turn left towards the Arco delle Due Porte, an arch that formed part of the city's 11th-century walls, passing a house on the left (No. 91–93) where Duccio (c.1260–1320) painted his famous *Maestà*. Turn right after the arch and follow the peaceful Via del Fosso di San Ansano to Piazza della Selva, where either the Via Franciosa or the Via Firolamo leads you to Piazza del Duomo or Piazza San Giovanni.

In Piazza San Giovanni you can visit the Battistero di San Giovanni (Baptistery) and then walk up the steps to your right to see the Duomo, Spedale di Santa Maria della Scalla.

WHERE TO EAT

The Nannini café at Banchi di Sopra 95–99 is a good place for a break, as is Bar Il Palio on Piazza del Campo (*tel 47 0577282055*).

THE VALLE UMBRA

This drive through undulating, fertile countryside, intersects with the Roman Via Flaminia, an ancient trade route that contributed to the prosperity of the towns that face each other across the valley. Saints, poets, and painters have all lived and left their mark in this area.

THE DRIVE

Distance: 122km (76 miles)
Allow: 4.5 hours driving time
Start/end: Piazza Garibaldi, Santa Maria degli Angeli, near Assisi

From Piazza Garibaldi take the road south for Foligno, following signs for Perugia and Roma. Pass under the *superstrada*, following signs for Costano and Bettona. The road now heads into open, flat countryside. Shortly after the *superstrada*, turn left at the intersection towards Bettona on the SP404 and head for Passaggio. Turn right at the roundabout (traffic circle) signposted for Bettona, Torgiano and Deruta and take a left, signposted for Bettona. Continue up the narrow SP403, with views to the north of the plain and Assisi, and drive through the terraced olive groves until you reach Bettona **1**. Go clockwise around the town and park by the town walls.

Overlooking the River Chiascio to the north, Bettona is an unspoiled town enclosed by medieval walls. It was the only Etruscan settlement on the east bank of the River Tiber.

Leaving Bettona, drive down the hill signposted for Torgiano. Turn right at the main road heading for Montefalco, Passaggio and Assisi, and continue to the roundabout at Passaggio. Go straight over the roundabout, towards Bevagna on the SP403. The road gently climbs as you approach the town. Park in the car park on the right in front of the large tower, with its arched entrance that leads into the town.

2 Bevagna's asymmetrical Piazza Silvestri is an extremely well-preserved example of medieval town planning. The 13th-century Palazzo dei Consoli, with its theatre and 12th-century Church of San Silvestro, are highlights of the town.

Drive out of Bevagna, following signs for Montefalco (7km/4.5 miles away), passing down an avenue of trees. About 100m (110yd) beyond the town limit sign, fork left onto the SP443, past vineyards and farmland dotted with trees. Turn right at the intersection and continue through Montepennino up towards Montefalco. Turn left at the intersection outside the town and at the walls bear right. Park in the large car park on your right.

With its panoramic views, Montefalco **3** (p.144) is known as the Balcony of Umbria and is renowned for its Sagrantino DOCG wine. The former Church of San Francesco (now the Museo Civico di San Francesco) contains world-famous Renaissance frescoes by the Florentine artist Benozzo Gozzoli.

From Montefalco, take the road for Spoleto and Terni which heads down through thick olive groves onto the SP445, with views of Trevi across the valley. Drive through Turrita, passing the ornate Madonna della Stella sanctuary on the left (8km/ 5 miles from Montefalco). Go straight across at the lights and at the intersection turn right onto a long straight road. Bear left at the next intersection at Mercatello. In Bruna go over the bridge and take the sharp left signposted for Trevi. Drive 7km (4 miles) along the SP457, across the valley floor and past Castel San Giovanni. Go straight across the roundabout, following the signs for Trevi. About 600m (650yd) farther along, turn left at the intersection onto the busy SS3, in the direction of Fano, Perugia and Foligno.

Shortly on the left, you will come to the ancient springs at Fonti del Clitunno **4** and the Tempio sul Clitunno, an excellent example of a Roman temple.

Continue north along the SS3 for a further 6.5km (4 miles), and at the traffic lights and service station turn right onto the road signposted for Parrano and Trevi. Drive up the SP425 past the Church of the Madonna delle Lacrime and the Bovara turning. Head through the gates of Trevi and circumnavigate the town towards the large car park above in Piazza Garibaldi.

5 Trevi (p. 156) is known as the City of the Olive, and the old town is surrounded by olive groves. In nearby Bovara there is an olive tree dedicated to St. Emiliano, which, at around 1,700 years old, is thought to be the oldest in Italy.

Leave Trevi, following signs for Foligno. Continue up the hill and turn left at the top. Drive down through Santa Maria in Valle towards the SS3. Follow the signs for Perugia at the roundabout, heading up onto the *superstrada* north. This fast road takes you past the industrial area around Foligno. About 8km (5 miles) from the roundabout, take the right towards Perugia onto the SS75. Come off the *superstrada* at the Spello exit. Turn right into the centre of Spello **6**. Park in Piazza Kennedy near the Porta Consolare at the south end of town, or around the corner on the Collepino road.

The winding alleyways of Spello (p. 155) are constructed from the local pink stone. There are more Roman remains here than in any other Umbrian town. The frescoes by Pinturicchio (1454–1513) in the Church of Santa Maria Maggiore are considered to be the artist's finest.

Take the road to the right of Porta Consolare and follow the signs for Collepino and Monte Subasio. Continue around the east side of town, branching up to the left after 1km (0.5 mile) to the town's Porta Montanara. Follow

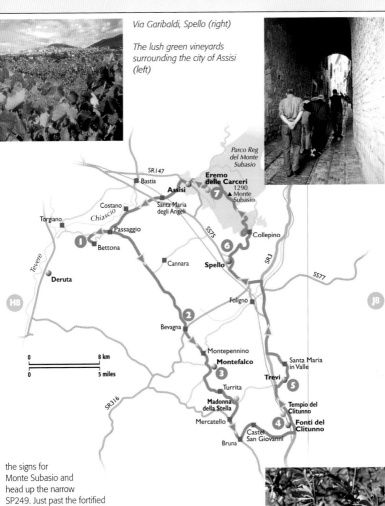

Via Garibaldi, Spello (right)

The lush green vineyards surrounding the city of Assisi (left)

the signs for Monte Subasio and head up the narrow SP249. Just past the fortified hamlet of Collepino, turn left at the Monte Subasio sign onto a so-called white (rough) road.

❼ St. Francis retreated to the Eremo delle Carceri on top of the massive limestone summit that forms the backdrop to Assisi. The top is 1,290m (4,232ft) above sea level, and 4.5km (3 miles) from the summit, the Eremo delle Carceri comes into view.

Continue down the hairpins of the SP251, past Assisi's 14th-century Porta Cappuccini. Turn left at the intersection at the bottom. Bear right past the service station towards Perugia along the SS147 and follow the road beneath the massive ramparts of the Basilica di San Francesco. Turn left to Santa Maria degli Angeli (3km/2 miles

from the intersection), cross the level crossing (grade crossing) and drive straight on towards the basilica until you arrive back in Piazza Garibaldi.

WHERE TO EAT

In the medieval hamlet of Relais La Corta di Bettona you can sit out on a terrace overlooking the plain towards Assisi. The Taverna del Guillare serves traditional Umbrian dishes such as home-made pasta with truffles *(Via Caterina, 2 Bettona, tel 075 987114, daily 12–2.30, 7.30–10 Easter–Nov; closed Mon in winter).*

   Other options include Da Nina *(Piazza Garibaldi 6, tel 0742 360161, closed Tue)* in Bevagna and Ristorante il Molino *(Piazza Matteotti 6–7, tel 0742 651305, closed Tue)* in Spello.

An olive tree in Spello

PLACES TO VISIT

Museo Civico di San Francesco
Via della Ringhiera Umbra,
06037 Montefalco
☎ 0742 379598
🕐 Daily 10.30–1, 3–7.30, Jul–Aug;
Tue–Sun 10.30–1, 2–6 Mar–May,
Sep–Oct; Tue–Sun 10.30–1, 2.30–5,
Nov–Feb
💶 €3

THE VALNERINA AND PIANO GRANDE

Beginning in Spoleto, this drive takes in the dramatic upper sections of the Nera Valley–the Valnerina, the lower Corno Valley and the Piano Grande on the southern edge of Monti Sibillini National Park.

THE DRIVE

Distance: 183km (114 miles)	
Allow: 4.5 hours driving time	
Start/end: Spoleto	
Overnight stop: Norcia	

From Piazza della Vittoria on the north side of Spoleto follow the signs for Flaminia SS3, and Norcia and Foligno. Continue along the SS3, following signs for Fano, Perugia and Foligno for 2.5km (1.5 miles) and then bear right towards Cascia and Norcia. Passing Eggi on your left, drive into the long tunnel. You will emerge in the Valnerina. Follow the signs for Norcia, heading along the SS209 and up the valley for 14.5km (9 miles). The breadth of the valley fluctuates, sometimes narrowing dramatically to a gorge. Poplars and oaks border the Nera, and fortified towers and settlements punctuate the sides of the valley, pointing to its turbulent past.

Castel San Felice ❶, with its lovely 12th-century Romanesque church, is up to your right. High up on the left above Borgo Cerreto stands Cerreto di Spoleto and its tower.

About 500m (550yd) past Borgo Cerreto, turn right at the intersection towards Norcia, over the elevated bridge into the tunnel. You will emerge on the SR320, which takes you along the narrow Corno Valley. The road cuts through tunnels and narrow gorges and passes under concrete galleries. At the sign for Cascia, where the main valley heads south, continue for a further 6km (4 miles) on the SR396 towards Norcia. The valley widens into a fertile bowl at the foot of the Sibillini Mountains, with the walled town of Norcia set on a mound before you (p. 144–145).

Park outside Norcia's city walls at Porta Romana, and walk into town ❷. Have a coffee in Piazza San Benedetto, or sample some of the best salami in Umbria.

Drive around the town walls clockwise and turn left towards Pescara, down a long straight avenue, following signs for Castelluccio. Turn left after 2.5km (1.5 miles) and head for Castelluccio, climbing up the SP477, enjoying views of the green valley below and the steep slopes of the Monte Sibillini foothills. Where the main road continues to the Adriatic, turn left for Forca Canapine and Castelluccio.

As you climb you can admire the dramatic views of Norcia below and the Monti Reatini to the south. Around 17km (11 miles) from Norcia the landscape becomes more rugged as you rise above the tree line. A little farther on, turn left towards Castelluccio, past a modern restaurant and over the brow of the hill. The massive slopes of Monte Vettore greet you, with the Piano Grande (p. 145) and the battered Castelluccio below. Cross the plain following the sign for Visso. Drive up into the village and park by the low wall facing the Sibillini.

Castelluccio ❸, the last outpost in Umbria, is famous for its wild lentils, collected from the valley floor.

From here, drive north towards Visso. After 5km (3 miles), from the pass above the village, there is a good viewpoint suitable for a picnic. As you continue into the Marche, down below the tree line the landscape becomes increasingly steep. Deep ravines cut through the white rock, and the conically shaped Monte Cardosa rises up on your left.

About 11km (7 miles) from Castelluccio ❹, just above the pretty village of Gualdo, turn left to Dell'Erborista Ristorante and Pizzeria, a good lunch stop. Continue down to Visso, bearing left onto the SP134 at Castelsantangelo sul Nera.

The small town of Visso ❺ with its sqaure towers nestles in a valley, surrounded by hills. The parish Church of Santa Maria contains some interesting remains of old frescoes.

Leaving Visso, follow the signs for Rome and Terni and drive out via Il Gole della Valnerina (a narrow gorge between high rocks) on the SR209, to emerge in a wild, narrow valley with overhanging rock formations. The valley floor opens up gradually as you drive on, and more settlements come into view. A further 11km (7 miles) down the Valnerina, take the turning left to Norcia if you are staying there for the night.

Otherwise continue on the SR209 past the tall, bleak towers of Triponzo that rise precariously from the cliff face. Ignore the turning to the right to Spoleto and continue in the direction of Terni through Scheggino, with its crumbling towers. Continue past Ceselli, where hamlets dot the hillside to the south. Slow down as you approach Sambucheto, and turn sharply right to San Pietro in Valle at the battered yellow sign just inside the village limits. Drive up the narrow lane past the cottages at Macenano and park in the car park down past the abbey.

❻ The Abbazia di San Pietro in Valle was founded in 720. Steeped in history, it contains some of the most important examples of Romanesque frescoes in Italy (p. 138).

Rejoin the main road, and continue south past Ferentillo as far as the intersection. Before turning right to Spoleto, make a detour and have a quick stop at Arrone to the left.

OUT AND ABOUT

Under a bridge across the river Nera, Valerina (left)

Paragliding at Monte Sibillini (right)

Lentils, Monte Sibillini

7 Arrone's church, Santa Maria Assunta, contains frescoes by Vincenzo Tomagni and Giovanni da Spoleto. The immaculate upper village has a medieval close with a tree growing out of the clock tower.

Return to Spoleto, crossing the SR209 and Via Montefranco on the SP4, a winding road with good views of the distant hills. Turn right onto the fast Flaminia SR3 and after 15.5km (9.5 miles) you will see Spoleto's unmistakable Rocca.

WHEN TO GO

The best time to see the Piano Grande is in May and early June, when the wildflowers are at their best. Check the weather with the tourist information office in Norcia before you head off *(tel 0743 816090, closed Wed Sep–May)*. Don't cross the Piano Grande in snow—Castelluccio can be cut off.

WHERE TO EAT

In Norcia; Cafe-bar Vignola *(tel 0743 817086)* and Ristorante Beccofino *(tel 0743 817031)* in Piazza San Benedetto.
Castelluccio; Bar del Capitano *(Via della Bufera Castelluccio 10, tel 0743 821159)*.
In Sant'Eutizio; Locanda Biancofiore *(Via Santa Caterina 8, Preci, tel 0743 9399319, closed Mon)*.
In Gualdo; Dell'Erborista Ristorante and Pizzeria *(Frazione Gualdo, Castelsantangelo sul Nera, tel 0737 98134, book at weekends)*.
In San Pietro in Valle; Ristorante Abbazia *(Abazia di San Pietro in Valle, SS 209 Valnerina, Loc. Macenano, 05034 Ferentillo, Terni, tel 0744 380011, closed in winter)*.

WHERE TO STAY

Hotel and Restaurant Grotta Azzura *(Via Alfieri 12, Norcia, tel 0743 816513)*.

TIPS

● It is better to break the journey up with an overnight stop in Norcia, concentrating on the upper circuit on the first day and Norcia and the lower circuit on the second.

OLD PERUGIA

From the medieval Via dei Priori this walk winds out to the northerly Porta Sant'Angelo and one of the oldest churches in Italy. You return to the city along the 13th-century aqueduct, past the dramatic arches of Via Maestà delle Volte behind the 'noble' Piazza IV Novembre.

THE WALK

Length: 3.7km (2.3 miles)

Allow: 2–3 hours

Start: Via dei Priori (from Palazzo dei Priori)

End: Piazza IV Novembre

Begin by walking down the Via dei Priori, the steep street that descends from Arco dei Priori beneath the Palazzo dei Priori tower. As you go down, passing the baroque Chiesa Nuova on your right, you will walk over a fragment of the 1st century AD *decumanus* pavement. As you continue, you will pass the Sciri tower and the Oratory of San Francesco on Via degli Sciri on your left.

The street now bends past the Piazzetta della Madonna della Luce, with its two churches. Stop and go inside the Church of Madonna della Luce to take in the miraculous *Vision of the Virgin* by Tiberio d'Assisi, and the cupola covered in frescoes by Giovan Battista Caporali.

Go down the steps to the left, through the Etruscan Porta Trasimeno, the old exit to Trasimeno and Tuscany, and turn right to enter Piazza San Francesco.

The Oratorio di San Bernardino, with its softly tinted façade, has a grassy area in front of it where students often relax in the sun—a good picnic spot on a sunny day.

Go back up Via San Francesco and take the next left up the steps along Via del Poggio. From here you can look down onto the front of the Church of San Francesco al Prato, built in 1230, and now undergoing restoration. Turn right up Via della Tartaruga, passing Piazza San Paolo on the right. At the top turn left and join Via Francolina towards Piazza Giuseppe Ermini and continue right onto Via del Verzaro. This narrow street, with tall buildings on both sides, runs along the

back of Teatro Morlacchi, built in 1778.

Before you emerge onto Piazza Morlacchi, part of the university, pass by the little Church of San Martino del Verzaro on your left (1163), which has frescoes by Giannicola di Paolo inside.

Bear left and you will come to Piazza Cavalotti. Cross over and walk down Via Baldeschi. Pass the steps marked Via Appia on your left and continue until you join Piazza Ansidei. Cross the square and walk down to the left along Via Ulisse Rocchi, following the signs to Arco Etrusco. As you continue down, go through the Etruscan Arch and cross the road with the big red 18th-century Università per Stranieri building on your left. Cross over to Corso Garibaldi.

This area is evidence of the city's expansion in medieval times, and is where the artisan quarters sprang up during the 13th and 14th centuries. On your right are Piazza Lupatelli and the Church of Sant' Agostino, with its pink and white checked front.

Continue walking along the Corso Garibaldi and you will pass a little *madonnina* (shrine) on your left and the Complesso della Mercanzia.

This 14th-century building belonged to one of the powerful guilds—you can still make out a granary sign above the door lintel. It was also used as a hospital for the poor.

As you wander along the Corso you pass a series of monastic settlements, each with its own church. The Benedictine Santa Caterina on your right was restructured by Galeazzo Alessi in 1547, and the Dominican monastery of Beata Colomba at No. 191 was where St. Francis and St. Dominic allegedly met in 1220.

Go straight on under a brick arch and you immediately find the graceful approach to Tempio Sant'Angelo, the oldest church in Umbria, to your right.

Stop and admire the views from this peaceful spot, which marks the end of the medieval boundary. You can see over towards the restored Convent of San Francesco del Monte outside the city walls. Cassero di Porta Sant'Angelo has a little museum and panoramaic terrace.

Return to Corso Garibaldi, passing the monastery of Santa Lucia. About halfway down, just after the Complesso della Mercanzia building, turn right down Via Domenico Lupatelli, a narrow street lined with houses and picturesque side alleys. At the end of Via Lupatelli turn right. Go along Via Fabretti until you come to Via dell'Aquedotto on the left. Walk along the aqueduct, looking down onto the houses and gardens below.

The aqueduct was built between 1254 and 1276 by Fra Bevignate to bring water down from Monte Pacciano to the city's Fontana Maggiore, 5km (3 miles) away. It became a pedestrian way in the 1830s after a new water supply was built. This is a popular spot with artists and photographers. Turn around to admire the rooftops and buildings behind you.

The ancient Via Appia merges with Via dell'Aquedotto, and 200 steps take you up through the arch of the aqueduct to Via Baldeschi. Return to Piazza Cavalotti and bear left up Via Maestà delle Volte.

A fresco of the Virgin and Child was painted on this dark medieval thoroughfare in 1297. The Maestà delle Volte Oratory was built in 1335 to protect the fresco, but was rebuilt in

The San Pietro church (left)

Perugia's Piazza IV Novembre, with the 15th-century Palazzo dei Priori and the 13th-century Fontana Maggiore (bottom)

Corso Venucci (above)

Città di Castello **H7**

Cortona **Gubbio** Fabriano **J7**
Macerata
Perugia
Assisi SS77
SS75 SS3

G8 Bagno Vignoni **Foligno** Parco Nazionale dei Monti Sibillini **Ascoli Piceno**
A1 E35 SR2 SS44B SS3
Pitigliano **Spoleto** **Teramo** Parco **K8**
SR74 **Terni** SS4
Viterbo Nazionale del Gran Sasso **K9**
E8 SS1 SS3 **Rieti** SR578 SS153
G9 SR2 **L'Aquila** E80
A12 E80
Civitavecchia **Tivoli** SS5 **Avezzano**
ROMA A24 A25
G10 Fiumicino Ciampino Frascati A1 E45 **Frosinone**
Velletri **J10**
Anzio **Latina** SS1

Bronze statues on the front of the Palazzo dei Priori (below right)

1576 after a fire. The medieval archway is a remnant of the portico, and Angelini built the fountain in the hollow beneath the church. On the right is a contemporary wall fresco by Beletti (1945).

Walk through the arches to Piazza IV Novembre, where you will find many cafés and bars selling ice cream.

WHERE TO EAT

Il Padrino serves fish dishes and is a good lunch stop *(Via Baldeschi 5, closed Sun and Aug)*. There is also the Osteria del Gambero *(Via Baldeschi 17, 075 5735461, daily 12.30–2.30, 7.30–11; closed Mon)*.

PLACES TO VISIT

Cassero di Porta Sant'Angelo
Porto Sant'Angelo
☎ 075 41670
🕐 Daily 11–1.30, 3–6.30, Jul–Aug; Wed–Mon 11–1.30, 3–6.30, Apr–Oct; Wed–Mon 11–1.30, 3–5, Nov–Mar
💶 €2.50
www.sistemamuseo.it

A CIRCUIT OF LAGO TRASIMENO

From Passignano this drive takes you anticlockwise around Lago Trasimeno, Italy's largest inland lake south of the River Po. You will pass by olive-studded slopes north of the lake, through the lowlands and marshy areas near the Tuscan border, and the gentle undulating countryside in the south.

THE DRIVE	
Distance: 80km (50 miles)	
Allow: 5.5 hours driving time	
Start/end: Passignano	

From the ferry pier drive west and north out of town, over the level crossing (grade crossing) on the old road (SR75) following signs for Tuoro and under the *superstrada*. After 6km (4 miles) turn right at the intersection and start climbing up, past the characteristic umbrella pines and cypress trees, to Tuoro ❶, which is approached up an avenue.

Park at the top and admire the view of Isola Maggiore from Piazza Municipio. This unassuming village is historically famous as the sight of the bloody massacre of the Roman legions by Hannibal at the Battle of Lago Trasimeno in 217BC.

Turn back down the hill, and after 300m (330yd) take a right, following the battle signs, then turn right again at the intersection to Castiglione del Lago. You will pass occasional signs for battle sites as the old road meanders past reed beds to the lake. Farther along from the intersection (at a bend in the road to the right), turn left following the signs for Borghetto, Chiusi and Castiglione del Lago. Drive over the level crossing, and under the dual carriageway (divided highway). At Borghetto, turn right onto the SR75 then turn left at the intersection onto the SR71. Continue for 8km (5 miles) across the low-lying country near the lake's shore as far as Castiglione del Lago, which can be seen jutting out into the lake. Turn left and drive up to the large intersection just outside the town and park by the ramparts.

This fortified town ❷ was originally an island on the lake in Etruscan and Roman times. Later, it was defended by the Tuscia Lombards against

Byzantine Perugia and subsequently fought over by Arezzo, Cortona and Perugia. Its present form dates from the middle of the 13th century.

Drive out from town on the SR71, following signs for Chiusi, and continue along the long straight road towards Citta della Pieve. Come off at the exit sign for Paciano and turn left onto the SP310, which goes under the main road. The landscape becomes more undulating and the fields widen to reveal vineyards, oaks and occasional redbrick houses. Approach Paciano up a road lined with cypresses and olives, turning left and driving up towards the centre. Park at the side of the road and walk up through the redbrick Porta Fiorentina. **Set among olive groves and oak woodland, Paciano ❸ is a quiet, well-preserved medieval village dating back to the 13th century. With its extensive views, this is a good base for walking and there are plenty of places to enjoy picnics in the surrounding countryside.**

Leave Paciano and return down the hill. Turn right onto the SP310 and shortly afterwards turn right again towards Panicale.

After 2km (1 mile) turn right at the intersection and up, past olive trees, to the attractive *borgo*. Park immediately outside Panicale, near the lace museum, and walk up through the gate.

Panicale ❹ once belonged to the Etruscan town of Chiusi, strategically important to the Perugians in controlling the Nestor Valley to the south as well as Lago Trasimeno. From its vantage point it provides lovely views over to Isola Polvese. The town's have developed in a circular pattern, with its three main squares on different levels.

Continue driving around the town; turn left at the intersection and drive northwest through Macchie. At the SR599 turn right for Magione. Go through Panicarola, past reed-fringed ditches, and the Sant'Arcangelo ferry stop on your left. After some 13km (8 miles), turn left for San Feliciano onto the SP316 and past San Savino. Follow the signs for the village, past the turning for the *traghetti* (ferries) to Isola Polvese, and park where you can or in the square.

San Feliciano ❺ is a traditional fishing village. This is highlighted in its fishing museum, the Museo della Pesca, which can be found at the end of a narrow cul-de-sac near the lakeside and boat yards.

Take the SP316 north out of the village, through Monte del Lago, and follow the signs for the resort of Torricella. Go over the level crossing and follow the signs for Passignano, which will take you up onto the fast *superstrada*. Come off at the next exit at Passignano Est, cross the level crossing and head back to the start point.

Fishing nets at San Feliciano, a hamlet on Lago Trasimeno

OUT AND ABOUT

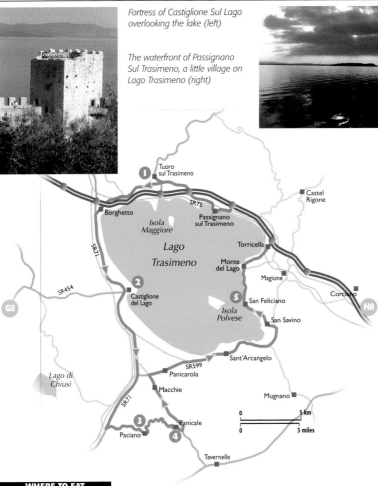

Fortress of Castiglione Sul Lago overlooking the lake (left)

The waterfront of Passignano Sul Trasimeno, a little village on Lago Trasimeno (right)

WHERE TO EAT

There are several café bars in Castiglione del Lago and the restaurant La Cantina (Lione del Lago, Centro Storico, Via Vittorio Emanuele 93, Castiglione del Lago, tel 0759 652463, daily 12.30–3.30, 6.45–11; closed Mon Oct–Mar). For refreshment in Panicale visit Bar del Gallo. About 2km (1 mile) south of San Feliciano is Da Massimo, specializing in lake fish (Via dei Romani 16, San Savino, tel 075 8476094/075 8476269, daily 11–11; closed Mon). Back in Passignano, Del Molo (Via A Pompili 7, San Savino, tel 075 827151, Tue–Sun 12.30–2.30, 7–10) is a reasonably priced Restaurant and there is a good Pizzeria opposite the ferry stop (Hotel Cavalieri, Via delle Ginestre, Passignano sul Trasimeno, tel 075 829292, daily 12.30–2.30, 7.30–10.30).

Street entertainment during a wine festival in Panicale

TIPS

● Time your drive to enjoy the evening views across the lake from the east and north.
● This drive is best arranged with a lunch stop at Castiglione del Lago or a picnic stop on the hill around Paciano.

PLACES TO VISIT

Museo della Pesca

Via Lungolago della Pace e del Lavoro 20, 06063 Magione

☎ 0758 479261

🕐 Daily 10.30–1,4–7, Jul–Aug; Tue–Sun 10–12.30, 3–6, Apr–Jun and Sep; Thu–Sun 10.30–12.30, 2.30–5.30, Feb–Mar and Oct; Sat–Sun 10.30–1,2.30–5.30, Nov–Jan

🎫 €3

THE CASTELLI ROMANI HILLS

From the frenetic centre of Rome to the quiet Albani hills, this route takes you past secluded villas, bustling towns and the serene lakes of Albano and Nemi. Wealthy Romans have escaped to the cool hills and lakes for centuries, and they remain a popular weekend retreat.

THE DRIVE

Distance: 76km (47 miles)	
Allow: 4 hours	
Start/end: Rome	

Leave Rome on the Via Appia Antica (p.180), the ancient road from the city lined with catacombs, where you will find the tomb of Romulus, legendary founder and first king of Rome. About 12km (7.5 miles) from the city centre you will pass the remains of an ancient Roman aqueduct on the right-hand side. After the turning for the airport (Ciampino) the road becomes the SS7. Continue along this road, following signs for Albano/Ciampino and you will soon see the town of Castel Gandolfo in the distance.

About 8km (5 miles) from the aqueduct take a left turning and join the SS140 for Castel Gandolfo, after which the route becomes quieter and rural. The road soon starts to climb and shortly you reach the outskirts of Castel Gandolfo ❶ (p. 183).

You won't be able to park in the heart of Castel Gandolfo, but it is worth the walk uphill into the middle to see the Church of San Tommaso di Villanova and the exterior of the Pope's summer residence,

Castel Gandolfo, the Pope's summer residence, from where he gives his Sunday blessings

and to admire the views over Lago Albano (p. 184).

Leave the town and continue along the Via Appia, following signs to Albano Laziale, home to a small museum and the tomb of the legendary warriors Horatius and Curiatii. From Albano it is about 2km (1 mile) to Ariccia, entered over a high bridge.

Ariccia ❷ **is a popular destination for Romans, who come here to enjoy al-fresco pizza on summer evenings. The town also contains the Palazzo Chigi, in which there is a museum.**

Leave Ariccia and follow the SS7. There are large villas on either side of the road and bushy umbrella pines that provide welcome shade in the summer months. After about 2km (1 mile) you reach the outskirts of Genzano, where you will see a large church on the left-hand side. Continue past a large sports stadium on the left, where the landscape has a more industrial appearance. Just outside Genzano, take a left turn for Nemi (it is easy to miss it) on to the Via Sardegna. At the next intersection, turn left in the direction of Nemi, and go right at the intersection, which brings you to the Piazzale Cina. Follow the SP76D, and after 1km 0.5 mile) you will approach the outskirts

of Nemi, with the lake of the same name down on the left-hand side.

The ancient Romans were so inspired by the still azure waters of Lago di Nemi ❸ that they named it Mirror of Diana and built a temple to the goddess on the lake's angled shores, surrounded by a sacred grove.

The road now winds uphill, and is lined with bars and restaurants. You will soon spot the town, which overlooks the lake, with its distinctive tower and narrow streets. If you want to explore further, park in the outskirts rather than in the crowded town.

❹ Nemi became famous in 1930 when the remains of a Roman ship were discovered at the bottom of its lake. See them in the Museo delle Navi Romane. Staircases run up and down this village, which is famous for its miniature straw-berries *(fragoline di Nemi)*, grown along the lake's shores. The tiny fruit, soaked in lemon juice and topped with fresh *panna* (cream), is a local treat in the bars lining the belvedere overlooking the water.

Leave Nemi, and about 1km (0.5 mile) from the middle of the town turn right. The road winds uphill and passes under a bridge. Follow the signs for Velletri/Roma. Shortly there is an intersection, where you turn left to join the SS217, a fairly busy, winding road. Turn right for Rocca di Papa, joining the SS218, which climbs uphill through rows of mature chestnut trees. After 2km (1 mile) you will reach Rocca di Papa, with broad views over Rome on the left. Continue and go left as the road forks and follow the SS218 into the heart of Rocca di Papa ❺. Once again it is best to park in the outskirts if you want to explore the town.

OUT AND ABOUT

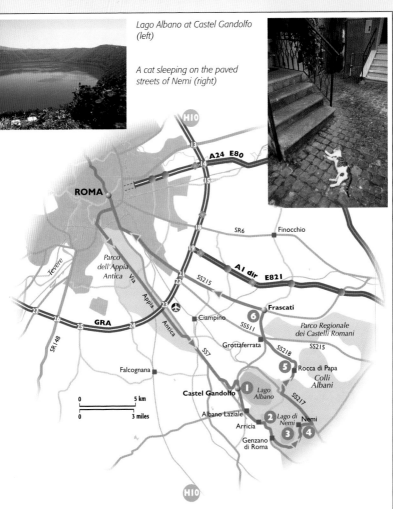

Lago Albano at Castel Gandolfo (left)

A cat sleeping on the paved streets of Nemi (right)

The narrow streets and houses of Rocca di Papa are built up around the hillside. From here it is possible to admire the 360-degree views of Rome, the Hannibal battlefields and the sea.

Now go downhill to leave the town, following the SS218 for about 4km (2.5 miles) to Grottaferrata, famous for its wine and 11th-century abbey. Leave Grottaferrata, following the SS218 until you reach Frascati **6** (p.184).

Frascati is the most famous of the Castelli towns, noted for its wine and sumptuous villas. The Villa Aldobrandini is occasionally open to the public and is particularly impressive with a large cascade in its grounds.

After exploring the town, follow the signs back to Rome.

WHERE TO EAT

Castel Gandolfo, Genzano and Frascati are full of restaurants and pizzerias. La Taverna da Rosa in Piazza Luigi Sabatini *(tel 06 9324381, closed Tue)* and La Volpe e L'Uva on Via Collegio Nazareno *(tel 06 9322251)* in Albano are both worth a try.

WHEN TO GO

Spring or autumn to avoid the summer crowds. This drive is popular with locals at weekends.

PLACES TO VISIT

Museo Civico
Via Risorgimento 3, Albano
☎ 06 9323490
🕐 Daily 9–1, Wed–Thu 9–1, 4–6.30
💶 €2.50

Museo delle Navi Romane
Via Diana, Nemi
☎ 06 9398040
🕐 Daily 9–7 in summer, 9–6 in winter
💶 Adult €2, child (under 18) free

Villa Aldobrandini
Villa Aldobrandini, Via Cardinal Massaia, Frascati, Tivoli
☎ 06 9420192
🕐 Gardens open daily except Sat pm, Sun and public holidays. Open Mon–Fri 9–1, 3–6. Closes at 5 in winter
💶 Free. Permits available for villa from visitor centre in Piazza G. Marconi

Palazzo Chigi
Piazza di Corte 14, Ariccia
☎ 06 9330053
🕐 Tue–Fri 11, 4 and 5.30, Sat and Sun 10.30, 11.30, 12.30. 4, 5, 6, 7
💶 €10

THE PARCO NAZIONALE DEL GRAN SASSO

This drive takes you through the breathtakingly beautiful Gran Sasso National Park (p. 202). Its unusual mountain landscape has earned it the name 'little Tibet'. With so much to explore en route you may want to take your time and spread it over two days.

THE DRIVE

Distance: 444km (276 miles)	
Allow: 8 hours	
Start/end: L'Aquila	
Roads: Although the route is full of tight mountain bends the road surface is generally good	

Take the motorway from L'Aquila (A24) in the direction of Teramo. Pass through the tolls and after 10km (6 miles) you will reach the Assergi Valley, where the area becomes fertile and green. Go through the tunnel, Traforo del Gran Sasso d'Italia, that cuts straight through the mountain. Exit the motorway at San Gabriele Colledara and follow the sign for Prati di Tivo. Drive through the middle of the resort following signs for Cima Alta. After 1km (0.5 mile) there is a parking place. From here walk about 200m (220yd) up the hill, where you can admire an extraordinary view over the mountain range that stretches right down to the sea.

Prati di Tivo ❶ is both a ski and summer resort at one of the highest points in the Gran Sasso mountain range. There are several bars and restaurants where you can find refreshments, and various places where you can ride horses or rent a bike.

From here take the ST43 in the direction of Ponte di Rio Arno Sotto. After 14km (9 miles) turn right onto the SS80 trunk road in the direction of Teramo. Ignore signs for the motorway marked Roma/L'Aquila, and continue along the main road following the signs for Castelli–San Gabriele.

Castelli ❷ sits 550m (1,805ft) above sea level under the picturesque Monte Camicia. This is a good starting point for trekking as you can cross over and climb the eastern face of the Gran Sasso Mountains from here. Castelli is renowned for its majolica ceramics, which

became famous in the 16th century. There are a number of ceramic shops and factories to visit in this pretty little village, where you can see the painters at work.

Drive through the village in the direction of Rigopiano.

On the left you will see signs for a steep path that leads 1km (0.5 mile) up to the tiny Church of San Donato in Martire ❸. It has a majolica ceiling dating back to 1615. If the church is closed, the caretaker who lives in the house opposite will let you in for a closer look. A further 500m (1,640ft) up the slope is the Castelli majolica museum, in a former Franciscan convent.

Fresh produce in the marketplace of the ancient city of L'Aquila

Take the southbound road to Rigopiano, which after 47.5km (30 miles) of bends takes you to Castel del Monte.

This is a tortuous road, but it is worth navigating all the hairpin bends for the scenery. Castel del Monte ❹ (p. 192) is another quaint stone village with a fortified quarter, Ricetto, and steep streets with flights of stone steps.

From Castel del Monte descend down the same road for 9km (6 miles) in the direction of Calascio/Rocca Calascio.

At 1,450m (4,757ft) above sea level, Calascio ❺ was one of the starting points of the migratory shepherds' trail, the Via della Transumanza. The shepherds would accompany their sheep from Abruzzo to the more temperate region of Puglia, farther south, in the winter, and then bring them back in the spring. They slept in stone huts, some of which are still visible en route.

From Calascio you can visit the 16th-century Church of Santa Maria Pietà or leave the car and climb up the scenic path that leads to the ruins of the 13th-century fortress of Rocca Calascio, a further 3km (2 miles) from the village. If you wish to drive, then bear in mind that the last 300m (330yd) are rough and the road is not surfaced, which can be treacherous in wet conditions. From this vantage point 1,464m (4,800ft) above sea level the eye can roam freely over the mountain peaks and valleys of the Maiella and Mount Sirente. The *rifugio* (mountain refuge) contains a small restaurant and has four charming rooms—an ideal place to stop for lunch or an overnight stay. Several panoramic trails start from here, suitable for all abilities during the warmer months, the longest going as far as Campo Imperatore (13km/8 miles).

Continue driving in the direction of Santo Stefano di Sessanio ❻, the last port of call on this drive.

This partially abandoned village lies 1,251m (4,104ft) above sea level. Its 120 inhabitants produce some of the country's best lentils, and you can buy them from one of the tiny shops. Grey stone houses

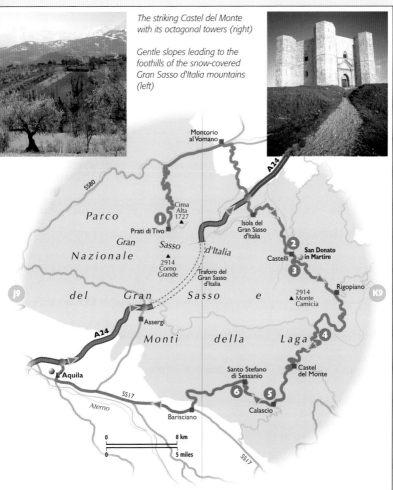

The striking Castel del Monte with its octagonal towers (right)

Gentle slopes leading to the foothills of the snow-covered Gran Sasso d'Italia mountains (left)

line the steep cobbled slopes, and at every turn there are views over the barren mountain range visible through the gaps in the narrow alleys.

From Santo Stefano di Sessanio descend to Barisciano and turn onto the SS17, which leads back into L'Aquila.

WHEN TO GO

Fine, dry weather is essential for this drive because of the hairpin bends. Avoid November to March, when the roads are icy. Spring and autumn are the prettiest months when the flowers are at their best, but high summer is refreshingly cool. Remember that August is the main holiday month for Italians and everywhere will be crowded.

WHERE TO EAT

There are many places to eat in Prati di Tivo and Castelli and plenty of good picnic spots. Rocca Calascio, Agriturismo al Borgo, is a mountain refuge that serves meals and snacks made from local produce (tel 0862 920423, open daily). Hotel Prati di Tivo is a hotel and restaurant that serves good local and Italian food (Località Prati di Tivo, Pietracamela, tel 0861 959636, only open when the hotel has guests). Ristorante Ostello del Cavaliere in Santo Stefano di Sessanio is a nice place to stop to sample traditional food at a moderate price (Via della Giudea, tel 0862 89679; closed Thu).

TIPS

● Some of the mountainous roads and tortuous bends are unmarked and the signposts are often hidden.
● Consider an overnight stop or divide the drive into two half-day itineraries: L'Aquila–Prati di Tivo–Castelli on the first day and L'Aquila–Santo Stefano–Calascio–Castel del Monte on the second day.
● It is possible to cut the drive short and return directly to L'Aquila from Castelli.

PLACES TO VISIT

Museo della Ceramica
Castelli
☎ 0861 979398
🕐 Daily 10–7, Jul–Sep; Tue–Sun 10–1, rest of year
💶 €2.60
www.castelliceramica.it

THE AMALFI COAST

This drive from the historical centre of Sorrento to the beautiful gardens and villas of Ravello follows a stretch of coastline in the middle of the protected marine area of Punta Campanella, stopping off at the enchanting Emerald Grotto along the way.

THE DRIVE

Distance: 32km (20 miles)
Allow: 7–8 hours
Start: Sorrento
End: Ravello

From Sorrento (p. 209) take the road for Massa Lubrense, passing the hotels Bristol and Brittania on your left. After 50m (55yd) you come to an intersection. Take the left-hand fork signposted Sant'Agata–Positano, a fairly wide but winding road. After 6km (4 miles) you reach Sant'Agata due Gulfi, with the Hotel Due Golfi on your left. Go straight on along the winding road with hairpin bends and after 4km (2.5 miles) you will come to an intersection at the end of the road with Ristorante Teresinella facing you. Turn right onto the main Positano–Amalfi road.

After 1km (0.5 mile) there is a good stopping place to view the Galli Islands ❶. Continue along the road to a wide lay-by (pull-off), with a prominent white statue of the Virgin Mary on the right. From here you can look down onto Positano and appreciate the view across the sea.

Shortly take the right-hand turn down a narrow one-way road with hairpin bends that leads into Positano. Ignore the first car park you see and continue along this road until you come to the service station and Mandara, which is the largest car park. If it's full, a few metres farther along on the right is the Di Gennaro car park. Park, walk past the second car park and a few metres along to the right is a pathway that leads to the beach.

❷ The path is fairly steep, but it is lined with a variety of small shops. After 150m (165yd), steps lead down to a square, to the left of which is the Church of Santa Maria Assunta with its imposing majolica dome. Take time to

see the 13th-century Byzantine painting known as *The Black Virgin* and the ceiling covered with frescoes. Opposite the church more steps lead down to another path. Turn left and you will pass through a narrower pathway, lined with shops whose outer walls are adorned with a variety of wares. At the end of the pathway is a terrace with steps leading down to the beach. It is worth walking part of the way down the beach to get a view of the houses above that seem to have tumbled over the edge of the cliff.

Return to your car and follow the one-way road out of Positano. When you reach the intersection, turn right onto the road that passes through the village of Praiano. You will soon come to the entrance to the Grotta di Smeraldo (Emerald Grotto) on your right (p. 209). There is parking here and two bars. Farther on, a tunnel leads down into the port of Amalfi (p. 209). There is a small island in the road here where a statue of Flavio Gioia, the inventor of the compass, stands. Turn right here into the car park.

Walk back to the statue and cross over into Amalfi's main square ❸. To the right is the cathedral, which dates back to the 11th century. Steps lead down under the right aisle to the crypt of Sant'Andrea, the patron saint of Amalfi (16th century), which contains some interesting Florentine mosaics. Continue up this street for 200m (220yd) and you will pass the papyrus

maker next to the bank (Monte dei Paschi di Sienna). The tourist information office is next to the post office, close to the statue on the road leading out of Amalfi towards Ravello.

Go back to your car and turn right in front of the statue onto the Ravello road. After 1km (0.5 mile) at the first intersection on your left go left and follow the road to Ravello. The car park is in front of you, with steps leading up to the main square.

Ravello ❹ is famous for providing refuge to the people of Amalfi when the Saracens landed in AD877. The Church of San Pantaleone stands in the square. At the top of the left aisle is a small altar with an ampoule containing the solid blood of the saint, which miraculously liquefies twice a year. To the right of the church you will find the entrance to the Villa Rufolo, dating back to the 11th century, with its beautiful gardens that overlook the coastline and the resort of Maiori. Wagner wrote *Il Parcifal* here (1879), and during the summer season the villa is the venue for Wagner concerts. Tickets are available from the villa or the tourist information office to the left of the church. Another villa with magnificent gardens is the 11th-century Villa Cimbrone.

Detail of the campanile, with its small towers and interwoven Arab-style arches dating from 1180– 1276, crowning the duomo in Amalfi

OUT AND ABOUT

A line of open boats drawn up the shore and the terracotta rooftops of buildings clustered around the harbour area in the resort of Sorrento (left)

WHERE TO EAT

If you walk along the seafront in Amalfi you will pass the Lido Azzurro, which serves good food at a reasonable price. The Compà Cosimo in Ravello also serves lovely food.

Golfo di Napoli

Torre Annunziata
SS18
A3

Castellammare di Stabià
Gragnano

Lattari

Vico Equense
SS145

K12

Monti 1444 ▲

Ravello ④
Minori
③
Amalfi
L12

Positano
SS163
Praiano ②

Sorrento ★

Massa Lubrense
San Pietro
Sant'Agata sui Due Golfi ①

Grotta di Smeraldo

Peninsola Sorrentina

Li Galli

Punta Campanella

0 ⸻ 5 km
0 ⸻ 3 miles

OUT AND ABOUT

PLACES TO VISIT

Villa Rufolo
Piazza Duomo, Ravello
☎ 089 857657
🕐 Daily 9–8, Apr–Sep; 9–6, Oct–Mar
🎫 €3

Villa Cimbrone Gardens
Via Santa Chiara 26, Ravello
☎ 089 857138/089 857459/
089 858072
🕐 Daily 9–1 hour before sunset
🎫 €5

Positano perched on a cliff (above left and right)

The town of Ravello, built high in rocky hills (right)

SORRENTO–MASSA LUBRENSE

On this walk, make the most of the rich scenery and memorable views over the Bay of Sorrento and the surrounding hills.

THE WALK

Length: 3.5km (2 miles)
Time: 1 hour
Start: Piazza Tasso, Sorrento
End: Massa Lubrense

From Piazza Tasso head down the Via Cesareo, a narrow, cobbled shopping street selling wood and leather goods and

shoulder to admire the view over the bay. Negotiate the bends by taking the three paths that act as a shortcut. Continue up on the road that climbs away from Sorrento. The road curves left but goes straight over onto the Via Priora, which is little more than a path. This takes you over a main road—beware of scooters.

the many pieces of art inside are paintings by Cardisco and Negroni. Noteworthy is the sacristy, with oval portraits of the bishops of Massa Lubrense and 18th-century wooden furniture.

Frequent buses run back to Sorrento from Massa Lubrense.

OUT AND ABOUT

liqueurs. Towards the end of the road you will see the Church of Sant'Annunziata on the left.

At the end of the road go right, then continue straight ahead and turn left at the parking sign, which leads to the restaurant Zintonio Mare. Here there is a slightly sloping road with a sheer rock face in front. Pass along the high walled path, which narrows and becomes a tight passage between two houses, one yellow and one pink. Walk up the steps, go around the railing, and you will find yourself on the busy main road.

At the International Camping sign, a little farther up on the right, turn left up the steep, cobbled road. Look over your

Looking down the hillside at people picnicking near Massa Lubrense (left)

Continue uphill to a shrine of the Madonna and Child and fork left.

You are now on a country trail in the middle of vineyards and lemon groves. It is around 600m (655yd) to the top of the hill. Continue on for another 400m (440yd) to a crossroads and join the Via Bagnulo. Pass under the arch below the white house and take the first right. Go down around two bends to an intersection and turn left, then take the first right heading straight towards Massa Lubrense.

The Church of Santa Maria delle Grazie, on Largo del Vescavado, stands on the foundations of the 16th-century Cathedral of Massa Lubrense. The original structure was completely rebuilt in 1760 by Bishop Bellotti when the Episcopio was added. Among

The resort of Sorrento on the Amalfi coast

WHEN TO GO

Don't attempt this walk in August, when it is intensely hot.

WHERE TO EAT

You can stop for refreshment either in Sorrento or at Massa Lubrense, but there is nothing on the walk itself. The Red Lion in Sorrento, despite its name, has typical local and national dishes on the menu at reasonable prices served in a pub-like atmosphere. Meals begin with a free tomato bruschetta and end with a free limoncello liqueur.

TIPS

● This walk is quite steep and isolated in some parts.
● Take plenty of water with you.

THE GARGANO PENINSULA

Spend a day touring the spur on Italy's 'boot', along the winding roads of the rugged coast and through the interior's limestone plateaux and forests that make up the Gargano National Park. Starting out near the old imperial city of Manfredonia, this tour takes you past medieval castles, pilgrimage churches, fishing villages, sandy beaches and the beautiful Foresta Umbra.

THE DRIVE

Distance: 208km (129 miles)

Allow: 1 day

Start: Santa Maria di Siponto (southwest of Manfredonia)

End: San Severo/A14 *autostrada*

From the A14 *autostrada*, take the Foggia exit and follow signs for Manfredonia on the SS89. Just before Manfredonia, follow the road as it forks right onto the SS159, past the Church of Santa Maria di Siponto.

Santa Maria di Siponto ❶ is a handsome 11th-century Romanesque church built over a fifth-century crypt.

Continue for 3km (2 miles) to Manfredonia ❷.

Manfredonia is a good place to shop for picnic refreshments. Its castle, built by King Manfred (1232–1266), now serves as a museum preserving the history of the Gargano Peninsula.

From Manfredonia, continue northeast on the SS89 and follow the road as it forks left towards Monte Sant'Angelo. The road winds north into the hills with several hairpin bends—beware of oncoming tour buses.

❸ Monte Sant'Angelo is a popular pilgrimage town, with many souvenir shops.

A souvenir stall in Monte Sant'Angelo, a sanctuary that dates back to the sixth century

It is celebrated for its Santuario di San Michele Arcangelo, a cave-shrine 90 steps down, where Archangel Michael appeared in the fifth century to the Bishop of Siponto.

Continue east towards the coast and Mattinata. Continue until you reach Baia di Zagare.

East of Baia delle Zagare is the Grotta Smeralda ❹, one of several grottoes along this stretch of coast.

A vast array of ceramics to choose from in a souvenir shop in Vieste

From Baia delle Zagare you can bypass some of the corniche's hairier bends by cutting inland to Testa del Gargano, heading back on the coast road towards Vieste.

❺ The peninsula's easternmost point, Vieste (p. 210) is a

pleasant resort with good sandy beaches, ideal for a swim.

The coast road from Vieste continues northwest to Peschici.

Peschici ❻ is a pretty fishing village perched on a promontory with good swimming on the sandy beach (p. 203).

Beyond Peschici, turn south off the coastal highway at the village of Valazzo and wind your way inland to Vico del Gargano ❼.

Vico del Gargano, with splendid views back over the Adriatic, has long been renowned for its olive oil.

From here, a narrow road winds up to the heart of the Foresta Umbra ❽.

The woodland road passes groves of beech trees, Foresta Umbra's pride (p. 194), as well as maple, hornbeam and birch. You may catch a glimpse rare orchids, deer or mouflon sheep on the limestone plateaux.

The SS528 continues south through the forest and meets the SS272 (west of Mont Sant'Angelo). Drive through San Giovanni Rotondo via San Marco in Lamis. This tour ends at the San Severo entrance to the A14 *autostrada* (73km/45 miles).

Vieste rises sheer from the rocks to overlook the sea (left)

Small boats on the sandy shoreline beneath the town of Peschici (right)

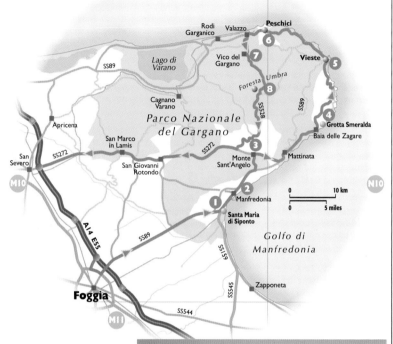

Right: The serrated, heavily wooded Adriatic coastline with steep limestone outcrops that form the many promontories of the Gargano Peninsula

WHERE TO EAT

The Locanda Dragone in Vieste is a good place to stop for lunch. *(Via Duomo 8, tel 0884 701212)*. Alternatively, you could wait and eat later at La Collinetta in Peschici *(Madonna di Loreto, tel 0884 964151)*.

PLACES TO VISIT

Parco Nazionale del Gargano
Tourist Information Office
• Piazza del Popolo 11, 61043 Manfredonia
☎ 0884 581998
🕐 Mon–Sat 9–1

Castello Manfredonia
Castello Svevo-Angioino, Manfredonia
☎ 0884 587838
🕐 8.30–7.30. Closed first and last Mon of month except Jul–Aug
🎟 €2.50

Santuario di San Michele Arcangelo
71037 Monte Sant'Angelo
☎ 0884 561150
🕐 Daily 8.30–6

THE SALENTINE PENINSULA

From the baroque town of Lecce, this drive traces the varied coastline around the rocky Salentine Peninsula. The cliff-top road occasionally descends to sea level, running along sandy shores, across creeks and through small fishing villages. At the tip of the heel of Italy, Capo di Santa Maria di Léuca, the road turns north to Gallipoli, with its medieval *centro storico*.

THE DRIVE

Distance: 150km (93 miles; plus 190km/118 miles) back to Lecce
Allow: 1 day
Start: Lecce
End: Gallipoli

❶ Enjoy Lecce's baroque jewels on the Piazza del Duomo, the Chiesa di Santa Croce and the Palazzi on Via Palmieri (p. 196).

On the east side of Lecce's ring-road, the Via della Libertà meets up with the SS543 highway to San Cataldo (7km/4miles). The highway to the coast passes through olive groves and past farmland and small fields reclaimed from the once malarial marshes on the coast. You will then pass the fine sands and pine woods of San Cataldo with its ancient Roman port, an area now known as the Lido di Lecce. From San Cataldo, turn back west for 1km (0.5 mile) on the SS543, then turn south onto the SS611 through the Riserva Naturale Le Cesine, past the Roca Vecchia towards Otranto.

The World Wildlife Fund's Riserva Naturale Le Cesine ❷ covers 620 hectares (1,532 acres) of pine and holm-oak woodland and shrub (myrtle, mastic, broom and juniper). The wetlands are the migratory home for herons, coots, mallards and moorhens.
The 14th-century castle ruin of Roca Vecchia has a grand cliff-top view of the sea and there is good swimming at Torre dell'Orso's sandy beach. West of the coast road is the fishing lake of Alimini Grande.
The fishing and ferry port of Otranto ❸ has a Norman-built Cattedrale, famous for its 12th-century mosaic (p. 202).

From the SS173 just outside Otranto, turn east onto the coast road that leads out towards Capo d'Otranto.

Capo d'Otranto ❹ is the Italian mainland's easternmost point, close to Albania. On a clear day you can see the island of Sazan and beyond to the Acrocerauni Mountains. Along the dramatic rocky coastline is Porto Badisco , a fishing hamlet where Aeneas, legendary hero of the Trojan Wars, is said to have landed in Italy.

Rejoin the SS173 at Porto Badisco. Continue south via Santa Cesarea Terme.

In the spa resort of Santa Cesarea Terme ❺ (recommended for respiratory ailments and tired bones), you can admire the art nouveau and Moorish-style Villa Sticchi over the thermal baths.

Continue to Castro ❻.

The ancient Roman cliff-top garrison-town of Castro overlooks a superb bay, where you can explore the subterranean Grotta Zinzulusa.

The SS173 continues south from Castro to Capo Santa Maria di Léuca ❼.

Capo Santa Maria di Léuca, is on the heel tip of Italy's boot. Its sanctuary, also known as Santuario de Finibus Terrae (Land's End), marks the point where St. Peter is said to have begun his mission to bring the Gospel to Italy.

Follow the coast road through Marina di Léuca, which winds its way past Punta Ristola northwest to Gallipoli. Punta Ristola is actually the boot's southernmost point. The coast road is punctuated by a series of Spanish-built watch-towers and modern beach resorts, notably Torre San Giovanni, Posto Racale and Baia Verde. Alternatively take a faster route inland along the SS274 (45km/28 miles).

The medieval *centro storico* of Gallipoli ❽ was originally an island. Now joined to the mainland by a causeway, it has a Byzantine *castello* and an elaborate baroque cathedral (see p. 194).

From Gallipoli, the SS101 returns north to Lecce.

The Roman amphitheatre in Lecce (second century AD)

OUT AND ABOUT

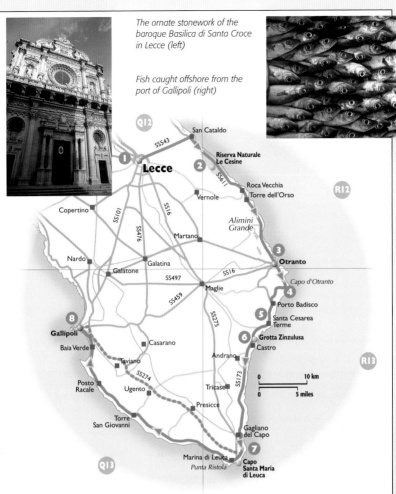

The ornate stonework of the baroque Basilica di Santa Croce in Lecce (left)

Fish caught offshore from the port of Gallipoli (right)

WHERE TO EAT

Try the Grotta del Conte (*Via Duca del Mare, tel 0836 943 859*) in Castro Marina.

PLACES TO VISIT

WWF Riserva Naturale delle Cesine
Approximately 5km (3 miles) away from Santo Catlado
☎ 0832 892264
🕓 All year round. Guided tours Sat–Sun 9.30–2.30

Grotta Zinzulusa
📌 The guided tours are organized from Castro Marina
☎ 0836 943812
🕓 Daily 9.30–7
💶 €3

A local fisherman mending his nets in Gallipoli (right)

SIRACUSA—
THE VALLE DELL'ANAPO

Drive through the rural countryside west of Siracusa, past the towns of the Monti Iblei Plateau to the valleys of the Anapo and Calcinara rivers, part of a large nature reserve.

THE DRIVE

Distance: 177km (110 miles)	
Allow: 7 hours (7.5 hours including the short walk)	
Start/end: Siracusa	

From the middle of Siracusa (p. 216) follows the SR124 in the direction of Solarino. At the entrance to the Parco Archeologico (Archaeological Park) of Neapolis turn west along Viale Paolo Orsi and follow the SR124 signposted to Floridia. The road is lined with evergreen trees and there is a huge cemetery on the right. The road then passes through orange and olive groves interspersed with some less attractive commercial premises, until you reach the unprepossessing town of Floridia.

On entering the town look for a sharp right-hand turn off the one-way system. From here, head towards the northwest, the limestone escarpments of the Monti Climiti can be seen in the distance from here. At the next intersection turn left at the sign to Sortino and Pantalica and then look for signs to Solarino, a further 3km (2 miles) away.

After reaching Solarino continue along the main street that climbs upwards through the town. Follow signs to the SR124 and the elegant baroque town of Palazzolo Acreide.

A fishing boat moored near Siracusa harbour

This road now passes through a landscape of old fields divided by limestone walls, olive groves and scattered farmsteads, with natural vegetation including the caruba or carob tree on some of the higher ground **❶**. After about 6.5km (4 miles) the beautiful valley of the Cava Monasterello can be seen to the left and, a little farther on, Mount Etna is visible towards the north on a clear day. The road now dips into a valley whose pleasant views are rather marred by pylons and a grain silo.

After about 6.5km (4 miles), Palazzolo Acreide comes into view, perched upon the hilltop ahead. As the road descends, watch out for the sharp bends. Cross the bridge just before entering Palazzolo Acreide **❷**. Continue uphill, turning right at the intersection. Follow the signs to the middle of town and try to park near the Piazza del Popolo.

It is only a short walk from here to the Museo Antonino Uccello, in Via Machiavelli, a fascinating museum of rural life and folklore. If time is not pressing, you can visit the Greek Theatre and other ruins to the southwest of the town, at the archaeological site of Akrai, founded by the Greeks of Siracusa around 664BC.

From the centre of Palazzolo Acreide continue on the SR124,

following the road downhill from the piazza to the next town, Ferla (signposted to Caltagirone). After about 8km (5 miles) the road forks; turn right off the SR124 and follow signs to Ferla. This road winds through mountainous limestone-covered slopes, alongside a gorge containing a tributary of the Anapo. Farther on, the landscape softens into olive groves, and after 6.5km (4 miles) you drive through Cassaro. Continue up the main street past Chiesa Madre on your right, following the SP10 to Ferla.

From Ferla, continue uphill along the main street and follow brown tourist signs on the right to Pantalica (ancient Hybla). As you enter this region, look for the ancient tombs cut into the limestone hillsides. The 12th-century BC ruins of the Castello del Principe can be found along a short, unmade track to the right, about 9km (6 miles) from Ferla.

Between the confluences of the Anapo and Calcinara rivers is the ancient Bronze Age settlement of Pantalica **❸**, the remains of a necropolis (burial chamber) that was part of the pre-Greek settlement of the Siculi, which flourished from around 1250BC until Greek domination in the eighth century BC. The enigmatic ruins of Castello del Principe (Prince's Palace or Anaktoron) have been described as dating anywhere from the 12th century BC to between the sixth to ninth centuries AD.

From the car park close to the Castello del Principe, it is possible to take a circular walk (2.5 hours) down to the river in the valley, returning along a winding path up the mountainside (p. 329). Continue for 1.5km (1 mile) to the end of the road, at the edge of the Valle del Calcinara.

Continued on page 328.

OUT AND ABOUT

Prehistoric cave tombs or burial chambers at the necropolis in Pantalica on Monte Iblei, all that remains of the Siculi civilization, which colonized the Calabrian mainland in the second century BC (left)

A spiral column adorning the Church of Annunziata in Palazzolo Acreide (below)

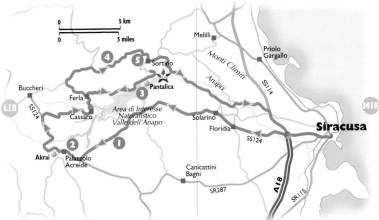

OUT AND ABOUT

PLACES TO VISIT

Museo Antonino Uccello
Via Machiavelli 19, Palazzolo Acreide
☎ 0931 881499
🕐 Daily 9–1, 3.30–7
🎟 Free
www.palazzoloacreide.com

Museo Civico dell'Opera dei Pupi
Piazza San Francesco 9, Sortino
☎ 0931 952079
🕐 Daily 9–1
🎟 Free. Shows €2 (2 hours)
www.comune.sortino.sr.it

WHEN TO GO

July and August are extremely hot and it is probably better to make this long car journey during the cooler months, especially if you are also considering doing the walk in the Valle dell'Anapo (p. 329).

WHERE TO EAT

Palazzolo Acreide has a reasonable choice of bars and restaurants, including Trattoria La Casareccia (*Ronco Cannarella 13, off Via Duca d'Aosta, closed Wed*). Ferla has less choice, but it is a more suitable place for lunch as it's halfway along the drive. Dell'Arco (*open daily, Via Arco Lantieri*) is an unpretentious but pleasant family-run trattoria and pizzeria. Another family concern, La Bomba (*Via Bordonali 2*), is a friendly and well-run restaurant and pizzeria. If you are visiting off-season and you want to linger in Pantalica, you may want to take a picnic, as the nearest restaurant, Ristorante Pizzeria Pantalica (*open May–early Oct only*), is about 5km (3 miles) back along the Ferla-Pantalica road. Sortino has a number of eateries and bars. Close to the Puppet Museum is a very good pizzeria, Pizzoleria (*Via Libertà 152, closed Mon*), while nearby

in Corso Umberto, Bar Arcadia serves excellent coffee and light refreshments.

TIP

● Parts of this drive are quite exposed and it is very hot in the summer. Carry plenty of water with you.

Iron railings mark the entrance to a short walk on the left, down to the stream and pool of the riverbed (1.6km/1 mile).

For those unwilling to clamber down the valley, walk a few steps beyond the railings to view the tombs of the 13th-century BC Necropolis Nord-Ovest, and the aptly named Grotta Pipistrelli (Bat Cave).

Return to Ferla and look for the right-hand turn to the SP10 and Sortino. This road winds through olive and oak trees. After about 4km (2.5 miles) turn right at the road intersection and continue to Sortino.

❹ Keep an eye out for the wonderful view of Mount Etna with the sprawl of Catania on its seaward base. To the right, and shortly before entering the town of Sortino, there is a lovely view of the Cava Cugni, a small river gorge leading to

The River Anapo that cuts through the Valle dell'Anapo near Ferla

the Cava Grande, the gorge of the Calcinara River.

Sortino is straight ahead of you on top of a cliff (not showing its best side). To enter the town, do not take the right-hand turn signposted Sortino, but take the left-hand turn signposted Siracusa and Carlentini.

❺ The Sicilian puppet museum, Museo Civico dell'Opera dei Pupi, in north-west Sortino, was founded by Don Ignazio Puglisi, whose father was also a master puppeteer, in 1996. Puppet theatre is a traditional form of entertainment for Sicilians that can be traced back to the first millennium AD, but some experts believe that the history of Sicilian puppet theatre goes back as far as the Hellenic period in Sicily. The themes of the Opera dei Pupi (puppet plays) are generally based upon the struggles of the Christian king Charlemagne and his knights (or paladins)

The ancient akrai. the Greek theatre in Palazzolo Acreide

against the Saracens, mixed with liberal amounts of folklore, comedy, romance and myth. The emphasis on the Christians' struggle against the Saracens very much reflects Sicily's own history, when the island was under Arab rule for around 200 years. The museum is famous for its collection of large puppets: Some are around 1.5m (5ft) tall and weigh up to 35kg (77 pounds). In May the theatre hosts the Festival delle Marionette, attracting groups of puppeteers from all over Italy.

Leave Sortino, following signs to Siracusa along Viale Mario Giardino. The road passes eastwards out of the town, with the large Municipio building set back from the road on the right.

Shortly after leaving the town look for the right turn onto the SP28 to Siracusa. This road roughly follows the course of the River Anapo, crossing and re-crossing it several times.

After about 18km (11 miles), it joins the SR114 to Siracusa. Ignore the turn-off to Siracusa Nord and continue along the SP114 to the Siracusa SR124 exit. Pass the large cemetery again on the outskirts of Siracusa, this time on your left.

At the next roundabout (traffic circle) keep left and follow the brown tourist signs that will direct you back to the Parco Archeologico della Neapolis.

ANCIENT PANTALICA—
THE VALLE DELL'ANAPO

This walk winds past remnants of an ancient age, through tall stands of wild fennel, thistle and myriad other plants, down to the floor of the Valle dell'Anapo. Birds, including blue-tits, goldfinches and stonechats, thrive in the tall vegetation, often heard rather than seen. Back on high ground, the views over the valley are spellbinding.

THE WALK

Length: 4km/2.5 miles (4.8km/3 miles with detour to Filiporto)

Allow: 2–3 hours

Ascent: 200m (655ft)

Start/end: Castello del Principe car park, 9.5km (6 miles) from Ferla along the Ferla-Pantalica road. Turn right off the main road and drive 200m (220yd) to the end of the unmade track.

Paths: Narrow, winding and sometimes steep. Slippery in parts

Parking: Castello del Principe

Lavatories: Old railway station (Stazione Ferroviaria) in the valley

From the car park, follow the path uphill to the tumbled blocks of stone marking the site of the Castello del Principe. Bear left down the hillside along the path towards the Necropolis Sud, passing the tomb chambers of the Grandi Tombe a Camere, a group of tombs that are part of the Necropolis Sud, dating from the ninth to eighth century BC, which you can see stretching out across the valley.

Part of the Monti Iblei mountain range, this limestone plateau bisected by the valleys of the Calcinara and Anapo rivers is famous for the ancient settlement of Pantalica.
Originally named Hybla, the town was founded during the middle of the second century BC by the Siculi, who colonized from mainland Calabria. The foundations of the Castello del Principe (Prince's Palace, or Anaktoron), once a thriving township, and the cave-like tomb chambers of Europe's largest *necropoli*, are virtually all that is left of this early civilization.

At the next intersection (300m/330yd) keep left and follow the path downwards. After 200m (220yd) you can take a short and rather overgrown detour on the right to the Church of Santo Nicolicchio.

The Byzantines who settled around Pantalica converted earlier tombs and chambers in the area into churches and dwellings, and constructed the tiny rock-church of Santo Nicolicchio here in the ninth century AD.

Continue for another 200m (220yd), keeping right where the path branches, and follow the steep, winding path down to the valley floor. Occasional red splashes of paint on the rocks help to define the route. On the valley floor, turn right and follow the broad dirt track, once part of the Siracusa–Vizzini railway line, for about 250m (275yd) to where the road briefly crosses the river.

The Stazione Ferroviaria

Near here on the left is a small, shady picnic area by the side of a citrus orchard. Continue along the track, which shortly re-crosses the river, and you will come across the old railway station building on your right, with a small grove of walnut trees opposite. Its lavatory blocks are clean if rudimentary, but do not rely on being able to find drinking water here. From the station, follow the right-hand curve of the track, flanked on the left by the river and abundant vegetation including blackberry, willow and holm-oak growing at the foot of sheer limestone cliffs.

This part of the Anapo is home to trout, freshwater crayfish and several varieties of dragon-fly, and along the river's calmer stretches water mint, water-cress and water iris are prevalent.

Approximately 800m (875yd) from the station house turn right off the track through a gateway in the stone wall and follow the path back up the mountainside. Look for splashes of red paint on the rocks, again marking the route. To begin with this path is fairly hard work as it zigzags steeply up through a swath of wildflowers including cistus, asphodel, wild salvia and broom. After about 450m (490yd) the path is bisected by another—the right leads back to Castello del Principe, the left to Filiporto.

Continue to Filiporto to see the necropolis, or the tiny Byzantine rock-tomb church of Santo Micidiario. A detour there and back adds approximately 1km (0.5 mile).

Turn right and enjoy the wonderful view of the valley from this vantage point. After 800m (875yd) the path rejoins the one from the Castello del Principe; keep left and continue back to the car park (300m/330yd).

TIP

● This is a strenuous walk and, with the exception of the valley floor, quite exposed, so cover up from the sun.

WHERE TO EAT

There are no bars or restaurants in the valley so it is essential to carry food and water. There is a small shady picnic area in the valley near the river.

WHEN TO GO

The best time to visit the Valle dell'Anapo is in spring (Mar–Apr), before the heat of summer, when most of the wildflowers are in bloom. To enjoy the valley at its best, avoid weekends and August crowds.

OUT AND ABOUT

Numerous companies specialize in organized tours across Italy. Whether you're an art lover, gourmand, fitness freak or thrill seeker, there is probably something to suit. You may want to seek some guidance to help you get the most out of your trip. Below are a few of the many tours led by expert tour guides who can help you get to grips with Italy's abundant attractions and long history.

For a virtual guided tour of Italy visit www.italytour.com. You'll find plenty of information on sports clubs, activities and cultural pursuits in Italy. They also have a searchable database of specialized tours and operators.

ART AND ARCHITECTURE
ACE Study Tours
tel 01223 835055 (UK)
www.study-tours.org
A long-established charity that organizes guided art and architecture trips and makes donations to restoration projects throughout the world.

British Museum Traveller
tel 020 7436 7575 (UK)
www.britishmuseum-traveller.co.uk
These cultural tours of Italy are led by British Museum experts.

Road to Italy
tel 1 800 848 8163 (Canada)
www.roadtoitaly.com
Escorted City breaks to Rome, Florence and Venice.

Eurogroups
tel 1 800 462 2577 (US)
www.eurogroups.com
10-day escorted rail tours, taking in the art and architecture of Rome, Florence, Pisa and Venice.

CYCLING AND WALKING
Charnes Tours
tel 866 6650324 (US)
www.charnestours.com
A US based company running fully supported bicycle and walking tours in Italy.

Headwater's
tel 01606 720099 (UK)
www.headwater-holidays.co.uk
Guided walking, cycling and culinary holidays in areas such as the Dolomites, Umbria, the Amalfi coast, Capri, Sardinia, Sicily and the major art cities.

Odyssey Tours
tel 06 77204019 (Italy)
www.odyssey-tours.com
This Rome-based tour operator runs guided walking and coach tours in popular tourist areas.

Ramblers Holidays
tel 01707 331133 (UK)
www.ramblersholidays.co.uk
Ramblers runs guided walking and sightseeing holidays throughout Italy.

FOOD AND CULTURE
JMB Opera Holidays
tel 01905 830099 (UK)
www.jmb-travel.co.uk
JMB's tours include tickets to music festivals and concerts in some of the great opera houses in Italy.

Kudu Travel
tel 01722 349 009 (UK)
www.kudutravel.com
A company running guided walking tours specilializing in culture, food, wine and music.

LUXURY
Benvenuto
tel 338 4040685 (Italy)
www.benvenutolimos.com
An Italian company providing exclusive chauffeur-driven half-day and full-day excursions

along the Amalfi coast, the Sorrento Peninsula and around Naples, Salerno, Livorno, Florence, Civitavecchia and Rome.

MOTOR RACING
Page and Moy
tel 08700 106212 (UK)
www.page-moy.com
A leading specialist with a varied choice of tours, city breaks and trips to Grand Prix motor racing.

Everlast Tour and Travel
tel 06 4741644 (Italy)
tel 06 4827625 (Italy)
www.italytourtravel.com
Everlast, based in Rome, caters to a range of interests. It runs gastronomic, cultural, language, cycling and walking tours as well as Formula 1 Grand Prix excursions.

MOTORCYCLING
CIMT (Central Italy Motorcycle Tours)
tel 06 6787870 (Italy)
www.cimt.it
Based in Rome, CIMT's specialist knowledge ensures that you will see the best of the country on two wheels.

Flavours of Italy
tel 02 2720 1556 (Italy)
www.mototouring.com
This Milan-based company runs guided motorcycle tours across Italy including gastronomic trips and an Italian Motorcycle factories tour. It can also help you organize motorcycle rental.

CULTURAL COACH TOURS
Archers, tel +44 (0)870 751 2000, www.archersdirect.co.uk
Citalia, tel +44 (0)20 8686 5533, www.citalia.co.uk
Consort Travel, tel +44 (0)845 345 0300
Crystal Italy, tel +44 (0)870 888 0024, www.crystalitaly.co.uk

Leger, tel +44 (0)800 018 9898, www.leger.co.uk
Magic of Italy, tel +44 (0)870 888 0228, magicofitaly.co.uk
Shearings, tel +44 (0)1942 824824, www.shearingsholidays.com
Woods, tel +44 (0)1243 868080, www.woodstravel.co.uk

OUT AND ABOUT

This chapter lists places to eat and to stay alphabetically by town within the book's regional divisions. In each town places to eat precede places to stay although many establishments provide both food and accommodation.

Eating and Staying

ITALIAN CUISINE

Eating is definitely one of life's pleasures in Italy. Families regularly gather en masse for restaurant Sunday lunch and the arrival of the year's 'first' is celebrated in food shops. Italian food is fresh, seasonal and, above all, regional. The diversity of the country is as apparent in its food as it is in its cities, culture and landscape. There's no such thing as Italian cooking, rather, there's Tuscan, Roman, Bolognese, Milanese, Neapolitan…and so on. Each region's cooking is dictated by its produce—so expect to find rice in the regions near the Po, truffles in Piemonte and Umbria and beans and pulses in Tuscany, and you will have to head for the coast if you want to eat fresh fish.

Gnocchi alla romana *(left)*, a well-stocked cellar in Lucca *(middle)* and some extremely rare and expensive truffles *(righ*

EATING AND STAYING

FRESH REGIONAL PRODUCE

Italian cooking is straightforward, its quality dictated by the superlative standard of ingredients. Italian cooks are obsessed with freshness and food shopping is a daily social event in smaller places. This is beginning to change in cities though, as huge supermarkets begin to take over. Outside the big cities, you're also unlikely to find restaurants serving anything other than local food, so don't expect to eat Venetian dishes in Tuscany, let alone exotic cuisine. If you're desperate for international cooking, head for Milan, Rome or Turin; cities this size are also the places to find regional restaurants specializing in food from all over Italy.

MEALS AND MEALTIMES

Many working Italians eat breakfast (*prima colazione*) in a bar—a *cappuccino*, strong coffee with plenty of hot milk, and a sweet pastry, *a brioche* or *cornetto*, a jam- or custard-filled croissant. Hotels catering for foreigners usually serve a buffet-style breakfast complete with fruit juice and a selection of cereal, cold meat and cheeses. The Italian day starts early, so if you are heading for breakfast in a bar, most open for business around 7–7.30; hotel breakfast normally starts at 8 or earlier in business hotels.

Lunch (*pranzo*) and dinner (*cena*) both follow the same pattern—though its unlikely that you will want to tackle the full menu twice a day. The first course is the *antipasto* (starter, but literally 'before the meal'), a selection of *crostini* (bread with a savoury topping), cold meats and salami, seafood or vegetable dishes. The next course, *il primo* (first course) is designed to fill you up and consists of pasta, soup or risotto. This is followed by the *secondo* (second course), a portion of a meat or a fish dish, served on its own—if you want vegetables (*contorni*) or a salad (*insalata*) order them separately. This is followed by a selection of puddings (*dolci*) or cheese (*formaggio*). The former is often a bowl of fruit, fruit salad (*macedonia*) or an ice cream (*gelato*), though fancier places will have desserts such as *tiramisù*, *zuppa inglese* (trifle) or something rich made with ricotta cheese or chocolate. There's no pressure to wade through the whole menu, and it's quite acceptable to order a primo and salad, or an antipasto and secondo. Italians drink water (*acqua minerale*) with every meal either sparkling (*frizzante* or *con gas*) or still (*senza gas*), accompanied by a relatively modest amount of wine or a beer. Excessive drinking is frowned upon in Italy, where it is rare to see anyone inebriated. Bread is automatically included with every meal. Restaurants normally open for lunch around 12.30 or 1 and stop serving at 3; they close for the afternoon and re-open for dinner around 7.30–8. Some restaurants may have non-smoking sections. People often smoke in restaurants and bars, but it is now technically illegal to smoke in public places.

WHERE TO EAT AND WHAT TO EXPECT

● **Trattorie** are usually family-run, serving home-style cooking (*casalinga*). They are generally simpler than restaurants. Sometimes there is no written menu and the waiter will reel off the list of the day's specials. They are open during lunchtime and in the evening.

● **Ristoranti** are more up-market and are not always open for lunch. The food and surroundings are usually more sophisticated than that of a *trattoria*. Both *trattorie* and *ristoranti* add a cover charge (*coperto*), which includes bread, and a service charge to the bill.

● **Pizzerie** specialize in pizzas, but often serve simple pasta dishes as well. Look out for the sign *forno al legno*, wood-fired pizza oven.

● **Osterie** can either be old-fashioned places specializing in home-cooked food or extremely smart, long-established restaurants.

PAYING THE BILL (IL CONTO)

Pay by requesting the bill (*'il conto per favore'*), and check to see whether service is included (*'il servizio è incluso?'*). Scribbled bills on scraps of paper are illegal; if you don't get one, say that you need a receipt (*'Ho bisogno di una ricevuta, per favore'*), which all restaurants, bars and shops are legally obliged to issue. Both they and you can be fined if you do not take this with you.

● Smaller establishments will normally expect to be paid in cash; you'll be able to use a credit card in more expensive establishments.

If service isn't included, it's customary to leave a small tip—some loose change will do.

● All restaurants have one official closing day a week, usually specified on a notice on the door or front window, but many places open every day during the summer.

SNACKS AND ICE CREAM

● **Bars** serve hot and cold drinks, alcohol and snacks throughout the day. It's customary to eat or drink standing up; you will pay a surcharge if you sit down either inside or at a table outside. In busier city bars make your request and pay at the cash desk, then take the receipt (*scontrino*) and go to the bar where you will be served. Snacks include *pannini* (filled rolls), *tramezzini* (sandwiches made on soft white bread), *mini-pizze*, toasted sandwiches (*toast*) and sometimes vol-au-vent. Smarter bars willl bring a saucer of olives, crisps or nuts with your drink if you're sitting down. All bars have lavatories (*toiletti*); you may have to ask for the key (*chiave*).

● **Alimentari** (general grocer) sell breads and will often make you up a *pannino* (filled roll).

● **Pizza,** Italy's own contribution to fast food, is available all over the country and served by the slice from tiny *pizzerie* to takeaway—look for the sign *pizza al taglio*. There are also a few international chains.

● **Távole calde** are stand-up snack bars that serve freshly prepared hot food; some have seating as well.

● **Forni** (bakers) sell *foccace*, flat oil and herb bread.

● **Rosticcerie** serve spit-roasted and ready-cooked food, particularly chicken, pasta and vegetable dishes to eat in or take away.

● **Gelateria** sell a range of varieties of ice cream, served in a cone (*cono*) or a tub (*coppa*) of varying sizes. The best ice cream is home-made on the premises; *produzione propria*. Many bars sell commercial ice cream.

● **Fast Food** Larger towns and cities have branches of McDonalds and Burger King.

● **International cuisine** is very limited in Italy. Chinese restaurants are becoming increasingly popular in middle- to large-sized towns, but you'll have to go to places such as Rome and Milan for a wider choice.

WHAT TO DRINK

● **Coffee** (*caffé*) is served in bars and cafés. Choose from either a small black coffee (*caffé* or *espresso*), a *cappuccino* (with frothy milk), *caffé con latte* (very milky coffee), *caffé macchiato* (an espresso with a drop of milk) or a *caffé corretto* with a slug of spirits. If you want weaker coffee, ask for a *caffé lungo* or an *Americano*. Decaffeinated coffee goes by the generic name Hag.

● **Tea** (*tè*) is generally served black; ask for *latte freddo* (cold milk) if you want milk. In summer *tè freddo* (ice tea), livened up with lemon or peach, is popular.

● **Hot chocolate** (*cioccalata calda*), often served with whipped cream (*panna*), is

available during the winter months.

● **Beer** (*birra*) is widely drunk, either bottled or draught (*alla spina*). Preferred Italian brands include Nostra Azzura, Peroni and Moretti, and imported beers are widely available.

● **Wine** is served in bars as well as in restaurants. Ask for white (*bianco*), red (*rosso*) or the less common rosé (*rosato*). House wine is either *vino de la casa or vino sfuso*, and can be very good. Bottled wines are locally produced, except in smarter restaurants; the best are DOCG wines (*Denominazione d'Origine Contollata e Garantita*); the label guarantees its origins. Many producers are marketing some superb wines as *vino da távola*, which are well worth sampling.

● **Spirits** are known by their generic names, and you will find all the usual ones on sale. Italians are also fond of *aperitivi* such as Martini, Campari, Cinzano and the artichoke-based Cynar, and firmly believe in settling the stomach after eating with a *digestivo*. Fiery *grappa* is the most common, but herb-based liqueurs (*amari*), such as Averna and Montenegro, are drunk everywhere and there are dozens of local varieties—Amaretto, based on almonds, Strega, made from herbs and saffron, and Limoncello, a lemon liqueur. Stock and Vecchia Romagna are Italy's preferred brandies.

● **Cocktails** are popular in Venice. Why not try a *bellini*, peach juice and sparkling wine, a *rossini*, strawberry juice and sparkling wine, or a *puccini*, mandarin juice and sparkling wine.

● **Soft drinks** such as coke and lemonade compete with native refreshments—*spremuta di aranci* (freshly pressed orange juice), *granita* (fruity crushed ice), *sugo di alicocca* (bottled apricot juice) and *frullata*, a type of milk shake.

To fully appreciate Italian cuisine you will need to venture away from the beaten track and the sanctuary of tourist resorts and sample the local dishes. If you don't speak Italian this can be a daunting prospect, but knowledge of a few key words will help you to work out what's on the menu, order what you want and avoid any embarrassing blunders. Below is a menu reader, to help you translate common words and familiarize yourself with dishes and ingredients that you are likely to see on an Italian menu.

Whole cheeses in Sulmona (left), lemon juice (middle) and freshly picked green olives (right)

Piatti–Courses
antipasti starter
stuzzichini appetizers
primi piatti first course
secondi piatti main course
contorni vegetables/side dishes
dolci desserts
spuntini snacks

Carne–Meat
agnello lamb
cacciagione game
coniglio rabbit
fegato liver
maiale pork
manzo beef
pancetta bacon
pollame poultry
pollo chicken
prosciutto cotto cooked ham
prosciutto parma ham
salsiccia sausage
tacchino turkey
vitello veal

Pesce–Fish
alici anchovy
baccalà dried salt cod
branzino sea bass
dorate bream
fritto misto mixed fried fish
merluzzo cod
pesce spada swordfish
sarde sardines
sogliola sole
tonno tuna
triglia mullet
trota trout

Frutti di Mare–Seafood
aragoste lobster
calamari squid
canestrelli scallops
cozze mussels
gamberetti prawns
granceola spiny spider crab
molluschi shellfish
ostriche oysters
seppia cuttlefish
vongole clams

Verdure–Vegetables
asparagi asparagus
carote carrots
carciofo artichoke
cavolfiore cauliflower
cavolo cabbage
cetriolino gherkin
cetriolo cucumber
cicoria chicory
cipolla onion
fagioli beans
fagiolini green beans
finocchio fennel
latuga lettuce
melanzane aubergines
  (egg plant)
patate potatoes
peperone red/ green pepper
  (capiscum)
piselli peas
pomodori tomatoes
spinaci spinach
verdure cotte cooked greens
zucchini courgettes
  (zucchinis)
broccolo brocolli

Metodi di Cucina–Cooking Methods
affumicato smoked
al forno baked
alla griglia grilled
arrosto roast
bollito boiled
casalingo home-made
crudo raw
fritto fried
frulatto whisked
ripieno stuffed
stufato stewed

La Pasta–Pasta
cannelloni baked meat or cheese filled tubes
conchiglie shell-shapes
farfalle butterfly shapes
fettucine wide strips
fusilli spiral-shapes
lasagne layers of pasta, meat sauce and béchamel or tomato sauce
linguine thin strips
pappardelle rippled strips
penne quill-shapes
ravioli pasta cushions filled with meat, cheese or spinach
tagliatelle thin ribbons or strips
tortellini little 'hats' with meat or cheese filling
trenette long narrow strips

Salsi/Sugi–Sauces
amatriciana bacon, tomato and onion

EATING AND STAYING

arrabbiata tomato and hot chilli
brodo broth
cacciatore sauce for meat: tomato, onion, garlic, wine
carbonara smoked bacon, egg, cream and black pepper
passata sieved tomatoes
pesto basil, garlic, pinenuts, olive oil and pecorino cheese
puttanesca tomato, garlic, hot chilli, anchovies, capers
ragù minced meat, tomato and garlic

Altri Piatti–Other Dishes
antipasto misto mixed cold meats: salami, ham etc.
frittata omelette
gnocchi small dumplings made from potato and flour or semolina
minestra soup
minestrone thick vegetable soup with pasta
risotto rice cooked in stock
risotto alla Milanese rissoto with saffron
zuppa soup

Bevande–Drinks
acqua minerale mineral water
birra beer
caffè corretto coffee with liqueur/spirit
caffè freddo iced coffee
caffelatte milky coffee
caffè lungo weak coffee
caffè macchiato coffee with a drop of milk
caffè ristretto strong coffee
digestivo after-dinner liqueur
dolce sweet
frizzante fizzy

Fresh fish in Gallipoli (left), fennel (middle) and oyster mushrooms, funghi di ostriche *(right)*

salsa sauce
salsa verde piquant/ vinaigrette
salsa di pomodoro tomato
sugo sauce
sugo di carne gravy

Specialità–Special Dishes
carpaccio thin sliced raw beef served with a cold vinaigrette. Invented in 1961 at Harry's Bar in Venice and named after the painter Vittore Carpaccio, noted for his use of red
pastiera Neopolitan Easter grain pie, filled with ricotta and seasoned with orange
peperonata sweet pepper and tomato stew
polpetti meatballs
saltimbocca veal escalopes with ham and sage cooked in white wine
scaloppini thinly-sliced veal cooked in white wine
stracotto beef stew
timballo baked meat and vegetable pie

Contorni–Side Dishes
insalata mista mixed salad
insalata tricolore mozzarella, tomato and fresh basil
insalata verde green salad
pane bread
patate fritte chips (french fries)
polenta maize meal dish

Dolci–Cakes/Desserts
cassata Sicilian fruit ice-cream
cioccolata chocolate
crema custard
gelato ice-cream
macedonia fruit salad
panna cream
una pasta a cake/pastry
semifreddo chilled dessert made with ice cream
tiramisù chocolate/coffee sponge dessert
torta tart
zabaglione egg, sugar and Marsala dessert
zabaione di Verduzzo custard pudding with Friuli wine
zuccotto ice-cream sponge
zuppa inglese trifle

Frutti–Fruit
arancia orange
fragole strawberries
lamponi raspberries
mele apples
melone melon
pere pear
pesca peach
pesca noci nectarine
uve grapes

Formaggi–Cheeses
fontina smooth, rich cheese
un formaggio di capra goat's cheese
un formaggio nostrano local cheese
parmigiano parmesan

ghiaccio ice
liquore liqueur
porto port wine
rinfreschi refreshments
secco dry
spumante sparkiling wine
succo di arancia orange juice
té tea
té al latte tea with milk
té freddo ice tea
vini da tavola table wines
vini pregiati quality wines
vino bianco white wine
vino rosato rosé wine
vino rosso red wine

Condimenti–Seasonings
aglio garlic
aromatiche herbs
basilico basil
capperi capers
pepe pepper
peperoncino chilli
prezzemolo parsley
rosemarino rosemary
sale salt
salvia sage
senape mustard
zucchero sugar

Il Conto–The Bill
IVA VAT value added tax
Paghi alla cassa pay at the till
servizio compreso service charge included
servizio non compreso service charge not included
coperto cover charge

STAYING IN ITALY

There is a wide range of accommodation all over the country, but central and northern Italy have a greater choice than the south. Choose from world-class deluxe hotels in historic buildings, ultra chic boutique hotels or family-run *pensiones* that haven't changed much in 30 years. On the whole, accommodation is more expensive in the major cities, central Italy, Tuscany and Umbria, the north, and the smarter coastal resorts during high season. In remoter areas, with fewer foreign visitors, you may be pleasantly surprised at the value for money, especially if you stay somewhere fairly simple; top-end prices are increasingly becoming standardized across the country.

HOTELS

Italian hotels (*alberghi*) are graded by regional authorities on a star rating of 1–5. These refer to the facilities provided—air conditioning, telephone and television, lift, swimming pool—rather than the character or comfort. You can expect 5-star hotels to be grand, with superb facilities and a high level of service; they will sometimes be in converted historic buildings, combining antique furnishings with 21st-century luxury. 4-star establishments will be almost as good and the accommodation first class. 3-star hotels are more idiosyncratic. Prices can vary enormously between them, as can the public areas, and staffing levels will be considerably lower, with often only one person manning the entire hotel. All 3-star rooms will have television, telephone, and sometimes air conditioning. One-and two-star hotels are relatively inexpensive, but are clean and comfortable, and rooms almost always have private bathrooms in 2-star places. Breakfast is usually included, but simpler hotels rarely have restaurants, and some do not provide breakfast. Breakfast can be very poor too, so consider a bar breakfast instead. During the high season at seaside resorts it's common to be forced to take half- or full-board (*pensione*), and single people may have to pay full price for a double if all singles are taken—though you may strike lucky and get a double for the price of a single.

PENSIONES AND LOCANDE

There's little difference between simpler hotels and *pensiones*. Both are usually family-run, and will provide spotlessly clean, comfortable rooms at a fair price. Some *pensiones* have failed to move with the times, and rooms may be dated but this is also the case in smaller hotels. Italy once had numerous *locande*, inns. These have virtually disappeared, and the word today frequently denotes something fairly up-market and quite expensive.

AGRITURISMI

The *agriturismo* scheme was started to enable farmers and landowners to conserve redundant farm buildings by converting them into holiday accommodation. This can take the form of a small and luxurious hotel, a self-catering apartment, or simply a handful of rooms in a converted barn. Accommodation can be on a weekly only basis, but many owners will let rooms by the night, and meals are often provided. *Agriturismi* are often in beautiful surroundings and frequently provide activities such as riding, escorted walking and mountain biking. Many have swimming pools and will serve their home-grown produce at meal times. The movement is particularly strong in Tuscany and Umbria. You'll need a car as *agriturismi* can be well off the beaten track. Most require advance booking, but a couple of days ahead will often be fine.

CAMPSITES

There are plenty of campsites, especially along the Adriatic coast, which are normally open between April and September. The better sites will have swimming pools, bars, children's play areas, restaurants and shops; these look more favourably on caravans (trailer houses) and camper vans (RVs), so if you're in a tent, stick to the smaller sites.

SELF-CATERING
There are a great number of old farmhouses and villas to choose from, particularly in the affluent north and in Tuscany and Umbria. You can also rent apartments or houses in many of the coastal resorts, but Italian families tend to snap these up for the whole summer season. Tour operators sell villa packages, which include flights and car rental, but if you want to be independent, contact the local visitor offices well in advance. There are also websites devoted to private house rentals: www.holidayrentals.com.

RIFUGI
If you're in the mountains hiking or climbing, you can stay in a network of *rifugi*, mountain huts, owned by the Club Alpino Italiano. Most are fairly sparse, and you'll probably find yourself in a dormitory bunk bed and washing in cold water, but all are very resonably priced and surrounded by wonderful countryside with spectacular views.

ROOMS TO LET
In popular areas you may see signs saying 'rooms', 'camere' or 'zimmer'. These are rooms to rent in private houses and are a good option if money is tight or you can't find a hotel. Local visitor offices keep a list.

RESERVATIONS
Book in advance in the main cities and popular resorts during the high season. In Rome, Florence and Venice you will need to book in advance all year round. Italians are on holiday during August, when you'll be competing with them for beds. If you're booking in advance from home, make certain you get written confirmation and take it with you. Without this, you may turn up and find all knowledge of your booking denied.

FINDING A ROOM
● If you haven't booked in advance, start looking around the main piazza or in the *centro storico*. In hilltop villages and towns it is also worth looking outside the *centro storico* or town walls. The local visitor information office will have lists and may be willing to book for you.
● Yellow signs direct you to hotels on the outskirts of towns and villages.
● In big cities, there is often a cluster of hotels near the railway station. Check them before you book as some are more respectable than others.
● It's perfectly acceptable to ask to see the room before you decide to stay somewhere.
● You will be asked to leave your passport at reception. Don't forget it when you leave.
● Check-out time is normally noon, but hotels will usually store your luggage till the end of the day.

PRICING
● Italian hotels are legally required to post rates for high and low season on the back of every bedroom door. Some only have one price.
● Rates vary according to the season, sometimes by as much as 25 per cent. Some hotels have high (*alta*) and low season (*bassa stagione*) rates; others charge the same rate year round (*tutto l'anno*).
● Agree a price before you make a reservation.
● Hotels often quote their most expensive rates; ask if they have cheaper rooms.
● City-centre hotels sometimes have reduced weekend rates.
● Smaller hotels can be open to gentle bargaining, particularly during quieter times.
● Hotels are often willing to put another bed in a room for an extra 35 per cent, ideal for families with children.

FURTHER SOURCES OF INFORMATION

HOTELS
● *Perfect Places to Stay in Italy*, published by the AA in conjunction with Touring Club Italiano, lists 500 recommended bed and breakfasts, farmhouses and townhouses across Italy (£14.99, www.theaa.com).
● The Touring Club Italiano, the Italian equivalent of the AA in Britain, publishes *Alberghi e Ristorante d'Italia*, which lists hotels in all price ranges. It comes out in early spring every year and is €20 (www.touringclub.it).
● An agency can reserve a room for you in the major cities, the Lakes, the Amalfi coast and Tuscany. Contact: Accomodation Line Ltd, 3rd Floor, 22–23 Princes Street, London W1B 2LT, tel 020 74091343, www.accomodationline.co.uk.

AGRITURISMI
Contact:
Agriturist
Corso V Emanuele 101,
00168 Roma
Tel 06 8521342
www.agriturist.com

Agriturist also publishes *Vacanza in Fattoria*, a guide to farm holidays in English.
The TCI publishes *Agriturismo e vacanze in campagna* annually at €40.

CAMPING
The TCI publishes an annual guide to campsites, *Campeggio e Villaggi Turistici* (€20).

VILLAS
CV Travel
High-standard villas, *palazzi* and farmhouses.
www.cvtravel.net
Tel 020 75912800

Magic of Italy
Villa rental packages.
www.magictravelgroup.co.uk/italy
Tel 0870 8880228

Vacanze in Italia
Farmhouses, villas and apartments, mainly in Tuscany and Umbria and the Lakes.
www.britishtravel.com/vacanze.htm
Tel 08700 780193

CHAIN HOTELS IN ITALY

Name of hotel chain	Description	Hotels in Italy	Website and phone number
Best Western	The world's largest group, with 4,000 independently owned hotels in 80 countries.	112	www.bestwestern.it tel 0800 393130
Boscolo Hotels	Seventeen luxury hotels in some of the most sophisticated cities in Italy.	11	www.boscohotels.com tel (0039) 049 8287777
Charming Hotels	The Charming Hotels group was founded in 1995, but its popularity has grown rapidly and they now have 60 luxury hotels world-wide.	53	www.charminghotels.it tel 840 707575 (in Italy) tel (00) 800 24276464
Golden Tulip (inc Tulip Inns)	This Netherlands-based company has around 440 hotels in 51 countries, branded as either Golden Tulip (4-star) or Tulip Inns (3-star).	10	www.goldentulip.com tel (31) 332544800
Hilton	This American-based chain of top-class hotels has almost 500 branches throughout the world.	4	www.hilton.com tel 08705 909090 tel 800 878346 (in Italy)
Ibis	Part of the French Accor group, Ibis is a fast-growing hotel chain, with more than 670 business and budget hotels world-wide.	9	www.ibishotel.com tel 0870 6090961
ITI Hotels	A group of 30 hotels, mostly in Sardinia, but also in Rome, South Central and North America.	10	www.itihotels.it tel (0039) 06 6781341
Jolly Hotels	Jolly has been running hotels in Italy since 1949, and now has establishments in 26 Italian cities.	41	www.jollyhotels.it tel (0039) 0445414018
Mercure	Part of the French group Accor, Mercure have 715 hotels in 45 countries, with accommodation to suit most budgets.	7	www.mercure.com tel 0870 6090965
Le Meridien	Le Meridien is a well established global hotel group with over 135 luxury hotels in 56 countries.	5	www.lemeridien.com tel 08000 282840
Novotel	Part of the French group Accor, Novotel have 373 hotels in 63 countries.	8	www.novotel.com tel 0870 6090961
Orient Express Hotels	There are three luxurious hotels under the Orient Express brand in Italy, including their flagship hotels, the Hotel Cipriani in Venice and the Hotel Splendido in Portofino.	3	www.orient-express.com tel 20 78055060
Quality Inn Comfort Inn	Quality Inns offer mid-priced accommodation, while Comfort Inns are a limited service chain.	10 7	www.choicehotels.com tel 0800 444444
Rocioli Hotels	A family-owned chain of prestigious 4-star hotels, all in the heart of Rome.	4	www.rosciolihotels.it tel 800 840000 (in Italy)
Rocco Forte Hotels	Rocco Forte have luxury hotels in key locations around the world, with one hotel in Florence and one in Rome.	2	www.roccofortehotels.com tel (0039) 05527351
Sina Hotels	Founded by the Bocca family in 1959, the Sina Hotels Group now have 6-, 4- and 5-star hotels in key cities throughout Italy.	9	www.sinahotels tel 800 273226 (in Italy)
Sofitel	Part of the French group, Accor, Sofitel is the company's premium brand, with 160 establishments around the world.	6	www.sofitel.com tel 0870 6090961
Starwood Hotels	Starwood is the name behind the prestigious hotel chains Sheraton, Westin and St. Regis, owning, leasing or managing around 750 hotels in 79 countries.	28	www.starwood.com tel 1 800 6255144 (US) tel 1 800 3253589 (US)
Utell International	The world's largest representative company, handling hotel reservations for nearly 5,000 luxury, business, and value hotels, resorts and apartments world-wide.	225	www.utell.com tel 08705 300200

EATING AND STAYING

EATING

Typical Milanese dishes are *risotto alla milanese*, rice simmered in saffron-flavoured stock, and the classic *osso buco*, slow-cooked shin of veal. Farther north the cooking is simpler; polenta, maize meal, and *bollitto misto*, mixed boiled meats, spiced up with Cremona's *mostarda di frutta* (pickled fruit with mustard).

Outside Milan the fertile farms of Lombardy produce the cheeses that are the main ingredient in the regions cooking; masacarpone, Bel Paese and Gorgonzola. Basil is the essential ingredient in Ligurian cuisine. The best pesto in Italy is made here, the famous basil, cheese and pine-nut sauce served with pasta. This is usually followed by seafood and fresh mixed salads. Try the local anchovies, served as an *antipasto*, *ciuppin*, fish soup, and *bacalá*, dried cod, a traditional sailors' dish. Local dishes often rely heavily on chickpeas, while *torta pasqualina*, a spinach-and-cheese pie, makes an excellent snack. Try white Cinque Terre wine, produced on the terraced cliff-top vineyards

Piemonte's forte is white truffles, whose intense taste enhances pasta and risoti, and sets off porcini mushrooms in autumn. This region borders France, so the food here has a touch of finesse and is beautifully presented. Good quality meats are served with sauces made from the excellent regional wines. *Bagna caoda*, a hot sauce made with anchovies, garlic, butter and cream, and used as a vegetable dip, is also worth trying. Be prepared to pay a lot for the illustrious red wines such as Barolo, Bardolino and Barbera. Asti is the area's major sparkling wine, best drunk well chilled, while Martini, Cinzano and Punt e Mes are all produced in and around Torino.

STAYING

Big-city pleasures and convenience are found in Milano and Torino, where you will find the full range of hotels that you'd expect to see in any prosper-ous town, but both are major business destinations, so prices can be steep and you should certainly book in advance. The same applies in Genoa—a cheaper option here would be to stay in one of the resort villages along the coast. East lies the Riviera de Levante and the Cinque Terre, and to the west is the Riviera di Ponente. The latter is a pleasant lower-key choice, patronized mainly by Italian families, while east lie the chic and glitzy ex-fishing villages of Portofino and Rapallo. North into Piemonte and the Valle d'Aosta you'll find hotels in the beautiful mountains of the Gran Paradiso. Mountains also form the backdrop to many of the popular places to stay in the east around Lake Como and Lake Garda. This is a holiday area par excellence and there are a wealth of watersports and activities to choose from in the area, so book ahead if you're planning a high-season trip. South from the Lakes lie the prosperous towns of Lombardy—Bergamo, Mantua and Cremona—good bases from which to explore the area.

AOSTA (GRAN PARADISO)

ⓘ VECCHIO RISTORO

Via Tourneuve 4, 11100 Aosta
Tel 0165 33238

You can still see the old machinery that used to drive the wheel in this restored mill, skilfully incorporated into a quietly elegant restaurant. Top notch cooking, with plenty of local recipes—try the *polenta con funghi* (polenta with wild mushrooms) or any dish containing them in autumn. There's an excellent *bollitto misto* (mixed boiled meat with sauce verte); or sample the *degustazione* menu for a full range of dishes. Great puddings; the amaretto-stuffed peaches with raspberry coulis shines. They have the best of Val d'Aosta wines and some good French varieties.

🕐 Tue–Sat 12.30–2.30, 7.30–10.30, Mon 7.30–10.30pm; closed Jun
🍷 L €30, D €40, Wine €12
Ⓢ Section

BERGAMO

ⓘ ANTICA HOSTERIA

Piazza Mercato delle Scarpe, 24129 Bergamo
Tel 035 247993

Antica is brimming with local specialities such as polenta with porcini mushrooms for just €8. Main courses are also great value at around €9. Choices include veal and rabbit, although the simple menu changes every week. A handful of famous Italian actors have been seen eating here, adding a bit of style to this Città Alta establishment. Within easy walking distance of the Piazza Vecchio.

🕐 Daily 12–2.30, 7–10.30pm, Jul–Aug; Tue–Sun 12–2.30, 7–10.30pm rest of year
🍷 L €25, D €40, Wine €10

ⓘ ALBERGO SAN VIGILIO

Via San Vigilio 15, 24129 Bergamo
Tel 035 253179
Fax 035 402081
www.sanvigilio.it

Great location overlooking the lower city of Bergamo from on top of San Vigilio hill. Only seven rooms are available, but each one has character. Despite being an old-fashioned *albergo*, all modern facilities are standard, from television to telephone to private bathroom. The hotel is run by Signora Franceschi, a painter and poet. She also looks after the excellent restaurant. Reserve early if you want to be sure to get a room.

🛏 €90–€120 excluding breakfast
Ⓘ 7

GENOVA (GENOA)

ⓘ LA MADALEINE

103 Via Maddalena, 16124 Genova
Tel 010 2465312

This tiny restaurant and bar comes highly recommended by trendy Genoese. Chalkboards advertize a daily menu of a small yet delicious range of modern Italian dishes, with

an emphasis on fresh local seafood. As with most of the city's simpler eateries, reservations aren't necessary—just turn up and find a table. Many guests just come for a drink (they have an impressive array of drinks on display) and to chat for hours on end.

🕐 Mon–Sat noon–3am; closed Aug
🍽 L €25, D €45, Wine €15
🚌 1, 2, 3, 4, 7, 8, 12 or 15 to the Porto Antico complex

🏨 ACQUAVERDE
Via Balbi 29, 12126 Genova
Tel 010 265427
www.hotelacquaverde.it
The rooms are spacious at this moderately priced hotel, with wooden floors and large

windows. The hotel owns a number of private parking spots nearby. A 10-minute walk brings visitors to the Via XX Settembre shopping area. The Porto Antico complex is a five-minute walk down the hill away from the Principe rail station.

🍽 €50–€80 excluding breakfast
🛏 30 (5 non-smoking)
🔄

🏨 SAVOIA CONTINENTAL
Via Arsenale di Terra 5, 16126 Genova
Tel 010 261641
Fax 010 261883
www.hotelsavoiagenova.it
The closest hotel to Genoa's Principe station. Despite renovation, the Savoia still has its original parquet floors and marble sinks. Spacious yet simple rooms have classic furniture, balconies and a plethora of television channels. The large if a little sedate public facilities are shared with its 4-star sister hotel next door, the Savoia Majestic. Many guests choose to avoid evening meals at the hotel and prefer to eat at one of the more inspiring restaurants in central Genoa.

💶 €150–€202
🛏 40
🔄 Ⓟ 🚪

LAGO DI COMO
🍴 RESTAURANT TERMINUS
Lungo Lario Trieste 14, 22100 Como
Tel 031 329216
www.albergoterminus.it
A fine restaurant (in the hotel of the same name) overlooking Lake Como. The decor is as elegant as it comes—brass fittings, comfy period chairs and a ceiling bedecked with painted fantastic scenes—yet the Terminus still manages a warm welcome for diners. First courses such as *penne arrabbiata* (pasta quills with a spicy tomato, onion and garlic

sauce) are priced at around €10. Main courses, including tiger prawns, are around €20. Only 10 carefully selected red wines are on the menu, and there are even fewer whites. In summer diners can enjoy views of the lake while seated outside on the large terrace.

🕐 Daily noon–2.30, 7.30–10pm
🍽 L €50, D €60, Wine €13

🏨 ALBERGO FIRENZE
Piazza Volta 16, 22100 Como
Tel 031 300333
www.albergofirenze.it
The English-speaking staff bend over backwards to help guests at this high-quality, affordable hotel in the heart of Como. Rooms are sleek after extensive renovation in 2001. The majority have wooden

floors, great views and are of more than ample size. Help yourself to cakes, coffee, bread and cheese at the buffet breakfast. The Albergo Firenze also has rooms specially fitted for use by people with disabilities.

💶 €120
🛏 44 (15 non-smoking)
🔄

LAGO DI GARDA

SPECIAL

🏨 🍴 GRAND HOTEL VILLA SERBELLONI
Via Roma 1, 22021 Bellagio
Tel 031 950216
www.villaserbelloni.it
Lakeside opulence without comparison. The illustrious

history of the Grand Hotel Villa Serbelloni—one of the most prestigious hotels on Lake Como for the last 100 years—is clearly visible in the period drawing rooms, magnificent guest lounges and colonnaded halls. Rooms are something special, many with old tiled floors, marble columns and period furnishings. Senior suites cost up to €800 per night. The attached restaurant, with its waterside terrace overlooking the lake, is one of the area's best. Experienced chefs cook up a mix of classic Italian and international dishes. Predominately meat-based, choices range from *carpaccio* (thinly sliced raw beef served with a cold vinaigrette) to succulent lamb and partridge. You can choose from several excellent Grand Crus wines. A jacket is required at dinner.

🕐 Daily 12.30–2.30, 8–10pm, Apr–Nov
🍽 L €100, D €140, Wine €15
🛏 81 (€310–€800)
🔄 🏊 Indoor and outdoor

AL FATTORE
Via Roma 8, 25015 Desenzano
Tel 030 9141937
www.alfattore.it
The crusty pizzas here are loaded with Italian goodies at bargain prices. One large pizza is €7—toppings include olives, roasted courgettes (zucchini), aubergine (eggplant), Parma ham, mozzarella and crispy Parmesan cheese. Fine dining in the restaurant's modern, mock-portico interior, with stylish wooden chairs and mellow lighting. There is plenty of room outside in the summer—jazzy tablecloths and steel tables. There's a small selection of inexpensive wines. Pasta first courses and meat main courses are also on the menu.
Daily noon–2.30, 7–11pm; Thu–Tue noon–2.30, 7–11pm rest of year
L €30, D €50, Wine €10

L'ARCIMBOLDO
Via Vittorio Emanuele 71, 25019 Sirmione
Tel 030 916406
Glass screens and outdoor heaters protect diners from the cold in the off-peak season at this restaurant on a terrace overlooking the lake. Simple dishes using the finest ingredients make up the short menu—highlights include beef, rocket (arugula) and Parmesan cheese, grilled swordfish or trout fillet in white wine. The restaurant's jazzy music makes this a lively place to eat. Found down a Tudor-style alley off the Via Vittorio Emanuele.
Wed–Mon noon–3, 7–11pm
L €30, D €55, Wine €14

FLAMINIA
Piazza Flaminia 8, 25019 Sirmione
Tel 030 916078
www.hotelflaminia.com
Stunning location in the middle of Sirmione. The wooden terrace built over the lake is perfect for swimming and sunbathing. Perhaps the most stylish hotel lounge on the lake—wooden floors, art deco tables and chairs, and comfy sofas to relax on after a day's sightseeing. The large bedrooms have similar furnishings. All rooms have a television, a telephone and private bathroom, and many have balconies overlooking the lake.

The hotel also has a restaurant and snack bar.
Tue–Sun 12.15–3, 7.30–11pm
L €30, D €80, Wine €12
41 rooms, 4 suites (30 non-smoking) (€119–€140)

BELLEVUE
Via Zanardelli 40, 25083 Gardone Riviera
Tel 0365 20235
www.hotelbellevuegardone.com
A small, quiet hotel brimming with amenities just 50m (164ft) from the lake. The ageing Bellevue with its terrace of flowers and trees is a pleasure to behold. The outdoor swimming pool never gets too busy, as the hotel has just 30 rooms. Large, uncluttered rooms are bathed in natural light, and most have balconies and wooden floors. Private parking to the rear of the hotel.
Apr–Sep
€100
30
12 rooms only   Outdoor

MIRAMAR
Via XXV Aprile 22, 25019 Sirmione
Tel 030 916239
www.hotelmiramar.it
Real value for money, especially in the low season, at this 1980s hotel five minutes from Sirmione's castle. Most rooms have balconies, and all are very modern—a television, new private bathroom, radio, telephone and a desk are standard. A huge (if slightly spartan) lounge and bar area caters for the surge of visitors in the summer and the gardens lead down to the water. Overall you get a great deal of service and decent facilities for very little money .
€37–€50 including breakfast
30

LA PAUL
26 Via XXV Aprile, 25019 Sirmione
Tel 030 916077
An ageing yet popular 3-star choice on the lakeshore, this hotel is a five-minute walk inland from Sirmione. Adventurous guests can rent rowing boats, marker buoys and bicycles. The more sedate can rent beach towels and sit round the pool. Refurbished rooms are big enough for a

giant, although they are spartan and the decoration lacks inspiration. Many have balconies overlooking the hotel grounds. Plenty of tea, fresh breads, fruit, cereals and is juice served at breakfast.
€72–€196
45
Outdoor

LAGO MAGGIORE
LA BAITA
Strada Cadorna 1, 28818 Piancavallo di Oggebbio
Tel 0323 587396
Overlooking Lake Maggiore from an altitude of 1,300m (4,265ft) is the town of Piancavallo with its La Baita mountaintop restaurant. The rustic two-storey cottage has a panoramic view over the surrounding area. The region is popular with hikers, bikers and foragers seeking out mushrooms, blueberries and chestnuts. Sample tagliatelle in a venison sauce, roe with polenta, or cheese from the local valleys along with a glass of one of more than 43 homemade grappa varieties.
Daily noon–2.30, 7.30–11pm, Jun–Oct; Wed–Mon noon–2.30, 7.30–11pm rest of year
L €40, D €60 by reservation only, Wine €6
Section

LA TERRAZZA
Via Mazzini 83, 28832 Belgirate
Tel 0322 7493
www.ristoranteterrazza.com
The fantastic La Terrazza restaurant sits on the shores of the lake in the village of Belgirate. Surrounded by trees and shrubs, and with a red-and-white awning covering the main dining area, it's a special place to enjoy views of the lake and delicious fish dishes. Menu items include smoked herring, Norwegian salmon and grilled lake fish. There is a great selection of white wines

to accompany the seafood dishes.

🕐 Thu–Tue 12.30–2.30, 7–10pm
🍽 L €30, D €36, Wine €12

⊖GRAND HOTEL DES ILES BORROMEES

Corso Umberto I 67, 28838 Stresa
Tel 0323 938938
www.borromees.it
Distinguished and wealthy guests have been staying at this 5-star luxury hotel since 1861. Commanding fine views of the lake from Stresa, the hotel offers watersports, mountain biking, horse riding and golf. Rooms have old-style comforts like fireplaces, giant balconies and huge baths. Even if you're not a guest, take the opportunity to pop in for an aperitif simply to appreciate the opulence.

💶 €266–€2,860
🛏 173 rooms, 15 suites (30 non-smoking)
♿ 🏊 ♨

⊖SPERANZA AU LAC

Piazza Marconi, 28838 Stresa
Tel 0323 31178
www.milanspteranza.it
Overlooking both the lake and the main square, this 4–star hotel with a slightly dated façade has the best location in town. The reception area is spacious and rooms have wide balconies. The buffet breakfast overflows with meats and cheeses. Modern rooms are equipped with large televisions, the latest telephones and private shower rooms. The hotel does have a recommended restaurant, although there are several places to eat within a minute's walk.

💶 €90–€180
🛏 86 rooms, 3 suites (10 non-smoking)
♿

EATING AND STAYING

MANAROLA
⊖MARINA PICCOLA

Via Lo Scalo 16, Manarola, La Spezia 19010
Tel 0187 920103
Fax 0187 920966
www.hotelmarinapiccola.com
Long before the Cinque Terre was 'discovered', the Marina Piccola was looking after the locals. Literally a stone's throw away from the sea, this is a simple seaside hotel, wit quirky elegance and touch of style. The rooms are plain and there's not much in the way of luxury—some have sea views—but it combines good taste with a totally relaxed atmosphere. Great restaurant overlooking the sea, serving nothing but fish.

🕐 Closed Nov
🍽 €80–€100
🛏 13
♿

🚗 Take the SS566 north from La Spezia, then head left on the SS370 to Manarola. You will need a permit from your hotel to take the car right into the village

MANTOVA (MANTUA)
🍴IL CIGNO-TRATTORIA DEI MARTINI

Piazza d'Arco 1, 46100 Mantova
Tel 0376 327101
Mantovan cooking returns to its roots in this long-established restaurant, once home to grand dishes and grand style. Today, the culinary excesses of the '80s are over and Tano, the owner, concentrates on the best of traditional food and wine, using 19th-century recipes. Homely dishes such as *tortelli di zucca* (pasta stuffed with pumpkin) and *maccheroni con pancetta e fagioli* (macaroni with pancetta and beans) are gorgeous. Main courses are seasonal—expect guinea fowl (*faraona*), pigeon, (*piccione*) and *rognone trifolate* (kidneys with garlic and herbs). Fantastic puddings and an excellent wine list.

🕐 12.30–1.45, 7.30–9.45 Wed–Sun; closed Aug and 1–5 Jan
🍽 L €60, D €90, Wine €13
🚫 Section

RECHIGI

Via Calvi, 30, 46100 Mantova
Tel 0376 320781
Fax 3762 220291
www.rechigi.com
The interior of this modern hotel has touches of quirkiness in the public areas. The owners are keen on contemporary art, so expect vibrancy, polished marble and interesting lighting. Bedrooms are functional, comfortable and well equipped, though you won't be able to spread out much in the bathrooms. Its good breakfasts, position (less than five minutes from the Palazzo Ducale) and friendly staff make this hotel a good choice.

💶 €140–€167
🛏 60 (10 non-smoking)
♿

🚗 From Parma take the SS343 to Mantova. Immediately before the station, turn right along Corso Vittorio Emanuele II and continue across the junction at Piazza Cavalloti into Corso Umberto I. At the end (Piazza Marconi) turn right into Via Calvi

MILANO (MILAN)
🍴BACI E ABBRACCI

Via de Amicis 44, 20123 Milano
Tel 02 89013605
www.bacieabbracci.it
Inter Milan striker Christian Vieri and AC Milan midfielder Christian Brocchi own this hi-tech but informal restaurant. All the profits from the

restaurant are donated to charity. The kitchen serves up a very light, traditional Italian menu. Octopus with potatoes, prawns in vinegar, and rice with pears and cheese all make an appearance, alongside more than 70 varieties of pizza. Sunday brunch is particularly well attended.

🕐 Mon–Fri 12.30–2, 6.30pm–2am, Sat–Sun 6.30pm–2am; closed Aug
🍽 L €45, D €75, Wine €15
🚇 Sant'Ambrogio

LE BICICLETTE

Via Torti angolo Corso Genova, 20123 Milano
Tel 02 8394177
www.lebiciclette.com

Housed in a former bicycle shop, this restaurant is decorated with modern paintings by emerging artists. Used to celebrate art and fashion events, it's not a bad place for celebrity-spotting. Ultra-busy at the end of the working day for aperitif time, when there is a giant buffet of pasta, sandwiches and tasty delights to accompany the €5 cocktails. The short menu includes artichoke salad, fish ravioli with black butter, and Argentinian steak.

🕐 Mon–Sat 8pm–2am, Sun 12.30–4, 8pm–2am; closed Aug
🍴 L €32, D €72, Wine €11.50
🚇 Santi Agosina
🚌 84

LA COZZERIA

Via Muratori 7, 20135 Milano
Tel 02 54107164

Gigantic portions at competitive prices are served at this seafood restaurant. The menu is almost entirely mussel-based—you'll find mussel soup, mussels with pepper, mussels with saffron, onions and cognac, and even curried mussels. All courses are based on a kilogram of mussels at €12, and are served with a side dish. This restaurant is quite small and the furniture is very simple, but it's certainly worth visiting.

🕐 Tue–Sun 7–11pm; closed Aug
🍴 D €45, Wine €10
🚇
🚇 Porta Romana

INNOCENTI EVASION 1

Via Privata della Bindellina 1, 20155 Milano
Tel 02 33001882
www.innocentievasioni.com

A small place with a wonderful, tiny garden where guests

can dine during the summer. Beautifully presented nouvelle cuisine at very affordable prices. This resataurant is ideal for couples or small groups, but there are only a few tables, so reservatons are a necessity. Four seasonal fixed-price menus are available, including one based on truffles. The restaurant is tricky to find, as it is on a street that looks like a private road.

🕐 Tue–Sat 8pm–10pm; closed Aug
🍴 D €70, Wine €11
🚇
🚇 Certosa

JUST CAVALLI

Viale Camoens, 20121 Milano
Tel 02 311817

Fashion designer Roberto Cavalli owns this glitzy restaurant and his style is reflected in the interior and the menu. Perch on huge leopard-skin sofas as you wait for your meal, while tropical fish swim about in the aquariums. The fusion of international and Italian styles is evident in dishes such as tuna with basmati rice, coriander (cilantro) and onion marmalade. Happy hour is from 7 to 8pm.

🕐 Daily 12.30pm–2am; closed Aug
🍴 L €100, D €120, Wine €10
🚇 Section
🚇 Cadorna

OSTERIA DEL BINARI

Via Tortona 1, 20144 Milano
Tel 02 89406753

This restaurant serves fixed-price meals, which diners select from the à la carte menu. The cooking style is traditional but extremely elegant. The more interesting choices include pumpkin ravioli and *risotto alla Milanese* (rice with saffron and Lombard sausage). The atmosphere is great, thanks to both the restaurant's rustic style and the beautiful garden. There is no parking for cars and no metro station nearby, so the best way to get here is by taxi.

🕐 Mon–Sat 7–11pm
🍴 D €72, Wine €13
🚇 Section
🚇 Porta Genova

PIXX

Via Maria Segreta 2, 20122 Milano
Tel 02 89015457
www.pixx.it

This classy take-away sandwich shop is a rare find in the middle of Milan. Tasty sandwiches, salads and other quick lunch options come at refreshingly low prices. The wide variety of salads includes couscous, Caesar and pasta. Sandwiches are filled with everything from chicken to prosciutto. Pastries and healthy desserts are also available. Most customers dash in and out, and eat their purchases in the nearby Piazza Duomo, sadly missing the stylish modern interior. No credit cards.

🕐 Mon–Sat 9–4
🍴 Sandwich or salad €3, pastry €1
🚇
🚇 Cordusio

PIZZERIA TRADIZIONALE

Ripa di Porta Ticinese 7, 20123 Milano
Tel 02 8395133

Find traditional Neapolitan pizzas at this pretty restaurant in the Nivigli dock area. The kitchen also serves up excellent seafood, which changes daily according to what's hot at the local market. Try the sautéed clams, octopus salad, or penne with prawns and courgette (zucchini) flowers. Larger dishes such as mixed grilled fish, swordfish, flat fish and squid are all excellent. The *margherita pizza* (cheese and tomato sauce), made with buffalo mozzarella, is also recommended. This restaurant only seats 22 people, so you will need to reserve a table.

🕐 Mon–Sat 8–10.30
🍴 D €160, Wine €19
🚇 Section 🚇
🚇 Porta Genova
🚋 Tram 29, 30, 2, 9
🚌 59

TANO PASSAMI L'OLIO

Via Vigevano 32a, 20144 Milano
Tel 02 8394139

Olive-oil bottles are everywhere in this creative little eatery. Dishes are made with one of the 40 types of oil in stock, ranging from ultra-light to heavy. Main courses are a mix between the creative and the traditional, including duck with truffles, king prawn tempura, and ravioli with ricotta. There is room here for only 22

diners at one time, so it's best to reserve a table.

🕒 Mon–Sat noon–3, 8–10.30pm
🍽 L €100, D €110, Wine €12
Ⓜ Porta Genova

🍴 ZEN

Via Maddalena 1, 20122 Milano
Tel 02 89013557
www.zenworld.it

Here at one of Milan's few sushi bars, you grab your rice, seaweed and raw fish as they revolve around the restaurant on a giant conveyor belt. A set lunch with drinks and a sushi selection costs €15. The evening menu is à la carte only. This Italian-run Zen establishment is fun and friendly. Japanese classics *sake* (rice wine) and Kirin beer are served, as well as a small selection of Italian wines.

🕒 Mon–Sat noon–3, 7–11.30pm, closed Aug
🍽 L €35, D €55, Wine €10
Ⓢ Section
Ⓜ Missori

🛏 BAVIERA

Via Castaldi 7, 20124 Milano
Tel 02 6590551
www.hotelbaviera.com

Comfortable if slightly behind the times, this extremely gracious hotel considers itself a business travellers' hotel. The pleasant, updated lounge has restful sofas and wooden floors. Rooms have old-fashioned bedding; some are larger than others, so ask for the biggest possible. They serve an high quality buffet breakfast of cereals, hams and fresh fruit. The hotel is within walking distance of the huge Stazione Centrale rail station.

🛏 €60–€210
🛏 50
Ⓢ
Ⓜ Repubblica

🛏 BRISTOL

Via Scarlatti 32, 20124 Milano
Tel 02 6694141
www.hotelbristolmil.it

Exit the Milano Centrale rail station via the stairs and you'll find yourself at the front door of this classic, stylish hotel. The style is refined Anglo-French, with modern amenities such as soundproofed rooms, direct-dial phones, in-room Jacuzzis and internet facilities. There is no restaurant on the premises, but the bar serves snacks and drinks until late at night. As with virtually all of Milan's hotels, most of the staff speak English.

🛏 €150–€200
🛏 68 (25 non-smoking)
Ⓢ
Ⓜ Centrale FS

🛏 CARLYLE BRERA HOTEL

84 Corso Garibaldi, 20121 Milano
Tel 02 29003888
www.carlylebrerahotel.com

The stylish Carlyle Brera is a cut above most business hotels. It provides free bicycles to use around town. The standard high-class buffet breakfast applies is served

here, where you help yourself to fresh bread, ham, cheese and coffee. The Moscova Metro station is a stone's throw away from the front door.

🛏 €170–270
🛏 94 rooms (2 suites)
Ⓢ
Ⓜ Moscova

🛏 MICHAELANGELO

Via Scarlatti 33, 20124 Milano
Tel 02 67551
www.milanhotel.it

The elegant 4-star Hotel Michaelangelo has a lot to recommend it. It's steps away

---

RESTAURANT AND HOTEL PRICES

🍴 **RESTAURANTS**
The prices given are for a two-course lunch (L) and a three-course dinner (D) for two people, without drinks. The wine price is for a bottle of house wine.

🛏 **HOTELS**
The prices given are for the lowest and highest for a double room for one night including breakfast, unless otherwise stated. Note that rates can vary depending on the time of year.

---

from Milano Centrale rail station, and direct buses to Milan's Malpensa and Linate airports leave from just outside its doors. They have hydrotherapy suites, opulent lounges and fine dining, and the guest rooms are vast. The majority of the wood and granite bathrooms have Jacuzzis.

🛏 €250–€350
🛏 300 rooms, 4 suites (69 non-smoking)
Ⓢ
Ⓜ Centrale FS

RIOMAGGIORE

🍴 BAR A PIE' DE MA'

Via dell'Amore, Riomaggiore 55, 19010 Riomaggiore
Tel 0347 7373985
www.cinqueterra.com

After a stroll along the Via dell'Amore, there's nowhere nicer to pause than this terrace bar, perched high above the sea. You can drop in for a drink, a snack or a full meal for a group if you book ahead. The emphasis is on fish, with whatever came off the boats that morning on the menu. Expect light meals such as *fritto misto* (mixed fried fish and shell fish) and *insalata di frutta di mare* (seafood salad with peppers, onions and piquant dressing). Wash it all down with Cinque Terre white wine, a flinty tipple.

🕒 Daily 10am–1am; closed Wed, Oct–Nov and Mar–Apr, closed mid-Nov–end Feb
🍽 L €20, D €35, Wine €6

SANTA MARGHERITA LIGURE

🍴 IL FRANTOIO

Via Giuncheto 23, Santa Margherita Ligure, 16038 Genova
Tel 0185 286667

When in Liguria eat basil and fish, and you'll find them both here; a delicate and intense *lasagne al pesto*, and a huge variety of *risotti*. Home-made pasta includes tagliolini served with a *sugo di pesce* (fish sauce), followed by simply grilled fish like *coda di rospe* (monkfish), *San Pietro* (John Dory) or scampi. Wild strawberry tart and a bittersweet *semifreddo al caffé* stand out on dessert menu. The huge wine list includes French labels.

🕒 Thu–Tue 2.30–2.30, 8–midnight; closed Nov
🍽 L €13, D €55, Wine €4.50
Ⓢ Section

🅘FINESTRE SUL PO

Lungo Po Caderna 1, 10100 Torino
Tel 011 8123633

With a view of the river, this restaurant has an elegant simplicity that is evident in its original flooring, heavy wine glasses and piano music. Meat and game are typical options in the main courses section of the menu, while *pappardelle* (pasta strips with rippled edges) and risotto make up some of the first courses. Countless dusty wine bottles rest on racks overlooking the tables.

🕐 Tue–Sun 7.30pm–2am; closed 10–25 Jul
🍷 D €55, Wine €10
Ⓢ Section🔁
🚌 11 and 12 to Piazza Vittorio Veneto

🅗LIDO PALACE

Via A Doria 3, Santa Margherita Ligure, 16038 Genova
Tel 0185 285821
Fax 0185 284708
www.lidopalacehotel.com

Redolent of gracious Edwardian days, the Lido Palace is on the seafront in the middle of town. All the rooms have sea views, many have balconies. Some are on the small side, but four-people

suites here are excellent value. The restaurant's seating is a bit cramped, but the staff aim to please.

🕐 Closed Nov–mid-Dec
🍷 €126–€232
🛏 54 (10 non-smoking)
🔁
🚗 From north exit the A12 at Rapallo and follow signs to Santa Margherita Ligure. The hotel is on the sea front opposite the marina

TORINO (TURIN)

🅘L'ABERO DI VINO

Piazza della Consolata 9, 10122 Torino
Tel 011 5217578
www.club2006.com

This restaurant is locally renowned for its selection of more than 300 different wines, many from the Piedmont region. Prices per bottle range from €9 up to €260. The sumptuous menu changes daily, and choices include duck, Alpine lamb and fillet of beef. There is a warm, snug dining area decorated in bold earth tones and outside seating on the piazza in the summer. There's often a fixed-price menu for lunch. Right in front of the imposing Santuario della Consolata.

🕐 Tue–Sat noon–3, 7.30pm–midnight
🍷 L €12, D €40, Wine €9
🚌 4, 11, 12 and 63 to Piazza della Repubblica

🅘TOSCANA

Via della Misericordia 4, 10122 Torino
Tel 011 5628953

Frequented by locals, this restaurant is as typical as they come in Turin. The emphasis is on fine fresh food rather than interior design, and hearty Tuscan classics, thick soups, stews and light pastas dominate the menu. *Saltimbocca* (veal escalope with ham and sage cooked in white wine), pasta with Gorgonzola and a buffet of *antipasti* are also worth a try. A small range of quality wines, including many Chiantis, makes up the wine list. Few people (staff included) speak English here.

🕐 Mon–Fri noon–2.30, 7.30–10pm, Sat 7.30–10pm; closed Aug
🍷 L €18, D €45, Wine €8.20
Ⓢ Section
🚌 4, 11, 12, 52, 56, 63, 67 and 72 to Piazza della Repubblica

🅗BOLOGNA

Corso Vittorio Emanuele 60, 10125 Torino
Tel 011 5620191
www.hotelbolognasrl.it

A convenient hotel under the porticoes opposite Porta Nuova rail station on the main street. Dusty and worn on the outside, the hotel is certainly passable on the inside. Most of the rooms have televisions, private bathrooms and telephones. It has no restaurant, but there are plenty of eating options nearby (a branch of

the restaurant chain Brek is round the corner). The bar is open to guests until late at night.

🍷 €72–€82
🛏 45
♿ 20 rooms only
🚉 Porta Nuova

🅗MONTAGNA VIVA

3 Piazza Emanuele Filiberto, 10122 Turino
Tel 011 5217882
www.montagnaviva.it

Montagna Viva's main ingredients are provided by a union of local farmers. One hundred local cheeses appear on the simple but delicious menu.

The owner has flown all over the world as a wine taster so the drinks menu is of an immensely high standard. Set menus of €25, €30 and €35 have local hams, mountain lamb and scores of *antipasti* to choose from. The owner also runs an *agrotourismo* hotel in the foothills of the Alps.

🕐 Mon–Fri noon–3, 7–10.30, Sat noon–3
🍷 L €35, D €50, Wine €9
Ⓢ Section
🚌 Buses to Piazza della Repubblica

🅗TURIN PALACE

Via Sacchi 8, 10128 Torino
Tel 011 5625511
www.thi.it

An elegant 4-star option. The Anglo–French-style rooms have giant beds and elegant lamps. The buffet breakfast is a rich spread of Piedmontese hams, cheeses and local Lavazza coffee. Turn left out of Turin's Porta Nuova rail station and you are right outside the hotel's doors.

🍷 €170–€244
🛏 125, 1 suite (20 non-smoking)
♿
🚉 Porta Nuova

EATING

The waters of the lagoon and the Adriatic yield an extraordinary variety of seafood and fish. Try *seppie* (cuttlefish) used, along with its ink, in risotto, *granceola* (spider crab) drizzled with oil and lemon, and *spaghetti all vongole verace* (spaghetti with clams). Fish to sample include grilled *sarde* (sardines), *dorata* (bream) and *branzino* (sea bass). Rice and polenta are the Venetian 'fillers'—try *risi e bisi*, made with rice and the season's first peas, and *pasta e fagioli*, a hearty stew of pasta and dried beans. Artichokes (*carciofi*), served raw, stewed or deep-fried, are another delicacy, while autumn visitors should try the intense, bittersweet *radicchio di Treviso*, a ruby-red leafy vegetable that's served braised or grilled.

Venetians often pop into a *bàcaro*; these are traditional Venetian bars selling wines by the glass and a range of *cicheti*, home-made snacks. Drinks on served will include *un'ombra*, Venetian slang for a glass of plonk, and the seemingly innocuous *spritz*, an aperitif made with wine, long drinks made with Campari, and sparkling water. Alternatively try a *bellini*, the classic mix of fresh white peach juice and *prosecco*, a champagne-like dry white wine from the Veneto.

STAYING

If you're spending a few days discovering Venice, stay in the heat of the city, though the Lido, with its sea and sand, can be a good bet for families. Within the city, decide where you want to be and book well ahead, particularly during Carnival or the summer. Most first-time visitors tend to stay in and around the *sestiere* of San Marco, but other areas worth considering are Dorsoduro, the city's most elegant residential area, Castello, where you'll pay a lot less for a 'room with a view' and Cannaregio, a wonderfully diverse *sestiere*. Across the Grand Canal, San Polo and Santa Croce have plenty of mid-range hotels and

pensione. Room prices are among the highest in Italy and wherever you stay, you'll find there's a hefty supplement for a view over the water. Bear in mind, too, that there are no door-to-door taxis and you may have to walk some distance carrying your luggage. If you're planning to stay for a week or so, self-catering is well worth considering.

BOOKINGS

The Associazione Veneziana Albergatori (Venetian Hoteliers' Association) has booths at the train station, the arrivals hall at Marco Polo airport and the Piazzale Roma car park. The official tourist board, the APT, publishes a list of all Venetian accommodation available at their offices at the train station, Marco Polo airport, Piazza San Marco 71 and Viale Santa Maria Elisabetta 6/A, Lido (www.provincia.venezia.it/aptve).

AI GONDOLIERI

Dorsoduro 366, Fondamenta Venier, 30123 Venezia
Tel 041 5286396

Despite its touristy name this restaurant, near the Peggy Guggenheim collection, is popular with locals and visitors alike. Specializing in traditional dishes from the Veneto hills,

you can choose from the impressive selection of expertly prepared meats and classic local vegetable dishes on the menu, such as ostrich, venison, horse meat (*carne di cavallo*), gnocchi and polenta.

Wed–Mon noon–3, 7–10pm; closed for lunch Jul–Aug
L €50, D €90, Wine €14.50
Section
Accademia

ALGIUBAGIO

Cannaregio 5039, Fondamente Nove, 30125 Venezia
Tel 041 5236084

Right on the Fondamente, this café with a small terrace has a striking view of the watery graveyard, San Michele. Many customers are locals and visitors awaiting vaporetti. It serves tasty pastries for breakfast and quick snacks throughout the day. It also has a gelateria, so on a summer's evening at low tide you can sit with an ice cream on the edge of the Fondamente and dangle your legs over the lagoon. No credit cards.

Daily 6.30am–8.30pm
Pastries €1, cone €2
Fondamente Nove

ALLA MADONNA

San Polo 594, Calle della Madonna, 30125 Venezia
Tel 041 5223824

If you ask any Venetian, this is one of the restaurants they're likely to recommend—but the queues of locals outside also hints at its popularity. In fact, the queuing is the only bad thing about it (there are no reservations). The food is fairly simple but tasty, the service charming, and the wine list small but well considered.

Thu–Tue noon–3, 7–10pm
L €50, D €80, Wine €10
Rialto

OSTERIA LA ZUCCA

Santa Croce 1762, Ponte del Megio, 30135 Venezia
Tel 041 5241570
www.lazucca.it

The predominantely vegetarian cuisine at Alla Zucca is cooked with style and imagination. The dishes marry pumpkin (la zucca), courgette (zucchini) flowers and fennel with a huge array of cheeses, enthusing those who have had very limited choice elsewhere. The place is great value for money and tends to fill up quickly, so you must reserve in advance.

Mon–Sat noon–2.30, 7–10.30pm; closed Aug
L €26, D €60, Wine €12.50

San Stae

EATING AND STAYING

AL MASCARON

Castello 5225, Calle Lunga Santa Maria Formosa, 30122 Venezia
Tel 041 5225995

When you find this place, in front of the Chiesa Santa Maria Formosa, don't be put off by the paper tablecloths and having to share a table with locals—the food is worth it. There are no airs and graces about Al Mascaron, just great *ciccheti* (Venetian tapas) and an anything-goes attitude. They also have a menu for pasta, risotto and salads if you fancy grazing a little longer.

Mon–Sat 11–3, 6.30pm–midnight; closed over Christmas and New Year

Cicheti for two €13, D €80 Wine/beer €1.50

San Zaccaria

ANTICA LOCANDA MONTIN

Dorsoduro 1147, Fondamenta di Borgo, 30123 Venezia
Tel 041 5227151
www.locandamontin.com

This family-run restaurant and hotel with faded façade and flower bedecked balconies overlooking the Eremite canal has attracted artists, writers and musicians for years, including Peggy Guggenheim, the flamboyant 20th-century socialite and art collector. The more-Mediterranean-than-Venetian menu will tempt you with many dishes, including an impressive beef steak tartare and a tantalizing *tiramisù*. Inside, the walls of the rooms and restaurant are lined with paintings, while the rows of tables outside allow you to enjoy fine food and wine in the leafy shade.

Thu–Mon 12.30–2.30, 7.30–10pm, (also open Wed Mar–Jun and Sep–Oct, Christmas and Carnivale); closed 2 weeks in Jan and 1 week in Aug

L €40, D €80, Wine €12

10 (double €110–€135)

Section

Accademia

CAFFÈ FLORIAN

San Marco 56/59, Piazza San Marco, 30124 Venezia
Tel 041 5205641
www.caffeflorian.com

The sumptuous surroundings of Caffè Florian have attracted the great and the good since 1720. Being well positioned on

the south side of Piazza San Marco, it is now mainly the haunt of Japanese and American visitors who are willing to pay €7 for a cappuccino —plus extra for the music— while they sit on seats once warmed by Goethe and Byron. The service is impeccable.

Sun–Fri 10am–11pm, Sat 10am–midnight, Mar–Nov; Thu–Tue 10am–11pm, rest of year

Coffee €7, spritz €7

Section

San Marco

CIPRIANI RESTAURANT

10 Giudecca, Hotel Cipriani and Palazzo Vendramin, 30133 Venezia
Tel 041 5207744
www.hotelcipriani.it

Reserve a table and the restaurant's private launch will collect you from San Marco, and take you back again later. But the free ride isn't the main reason for coming here— there's also the exclusive location, the dining terraces, the superior service and the matchless regional Italian

cuisine. The menu and wine list are very carefully thought out; indeed, every aspect of the experience is delivered with care and attention to detail. A memorable meal.

Daily noon–11pm; closed early Nov–early Apr

L €120, D €220, Wine €39

Giudecca

DA FIORE

San Polo 2202A, Calle di Scaleter, 30125 Venezia
Tel 041 721308
www.dafiore.com

Perhaps better known for its fine cellar, Da Fiore is considered one of the best restaurants in Venice. Even so, dining here may not incur as much damage to the bank balance as some of the other top spots in town. The chef brings an international twist to

ANTICHE CARAMPANE

San Polo 1911, Rio Terra delle Carampane, 30125 Venice
Tel 041 5240165

Not just another fish restaurant. In fact, its one of Venice's best-kept culinary secrets. Carampane is dedicated to the history of Venetian cooking, but isn't afraid to use different ingredients and add a modern twist here and there. Renaissance dishes and Medieval dishes are cleverly reinterpreted—try

the *caperosolli Savanarola* (shellfish with olive oil and Parmesan) or the *filetto di San Pietro con radicchio trevigno* (filleted St. Peter's fish with Treviso chicory). Let the experts choose your meal and recount the stories behind each dish. Enjoy for example the recipes taken from the book of Bartolomeo Scoppi, cook of Pope Pious V. Don't miss the home-made biscuits—a delicous conclusion to your meal.

Tue–Sat 12.30–3.30, 7.30–10.30pm

L €38, D €95, Wine €12

San Silvestro

Venetian cooking. If you want to dine here beside Venice's glitterati, it's advisable to make a reservation.

Tue–Sat 12.30–2.30, 7.30–10.30pm; closed Aug

L €100, D €200, Wine €19

San Stae

🍴 GAM GAM

Cannaregio 1122, Fondamenta
Cannaregio, 30125 Venezia
Tel 041 715284
www.jewishvenice.org/food/gamgam

For some genuine Venetian
cuisine (there has been a
Jewish community resident
here since the 14th century),
try Gam Gam (meaning 'More!
More!'), the famous kosher
restaurant in the Ghetto north
of the Guglie vaporetto stop.
After washing your hands in
the fountain, sit in pleasant
pastel surroundings and enjoy
some excellent *cholent*, *couscous* and *bourekas*. The wine
list is kosher, too, and includes
Golan and Bartenura.

🕐 Sun–Thu 12.30–10pm, Fri–Sat
12.30–dusk
🍴 L €25, D €50, Wine €13
💳
🚤 Guglie

🍴 HARRY'S BAR

San Marco 1323, Calle Vallaresso, 30124
Venezia
Tel 041 5285777

If you're going to push the
boat out in Venice, you'll get
your money's worth at the
world-famous Harry's Bar. This
stylish yet understated restaurant is swamped with
Americans, who feel at home
here. It also draws visiting
celebrities. Harry's Bar is
famous for its *bellinis*
(sparkling *prosecco* wine with
white peach juice) and its
carpaccio of beef (razor-thin
slices of sirloin). Both deserve
the hype.

🕐 Daily 10.30am–11pm
🍴 L €80, D €190, Wine €24
💺 Section
💳
🚤 San Marco

🍴 HARRY'S DOLCI

Giudecca 773, Fondamenta San Biagio,
30133 Venezia
Tel 041 5224844
www.cipriani.com

For summer dining, Harry's
Dolci has a little more than its
counterpart, Harry's Bar, at San
Marco—and at slightly more
agreeable prices. Its dining terrace on the green overlooks
the Zattere and the boats passing by on the canal—a great
location with memorable
views. The light pasta and fish
dishes are highly recom-
mended, and leave room for
the sublime puddings that jus-

tify this restaurant's reputation.

🕐 Wed–Mon 10.30–10.30, Easter–Oct
🍴 L €60, D €120, Wine €20
🚤 Palanca

🍴 NICO

Dorsoduro 958, Zattere, 30123 Venice
Tel 041 5225293

In the summer, Fondamenta
Zattere, right on the waterfront, is a perfect spot for
sitting and enjoying an ice
cream and looking out over
the shimmering water to
Giudecca. The *gelati* and
frozen yoghurt are beautifully
made, and there are some
unusual tastes if you're feeling
adventurous. Try the hazlenut-
and-chocolate. Drinks served
here include *spritz* and *prosecco*. No credit cards.

🕐 Daily 8am–10pm
🍦 Cone €2.50
🚤 Zattere

🍴 OSTERIA OLIVA NERA

Castello 3417/18, Calle della Madonna,
30122 Venezia
Tel 041 5222170

This is one of a new breed
challenging the old school of
Venetian restaurateurs. Its
menu, full of interesting quirks
yet executed confidently,
shows that Venetian cooking

can be given a contemporary
edge. Delicious examples
include scallops with wild
mushrooms, octopus salad,
and lamb cooked in thyme.
The dessert menu includes
pannacotta with wild fruits and
a rich mascarpone cheesecake.
The uncomplicated decor and
unpretentious staff make lunch
or dinner here a treat.

🕐 Fri–Tue noon–2.30, 7–10pm
🍴 L €50, D €85, Wine €9
💳
🚤 San Zaccaria

🛏 AL PONTE ANTICO

Cannaregio 5768, Calle dell'Aseo, 30131
Venezia
Tel 041 2411944

www.alponteantico.com

This magnificent 15th-century
palazzo has been well
appointed with antiques, chandeliers, frescoes and preserved
beamed ceilings. Public rooms
have large windows with stunning views of the Canal
Grande. Take breakfast and
later sip *aperitivi bellini* on the

terrace or in the narrow, light
and elegant salone. Guest
rooms and junior suites have
Venetian decorative flourishes
and modern private bath-
rooms. Other facilities include
safe, television, minibar, hair-
dryer, internet connection,
room service and hydromassage bath.

🍴 €207–€517
🛏 8 (non-smoking)
💳
🚤 Rialto

🛏 ANTICA LOCANDA AL GAMBERO

San Marco 4687, Calle dei Fabbri, 30124
Venezia
Tel 041 5224384
www.locandaalgambero.com

This is a comfortable, well-run
hotel between Rialto and San
Marco. Public areas have dark
wood furniture and marble
flooring. Immaculate private
bathrooms add to the good
value here. Other amenities
include television, telephone,
safe, internet connection, hair-
dryer and minibar. As with its
sister hotel the Locanda
Sturion (p.350), there are
tea/coffee-making facilities in

EATING AND STAYING

each room. Discount meals are available in the excellent Le Bistrot downstairs.

🏨 €110–€170
🛏 6 (non–smoking)
💲
🚇 San Marco

◉BISANZIO

Castello 3651, Calle della Pietà, 30122 Venezia
Tel 041 5203100
www.bisanzio.com

The Busetti family have run this restored 16th-century palazzo hotel, near the so-called Chiesa di Vivaldi, since 1969. Guest rooms have parquet flooring, beamed ceilings and unfussy Venetian touches. The most sought-after and

expensive rooms have charming balconies with rooftop views. All have telephone, satellite television, hair-dryer and minibar. The Brown Lounge, bar and breakfast room share a functional, understated appearance. Continental breakfast is included and may be taken in the old courtyard.

🏨 €110–€320
🛏 50 (20 non–smoking)
💲
🚇 San Zaccaria

◉LA CALCINA

Dorsoduro 780–783, Fondamenta Zattere ai Gesuati, 30123 Venezia
Tel 041 5206466
www.lacalcina.com

A perennial favourite along the Zattere, this restaurant has wonderful views of Giudecca. Follow in the footsteps of English critic John Ruskin, who stayed here in the 1870s when it was a two-storey inn. Simple rooms have parquet flooring and attractive period touches. Each has a private bathroom, telephone, hair-dryer and safe. There are no televisions or minibars in the bedrooms. A plush suite is available in the

annexe. Take breakfast on the canalside platform, then relax on the roof terrace. La Piscina bar/restaurant serves unfussy Venetian fare.

🏨 €90–€182
🛏 29 (non-smoking)
💲
🚇 Zattere

◉CA' PISANI

Dorsoduro 979/a, Rio Terra dei Foscarini, 30123 Venezia
Tel 041 2401411
www.capisanihotel.it

Ca' Pisani quietly shook up the Venetian hotel world on its opening in 2000. They have traded in the ubiquitous and heavy Venetian glitz, for stylish '30s and '40s inspired interiors. Smooth lines, exposed beams and art deco furnishings mix with modern minimalist touches. Each room is individually designed and has a relaxing, sophisticated charm. The facilities, including sauna, are excellent and the bathrooms are the most

contemporary in town. La Rivista restaurant continues the modern theme with simple contemporary and classic Italian cuisine.

🏨 €204–€285
🛏 29 (4 non-smoking)
💲 ⬛ Access
🚇 Accademia

◉DANIELI

Castello 4196, Riva degli Schiavoni, 30122 Venezia
Tel 041 5226480

www.danieli.hotelinvenice.com

An expansive, spellbinding lobby and a rooftop terrace overlooking the lagoon give the Danieli luxury status and celebrity appeal. This former home of Doge Dandolo, patronized by writers Charles Dickens and d'Annunzio, is dramatically lit and filled with marble and antiques. Dine Venetian-style at the pricey Terrazza Restaurant, then sip a spritz at the Dandolo Piano Bar. Guest rooms vary immensely, but most have flowery furnishings and excellent amenities. Suites range from dark-wood elegance to Murano-glass glitz.

🏨 €482–€2,400
💲
🛏 233 rooms (43 non-smoking)
🚇 San Zaccaria

◉LA FENICE ET DES ARTISTES

San Marco 1936, Campiello della Fenice 193, 30124 Venezia
Tel 041 5232333
www.fenicehotels.com

This is popular with musicians and opera aficionados as it's close to the famous La Fenice. Exposed beams, classic seating, antique furnishings and marble give it a refined yet comfortable character. The evocative Angolo Bar resembles an early 20th-century theatre bar. The best rooms have balconies and unusual

artwork. Facilities include telephone, television, private bathroom, hair-dryer and safe. La Taverna restaurant serves traditional Venetian dishes.

🏨 €135–€218
🛏 67 rooms, 1 suite (34 non-smoking)
💲
🚇 San Angelo or San Marco

◉LOCANDA ART DECO

San Marco 2966, Calle delle Botteghe, 30124 Venezia
Tel 041 2770558

www.locandaartdeco.com

Lovers of the belle-époque will enjoy the mood at the Locanda Art Deco, found near the Accademia bridge and Campo Santo Stefano. Public rooms and bedrooms are filled with art deco antiques. Each attractive guest room has an orthopaedic mattress, private bathroom, kettle, television, hair-dryer and phone.

📶 €100–€170
🛏 6 (2 non-smoking)
♿
🚤 Accademia

🏛 LOCANDA LA CORTE

Castello 6317, Calle Bressana, 30122 Venezia
Tel 041 2411300
www.locandalacorte.it

Within easy reach of many shops, restaurants and entrtainment venues, this pleasant hotel is in an attractive part of the Castello Sestriere, near the huge bulk of Chiesa Santi Giovanni e Paolo. The rooms in this former 16th-century palazzo, with their high ceilings and exposed beams, have been completely restored and refurbished using rich fabrics

and luxury Venetian furniture. Facilities include private bathroom, television, hair-dryer and phone. The secluded courtyard full of trees and flowers at the heart of the hotel is a great place to relax and enjoy the buffet breakfast.

📶 €115–€180
🛏 16 (non-smoking)
♿
🚤 San Zaccaria or Fondamenta Nuove

🏛 LOCANDA SAN BARNABA

Dorsoduro 2785–2786, Calle del Traghetto, 30124 Venezia
Tel 041 2411233
www.locanda-sanbarnaba.com

A wonderful 16th-century palazzo near the Ca' Rezzonico vaporetto stop in the university quarter. The impressive

marble-floored and ornately appointed hall hints at wealth and history. Savour the views on the terrace or relax in the courtyard. The unfussy bedrooms have white walls, dark parquet floors, understated period furniture and exposed beams. Each has an amusing name: Lovers' Nest, Philosopher's Refuge, Playwright's Chamber. Superior rooms have 18th-century ceiling frescoes.

📶 €120–€170
🛏 13 (non-smoking)
♿
🚤 Ca' Rezzonico

🏛 LOCANDA STURION

San Polo 679, Calle del Sturion, 30125 Venezia
Tel 041 5236243
www.locandasturion.com

Convivial Italo-Scottish management welcomes visitors to this well-run hotel. Once frequented by Rialto merchants, it appears in Vittore Carpaccio's *Miracle of the Cross*, painted in 1494, housed in the Accademia. Marble floors and dark wood dominate. Most rooms face a quiet *calle* and

each has a television, safe, hair-dryer, minibar and even a kettle! The luminous breakfast room and the most sought-after bedrooms have views of the Rialto. There is no lift—the stairs prove challenging with heavy bags.

📶 €100–€260
🛏 11 (non-smoking)
♿
🚤 San Silvestro Rialto

🏛 LONDRA PALACE

Riva Degli Schiavoni, 4171 Castello, 30122 Venezia
Tel 041 5200533
www.slh.com/londra

This handsome 19th-century palazzo along the busy Riva was renovated in 1999. In 1877, Tchaikovsky composed

his fourth symphony in room 106, while gazing out towards San Giorgio Maggiore. Dark wood furniture and marble floors blend with the light walls and modern lighting, creating an air of calm and restrained elegance. Enjoy the stunning views from the terrace while you dine at Do Leoni, which serves Chianina beef and other regional dishes. Rooms vary in size and are comfortable, but they are a little characterless, but the ample pink marble bathrooms come with bathrobe, shower and jacuzzi.

📶 €270–800
🛏 53
♿
🚤 San Zaccaria

🏛 METROPOLE

Castello 4149, Riva degli Schiavoni, 30122 Venezia
Tel 041 5205044
www.hotelmetropole.com

This hotel is handy for San Marco. Rooms with views face the bustling Riva and may be noisy. Oddities and antiques including crucifixes, nutcrackers and corkscrews fill the sumptuous lounge and busy Bar Zodiaco. Vivaldi taught orphans in the chapel, and Freud stayed here when it was Casa Kirsch. Rooms have chandeliers and elegant fittings, and some of the suites have canopied beds and the bathroom floors are heated. Don't miss the live dinner-time music in

EATING AND STAYING

courtyard restaurant.

🛏 €210–€465
🛌 56 rooms, 14 suites (10 non-smoking)
🔆
🚤 San Zaccaria

⊖NOEMI
San Marco 909, Calle dei Fabbri, 30124 Venezia
Tel 041 5238144
www.hotelnoemi.com
An attractive and well-managed hotel in the long, straight Calle dei Fabbri, near Piazza San Marco. Marble floors, elaborate carpets and dainty furniture fill the bright public areas. Some of the well-appointed bedrooms have exposed beams, and half of them have a private bathrooms. Expect Venetian-style patterned fabrics, wallpaper and period furniture. Facilities include television, telephone and safe. Air-conditioning available on request.

🛏 €50–€150
🛌 15 (non-smoking)
🔆 10 rooms only
🚤 San Marco–Vallaresso

⊖PAUSANIA
Dorsoduro 2824, Fondamenta Gherardini, 30123 Venezia
Tel 041 5222083
www.hotelpausania.it
This 14th-century palazzo, complete with quadruple lancet windows, stunning staircase and an original well, was refurbished in 2002. Public areas have marble floors, understated furnishings, Murano glass chandeliers and frescoed ceilings. The similarly decorated bedrooms are spacious and well equipped, all with a private bathroom, telephone, television, radio and minibar. The buffet breakfast is served in a room overlooking the wonderful garden—a rarity in Venice. Make sure you reserve a room early as this is a very popular hotel.

🛏 €130–€250
🛌 26 (5 non-smoking)
🔆
🚤 Ca' Rezzonico

⊖LA RESIDENZA
Castello 3608, Campo Bandiera e Moro, 30122 Venezia
Tel 041 5285315
www.venicelaresidenza.com
This handsome palazzo once owned by the influential Gritti family is reasonably priced for Venice. The Gothic façade, with its 10th-century sculptural details, overlooks the peaceful

Campo Bandiera e Moro to the south. The wonderful lobby has elegant furnishings amidst ornate ceilings and walls. Request one of the refurbished rooms, which have a fresh, bright feel and period pieces. Facilities include private bathroom with shower, television, safe and minibar.

🛏 €100–€155
🛌 15 (non-smoking)
🔆
🚤 Arsenale

⊖SAN SAMUELE
San Marco 3358, Salizada San Samuele, 30124 Venezia
Tel 041 5228045
www.albergosansamuele.it
This above-average one-star hotel is in a wonderful location near the San Samuele vaporetto stop. Staff are friendly and the hotel is tidy and well run. The lounge area has the usual Venetian trappings: patterned wallpaper, marble floors, antiques and chandeliers. For this price, the rooms are nothing special, but in contrast to the competition they are clean and comfortable. Most have shared bathrooms and basic facilities. No credit cards.

🛏 €50–€105
🛌 10
🚤 San Samuele

⊖WESTIN EXCELSIOR VENICE LIDO
Lido 41, Lungomare Marconi, 30126 Venezia
Tel 041 5260201
www.starwood.com
A Moorish building, with fountains and lemon trees in the courtyard, once frequented by the belle-époque set. The terraces lead down to a swimming pool. Facilities include television, safe, dry-cleaning and 24-hour concierge service. Dine in the elegant Tropicana salon or

Terrazza restaurant, then sip cocktails in the Blue Bar. Clay tennis courts, watersports and a beauty parlour are available.

🕐 Mid-Mar–Nov
🛏 €2960–€846
🛌 197 rooms and suites (10 non-smoking)
🔆 🚤 Outdoor
🚤 Lido Casino

SPECIAL

⊖PENSIONE ACCADEMIA
Dorsoduro 1058, Fondamenta Bollani, 30123 Venezia
Tel 041 5210188
www.pensioneaccademi.it
Verdant courtyard gardens, Grand Canal views and helpful staff complement this hotel that is in a great location for art lovers. Once called Villa Maravege, it is a former Russian embassy. The stately rooms have wooden floors, 19th-century furniture and chandeliers. Private bathroom, television and phone in all the rooms. Continental breakfast spread provides a bountiful choice and can be enjoyed on the tranquil canalside terrace. Early reservations are recommended.

🛏 €130–€275
🛌 27
🔆
🚤 Accademia

EATING

It's generally accepted that you eat better in Emilia-Romagna than anywhere else in Italy. The quality of the food is exceptional in the home of world-famous dishes such as *parmigianino-reggiano* (parmesan cheese), *prosciutto di Parma* (Parma ham), *ragù* (rich sauces) and egg pasta. Both butter and cream are lavishly used, particularly in the delicate home-made pasta, stuffed with ricotta and spinach, pumpkin, and subtly spiced meats. Meat dishes include *bollito misto* (mixed boiled meats) and *zampone*, a stuffed pig's trotter usually served with lentils. Emilia's big-name wine is Lambrusco, golden and intensely scented.

Cooking in Trentino-Alto-Adige is geared towards long, cold winters. You'll find hearty soups rather than pasta, dumplings (*canerderli*), spicy smoked meat (*speck*), game and rabbit, while puddings are based on locally grown apples, plums and pears. Farther north, the German influence is evident; goulash, sauerkraut and appel strudel all finding their way onto the menu, and coffee getting weaker and creamier by the kilometre. More DOC wine is produced in the region than anywhere else in Italy—look out for Pinot Grigios and Chardonnays.

Friuli-Venezia Giulia's cuisine relies heavily on yoghurt and rye bread, piccant sweet-sour dishes and fish broths spiced with cumin and fennel. The region borders Yugoslavia and some of the cooking has Slav influences and the pasta fillings are heavily spiced. The famous San Daniele ham is produced here, delicious with the local wines such as Tocai, Verduzzo and Pinot Nero.

STAYING

You'll find plenty of accommodation choice in the northeast and Emilia-Romagna, an area of immense diversity. If you're on the artistic and cultural trail, it's likely you'll be heading for Emilia-Romagna and Bologna. Many hotels in the regional capital are aimed at business

visitors and can be busy, but you should have no trouble in the region's smaller cities of Padua, Ravenna, Verona, Parma and Vicenza. Heading east into Friuli-Venezia Giulia, whose main towns are Trieste and Udine, there is plenty of accommodation. Northwest lies the scenic splendour of the mountains of the high Veneto and Trentino-Alto-Adige, where you're more likely to find yourself staying in an Austrian-style chalet than a splendid palazzo. Except for the peak months of July and August, you should have no trouble finding somewhere to stay, but remember that German is the first language in the Alto-Adige. Good areas for a few nights include the valleys of the Dolomites and the beautiful, historic town of Trento.

BOLOGNA

ⓘ BROCCAINDOSSO
Via Broccaindosso 7/a , 40125 Bologna
Tel 051 234153
At an unmarked door in a quiet street, a small sign and bell tell you this is the right place. The rustic interior has rough tables and long wooden benches. They only serve one course and desserts, and there is no menu; although you can order pasta, it's better to wait and see what the staff bring you. Pace yourself—the first three desserts that arrive are just the beginning!
Reservations essential. No credit cards.
🕐 Mon–Sat 8.30pm–2am; sometimes closed Aug
🍴 D €50, Wine €10
🚋 14, 27

ⓘ CAFFÉ ZAMBONI
Via Zamboni 6, 40124 Bologna
Tel 051 231703
A stylish café on the edge of the university district, right by the two towers. Frequented by both students and older Bolognese dropping in for their Sunday hot chocolate. They have three separate drink menus: one for tea, one for coffee and one for chocolate. The chocolate menu alone has 31 different types! They also serve snacks, salads and aperitifs.
🕐 Daily 6am–10pm, Oct–May
🍷 Drinks from €2

ⓘ C'ENTRO
Via dell'Indipendenza 45, 40100 Bologna
Tel 051 234216
On the main road running from the middle to the rail station, this modern, clean restaurant has an excellent range of local dishes and salads—all at very reasonable prices. C'entro is a safe haven for vegetarians, who can pile up as many of the raw ingredients as they like on their plates. This restaurant is popular with locals and tourists alike and there are tables outside in the summer too.
🕐 Mon–Sat 11.45–3, 6.30–9pm
🍴 L €16, D €25, Wine €7
🚭
🚋 20, 27

ⓘ CESARI
Via de' Carbonesi 8, 40123 Bologna
Tel 051 237710
www.da-cesari.com
Stately establishment, five minutes' walk south of the main square, that has long been a star in Bologna's gastronomic sky. The service is friendly and efficient and the staff

occasionally reach up to get a dusty bottle from the wines that line the walls. The interior is dominated by a large iron chandelier. Specialities include home-made ravioli stuffed with rabbit and white truffle with celery and Parmesan. The wine list is extensive and good and includes wines produced by the owner. Reservations essential. Air-conditioned.
🕐 Mon–Sat 12.30–3, 7.30–10.30pm; closed Sat in Jul and Aug
🍴 L €50, D €60, Wine €12
🚋 20, 21

ⓘ FANTONI
Via del Pratello 11, 40122 Bologna
Tel 051 236358
This small, lively trattoria 10 minutes' walk west from the heart of town, on a street

known for its bars, is great value for money. Red-and-white checked tablecloths and walls festooned with caricatures. They serve simple local dishes with home-made pasta and wines and fresh fish from Thursday to Saturday. Its great reputation means it's packed with families, so be prepared to queue at the door if you haven't made a reservaton. The small menu changes daily. Specials include baked *maccheroni* as a first course. You can sit out on the terrace in summer. No credit cards.

🕐 Tue–Sat 12–2.30, 8–10.30pm, Mon 12–2.30; closed Aug
🍴 L €20, D €32, Wine €8
🚻 Section

🅴CENTRALE
Via della Zecca 2, 40121 Bologna
Tel 051 225114
Small central third-floor hotel with lift. Best-value and most pleasant of the city's cheaper hotels. Large guest rooms but occasionally a lingering smell of cigarettes. You can choose a room with or without your own bathroom. The hotel is simply furnished, but it has large beds and there is a television in all the rooms. Some upper-floor rooms have views over the rooftops. Close to a main road (Via Ugo Bassi), so there is some traffic noise, but rooms overlooking it have double-glazing. Breakfast room/bar.

🛏 €92 excluding breakfast
🚪 20
🚻

🅴GRAND HOTEL BAGLIONI
Via Indipendenza 8, 40121 Bologna
Tel 051 225445
www.baglionihotels.com
Housed in the Palazzo Ghisilardi Fava, near the central piazzas, the Baglioni has areas that date back to the 16th century. Beyond its discreet entrance you discover a magnificent lobby. Rooms are all luxuriously furnished and superbly equipped, with 24-hour room service, adjustable heating and air-conditioning, satellite television, minibar and safe. Cheaper rooms have showers, no bath. Rooms on the street side are well sound-proofed. Restaurant sumptuously decorated with frescoes by the Carracci school.

Parking is available and there is computer access.

🛏 €319–€390
🚪 125 (20 non-smoking)
🚻

🅴OROLOGIO
Via IV Novembre 10, 40124 Bologna
Tel 051 231253
www.bolognahotel.it
In the city's heart, facing the Palazzo Comunale on a small,

quiet street with little traffic, this welcoming hotel provides excellent service. Public rooms are graceful, guest rooms elegant and well equipped with television, hair-dryer, safe and internet access. Some have views across to Bologna's famous towers. Buffet breakfast. Pets allowed. Bicycles available. Garage parking. Reservations essential.

🛏 €180–€341
🚪 34 (5 non-smoking)
🚻

CANAZEI
🅴🍽HOTEL ASTORIA E RISTORANTE DE TOFI
Via Roma 92, Canazei, 38032 Trento
Tel 0462 601 302
www.hotel-astoria.net
Good restaurants are few and far between in this holiday area, and locals consider the restaurant at the Hotel Astoria to be the pick of the bunch. The dining room is slightly clinical and mealtimes are short, but the food makes up for it, with local dishes, a vegetarian menu and immense trouble taken over personal requirements. Local dishes include *polenta al ragù* (maize meal with meat sauce), *funghi* (mushrooms) in autumn and some game. The huge portions are aimed at outdoor enthusiasts.

🕐 Daily 12.30–1.30, 7–8.30; closed May–mid-Jun and Oct–Nov
🍴 L €20, D €45, Wine €9
🚪 39 (€104–€292)

🚻
🚗 From the A22 (Brennero) exit Egnaora then follow signs for Cavalezei and Val di Fassa. From here follow signs to the hotel

CIVIDALE DEI FRIULI
🍽ANTICA TRATTORIA DOMINISSINI
Stretta Jacopo Stellini 18, Cividale dei Friuli, 33043 Udine
Tel 0432 733763
www.anticatrattoriadominissini.it
Make your way through the bar area and down a couple of steps into this traditional restaurant, lined with old dressers decorated with local pottery. The menu is faithful to straightforward Friulian cooking, so you'll be able to try traditional cheese and potato cakes, thick vegetable soups and grilled meat. The owner doubles as the waiter and he is passionate about wine; ask his advice on local vintages or try the smooth white Tocai bursting with depth.

🕐 Tue–Sun 10.30–3, 6–11, May–Oct; Tue–Sat 10.30–3, 6–11 rest of year
🍴 L €30, D €44, Wine €7
🚻

🍽🅴LOCANDA POMO D'ORO
Piazza San Giovanni 20, Cividale dei Friuli, 33043 Udine
Tel 0432 731489
Fax 0432 701257
www.alpomodoro.com
Just behind Cividale's duomo you'll find the pink-painted façade of this lovely old hotel, run by the Picotti family for several generations. The earliest parts of the building date from the 11th and 12th centuries, but inside modern comfort, on a provincial scale, reigns. There are plenty of traditional touches—wooden panelling and old beams—but the bathrooms are very modern and the rooms are spacious. Downstairs there is a series of rooms used for breakfast and the above average restaurant.

🕐 Thu–Tue 12–2, 7–10pm
🍴 L €30, D €44, Wine €6.50
🚪 17
🛏 €60
🚗 From the north exit the A23 at Udine and follow signs to Cividale dei Friuli (S54). Turn right opposite the station and follow signs into town and the hotel. From the south exit A23 Udine Sud and follow signs to Cividale (S54).

MERANO (MERAN)

🔟 FLORA
Via Portici 75, Merano, 39012 Bolzano
Tel 0473 231484

Merano's 15th-century Palace
of Justice is home to this intimate restaurant, panelled in
dark wood. Cooking here is
remarkably varied–the chef
has worked abroad–but the
accent's Italo-Austrian, with all
pasta home-made and ingredients locally sourced. The *pasta
bianca e nera con gamberi e
erbe* (black and white pasta
with prawns and wild herbs) is
a signature dish; try the
aragostina (crayfish) too.
Secondi include excellent
filetto d'agnello (lamb fillet).
They have a huge Italian and
international wine list.

🕐 12.30–2.30, 8–12; closed Sun, Mon
lunch and mid-Jan–Mar
🍴 L€ 35, D €50, Wine €14
Ⓢ Section

⊖ EINSIEDLER EREMITA
Via Val di Nova 25, Merano, 39012
Bolzano
Tel 0473 232191
Fax 0473 211575
www.einsiedler.com

Alpine in style, with geranium
window boxes, this great-value
hotel stands amid vineyards
and woods overlooking
Merano and the mountains.
There's a good bus service into

town 5km (3 miles) away and
a cable car within 300m
(912ft). This makes a good
base for families, with tennis
courts, a sauna and a playground for young children.
Expect big rooms, puffy
Austrian duvets, gargantuan
breakfasts and a welcome that
combines professionalism with
genuine friendliness.

🕐 Apr–Nov
💶 €30–€50
ⓘ 37
🏊 Outdoor and indoor
🚗 Exit the A22 at Merano Sud. The city
is divided into 6 hotel zones. The

Einsiedler is in the yellow zone, so follow the yellow arrows to the correct
zone, where you will pick up signs
directing you to the hotel

PADOVA (PADUA)

🔟 ANFORA
Via Solcin 13, 35122 Padova
Tel 049 656629

This is a lively place in the narrow streets of the old Jewish
Ghetto near the Piazza
dell'Erbe. Its bohemian air is
appreciated by the student
crowd, who often take the
party outside as the weather
gets warmer. Anfora concentrates its efforts on local
produce and fish dishes, and
its prices are very reasonable.
Outside of restaurant hours it
operates as a bar. It is worth
making a reservation or
arrive early.

🕐 Mon–Sat 12.30–3, 8–10.30pm
🍴 L €20, D €40 Wine €9
Ⓢ

🔟 BELLE PARTI
Via Belle Parti 11, 35122 Padova
Tel 049 8751822

A charming restaurant in the
old town with wooden beams
across the high ceiling,
starched white tablecloths and
art nouveau stained glass.
Elegant furniture and subtle
lighting add to the appeal of
this calm, compact establishment. Service is excellent. The
menu includes regional and
international dishes. Choose
from dishes such as steamed
mullet with potatoes and
olives, cuttlefish with polenta,
bigoli pasta with duck *ragù*
and foie gras, and risotto with
prawns and saffron. They have
an excellent wine list.
Reservations advisable.

🕐 Mon–Sat 12.30–2.30, 8pm–2am
🍴 L €60, D €80, Wine €14
Ⓢ Section Ⓢ

🔟 NANE DELLA GIULIA
Via Santa Sofia 1, 35121 Padova
Tel 049 660742

This *osteria*, reputed to be the
oldest in town, is in the university quarter and students
gather to enjoy the relaxed
atmosphere. The menu is
strong on the cooking of the
Veneto region and vegetarian
dishes, making good use of
local cheeses and vegetables;
all items are very reasonably
priced. Popular dishes include
pasta with beans. There's live

piano music on Wed and Thu
evenings. Gay friendly. No
credit cards.

🕐 Tue–Sun 11.30–2.30, 7–midnight
🍴 L €16, D €40, Wine €8
Ⓢ Section

🔟 OSTERIA DEI FABBRI
Via dei Fabbri 13, 35122 Padova
Tel 049 650336

This central *osteria* is just off
Piazza dell'Erbe in the old
Jewish Ghetto. The interior is
attractive with dark wooden
tables and rustic furnishings.
The menu has simple local
pasta and polenta dishes, such
as *pasta e fagioli* (pasta with
beans) and grilled meats,
including rabbit and beef.
Reservations are advisable.

🕐 Mon–Sat 12.30–2.30, 7.30–midnight
🍴 L €24, D €60, Wine €7.50

🔟 PEPEN
Piazza Cavour 15, 35100 Padova
Tel 049 8759483

A large pizzeria right in the
heart of the old town, with
outdoor seating in the square
in summer. There's a wide
range of pizzas, as well as
other dishes. Try the fish and
puff pastry with cream cheese,
barley and candied fruit. A
reservation is essential, even at
lunch-time, as office workers
from the surrounding banks
and businesses make a
beeline here.

🕐 Mon–Sat noon–3, 7–11pm; closed
Aug
🍴 L €25, D €70, Wine €10
Ⓢ Section Ⓢ

⊖ CITTÀ DI PADOVA YOUTH HOSTEL
Via Aleardo Aleardi 30, 35122 Padova
Tel 049 8752219
www.ctgveneto.it/ostello2

This is a friendly and busy hostel in a modern building 10
minutes' walk southwest of
the middle of town. It is in a
quiet district and some of the
rooms overlook the courtyard
garden. The spacious public
areas are sparsely and func-
tionally decorated and the
large common area upstairs is
dominated by a television.
Rooms vary from 2 to 16 beds
(bunk-beds). Laundry
machines are available and
bicycles can be hired. Check-in
from 4pm, curfew 11pm. It's
advisable to reserve from May
to October. Membership is
required.

EATING AND STAYING

⊘ Closed 20 Dec–6 Jan
🛏 €13.50–€15.50 per bed including breakfast
🛌 220 beds
🚌 3, 8, 12, 18 from Bay 3 at the rail station

🏨 MAJESTIC TOSCANELLI

Via dell'Arco 2, 35122 Padova
Tel 049 663244
www.toscanelli.com

This hotel is in the old Ghetto district of central Padova, just south of the main market square and within easy walking distance of the sights. This is the nicest of the city's 4-star hotels. The entrance hall is sumptuous and the rooms

stylish, decorated in mock 18th-century English or Venetian baroque style. Guest rooms are equipped with satellite television and a safe. Other services include laundry and child minding.
🛏 €150–€171
🛌 34 (22 non-smoking)
🅿 🔄

🏨 SANT'ANTONIO

Via San Fermo 118, 35137 Padova
Tel 049 8751393
www.hotelsantantonio.it

The Sant'Antonio is an inexpensive but well-positioned hotel on the northern edge of the town. It overlooks the old stone bridge that spans the river, itself a rather uninspiring sight. Rooms are large and pleasant, although their modern furnishings are past their prime, and are available with

or without bathroom. There is a bar and a lift. Pets are welcome.
🛏 €68–€78 excluding breakfast
🛌 33
🔄

PARMA

🍴 SANTA CROCE

Via Pasini 20, 43100 Parma
Tel 0521 293529
www.ristoratori.it/santacroce

Restrained elegance in three rooms—glowing damask, polished wood floors and fresh flowers, all warm and welcoming. They serve up authentic Parma cuisine with a twist; try the mixed *salumi* to sample Parma ham in its birthplace, or delicate *rouleau al granchio* (crab roulade), then move to seasonal dishes (*cappone*, capon, particularly in autumn), prime fillet steak and mousses and *semifreddi* for dessert. The huge wine list has foreign labels as well as wines from all over Italy.
⊘ Mon–Fri 12.30–2, 8–10, Sat 8–10; closed last 3 weeks in Aug
🍷 L €40, D €60, Wine €10
🔄 Section 🔄

🏨 VERDI

Via Pasini 18, 43100 Parma
Tel 0521 293 539
Fax 0521 293 559
www.hotelverdi.it

An early 19th-century, four-storeyed, pink-painted villa on the edge of the Parco Ducale. A stylish Italian hotel of the old school, the lofty public rooms are crammed with antiques, hung with pictures and chandeliers and carpeted with the best Persian rugs—even the breakfast china's Ginori. The bedrooms have clean lines, with comfy armchairs, writing tables and good sized wardrobes; the bathrooms are marble-clad and luxurious. Private parking and a good, if expensive, restaurant top off the whole package.
⊘ Closed 2 weeks in Aug and over Christmas
🛏 €145–€185 excluding breakfast
🛌 20
🔄
🚗 From Mantova, Bologna, Piacenza or Milan take the viale that circles the *centro storico*. Via Pasini is the section opposite the Parco Ducale

🍴 BIZANTINO

Market Hall, Piazza A. Costa, 48100 Ravenna
Tel 054 432073

The Bizantino is a self-service restaurant on the big market square in the centre of old Ravenna. It's a large, airy, modern space on two floors, ideal for a quick bite to eat while you're out sightseeing. Expect good, simple food with plenty of fresh produce. The clientele are a mix of students, visitors and locals visiting the market. No credit cards.
⊘ Mon–Fri noon–3
🍷 L €13, Wine €1.60
🔄

🍴 CA' DE VEN

Via Corrado Ricci 24, 48100 Ravenna
Tel 0544 30163

This 'House of Wine' (in the local dialect) is a centrally placed *enoteca* in a former hostel where Dante is reputed to have stayed. Peeling ceiling frescoes, large wooden cabinets and panelled walls create a marvellous setting. The long tables are often crowded with locals. They have a large selection of wine including local sweet varieties. The simple menu has salads, cold meats, fresh pasta and the local dish, *piadine*: a round flat bread filled and rolled up.
⊘ Tue–Sun 11–2, 6–10pm
🍷 L €20, D €40, Wine €10
🔄 Section

🍴 LA GARDELA

Via Ponte Marino 3, 48100 Ravenna
Tel 0544 217147

A bustling and friendly restaurant that's close to the main visitor attractions. Its traditional interior has a main dining area and a gallery. It has an excellent reputation as one of the best restaurants in town. They specialize in home-made pasta, such as *tortelloni della casa* with ricotta, cream, spinach, tomatoes and herbs, tagliatelle with porcini mushrooms, and ravioli stuffed with truffles. If you fancy something more substantial they also serve grilled meats, fresh fish and vegetables. The menu changes regularly. Reservations advisable
⊘ Fri–Wed noon–2.30, 7–10pm
🍷 L €20, D €30, Wine €7.50

EATING AND STAYING

🍴L'OSTE BACCO

Via Salara 20, 48100 Ravenna
Tel 0544 35363

A small, family-run *trattoria* in the middle of old Ravenna, near the main visitor attractions. A floral green-and-cream theme complements the light and simple interior. Tasty traditional Romagnolo cuisine is on the menu—good fish and *antipasti*. The wine list is also good—Oste Bacco means 'Your host is Bacchus', the ancient wine god. It is worth reserving a table.

🕐 Wed–Mon noon–2.30, 7.30–10.30pm
🍴 L €20, D €32, Wine €7
⛔

🍴AL RUSTICHELLO

Via Maggiore 21/23, 48100 Ravenna
Tel 0544 36043

Just outside the old town walls west of the town, the Rustichello has gained a reputation for both the quality of its food and the size of its

portions. The restaurant has a modern, light and elegant interior. English is spoken and the owner comes and tells you what's on the menu. Top dishes include a marvellous *cappelletti* (a type of meat-filled ravioli) with asparagus. It draws a mainly local crowd, both young and old. Reservations recommended. No credit cards.

🕐 Mon–Fri noon–2, 7–10pm, Sat 7–10pm
🍴 L €40, D €50, Wine €6
⛔

🏨ALBERGO CAPPELLO

Via IV Novembre 41, 48100 Ravenna
Tel 0544 219813
www.albergocappello.it

An elegant, small, mid-price hotel in a 15th-century palazzo in the heart of the old town near the market hall. Very stylish rooms—old frescoes, panelled ceilings, designer fur-

nishings—but they only have seven rooms, including two doubles, two junior suites, and two suites. All have television, hair-dryer, safe and adjustable air-conditioning. Some rooms are accessible for guests with disabilities. There is also an excellent restaurant attached. There is a lift, and babysitting service is available on request.

🛏 €110–€165
🚪 7 (4 non-smoking)
⛔

🏨RESIDENZIA GALLETTI ABBIOSI

Via di Roma 140, 48100 Ravenna
Tel 0544 215127

Smarter and more central than the other youth hostel in town. Housed in an 18th-century palazzo, it lies midway between the station and the middle of town. The rooms are large and simply equipped. Some of the bigger ones have fine frescoes on the ceilings. Rooms for one, two, three or more people. Lifts to upper floors. Television room.

🛏 €90
🚪 30 rooms, 70 beds
⛔

TRENTO

🏨ANDES

Piazza Europa Vigo di Fassa, 38039 Trento
Tel 0462 764575
Fax 0462 764598
www.hotelandes.com

The owners are eager to look after you at this chalet-style hotel, which provides everything that holidaymakers might want. The in-house health and beauty centre is great, the bar is inviting, there's a kids' playground and a disco for teenagers during the skiing season. The rooms are a good size with ample cupboard space; front rooms have balconies with mountain views.

🕐 Closed end Oct–30 Dec
🛏 €60–€106 excluding breakfast
🚪 31
🍴

🚗 From SS 48 take the N242 to Vigo di Fassa. Turn left in village to Funivia Catinaccio; hotel is on left

TRIESTE

🍴ANTICA TRATTORIA SUBAN

Via Comici 2, 34100 Trieste
Tel 040 54368

Eat in or outside at this wonderful old coaching inn, well

🏨VILLA MADRUZZO

Via Ponte Alto 26, Cognola, 38050 Trento
Tel 0461 986220
Fax 0461 986 361
www.villamadruzzo.it

If you don't have a car, there are regular buses up the hill from the town to this beautiful 18th-century villa set in parkland, overlooking both the town and surrounding mountains. The gardens are lovely, but the villa itself steals the show, with antique furnishings and old country house style and elegance. Bedrooms are classy and the rooms airy and well-equipped. The restaurant is excellent and good value, and the staff are professional and friendly.

🛏 €85–€95
🚪 51 (non-smoking)
⛔

🚗 Exit the A22 at Trento or Trento Nord and follow signs to Padova. Climb the hill and go through the tunnel, then turn almost immediately left towards Cognola. At the roundabout trun right to Via Ponte Alto, continue for about 100m (304ft) then take the sharp right between the walls into hotel

worth the trip out to the suburbs. The food is the best in Trieste, with all the central-European touches you'd expect. Try the *jota carsolina*, a soup filled with beans, ham and sauerkraut, or the *risotto alle erbe del Carso*—risotto with wild local herbs. Follow it up with veal simmered in wine and a thoroughly modern chocolate soufflé. Terrano is the local house special wine, a deep and intense taste.

🕐 Wed–Sun noon–3, 7–10.30; Mon 7–10.30; closed Tue
🍴 L €30, D €60, Wine €10
⛔ Section
🚪 35

🏨DUCHI D'AOSTA

Piazza Unità d'Italia 2, 34121 Trieste
Tel 040 7600011

Redolent with central-European grandeur, the Piazza Unità d'Italia is one of Europe's great squares; the Duchi d'Aosta an essential part of its architectural appeal. Inside, are wonderful furnishings, beauti-

EATING AND STAYING

ful fabrics—sedate but relaxing elegance. The staff are highly professional and provide first-class service, a great combination of old-world style and modern comforts make it Trieste's top choice.

🏷 €253–€285
🛏 55 (12 non-smoking)
♿
🚗 Follow the signs to *centro citta*; the hotel is on the main piazza facing the sea

UDINE

🍴🛏 LA' DI MORET

Viale Tricesimo 276, 33100 Udine
Tel 0432 545096
Fax 0432 545096
www.ladimoret.it

The Marini family have been in the hotel business since the 1800s, and they built this modern hotel in 1967. Outside, it is dull and functional, but the interior is surprisingly traditional and immensely comfortable, with natural stone in the public rooms and classically simple, large bedrooms. The hotel combines top-rate business facilities with charming staff and one of the region's best restaurants—if you need to exercise off your over-indulgence, they'll even provide you with a free bicycle.

🕐 Tue–Sat 12–2, 7.30–10pm, Mon 7.30–10pm, Sun 12–2
🍽 L €40, D €70, Wine €15
🏷 €100–€125
🛏 82 (15 non-smoking)
♿ 🏊 Outdoor and indoor
🚗 Exit the A23 at Udine Nord and follow signs to Tarvisio, then Udine – Cividale; the hotel is on the right at the second set of traffic lights.

VERONA

🍴 AL CARRO ARMATO

Vicolo Gatto 2/a, 37121 Verona
Tel 045 8030175
www.carroarmato.it

Delightful bar/restaurant near the Gothic church of Santa Anastasia, with its mysterious name meaning 'armoured car'. Delicious *antipasti* are served from the narrow bar or on large trestle tables in the adjoining high-ceilinged hall. The good-humoured staff occasionally burst into song. Wines are served either from the barrel or by the bottle. Card games are often played here, and there's occasional live music. Young clientele. No credit cards.

🕐 Thu–Tue 11–3, 6pm–2am, Sun 1–5, 6pm–midnight
🍽 L €20, D €50, Wine €5
♿

🍴 LA BOTTEGA DEL VINO

Via Scudo di Francia 3, 37121 Verona
Tel 045 8004535
www.bottegavini.com

A major player on the Veronese gastronomic scene for more than a hundred years, right in the old town, just off Via Mazzini. This elegant restaurant with its flamboyant interior, proves to be a winner with visitors and locals alike. It is always crowded and bustling, but the service is slick and professional. As the name suggests, they have a very good wine list with more than 1,000 labels—some are extremely expensive, such as three excellent Amarone wines, including one from the Masi vineyard. Excellent Italian cheese served with honey.

🕐 Daily 10.30–3, 6pm–midnight, Jul–Aug; Wed–Mon 10.30–3, 6pm–midnight rest of year; open til 3am on opera nights
🍽 L €60, D €100, Wine €17

🍴 CAFFÈ COLONIALE

Piazza Viviani 14/c, 37121 Verona
Tel 045 8012647

This colonial-style, central café has a relaxed feel. It appeals to a broad clientele, and the terrace is a great place for watching Verona's Carnival procession on the last Friday before Lent. You'll find a range of drinks—cocktails, wines, beers, teas, coffees and the best hot chocolate in town—as well as snacks and sandwiches.

🕐 Tue–Thu 7.45am–midnight, Fri–Sat 8am–1am, Sun 10am–midnight
🍽 L €15, D €30, Wine €13
♿ Section

🍴 OSTERIA LA PIGNA

Via Pigna 4, 37121 Verona
Tel 045 8004080
www.osteriapigna.it

Large and elegant restaurant divided into three large rooms, near the duomo. Diners are given a glass of sparkling *prosecco* while they peruse the menu. The service is excellent and attentive. A good range of wines is available, as well as other drinks. Try the duck *pappardelle* (duck with pasta strips with rippled edges),

risotto with Amarone wine or *stracotto* (beef stew) and Amarone wine.

🕐 Mon–Sat noon–3, 7–11pm; closed Aug
🍽 L €30, D €50, Wine €10
♿ ♿

🍴 TRATTORIA ALLA COLONNA

Largo Pescheria Vecchia 4, 37121 Verona
Tel 045 596718

Five minutes' walk southeast of Piazza dell'Erbe, this very popular establishment takes its name from the large column in the middle of the room. It's packed with locals, so if you haven't reserved make sure you get arrive before 9pm for dinner. Expect excellent regional cooking that is good-value for money. Top dishes include horse meat, rabbit and bigoli pasta. The wines served are from the Veneto region. There is a fixed-price menu available for €13.

🕐 Mon–Sat 12–2.30, 7.30pm–2am
🍽 L €24, D €50, Wine €9
♿ Section

🍴 LA VECETE

Via Pellicciai 32A, 37121 Verona
Tel 045 594748
www.grupporialto.it

The best bar in town for tasting a very wide selection of wines. Five minutes' walk north from Piazza Bra, it's simply decorated with an enormous array of bottles to choose from, which the bar staff seem to know intimately and they delight in offering detailed recommendations of what to drink. Wine prices are reasonable to very expensive; all can be ordered by the glass. They also have excellent food, both snacks and full meals, served at the bar or at tables. It is advisable to make a reservation during July and August.

🕐 Mon–Sat 9am–midnight; til 3am during opera season (Jul–Aug)
🍽 L €28, D €60, Wine €13
♿ Lunch only

🛏 COLOMBA D'ORO

Via Carlo Cattaneo 10, 37121 Verona
Tel 045 595300
www.colombahotel.com

A luxury hotel in the heart of Verona, close to the Arena. The building dates back to medieval times and has been a hotel since the early 19th century. The entrance hall has magnificent frescoes, and there is beautiful antique furniture in many of the rooms. The elegant guest rooms have minibars and satellite Television. The marble bathrooms all have hair-dryers and towel warmers. There is also a conference room, a breakfast room where the breakfast buffet is served and a bar. Parking is free or you can pay €18 to park in the hotel garage.

🍴 €152–€197
🛏 39 rooms, 10 suites (11 non-smoking)
♿

⊖ HOTEL DUE TORRE
Piazza Sant'Anastasia 4, 37121 Verona
Tel 045 595044
www.baglionihotels.com
This luxurious hotel occupies a 14th-century palazzo in central Verona, right next to Sant'Anastasia church, between the river and the central squares. It's spread over five floors, and the rooms all have a television, minibar, hair-dryer and safe. Both the public areas and the guest rooms are furnished magnificently, with pieces ranging from Louis XVI to Empire and Biedermeier. There is a restaurant and a bar on the premises.

🍴 €231–€495
🛏 90 (non-smoking)
♿

⊖ IL TORCOLO
Vicolo Listone 3, 37121 Verona
Tel 045 8007512
www.hoteltorcolo.it
This is a very friendly, small hotel on a quiet street, just one block away from Piazza Bra and close to the Arena. The well-proportioned rooms are

simply equipped but elegantly furnished and include a television and a refrigerator. In the summer, you can have breakfast on the terrace in front of

the hotel. There is a lift, and parking is available at €8 per day.

🍴 €90–€100 excluding breakfast
🛏 19 (non-smoking)
♿

⊖ VICTORIA
Via Adua 8, 37121 Verona
Tel 045 590566
www.hotelvictoria.it
This friendly hotel just southwest of the heart of the city. The flashy modern lobby leads into the older parts of the hotel, which contain the guest rooms. They are equipped with satellite television, phone, safe and minibar (whirlpool baths on request). The superior class rooms are magnificent. The hotel has a bar and lounge area, and a sauna and solarium. There is a laundry service available. Garage parking costs €20 per night, but advanced booking is recommended.

🍴 €190–€270
🛏 66
♿ 🍽

⊖ VILLA FRANCESCATTI YOUTH HOSTEL
Salita Fontana del Ferro 15, 37129 Verona
Tel 045 590360
www.ostellionline.org
A youth hostel in a beautiful 16th-century villa across the river from the town and a small climb up the hill. The older rooms have frescoes. The dorms are in the newer wing. This is a large, yet friendly place with more than 200 beds, so even though you cannot reserve, there is likely to be space. Staff are on hand 24 hours a day. The curfew is 11.30, but allowances are made if you have tickets for the opera. They serve good, cheap evening meals. Membership is not essential. No credit cards.

🍴 €12.50 including breakfast
🛏 223 beds

VICENZA

🍴 ANTICA TRATTORIA TRE VISI
Corso Palladio 25, 36100 Vicenza
Tel 0444 324868
www.trevisi.vicenza.com
This lovely 15th-century building has a great team of staff making this a particularly enjoyable place to eat. The food is firmly mainland

Venetian, made with top-quality seasonal ingredients, raised and grown locally. Try *porca l'Oca in pignatti con funghi*, a traditional dish of long-simmered goose with wild mushrooms, or *bigoli al radicchio di Treviso con acciughe*, the bitter-sweet long red radicchio from Treviso served with home-made pasta and anchovie—an intense and rich dish. The wine list consists of some good, mainly local, wines.

🕐 Tue–Sat 12.30–2.30, 7.30–10.30pm, Sun 12.30–2.30
🍴 L €30, D €60, Wine €12
♿ Section

⊖ CRISTINA
Corso SS Felice e Fortunato 32, 36100 Vicenza
Tel 0444 324297
Fax 0444 543656
Prosperous little Vicenza is well-used to looking after visitors and this modern, family-run hotel is ideal for an overnight stay. A stroll away from the *centro storico*, it has its own parking, a real bonus, and a good level of slightly impersonal comfort. There's plenty of parquet flooring, marble-clad walls and deep sofas in the public areas and the bedrooms are well-equipped. Ask to see your room before you confirm—some are a little on the small side.

🕐 Closed 24 Dec–2 Jan
🍴 €81–€106
🛏 33 (10 non-smoking)
♿
🚗 From the A4 follow signs to the city; you will arrive on the Corso SS Felice e Fortunato

RESTAURANT AND HOTEL PRICES
🍴 **RESTAURANTS**
The prices given are for a two-course lunch (L) and a three-course dinner (D) for two people, without drinks. The wine price is for a bottle of house wine.
⊖ **HOTELS**
The prices given are for the lowest and highest for a double room for one night including breakfast, unless otherwise stated. Note that rates can vary depending on the time of year.

EATING

Florentine cooking is Tuscan, simple food prepared with good-quality ingredients. Although on offer in every restaurant and *trattoria*, pasta is not a traditional staple, though *pici*, a local variety of thick spaghetti, is a well-known Florentine *primo*. Bread is a favourite ingredient, toasted with a drizzle of olive oil in the form of bruschetta, spread with savoury toppings and served as *crostini*. The excellent vegetable soups (*ribollita*) made the day before they are eaten, are well worth trying. Beans are another local treat, appearing in soups or served as a *contorno*, livened up with olive oil and sage. Grilled meat (*alla Fiorentina*) is popular—the first choices here are the *bistecca alla fiorentina*, a prime-quality steak slowly char-grilled over log embers, or *tagliata*, T-bone steak sliced across the grain and served with rocket and Parmesan cheese.

If you just want something light, head for a *vinaio*, a cross between a wine cellar and a snack bar. Wines to try include Chianti, Brunello and Vino Nobile di Montepulciano; Sfuso wine can be excellent, usually made from the locally favoured Sangiovese grape.

STAYING

To get a genuine feel for Florence and its treasures you should aim to stay for three to four days. It is essential to book well in advance. The heart of the city is surprisingly small, and most accommodation is within easy walking distance of the main sights. Florence is home to some of Italy's greatest hotels, with superb standards of luxury and service, but hotel prices are high, and breakfast is rarely included in the room price. More modest hotels and *pensioni* often occupy one or two floors of a much larger building and rarely have much in the way of public areas, courtyards or gardens. It's worth paying more for some extra space, quiet surroundings and air conditioning during the summer. If you are making

Florence part of a touring holiday, consider staying outside the city, possibly in Fiesole, Prato or Pistoia, and using public transport to travel into Florence. Visitors on a budget can stay in one of the clean and relatively cheap hostels. Some of the best are run by religious orders.

BOOKINGS

Branches of Florence's APT can be found at Via Manzoni 16, Via Cavour 1r and Piazza Mino 7, Fiesole. They publish complete lists of accommodation, but do not make bookings. The Consorzio Informazioni Turistiche Alberghiere (Hoteliers' Tourist Information Consortium) have offices at the train station, at the AGIP service station in Peretola on the A11 Firenze-Mare Autostrada, at the Chianti Est service station on the A1 Autostrada del Sole and at Vespucci airport. The station office will book rooms for personal callers only; the others only have lists of accommodation (www.firenze.turismo.toscana.it/).

L'ANTICO RISTORO DI CAMBI
Via Sant'Onofrio 1r, 50124 Firenze
Tel 055 217134
This eatery, in the wonderful Oltrarno district near the Ponte Vespucci and Piazza del Tiratoio, is a top lunch-time choice with the locals. The menu concentrates on fresh ingredients and largely steers

away from stodge. Try one of the excellent salads or platters, which are pilled high with fresh produce including basil, rocket (arugula), pecorino cheese, *mozzarella di bufala* (buffalo mozzarella) and cured meats.
🕐 Mon–Sat 12.30–2.30, 7.30–10.30pm

🍴 L €30, D €60, Wine €12
Ⓢ Section Ⓢ
🚌 D, 6

BALDOVINO
Via San Giuseppe 22r, 50122
Tel 055 241773
www.baldovino.com
A bustling yet relaxed *trattoria* not far from Piazza Santa Croce. It's run by a Scotsman with some famous pals from the world of entertainment, who often drop in when they're in town. Especially good for those with children, as they serve great pizzas from a wood-burning oven. The changing menu includes lots of soups, beef, various grilled meats and some inventive plates of *pastasciutta*, including *tagliatelle agli asparaghi*. The wine list will satisfy most tastes and includes many Tuscan classics.
🕐 Daily noon–2.30, 7pm–midnight, Mar–Oct; Tue–Sun noon–2.30, 7pm–midnight, rest of year
🍴 L €30, D €55, Wine €14
Ⓢ Section
🚌 C, 14

BECCOFINO
Piazza degli Scarlatti 1r, 50125 Firenze
Tel 055 290076
www.beccofino.com
This restaurant has an international following who enjoy such delights as *gnocchi al nero di seppia* (small dumplings in squid ink) and *faraona alle olive* (roast guinea-fowl with black olives). An alternative menu has lots of salads, pasta and risotto dishes. As you'd expect from an *enoteca* (Italian-style wine bar), there's lots of wine in the cellar. The 500-strong list has a superb range of Tuscan and Piemontese vintages.
🕐 Tue–Sat 7–11.30pm, Sun 12.30–3
🍴 L €50, D €95, Wine €15
Ⓢ Section Ⓢ
🚌 6, 11, 36, 37

OSTERIA DEL CAFFÈ ITALIANO
Via Isola dell Stinche 11/13r, 50122 Firenze
Tel 055 289080
www.caffeitaliano.it
The service may be slow at times, but the rustic charm and superb food make it a pleasure to linger a little longer than usual here. You can enjoy the classic Tuscan fare in the

14th-century Salviati Palace, full of wonderful antiques. Carnivores should try the *cinghiale* (wild boar) and there's an excellent choice of pasta dishes and chunky soups full of the freshest seasonal ingredients. The wine list includes lots of Chiantis and 'Super Tuscans'.

🕐 Tue–Sat noon–1am
🍽 L €40, D €100, Wine €14
🚇 Section
🚌 A

🏛 CAFFÈ RICCHI

Piazza Santo Spirito 8–9r, 50125 Firenze
Tel 055 215864
www.caffericchi.it

Oltrarno's stylish set makes up the bulk of the crowd here. Choose to eat alfresco in the gloriously leafy Piazza Santo Spirito, or opt for the clean, contemporary dining rooms. The menu is crammed with traditional Tuscan dishes like *maltagliati* pasta with scampi, and *viareggina* fish soup—all the fish is fresh. There are a lot of meat dishes as well as imaginative salads and vegetables for the less bloodthirsty.

🕐 Mon–Sat 7.30pm–2am; closed last 2 weeks Aug
🍽 D €70, Wine €15
🚇 Section
🚌 D, 11, 36, 37

🏛 CAFFÈ RIVOIRE

Piazza della Signoria 5r, 50122 Firenze
Tel 055 214412

Now a Florentine institution, the Rivoire was opened in the 1870s and is a must for the first-time visitor and chocolate connoisseur. Produces arguably the best chocolate in town, some of which is shaped into the many intriguing figures on view. Eat one of their exquisite *gelati* or sample the famous hot chocolate while seated at one of the tables in the Piazza della Signoria or Loggia dei Lanzi. It costs much more to sit down.

🕐 Tue–Sun 8am–midnight; closed for 2 weeks in Jan
🍽 Cappuccino €5, ice cream from €5.50 to eat in
🚇 Section
🚌 A, B

🏛 CAPOCACCIA

Lungarno Corsini 12–14r, 50123 Firenze
Tel 055 210751
www.capocaccia.com

This upper-crust café-bar also has branches in Geneva and Monte Carlo. It's one of the places to be seen eating a snack or meal, or indulging in a brandy. It is famed for its sumptuously filled panini and American-style brunch menu. Indulge in style in the smoke free frescoed salone or opt for the bar area overlooking the Arno. There are more than 200 different wines available,

including Brunello di Montalcino and a host of 'Super Tuscan' varieties.

🕐 Tue–Sun noon–2am, Mon noon–4pm
🍽 Filled panini €4.50–€12, smoked salmon and salad €15.50
🚇 Section
🚌 B

🏛 CARABÈ

Via Ricasoli 60r, 50121 Firenze
Tel 055 289476
www.gelatocarabe.com

This *gelateria Siciliana* sells ice cream reminiscent of the first ice dessert recipes that arrived in southern Italy from the ancient Arabic world. The more natural tastes of pistachio, fig, apricot and vanilla makes for a stimulating change. Worth trying are the refreshing *granite* (crushed ice with fruits and sometimes cream) and *sorbetti* (delicate ice crystals: sorbet). No credit cards.

🕐 Daily 10am–1am
🍽 Ice cream cone €1.70–€5.50
🚌 1, 6, 11, 14, 17, 22

🏛 DA BENVENUTO

Via della Mosca 16r, 50122 Firenze
Tel 055 214833

Lots of solid Tuscan food to choose from at this quirky establishment in Santa Croce. Walls are adorned with eclectic artworks, and the place is invariably packed with equally intriguing local characters. Among the good-value offerings is pasta with a meaty *ragù* sauce. Ask about the latest beef and pork dishes, which are seasoned with herbs and may be accompanied by crunchy vegetables and potatoes. The house red goes down very well.

🕐 Mon–Sat 12–2.30, 7–10.30pm
🍽 L €30, D €45, Wine €8
🚇
🚌 B, 23

🏛 ENOTECA PINCHIORRI

Via Ghibellina 87, 50122 Firenze
Tel 055 242777
www.enotecapinchiorri.com

This French-influenced establishment is one of Italy's best. The magical rose-scented *cortile* (courtyard) and elegant dining areas are a fitting complement to the exquisite nouvelle cuisine and unrivalled wine list. Meat-lovers will delight in the imaginative dishes of liver and pigeon. They have some sumptuous sweets and the service is impeccable. All of this does not come cheap, but the prices don't discourage the crowds, so make a reservation.

🕐 Thu–Sat 12.30–2, 7.30–10pm, Tue–Wed 7.30–10pm; closed Aug, 24–25 and 31 Dec
🍽 L €130, D €210, Wine €25
🚇 Section 🚇
🚌 A, 14

🏛 IL LATINI

Via de' Palchetti 6r, 50123 Firenze
Tel 055 210916
www.illatini.com

A traditional rustic *osteria* with large, hearty helpings of Tuscan classics that attract a loyal crowd to the long communal tables. Highlights include a traditional *zuppa di farro* (a meat, grain and vegetable soup) and the wild boar *dolceforte* stew. The *tiramisù* is outstanding, although by the time you finish its rich layers you may find it difficult to move! The Latini family produce some fine wines and delicious olive oil.

🕐 Tue–Sun 12.30–2.30, 7.30–10.30pm
🍽 L €24, D €50, Wine €10
🚇 Section
🚌 A, 6, 14, 17, 26

EATING AND STAYING

OLIVIERO

Via delle Terme 51r, 50123 Firenze
Tel 055 287643
www.ristorante-oliviero.it
Soft, fabric-filled interior, excellent service and superb Tuscan food are the main characteristics of Francesco Altomare's dinner-only eatery. Meat-lovers have a lot to choose from, including wild boar, guineafowl and rabbit. Sublime

soups, exquisite vegetables and innovative pasta creations make up the rest.

Mon–Sat 7.30pm–1am; closed Aug
D €90, Wine €17
Section
A, B, 6, 11, 36, 37

OSTERIA SANTO SPIRITO

Piazza Santo Spirito 16r, 50125 Firenze
Tel 055 2382383
A trendy *osteria* which excels in creating adventurous, mountainous salads—chunks of Parmesan and *prosciutto crudo* ham are mixed with pine nuts and various leaves such as rocket (arugula). There's a superb choice of cheeses and a decent wine list. You can also dine in the piazza, weather permitting.

Daily 12.30–11.30pm
L €20, D €60, Wine €12
D, 11, 36, 37

PERCHÈ NO!

Via dei Tavolini 19r, 50122 Firenze
Tel 055 2398969
Customers can sit down in this ice cream parlour, which is a welcome bonus. There are plenty of new tastes to discover. Try the favourite Malaga, which is dotted with rich wine grapes. It's worth asking for *due palline* (two scoops)—point at the *meringa gelata* (meringue ice cream) and wait for the waitress to ask for confirmation before exclaiming 'Perchè no!' (meaning 'Oh, why not!'). No credit cards.

Wed–Mon 11am– 12.30am, Mar–Oct; Wed–Mon 12–7.30pm, Dec–Feb; closed Nov
Ice cream cone €2
6, 17, 23

RISTORANTE PERSEUS

Piazza Mino da Fiesole 9, 50014 Firenze
Tel 055 59143
One of the best for sampling the famous *bistecca alla Fiorentina* (Florentine steak). Choose a huge chunk of beef by weight—a 1-kilo (2.2lbs) slab will feed two hungry mouths—or a thinner version cooked in balsamic vinegar. All dishes are accompanied by delicious salads, Tuscan cannellini beans and cooked vegetables. Try the *pannacotta* (set cream pudding) with forest fruits or the sublime cheesecake. They have a decent wine list and a wonderful terrace facing the Teatro Romano. This is a good place to bring children.

Daily 12.30–3, 7.30–11.30pm Jun–Sep; Wed–Mon 12.30–3, 7–11pm in winter
L €30, D €50, Wine €13
Section
7

SABATINI

Via dei Panzani 9a, 50123 Firenze
Tel 055 282802
www.ristorantesabatini.it
This elegant, wood-filled restaurant is a respected Florentine choice. The solid Tuscan dishes have international touches. Meat-eaters can devour an excellent *bistecca alla Fiorentina* (Florentine steak), while seafood enthusiasts can opt for the *risotto con scampi*. As you would expect there is an excellent wine list and the service is professional.

Tue–Sun 12.30–3, 7–11
L €80, D €140, Wine €14
Section
A, 1, 4, 7, 10, 11, 22, 23, 36, 37

TARGA BISTROT FIORENTINO

Lungarno Cristoforo Colombo 7, 50136 Firenze
Tel 055 677377
www.targabistrot.net
Enjoy international cuisine at its finest amid sleek contemporary surroundings along the River Arno. There are lots of innovative delights to savour

and some inspiring uses of typically southern European ingredients. The menu has such highlights as *tortiglioni con pesce spada* (pasta with swordfish) and a scampi risotto. There are many cheeses to try, a detailed wine list and some delectable *dolci* (desserts). Make sure you reserve a table well in advance.

Mon–Sat 12.30–2.30, 8–11pm; closed Aug and 1–8 Jan
L €40, D €90, Wine €19
Section
14, 31, 32

TRATTORIA ANTICHI CANCELLI

Via Faenza 73r, 50123 Firenze
Tel 055 218927
Hearty Tuscan food is the mainstay of this good value-trattoria in central Florence. Feast on hearty soups and bruschetta topped with sweet tomatoes and extra virgin olive oil. The menu changes according to the seasonal produce, and there's always a meat or fish dish that satisfies. Vegetarians have a variety of *contorni* (side dishes) to choose from and the classic *spaghetti al pomodoro e basilico* is tasty. The house wine is very reasonable. There is a set menu for €12.

Daily noon–2.30, 7.30–10.30pm
L €20, D €40, Wine €6
Section
4, 7, 10, 12, 13, 25, 31, 32, 33

VIVOLI

Via Isole delle Stinche 7, Firenze
Tel 055 292334
www.vivoli.it
The Vivoli family have been making ice cream since the 1930s, and this is Florence's most famous *gelateria*. If you don't mind queuing, the rewards are delicious. Lots of varieties to choose from, including an extra-creamy *mousse di amaretto*. All are served in *coppette* (cups of different sizes): Vivoli is a no-cone zone. No credit cards.

Tue–Sat 7.30am–1am, Sun 9am–1am; closed last 3 weeks in Aug and 1 week in Jan
Ice cream from €1.50
A, 14, 23

🍴ZIBIBBO

Via di Terzollina 3r, 50139 Firenze
Tel 055 433383
www.zibibbonline.com

Zibibbo's forte is fish and they have a deservedly good reputation. But there are also tasty vegetable *contorni* (side dishes) and typically Tuscan creations such as tagliatelle with duck *ragù*. A superb choice of fish includes *tagliatelle ai gamberi e zucchine* (prawns and courgettes/zucchini) and *spaghetti al pesce spada* (spaghetti with swordfish). There's plenty of *vini toscani* and *dolci* (dessert) enthusiasts have a wide choice that includes chocolate cake.

🕐 Mon–Sat 12.30–3, 7–11pm; closed Aug
🖐 L €50, D €80, Wine €14
Ⓢ Section 🔁
🚍 14c, 40

🏛ANNALENA

Via Romana 34, 50123 Firenze
Tel 055 222402
www.hotelannalena.it

This building, close to the best restaurants of Oltrarno, has housed all manner of guests over the years from tragic young widows during the Medici era right up to Mussolini's fascist police. The accommodation is simple and clean—one room has a terrace, others look out onto the gar-

den. Each room has a private bathroom, with either a shower or bath, plus television and telephone. A wonderfully peaceful place after a busy day at the art galleries.

🖐 €120–€177
ⓘ 20
Ⓢ
🚍 D, 11, 36, 37

🏛BELLETTINI

Via de' Conti 7, 50123 Firenze
Tel 055 213561
www.hotelbellettini.com

Close to the duomo, this hotel

dates from the 15th century and is one of the oldest and friendliest and best-run in the city. There are some lovely Tuscan touches in the decor, and rooms come in varying sizes, making it perfect for families. The facilities are good and include private bathroom (optional), television, telephone, internet access and safe. Breakfast should not be missed, as the owners' excellent home baking forms part of the feast.

🖐 €125–€159
ⓘ 28, 5 suites
Ⓢ
🚍 1, 4, 6, 7, 10, 11, 14, 17, 23

🏛CASCI

Via Cavour 13, 50129 Firenze
Tel 055 211686
www.hotelcasci.com

This family-run hotel, just a short stroll from the duomo, was once the home of the opera composer Rossini. There are some original 14th-century touches, but overall it has been thoroughly modernized. The present owners, the Lombardis, maintain the immaculate, functional rooms. The triple-glazed windows deaden the noisy throng outside. This is especially good for families and people with special needs. Many of the simple but comfortable rooms have a

balcony. Facilities include private bathroom, telephone, cable television and minibar.

🖐 €90–€140
ⓘ 25 (8 non-smoking)
Ⓢ
🚍 1, 6, 7, 10, 11, 17, 31, 32

🏛CRISTINA

Via della Condotta 4, 50122 Firenze
Tel 055 214484

This friendly, small hotel with largish rooms is a great place for families, as the owners go out of their way to make children and their parents feel

comfortable and at home. The rooms are clean and spacious, and four have private bathrooms. Most have high ceilings, simple dark wood furniture and views of Florentine street life. Hotel Cristina is great value for money, so you'll need to reserve well in advance. No credit cards.

🖐 €55–€88
ⓘ 9
🚍 A, 14, 23

🏛GALLERY HOTEL ART

Vicolo dell'Oro, 50123 Firenze
Tel 055 27263
www.lungarnohotels.com/gallery/

The Tuscan capital's finest for sleek modernity and stylish comfort. Public spaces have an intriguing mix of exhibits, from ethnic art to sculpture, and there's a superb library. The rooms are improved by designer furniture, subtle lighting and state-of-the-art technology. The penthouse includes linen sheets and cashmere blankets. Facilities include a chauffeured car service, laundry service, telephone, safe, room service and television. The Fusion Bar Shozan, with views over the Ponte Vecchio, serves light meals and drinks.

🖐 €315–€909 including breakfast
ⓘ 74 rooms, 9 suites (47 non-smoking)
Ⓢ
🚍 B

🏛GOLDONI

Borgo Ognissanti 8, 50123 Firenze
Tel 055 284080
www.hotelgoldoni.com

Hotel Goldoni is great value for money. Mozart was a guest here in 1700, and many others have stayed here to visit the

nearby sites of the Uffizzi, Ponte Vecchio and the green waters of the River Arno. The rooms have a smart, Parisian feel to them and are very well

EATING AND STAYING

tended, and the hotel has some excellent period pieces of furniture throughout.
Each guest room has a private bathroom, telephone, internet point, television and safe.
📖 €110–€190
🛏 20 (5 non-smoking)
💲
🚪 A, B, 6, 11, 36, 37

🏨 HELVETIA & BRISTOL
Via dei Pescioni 2, 50123 Firenze
Tel 055 287814
www.thecharminghotels.com
Once popular with English ladies on the Grand Tour, this hotel preserves the refined air of the 19th century and has provided hospitality for European royalty and eminent artistic figures such as Stravinsky and Pirandello. Each room has been carefully

designed by architects Gaetani and Ruspolito. Modern amenities such as private bathroom, hair-dryer, television, telephone, minibar and safe are carefully blended into the Old World ambience. The hotel's Bristol restaurant serves contemporary Tuscan food. Breakfast is served in the enchanting Winter Garden.
📖 €286–€517 excluding breakfast
🛏 67 (30 non-smoking)
💲
🚪 A, B, 6, 11, 22, 36, 37

🏨 JOHANNA I
Via Bonifacio Lupi 14, 50129 Firenze
Tel 055 481896
www.johanna.it
The owners of this guest house and its sister establishment, Johanna II, are making their mark on the Florence hotel scene. Knowledgeable and enthusiastic staff help to create a laid-back feel. The rooms are small but beautifully furnished, and there is a comfortable communal room with a fridge. You will get a private bathroom, coffee- and tea-making

facilities, a television and telephone.
📖 €85
🛏 11
🚪 8, 11, 12, 20

🏨 LOGGIATO DEI SERVITI
Piazza Santissima Annunziata 3, 50122 Firenze
Tel 055 289592
www.loggiatodeiservitihotel.it
This former Servite monastery, with vaulted ceilings, dark wood antiques and rich fabric, is in a charming square. The refurbished rooms are enlivened by bright curtains and throws. Many look onto Tacca's equestrian statue and the Brunelleschi-designed arcades of Piazza Santissima Annunziata. Indeed, the building's façade mirrors the architect's Ospedale degli Innocenti opposite. Rooms have a private bathroom, telephone, minibar, safe, hair-dryer and television. The breakfast room and bar look out over the Accademia gardens.
📖 €130–€205
🛏 29
💲
🚪 C, 6, 31, 32

🏨 MALASPINA
Piazza Indipendenza 24, 50129 Firenze
Tel 055 489869
www.malaspinahotel.it
Right on the beautiful Piazza

Indipendenza, the elegant Malaspina Hotel was built in the 14th century. The sound-proofed rooms are quite modern but they have kept some of their traditional touches and are spotless. All have a television, minibar, safe and telephone.
🕐 Closed 5–25 Aug
📖 €150–€195
🛏 31 (9 non-smoking)
💲
🚪 7, 10, 20, 25, 31, 32, 33

🏨 MONNA LISA
Borgo Pinti 27, 50121 Firenze
Tel 055 2479751
www.monnalisa.it
This 15th-century palazzo and former residence of the Neri family is a wonderful mix of old and contemporary design. The overall 19th-century style includes period paintings and work by the sculptor Giovanni Dupre. The reception has stuccoed walls and a striking

staircase. Many rooms have elaborate ceilings, wall hangings and antiques. Facilities include private bathroom, hair-dryer, television, telephone, minibar and safe. Perhaps the loveliest thing about this hotel is its flower-filled garden, perfect for relaxing in and sharing a 'Super Tuscan' wine.
📖 €180–€284
🛏 55
💲
🚪 14, 23

🏨 RIVOLI
Via della Scala 33, 50123 Firenze
Tel 055 27861
www.hotelrivoli.it
Close to Santa Maria Novella, the Rivoli is a beautifully renovated Franciscan monastery. The public spaces have cross vaults, arches and pillars, which recall its serene and austere past. The rooms are simple with large marble bathrooms, and some have a balcony or terrace. Services and amenities include 24-hour room service, laundry, coffee- and tea-making facilities, television, radio, telephone and trouser press. On fine days, breakfast is served on the flower-filled patio.
📖 €150–€320
🛏 69 (12 non-smoking)
💲 🏊 Outdoor heated whirlpool
🚪 A, 11, 36, 37

SAVOY

Piazza della Repubblica 7, 50123 Firenze
Tel 055 27351
www.roccofortehotel.it

This 19th-century building had a massive renovation in 2000 and is now a top boutique hotel. Parquet flooring and natural fabric carpets give it an air of comfort and luxury, while sleek furniture, cool photography and sculpture give the rooms a designer edge. The

private bathrooms have deep tubs, marble fittings and mosaics. The facilities include hair-dryer, satellite television, telephone, minibar and safe. You can enjoy a meal at L'Incontro restaurant downstairs for fine food in the company of the Florentine glitterati. End the evening with a nightcap in the handsome bar.

€264–€495 excluding breakfast
107 (64 non-smoking)
A, 6, 22

SCOTI

Via dei Tornabuoni 7, 50123 Firenze
Tel 055 292128
www.hotelscoti.com

This impressive 15th-century building stands opposite the

Palazzo Strozzi in the shopping Mecca of Via Tornabuoni. It is small with simple but light-filled bedrooms. None of the rooms have private bathrooms. The lounge area has some beautiful 18th-century frescoes

depicting an Arcadian landscape. Electric fans are available in the summe months.

€60–€85
11
A, 6, 11, 36, 37

TORRE GUELFA

Borgo Santi Apostoli 8, 50123 Firenze
Tel 055 2396338
www.hoteltorreguelfa.com/

Here you can sleep in a 13th-century tower and enjoy some

excellent views. The building was once home to the extremely wealthy Acciaiuoli family. Inside you're aware of the loftiness of the building, with high ornate ceilings giving it an airy feel. Some rooms have canopied beds and balconies. The facilities include telephone, private bathroom, minibar, safe and television. The rooftop terrace is another reason why guests return year after year, so make sure you reserve well in advance.

€150–€180
20
B, D, 11, 37

SOGGIORNO ANTICA TORRE

Piazza della Signoria 3, 50122 Firenze
Tel 055 216402
www.anticatorre.com

The Soggiorno Antica Torre is beside the Piazza della Signoria, the venue for many of the city's most notable historical events. The hotel is part of a tower that was built in the 11th century. The building has undergone extensive refurbishments and countless renovations, but the original ceilings remain intact and they are complemented by handsome parquet floors. The rooms are beautifully furnished and have a distinctly Florentine feel about them. Each one has its own private bathroom (with shower or bath), heating, hair-dryer, minibar, television and telephone.

€114–€140 excluding breakfast
6
A, B

WESTIN EXCELSIOR

Piazza Ognissanti 3, 50123 Firenze
Tel 055 264201
www.westin.com

If you like old-fashioned opulence and enjoy being gently fussed over, the Excelsior will appeal. The splendour of the reception area continues throughout the hotel, with marble-laden rooms, beautiful frescoes and numerous antiques and pieces of artwork on the walls. Many rooms have picture-postcard views from their windows of the Arno and the city. There are excellent amenities, including private bathroom, telephone, hair-dryer, television, minibar and safe. The fine Il Castello restaurant and downstairs Bar Donatello will tempt you to eat in.

€546–€790 excluding breakfast
161
Nearby gym available to residents
B, C, 9

EATING

Tuscan food is simple and straightforward, with an emphasis on local ingredients. Regional dishes include *cinghiale*, a robust wild boar casserole, *coniglio alla vernaccia*, rabbit cooked with white wine and herbs, and pheasant when in season. Southern Tuscany produces excellent *pecorino*, sheep's-milk cheese, while Siena's *panforte*, a spicy nut and fruit flat cake, and *cantuccini*, hard almond biscuits traditionally dipped into sweet Vinsanto wine, will satisfy a sweet tooth.

You will see Chianti everywhere; other local wines include Brunello from Montalcino, Montepulciano's Vino Nobile and Vernaccia, an interesting white from San Gimignano.

Umbrian cooking has much in common with Tuscan food, where quality and simplicity is again the keynote. Worth seeking out are any of the truffle-based recipes for which Umbria is renowned, while the area around Norcia is particularly noted for its wonderful range of prosciutto and salami. Mountain food, such as tiny lentils from Castelluccio and local cheese, is excellent in the east of the region. Umbria's best-known wines are the whites from Orvieto, but Montefalco produces some superb red wines. The Greccheto grape is unfailingly reliable.

STAYING

There are dozens of lovely places to stay throughout Tuscany and Umbria, Italy's top destination for foreign visitors, from 5-star opulence to *agriturismo*. Tuscany's main towns are Siena, Pisa, Lucca and Arezzo, all with a wide range of accommodation. Book ahead in summer, and remember that rooms will be reserved months in advance in Siena during the July and August Palio. If you're driving, you'll find an excellent choice in the Chianti villages, San Gimignano and the southern Tuscan hill towns. Umbria's main town is Perugia, where you should aim to stay in the *centro storico*. Like Tuscany, Umbria has a clutch of appealing small towns and villages with excellent accommodation— book ahead if you want to stay in Orvieto and Assisi during high season, but two to three days in advance should be sufficient for the towns of Todi, Gubbio, Spello and Norcia. The Lago di Trasimeno is busy on summer weekends and during July and August, and Spoleto is packed during its summer festival.

AREZZO

ⓘ BUONO & SANO

Largo 1 Maggio 23, 52100 Arezzo
Tel 0575 26405

A family run, small vegetarian and organic restaurant that is a refreshing change from all the meat-orientated Tuscan eateries. The creative chef devises meat-free versions of local dishes that attract a loyal local following. Within walking distance of the town, it's in a prime location.

🕐 Fri–Sat noon–2.30, 7.30–9.30pm, Mon–Thu noon–2.30; closed Aug
🍽 L €20, D €40, Wine €7
🅢

ⓘ LE TASTEVIN

Via de Cenci 9, 52100 Arezzo
Tel 0575 28304

Le Tastevin is buzzing with local life. One room resembles a traditional trattoria, another, with pictures of film stars, is a

jazz bar where the owner performs at weekends. There's also outside seating in summer. The restaurant claims Roberto Benigni, among other celebrities, as a regular. The food is traditional with some modern additions such as truffle and asparagus risotto. It is so popular that it is advisable to make a reservation.

🕐 Tue–Sun 12.30–2.30, 7.30pm–11.30pm
🍽 L €40, D €65, Wine €10
🅢

Grilled polenta with vegetables

🚻LA TORRE DI GNICCHE

Piaggia San Martino 8, 52100 Arezzo
Tel 0575 352035

This small bar seats just 30 people, but there is a terrace with more seating overlooking the Piazza Vasari in summer. A menu is available, but regular customers here trust the staff to decide between the snacks,

sandwiches and local main dishes, which change regularly with the seasons. They also have a good selection of cheeses made in the area and a great wine list, including the local Colli Aretini.

🕐 Thu–Tue noon–3, 6pm–1am
🍴 L €12, D €40, Wine €12
💲

ASSISI

🚻RISTORANTE MEDIO EVO

Via Arco dei Priori 4, 06081 Assisi
Tel 075 813068

This is a good option if you want to try out Umbrian delicacies. Truffles and wild boar turn up on the list of hearty local dishes. The fabulous grilled beef fillet with truffles as a main course costs €15, and the tasty home-made *strangozzi* spaghetti with tomatoes is €9.50 as a first course. Dust from the 13th-century roof covers the vast range of wines, some of which are priced up to €60 and beyond.

🕐 Thu–Tue noon–2.30, 7.30–10.30pm
🍴 L €20, D €55, Wine €10
💲

🚌 The Linea A bus runs the 3km (1.9 miles) from Assisi's rail station into Piazza Unità d'Italia every half hour

🛏FONTEBELLA

Via Fontebella 25, 06081 Assisi
Tel 075 812883
www.fontebella.com

This slightly crumbling, 16th-century palazzo can be found between the Piazza del Pool and the Basilica di San Francesco. Golden swags, old paintings and tapestries cover

the walls; and the rooms are traditionally furnished. The garden restaurant is the perfect place for dining if you don't fancy venturing farther afield.

🛏 €99–€230
🛏 46
💲

🛏SAN FRANCESCO

Via San Francesco 48, 06082 Assisi
Tel 075 812281
www.hotelsanfrancescoassisi.it

This hotel, opposite the basilica, is perfectly positioned for exploring Assisi. There are both spacious and cramped rooms in this old building so chose your room wisely, but they are

all comfortable and cheerful. The owners take great delight in making you feel welcome, and make a particular effort to ensure you start the day well fed. Don't miss the views over the rooftops from the terrace upstairs.

🛏 €110–€155
🛏 44
💲

🛏WINDSOR SAVOIA

Viale Marconi 1, 06082 Assisi
Tel 075 812210
www.hotelwindsorsavoia.it

Right by the city walls, the Windsor Savoia is slightly removed from the hubbub of the town yet within strides of the basilica. The terrace has panoramic views of the Umbrian valleys. Built at the turn of the last century, the hotel has a stylish feel and

makes much use of marble and wood. The rooms are tiled and have large windows, with many that open out onto the little balconies.

🛏 €100–€115
🛏 34 (17 non-smoking)
🚌 Take the Linea A bus to the basilica
💲

CORTONA

🛏RELAIS VILLA BALDELLI

San Pietro a Cegliolo 420, 52044 Cortona
Tel 0575 612406
www.villabaldelli.com

Dating from the 1600s, this 4-star country villa built of *pietra serena* (the local grey

stone) sits in peaceful parkland. Rooms are simple but elegant with beamed ceilings, wrought-iron beds and wooden furnishings. The shared lounge has a large, original fireplace. Facilities include a bar and wine-tasting room. Traditional breakfasts are served on the terrace in summer. Walks, horse riding and excursions can be arranged. There is also an on-site golf academy and driving range.

🛏 €200–€300
🛏 15
💲 🏊 Outdoor
🚕 Camucia, then taxi 2km
🚌 Take the Valdichiana exit on the A1 and follow signs for Cortona. At Camucia take the SS71 in the direction of Arezzo. The Villa Baldelli is on the right just after Sodo, 2km (4 miles) from Arezzo

EATING AND STAYING

GREVE (IN CHIANTI)

🅐 TRATTORIA DEL MONTAGLIARI

Via Montagliari 29, Panzano in Chianti, 50020 Firenze
Tel 0558 52014
www.montagliari.it

An idyllic wine estate, founded in 1720, 5km (7 miles) from Greve. It has a big dining room, with a beamed ceiling, checked cloths and old prints; tables outside in summer. Go for the *pappardelle al cinghiale* (wide pasta ribbons with a rich wild boar sauce), the home-made ravioli or the *faraona al vinsanto* (guinea fowl with an intense wine sauce). Wines are serious; the estate produces Chianti Classico and Riserva, grappa, Vinsanto and Amaro—you can buy them in the estate shop.

🕐 12.30–2.30, 7.30–9.30; closed Mon and Jan 7–Feb 10
🍴 L €24, D €50, Wine €7
Ⓢ Section
🚌 Take the SS222 from Firenze. The restaurant is on this road, at the 28.800km (0.6 mile) marker, 1km before Panzano

🅓 DEL CHIANTI

Piazza Matteotti 86, Greve, 50022 Firenze
Tel 0558 53763
Fax 0558 53763

Greve is a classic Chianti village and this historic hotel (parts of the building are nearly 1,000 years old) is right on the central piazza. Bedrooms are light and airy, with wrought-iron bedheads and cool white drapes, while downstairs there are terracotta floors, white walls and a mix of modern and antique furniture. The vine-shaded eating area under a pergola in the garden is a bonus.

🕐 Mar–Nov and 15 Dec–7 Jan
🛏 €90–€95
🔢 16
🅗 🅧 Outdoor
🚌 Greve is on the SS222, the old Via Chiantigiana that links Florence and Siena

LAGO TRASIMENO

🅐 ALBERGO SAURO

Isola Maggiore, 06060
Tel 075 826168

This little hotel is tucked away on the traffic-free island of Isola Maggiore, on Lake Trasimeno. Daily ferries run from Castiglione del Lago and

Passignano, but these are the only reminders of the outside world. The hotel has its own small beach and peaceful gardens, and a restaurant that serves home-style cooking and dishes made from fish caught earlier that day in the lake. The rooms are large, airy and unpretentious.

🛏 €60–€65
🔢 12
Ⓢ

LUCCA

🅐 BUCA DI SAN ANTONIO

Via della Cervia, 56100 Lucca
Tel 0583 55881

This is one of the oldest and most popular restaurants in Lucca. The à la carte menu focuses on Lucchese cuisine and changes with the season. Offerings generally include grilled and roasted meats such as filleted and stuffed oven-cooked rabbit, pork with rosemary and garlic, and

grilled beef with rocket (arugula) and parmesan. The waiters are happy to recommend something from the extensive wine list. Reservations recommended for dinner.

🕐 Tue–Sat 12.30–2.30, 7.30–11, Sun 12.30–2.30
🍴 L €50, D €80, Wine €13
Ⓢ Section

🅐 RISTORANTE GAZEBO

Via Nuova per Pisa 1952, 55050 Massa Pisana
Tel 0583 379737
www.locandalelisa.com

In the stately conservatory of the 5-star Locanda l'Elisa hotel, Il Gazebo prides itself on using local produce in its menu of classic regional dishes. Main courses like *costolette d'agnello al rosmarine con purea di patate al tartufo* (lamb with rosemary served on mashed potato with truffles) reflect the chef's aim to serve traditional

country food with a modern twist. Reservations essential.

🕐 Daily 12.30–2.30, 7.30–10pm; closed Jan
🍴 L €35, D €100, Wine €20
Ⓢ
🚌 From Pisa during the day
🚗 A11 Firenze/Pisa Lucca exit, drive towards San Giuliano Terme/Pisa.

🅗 ALBERGO SAN MARTINO

Via della Dogana 7/9, 55100 Lucca
Tel 0583 469181
www.albergosanmartino.it

This 3-star hotel in Lucca's old town is only a brief stroll from

the cathedral from which it takes its name. Bedrooms are comfortably furnished and have a television and refrigerator. An English speaker pops into the hotel at 6pm every evening to give guests a talk on what to see and do in Lucca. The talk comes with a complimentary afternoon tea or summer drinks. Parking is €10 per day and bicycle hire is also available.

🛏 €100–€120
🔢 9
🅗
🚉 300m (984ft) from the central rail station
🚗 Drive into the old city through Porta Eliza. Turn left at Via dei Fosso until you get to Corso Garibaldi where you take the first left

VILLA ROMANTICA
Via Barbantini 246, 55100 Lucca
Tel 0583 496872
www.villaromantica.it

Villa Romantica is an imposing townhouse surrounded by trees and urns filled with flowers, only a few minutes' walk from Lucca's famous walls. The rooms are brightly decorated with busy fabrics in the fashion

of the period. For a romantic trip, book into the suite with its four-poster bed, living room and terrace. There is a shuttle service to the town that runs four times an hour. You can also park here for free and rent a bicycle.

€98–€138 excluding breakfast
4 (1 junior suite, 1 suite)
Outdoor
5 minutes' walk from Lucca. At the city walls, just before the football stadium, turn right into Via dello Stadio. The hotel is at the end of the road

VILLA LA PRINCIPESSA
Via Nuova per Pisa 1616, 55050 Massa Pisana
Tel 0583 370037
www.hotelprincipessa.com

At the base of the hills surrounding Lucca, this vine-covered villa is the former home of Castruccio Castracani, lord and duke of Lucca. Castracani was famed for being the inspiration for Machiavelli's *The Prince*. Today this 4-star hotel is one of the most elegant lodgings in Tuscany. The luxurious guest rooms are decorated with

GRANARO DEL MONTE
Via Alfieri 12, Norcia, Perigia 06046
Tel 0743 816513

The Granaro del Monte was once a tithe barn for offerings to the church. Today its lovely vaulted rooms are a national monument and home to one of Umbria's best restaurants. Every local dish appears on the menu—mountain lentils from Castelluccio, pork products and hams from the town, black truffles and *funghi* from the wooded valleys. *Degustazione* menus let you sample the lot. The wine list is serious, the welcome friendly, and there's a roaring log-fire where you can watch your grilled meat cooking.

12.30–2.30, 7.30–10
L €24, D €40, Wine €10
Section

antiques and period furnishings. Facilities include a lounge, bar and restaurants. Bedrooms come equipped with telephone, satellite television and minibar.

€240–€290
42
Outdoor
Regular buses run from both Lucca and Pisa. From Pisa, there is a stop near the hotel

MONTALCINO

GRAPPOLO BLU
Via Scale di Moglio, Montalcino, 53024 Siena
Tel 0577 847150

Down some steps from the main piazza you'll find this great little restaurant, serving up real Montalcino cooking. Terracotta floors, scrubbed tables and rush-seated chairs marry happily with the white walls and beamed ceiling—true Tuscan style. Try the *zuppa di fagioli* (Tuscan bean soup) *crostini* (toasted bread with different toppings) and *stinco all'aceto balsamico* (shin of beef in balsamic vinegar)—but leave room for the delicious *crostata di limone* (lemon tart). The local wines are excellent value.

12–3, 7–10; closed Fri and mid-Jan–mid-Feb
L €30, D €40, Wine €8
Section

DEI CAPITANI
Via Lapini 6, Montalcino, 53042 Siena
Tel/Fax 0577 847227
www.deicapitani.it

Almost all the rooms in this beautifully converted late medieval building have sweeping views over the archetypal Tuscan landscape of the Val d'Orcia. The bedrooms are lofty and come in cool shades with lovely beamed ceilings and plenty of space; some are outside the main building. Family-run, the hotel prides itself on personal service. The breakfast buffet could keep you going all day, and if the private parking's full, they'll help you find a space in town.

Closed 5 Jan–15 Feb
€103
29
Outdoor
Exit the Autosole at Firenze Certosa from the north, Chiusi Chianciano from the south, and follow signs to Montalcino. On arrival follow the yellow signs to the hotel in the *centro storico*

MONTEPULCIANO

ALBERGO DUOMO
Via San Donato 14, Montepulciano, 53045 Siena
Tel/Fax 0578 757473
www.albergoduomo.it

Apart from the breakfast room, there's not much in the way of public rooms here, but the

hotel's position, right opposite the duomo at the town's highest point, and the bedrooms make up for this. Run by the same family for many years, this lovely old building has been sensitively restored in true Tuscan style, the beamed ceilings untouched, the furniture kept simple and traditional. Room sizes vary; try and get one of the huge first-floor ones at the front.

€85–€100
13
Exit the Autosole at Firenze Certosa from the north, Chiusi Chianciano from

the south and follow signs to Montepulciano. On arrival follow yellow signs to the hotel in the *centro storico* at the highest point in town

NORCIA
⊖ GROTTA AZZURRA
Via Alfieri 12, 06046 Norcia
Tel 0743 816513
The building's beautiful stuccoed walls, cavernous rooms and fabulous furnishings create surroundings that do not disregard comfort. Suits of armour preside over those eating in the impressive dining rooms, where local roast lamb is served. Most of the bedrooms are fairly simple, but the slightly pricier rooms look like film sets and are worth paying extra for.
€35–€120
46 (4 non–smoking)
Follow signs for the hotel from Spoleto

ORVIETO
ⓘ GROTTE DEL FUNARO
Via Ripa Serancia 41, 05018 Orvieto
Tel 0763 343276
Orvieto has no more stunning restaurant than the Grotte del Funaro. This giant cellar with views over the Umbrian valleys below has been open for business for more than 20 years. Several chambers with hefty

stone walls are great for groups. More than 1,000 wines are stacked up in front of the huge casks. Sliced wild boar with truffles on toast is a first course at €10. Suckling pig, roasted on an open fire, is €8.50.
Tue–Sun noon–2.30, 8–midnight
L €45, D €55, Wine €9
No smoking section
Five minutes' walk from the funicular rail station at Piazza Cahen. The funicular connects the *città alta* with Orvieto's main rail station

ⓘ RISTORANTE DELL' ANCORA
Via di Piazza del Popolo 9, 05018 Orvieto
Tel 0763 342766
This restaurant is off the beaten track near Piazza del Popolo, a square that occasionally hosts live music events in the evening. Choose between the quiet, classic front room, the outdoor terrace, a lively second dining area or the square dining room with its huge wood-fired oven. Chef's specials include salmon with rocket as a starter or devilled chicken as a main, and there is a solid range of red wines.

Daily 12.30–2.30, 7.30–10.30; closed Thu, winter
L €40, D €36, Wine €10
Section
Five minutes' walk from the funicular rail station at Piazza Cahen. The funicular connects the *città alta* with Orvieto's main rail station

ⓘ RISTORANTE IL GIGLIO D'ORO
8 Piazza del Duomo, 05018 Orvieto
Tel 0763 341903
Opposite the duomo, this is one of Orvieto's finest restaurants. Although the building is over 500 years old (formerly home to the builders of the

duomo), the interior is ultramodern and awash with fresh flowers. Meat mains such as beef with truffles are excellent, and the setting (especially the alfresco summer dining) is

unsurpassed. The huge four-course set menu is €40, and the enormous wine list is organized by region.
Thu–Tue noon–3, 7–11
L €60, D €80, Wine €10
Section
Five minutes' walk from the funicular rail station at Piazza Cahen. The funicular connects the *città alta* with Orvieto's main rail station

ⓘ RISTORANTE ZEPPELIN
28 Via Garibaldi, 05018 Orvieto
Tel 0763 341447
This fine establishment serves great food and runs Italian cookery lessons. The prices in this well-staffed restaurant

away from the busy sightseeing areas are good value considering the high quality of food served. Chianina beef with black truffles is €17, while the rabbit with fennel and herbs (an Orvietan dish) is €12. They also make their own bread and pasta on site. Popuar with the locals, it is tremendously busy at Sunday lunchtimes.
Daily 12–3, 7.30–10.30
L €45, D €55, Wine €10
Section
10 minutes' walk from the funicular rail station at Piazza Cahen. The funicular connects the *città alta* with Orvieto's main rail station

⊖ VIRGILIO
Piazza del Duomo 5, 05018 Orvieto
Tel 0763 341882
www.hotelvirgilio.com
You won't find better value in one of Orvieto's most popular areas. The sound of church bells can always be heard in this hotel, set right on the main piazza, never letting you forget you're in a small Italian town. The rooms are small but cared for, and every room has private facilities. Try to get a room with a view of the magnificent duomo. The breakfasts are simple but tasty.

Ⓧ Closed Feb

Ⓔ €52–€85

ⓘ 13

Ⓡ Funicular from railway station and then take a taxi or hop on the city-circuit bus

PERUGIA

Ⓡ CANTINONE

Via Ritorta 6, 06123 Perugia

Tel 075 5734430

A stunning restaurant in a 500-year-old dining hall with brick ceilings, stained with decades of wine residue, as this cellar was once used as a fermentation area. Several small rooms

provide private dining away from the huge main medieval chamber. Chicken in white wine and the beef with Umbrian truffles are great main courses. A wide range of cheeses and more than 50 wines are available. No credit cards.

Ⓣ Wed–Mon 12.30–2.30, 7.30–10.30pm

Ⓔ L €20, D €36, Wine €6

Ⓢ Section

Ⓑ 6, 7, 9, 11 to Piazza Italia

Ⓔ ETRUSCAN CHOCOHOTEL

Via Campo di Marte 134, 06124 Perugia

Tel 075 5837314

www.chocohotel.it

The theme of this hotel celebrates Perugia's passion for all things chocolate. The hotel restaurant presents an enlightening array of treats and recipes that mean you can eat chocolate at every course, for example, duck breast with chocolate sauce. They also recommend which wine is best to accompany these unusual dishes. As you would expect, the wonderful shop sells freshly made praline. The pretty rooms have hand-painted murals on the walls and you can relax and enjoy the views over Perugia from the swimming pool.

Ⓔ €88–€120

ⓘ 94 (4 non-smoking)

Ⓢ ⓩ Outdoor

Ⓔ 2, 13D

Ⓡ Perugia

Ⓡ Take the Preppo exit off the Perugia bypass

Ⓔ SANGALLO PALACE

Via Masi 9, 06100 Perugia

Tel 075 5730202

www.sangallo.it

This modern hotel is in Perugia's old heart. Almost all rooms have balconies, allowing guests to enjoy splendid views of the city and the hills that surround the property.

The guest rooms are a bit generic since they are geared towards business visitors, but they have every standard amenity. There is a state-of-the-art gym and an impressive indoor pool.

Ⓔ €100–€170

ⓘ 94

Ⓢ ⓩ Indoor

PIENZA

Ⓔ RELAIS IL CHIOSTRO DI PIENZA

Corso Rossellino 26, Pienza, 53026 Siena

Tel/Fax 0578 748400

www.relaisilchiostrodipienza.com

Walk through the luminous cloister of this 15th-century ex-monastery to one of southern Tuscany's most atmospheric hotels. The restoration has been beautifully done, leaving the vaulted ceilings, beams and architectural details untouched, while sensitively adding 21st-century comfort. The bedrooms are big and antique pieces enhance the public areas. A good restaurant, dreamy terraces and geraniums add to the magic, all a minute's walk from Pienza's main piazza.

Ⓣ Closed 7 Jan–15 Mar

Ⓔ €180–€220

ⓘ 37

Ⓢ ⓩ Outdoor

Ⓡ Exit the Autosole at Valdiciana from the north, Chiusi Chianciano Terme from the south, and follow signs to Pienza. The hotel is inside the town walls on the right.

PISA

Ⓡ DA BRUNO

Via Luigi Bianchi 12, 56100 Pisa

Tel 050 560818

www.pisaonline.it/trattoriadabruno

The self-proclaimed best restaurant in Pisa, Da Bruno serves traditional Pisan cuisine within walking distance of the Leaning Tower. The two dining rooms have wood-beamed

ceilings, long, elegant tables and whitewashed walls covered with photos of famous people who have dined here. The menu is made up of rustic country dishes such as *baccalà con i porri* (salt cod cooked with leeks and tomatoes) and a variety of grilled fish dishes. Booking is recommended.

Ⓣ Wed–Sun noon–3, 7–11, Mon noon–3

Ⓔ L €40, D €50, Wine €10

Ⓡ LA BUCA

Via G. Tassi 6/B, Via Santa Maria 171, 56100 Pisa

Tel 050 560660

www.labuca.org

Within walking distance of Piazza dei Miracoli and the Orto Botanico. La Buca draws the crowds with its pleasant outdoor terrace and fixed-price lunch menu, which serves Tuscan and home-made cuisine at a reasonable price. Dinner is a little more formal with à la carte menus and attentive waiters, but the dishes are nothing unusual for Pisa, with lots of pizza and pasta choices.

Ⓣ Sat–Thu noon–3, 7–11pm

Ⓔ L €20, D €35, Wine €9

Ⓢ Section

OSTERIA LA MESCITA

Via Cavalca 2, 56100 Pisa
Tel 050 544294
Family-run restaurant and *enoteca* in central Pisa which serves traditional but light Tuscan cuisine strongly influenced by local and seasonal produce. The menu changes weekly depending on what's for sale in the market, but generally includes *spaghetti al mescita* (spaghetti flavoured with pork fat), light salads of wild fennel and ricotta cheese, and fresh fruit desserts. The *enoteca* has a cellar of more

than 300 varieties of wine. The restaurant is small, but reservations aren't usually necessary.
Tue–Sun 12.30–3, 7.45–10.45pm; closed 3 weeks in Aug
L €30, D €70, Wine €12
Section
3, 5, 7

LA PERGOLETTA

Via delle Belle Torri 36, 56127 Pisa
Tel 050 542458
La Pergoletta, inside an attractive medieval tower, has a menu that combines Tuscan rustic cuisine with modern flair. Specialities include *minestra di farro* (minestrone with farro grain), *arosto dagnello* (roast lamb with rosemary and garlic) and a

fresh fish of the day. The chefs spacial is pasta stuffed with pears. Booking recommended for evening meals.
Tue–Fri and Sun 8–11.30, Sat

12.30–2.30, 8–11.30; closed 1 week in Aug
L €50, D €60, Wine €10

FRANCESCO

Via Santa Maria 129, 56126 Pisa
Tel 050 554109
www.hotelfrancesco.com
Close to the Leaning Tower and the botanical gardens, this small hotel and restaurant is in the heart of Pisa. Rooms are whitewashed, with wooden furnishings, and, in most cases, have panoramic views. Reserve early to get the one room that has a private terrace. Breakfast

is served alfresco on the hotel's main terrace. Bedrooms have a television and minibar. Facilities include a family-run pizzeria, bicycle hire and a courtesy airport shuttle.
€95–€120
13

4

RADDA IN CHIANTI

RELAIS FATTORIA VIGNALE

Via Pianigiani 8, Radda in Chianti, 53017 Siena
Tel 0577 738300
Fax 0577 738592
www.vignale.it
Fattoria Vignale started life as the manor house of a big wine estate; today, it's one of Italy's

top hotels, aimed at well-heeled foreigners. The conversion is very successful—expect traditional Tuscan architecture, well-polished

antiques, fireplaces big enough to roast an ox and huge sofas. The bedrooms, some with private terraces, are opulent and luxurious, with service to match. The vaulted wine cellars house a taverna, and there's a smarter restaurant 200m (656ft) from the main building.
Open mid-Mar–Nov and Christmas–Jan 6
€165–€235
42 (10 non-smoking)
Outdoor
From the Autosole (A1): from the north exit Firenze Certosa, take the superstrada Firenze–Siena towards Siena. Exit at S Donato (22km/14 miles) and follow signs to Radda in Chianti. From the south exit at Valdarno, take the N408 to Gaiole in Chianti. After 17km (11 miles) take the road to Radda in Chianti. The hotel is signposted (yellow signs) and is in the middle of Radda

SAN GIMIGNANO

RISTORANTE DORANDÒ

Vicolo dell'Oro 2, 53037 San Gimignano
Tel 0577 941862
www.ristorantedorando.it
This restaurant is tucked away in the heart of San Gimignano, between Piazza del Duomo and Piazza della Cisterna. Its three stone-walled dining rooms date from the 14th century. Some of the dishes on

the menu are based on recipes from the Middle Ages and Etruscan times. Meals are given a modern twist, each accompanied by an intriguing story. The home-made desserts are also delicious. It is essential to book in advance.
Daily 12.30–2.30, 7.30–9.30, Jan–Oct; Tue–Sun 12.30–2.30, 7.30–9.30, Nov–Dec; closed 6 Jan–1 Mar, 10 Dec–26 Dec
L €60, D €90, Wine €10
Section

ⓘLE TERRAZZE

Albergo la Cisterna, Piazza della
Cisterna 24, 53037 San Gimignano
Tel 0577 940328
www.hotelcisterna.it

In the Braccieri's Palace Hotel, this restaurant has amazing views over the town's striking towers and defensive walls. Although the restaurant does not have outdoor seating, one wall in the 14th-century dining room is all glass, giving the impression of alfresco dining all year round as well as providing magnificent panoramic views. Traditional Tuscan and San Gimignano cuisine and a wide selection of wines, both local and national.

🅒 Fri–Mon 12.30–2.30, 7.30–9.30pm, Wed–Thu 7.30–9.30pm; closed Jan–Feb
🍴 L €28, D €56, Wine €10
🅢 Section 🅢

🅤L'ANTICO POZZO

Via San Matteo 87, 53037 San
Gimignano
Tel 0577 942014
www.anticopozzo.com

This is a superbly restored 15th-century, 3-star townhouse hotel in the middle of San Gimignano. The building sits on a cobbled street near the Piazza della Cisterna. The interior is medieval in

character and contains a well-preserved lobby with a high, vaulted ceiling. There's an atmospheric bar in the brick cellar and a first-floor garden terrace. Rooms have satellite

television, minibar and safe. Guests get a discount when parking in lot 3.

🅒 Closed Dec–mid-Jan
🍴 €130–€150
ⓘ 18
🅢
🚆 From Florence, Siena, Volterra
🚆 Poggibonsi then take a bus to San Gimignano
🚗 Take the Poggibonsi Nord exit of the Firenze/Siena highway and follow signs to San Gimignano

🅗HOTEL RELAIS SANTA CHIARA

Via Matteotti 15, 53037 San Gimignano
Tel 0577 940701
www.rsc.it

A short walk from the medieval hill town of San Gimignano, the 4-star Relais Santa Chiara combines

contemporary architecture with superb views. To ensure the best outlook, request a room with a balcony when you make your reservation. The hotel has no restaurant, but a generous breakfast is served. There is also a cocktail bar and meeting room on site. The rooms have satellite television and a minibar.

🍴 €140–€200
ⓘ 41
🅢 🚗 Outdoor
🚗 On arrival at San Gimignano turn left at the roundabout in the direction of Volterra, then take the next right. The hotel is 450m (1500ft) south of Porta San Giovanni, outside the city walls

SIENA

ⓘAL MARSILI

Via del Castoro 3, 33100 Siena
Tel 0577 47154
www.ristorantealmarsili.it

This restaurant in Siena's old town occupies a medieval building dating from the 14th century and is furnished with traditional heavy wood. There's a large main dining room and smaller brick niches with banqueting tables for larger

parties. The wine bar is in a cellar carved out of rock below the Marsili Palace. Classical Tuscan cuisine is on the menu, including *gnocchetti* (little potato dumplings) with duck,

homemade *crespelle* (crêpes) and vegetarian options.

🅒 Tue–Sun 12.30–2.30, 7.30–9.30
🍴 L €45, D €80, Wine €10
🅢 Section

🅗GRAND HOTEL CONTINENTAL

Via Banchi di Sopra 85, 53100 Siena
Tel 0577 56011
www.ghcs.it

This luxurious hotel in a former aristocratic home is a part of Siena's cultural heritage. It has been faithfully restored to its former glory

right down to the magnificent frescoes, a wall painting of St. Christopher dating from the 15th century, and the ornamental motifs from the 19th century. A covered courtyard has been coverted into a winter garden. Full leisure facilities are available at the nearby Park Hotel via a courtesy bus service.

🍴 €394–€730
🅢
ⓘ 51 (20 non-smoking)
🚆 3, 9, 10, 5 from Florence to La Lizza

EATING AND STAYING

MINERVA

Via Garibaldi 72, 53100 Siena
Tel 0577 284474
www.albergominerva.it
A 10-minute walk from Piazza del Campo and the rail station,

this 3-star hotel has good views over the city and hills beyond. Good value (especially for single visitors with single rooms from €68), with modern, fully equipped bedrooms.

💶 €80–€122
🛏 59 (15 non-smoking)
♿
🚍 3, 4, 7, 8, 10, 17, 77

SANGALLO PARK HOTEL

Strada di Vico Alto 2, 53100 Siena
Tel 0577 334149
www.sangalloparkhotel.it
This hotel is just outside the town walls, on the Vico Alto

Hill. It has all modern amenities, but lacks the character of the hotels in the heart of town. Despite this, the rooms at the front of the building and the restaurant where breakfast is served have panoramic views and its quiet setting and relaxing gardens are in its favour.

💶 €80–€140
🛏 50
♿ 🏊 Outdoor
🚍 7, 77, 15
🚗 Close to motorway, from centre follow signs for hospital Le Scotte and turn left just before entrance, the hotel is on the left. 1.5km (1mile) from centre

SPELLO

PALAZZO BOCCI

Via Cavour 17, Spello, 06038 Perugia
Tel 0742 301021
Fax 0742 301464
www.emmeti.it/pbocci.it
Built in the 18th century and renovated in the 1990s, this romantic hotel is set in the heart of one of Umbria's prettiest towns. You'll find high frescoed ceilings, public rooms with deep sofas and terracotta floors scattered with Persian rugs, a pretty breakfast room and terraces with views over the plain below. The bedrooms are all different and spacious, with luxury fabrics, huge beds and state-of-the-art bathrooms. The staff are charming, efficient and multi-lingual.

💶 €130–€150
🛏 23
♿
🚉 Spello old town is a short walk from the rail station
🚗 Exit the Autosole (A1) from the north at Valdichiana, from the south at Orte, and follow signs to Spello. Follow the signs to *centro storico* and then the yellow hotel signs. The hotel is on left up main street

SPOLETO

PALAZZO DRAGONI

Via Del Duomo 16, 06049 Spoleto
Tel 0743 222220
www.palazzodragoni.it
Next to the cathedral, this 14th-century building was the home of the Dragoni family, who more than contributed to the prosperity of Spoleto. Now owned by the local bakers, the Diotallevi family, it has kept much of its original charm with the added bonus of modern facilities and the best breakfast pastries in town. The rooms are all different, but each is comfortable and well-tended. The dining area has wonderful views of the city.

💶 €119–€145
🛏 15 (3 non-smoking)
♿
🚉 CA from station

TODI

UMBRIA

Via S Bonaventura 13, Todi, 06059 Perugia
Tel 075 8942737
This family-run restaurant has a huge open fire in winter. They also have a terrace for dining in the summer. The menu consists of traditional Umbrian recipes, authentically prepared. You can eat truffles year-round—try the classic *tagliatelle al tartufo*, grated black truffles on egg pasta, or sample *funghi porcini* (ceps), cooked with garlic and oil, in autumn. Start with the delicate *zuppa di farro*, a soup made from the ancient spelt grain, and follow it up with plainly grilled meat and piquant salad, accompanied by one of the Umbrian wines.

🕐 Wed–Mon 2.30–2.30, 7.30–10.30
🍴 L €40, D €80, Wine €12

FONTE CESIA

Via L Leony 3, Todi, 06059 Perugia
Tel 0758 943737
Fax 0758 944677
www.fontecesia.it
The Fonte Cesia was originally an 18th-century palazzo, complete with private

chapel—today, it's a top-class luxury hotel with 21st-century facilities. Bar, breakfast room and lounge all retain their brick vaulting, the perfect setting for squishy sofas, soft lighting and antique furnishings. The bedrooms are decorated with heavy brocades and have ultra-comfortable beds and marble bathrooms. The staff are friendly, they serve an excellent breakfast, and there's a, smart, expensive restaurant on the premises. Free parking.

💶 €130–€152
🛏 32 bedrooms, 5 suites
♿
🚉 Ponte Rio (Terni/Perugia line)
🚍 Route C
🚗 Exit the Autosole at Orvieto and take the SS448 to Todi. Follow the yellow signs to the hotel in *centro storico*

EATING

Roman cuisine has a very distinct style based on gutsy down-to-earth foods, with more than a touch of Jewish flavour. Dishes are strong in taste—try *spaghetti aglio e olio* (garlic and oil), or *alla carbonara* (with pancetta cubes, cheese and beaten eggs). Romans are particularly fond of offal in all its guises, and you'll see *lingua* (tongue), *milza* (spleen), *rognone* (kidneys) and *trippa* (tripe) on the menu. If that's a bit daunting, other local dishes include *abbacchio*, meltingly tender milk-fed lamb, and the delicious *saltimbocca alla romana*, thin veal slices wrapped in prosciutto and seasoned with sage. Artichokes (*carciofi*) are deep-fried *alla giudea*, Jewish style, peas are tossed through pasta with delicate pasta sauces and you can try tender courgette flowers, stuffed with mozzarella, dipped in light batter and fried until crisp. Local wines include Frascati from the Castelli Romani and Est! Est! Est! from Montefiascone—it gets its name from the words Est! Est! Est! (Here it is! Here it is! Here it is!) that were scribbled on an *enoteca* door by a medieval papal envoy, sent to find the best wine shop in the town.

STAYING

Rome's busiest months are from Easter to the end of October, but, for peace of mind and better choice, it's worth booking in advance whenever you visit the capital. There's a good range of accommodation in the *centro storico*, Rome's tightly packed heart, west of the Via del Corso. From here, there's plenty to see within walking distance, with the bonus of a wide choice of bars and restaurants. Heading farther east, classy hotels are clustered around the Piazza di Spagna and towards the Via Vittorio Veneto, with plenty of mid-range options to the southwest between the Quirinale and the Forum. You could also consider staying across the River Tiber in the pleasant district of Prati, near the Vatican and St.

Peter's, or check in somewhere in the vibrant Trastevere area. Budget hotels are mainly found near the Stazione Termini; pick carefully here—some are distinctly unappealing. If money's tight, consider a stay at one of the well-appointed convents run by the religious orders.

BOOKINGS

Rome's APT offices will not book accommodation for you, but they do have lists of hotels. The main office is five minutes' walk from Stazione Termini at Via Parigi 5 (Mon–Fri 8.15–7.15, Sat 8.15–1.45, tel 06 48899253, www.romaturismo.com or www.provincia.roma.it).

🍴 ALBERTO CIARLA

Piazza San Cosimato 40, 00153 Roma
Tel 06 5818668
www.albertociarla.com
You will find this internationally reputed fish restaurant on

the market piazza of San Cosimato in the district of Trastevere. It is currently undergoing a transformation from its rather retro and formal red-and-black mirrored interior into something more minimalist in style, but the innovative menu and supreme skills of master chef Alberto Ciarla remain. Bean soup with seafood and lentils from Ponza with lobster are just a coupple of the highlights. There are six different tasting menus available and they have a vast wine cellar.
🕐 Mon–Sat 8.30pm–midnight
🍷 D €120, Wine €20
🔲 Section
🏠 H to Piazza Santa Maria in Trastevere
🚋 Tram 3, 8

🍴 ANTONIO AL PANTHEON

Via dei Pastini 12, 00186 Roma
Tel 06 6790798
A family-run restaurant in a pedestrian street near the Pantheon. You can be sure of

good food and a warm welcome. The large, brick-vaulted room has 1960s paintings on the walls. Food is quintessentially Roman and the clientele reassuringly local. Try the fresh fettuccine with creamy walnut sauce and for a main course the calves' liver cooked in chilli, olive oil and wine. The portions are very generous and the service is outstanding.
🕐 Mon–Sat noon–3, 7–11; closed 2 weeks in Aug
🍷 L €20, D €50, Wine €8
🚌 30, 40, 46, 63, 116,

🍴 AL BRIC

Via del Pellegrino 51, 00186 Roma
Tel 06 6879533
This is a very stylish *osteria* and wine bar. There are many small tables in the large room overlooking Via del Pellegrino, near Campo dei Fiori. The wine list is huge, with more than a thousand labels to choose from, while the menu has a wide selection of creative dishes matched perfectly with the wine suggestions. Try spaghetti with anchovies and pecorino or pears with Gorgonzola cheese. Among the home-made desserts, don't miss the strudel with cinnamon ice cream. The bread is home-made, too.
🕐 Daily 7.30–11.30pm, May–Oct; Tue–Sun 7.30–11.30pm, rest of year
🍷 D €80, Wine €8
🚌 64, 87, 492 to Largo Argentina
🚋 Tram 8

BAIRES

Corso Rinascimento 1, 00186 Roma
Tel 06 6861293
www.baires.it

Vibrant walls and floors and
the sounds of the tango, create
a South American mood just

behind Piazza Navona.
Argentinian grilled meat served
with various sauces is the obvious dish of choice. First
courses include Argentinian-
style marinated chicken (*pollo
all'escabeche*) and there's a
choice of salads and soups.
The wine list similarly focuses
on Argentinian varieties. The
house red and white are
both organic.

🕐 Daily 12–3.30, 7–midnight
🍽 L €40, D €60, Wine €12
🚌 87, 116, 492

IL BOOM

Via dei Fienaroli 30a, 00153 Roma
Tel 06 5897196
www.ilboom.it

This restaurant is dedicated to
the Italian 1960s, with retro-
style chairs, an original jukebox
and photos of La Dolce Vita
celebrities hanging on the
walls. The *granmisto* has a
selection of different first
courses, from fried vegetables
to creative *bruschette* (toasted
bread). Sardines with rocket
(arugula) and ricotta is the
chefs special. The wine list
focuses on southern Italy.
Passiti and Malvasie complement the homemade desserts.

🕐 Mon–Sat 7.30–midnight
🍽 D €50, Wine €8.50
Ⓢ Section
🚌 H, 44, 780
🚋 Tram 3, 8

I BUONI AMICI

Via Aleardo Aleardi 4–6–8, 00185 Roma
Tel 06 70491993

One of the best-value restaurants in Rome, with Richard
Gere and Sly Stallone as customers. Tables with traditional
red-and-white chequered

tablecloths are stacked with an
array of delicious antipasti
including aubergine (egg-
plant), courgette (zucchini),
sweet peppers, spinach and
squid salad. Try the fresh pasta
with lobster and chargrilled
fish to follow, or the roast
lamb. Leave room for the
home-made *tiramisù* and *pannacotta*. The Cannonau red
from Sardinia is a steal at only
€8 a bottle.

🕐 Mon–Sat 12.30–3, 7.30–11pm
🍽 L €24, D €45, Wine €4
Ⓜ Manzoni
🚌 16, 81, 87, 117, 714

CAFÉ CAFÉ

Via de' SS Quattro 44, 00184 Roma
Tel 06 7008743

Escape the tourist traps encircling the Colosseum and relax
in bohemian elegance at Café
Café. The Swedish owner
serves up coffee, cakes, fresh
juice, home-made ice cream
and light Italian fare. Expect
bright walls and soft jazz. The
tiny establishment fills up
quickly for Sunday brunch, a
€12 buffet of crunchy salads,
bruschette, cheese and prosciutto. This restaurant comes
highly recommended for vegetarians, vegans and single
visitors, who will not feel
uncomfortable sitting on there
own with the generous pile of
newspapers for company.

🕐 Tue–Sun 10am–2am; closed Aug
🍽 L €16, D €15, Wine €12.50
🚌 3, 60, 75, 87, 117
Ⓜ Colosseo

ANTICO CAFFÉ GRECO

Via dei Condotti 86, Roma
Tel 06 6791700

This famous old café was
founded in 1767 by a Greek,
hence the name. It has always
been popular with the rich and
famous, and English poets
John Keats, George Byron and
German poet and scientist
Johann von Goethe have all
sought refreshment here. Look
out for the pictures of some of
the café's well-known past
customers in the back room.

🕐 Daily 8–8
🍽 Table service: coffee €4.75,
capuccino €5.20, cake €6.20
🚌 119 to Piazza di Spagna, or 52, 53,
58, 61, 71, 85, 160 to Piazza San
Silvestro
Ⓜ Spagna

CUL DE SAC

Piazza Pasquino 73, 00186 Roma
Tel 06 68801094

Very close to Piazza Navona,
this was originally just a wine
bar, but Cul de Sac gradually
built a reputation for its food

as well, particularly its pâtés.
Try the sweet and sour wild
boar pâté and the veal and
Tabasco pâté (€8). The interior
is reminiscent of a 1950s train,
furnished in white wood. There
are thirty-five wines available
by the glass and more than
1,400 wines in stock.

🕐 Daily noon–4, 7pm–12.30am
🍽 L €25, D €37, Wine €8
🚌 46, 62, 64, 87, 116, 492

DA BAFFETTO

Via del Governo Vecchio 114, 00186
Roma
Tel 06 6861617

Eat early or prepare to queue
like a Roman, joining the
messy, exuberant mob outside
one of the capital's best pizzerias. Sixties radicals
popularized Da Baffetto—now

the whole world vies for a seat
at this straightforward establishment. Don't miss the
savoury *bruschetta al
pomodoro* (toasted bread
topped with tomato, basil and
olive oil). Be prepared for
more genial jostling for the
outdoor tables. No credit
cards.

🕐 Daily 6.30pm–1 am
🍽 D €30, Wine €5
🚌 46, 62, 64, 87, 116, 492

🟦DA VITTORIO

Via di San Cosimato 14, 00153
Tel 06 5800353

The Neapolitan pizzas served here are endearingly heart-shaped and incredibly tasty. Start with the mixed antipasti and unadorned oil-drenched pizza base, called *pizza bianca*. Many dishes offer the latter sprinkled only with mozzarella, but Vittorio also indulge customers craving sauce, with the festive tangle of rocket (arugula) and cherry tomatoes on their pizza margherita. Reservations are crucial, as the tiny, blue-lit nook fills up quickly. Look for Sophia Loren among the celebrity photos on the walls. Diners and American Express credit cards only.

🕐 Mon–Sat 7. 30pm–midnight
🖐 D €20, Wine €4
🚌 H, 63, 75

🟦L'EAU VIVE

Via Monterone 85, 00186 Roma
Tel 06 68802101, 06 68801095

This restaurant is run by an international order of nuns in a Renaissance building with frescoed vaulted ceilings. The cuisine is mainly French in origin. Classical music plays in the background. The wine list is excellent. Profits from the restaurant help the nuns raise funds for Third World missions. You are welcome to join the sisters for evening prayer at 10pm—an optional extra.

🕐 Mon–Sat 12.30–4, 7.30–11pm; closed Aug
🖐 L €50, D €80, Wine €6
🚇
🚌 87, 492
🚊 Tram 8

🟦F.I.S.H.

Via dei Serpenti 16, 00184 Roma
Tel 06 47824962
www.f-i-s-h.it

An Australian-inspired sushi restaurant that has echoes of Sydney harbour. Try an aperitif with oysters in the bar, then

head into the restaurant, with a view of the kitchen. Oakwood alternates with glass and iron chairs and tables. Select from three very contrasting menus: Mediterranean, Oriental and Antipodean. Finish with the crème brulée with coconut and dates or a sashimi of exotic fruits.

🕐 Tue–Sun 1–3, 8pm–2am; closed 10 Aug–2 Sep
🖐 L €70, D €80, Wine €12
🚇 Section
🚇 Cavour or Colosseo
🚌 117

🟦GELATERIA DELLA PALMA

Via della Maddalena 20, 00186 Roma
Tel 06 68806752

Close to the Pantheon, this ice-cream shop has a great number of varieties to choose from, including 20 different kinds of chocolate. There are also mousses and ice cream with meringues on sale. If you prefer fruit, the raspberry ice-cream is unforgettable. There are two wooden benches

inside, though the best idea is take a stroll down to Piazza della Rotonda in front of the Pantheon and eat your ice-cream there, as it gets extremely crowded. No credit cards.

🕐 Daily 8am–2am
🍦 Ice creams from €2
🚇
🚌 64, 87, 492
🚊 Tram 8

🟦IL GURU

Via Cimarra 456, 00184 Roma
Tel 06 4744110

Craving a curry? Excellent Indian food can be found in the heart of Rione Monti, near the Colosseum. Every detail of the ethnic interior is designed to recreate a little corner of India. You can order tandooris and curries of varying strengths or choose from one of three fixed-price menus—vegetarian

(€15), meat (€18) or fish (€19)—or order à la carte. Traditional desserts are available along with Indian beer and the staff are very welcoming.

🕐 Daily 7.30pm–1am
🖐 D €40, Wine €6
🚇
🚇 Cavour
🚌 68

🟦IL MARGUTTA

Via Margutta 118, 00187 Roma
Tel 06 32650577
www.ilmargutta.it

This is the only real vegetarian restaurant in the city, a large,

futuristic space with traditional touches. Art is exhibited on the walls. They have a lunch buffet, but it is more intimate in the evening. There are more than 40 vegetarian dishes and 120 wines to choose from, all at reasonable prices. They have a very good dessert wine list.

🕐 Daily 12.30–3.30, 7.30–11pm; closed 2 weeks in Aug
🖐 L €15–€25, D €60, Wine €15
🚇 Section
🚇 Flaminio or Spagna
🚌 116, 117

🟦PIERLUIGI

Piazza de' Ricci 144, 00186 Roma
Tel 06 6861302
www.pierluigi.it

This excellent fish restaurant is reasonably priced considering its quality and setting—on the edge of a piazza, with plenty of tables outside. Inside, the spotlights pick out the cool

terracotta floors, brick arches and chunky medieval beams. The scampi risotto is fantastically smooth and tasty, as is the *carpaccio* of tuna or swordfish. The fresh fish of the day are displayed behind a glass cabinet. A carafe of house wine is €7 and you can ask to see the wine cellar.

Tue–Sun noon–3, 7.30pm–midnight
L €42, D €80, Wine €14
46, 62, 64, 87, 116, 492

PIZZARÉ
Via Lucullo 20, 00187 Roma
Tel 06 42013075
www.pizza-re.it
This restaurant is in a Liberty-style building, surrounded by palm trees, just a short walk from Via Veneto. They serve the best-loved pizzeria in the heart of Rome. Try the real Neapolitan pizza with buffalo mozzarella, which arrives daily from Battipaglia. Try *ripieno fritto*, a folded and fried pizza with tomato, mozzarella, ham and ricotta filling, or *pizzare*, with tomato sauce, fresh Sicilian cherry tomatoes and buffalo mozzarella. Round off your meal with a traditional home-made Neapolitan cake. Make a reservation to avoid disappointment. Lunch specials start from €8.

Daily 12.30–2.30, 7.30pm–midnight
L €15, D €20, Wine €6
Section
Barberini

ROOF GARDEN 'LES ETOILES'
Via dei Bastioni 1, 00193 Roma
Tel 06 6873233
www.atlantehotels.com
For unparalleled views of St. Peter's and food to match, this roof terrace restaurant is a must. High-backed upholstered dining chairs and candlelit tables complement the sumptuous Mediterranean cuisine, including a raw tuna and tomato pasta and château

filet with foie gras and sliced truffle. They have an imaginative wine list that includes one of Umbria's best-kept secrets, the red Sagrantino di Montefalco.

Daily 12.30–2.30, 7.30–10pm
L €60, D €145, Wine €15
Ottaviano
70, 492

SORA LELLA
Via di Ponte Quattro Capi 16, 00153 Roma
Tel 06 6861601
This family-run restaurant was established in 1943 by the sister of the famed actor Aldo Fabrizi. Sitting on Isola Tiberina, near Trastevere, it is

possibly one of the most unusual locations to eat in the city. Here you will find Roman cuisine at its best with a view of the Tiber, if you're lucky enough to sit near the window. All the typical dishes, from oxtail with cinnamon, cloves, raisins and pine nuts to some memorable *carciofi alla Giudia* (fried artichokes). Reservations recommended.

Mon–Sat 12.30–2.30, 8–11pm; closed Aug
L €40, D €100, Wine €13
23
Tram 8

T-BONE STATION
Via Crispi 29/31, 00186 Roma
Tel 06 6787650
The trendiest steakhouse in

Rome, between Piazza di Spagna and Piazza Barberini. Black-and-white movie stills and hi-tech design liven up the place. Steaks dominate the menu, but the salads are huge and appetizing too, especially the fresh crispy spinach and the classic chicken Caesar with Parmesan topping. They also have some excellent cocktails.

Daily 12.30–3, 7.30pm–1.30am; closed 1 week mid-Aug
L €20, D €60, Wine €12
Barberini
52, 53, 61, 62, 63, 80, 95, 16, 119, 175, 492, 590

ALIMANDI
Via Tunesi 8, 00192 Roma
Tel 06 39723948
www.alimandi.org
This is a superior 3-star, family-run hotel that is very good value for money. Close to the Vatican Museum and totally refurbished, the 19th-century building has kept some original features, including elegant Venetian stucco work. Rooms are spacious with modern furnishings and pastel hues. All

have satellite and pay television, roomy bathrooms with hair-dryer, and internet connection. They cater very well for visitors with disabilities. The continental buffet breakfast is served on the roof terrace or in the dining room. They provide a free airport shuttle and garage parking is available.

Closed 10 Jan–10 Feb
€130–€150
35
Cipro-Musei Vaticani or Ottariano
81, 95, 492

ANNE AND MARY
Via Cavour 325, 00184 Roma
Tel 06 69941187
www.anne-mary.com
This welcoming bed-and-breakfast occupies an elegant

SPECIAL
⊜LANCELOT

Via Capo D'Africa 47, 00184 Roma
Tel 06 70450615/6
www.lancelothotel.com

Don't let the high rise appearance of this hotel put you off this welcoming, family-run hotel just above the Colosseum. The entrance hall and dining room have period furniture and Murano glass chandeliers. There is a bar, library and a delightful courtyard. The rooms are spacious

and most have wooden floors and pastel walls. All the rooms have bathrooms with a shower, a safe and satellite television. Some of the guest rooms have terraces or you can enjoy a glass of wine on the roof terrace. Continental breakfast.

🖐 €145
ⓘ 60
🅢
🅠 Colosseo, San Giovanni
🚌 81, 85, 87, 117; tram 3

19th-century building near the Colosseum. Rooms are simple but they are dramatically appointed, with clean lines and swooping curtains. Each has a small private bathroom with an enclosed shower. Via Cavour is a large, somewhat frantic road, but the proximity of this hotel to the major sights means it is worth putting up with the muted noise.

🖐 €100–€125
ⓘ 6 (non-smoking)
🅢
🅠 Cavour, Colosseo
🚌 75, 81, 85, 87, 116, 117

⊜ATLANTE STAR

Via G Vitelleschi 34, 00193 Roma
Tel 06 6873233
www.atlantehotels.com

Nestled between the Vatican City and the Castel Sant'Angelo, this establishment exudes class and nobility, with richly upholstered sofas, heavy drapes, stuccoed ceilings and plush carpets in gold, red and blue. The guest rooms are equally lush and spacious. Half of them have whirlpool baths. There is a bar and renowned

gourmet restaurant and you can enjoy views of the Basilica di San Marco over the American buffet breakfast. The hotel provide a free airport shuttle service.

🖐 €170–€299; children under 12 free
ⓘ 80 (15 non-smoking)
🅢
🖥 32, 81, 492
🅠 Ottaviano–San Pietro

⊜CAPO D'AFRICA

Via Capo d'Africa 54, 00184 Roma
Tel 06 772801
www.hotelcapodafrica.com

This is a handsome 19th-century building close to the Colosseum in a trendy district. The hotel is a fusion of contemporary and classic design with Japanese touches. The rooms are a joy to behold, with warm ochre and saffron shades and perfectly fitted bathrooms in marble and wood. The breakfast room on the roof looks out over the Collosseo. There's a large,

well-equipped gym and a solarium. The hotel is accessible for guests with disabilities. There is one non-smoking floor. American buffet breakfast.

🖐 €265–€280
ⓘ 65 (20 non-smoking)
🅢 🍽
🅠 Colosseo, San Giovanni
🚌 81, 85, 87, 117
🚋 Tram 3

⊜GENIO

Via G Zanardelli 28, 00186 Roma
Tel 06 6832191/6833781
www.LeonardiHotels.com

This is a hotel with a nice touch of the Old World about it. Antique furniture and rich red carpets throughout give it a regal air. The high-ceilinged rooms are a good-size, with embroidered armchairs and marble-fitted bathrooms. The bar and roof terrace have fine

views of the Basilica di San Marco and Castel Sant'Angelo. It is very convenient for the Renaissance quarter of Rome and just seconds away from Piazza Navona. A free airport shuttle is available.

🖐 €200–€232
ⓘ 60
🅢
🖥 70, 81, 87,116, 492

⊜HOTEL DE RUSSIE

Via del Babuino 9, 00187 Roma
Tel 06 328881
www.roccofortehotels.com

In the heart of the city amidst all the top designer shops, this

EATING AND STAYING

is one of the top hotels in Rome. The Bonaparte brothers lived and died here. It's a unique blend of contemporary and classic styles. The guest rooms have high ceilings and are well furnished. The bathrooms are a work of art with all the amenities. If that's not enough there is a spa with a hydropool, sauna, Turkish baths and beauty treatments. The first-class restaurant is elegant and, when open onto the gardens, one of the most romantic spots in Rome. Buffet breakfast €25.

🛏 €572–€798 excluding breakfast
🛌 129 (37 non-smoking)
♿ 🐕
🚇 Flaminio
🚌 117

HOTEL D'INGHILTERRA
Via Bocca di Leone 14, 00187 Roma
Tel 06 69981
The wealthy Torlonia family built this palazzo, now a sumptuous hotel near the boutique-lined Via Condotti. The exterior has an imposing golden façade, supported by arches. A black-and-white spotted carpet runs through the lobby, punctuated by delicate antiques and plump red sofas. The guest rooms are less dramatic but pleasant, with thick carpeting, carved bed frames and carefully chosen paintings and prints. Round-the-clock room service. Breakfast €25.

🛏 €325–€445 excluding breakfast
🛌 98 (20 non-smoking)
♿
🚇 Piazza di Spagna

INTERNAZIONALE
Via Sistina 79, 00187 Roma
Tel 06 69941823
www.hotelinternazionale.com
Wisteria winds up the front of this palazzo, which was as a convent in the 16th and 17th centuries. The breakfast lounge is swathed in soothing pastel shades of blue and mauve. The scheme continues throughout the hotel, from the cupids in the cupola to the moiré wall coverings in the bedrooms.

🛏 €212–€235
🛌 42
♿
🚇 Piazza di Spagna
🚌 62

ITALIA
Via Venezia 18, 00184 Roma
Tel 06 4870919
www.hotelitaliaroma.com
This inexpensive, family run hotel is very central and just off

the second-largest shopping street in town. The reception is on the first floor. The 19th-century building was refurbished simply in 2002. The rooms are functional with television, minibar, air-conditioning (€7.75 extra per day), bathroom and hair-dryer. The hotel has a bar and a safe at the reception. Continental buffet breakfast.

🛏 €75–€114
🛌 32 (15 non-smoking)
🛁 15 rooms (€8 extra)
🚇 Repubblica
🚌 64

LOCARNO
Via della Penna 22, 00186 Roma
Tel 06 3610841
www.hotellocarno.com
Artists and intellectuals such as Umberto Eco, author of *The Name of the Rose*, favour this art deco refuge on a sleepy street near the Piazza del Popolo. The 1925 building still has some original features, including a cast-iron elevator. The decorating is delicate and deft, using period lamps, furniture and fabrics. Each room is different. Free use of the business facilities, and vintage bicycles.

🛏 €190–€310
🛌 66 (6 non-smoking)
♿
🚇 Flaminio
🚌 117

LORD BYRON
Via Giuseppe de Notaris 5, 00197 Roma
Tel 06 3220404
www.lordbyronhotel.com
The Lord Byron is a romantic hideaway in pastoral Parioli, overlooking the Villa Borghese. The art deco villa has been

restored elegantly, with scarlet sofas, lacquered furniture, gilded mirrors and marble bathrooms. Rooms 503, 602 and 603 have spectacular views. Its restaurant, Relais Le

Jardin, is considered to be one of Italy's finest.

🛏 €300–€440
🛌 37 (12 non-smoking)
♿
🚇 Flaminio
🚌 117
🅿 West side of Via Giuseppe de Notaris 5, just north of Via Mangili

NAZIONALE A MONTECITORIO
Piazza Montecitorio 131, 00186 Roma
Tel 06 695001
www.nazionaleroma.it
This hotel is next to the Parliament buildings, close to the Fontana di Trevi and the Scalinata di Trinita dei Monti. It has dark wood panelling and

marble floors and columns in the lobby. The moderately-sized rooms, with high ceilings and period furnishings, are decorated in gold and brown shades. All have private bathrooms, satellite/pay television, minibar and a safe. They have a nice old-fashioned bar and restaurant with marble floors and a Renaissance ceiling, serving Italian and Continental cuisine.

🛏 €321–€500
🛌 92
♿
🚌 46, 62, 116

PORTOGHESI
Via dei Portoghesi 1, 00186 Roma
Tel 06 6864231
www.hotelportoghesi.com
This hotel is tucked away in the labyrinth of the Tor di Nona area, north of Piazza Navona. From here you can feel the heartbeat of Rome as mopeds sputter and locals chatter nearby. It's easy to miss the unassuming entrance, flanked by potted evergreens. Keep an eye out for the row of dainty flags. Highlights include the sunny breakfast room and the roof terrace overflowing with flowers.
🛏 €170–€190
ℹ 28
⛔
🚇 Spagna
🚌 116, 280

PRINCIPESSA TEA
Via Sardegna 149, 00187 Roma
Tel 06 4744243
www.hoteltea.com
The Principessa Tea presides over the Via Veneto and the Villa Borghese. It has true elegance—traditional and elaborate without being fussy. Oriental carpets, gilt mirrors and mauve upholstery add to the sense of gentility. The Ludovici Group deserves high praise for preserving the style of this grande hotel. There is an American bar and a traditional *trattoria*. Indoor parking on request.
🛏 €90–€140
ℹ 35
⛔
🚇 Piazza di Spagna

RAPHAEL
Largo Febo 2, 00186 Roma
Tel 06 682831
www.raphaelhotel.com
Day or night, the ivy-covered façade of this hotel, a short distance from Piazza Navona, always looks romantic. The antique-filled lobby, golden velvet sofas and gilt tables give

it a period feel. The rooms are littered with objets d'art and furnished in the Imperial style. There are plenty of modern facilities though; satellite television, a safe and a minibar. The restaurant has an international reputation and a roof terrace where you can have breakfast (€18), with unparalleled views of the city.
🛏 €390–€420 excluding breakfast
ℹ 47 (5 non-smoking)
⛔ 🍽
🚌 40, 62, 64, 87, 116, 492, 628 to Piazza Navona

SCALINATA DI SPAGNA
Piazza Trinità dei Monti 17, 00187 Roma
Tel 06 6793006
www.hotelscalinata.com
Reserve months—if not years—in advance at this boutique

hotel atop the Scalinata di Trinita dei Monti. La Scalinata's 16 rooms are highly coveted (especially numbers 10 and 12). The breakfast terrace, overlooking the red-tiled roofs and cupolas, is a riot of blossom. Active visitors can jog in the nearby Villa Borghese park, which also has a modern underground gym. Plug in your laptop, or try the free internet television with e-mail.
🛏 €350
ℹ 16 (5 non-smoking)
⛔
🚇 Spagna
🚌 116

THE DUKE
Via Archimede 69, 00197 Roma

Tel 06 367221
www.thedukehotel.com
The Duke is in the heart of the well-heeled Parioli district, between the parks of the Villa Borghese and the Villa Gloria. Inside, it looks like an English country-home with classical flourishes and there is a delightful art nouveau glass cupola in the Polo lounge. The rooms are luxurious and intimate, spacious and light, with minibar, safe, satellite television and a games console. The large marble bathrooms are very luxurious. Children get welcome packs and free tickets to the zoo.
🛏 €285–€380
ℹ 78 (38 non-smoking)
⛔ 🍽
🚇 Flaminio
🚌 910
🚆 From Piazza del Popolo, train to Viterbo, 1st stop–Termini

STARGATE HOSTEL & HOTEL
Map 258 H4
Via Palestra 88, 00185
Tel 06 445 7164
www.stargatehotels.com
A very clean and efficient hos-

tel/ hotel near Termini station, that is extremely good value for money. The hostel has dormitory rooms sleeping four to six people. These are spacious, with bunk-beds, desks, chairs, wardrobe, washbasin, TV and internet access. There is also an internet lounge and a kitchen. Other rooms come with their own shower, but there is a communal shower on each floor. Towels and linen are provided and there is a launderette. No curfew is imposed. The hotel rooms are similar but more private. An Italian breakfast of coffee and brioche is included.
🛏 Hostel €10–20, hotel €40–90
ℹ Hostel 20, hotel 20
🚇 Castro Pretorio or Termini
🚌 492

EATING

The cooking in Lazio is very like that of Rome, and you'll find many of the same dishes that are served in the capital. Along the coast, there's plenty of seafood and fish, appearing as crisp *fritto misto*, tiny mixed fried fish, *alla griglia*, grilled, or *al forno*, baked. A popular antipasto is *insalata frutta di mare*, mixed shellfish and squid in a piquant salad. In summer look out for *gelaterie* selling homemade ice-cream (*prodizione propria*) and sample the wonderful range of fresh fruit ices.

The rural region of the Marche is renowned for its tradition of real country cooking—rabbit (*coniglio*), baby lamb (*agnello*) and *porchetta*, a whole roast suckling pig stuffed with a secret blend of wild herbs and spices. Don't miss the chance to try olive *ascolani*, huge meat-stuffed olives coated with egg and breadcrumbs and deep-fried. The luscious *vincisgrassi*, layered pasta with *ragù* and béchamel is another local special and along the coast you'll come accross *brodetto*, a delicate fish soup. The best wine in the Marche is Verdicchio, while Rosso Conero, also from the Marche, is one of Italy's finest red wines.

STAYING

Apart from the hill towns around Rome—Albano, Frascati and Tivoli—much of Lazio, and certainly the Marche, is relatively untouched by tourism. If you are heading east across the Apennine, Tivoli is a good overnight stop. North along the Lazio coast from Rome, Tarquinia is a good base from which to explore the Etruscan sites. Inland from here is Viterbo and the placid Lago Trasimeno, a cool oasis in the summer with plenty of hotels around the lake. Heading south from Rome, the coast around Monte Circeo and Terracina is a picturesque place to stay, but busy in summer, so book in advance if you want to saty in high season. East into the Marche, the main focal points are Urbino and the compact Ascoli Piceno in the Tronto valley; both have good hotels and restaurants. If you're looking for a typical Italian resort, head for Pésaro or Fano, both of which have plenty of family-run hotels.

ALBANO

🍴 LA VOLPE E L'UVA
Via Collegio Nazzareno 14, 00042 Albano
Tel 06 9322251
Beside Albano's duomo, this restaurant-wine bar is a harmonious blend of good food, wine and art. The fixed menu changes weekly, with dishes paired with their complementary wines. An ample list of Italian wines is also available, including vintage Barolo. This is the best place in Castelli Romani for food and wine. There is a limited number of tables. so reservations are essential. No credit cards.
🕐 Tue–Sat 7–11.30pm, Sep–Jun
🍴 D €40 including wine, Wine €6

ASCOLI PICENO

🍴 GALLO D'ORO
Corso Vittorio Emanuele 54, 63100 Ascoli Piceno
Tel 0736 253520
Opened by Giuseppe Mazzitti in 1960 and now in his son's capable hands, the 'Golden Rooster' is Ascoli's premier culinary institution, just steps away from the central duomo. The cuisine is based on the area's marriage of tastes from *mare e monti* (sea and mountains). First courses include fried calamari, while main courses are topped with truffles or wild porcini mushrooms. The house special is *fritto misto* with fried olives, lamb cutlet, veal brain and courgettes (zucchini). A tourist menu is available for €20.
🕐 Mon–Fri noon–4, 7.30pm–12.30am, Sat noon–4
🍴 L €20, D €50, Wine €10
🚇 Section 🚇

🍴 GASTRONOMIA ENOTECA MIGLIORI
Piazza Arringo 2, 63100 Ascoli Piceno
Tel 0736 250042
Ascoli Piceno's most famous foodstuff is the *oliva ascolane*: pitted giant green olives stuffed with spiced meat, breaded and deep-fried until a thick, golden crust is formed. Any restaurant in Ascoli will proudly serve them, and you can order them by the plateful, but nobody makes them better than the Enoteca. This is a great place for cocktails or afternoon snacking, and it has a vast wine selection.
🕐 Tue–Sat 9–9, Sun 9–3
🍴 L €22, Wine €3
🚇

🏨 GIOLI
Viale A de Gasperi 14, 63100 Ascoli Piceno
Tel 0736 255550
This is Ascoli Piceno's most highly recommended hotel, although it loses points for sketchy service. It is just steps away from the busy Piazza Arringo and the tower-lined Piazza del Popolo. It even has a small garden, which adds a

refreshing touch of green. The interior is light and modern but comforting and classy, with fresh cut flowers and newly plumped pillows. There is 24-hour room service and parking is available.
🏨 €100
🛏 56
🚇
🅿 2, 3
🚉 Ascoli Piceno; train to San Benedetto del Tronto and change for Ascoli Piceno
🚗 From the A14 take the San Benedetto del Tronto exit and follow signs to Ascoli Piceno and then to *centro storico*; from Roma take the Via Salaria

🏨 MARCHE
Viale Kennedy 34, 63100 Ascoli Piceno
Tel 0736 45575
This hotel is near the Piazza Immacolata, 10 minutes' walk from the city. Built about 20 years ago, the Hotel Marche offers its guests all the modern amenities needed for a comfortable stay. Guest rooms are large and contemporary, and a tasty breakfast with fresh country jams is served every morning. A hotel school is

located in the building, and many of its students are also employed here, adding a touch of energy to the service.

🖐 €67
🛏 32

FRASCATI

🍴 CANTINA TRINCA

Piazza San Rocco 4, 00044 Frascati
Tel 06 9409246, 338 8181955 (mobile)
www.cantinatrinca.it

Come here for a taste of local life. *Fraschette* are Frascati's most typical eateries, generally selling local wine and sand-wiches. Cantina Trinca is just one of the more popular in town. Paper tablecloths and wood benches add a touch of rustic charm. Ask the owner for a selection of prosciutti, salami, cheeses, olives and the delicious *porchetta di Ariccia* (roast pork served cold). All the wine is produced by the owner and his family. No credit cards.

🕐 Daily 4pm–midnight, Jun–Sep;
Tue–Sun 11–11, Oct–May
🖐 €9–€12 per person including wine
🚇 Metro A: Anagnina, then bus to Frascati
🚆 From Termni Station

🍴 GELATERIA TRIS

Piazza San Pietro 4, 00044 Frascati
Tel 06 9416434

Head for Gelateria Tris to sam-ple the best ice cream in Frascati, made by the owners in the traditional way. There are a huge number of different creamy and fruity varietie—don't miss zabaglione. They also have soy ice cream, fruit and milk shakes, coffee and fruit *granita*. There are no tables or seats, but you can walk down the belvedere with your take-away. As it's popular, it may be a bit of a battle to get to the counter in the evenings. No credit cards.

🕐 Daily 11am–3am
🖐 Ice cream €1–€3
🚫
🚇 Metro A: Anagnina, then bus
🚆 Train from Termini Station

🍴 RISTORANTE ZARAZÀ

Viale Regina Margherita 45, 00044 Frascati
Tel 06 9422053

This is the place to enjoy traditional Roman cuisine and the menu is adapted to make the most of seasonal produce. Among the typical dishes are *pasta all'amatriciana* (spicy tomato and bacon) and *coda alla vaccinara* (oxtail cooked with a vegetable sauce). There's also a selection of creative dishes including a mouth-watering guinea fowl served with nuts and orange sauce. Most wines are from Lazio and, of course, Frascati. Finish off the meal with one of the restaurant's homemade pastries. You can enjoy the view from the terrace in the summer, overlooking Rome and Valle Tiburtina, but be sure to book in advance.

🕐 Tue–Sun 12.30–2, 8–10, Oct–May; closed Sun 8–10
🖐 L €50, D €50, Wine €5
🚫
🚇 From Roma take Metro A to Anagnina then bus
🚆 From Termini Station to Frascati

🏨 BELLAVISTA

Piazza Roma 2, 00044 Frascati
Tel 06 9421068
www.hbellavista.it

Occupying one of the most important palaces in town, Palazzo Senni, this hotel looks out over Frascati's main square. The rooms are com-fortable and simply furnished, designed to make the best of the original architecture. They have televisions and tele-phones and a tiny bathroom with a shower. There is a breakfast room. Private parking in the courtyard.

🖐 €80–€103
🛏 18
🚫 ♿ 5 rooms
🚇 From Roma take Metro A: Anagnina, then bus
🚌 Blue bus from Roma to Frascati
🚆 Train from Termini Station to Frascati

🏨 FLORA

Viale Vittorio Veneto 8, 00044 Frascati
Tel 06 9416110
www.hotel-flora.it

Divided into two Liberty-style buildings, this hotel was once home to local nobility. There is antique furniture and prints in the refined and spacious rooms. Some rooms in the main building have a terrace overlooking Rome or the Villa Aldobrandini (request when making your reservation). A few smaller and cheaper rooms are in the basement—despite private patios, they can be a bit dark. The Continental breakfast is served on the veranda and terrace and they have a roof garden. There is satellite television in the guest

rooms. Airport transfers are available on request.

🖐 €125–€180
🛏 37
♿
🚇 From Rome take Metro A: Anagnina, then bus
🚌 Blue bus from Roma to Frascati
🚆 Train from Termini Station to Frascati

SAN LEO

🏨🍴 CASTELLO

Piazza Alighieri 11, San Leo, Pesaro e Urbino 61018
Tel 0541 916214

This 16th-century palazzo, on one side of San Leo's main square, is the town's only hotel, its best restaurant and a popular meeting place for locals. The friendly bar spreads back into the dining room, where genuine local dishes are served—all the pasta's freshly made *a casa* (in house), and the *coniglio alla porchetta* (rabbit boned and spit-roasted with wild herbs) is a local treat. Upstairs, the simple and spot-less bedrooms are peaceful.

🕐 Closed 2 weeks in Nov and Jan
🖐 L €32, D €40, Wine €6
🛏 14 (€50–€63)
🚫 Section
🚌 From Rimini
🚌 From Rimini take the SS258 west and turn left at Pietrocuta for San Leo

SPERLONGA

⊜LA SIRENELLA

Via Colombo 25, Sperlonga, Latina
04029
Tel 0771 549186
Fax 0771 549189
www.lasirenella.com

A typical, family-run, good-value holiday hotel, right on the beach in one of Lazio's prettiest villages. The clean, simply furnished rooms have more-than-adequate bathrooms and there is a lovely terrace overlooking the beach. The rooms at the front have sea views and the hotel has access to the private beach (Blue Flag rated). This is an Italian family holiday favourite, so expect friendliness and few foreigners. Half- or full-board is compulsory and only full-board is available in July and August, but the food is fine and a three-day package is excellent value for money.

🕒 Closed Dec
🛏 €110–€152 (half-board) €158–€190 (full board)
🚪 40
🚭
🚆 Fondi Sperlonga (Roma/Napoli line) then bus
🚗 Exit the Autosole at Ceprano and take the N82 toSperlonga. The hotel is on the seafront

TIVOLI

⑪RISTORANTE ANTICHE TERME DI DIANA

Via dei Sosii 19, 00019 Tivoli
Tel 0774 335239
www.termedidiana.it

Here you can eat in a Roman dining room, under barrel vaults, beside columns made of travertine. This underground restaurant is within the ruins of a thermal complex dedicated

to Diana, ancient goddess of the hunt. The choice is vast and appetizing, but don't miss the fresh egg pasta, made on the premises. There is a lovely garden for summer dining.

🕒 Tue–Sun 12.30–2.30, 7.30–10pm
🍷 L €20, D €50, Wine €7
🚭
🚆 33km (21 miles) from Roma: Follow the Via Tiburtina or the Gran Raccordo Anulare (GRA). Turn off at Tivoli Citta and follow signs for Villa d'Este; from the A24 (Rome/L'Aquila) take the exit for Tivoli (3km/2miles)

⑪RISTORANTE SIBILLA

Via della Sibilla 50, 00019 Tivoli
Tel 0774 335281
www.ristorantesibilla.it

At Restorante Sibilla you can eat on the terrace around the Temple of Vesta in spring and summer, surrounded by lilac, wisteria and violets. Inside, the rooms of this 18th-century restaurant are finely decorated. They serve typical Roman cuisine, home-made pasta and succulent grilled meat. Popes, princes and other celebrities

such as Goethe and Gabriele d'Annunzio have eaten here, adding to its allure. You will need to make a reservations if you want to have a meal here at the weekend.

🕒 Tue–Sun 12.30–3, 7–10.30pm
🍷 L €30, D €60, Wine €8
🚭
🚆 33km (21 miles) from Roma: Follow the Via Tiburtina or the Gran Raccordo Anulare (GRA). Turn off at Tivoli Citta and follow signs for Villa d'Este; from the A24 (Rome/L'Aquila) take the exit for Tivoli (3km/5 miles)

⊜LA PANORAMICA

Viale Arnaldi 45, 00019 Tivoli
Tel 0774 335700
www.villadestetivoli.it

Rooms in this 19th-century building are all comfortable, with private bathroom (though in some cases it is outside the room) and television. Double rooms with extra bunk-beds are available for families. In summer, breakfast is served on the terrace, which has a splendid view of Rome. The sitting room has a piano and a tele-

⊜SIRENE

Piazza Massimo 4, 00019 Tivoli
Tel 0774 330605
www.hotelsirene.com

This is a 19th-century villa, just 10 minutes' walk from the Villa d'Este. The rooms are spacious and gracefully decorated. All have private bath and satellite television. Some have a private terrace (request when making a reservation). There is fine view of the Aniene valley, the waterfalls and the remains of the Temple of Vesta from here. They have a restaurant and café with a panoramic terrace—local cuisine and sophisticated presentation. Famous guests include Sir Winston Churchill. Airport transfers are available and there is a laundry service.

🛏 €120–€135
🚪 35 (2 non-smoking)
🚭
🚇 Ponte Mammolo or Rebibbia, then bus
🚆 33km (21 miles) from Roma: Follow the Via Tiburtina or the Gran Raccordo Anulare (GRA). Turn off at Tivoli Citta and follow signs for Villa d'Este; from the A24 (Rome/L'Aquila) take the exit for Tivoli (3km/2 miles)

scope. The owners are happy to give advice on where to go

and what to do—the hotel is only 200m (656ft) from Villa d'Este.

🛏 €52
🚪 10 (non-smoking)
🚇 Ponte Mammolo or Rebibbia, then bus for Tivoli
🚆 33km (21 miles) from Roma: Follow the Via Tiburtina or the Gran Raccordo Anulare (GRA). Turn off at Tivoli Citta and follow signs for Villa d'Este; from the A24 (Rome/L'Aquila) take the exit for Tivoli (3km/2 miles)

EATING AND STAYING

URBINO

🍴 L'ANGOLO DIVINO

Via Sant'Andrea 14, 61029 Urbino
Tel 0722 327559
www.mediaworks.it/divino.htm

The Renaissance City may have many 'divine angles', but this place, inside a historic palazzo near the Porta Lavagine, is the *angolo divino* for truffle-lovers. Casciotta d'Urbino cheese and *salame matto* (spicy salami) will whet your appetite, and the *agnello all'aceto balsamico con governa di tartufo* (lamb in a balsamic vinegar and truffle reduction sauce) will satisfy. All meals are served with plenty of the fist-sized white and black truffles that Urbino is famous for.

🕐 Tue–Sat 12–4, 7pm–midnight, Sun 11.30–4
🍽 L €24, D €50, Wine €7.80
🔲 🔲
📮 From Pesaro and Roma
🚌 Pesaro then frequent local bus service

🍴 TAVERNA LA VECCHIA FORNARINA

Via Mazzini 14, 61029 Urbino
Tel 0722 320007

Considered to be Urbino's last culinary secret, the Taverna is where to go to find rustic charm, a local clientele and hearty food served in generous portions and smothered in decadent sauces. Two popuar dishes are the *strozzapreti alla*

fornarina (long pasta with a meat *ragù* sauce) and *coniglio alla duchessa* (stewed rabbit). The house red wine is surprisingly good. No credit cards.
🕐 Wed–Mon noon–2.30, 7–10.30pm
🍽 L €24, D €50, Wine €8
🔲

🍴 LA VECCHIA URBINO

Via dei Vasari 3/5, 61029 Urbino
Tel 0722 4447
www.vecchiaurbino.it

This is a gastronomic wonderland, run by Gabriele and Eugenia Monti. A spectacular wood ceiling and hanging ducal-star lamps form the backdrop to a cornucopian display of fresh pasta and vegetables. This is one of the

most famous restaurants in the Marche and should not be missed. Dishes to look out for are *delizia del Montefeltro* (ravioli with white truffles) and *vincisgrassi alla Federico* (lasagne with a cheese crust). There is a Sommelier on call and they have an encyclopaedic wine list.
🕐 Wed–Mon noon–3, 7.30–midnight
🍽 L €40, D €60, Wine €11.50
📮 To Porta Lavagine

🏨 BONCONTE

Via della Mura 28, 61029 Urbino
Tel 0722 2463
www.viphotels.it

Without a doubt, Urbino's most luxurious option. Embedded in the thick southern walls of the city, with cityscapes to the north, and the Marche's most beautiful cypress-lined hills to the south. Breakfast is served in a lush garden, and they have a good restaurant serving local cuisine.
🏨 €95–€156
🛏 23
🔲
🚗 Exit A14 at Pesaro/Urbino and then follow signs to *centro storico*. From here follow signs for hotel

🏨 RAFFAELLO

Via Santa Margherita 40, 61029 Urbino
Tel 0722 4784
www.albergoraffaello.com

Named after the Renaissance master, this hotel is in 14th-century palace that's just steps away from Raphael's birthplace. The three-floor brick building is on a hill that dominates this corner of the historic heart. The top-floor rooms look out over San Francesco's bell tower and the Palazzo Ducale. What this hotel lacks in luxury it makes up for with friendliness and willing staff. Diners Club and American Express credit cards are not accepted.
🏨 €90–€114
🛏 14
🔲
🚗 Exit A14 at Pesaro/Urbino and then follow signs to *centro storico*. From here follow signs for hotel

🏨 SAN GIOVANNI

Via Barocci 13, 61029 Urbino
Tel 0722 2827

This is two-star hotel is a great option for shorter stays. It has the added attraction of an excellent restaurant/pizzeria on the premises. The exterior of the 15th-century building has been preserved, but the interiors have been refurbished with nondescript modern furniture. You can catch a glimpse of the Palazzo Ducale and the surrounding cityscape from the upper floors. The chiming church bells will probably wake you in the morning. No credit cards.
🕐 Closed Jul
🍽 €34–€50
🛏 31
🚗 Exit A14 at Pesaro/Urbino and then follow signs to *centro storico*. From here follow signs for hotel

EATING

Home of the pizza, Naples has some of Italy's best cooking—tasty, fresh and imaginative. Try the ultra-thin classic *pizza marinara*, and other food-to-go such as *arancini*, fried rice balls, and *fiorilli*, stuffed and battered courgette flowers. Expect mounds of pasta, simply served with tomato and basil sauce, superb fish and seafood with fresh mozzarella and vegetables such as peppers, aubergines and courgettes. Neapolitans are also famed for their pastries, often stuffed with sweetened ricotta and candied fruit.

The Puglian countryside yields huge quantities of wine, olive oil and vegetables, much used in local dishes. Short, thick pasta is mixed with bitter vegetable sauces, while lamb, roasted with thyme and rosemary, is the favourite meat dish. The cheeses, particularly the fresh milk varieties such as mozzarella and ricotta, are delicious—look out for *caprini*, goat's milk cheese preserved in olive oil, and *fagottini*, smoked cheese. Puglian wines are on the up—pick of the bunch are Salice Salentino and Primitivo di Manduria, huge reds with a deep taste made using the best of modern New World technology.

Calabria and Basilicata are still relatively poor regions. Despite this the food is full of variety. Local cooking predominantly consists of homemade pasta and sauces made from local produce including tomatoes, pimentos, chillies, aubergines, pine kernels and olive oil, livened up with plenty of garlic, ginger and spices. In remote areas, menus will be limited, but the freshness and quality of the ingredients still shines through.

STAYING

Naples, the Amalfi coast and the Sorrento peninsula have something to suit everyone, all within easy reach of Naples, the great classical ruins of Pompei, and the off-shore islands of Capri and Ischia. Across the Apennines lies the Gargano peninsula, a well-kept secret with pretty villages and comfortable hotels. This is a great place from which to explore south into Puglia. Vibrant Bari is Puglia's capital, but the best place for accommodation is in the *trulli* country round Alberobello and baroque Lecce. Further south again in the regions of Calabria and Basilicata, there are some good hotels in Matera and Maratea, and there are many simple, family-run establishments along the coast and in the other main towns.

SPECIAL

ⓗ CARAVELLA

Via Camera 12, 84011
Tel 089 871029
www.ristorantelacaravella.it

Consistently awarded a very high rating by L'Espresso magazine, Caravella has been producing excellent cuisine that marries traditional elements with innovative twists, since 1959. The maritime heritage is reflected in the menu with plenty of seafood dishes to choose from and lightly boiled filleted fish with freshly squeezed lemon. Simplicity is the key, using fresh local ingredients. The service is first class and the choice of wines is equally exemplary.

🕐 Wed–Mon 12–2.30,
7.30–10.30pm; closed 10 Nov–25 Dec
🍴 L €80, D €130, Wine €16
🔲 🔲

ⓗ DEI TRULLI

Via Cadore 32, Alberobello, 70011 Bari
Tel 080 4323555
Fax 080 4323560
www.hoteldeitrulli.it

Sample the full *trulli* experience in this deluxe hotel converted from a group of Alberobello's distinctive conical stone houses. Totally traditional from the outside, the interior has been skillfully converted to provide the comfort that its numerous foreign guests expect. This hotel is popular with group tours, but the gardens and pines provide a calm setting and the bedrooms' white-washed walls, simple decoration and well-equipped bathrooms are oases of tranquility. Rooms are available on a half-board basis only.

🛏 €140–€160
🛎 48
🔲 🏊 Outdoor
🚌 From Bari
🚉 Alberobello from Bari
🚗 Exit the A14 at Bari Nord and follow signs to Alberobello, then follow signs to the hotel

AMALFI

🍴 TARI
Via Capuano, 84011 Amalfi
Tel 089 871832
This family-run restaurant is an intimate place to dine on quality traditional cookery. Intriguing artworks and vibrant tiles make it a relaxing change from the formality of some gastronomic establishments. Expect some wonderful pasta and seafood creations using the freshest of produce, or simply opt for a delicious pizza for €6. The wine list has something to suit most tastes and includes lots of good local labels.

🕐 Wed–Mon 11.30–3, 8–11pm; closed Nov
🍽 L €14, D €70, Wine €6
💺 Section ♿

🛏 LA BUSSOLA
Lungomare dei Cavalieri 16, 84011 Amalfi
Tel 089 871533
www.labussolahotel.it
This former mill and pasta factory is on the outskirts of Amalfi, near the fabulous duomo. Its attractions include a small private jetty and a large terrace with great views of the azure waters below. The restaurant serves a very good selection of regional dishes. The lobby has a 1970s feel, while the lounge area has some elegant 18th/

19th-century period furnishings. Guest rooms are simply furnished with amusingly kitsch artworks, and have basic facilities. They have a private car park (€10 a day).
🍽 €94–€154
🛏 62
♿ 12 rooms only

🛏 LIDOMARE
Largo Piccolomini 9, 84011 Amalfi
Tel 089 871332
www.lidomare.it
The Lidomare is in a

14th-century building just off the main piazza. It is good value for this part of the world, and the Camera family are amiable hosts. Many of the rooms have high ceilings, bright tiled floors, and a mixture of modern and dark-wood furniture. Facilities include private bathroom with shower or bath, television, safe, heating and telephone. There's a pleasant terrace with superb views where you can take breakfast, which is served until late morning.
🍽 €96–€106
🛏 15
🚆 From Naples or Salerno
🚌 Salerno then bus to Amalfi
🚗 Take the A3 from Napoli then turn right to Amalfi and follow signs for *centro*

BARI

🍴 AI DUE GHIOTTONI
Via Putignani 11, 70121 Bari
Tel 0805 232240
Old stone walls and modern design combine to give this buzzing restaurant a great sense of style. They serve genuine Puglian cooking, with lots of fresh fish, seafood and high-quality vegetables. Try the *risotto ai due ghiottoni*, a rich rice dish with spinach, cream, ham and fontina cheese, then move on to simply grilled fish, or *branzino al sale* (sea bass baked in salt). There is an excellent *macedonia* (fruit salad) along with some creamier treats on the dessert menu. Italian and foreign wines.
🕐 Mon–Sat 12.30–3.30, 7.30–12
🍽 L €40, D €70, Wine €12
💺 Section ♿

🛏 VICTOR
Via Nicolai 71, 70100 Bari
Tel 0805 216600
Fax 0805 212601
www.victorservice.com
Bari can be noisy and chaotic, so the sound-proofed rooms

here are a real bonus. This is a modern and efficient hotel, aimed at business visitors and sightseers alike, and it wins for its position and parking—a nightmare in Bari. The rooms are comfortable and well-equipped. There's an extravagant breakfast buffet and the staff will do all they can to help.
🍽 €100–€110
🛏 77
♿
🚆 From Roma, Napoli, Milano, Lecce
🚌 Bari from Roma, Napoli, Milano, Lecce
🚗 From the north, exit Bari Nord and fork left towards Bari Fiera on tangenziale SS16, take exit 4 Fiera Porto–Via Napoli. From the south take exit 4

CAPRI

🍴 CAPANNINA
Via le Botteghe 12/14, 80073 Capri
Tel 081 8370732
www.capannina-capri.com
Some of the world's great beauties—from Sofia Loren to

Liz Hurley—have graced this prestigious establishment. Highlights include *ravioli alla caprese*, aubergines stuffed with ricotta cheese, luscious avocados and prawns and fresh local lobster. The wine list has more than 200 labels, and the desserts are devilishly rich—not for those counting the calories. There is a wine bar opposite and an *enoteca* (Mon–Sat) selling wines, liquers and grappa. Reservations are required.

🕐 Daily 12.30–3.30, 8–11; closed Wed, Nov–Mar 15 except Christmas period
🍽 L €100, D €100, Wine €12

🍴 DA GEMMA
Via Madre Serafina 6, 80073 Capri
Tel 081 8370461
www.dagemma.com
Gemma's, named after its former proprietor and society darling, has been the hangout of the *bella gente* since the 1930s. Savour the wonderful *pizza napoletana* and soak up the history documented on the walls. Highlights include fisherman's risotto, *ravioli alla caprese* and *maccheroncelli* with potatoes and mussels. The *carpaccio* with porcini mushrooms is another perennial pleaser. There is an *antipasti* buffet and dessert-lovers have a mouth-watering choice, including traditional or fruit-laden *tiramisù*. The wine list is excellent.
🕐 Daily noon–3.30, 7–midnight; closed 3 weeks in Jan
🍽 L €35, D €60, Wine €10
🚭 Section 🔲

🍴 DA TONINO
Via Dentecalla 12, 80073 Capri
Tel 081 8376718
For quality wine and traditional southern Italian fare, look for Tonino's, near the Arco Naturale. They have hundreds of wines from Campania and Puglia, as well as the rest of the world. Of particular note is the *millefoglie d'alici* (delicate pastry with anchovies) served with peppers and potatoes mixed in a pesto sauce. The quail with chestnuts is also good. Afterwards, enjoy iced *zabaione di Verduzzo* (a custard pudding made with Friuli wine).
🕐 Daily 12.30–2.30, 7–10.30pm; closed 6 Jan–15 Mar
🍽 L €20, D €70, Wine €8.50

🏨 BELSITO
Via Matermania 11, 80073 Capri
Tel 081 8370969
www.hotelbelsito.com
The Belsito is housed in an attractive, red-hued, 18th-century villa. It is in an excellent spot, only a short stroll from the Piazzetta di Capri and Arco Naturale. Some of the light and cheery guest rooms have balconies that overlook the Marina Piccola. The white walls blend well with bright modern

furnishings. The terrace restaurant serves traditional Neapolitan dishes, including tasty seafood dishes, and there are some enchanting views of the island from here.
🍽 €80–€155
🛏 13
🚡 From Napoli and Sorrento then funicular to town (also from Salerno and Positano in Aug). Hotel is 10 minutes from the middle

🏨 DA GELSOMINA MIGLIERA
Via Migliara 72, 80071 Anacapri
Tel 081 8371499
www.dagelsomina.com
This hotel provides good-value accommodation in Anacapri, near the sublime Migliera cliff-top vantage point. Originally opened as a café nearly 50 years ago, it now has excellent facilities and a wonderful restaurant. The rooms are decorated in the customary Caprese style: cool hues and tiled floors. All have television, telephone, minibar, hair-dryer and private bathroom. There are jaw-dropping views from each balcony and a large swimming pool and sundeck.
🍽 €105–€125
🛏 5
🏊 Outdoor
🚡 From Capri town
🚡 From Napoli and Sorrento then funicular to town (also from Salerno and Positano in Aug)

🏨 GRAND HOTEL QUISISANA
Via Camerelle 2, 80073 Capri
Tel 081 8370788
www.quisi.com
Marble floors, elegant statues, chesterfield sofas and chandeliers greet you in the lobby of this well-established luxury hotel, opened in 1845. Exclusivity, quality and service are the watchwords here. The rooms are filled with a blend of cool and warm pastel shades, and a mixture of comfy modern and elegant Venetian-style furnishings. There are superb views throughout and top-class facilities, including a spa and a first-rate restaurant.
🕐 Closed Nov–mid-Mar
🍽 €300–€700
🛏 150
🏊 Indoor and outdoor 🔲

🏨 LA TOSCA
Via Birago 5, 80073 Capri
Tel 081 8370989
www.latoscahotel.com

This is a lovely little hotel with wonderful views of the Monastery of San Giacomo and the distinctive Faraglioni rocks. The bright and cheerful entrance is mirrored in the

comfortable rooms, which are generally white, light and airy. Facilities include private bath in most rooms and telephone. Breakfast costs an additional €8 per person, and can be taken on the terrace.
🍽 €60–€110
🚡 From the port take the furnicular to Piazatta di Capri (Piazza Umberto VII and la Tosca is a five-minute walk away
🔲

GARGANO PENINSULA

🍦 GELATERIA ARTIGIANALE MAGGIORE
Via Deputato Petrone & Via Santa Maria di Merino 40, 71019 Vieste
The best ice cream in the area can be found at a couple of

small *gelaterie* in the middle of town. Ask the friendly staff to guide you through the many choices: try a combination of fruits like *arance* (orange), *limone* (lemon), *frutti del bosco* (forest fruits) and the creamy, *decadent cioccolato* (chocolate). Also worth trying are the fabulous *granite* (ice crystals with natural fruit and sugar), sorbets and milk-shakes. No credit cards.
🕐 Daily 10–10
🍦 Ice cream from €3.50
🔲

EATING AND STAYING

🍴 MEDIEVO
Via Castello 21, 71013 Monte
Sant'Angelo
Tel 0884 565356
www.ristorantemedievo.it
Pilgrims often miss this wonderful restaurant in Monte
Sant'Angelo. Savour food
inspired by the best elements
of la *tradizione Garganica*.
Start with some of the region's
best salumi and cured meats
and order from the small but
excellent wine list. You can't
leave Puglia without sampling
the local ear-shaped *orecchiette* pasta. Here they combine
this Puglian dish with a meaty
lamb sauce. The dried figs with
almonds bathed in rum must
be tasted.
🕐 Daily 12.30–3.30, 8–10pm,
Aug–Sep; Tue–Sun 12.30–3.30,
8–10pm, rest of year. Closed 2 weeks in
Nov
🍴 L €24, D €50, Wine €7
🚭

🏨 ALBA DEL GARGANO
Corso Matino 102, 71030 Mattinata
Tel 0884 550771
www.albadelgargano.it
For great value on the Gargano
coast, this is a sure-fire hit.
Public areas are functional yet
comfortable. The guest rooms
are simply furnished with
modern fittings, and facilities
include a television, telephone
and compact bathroom with
shower. The restaurant serves
decent regional cooking in
attractive outdoor and indoor
surroundings. The hotel's wonderfully sandy private beach
(2km/1.25 miles away) is
equipped with the usual paraphernalia, including
complementary parasols and
deck-chairs.
🍴 €56–€82 Jun–Jun; €128 half-board
rate only during Aug
🛏 40 (non-smoking)
🚭 (10 rooms)
🚌 Bari to Foggia
🚂 Foggia then local bus
🚗 A14 to Foggia exit then SP89 to
Mattinata

🏨 HOTEL DEI MANDORLI
Località Montagna, 71043 Ruggiano
Tel 0884 530400/1
www.hoteldeimandorli.it
Set in the verdant surroundings of the Gargano National
Park, this hotel is a good base
for exploring the area and visiting San Giovanni Rotondo and
Monte Sant'Angelo. The lobby

is full of light wood, marble
and warm hues. The rooms
have a 1970s functional feel,
but are comfortable. There is a
decent restaurant serving pizza
from a wood-burning oven.
Horse riding can be arranged,
and there are plenty of outdoor activities and beach
options to occupy the active
(and the less so).
🍴 €52
🛏 19 (non-smoking)
🚭
🚌 Bari to Foggia
🚂 Manfredonia then local bus to
Ruggiano
🚗 Take the SP89 from Foggia and turn
left at Manfredonia

LECCE

🍴 PICTON
Via Idomeneo 14, 73100 Lecce
Tel 0832 332383
Deep in the heart of the
baroque city is Lecce's finest
restaurant. You'll find a menu
largely filled with traditional
Puglian meals and the odd
surprise. Seafood dominates
the *antipasti* and pastas. The
potato gnocchi with swordfish
is outstanding. *Bistecche di
manzo* (beef steaks) and other
meat choices sit alongside
main course fish dishes. Divine
dolci and excellent regional
wines complete this greatvalue culinary journey.
🕐 Tue–Sun 12.30–3.30, 8–11pm
🍴 L €40, D €70, Wine €10
🚭 🚭

🏨 CENTRO STORICO B&B
Via Andrea Vignes 13, 73100 Lecce
Tel 0832 242727
www.bedandbreakfast.lecce.it
On the second floor of a
16th-century palazzo in the old
town, this hotel is well worth a
reservation for its excellent
value and comforts. Just a
short walk from the rail station
and the splendid Piazza San
Oronzo. The hotel has vaulted
ceilings and is decorated with
attractive artwork. The guest
rooms are simply furnished
and clean. The suite has space
for two to three people, with a
large bathroom and kitchen
area. Enjoy the baroque
cityscape from the terrace. No
credit cards.
🍴 €52–€80
🛏 6 (non-smoking)
🚭
🚌 From Bari, Napoli, Taranto
🚂 Lecce

🏨 PATRIA PALACE
Piazzetta Riccardi 13, 73100 Lecce
Tel 0832 245111
www.pregiohotel.it
Lecce's first 5-star hotel is in
the 17th-century baroque
Palazzo D'Anna, deep in the
centro storico district. Antiquefilled public areas have original
architectural features. The
guest rooms, decorated in
warm hues, are immaculate
and refined—elegant darkwood furniture blends with
artwork on the walls. The
excellent facilities include private bathroom, television,
telephone, 24-hour concierge
service and a fitness room.
Feast on quality *cucina
Pugliese* served in the evocative restaurant, or enjoy a drink
in Danny's Bar.
🍴 €150–€220
🛏 67
🚭

MARATEA

🍴 TAVERNA ROVITA
Via Rovita 63, Maratea, 85046 Potenza
Tel 0973 876588
On one of old Maratea's most
picturesque streets is the
Rovita, an elegantly laid-back
establishment with touches of
rustic charm and antique furniture. The cooking is regional,
the bread and pasta homemade. Expect dishes like
*risotto di cedro e profumo di
mare*, a delicate citron-spiked
seafood risotto, plainly grilled
fish and fruit-studded *cassata*
(ice cream *bombe* with crystallized fruit and nuts). Some
French wines augment the
local and Italian list.
🕐 Daily 12.30–2, 7–11pm, Apr–Sep;
Wed–Mon 12.30–2, 7–11pm, Oct,
Jan–Mar
🍴 L €30, D €70, Wine €4
🚭 Section

🏨 VILLA DEL MARE
Acquafredda, Maratea, 85046 Potenza
Tel 0973 878007
Fax 0973 878102

EATING AND STAYING

www.hotelvilladelmare.com
A week or more can be happily spent at this headland resort hotel on Basilicata's rocky west coast. Inside, the style is Mediterranean; cool and white, with shady, flower-filled terraces for relaxing and dining and comfortable, traditional bedrooms, many big enough for families. There's a crèche for kids and you can take excursions on the hotel's private yacht. A lift will whisk you down to the private beach. If you want total peace, check when the in-house disco operates. Parking.

🎬 Closed Nov
💶 €110–€190
🛏 75 (12 non-smoking)
♿ 🏊 Outdoor
🚆 Sapri (Napoli/Reggio di Clabria line) then bus to Acquafredda
🚗 Exit the Autosole at Lagonegro-Nord and follow the Valle del Noce superstrada to the Sapri exit. At Sapri, turn left on to the N18 towards Maratea. The hotel is 6km (9.6 miles) along this road

MATERA

🍴 DA MARIO
Via XX Settembre 14, 75100 Matera
Tel 0835 336491
www.ristorantedamario.net

Mario's is a *rosticceria*, bar, *pizzeria* and little restaurant serving local food at low prices. A brick-lined vaulted hall, once a storage room of a grand palazzo, sets the tone; full of locals with tributes to the chef prominently displayed. Various set menus include local dishes such as *strascinate con rape*, turnip tops with home-made pasta, and *orecchiete con funghi*, pasta 'ears' with wild mushrooms. Meat is simply grilled or *en brochette* and the vegetables are fresh.
🎬 Mon–Sat 2–3, 8–midnight; closed 10–17 Aug
💶 L €20, D €55, Wine €8
🅢 Section

🏨 ITALIA
Via Ridola 5, 75100 Matera
Tel 0835 333561
Fax 0835 330087
www.albergoitalia.com
Ask for a room overlooking the *sassi* when you book here, for unforgettable views of the townscape. Hotels as comfortable as this are thin on the ground in Basilicata, and you'll find rooms and amenities well up to northern standards. The building is an old palazzo, so there are high ceilings, marble and flagged floors and gracious architecture. Bedrooms are big, and the friendly and helpful staff will happily add a couple of beds to your room for the kids.
💶 €980
🛏 45
♿
🚆 From Napoli, Bari, Taranto and Potenza
🚗 Exit the A14 at Taranto Nord and take the N7 west to Matera. From the town outskirts follow yellow signs to the hotel

NAPOLI (NAPLES)

🍴 DORA
Via Ferdinando Palasciano 30, 80122 Naples
Tel 081 680519
Traditional fish dishes make up the bulk of the impressive menu here, where the staff often treat diners to an eccentric performance at the end of the evening. Well worth trying is the famous *pasta alla Dora* (pasta with a tomato sauce and shellfish), but the menu also offers a choice of grilled and baked fish dishes. Some very good wines are available and dessert is worth saving room for.
🎬 Mon–Sat noon–3, 8pm–midnight; closed 3 weeks in Aug
💶 L €80, D €120, Wine €13
🚆 Piazza Amedio
🚌 C18, 1, 150

🍴 GRAN CAFFÈ LA CAFFETTERIA
Piazza dei Martiri 26, 80121 Napoli
Tel 081 7644243
This café lies amidst the refined surroundings of Piazza dei Martiri. It's a great choice if you like to sit outside and people-watch. Inside there's a smart tearoom where you can sit and relax. Many of the locals take their espresso with a small Neapolitan pastry.

A good place to start is with one of their *baba* cakes or a crispy *sfogliatelle* pastry. This is a child-friendly establishment.
🎬 Sat–Sun 7.30am–midnight, Mon–Fri 7.30am–10pm
💶 Cappuccino €1.70, sandwich €3.50
🚌 102, 128

🍴 TRATTORIA SAN FERDINANDO
Via Nardones 117, 80132 Napoli
Tel 081 421964
This welcoming place is full of artwork evocative of the nearby San Carlo theatre. Choose from a dozen excellent first and second courses: The

delicious peppers and buffalo cheese and penne pasta with courgettes stand out. There is a great selection of desserts and the wine list is faithful to local producers.
🎬 Mon and Sat 12–3, Wed–Fri 12–3, 8–11.30
💶 L €30, D €50, Wine €8
🚌 C4, C22

🏨 HOTEL IL CONVENTO
Via Speranzella 137/A, 80132 Napoli
Tel 081 403977
www.hotelilconvento.com
This handsome 17th-century palace, next to the convent of Santa Maria Francesca, is newly renovated and has subtle lighting, wood details and attractive antique furniture. The small roof garden is a relaxing place to enjoy breakfast. Two spacious junior suites have balcony views, but all the rooms have excellent,

EATING AND STAYING

up-to-date amenities including telephone, radio, minibar and television.

💶 €90–€160
🛏 10 rooms, 4 suites
♿
🚆 R2 from the Napoli train station

🅿 🅸 EXCELSIOR
Via Partenope 48, 80121 Napoli
Tel 081 7640111
www.excelsior.it

The Hotel Excelsior's restaurant, La Terrazza, is hard to beat, with its stunning views, exquisite food and luxurious

touches. The wine list has been compiled by a professional sommelier, so you can expect top quality. There are some inventive pasta creations and a superb mixed grill garnished with mussels. The desserts are heavenly, but there is no cheese platter. On Sunday only the first floor is used for dining. Set in the Santa Lucia waterfront district the rooms have great views of Castel dell'Ovo and Vesuvio. Marble, chandeliers and Neapolitan painted scenes give it the air of a 19th-century *nobilita napoletana* residence. Guest rooms have individual belle Èpoque decorative flourishes plus all the facilities you'd expect from a top-class hotel. A very professional concierge service is always available. Around half the rooms have sea views.

🍴 Mon–Sat 12.30–3, 8–11pm
🍴 L €80, D €130, Wine €14
🚆 152
💶 €300–€330
🛏 124 (15 non-smoking)
♿
🚆 C52, E5, 140, 152

🅿 EUROPA
Corso Meridionale 14, 80143 Napoli
Tel 081 267511
www.sea-hotels.com

A convenient location and decent service make this a

good bet for accommodation near the *centro storico*. The 19th-century classical-style façade is reminiscent of the Bourbon royal palace nearby. Plants and frescoes fill the library and other public areas. Most of the soundproofed rooms have cheerful paintings hung on whitewashed walls. Facilities include television, phone, safe, hair-dryer and minibar. Traditional music is often played in the adjoining La Grande Abbuffata restaurant.

💶 €68–€180
🛏 80 (60 non-smoking)
♿
🚉 Piazza Garibaldi
🚆 ALIBUS to Piazza Garibaldi

🅿 GRAND HOTEL VESUVIO
Via Partenope 45, 80121 Napoli
Tel 081 7640044
www.vesuvio.it

Many notable figures such as Grace Kelly and tenor Enrico Caruso have passed through the doors of the Grand Hôtel du Vesuve since it opened in 1882. Public rooms and guest rooms are filled with antiques and exquisite fabrics. Services are comprehensive: limousine service and even a boat to

whisk you away. Dine in style at Caruso, the rooftop restaurant, or take advantage of the fitness, health and beauty facilities available at the Echia Club.

💶 €370
🛏 163 rooms, 16 suites (20 non smoking)
♿ 🏊
🚆 C52, E5, 140, 152

🅿 MARGHERITA
Via Cimarosa 29, 80127 Napoli
Tel 081 5567044

The Margherita is a decent budget option near the San Martino museum and gardens. There is a small, functional reception and the staff are welcoming. Some of the rooms are a little dark, but they are kept clean and tidy. Most doubles have two single beds put together. There are no fancy facilities, and bathrooms are shared. A far better choice than one of the shabby 1-star hotels near the Napoli Centrale station. No credit cards.

💶 €62 excluding breakfast
🛏 19
🚆 C28, C31, C32
🚡 Montesanto Funicular railway to Via Cimarossa

🅿 MIRAMARE
Via Nazario Sauro 24, 80132 Napoli
Tel 081 7647589
www.hotelmiramare.com

An aristocratic villa in the 19th century and the American consulate in the 1950s, this beautiful building has been transformed into an attractive hotel. Inside you will find quirky paintings and art nouveau furnishings. The bedrooms come with all modern comforts—satellite television, video player (with free video rental), trouser press, tea/coffee maker, minibar and hair-dryer. You can relax and enjoy the sublime vistas on the terrace.

💶 €150–€200
🛏 31
♿
🚆 152

POMPEI

🅸 DE VIVO
Via Roma 36/38, 80045 Pompei
Tel 081 8631163

This superb bar/ice cream parlour/pastry shop has a good range of beverages and snacks, including small pizzas and

filled flat-bread sandwiches and panini. For the sweet tooth, there are lots of pastries and cakes including Neapolitan *pastiera* (Easter orange and ricotta-filled grain pie), *sfogliatelle* (crunchy pastry wth a custard filling) and *babà al limoncello* (a soft cake with limoncello liqueur). You can even order a large cake, including the wonderful almond cake. The *gelati*, *sorbetti* and *semifreddi* will delight kids after a long day walking around the Scavi. No credit cards.

🕐 Daily 9am–10pm, Aug, Wed–Mon 9am–10pm, rest of year; closed 2 weeks in Jul

🍴 Pastries from €1, ice cream from €1.30

🍴 RISTORANTE-PIZZERIA CARLO ALBERTO

Via Carlo Alberto 15, 80045 Pompei
Tel 081 8633231

A small, well-designed eatery not far from the excavations. Choose from a wide selection of pastas and pizza. Delicious creations include seafood served in a tangy, slightly spicy lemon sauce. The wine list is okay for all but the very fussy, and the desserts are top notch. Polish off the meal with a drop of *grappa del vesuvio*, made from the Lacrima Christi grape that grows on the slopes of the dormant volcano.

🕐 Daily 12–3, 7–11.30pm
🍴 L €20, D €40, Wine €5
🔳 🔳

🍴 PRESIDENT

Piazza Schettino 12, 80045 Pompei
Tel 081 8507245
www.uniplan.it/president

This is an excellent choice for seafood-lovers. The fish is freshly caught and of the highest quality—the choice catches of the day are cooked in the oven using traditional methods. The choice of *antipasti* includes calamari served in a

subtle sauce and there is a superior selection of wines. There is also a water and an oil list (24 oils!).

🕐 Tue–Sun 12.30–3.30, 8–11; closed from 10–25 of Aug
🍴 L €80, D €80, Wine €11

🍴 AMLETO

Via Bartolo Longo 10, 80045 Pompei
Tel 081 8631004
www.hotelamleto.it

L'Amleto is a great base from which to explore the ruins of Pompei, Herculaneum (Ercolano) and the brooding menace of Vesuvio. The rooms are brightened up with artworks, mosaics and classical furnishings. The marble floors, subtle lighting and fresh, vibrant walls give the hotel an air of spacious tranquillity. The roof garden and solarium have bird's-eye views of the petrified Roman town. Free parking.

🍴 €95
🚪 26
🔳
🚆 Circumvesuviana train to Pompei

POSITANO
🍴 CAPITANO

Via Pasitea 119, 84017 Positano
Tel 089 811351

A feeling of elegant refinement pervades the Capitano. Dine under the pergolas on the terrace, where magical sea views complement the exceptional fare. First courses include a delicious calamari and scampi salad. Seafood dishes dominate. You shouldn't leave this part of the world without trying fried prawns with orange mayonnaise. The desserts are wonderful and the wine list is of a very high standard. Reservations are recommended.

🕐 Daily 12.30–3.30, 7.30–11pm
🍴 L €50, D €80, Wine €14

🍴 AL PALAZZO

Via dei Mulini 23, 84017 Positano
Tel 089 875177
www.palazzomurat.it

This refined restaurant in the Palazzo Murat hotel is covered in luxuriant foliage. The service may be a bit aloof for some but the food more than makes up for it. Of particular note is the spaghetti *al frutti del*

mare—a perfect marriage of various types of seafood and pasta. Their Neapolitan specials, aubergine (eggplant) *parmigiana*, is alive with the fresh essential tastes of this fertile region.

🕐 Daily 7.30–11; closed Nov–Easter
🍴 D €150, Wine €18

🍴 LA SPONDA

Via Cristoforo Colombo 30, 84017 Positano
Tel 089 875066
www.sirenuse.it

Lemon trees and bougainvillaea fill the air with scents in the summer months. The Sersale family are famed for their classic Neapolitan pasta

dishes and produce a very special *spaghetti al pomodoro e basilico* (tomato and basil). Also of note is the pasta with courgettes (zucchini). Try the *babà* and *pastiera* pastries. The wine list complements the dishes perfectly.

🕐 Daily 1–3.30, 8–10.30pm, Mar–Nov
🍴 L €80, D €175, Wine €30
🚆 Train from Napoli to Sorrento then local bus

⊖ALBERGO CASA ALBERTINA
Via Tavolozza 4, 84017 Positano
Tel 089 875143
www.casalbertina.it
A flight of 60 steps descending from the road leads to this

family-run hotel perched on the cliffs above Positano. Whitewashed vaulted ceilings and cool, blue-tiled, majolica flooring create a relaxing air. There are antique furnishings and fittings throughout and first-rate facilities in the guest rooms—some rooms have hydro-massage baths and all have a private terrace with a sublime panorama. There is a twisting route down to the beach by way of the *scali-natella* path. The restaurant serves excellent seafood and traditional Neapolitan dishes. Parking available.

🍴 €220–€250. Rooms are available on a half-board basis only
🛏 20 (non-smoking)
♿
⛴ Hydrofoil from Napoli Jun–Sep

⊖LA FENICE
Via Marconi 4, 84017 Positano
Tel 089 875513
A small hotel with spectacular views on the beachside. Cheery tiling, simple furnishings and intriguing artworks make the guest rooms beguiling, although the facilities are basic. Exuberant bougainvillaea surrounds the seawater pool and jacuzzi, and there is a wonderful private beach. Private boat tours can be booked from here, too. The hotel's paths are rather steep and the traffic can be noisy—not ideal for vertigo sufferers or light sleepers.

🍴 €100–€125
🛏 13 (2 suites)
⛱ Outdoor

⊖HOTEL DI SAN PIETRO
Via Laurito 2, 84047 Positano
Tel 089 875455
www.ilsanpietro.it
This luxury hotel (a member of the Relais & Châteaux alliance) is famed for its views, facilities, sumptuous suites and celebrity guests (it was Fellini's top choice). It has its own 17th-century church, perched among the dramatic cliffs just outside Positano. Each room has a huge marble bathroom and a private terrace. Antiques are carefully placed in common areas and guest rooms. Relax in the tran-

quil gardens and dine in the first-rate terrace restaurant. There is a private beach, a swimming pool overlooking the town of Praiano and a tennis court.

🍴 €420–€480
🛏 62 (8 non-smoking)
♿ ⛱ Outdoor
🚗 Take the A3 from Napoli and follow signs for Sorrento, then pass Positano and follow signs for the hotel (1.5km/2.4miles) on the SS163 towards Amalfi

⊖VILLA FRANCA
Viale Pasitea 318, 84017 Positano
Tel 089 875655
www.villafrancahotel.it

The cool blue-and-white façade hints at the relaxing qualities of this hotel's interior. Tiles, urns, plinths and green fronds fill the elegant public areas. Guest rooms vary in size,

but all have subtle shades and bright decorative touches. The pool and terrace overlook the beach and the terrace restaurant serves an excellent choice of Neapolitan food. Facilities include a health club and gym complete with Roman-style steam room and a state-of-the-art solarium.

🍴 €190–€310
🛏 37
♿ ⛱ Outdoor 🚗

RAVELLO

⊕CUMPÀ COSIMO
Via Roma 44/46, 84010 Ravello
Tel 089 857156
A magnet for visitors thanks to its great-value dishes and famous matriarch, Netta Bottone, who is something of a celebrity in the area. If you want to try a mixture of pasta shapes, usually served with pesto, opt for the *pasta mista*. The spicy *penne all'arrabiata* is particularly tastebud-tingling. Main courses include catches of the day from land and sea. There is a limited selection of wines. The home-made ice cream is excellent.

🕐 Daily 12.30–3.30, 8–11pm, Apr–Oct; Tue–Sun 12.30–3.30, 8–11pm, rest of year
🍴 L €35, D €60, Wine €9
♿ Section ♿

⊕ROSSELLINIS
Via San Giovanni del Toro 28, 84010 Ravello
Tel 089 818181
www.palazzosasso.com
Consistently awarded a very high rating by L'Espresso magazine, this restaurant is perched 300m (984ft) above the sea. They produce beautifully crafted dishes to delight

most palates. Look out for the asparagus *raviolini* with artichoke and carrot sauce, and the classic aubergine (eggplant) cannelloni. There are wonderful fish dishes and an irresistible dessert selection, including *sanguinello* (blood orange) and basil consommé accompanied by *cacao crostini* biscuits (cookies). The wine list is exceptional.

Ⓒ Daily 7.30–10.30pm; closed Nov–Mar

Ⓔ D €180, Wine €38

Ⓢ

⊖VILLA AMORE

Via Santa Chiara, 84010 Ravello
Tel 089 857135

A peaceful hotel just a short stroll from Piazza Duomo that is good value in the chic, pricey town of Ravello. There are spellbinding views from the terrace and a very good bar/restaurant serving traditional local dishes. Guest rooms are compact with modern furnishings and have original vaulted ceilings. Most have views of the gardens and beyond to the Thyrrhenian Sea. Reserve your place at this bargain hotel well in advance.

Ⓔ €68–€82

Ⓘ 12

⊖VILLA MARIA

Via Santa Chiara 2, 84010 Ravello
Tel 089 857170
www.villamaria.it

Villa Maria has whitewashed interiors that blend well with antiques and vibrant tiling. The gardens and many of the rooms provide great views of the Vallone del Dragone. Guest rooms have dark wood furniture, tiled floors and are equipped with private bathroom, telephone and television. The restaurant has an expansive terrace and lots of art nouveau touches. The Palumbo family also run cooking courses from here.

Ⓔ €210–€480

Ⓘ 23

Ⓢ

🚗 Turn off the A3 Napoli/Salerno road at junction Vietri S.Mare. Follow signs for Ravello and then signs for the hotel. Hotel guests can be escorted from Napoli by prior arrangement

SORRENTO

ⓘBUCO

Rampa Seconda Marina Piccola 5, 80067 Sorrento
Tel 081 8782354
www.ilbucoristorante.it

Buco is a former Teatini monastery, right in the middle of Sorrento. The food here

marries tradition with innovation, and the service is superb. Of particular note is the *fusilli al ragù* Genovese (pasta in a lamb sauce). Fish dishes include red mullet served on a

bed of orange slices and pecorino cheese. There are pleny of decent wines and some scrumptious desserts, which you can enjoy on the outside terrace.

Ⓒ Thu–Tue 12.30–2.45, 7–11pm; closed Jan

Ⓔ L €40, D €88, Wine €13

Ⓢ Section Ⓢ

ⓘCARUSO

Via Sant'Antonino 12, 80067 Sorrento
Tel 081 8073156
www.restorantemuseocaruso.com

This restaurant is named after the celebrated tenor and gastronomic genius. One room is crammed with photos and oddities documenting Caruso's life. The gramophone plays crackling classics by the maestro in the background. The menu has lots of vegetable and seafood dishes. Ask about the catch of the day, fried scampi with anchovy salsa, roasted peppers and the mouth-watering seafood platter. For dessert, try the *torta Caruso* made with orange and nuts.

Ⓒ Daily 12–3.30, 7.30–11.30pm; closed Mon in Jan

Ⓔ L €82, D €110, Wine €15

Ⓢ Section Ⓢ

ⓘLA FAVORITA–O' PARRUCCHIANO

Corso Italia 71, 80067 Sorrento
Tel 081 8781321
www.parruchiano.it

Dining is quite an event in this cavernous Victorian greenhouse filled with luxuriant foliage and trees. It was opened in the late 19th century by a local priest. Culinary highlights include the traditional *Sorrentine peperoni*

ripieni (stuffed peppers) and *ravioli caprese* filled with mozzarella, sweet pomodoroni tomatoes and basil. For dessert, try the scrumptious profiteroles, Neapolitan pastries or a choice of *gelati* and *semifreddi*. There is a good selection of regional vintages.

Ⓒ Daily 12.30–3.30, 8–11pm, Apr–Oct; Thu–Tue 12.30–3.30, 8–11pm, rest of year

Ⓔ L €24, D €62, Wine €6

⊖GRAND HOTEL EXCELSIOR VITTORIA

Piazza Tasso 34, 80067 Sorrento
Tel 081 8071044
www.exvitt.it

This magnificent hotel first opened in 1834, brimming with Victorian style. Within the lush grounds are 2ha (5 acres) of citrus trees and many rare plants, as well as a sizeable swimming pool. The guest rooms and suites have lots of belle époque decorative touches and top-class facilities. Many have terraces with views of the gardens or sea. There are self-catering apartments also available. At the restaurant you can dine in style under a celestial 19th-century ceiling or by candlelight on one of the terraces.

Ⓔ €310–€400

Ⓘ 98 (non-smoking)

Ⓢ 🏊 Outdoor

🚢 From Napoli and Sorrento

⊖IMPERIAL TRAMONTANO

Via Vittorio Veneto 1, 80067 Sorrento
Tel 081 8781940
www.tramontana.com

This 16th-century palazzo, opened its doors as a hotel in 1812 and has been the choice of royalty as well as literary icons such as Byron, Shelley and Goethe. The winter garden has luxuriant fronds and antique items; and the lobby has antiques and Old World panache. Most guest rooms have parquet flooring and elegant furnishings. Many of them have magnificent views, and there is access to a private beach and swimming pool.

Ⓒ Closed Jan–Feb

Ⓔ €260

Ⓘ 116

Ⓢ 🏊 Outdoor

EATING

Sicilian cooking reflects the influence of the island's foreign invaders; Greek, Arab, Norman and Spanish. Like southern Italy, street food is popular in the shape of pizza, *arancini*, croquettes and fritters, and there's a plethora of sweets—don't miss *cannoli*, fried pastries stuffed with ricotta, candied fruit and chocolate, or cassata ice cream and ultra-realistic marzipan fruit. Fish is everywhere, particularly swordfish and tuna, and the quality and variety of fruit and vegetables is superlative. Marsala, a sweet fortified wine, is made here; for mealtime drinking, pick one of the excellent Corvo wines. Sicilian pastries are feather-light and traditionally livened up with lemon or orange flower water.

Sardinia's landscape is not romantic like Siciliy and mainland Italy. Despite its rocky and arid appearance it has a primordial beauty and simplicity that is reflected in its cuisine. There is very little pasta. Roasted vegetables, meats and fish dominate the menu instead. Cooking relies heavily on fish, often made into Spanish-influenced stews spiked with saffron. There are some excellent local cheeses—look out for the salty pecorino Sardo. Carnivores will find plenty of suckling pig and young lamb on the menu, best enjoyed with Cannonau di Sardegna, a punchy, full-bodied red wine. Another delicious meal is Bottarga, mullet-egg caviar; it's often served with the papery, crisp *carta di*

musica, just one of Sardinia's excellent breads. Look out for the delicate gnocchetti, made from durum wheat tinted with saffrona, unique to the island.

STAYING

Unless you're visiting Sicily for a seaside holiday, the chances are you'll be touring, staying just a couple of nights at different bases. Most visitors take in Palermo, the capital, where there's plenty of choice, before heading on. Good options include historic Siracusa, Agrigento for the classical sites, and picturesque Erice on the west coast. Taormina is Sicily's prime resort town, but Cefalù, on the north coast, has a lot going for it, while Enna, high in the interior mountains, makes a great stopover. The off-coast island groups, the Egadi and Aeolian, are popular holiday destinations in summer, and it is advisable to book in advance.

Sardinian possibilities include Olbia, handy for the Costa Smeralda, the lovely west-coast Cala Gonone and Alghero, the island's main holiday destination, on the east coast. Cagliari is the capital and you should aim to stay in the old Castello quarter to experience the city at its best.

AGRIGENTO

🍴 BLACK HORSE

Via celauro 8, 92100 Agrigento
Tel 0922 23223

Climb the steep steps from 'new' Agrigento's main drag to discover this tiny eating house, packed with hungry locals. Tables in the two small rooms

are cramped and close together, but you'll forget this as you are served some of the best food that Sicily has to offer. Everything's home-made and the staff are incredibly helpful. Try *spaghetti con le sarde* (spaghetti with sardines), pasta with *melanzane* (pasta with aubergines, tomato and melted mozzarella), *ricotta salata* (aubergines and intensely-seasoned salted ricotta), plain grilled fish and *caponata* (mixed vegetables with a hint of sweet and sour).

🕐 Mon–Sat 2.30–2.30, 7.30–10pm; closed 1 Jan
🍷 L €14, D €30, Wine €4.50

🍴 KAOS

Villagio Pirandello, 92100 Agrigento
Tel 0922 598622
Fax 0922 598770
www.atenahotels.com
This 18th-century villa, once the property of a local landowning family, has been sensitively converted into one of the area's nicest hotels, nestling among ancient olive groves. The rooms are big and cool, the public areas well thought out and there's plenty to do, with tennis, spacious grounds and a private beach. At only 2km (3 miles) from the Valley of the Temples, it's a great place to stay to escape the crowds.
💶 €130–€150
🛏 111 (non-smoking)
🏊 Outdoor
🚗 From Catania and Palermo
🚌 Agrigento from Catania and Palermo
🚙 Take the A20 from Messina to Palermo and the Caltanissetta exit. Follow the signs to Agrigento on the SS640, then take the SS189 to Agrigento and follow signs to the hotel

CEFALU

🍴 OSTARIA DEL DUOMO

Via Seminario 5, Cefalu, Palermo 90015
Tel 0921 421838
You can eat outside in the shadow of the magnificent duomo or in the welcoming interior on cooler evenings. The grilled fish, seafood, pasta and *antipasti* are particularly good—choose from a selection of local sweet-sour dishes, *caponata* (spicy vegetable pickled salad), white anchovies and tiny fried fish. It can be

SPECIAL

⊖MODERNO
Via Vittorio Emmanuele 63, Èrice,
91016 Tràpani
Tel 0923 869300
Fax 0923 869139
www.pippocatalano.it
You're in for a treat at this
lovely hotel, a sensitively converted 18th-century house.
The bedrooms have white
walls, white linen and gleaming mahogany pieces, while
the public areas are scattered
with squishy sofas. There is a
lovely courtyard for breakfast
and an excellent restaurant,
which stresses the multicultural side of Sicilian cuisine.
€95–€115
40
From Trapani (10km/16 miles)
Take the A29 from Palermo and
exit at Trapani, then follow signs to
Erice and yellow signs to the hotel

busy at lunchtime, but it is
worth waiting to get a table
here. There is a selection of
Sicilian and Italian wines—try
Corvo, an excellent red.
Daily 12.30–3, 7–midnight,
May–Sep; Tue–Sun 12.30–3, 7–
midnight, rest of year
L €30, D €56, Wine €10

⊖KALURA
Via V Cavallaro 13, Cefalù, 90015
Palermo
Tel 0921 421354
Fax 0921 423122
www.kalura.it
Nearly all the big, airy rooms
here have balconies overlooking the sea, as does the
outdoor dining terraces and
bar. One of the most beautifully positioned hotels in Sicily,
with lovely gardens, tennis
courts and a children's playground; steep steps lead down
to the beach. Efficiently run by
a Sicilian family, there's a winning combination of laid-back
charm and attention to detail
here. It is peaceful and quiet,
except at weekends, when it's
a favourite spot for weddings.
€120–€196
50 (40 non-smoking)
Outdoor and private beach
From Palermo
Cefalu then bus
From Palermo or Messina take the
A20 and exit at Cefalu Ovest. Follow the

yellow hotel signs to the hotel; approx
1.5 km (1 mile) east of the old town on
the coast

LIPARI

⊕FILIPPINO
Piazza Municipio, Lipari, Isole Eilie,
Messina
Tel 0909 811002
A big, bustling restaurant full of
locals and holidaymakers;
white walls with bright tiles,
ceramics and greenery set the
tone. The signature dishes
here include *maccaruna, tre-
cette orchidee delle Eolie*, a
local pasta dish with a caper,
almond, basil, pecorino and
anchovy sauce, and sea bass-
stuffed ravioli (*ravioli di
cernia*). There is fish from the
family boats, and friendly
service—leave room for the
semifreddo with hot
chocolate sauce.
Daily 2.30–2.30, 7.45–10.30pm,
Apr–Oct; Tue–Sun 2.30–2.30,
7.45–10.30pm, Oct–9 Nov and 27
Dec–May; closed 10 Nov–26 Dec
L €40, D €60, Wine €10
Section

⊖GATTOPARDO PARK
Via Diana, Lipari, 98055 Messina
Tel 0909 811035
Fax 0909 880207
www.netnet.it/hotel/gattopardo/index
The main building, a villa in a
beautiful setting, dates from
the 18th century, but the
rooms to go for are in the private dwellings that nestle in
the flowery garden away from
the villa. There are great views
from the breakfast terrace, the
service is friendly and helpful
and its close to some of the
island's best beaches.
Closed Nov–Feb
€110–€240
50 (non-smoking)
From Messina, Naples and Palermo
May–Oct
Take a taxi from the port

PALERMO

⊕FRUTTI DI MARE
Via Messina Marine 204, 90100 Palermo
Tel 091 471699
Overlooking the Mediterranean
Sea, this well-known seafood
restaurant beautifully prepares
the catch of the day. It's worth
visiting for the *vongole e faso-
lari zuppetta* (mussel and clam
soup) as well as the spicy
seafood spaghetti. The wine
list is pretty basic, but the
house wines are good enough

to rely on. Overall this restau-
rant is great value for money.
No credit cards.
Daily noon–3, 7–midnight
L €30, D €40, Wine €8
Section
101, 212, 250

⊕OSTERIA DEI VESPRI
Piazza Croce Dei Vespri 6, 90133
Palermo
Tel 091 6171631
Considered one of Sicily's
finest restaurants, this intimate
eatery is where locals come for
a romantic feast. The *caponata*
(salad made with
aubergine/eggplant) and
penne pasta with tuna sauce
are recommended. In summer,
you can eat outdoors in the
beautiful piazza. Be sure to
reserve well in advance, as
tables here are constantly
in demand.
Mon–Sat noon–3, 8–midnight,
Sep–Jul; Mon–Sat 8–midnight, rest of
year; closed 1 week in Aug
L €40, D €70, Wine €10
Section
101, 122, 220

⊖PRINCIPE DI VILLA
FRANCA
Via Giuseppina Turrisi Colonna 4, 90140
Palermo
Tel 091 6118523
www.principedivillafrance.it
Villa Franca is in a smart district
near the Teatro Politeama. The
large guesthouse showcases
Sicilian craftsmanship, from
the bed spreads to the furniture, and pride and care have
been taken in every detail. The
restaurant is worth a visit for
its traditional cooking, which
makes the most of the island's
abundant produce.
€180
34 (3 non-smoking)
101, 107, 614

SIRACUSA
⊕DON CAMILLO
Via Maestranza 96, 96100 Siracusa
Tel 0931 67133
www.ristorantedoncamillosiracusa.it
This busy, highly regarded
restaurant has a creative
approach to the bounty of
seafood available to it. The raw
shrimp, octopus and squid are
top choices, as is the *piselli e
vongole* (mussels with peas).
The chef, Giovanni, has won
the Premio Caseus, an award
for promoting gourmet and

EATING AND STAYING

artisan cheeses, so check out the cheese board. Try a slice of lemon torte for dessert. A complimentary bus service runs on a circular route from the parking area near the restaurant to the middle of the city.

🕐 Mon–Sat noon–3, 7–10pm; closed 2 weeks in Nov, and 23–27 Dec
🍴 L €24, D €75, Wine €12
Ⓢ section Ⓢ
🅿 1

🍴 JONICO A RUTTA 'E CIAULI
Riviera Dionisio il Grande 194, 96100 Siracusa
Tel 0931 65540

Stylish art nouveau surroundings and a terrace with beautiful views over the Mediterranean complement the carefully prepared food here. The menu offers plenty of opportunity to be adventurous, with fresh pasta and marinated octopus, or fragrant roasted aubergines (eggplants) with sardines. The staff are very helpful and happily accommodate fussy customers. Make room for a dessert—sample the creamy *gelato* (ice cream) or the rich *zuppa inglese* (trifle).

🕐 Wed–Mon noon–3, 8–10.30pm
🍴 L €20, D €50, Wine €11
🅿 1

🍴 RISTORANTE GIOIA
Via dei Tolomei 5, 96100 Siracusa
Tel 0931 66386

This well-known restaurant is just a few steps away from the cathedral, and is appreciated by both locals and visitors who enjoy great food at low prices. The *gambieri al menta* (minted prawns) are unusual but delicious. The pastas with seafood and vegetables are fresh-tasting and plentiful.

🕐 Tue–Sun 12.30–3, 7.30–midnight
🍴 L €40, D €60, Wine €10
🅿 1

🛏 DOMUS MARIAE
Via Vittorio Veneto 76, 96100 Siracusa
Tel 0931 24858
www.sistema.it/domusmariae

The small and efficient Domus Mariae, with its fantastic location on the promontory of Ortigia, is good value for money. Set right on the seafront, the terrace has mesmerizing views of Mount Etna smoking in the distance. The rooms are spacious and have big beds, balconies and tidy little bathrooms. The restaurant serves a good selection of Sicilian dishes.

🛏 €130–€150
🛏 12 (non-smoking)
Ⓢ
🚌 Circolare 1, 8, 20
🚂 Siracusa from Milano, Roma, Napoli and Palermo

🛏 GRAND HOTEL VILLA POLITI
Via Politi 2, 96100 Siracusa
Tel 0931 412121
www.villapoliti.com

Once a haunt of the island's great: Winston Churchill chose this hotel as a retreat, where he spent many hours painting Ortigia. Its carefully preserved 18th-century elegance sets it apart from other hotels, and the level of service ensures that guests return year after year. The bedrooms have a sense of grandeur, but have a number of modern touches.

🛏 €186
🛏 100 (20 non-smoking)
Ⓢ 🏊 Outdoor
🚌 Circolari 1, 3

🛏 GUTKOWSKI
Lungomare Vittorini 26, 96100 Siracusa
Tel 0931 465830
www.guthotel.it

Free of frills, the Gutkowski is appealing in its simplicity. The rooms are fresh and airy and have clean, tiled bathrooms. Take your breakfast on the terrace and soak up the dazzling Mediterranean views before exploring the local sights, such as the Tempio di Apollo and the duomo, which are within minutes of the hotel.

🛏 €85–€90
🛏 27 (4 non-smoking)
Ⓢ
🚌 Circolare 20
🚗 Take the Catania–Siracusa motorway and exit at Siracusa Sud. Follow this to the *centro storico*. The hotel is on the east coast of the Isla di Ortiga

🛏 TENUTA DI ROCCADIA
Strada Provinciale Carlentini-Villasmundo, Carlentini, 96013 Siracusa
Tel 0959 90362
www.roccadia.com

Count Roccadia gave this ancient parcel of land to a group of Cistercian monks, who built a monastery here. Now converted into an *agritourism* hostel, it provides guests with the opportunity to experience the beauty of rustic

Sicily. The hostel arranges a wide range of outdoor activities such as horse riding and archaeology tours. The rooms, which are more stylish than in most hostels, sleep two to four and even have private bathrooms. A car is essential here.

🛏 €60–€80
🛏 20
Ⓢ 2 🏊 Outdoor
🚂 Train to Lentini
🚗 Take the Catania–Siracusa motorway and exit at Brucoli–Carlentini, 30km (19 miles) from Siracusa

TAORMINA

🍴 CASA GRUGNO
Via Santa Maria de' Greci, 98039 Taormina
Tel 0942 21208
www.casagrugno.it

In the medieval part of the city, close to the duomo, this restaurant has been artistically decorated using flattering, warm hues of orange and yellow. The sumptuous fare includes shellfish doused in Cognac and freshly made ravioli filled with goat's cheese. The staff will help you choose a wine from the exhaustive list.

🕐 Mon–Sat noon–2.30, 7–10.30pm, Dec–Jan, Mar–Apr and Oct; Mon–Sat 7–10.30pm, May–Sep; closed Feb and Nov
🍴 L €60, D €100, Wine €16
Ⓢ Section

🍴 PORTA MESSINA
Largo Giove Serapide 4, 98039 Taormina
Tel 0942 23205

Next to the city walls, this restaurant overlooking a little piazza is an inexpensive option at €7. The menu is comprehensive, with pizza, seafood and pasta choices. The simply grilled catch of the day with a spicy dressed salad stands out, as do the traditional Sicilian puddings and simple but wonderfully refreshing *granita* (fruity crushed ice).

🕐 Daily noon–2.30, 7–midnight,

Jul–Aug; Thu–Tue noon–2.30, 7–midnight, Sep–Dec and Feb–May; closed Jan

🍴 L €20, D €50, Wine €10
Ⓢ Section

🍴 RISTORANTE LA GRIGLIA
Corso Umberto 54, 98039 Taormina
Tel 0942 23980

Taormina can be crowded during summer, but you can escape the hordes here. Sit outside and enjoy a traditional meal under the covered terrace. You'll find local dishes on the menu including spit roasted pig. Look out for raw scampi with lemon, and pasta with aubergine (eggplant) and basil. The desserts are worth a mention too, with *crêpes all cassata* stealing the show.

⏰ Wed–Mon noon–2.30, 7.30–10.30pm
🍴 L €30, D €70, Wine €16
Ⓢ Section 🔲

🏨 GRANDE ALBERGO CAPOTAORMINA
Via Nazionale 105, 98039 Taormina
Tel 0942 572111
www.capotaorminahotel.com

With rooms as bright as Sicilian pottery, inspiring views and a lift descending to the hotel's private caves, beach and saltwater pool, this Minoletti-designed hotel has a lot to recommend it. Every room has a balcony or sea view terrace. Downstairs, there is a piano bar and three restaurants.

⏰ Closed Oct–Mar
🛏 €208–€300
🛌 206 (13 non-smoking)
🔲 🏊 Outdoor 🎾

SPECIAL
🍴 RISTORANTE DA LORENZO
Via Roma 12, 98039 Taormina
Tel 0942 23480

This restaurant has a beautiful open-air terrace overlooking the Ionian Sea. Squid and fish are imaginatively prepared and served with roasted vegetables or fresh pasta. Make room for the *tiramisù* or the local perfumed strawberries and a glass of Marsala.

⏰ Thu–Tue noon–3, 7–11pm; closed 10 Jan–10 Feb
🍴 L €30, D €60, Wine €7.50
Ⓢ Section

🏨 VILLA BELVEDERE
Via Bagnoli Croce 79, 98039 Taormina
Tel 0942 23791
www.villabelvedere.it

One of Taormina's first hotels, this establishment remains one of the area's best places to stay, and is the perfect base from which to enjoy the history and architecture of the town.

The beautiful garden pool, where flowers drop into the water, is a relaxing place to enjoy a drink. The rooms are fresh and clean with small balconies, many of which look out over the Ionian Sea or Mount Etna.

⏰ Closed Nov–Mar
🛏 €164–€198
🛌 49 (10 non-smoking)
🔲 🏊 Outdoor

🏨 VILLA FIORITA
Via Pirandello 39, 98039 Taormina
Tel 0942 24122
www.villafioritahotel.com

Built on the side of a cliff and close to the Teatro Greco, this old inn has a number of interesting features, from the Greek tomb in the garden to its many staircases. Each room has a terrace, and when the Sicilian sun gets a little too much there is a garden with shady areas and a pool.

🛏 €120
🛌 25
🔲 🏊 Outdoor
✈ From Catania airport 40km (25 miles)
🚂 Taormina, then local bus or taxi
🚗 Exit Taormina from the A18 and head for *centro storico* and follow signs for hotel

SARDINIA

ALGHERO
🍴 AL TUGURI
Via Maiorca 113, Alghero, 07041 Sassari
Tel 0799 76772
www.altuguri.it

Benito Carbonella cooks true Sardinian food in this tiny and elegant restaurant on two floors—head upstairs and watch the food being prepared in the kitchen. Fish is king here, and the menu changes constantly, dictated by season, freshness and availability. To sample it properly go for the *menu degustazione* or try *acciughe marinate* (white marinated anchovies), *conchiglie con aragosta e broccoli* (pasta shells with a lobster and broccoli sauce), Catalan-influenced chicken with peppers (*pollo e peperoni*) and *crema catalan*, vanilla custard with a caramelized topping.

⏰ Mon–Sat 2.30–2, 8–10.30pm; closed 20 Dec–20 Jan
🍴 2 courses minimum: L €50, D €56, Wine €13
🔲

🏨 CONTINENTAL
Via F.lli Kennedy 66, Alghero, 07041 Sassari
Tel 0799 75250
Fax 0799 81046
www.hotelcalabona.it

Outside the city but with a regular bus service into town, this makes a good choice if you want to escape the crowds. Very much a family affair, this is a typical Italian summer hotel, with good-sized rooms, some with balconies, and adequate bathrooms. It is superb value, and you can use the facilities of its more expensive sister hotel, the Calabona.

⏰ May–Sep
🛏 €67–€108
🛌 35
🏊 Use of pool and private beach at Hotel Calabona (800m/2,624ft)

CAGLIARI
🍴 ANTICA HOSTARIA
Via Camillo Benso Cavour 60, 09124 Cagliari
Tel 070 665870

This is the restaurant of choice for the Sardinian glitterati. Staff are formally dressed and there is an air of grandness about the place. High on the menu are the mussels and lobster cooked in local white wine and *burrida* (fish marinated in walnut and garlic sauce). The wine list is limited but excellent.

⏰ Mon–Sat 1.30–3, –11pm; closed Aug and 23 Dec–6 Jan
🍴 L €40, D €60, Wine €10
🔲
🚌 1, 6, 7

CORSARO
Viale Regina Margherita 28, 09125
Cagliari
Tel 070 664318

This elegant dining room gets top marks for service and style and the food is worth the high prices. Start your meal with hot Sardinian *carasau* (thin, crispy bread) with a trickle of olive oil. Notable dishes include *saccaia* (lamb with broth) and pasta stuffed with ricotta and vegetables. There is an excellent wine list.

🕐 Mon–Fri 12.30–3, 7.30–11pm, Sat 7.30–11pm; closed 2 weeks in Aug and 23–27 Dec
🍴 L €50, D €80, Wine €17
🅢 Section 🅢
🚌 5, 6

FLORA
Via Sassari 45, 09124 Cagliari
Tel 070 664735

This charming little *trattoria* in the Stampace area has a courtyard with a banana tree and scented flowering shrubs. It serves a number of inventive dishes: Worth trying are the tagliatelle with sea anemone, pasta with *bottarga* (sun-dried fish roe) and *fregola* (Sardinian couscous). This place heaves with locals almost every night of the week, so reserve your table early.

🕐 Mon–Sat 1–4, 8–midnight; closed 2 weeks in Aug and 25 Dec
🍴 L €40, D €60, Wine €12
🅢 Section
🚌 1, 5, 6, 7

FORTE VILLAGE
Santa Margherita di Pula, 09010 Cagliari
Tel 070 92171
www.fortevillageresort.com

This sprawling, 5-star resort is the ideal place to be pampered in the Sardinian sun. An extensive range of accomodation, bars and restaurants are available throughout its exotic gardens. The famous Thermae del Parco Spa, used by international footballers recuperating from injuries, was prized with the prestigious World's Leading Spa award in 2003. The resort has plenty of sport and recreation facilities to choose from such as golf, go-karting and outdoor ice-skating.

🕐 Mar–Oct
🍴 €167–€2,000. Rooms available on a half-board only basis

🛏 771 rooms, suites and bungalows
🅢 🏊 Outdoor 🅥
🚆 From Piazza Matteotti rail station and Elmas bus from the airport on request
🚗 Follow road SS195

CALA GONONE

AL PORTO
Piazza del Porto 2, Cala Gonone, 08020 Nuòro
Tel 0784 93185

This is a local favourite with views over the port from the pretty terrace. Fish and seafood dominate, but there are nice touches such as the traditional paper-thin bread, *carta di musica*, and good local wines. Try the *Zuppa di pesce all'aragosta* (fish soup with lobster*), scampi, insalata di mare* (fish and seafood antipasto), *fritto misto* (mixed fried fish) or the the day's catch *alla griglia* (charcoal-grilled).

🕐 12.30–3.30, 7.30–11.30; closed first 2 weeks in Dec and last 2 weeks in Jan
🍴 L €30, D €36, Wine €11
🅢 Section

CALA LUNA
Lungomare Palmasera 6, Cala Gonone, 08020 Nùoro
Tel 0784 93133
Fax 0784 93162
www.hotelcalaluna.com

Cala Gonone has some of the loveliest stretches of coastline on the island, and this good-value hotel stands less than 50m (164ft) away from the beach. Italian-seaside in style, the rooms have good beds, though they're plain and simply furnished. Don't expect great interiors, but the staff are friendly—the family have run the place since the 1960s.

🍴 €57–€78
🛏 26
🚗 Take the SS125 north from Cagliari. Turn right down to Cala Gonone just before Dorgali

PORTO ROTONDO

DA GIOVANNINO
Piazza Quadrata, Porto Rotondo, 07020 Sàssari
Tel 0789 35280

Push the boat out and eat at this elegant restaurant, as renowned for its wines as its food. In summer you can enjoy fish and seafood, but come autumn game and wild mushrooms make up the menu. All pasta is home-made; try *mac-*

carones de busa with chicken sauce, perhaps a *fritto misto* (mixed fried prawns, shrimp and scampi) or *filetti al limone*, fish with lemon sauce. They have some tasty desserts including a superb *crema catalana*. (Catalan cream dessert).

🕐 Daily 12.30–2.30, 8–10.30pm, Apr–mid-Nov; Tue–Sat 12.30–2.30, 8–10.30pm, Sun 12.30–2.30pm mid-Nov–Mar
🍴 L €100, D €120, Wine €15
🅢 Section 🅢

GREEN PARK
Località Aldia Manna, Porto Rotondo, 07020 Sàssari
Tel 0789 380100
Fax 0789 380043
www.progest.net

Stay in the main building, with more expensive rooms, or opt for one of the cheaper, single-storey dwellings scattered around the grounds—they all have a balcony or terrace with a sea view and the beach is less than 1km (0.6 mile) away. The rates are good for the Costa Smeralda and there are plenty of sporting activities laid on. The complex is totally geared to holidaymakers and the full board includes Sardinian specials and wine.

🕐 Closed mid-Oct–mid-Apr
🍴 €76–€150 full board; €70–€142 half-board
🛏 50
🅢 🏊 2 outdoor
🚗 Take the 125 north from Olbia then after 9km (5.6 miles) turn right to Porto Rotondo and follow signs to the hotel
🚕 Olbia then taxi; hotel will arrange transfer

RESTAURANT AND HOTEL PRICES		

RESTAURANTS
The prices given are for a two-course lunch (L) and a three-course dinner (D) for two people, without drinks. The wine price is for a bottle of house wine.

HOTELS
The prices given are for the lowest and highest for a double room for one night including breakfast, unless otherwise stated. Note that rates can vary depending on the time of year.

Planning

CLIMATE AND WHEN TO GO

Contrary to the picture-postcard image of perpetual sunshine and blue skies, Italy has variable weather. Apart from the summer months, when temperatures soar and the sun shines all day, this mountainous country has the full range of conditions. The climate is predominantly Mediterranean, with the far north experiencing Alpine trends and the far south arid and hot. Spring is pleasant everywhere, but there's frequent rain right through into May, and temperatures north of Rome only start to climb in June. Farther south, April and May see the start of summer. Italy's hot months are from July to September, when average temperatures are around 30°C (86°F) and the sirocco, a hot wind from Africa,

pushes the humidity up. In summer, the area around the Alps experiences numerous thunderstorms, which regularly help clear the air, but inland parts of southern Italy suffer extremely hot nights, often making sleeping difficult. As in the spring, the sirocco may well bring very high temperatures to parts of Italy during the autumn, accompanied by high humidity. Temperatures start to drop everywhere towards the end of September, with increasingly frequent bouts of rain and the first frosts in the Alps. Winter in the north is cold, with snow in the mountains, heavy frosts and thick fog on the plains. These conditions are also found to an extent in central Italy, with Tuscany and Umbria both experiencing bitter spells during the winter months. Winter is the wettest season in the south, and average daytime temperatures range from 7°C to 13°C (45°F to 55°F). November is dank and wet everywhere, though things improve around Christmas, when you can hope for some crystal-clear, cold, sunny weather. Mountain regions are colder with heavy winter snowfalls (see below).

WEATHER REPORTS

BBC world news and CNN news have websites and broadcast regular global weather updates in English, and The Weather

Channel and the Met Office in the UK have global weather websites too (www.bbc.co.uk, www.CNN.com, Weather Channel—www.weather.com, www.metoffice.com).

MOUNTAINOUS AREAS

The weather can change dramatically very quickly in the mountains throughout the year,

TIMES ZONES		
City	Time difference	Time at 12 noon in Italy
Amsterdam	0	noon
Auckland	+11	11pm
Berlin	0	noon
Brussels	0	noon
Cairo	+1	1pm
Chicago	-7	5am
Dublin	-1	11am
Johannesburg	+1	1pm
London	-1	11am
Madrid	0	noon
Montreal	-6	6am
New York	-6	6am
Paris	0	noon
Perth, Australia	+7	7pm
San Francisco	-9	3am
Sydney	+9	9pm
Tokyo	+8	8pm

Italy is one hour ahead of GMT/UTC. The clocks are moved forward an hour for daylight saving time on the last Sunday in March. The clocks go back an hour on the last Sunday in October. The chart shows the time differences from Italy.

WEATHER STATIONS

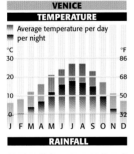

Venice 6m 20ft

Milan 210m 689ft

ROMA 3m 10ft

Palermo 34m 112ft

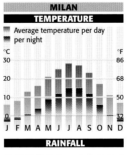

VENICE

TEMPERATURE

■ Average temperature per day
■ per night

MILAN

TEMPERATURE

■ Average temperature per day
■ per night

ROME

TEMPERATURE

■ Average temperature per day
■ per night

RAINFALL

Average rainfall

RAINFALL

Average rainfall

RAINFALL

Average rainfall

PLANNING

ITALIAN EMBASSIES AND CONSULATES ABROAD

Country	Address	Website
Australia	12 Grey Street, Deakin ACT 2600, Tel 02 6273 3333	www.ambitalia.org.au
Canada	275 Slater Street, 21st Floor, Ottawa (ON), KIP 5HP, Tel 1 613 2322401	www.italyincanada.com
Ireland	63/65 Northumberland Road, Dublin 4, Tel 1 6601744	www.italianembassy.ie
New Zealand	34–28 Grant Road, PO Box 463, Thorndon, Wellington, Tel 4 4735339	www.italy–embassy.org.nz
South Africa	796 George Avenue, Arcadia 0083 Pretoria, Tel 012 4305541/2/4/4	www.ambital.org.za
UK	No. 14 Three Kings Yard, London W1Y 2EH, Tel 020 73122200	www.embitaly.org.uk
USA	3000 Whitehaven Street NW, Washington DC 20008, Tel 202/612-4400	www.italyemb.org

so prepare for all eventualities. Always carry waterproofs and extra layers, as sudden drops in temperature and changes in conditions are common even in summer. Remember to carry enough water when you are in remote areas. At high altitudes the sun can be fierce and it is magnified in winter when it reflects off the snow, so cover up and wear plenty of sun block. Most ski resorts monitor the avalanche reports and close runs that are at risk, but if you intend to go off piste or climb in remote areas without a guide, you should check the weather and avalanche reports beforehand. (www.eurometeo.com www.csac.org).

NATURAL HAZARDS

These include landslides, avalanches, mudflows and flooding, mainly in the winter months. Earthquakes are occasionally felt in many parts of the country. Northern and central Italy may experience bad flooding in the winter months and shorter periods of localized flooding during the dramatic summer thunderstorms,

DUTY-FREE AND DUTY-PAID GUIDELINES

Anything that is clearly for personal use can be taken into Italy free of duty, but it is worth carrying receipts for valuable items in case you need to prove that they haven't been bought in Italy.

Duty-paid allowances for US citizens

US citizens can bring home up to $800 of duty-paid goods, provided they have been out of the country for at least 48 hours and haven't made another international trip in the past 30 days. This limit applies to each member of the family, regardless of age, and allowances may be pooled.

•1 litre of alcohol	•100 cigars (non-Cuban)
•200 cigarettes	•1 bottle perfume (if trademarked in the US)

For the most up-to-date information, see the US Department of Homeland Security's website: www.customs.treas.gov.

Duty-paid guidelines for EU citizens

You cannot buy goods duty-free if you are journeying within the EU. You can take home unlimited amounts of duty-paid goods, as long as they are for your own personal use. H. M. Customs and Excise considers anything over the following limits to be for commercial use.

Whatever your entitlement, you cannot bring back goods for

•3,200 cigarettes	•3kg of tobacco
•400 cigarillos	•200 cigars
•110 litres of beer	•10 litres of spirits
•90 litres of wine	•20 litres of fortified wine (such as port or sherry)

payment (including payment in kind) or for resale. These goods are considered for commercial use, and duty is payable.
For the most up-to-date information, see the H. M. Customs and Excise website: www.hmce.gov.uk

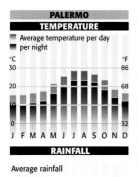

PALERMO

TEMPERATURE

■ Average temperature per day
■ per night

RAINFALL

Average rainfall

particularly around the northern lakes. Flooding and land subsidence is an ongoing problem in Venice. In autumn, especially in October and November, the tide rises in the city, flooding houses, churches and shops, causing damage to businesses and affecting visitors and residents alike. Parts of southern Italy lie on a major seismic fault line, and minor tremors and earthquakes are almost a daily occurrence. There has been renewed volcanic activity on Mount Etna in Sicily. The eruptions themselves appear to have subsided for the

meantime, but if you plan to climb Etna you should always follow the advice of guides near the summit and keep to the designated routes at all times. There is ongoing volcanic activity on the island of Stromboli.

WHAT TO TAKE

You will need lightweight cottons and linens to wear during the summer, except in the mountains where sudden drops in temperature and changes in weather conditions are common. Natural fabrics are more comfortable in humid conditions. Light- to medium-weight clothing

PLANNING

is worn in the south during winter, while warmer clothes are worn elsewhere. Alpine wear is needed during winter in the mountain resorts.

In the fashion-conscious cities such as Rome, Milan and Venice, people tend to dress smartly at all times. Bring clothes that cover your shoulders and knees if you are intending to visit churches or other religious buildings.

REMEMBER TO PACK…
- Waterproofs.
- A folding umbrella.
- A small bag for daily use, such as a shoulder bag that can be worn across the body, or a money belt.
- Your driver's licence.
- Comfortable shoes.
- A compass.
- Your address book, for emergency contacts or postcards.
- Photocopies of all important documents: passport, insurance details, credit card, debit card and passport numbers and registration numbers for mobile phones, cameras and other expensive items.
- A torch (flashlight) and binoculars.
- A first aid kit, including plasters (Band Aids), antiseptic cream, painkillers and any prescribed medication.
- An Italian phrasebook—any attempt at Italian is appreciated.
- Toiletries and sunscreen in screw-top containers inside plastic bags to guard against leakage caused by variable pressure in aircraft luggage holds.

LUGGAGE ALLOWANCES
On international flights within Europe, the IATA allowances are 20kg (44 pounds) for economy class and 30kg (66 pounds) for first class, but ask your airline before you fly as there may be restrictions (particularly budget airlines) and you may have to pay excess baggage charges. You can take more luggage on transatlantic flights as you are only restricted to 2 pieces of luggage no larger than 170cm (67 inches) across.

PASSPORTS
Officially visitors from EU countries only need a national identity card to enter Italy. In practice, you will need a passport. All other foreign visitors to Italy will need a passport,

which should be valid for at least another six months from the date of entry into Italy. If you lose your passport, you should contact your embassy (see p. 411).
- Keep a note of your passport number or carry a photocopy of the information page separately from your passport.
- Alternatively, scan the information pages of your passport and any other important documentation and email them as attachments to a web-based email account that can be accessed from anywhere in the world.
- If you intend to work or study in Italy, make sure your passport is stamped with your date of entry. You will need it to apply for a *permesso di soggiorno* (see below).

VISAS
If you are an EU national, or from Australia, Canada, New Zealand or the United States, you do not need a visa for stays of up to 90 days. To extend your visit you can, one time only, apply to any police station for an extension of a further 90 days. This extension cannot be used for studying or employment, and you will have to prove that you can support yourself financially. Regulations can change at short notice so check before making your travel arrangements. If you are a citizen of a country other than those mentioned above, you should contact the Italian Embassy in your home country to check visa requirements.

WORKING IN ITALY
EU citizens do not need permits or visas to work in Italy but you must register at the police station and apply for a *permesso di soggiorno*, essential if you intend to live, work or study in Italy. This will necessarily involve an experience of Italian bureaucracy—ir can be a lengthy process. The documentation you need changes every year, but will usually include your passport (with your date of entry into the country stamped inside), four passport photographs and proof that you will be able to support yourself financially. You can apply for a *permesso di soggiorno* at the foreigners' bureau (*ufficio stranieri*) at any police station.

Non-EU citizens have to apply for a *permesso di lavoro*, and the procedure differs depending on whether you will be working for an Italian company or a not.

If you are working for an Italian company, it will organize the permit and forward the documents to your home country's Italian consulate, which will then issue you with a visa. If you are going to work for a non-Italian company (or if you are self-employed or paid in a foreign currency), you will have to organize the permit yourself through the Italian consulate in your own country. Allow plenty of time—the process can take several months.

STUDYING IN ITALY
EU citizens will need a *permesso di soggiorno* (see above).
Non-EU citizens will need a visa. You should apply to the Italian consulate in your home country, who will need proof of your enrolment, proof of payment of fees and evidence of your financial support. The visa will only cover you for the length of your course.

TRAVEL INSURANCE
Take out your insurance as soon as you book your trip. If you leave it too close to your departure date you may not be covered for delays. Most policies cover cancellation, medical expenses, accident compensation, personal liability, and loss of personal belongings (including money). It should cover the cost of getting you home in case of medical emergency. An annual travel policy may be the best value if you intend to make several trips away from home a year, but long trips abroad may not be covered. If you have private medical cover, check your policy, as you may be covered while you are away.

HEALTH DOCUMENTS
Take photocopies of important documents, such as your travel insurance or health insurance policy and passport information page and keep them seperate from the originals. Alternatively, scan them and send them to a web-based email account that can be accessed worldwide.

PRACTICALITIES

ELECTRICITY

Electricity in Italy is on 240 volts, and electrical appliances are fitted with sockets that have two round pins. If your appliances are manufactured for 240 volts, you just need a plug adaptor. If your voltage is different (eg in the US), you need an adaptor and transformer.

LAUNDRY

Most visitors trust their cleaning to their hotel, where your clothes are returned to your room and the (often high) charge added to your bill. Self-service launderettes *(la lavandaria automatica)* are few and far between, but they are emerging in the larger cities. A wash will cost around €4. Dry cleaning *(lavasecco)* starts from around €3 for a shirt up to €7.50 for larger items such as jackets and coats, but the quality of the service varies immensely.

MEASUREMENTS

Italy uses the metric system, with all foodstuffs sold by the kilogram or litre. They also use the *ettogrammo* (100g), usually abbreviated to *etto*.

PUBLIC LAVATORIES

There are public lavatories at railway stations and in larger museums, but otherwise they are rare. You will probably end up using the facilities in a bar or café. Café/bar owners may let you use their facilities if you are not a patron, but obviously they prefer you to buy something first. Facilities can be basic, to say the least. Toilet paper may or may not be provided, and sometimes there is only one lavatory for both men and women. In some places there is a dish for gratuities—you should tip around 25c. Where separate facilities exist, make sure you recognize the difference between *signori* (men) and *signore* (women).

SMOKING

● Smoking is very common in Italy, and is still permitted in many hotels and restaurants. Non-smoking areas are rare.
● Smoking is not permitted on public transport, inside airport buildings and in most public offices and buildings.
● Smoking will soon be banned

CLOTHING SIZES

Clothing sizes in Italy are in metric. Use the chart below to convert the size you are at home into metric.

UK	Metric	USA	
36	46	36	
38	48	38	
40	50	40	
42	52	42	SUITS
44	54	44	
46	56	46	
48	58	48	
7	41	8	
7.5	42	8.5	
8.5	43	9.5	
9.5	44	10.5	SHOES
10.5	45	11.5	
11	46	12	
14.5	37	14.5	
15	38	15	
15.5	39/40	15.5	
16	41	16	SHIRTS
16.5	42	16.5	
17	43	17	
8	36	6	
10	38	8	
12	40	10	
14	42	12	DRESSES
16	44	14	
18	46	16	
20	48	18	
4.5	37.5	6	
5	38	6.5	
5.5	38.5	7	
6	39	7.5	SHOES
6.5	40	8	
7	41	8.5	

CONVERSION CHART

From	To	Multiply by
Inches	Centimetres	2.54
Centimetres	Inches	0.3937
Feet	Metres	0.3048
Metres	Feet	3.2810
Yards	Metres	0.9144
Metres	Yards	1.0940
Miles	Kilometres	1.6090
Kilometres	Miles	0.6214
Acres	Hectares	0.4047
Hectares	Acres	2.4710
Gallons	Litres	4.5460
Litres	Gallons	0.2200
Ounces	Grams	28.35
Grams	Ounces	0.0353
Pounds	Grams	453.6
Grams	Pounds	0.0022
Pounds	Kilograms	0.4536
Kilograms	Pounds	2.205
Tons	Tonnes	1.0160
Tonnes	Tons	0.9842

which may not be as clean as you are used to, can make things difficult for people with very young children.

● Italian children stay up late—if parents are eating out, the kids go too. This means that most hotels do not offer a baby-sitting/listening service.
● Put on the high-factor sunscreen and keep children covered up until they acclimatize to the sun. If they're swimming, persuade them to cover up and swim in a T-shirt.
● Children are susceptible to heat stroke, so seek shade in the middle of the day and keep their heads and necks protected.
● Most hotels will put up to three or four beds in a room so families can stay together; the add-on cost is around 30 per cent of the room price.
● Italian hotels are unheated until the end of October, and, in the south, some remain so.
● If you are bottle-feeding your baby, you might want to bring the formula with you.
● Children between 4 and 12 qualify for a 50 per cent discount on trains; those under 4 go free.
● Books with ideas on how to keep children occupied are available in Rome, Florence and Venice bookshops, and local tourist information offices are also able to help.
● Strollers and pushchairs can be hard work on cobbled streets in hill towns.

in all public places in line with EU regulations, but it remains to be seen how strictly the law will be enforced.
● Cigarettes and other tobacco products can only legally be sold in *tabacchi* (tobacconists) to those over 16. The stand-alone *tabacchi* are only open during normal shop hours (p. 413). Those attached to bars stay open longer.

VISITING ITALY WITH CHILDREN

Children are welcomed at most hotels and in almost all restaurants. Disposable nappies (diapers) and baby foods are available in many food shops *(il negozio di alimentari or il supermercato)*. On the down side, the lack of public lavatories and changing facilities, most of

PLANNING

VISITORS WITH DISABILITIES

Wheelchair access is improving in the larger cities, but it is virtually non-existent in the rest of the country. It is always worth asking individual establishments what access is like. The narrow, cobbled streets and lack of pavements (sidewalks) in many of the old towns can prove difficult and places like Venice present their own unique set of problems for people with mobility issues (p. 64).

● Holiday Care in the UK publishes information on accessibility on holiday (Holiday Care, 7th Floor, Sunley House, 4 Bedford Park, Croydon, Surrey CR0 2AP,
tel 0845 1249971, fax 0845 1249972,
www.holidaycare.org.uk).

● In the US, SATH (Society for Accessible Travel and Hospitality) has lots of tips for holidaymakers with visual impairment or reduced mobility (**www**.sath.org).

PLACES OF WORSHIP

If you are Catholic you will have no problem finding somewhere to celebrate your faith in Italy. You will find Catholic churches in even the smallest towns and villages and there are plenty of famous pilgrimage sites to track down. Religious festivals are celebrated enthusiastically throughout the year (p. 413). Every Wednesday at 11am the Pope leads Mass in St. Peter's or Aula Paolo VI in Vatican City (www.vatican.va).

There is a large Jewish community in Italy too. Rome has a Jewish quarter and the religion is widely practised in Venice, Florence, Ferrara and the north. To find synagogues and Jewish community centres in Italy, go to www.kosherdelight. com or www.maven.co.il.

There are few mosques in Italy, but the main centre for Islam is in Milan. For information contact the Unione delle Comunite ed Organizzazione Islamiche in Italia (UCOII) (Via Padova 38, 20127 Milano, tel 01 83660253) or the Islamic Cultural Society Milano (Via Staro 5, Milano, fax 02 26413204). For details of mosques, halal restaurants and Muslim shops in Italy visit **www**.muslimtraveller. com.

MONEY

A bancomat, the Italian name for a cash machine

Italians traditionally use cash, but this is changing. Credit and debit cards are widely accepted, but not for small sums. Food bills are paid for in cash and market traders don't take cards.

CREDIT AND DEBIT CARDS

MasterCard, Diners Club and Visa are widely accepted, as well as Eurocheque cards. Credit cards *(carta di credito)* are now becoming more widely accepted, but some smaller establishments still do not take them. Look for the credit card symbols in the shop window or check with the staff. You can also use your credit card to make cash withdrawals, although your credit card company will charge it as a cash advance. Contact your credit card company to get a PIN number.

ATMs

Cash machines, called bancomats in Italy, are plentiful and many are accessible 24 hours a day. Most have instructions in English and other languages. You avoid commission and the exchange rates are better when you withdraw cash with a debit card (Cirrus/Maestro/Delta) from ATMs rather than using a bureau de change. Check with your bank before leaving home that you will be able take cash out with your card while in Italy.

LOST/STOLEN CREDIT CARDS	
American Express	
06 7228 0371	
Diners Club	
800 864064	
MasterCard/Eurocard	
800 870866	
Switch	
+44 870 6000 459	
Visa/Connect	
800 877232	

TRAVELLERS' CHEQUES

Travellers' cheques are accepted almost everywhere. To avoid additional exchange rate charges, take travellers' cheques in euros, pounds sterling or US dollars.

CURRENCY EXCHANGE

Travellers' cheques, cheques and foreign money can be changed at banks, railway stations and airports, and very often at major hotels (generally at a poorer rate). Many banks in you home country have differing exchange rates depending on the denominations of currency being bought or sold. Check with banks for details and shop around before you buy.

10 EVERYDAY ITEMS AND HOW MUCH THEY COST	
Sandwich	€2.50
Bottle of water	50c
Cup of tea or coffee	€1.50–€4
0.5 litres of beer	€3.20–€6.50
Glass of wine	85c–€4.50
Daily newspaper	90c–€3
Roll of camera film	€5
20 cigarettes	€2.50
An ice cream cone	€2
A litre of petrol (gas)	€1.05

BANKS AND POST OFFICES

The largest banks in Italy are Unicredito and Intesa-BCI. Most major banks have cash machines and exchange facilities, although they are often very busy. Banks are usually open from 8.30 until 1 or 1.30, and again for a short time in the afternoon. Some open on Saturday morning. Central post offices usually have a currency exchange that is open throughout the day until 6.30.

BUREAUX DE CHANGE

There are bureaux de change (cambio) in all the main cities, usually open throughout the day until around 7.30. They often change money commission free, but the exchange rates are not as good as those from banks.

CURRENCY RESTRICTIONS

Import and export of local and foreign currency is limited to €10,329.14, but check with your embassy before departure if you need to bring large sums into the country. Amounts greater than this should be declared and validated in Italy.

WIRING MONEY

Wiring money is quite a lengthy process and the bureaucracy involved means that it is probably not worthwhile unless you are planning to spend quite a long time in Italy. Ask your bank at home for a list of affiliated banks. You can get money wired out to any bank from home, but if your bank is already in contact with certain banks in Italy it will make the process a lot easier. Always ask

for a separate letter, telex or fax confirming that the money has been sent and ask that it be sent to Swift. It can take up to a week for the money to transfer. If you have a bank account in Italy and at home, you can transfer money directly if both the banks are part of the Swift system of international transfers. Again it takes about 5–7 days, if not longer. American Express Moneygram and Western Union Money Tranfers are faster from the US, but more expensive. Citibank can transfer money for a flat fee of $10 to anywhere in the world (www.c2it.com). Do not wire more money than you need; you can only export just over €10,300.

TAX REFUNDS

All non-EU shoppers are entitled to an IVA (sales tax) refund on major purchases. Ask for a fattura when shopping, then present this at customs for stamping when leaving the EU. Return the stamped invoice to the store within four months of the date of purchase and the shop will refund the IVA direct.

BANKNOTES AND COINS

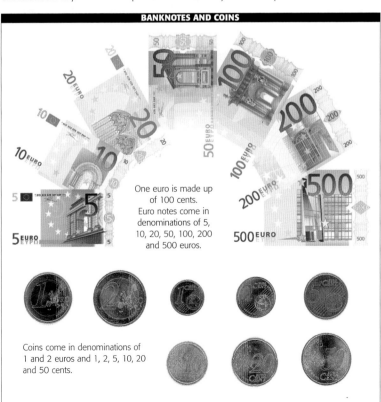

One euro is made up of 100 cents. Euro notes come in denominations of 5, 10, 20, 50, 100, 200 and 500 euros.

Coins come in denominations of 1 and 2 euros and 1, 2, 5, 10, 20 and 50 cents.

PLANNING

HEALTH

A green cross outside a shop denotes a pharmacy

BEFORE YOU GO

No vaccinations are necessary for a trip to Italy, unless you are coming into the country from an infected area. If you have any doubts, contact your doctor before you leave.

You should always take out health insurance, and most people do so as part of their travel insurance (p. 402). You should ensure that it covers the cost of getting you home in an emergency. If you already have health insurance to cover treatment at home, check with your insurer before you leave that you will be covered while abroad.

In addition to health insurance, European citizens should carry an E111, available from post offices, health centres and social security offices. Italy has a reciprocal health agreement with the rest of the EU, Iceland, Liechtenstein and Norway, which allows reduced-cost dental and medical (including hospital) treatment on presentation of the E111 form. One form covers the whole family for an indefinite period. A fee must be paid, though, plus part of the cost of any prescribed medicines. For specialist treatment you will need medical insurance.

For up-to-date information, see the Department of Health's website on www.doh.gov.uk (in the UK) or the National Center for Infectious Diseases on www.cdc.gov/travel in the US.

MEDICAL ASSISTANCE
Ambulance (emergencies)
118

HEALTHY FLYING

● People visiting Italy from as far as the US, Australia or New Zealand may be concerned about the effect of long-haul flights on their health. The most widely publicized concern is deep vein thrombosis, or DVT. Misleadingly known as economy class syndrome, DVT is the forming of a blood clot in the body's deep veins, particularly in the legs. The clot can move around the bloodstream and could be fatal.

● Those most at risk include the elderly, pregnant women and those using the contraceptive pill, smokers and the overweight. If you are at increased risk of DVT, see your doctor before departing. Flying increases the likelihood of DVT because passengers are often seated in a cramped position for long periods of time and may become dehydrated.

To minimize risk:
drink water (not alcohol)
don't stay immobile for hours at a time
stretch and exercise your legs periodically
do wear elastic flight socks, which support veins and reduce the chances of a clot forming
a small dose of aspirin may be recommended; this thins the blood before the flight.

EXERCISES

1 ANKLE ROTATIONS	2 CALF STRETCHES	3 KNEE LIFTS

Lift feet off the floor. Draw a circle with the toes, moving one foot clockwise and the other anticlockwise

Start with heel on the floor and point foot upward as high as you can. Then lift heels high keeping balls of feet on the floor

Lift leg with knee bent while contracting your thigh muscle. Then straighten leg, pressing foot flat to the floor

Other health hazards for flyers are airborne diseases and microbes spread by the plane's air-conditioning system. These are largely unavoidable but seek advice from a doctor before you leave if you have a serious medical condition.

WHAT TO TAKE WITH YOU

It is a good idea to take photocopies of all important documentation, such as travel insurance and your E111, which should be kept separate from the originals. You could scan the photocopies and send them to an email address that can be accessed anywhere in the world.

If you are on regular medication, you should ensure that you have adequate supplies for your trip. Make a note of the chemical name (rather than the brand name) in case you need replacement supplies.

HOW TO GET A DOCTOR (UN MEDICO)

● To get in touch with a doctor, ask at your hotel or consult the Yellow Pages *(Pagine Gialle)* under *Unità Sanitaria Locale.*
● For an ambulance, call 118.
● If you need emergency treatment, go directly to the Pronto Soccorso (casualty department/emergency room of the nearest hospital)

PLANNING

HOW TO GET TREATMENT WITH YOUR E111

● If you need medical treatment while you are away, take your E111 to the USL (Unità Sanitaria Locale) office, which will give you a certificate of entitlement.
● Take this to any doctor or dentist on the USL list to receive free treatment. If they need to refer you to a hospital, they will give you a certificate that entitles you to free treatment.
● If you go to hospital without being referred by a doctor, you should give the E111 to them.
● If you do not have a USL certificate, you will have to pay for treatment and it may be difficult to get the money back afterwards, and then you will probably only receive a partial refund.
● If you are charged in full for medicines, keep the price tags or receipts—you will not get a refund without them.
● It is advisable to carry a photocopy of your E111, as some doctors and hospitals keep the form. If they do, you can pick up another form when you get home.

HOW TO GET TREATMENT WITH INSURANCE

● If you have health insurance at home it is likely that it will cover you for medical treatment abroad. Check your policy before you leave home.
● Take a copy of your insurance documents to the doctor or hospital—they may be able to bill your insurance company direct.
● If you have to pay for treatment, keep all of your receipts for your insurance claim.

PHARMACIES (FARMACIA)

Pharmacies sell toiletries as well as a wide range of over-the-counter medicines. Pharmacists are well-trained and can deal with minor ailments. Most pharmacies are open during normal shop hours, but a rota system operates in major cities such as Rome so that there is at least one open at all times—a copy of the rota is displayed in pharmacy windows.

DENTAL TREATMENT (UN DENTISTA)

If you have an E111, contact the USL, as above. If you do not have an E111, contact a private dentist (in the Yellow Pages

Enjoying the sun near the fortress of Rocca Scaligera in Sirmione on Lake Garda

under *Dentista*). Again, take a copy of your insurance details and keep your receipts.

OPTICIANS

Opticians can usually carry out minor repairs to your glasses, such as replacing screws, on the spot, for little or no charge. Lenses can often be replaced overnight. If you really cannot survive without your glasses or contact lenses, bring a copy of your prescription with you so that you can have replacements made up if necessary.

FOOD AND DRINK

Italy's tap water is generally safe to drink, but you should look out for signs that say *acqua non potabile*, which means the water

is not drinkable. Local meat, dairy products, poultry, seafood, fruit and vegetables are all safe to eat.

SUMMER HAZARDS

From April to the end of September the sun is extremely strong and you will need to wear a high-factor sunblock (broad spectrum of factor 15 or above is recommended).

Insect bites are irritating rather than dangerous. There are no malaria-carrying insects in Italy, but there is an ongoing mosquito problem across the country even in inland towns—Milan is particularly bad. Use plenty of insect repellent or a mosquito net at night in the summer months and be vigilant near water and woodland areas.

SELECTED HOSPITALS WITH EMERGENCY DEPARTMENTS

CITY	Address	Telephone
ROME		
Policlinico Gemelli	Largo Gemelli 8	06 68371
FLORENCE		
Santa Maria Nuova	1 Piazza Santa Maria Nuova	055 27581
VENICE		
San Giovanni e Paolo	Campo San Giovanni e Paolo	041 529 4111

ALTERNATIVE MEDICAL TREATMENTS

You can buy homeopathic remedies in most pharmacies. For more detailed advice, contact one of the following associations for practitioners in your area:

Italian Medical Association of Acupuncture (AMIA), Piazza Navona 49, 00186 Roma, tel 06 6868 556

Associazione Terapie Naturale (A.Te.Na), Piazza Wagner 8, 20145 Milano, tel 02 468798.

Research Institute in Clinical Homeopathy, Acupuncture and Psychotherapy (CSOCAP), Via Sabotino 2, 00195, tel 06 3751 6391

PLANNING

COUNTRY CODES FROM ITALY	
Australia	00 61
Belgium	00 32
Canada	00 1
France	00 33
Germany	00 49
Greece	00 30
Ireland	00 353
Netherlands	00 31
New Zealand	00 64
Spain	00 34
Sweden	00 46
UK	00 44
USA	00 1

USEFUL TELEPHONE NUMBERS

International operator-assisted service and Italian operator: **170**

Italian directory enquiries: **12**

Information in foreign languages: **176**

Information on addresses from phone numbers: **1412**

AREA CODES FOR MAJOR CITIES	
Bologna	051
Brindisi	0831
Florence	055
Genoa	010
Milan	02
Naples	081
Palermo	091
Perugia	075
Pisa	050
Rome	06
Siena	0577
Turin	011
Venice	041
Verona	045

Calling Abroad
A call from outside Italy would be dialled as 0039 + 06 (code for Rome) + phone number.
A call from Rome to the UK would be dialled as 0044 + the area code missing off the first 0 (eg: 01780–1780) + the number. A call from Rome to the US would be dialled as 001 + the area code + the number.
For all calls within Italy, local and long distance, you must dial the regional area code *(prefisso)*, which begins with a 0, as 06 for Rome, 041 for Venice.

Public phones can be found on the streets and in train stations, larger stores and call centres

CALL CHARGES

Free phone numbers *(numeri verde)* usually begin with 800 and national call rate numbers begin with 848 or 199. Hotels tend to overcharge for long-distance and international calls, so it is best to make calls from public phones, using telephone cards. Rates are lowest on all day Sunday and between 10pm and 8am on weekdays and Saturday.

REVERSE-CHARGE (COLLECT) CALLS

From major Italian cities, you can place a direct call abroad by reversing the charges or by using a phone credit card number. To reverse the charges, call the International Operator on 170 or, for a cheaper alternative, dial the country's operator direct on one of the following free numbers:
 Australia (Optus): 800 172 611
 Australia (Telstra): 800 172 601
 Canada: 800 172 213
 France: 800 172 226
 New Zealand: 800 172 641

UK: 800 172 440
USA (AT&T): 800 172 444
USA (MCI): 800 905 825
USA (Sprint): 800 172 405

PUBLIC TELEPHONES

If you are calling from a public phone you must deposit a coin or use a phone card to get a dial tone. Note that some pay phones will only accept coins and others only *carta telefonica* (phone cards). Phones that only take coins tend to be less reliable than phone card phones. Call-centre telephones are a better bet than the often poorly maintained public telephones. Here you are assigned a booth to make your call and you pay for the call when you have finished.

PHONE CARDS

Prepaid *carte telefoniche* (phone cards) are used widely. You can buy them from post offices, tobacconists, newsstands and bars. Tear off the corner of the card and insert it in the slot of the public phone. When you dial, its value appears in the window. After you hang up, the card is returned so you can use it until it runs out. The Time phone card is good value, allowing you to call

Europe and the United States at 28c per minute during peak time, but if you are calling between 10pm and 8am, or all day Sunday, conventional phonecards are cheaper.
 You can also make cheap international calls from the call centres which exist in all major cities.

MOBILE PHONES

It can be very expensive to use your mobile phone abroad and you will often be charged to receive calls as well as make them. If you travel abroad frequently and intend to use your phone, consider swapping your SIM card to a card from an alternative provider—either a foreign network or a dedicated provider of international mobile phone services. You can buy these at mobile phone shops before you leave.
 Text messages are often a cheaper alternative to voice calls, but check the charges for making calls and text messages with your service provider. Italian mobile numbers begin with 330, 335, 347, 368 etc.

PLANNING

INTERNET CAFES

These are relatively widespread across Italy and reasonably cheap—you can expect to pay around €5 an hour. The netcafeguide.com website (www.netcafeguide.com/countries/italy.htm) has an impressive searchable directory of Internet cafés in Italy and throughout the world. You do need a web-based email account if you want to send or receive email from abroad (hotmail, yahoo etc.).

Remember to log out once you have finished browsing or emailing at an Internet café and close the browser completely to dump your session cookies (temporary files where your personal info is sometimes stored). These are shared computers and you don't want someone else reading your mail or accessing your personal files.

LAPTOPS

If you intend to use your own laptop in Italy, remember to bring a power converter to recharge it and a plug socket adaptor. A surge protector is also a good idea. To connect to the internet you need an adaptor for the phone socket.

If you use an international internet service provider, such as AOL or Compuserve, it's cheaper to dial up a local node rather than the number in your home country. Wireless technology, such as Bluetooth, allows you to connect to the internet using a mobile phone. Dial-tone frequencies vary from country to country, so set your modem to ignore dial tones.

A post box in Naples

POSTAL SERVICES

Poste Italiane have 14,000 post offices (*posta, ufficio postale or PT*) across Italy. You can buy stamps and send letters and packages from here and send faxes and telegrams from larger post offices. Although notoriously

INTERNET CAFES	
Region/Town	**Popular Internet Cafés**
The Northwest	
Milan	Gr@zianet, Piazza Duca d'Aosta 14, Staz. Centrale, tel 02 670 0543
	Phone@Point, Via le Sabotino 5, tel 02 5830 7274
Turin	BU.NET, Internet Wine Café, Via S.Quintino 13f, tel 0114407517
Venice	TheNetgate, Crosera San Pantalon, Dorsoduro 3812a, tel 041 244 0213
Northeast and Emilia-Romagna	
Bologna	Net Arena, V. de' Giudei 3/b, tel 051 220850
Padua	Bowling padua, Via Venezia 124, tel 049 776465
Ravenna	Bowling, Via Romea Nord 231 Savio-Cervia, tel 0544 927982
Verona	Internet Idea, Via Sforza 1, tel 045 8550545
Florence	Internet Point, Via del Moro 58, tel 055 265 8221
Tuscany and Umbria	
Gubbio	Gubbio On Line, Via Madonna di Mezzo Piano 25, tel 075 922 3000
Perugia	The NetGate, Via Cesare Battisti 19, tel 075 572 0771
Pisa	Internet Planet, Piazza Cavallotti, tel 050 830702
Rome	TreviNet Pl@ce Internet Point, Via Arcione 103 (Fontana di Trevi), tel 06 6992 2320
	Excape, Via Somalia 227, tel 06 8632 9492
	Stargate I-Café, Via Marrucini 12, tel 445 4953
The South	
Capri	Capri Internet Point, Marina Grande, tel 081 837 8518
Naples	I-cafe Piazza Garibaldi 73 - Staz. Centrale, tel 081 563 4836
	InternetNapoli, Piazza Cavour 146, tel 081 298877
Sicily	
Palermo	Everalways, cso Tukory 198, tel 091 217652
Siracusa	Fermento SRL, Via del Crocifisso 44/46, tel 0931 60762
Sardinia	
Cagliari	Intermedia Point, Via Eleonora d'Arborea 4, tel 070 652201

POSTAGE RATES		
Airmail (*via aerea*)	**Letter (20g)**	**Delivery time**
Europe	€0.41	up to 2 weeks
USA	€0.77	up to 2 weeks
New Zealand and Australia	€0.77	2–3 weeks
Posta Prioritaria	**Letter(20g)**	**Letter(21–100g)**	**Delivery time**
Europe	€0.62	€1.25	3 days
USA, Africa, Asia	€0.77	€1.55	4–8 days
New Zealand and Australia	€0.77	€1.55	4–8 days

COURIERS	
DHL	800 345345
Federal Express	800 833040
UPS	199 199 345
EMS–International Express Courier (Italian postal service)	800 009966

unreliable, the introduction of a priority mail service *(posta prioritaria)* has provided a more efficient alternative, relieving the pressure on the old state post service, which has improved.

The Vatican has its own postal service, which is more efficient than the Italian state system. There is a Vatican post office in the square in front of the Basilica di San Pietro.

Stamps *(francobolli)* are also available from tobacconists, denoted with an official *tabacchi* sign, a large 'T'. The value of the stamps they sell you for a letter will be an approximation of the delivery cost. If you need to send a heavy letter or a package, you are better off taking it to a post office where it can be weighed.

For information on all Italy's postal services, contact Poste Italiane (tel 800 222666, www.poste.it). In general, post offices are open Mon–Fri 8.15–2, Sat 8.15–noon or 2.

POSTCARDS

These are classed as low-priority post, so if you want them to arrive at their destination within a couple of weeks, send them *priorità.*

SENDING ITEMS OF VALUE

You can use the registered post *(raccomandato)* to send valuable items; add €2.60 on top of the price of normal postage. The cost of insured mail *(assicurato)* depends on the value of the items (€5.15 for packages up to €55.65 in value). Insured mail services are not available to the US.

RECEIVING POST IN ITALY

Poste restante, or general delivery, is known as *fermo posta.* These letters are held at the *fermo posta* counter in the main post office of the town to which the letter is addressed. To pick them up you must present your passport as identification and there is a small charge. *Fermo posta* letters should be addressed in the following way:

> Rebecca Brown,
> Fermo Posta,
> 00185 Roma,
> Italy

If you are receiving items in Italy via courier, you may have to pay IVA of up to 20 per cent to pick up the package.

FINDING HELP

An Italian municipal policeman (vigile urbano) *giving directions*

PERSONAL SECURITY

Though levels of crime are low, you should take care around railway stations, on public transport and in crowded areas in the larger cities where pickpockets and bag snatchers may be operating. Be particularly wary of groups of children who may try to distract your attention while stealing from you. Passports, credit cards, travel tickets and cash should not be carried together in handbags or pockets. Only carry with you what you need for the day and consider making use of safety deposit facilities in hotels. An increasing number of robberies are taking place from cars at rest stops/service stations on the motorways. You should treat with caution offers of help if you find yourself with a flat tyre, particularly on the motorway from Naples to Salerno, as sometimes the tyre will have been punctured deliberately.

● Lock your vehicle and never leave valuables in the vehicle even if you will only be away for a short time or are nearby.

Recently cars containing luggage have been the targets of car thieves, so avoid leaving luggage in cars overnight or for any length of time.

● Be vigilant when on sleepers/night trains as thieves sometimes operate on the trains and may take the opportunity during the night to rob sleeping passengers. Theft can also take place on trains during the day, so do not leave bags containing valuables unattended.

● Never carry money or valuables in your back pocket. Always keep them secure in a money belt or similar.

● Do not flaunt your valuables. Leave valuable jewellery in hotel safes and, if you are a woman walking around on you own, consider turning any rings with stone settings or similar around so that only the band is visible and not the jewels.

● Never put your camera or bag down on a café table or on the back of a chair, from where it could be snatched.

● Carry bags or cameras on the side of you that is farthest away

Credit Card/Travellers' Cheques

American Express	tel 06 7228 0371
Diners Club	tel 800 864064
Eurocard/CartaSi (including MasterCard and Visa)	tel 800 870866
MasterCard	tel 800 870866
Visa	tel 800 877232
American Express traveller's cheques	tel 800 872000

from the road, to minimize the risk from bag snatchers.

● Keep a close eye on your bags and possessions in crowded areas.

● Wear handbags across your body, rather than just over your shoulder, from where they can be easily snatched.

● If you have a programmable safe in your hotel room, do not use your date of birth as the code. It is on your passport and your hotel registration.

LOST PROPERTY

ATAC had lost property offices for articles left on buses or trams, as do FS trains for anything left on their trains.

● If you will be making an insurance claim, you need to report the loss to the police to get a statement *(denuncia)*.

● If your passport is lost or stolen, report it to the police and your consulate. The whole process of getting a replacement is easier if you have kept a copy of your passport number or a photocopy of the information page safe (p. 402).

● If your credit card or bank card is stolen, report it to the police and phone the appropriate bank card/credit card emergency number to cancel your card. All are open 24 hours a day and have English-speaking staff.

● If your travellers' cheques are stolen, notify the police, then follow the instructions given with the cheques.

REPORTING THEFT

Report thefts to a police station, where you will need to make a statement. It is unlikely that you will get your belongings back, but you need the statement *(denuncia)* to make a claim on your insurance. You can find the address and contact details of your nearest police station in the Yellow pages *(Pagine Gialle)* under *Commissariato, commando di polizia* or *stazione dei carabinieri*.

POLICE

There are three branches of the police in Italy, any of whom should be able to help you if you are in difficulty.

The *carabinieri* are military police, easily recognizable by the white sash they wear across their bodies. They deal with general crime, including drug control.

The *polizia* is the state police force, whose officers wear blue uniforms. They too deal with general crime, and if you are unfortunate enough to be robbed (or worse) they are the ones you will need to see.

The *vigili urbani*, the traffic police, wear dark blue uniforms and white hats.

WHAT TO DO IF YOU ARE ARRESTED

If you are taken into custody by the police, you could be held for up to 48 hours without appearing before a magistrate. You can also be interviewed without a lawyer present. You do, however, have the right to contact your consul, who is based at your country's embassy, but you are still bound by Italian law. Your consul will not be able to get you out of prison, but they will visit you and put you in touch with English-speaking lawyers and interpreters, offer advice and support and contact your family on your behalf. Try to keep hold of your passport and contact your travel insurance company, as your insurance may cover you for legal costs.

EMBASSIES AND CONSULATES

Lists of embassies and consulates are available from tourist offices. You can also look under *Ambasciate* or *Consolati* in the phone book or visit www.embassyworld.com.

EMBASSIES AND CONSULATES

Australia		
Embassy	Via Alessandria 215, 00198 Roma	tel 06 852721
Consulate	25c Corso Trieste, 00198 Roma	tel 06 852721
Consulate	3rd Floor, Via Borgogna 2, 20122 Milano	tel 02 7770 4217
	www.australian-embassy.it	
Canada		
Embassy	Via G B de Rossi 27, 00161 Roma	tel 06 445981
Consulate	Via Vittorio Pisani 19, 20124 Milano	tel 0267581
Ireland		
Embassy	Piazza di Campitelli 3, 00186 Roma	tel 06 697 9121
Consulate	Piazza F Pietro in Gessate 2, 20122 Milano	tel 02 5518 7569
New Zealand		
Embassy	Via Zara 28, 00198 Roma	tel 064 417171
Consulate	Via Guido d'Arezzo 6, 20145 Milano	tel 02 4801 2544,
		fax 024801 2577
USA		
Embassy	Via Vittorio Veneto 119a–121, 00187 Roma	tel 06 46741,
	www.usis.it	
Consulate	Lungarno Ameriggo Vespucci 38, 50123 Firenze	tel 055 239 8276
Consulate	Largo Donegani 1, Milano	tel 02 290351
Consulate	Piazza della Repubblica, 80122 Napoli	tel 081 583 8111
Consulate	Via Vaccarini 1, 90141 Palermo	tel 091 625 2426
Consulate	Via Dante 2/43, 16121 Genova	tel 010 584492
UK		
Embassy	Via XX Settembre 80a, 00187 Roma	tel 06 4220 0001
Consulate	Lungarno Corsini 2, 50123 Firenze	tel 055 284133,
		fax 055 219112
Consulate	Via S Paolo 7, 20121 Milano	tel 02 723001,
		fax 02 720 20153
Consulate	Via dei Mille 40, 80121 Napoli	tel 081 423 8911,
		fax 081 422434
Consulate	Palazzo Querini, Dorsoduro 1051, 30123 Venice	tel 041 522 7207,
		fax 041 522 2617
Consulate	Via Dalmazia 127, Bari	tel 080 554 3668

MEDIA

MAGAZINES

Most Italian magazines are adorned with pictures of scantily clad women, but this isn't necessarily a reflection of their content (although it can be).

Amica is a stylish Italian read with articles on all that is fashionable and cutting edge in Italy. English language magazines are few and far between, but if you read a little Italian, magazines such as *Panorama* and *L'Espresso* are good for news, while *Oggi* is a slightly more light hearted alternative with more of a focus on celebrity gossip and lifestyle. *L'Espresso*, renowned for its restaurant reviews and accreditations, is highly respected in Italy. *Roma C'è* (Fridays) and *Time Out Roma* (monthly) both have English-language sections. *Wanted in Rome* is aimed at resident English-speakers, but also has what's-on listings for the city.

There is a vast array of listings magazines and newspapers to choose from at most newsstands

ENGLISH-LANGUAGE NEWSPAPERS

You can usually buy major international newspapers at three times their home cover price the day after publication, from about 2pm, at larger newsstands. In Milan and Rome you may occasionally find them on the day of publication, particularly titles such as *The Times, The Financial Times, The Guardian, The European, The New York Times, The Wall Street Journal* and *The International Herald Tribune*. There are also some Italian newspapers available in English, namely *International Herald Tribune*) and *Il Sole/24 Ore* (economic and financial news from FT.com).

ITALIAN-LANGUAGE NEWSPAPERS

La Repubblica has a good what's-on section on Thursdays and a glossy magazine supplement on Saturdays called *La Repubblica delle Donne* with excellent articles reflecting all aspects of Italian life and society. There are two daily sports papers published in Italy—*La Gazzetta dello Sport* (pink paper) and the *Corriere dello Sport*—mainly dominated by football and motor sport news. *La Gazzetta dello*

Sport also publishes a supplement on Saturday called *Sport Week,* which tends to cover a wider range of sports and contains excellent full-colour photos and features on the week's events.

Il Messaggero is a local paper, popular with Romans. *La Repubblica, Corriere della Sera, La Stampa* and *Il Sole/24 Ore* are the main national newspapers. *La Repubblica* and *Corriere della Sera* both print special editions in Rome.

TELEVISION

Italy has three state-run television stations (RAI-1, -2 and -3), which broadcasts some worthy entertainment, three stations run by Berlusconi's Mediaset group (Italia Uno, Rete Quattro and Canale Cinque) and a number of local channels. RAI-3 has an international news broadcasts, which includes an English-language section. It starts at 1.15am. Italian television is generally pretty frivolous, usually comprising a mixture of soaps, chat shows and American imports dubbed into Italian. Quiz shows are almost always accompanied by skimpily dressed women. Moves are

under way to change this, with a view to making 'respectful references to the image of women', but game show girls are as popular as ever.

Most hotels, from mid-range upwards, have satellite television, so you can keep up-to-date with the news and sport on BBC World, CNN and Eurosport.

RADIO

RAI Radio 1, 2 and 3 (89.7FM, 91.7FM and 93.7FM), the state-run stations, have a mixture of light music, chat shows and news—all in Italian. If you are in Rome, Radio Vaticano (93.3FM) broadcasts news in a number of languages, including broadcasts in English at 5.10pm and 9.50pm daily. Radio Italia Network (90–108FM) is the best national radio station for dance music and Radio Deejay (99.7–107FM) plays a variety of popular music and chat shows. You can get BBC radio stations including Radio 1, Radio 2, 5 Live and 6 Music on the Internet via www.bbc.co.uk. The BBC World Service frequencies in Italy are MHz 12.10, 9.410, 6.195 and 0.648. Visit www.radio-locator.com to find US radio stations online.

OPENING TIMES AND TICKETS

OPENING TIMES

Banks
Mon–Fri 8.30–1.30. Some larger branches might open on Saturdays.

Post Offices
Mon–Fri 8.15–2, Sat 8.15–noon or 2.

Pharmacies
Pharmacies are usually open the same hours as shops, but take it in turns to stay open during the afternoon and late into the evening. Look for the list displayed in the shop window providing details of other pharmacies in the area and their opening times.

Museums and Galleries
The opening times for museums and galleries vary greatly, according to the season and the location. Some are open all day, while others close at lunchtimes. Many close one day each week, usually Mondays. Check the Sights section of this book, or contact the museum or gallery concerned for the most up to date information.

Churches
Most churches open early in the morning for Mass, often around 7. They close at lunchtime, opening again around 4 and closing at 7. Some of the larger churches are open all day, and some may be closed to visitors during services. Check the Sights section of this book (p. 65–220) for specific opening times or contact the church.

Cafés and Bars
The hours kept by Italy's cafés and bars vary considerably from establishment to establishment and according to the season. Some are open for breakfast, others open in time for lunch, and some are only open in the evenings. Wine bars usually close at midnight or later. See the What to Do section of this book for specific opening times (p. 221–276).

Restaurants
Restaurants that serve lunch open from 11am and usually close during the afternoon. They reopen, along with those that only serve dinner, sometime after 7pm and stay open late. Pizzerias are usually only open in the evening.

Many restaurants close for the whole of August—look for the sign *Chiuso per ferie*. See the Eating and Staying section of this book for specific opening times (p. 331–398).

Shops
Traditionally, shops open in the morning between 8 and 9 and close for lunch at around 1. They reopen in the afternoon at 3.30 or 4 and close at 8. Most are closed Sundays and Monday mornings, but shops in the larger cities are beginning to stay open all day—look for the sign *Orario continuato*. See the What to Do section of this book for specific opening times (p. 221–276).

NATIONAL HOLIDAYS
Shops and banks generally close on public holidays. The road and rail network are usually very busy at this time. There is a limited public transport service on Labour Day and the afternoon of Christmas Day. However, with the exception of Labour Day, the Assumption and Christmas Day, most bars and restaurants remain open.

ENTRANCE FEES
Admission to churches tends to be free, but you may be asked to give a small donation or pay to see inside a church, or part of a church, that is of particular artistic or historic interest; the dome of St. Peter's in Rome, for example. You should expect to pay around €2, but it can be as high as €8 for the main attractions and pilgrimage sites. Museums charge for admission. Expect to pay €5–€10, but discounts are almost always available (see below). Larger archaeological sites have an entrance fee of around €5, but expect to pay up to €10 for the larger sites such as Pompeii. Entrance fees sometimes include a guided tour.

Combined Tickets
If you are intending to do a lot of sightseeing in a particular area, it is worth enquiring about combined tickets. For example, in Venice, you can buy a combined ticket for the 15 churches in the CHORUS group of artistically important churches for €8: If you went to see all of them and paid separately it would cost you €30. You can purchase a *Carta Musei* in Umbria, and Siena has a combined ticket incorporating all of its museums, again providing significant savings. Most major tourist towns or regions have combined tickets covering museums and areas of cultural interest. Further details of these are available from tourist offices.

Discounts
Discounts are rarely available where there is an admission charge for churches, but all other museums and attractions have concessions for students (with an international student card), and European Union citizens over 65 and children under 5 or 6 who are generally admitted for free. Occasionally children under 10 are admitted for free, but there tend to be discounts available for youngsters up to the age of 18, and this is sometimes extended to those under 20. Some attractions admit disabled people and a carer for free and charge less for groups of more than 15, teachers and visitors from EU countries.

PLANNING

TOURIST OFFICES

TOURIST OFFICES

Most major towns have a tourist office within their main railway stations and airports. Known as Azienda Promozione del Turismo (APT), they tend to keep normal shop opening hours (p. 413). They have maps and information and provide help and advice in finding accommodation. They may also book accommodation and tours for you.

The Ente Provinciale per il Turismo (EPT) is usually devoted more to the bureaucracy of tourism rather than providing information for tourists. Villages may have a small office known as a Pro Loco, but they often have limited opening hours.

The table below shows the addresses and contact details for the main regional tourist ofices across Italy.

Tourist offices provide free maps, guides and leaflets for visitors

OVERSEAS TOURIST OFFICES	
Italian State Tourist Offices Overseas (ENIT)	
www.enit.it or www.piuitalia2000.it	
Australia	Level 45, 1 Macquarie Street, Sydney 2000, NSW, tel 02 9392 7900
New Zealand	36 Grant Road, Thorndon, Wellington, tel 04 736065 or 04 4735339
Canada	1 Place Ville Marie, Montréal, Québec H3B 3M9, tel 514 8667667
UK	1 Princes Street, London W1 8AY, tel 020 7408 1254
US	630 5th Avenue, Suite 1565, Rockefeller Center, NY 10111, tel 212/ 245-5618

TOURIST OFFICES

THE NORTHWEST

Genoa
Via Acqua Verde–Stazione Piazza Principe, tel 010 576791, fax 010 581408,
www.apt.genova.it

Turin
Palazzo Madama, tel 011 535901, fax 011 530070,
www.turismotorino.org

Como
Piazza Cavour 17, tel 031 269712, fax 031 240111,
www.lakecomo.org

Mantua
Piazza Mantegna 6, tel 0376 328253, fax 0376 363292,
www.aptmantova.it

Milan
Via Marconi 1, tel 02 7252 4301, fax 02 7252 4350,
www.milanoinfotourist.com

Venice
Castello 4421, tel 041 5298711, fax 041 5230399,
www.tourismovenezia.it

THE NORTHEAST AND EMILIA-ROMAGNA

Padua
Riviera dei Mugnai, tel 049 876 7911, 049 650794,
www.padovanet.it

Verona
Piazza Bra,Via Alpini 11, tel 045 8068680, fax 045 800 3638,
www.tourism.verona.it

Vicenza
Piazza Duomo 5, tel 0444 544122, fax 0444 325001,
www.ascom.vi.it/aptvicenza

Bologna
Palazzo Podesta, Piazza Maggiore 1, tel 051 246541, fax 051 639 3171,
www.comune.bologna.it/bolognaturismo

Ravenna
Via Salara 8–12, tel 0544 35404, fax 0544 482670,
www.turismo.ravenna.it

Florence
Via Manzoni 16, tel 055 23320, fax 055 234 6285,
www.firenzeturismo.it

TUSCANY AND UMBRIA

Lucca
Piazza S. Maria, tel 0583 919931, fax 0583 91663,
www.lucca.turismo.toscana.it

Pisa
Via Pietro Nenni, tel 050 929777, fax 050 929764,
www.pisa.turismo.toscana.it

Siena
Piazza del Campo 56, tel 0577 280 551, fax 0577 281041,
www.siena.terresiena.it

Assisi
Piazza del Comune, tel 075 812 450, fax 075 813727,
www.bellaumbria.net/assisi

Perugia
Piazza IV Novembre 3, tel 075 573 6458, fax 075 572 0988,
www.umbria-turismo.it

Rome
Via Parigi 5, tel 06 488991 or 06 3600 4399, fax 06 481 9316,
www.romaturismo.com

LAZIO AND THE MARCHE

Ascoli Piceno
Piazza del Popolo 1, tel 0736 253045, fax 0736 252391,
www.turismo.marche.it

Tivoli
Largo Garibaldi, tel 0774 334 522, fax 0774 331294,
www.comuneditivoli.it

THE SOUTH

Capri
Piazza Umberto I 19, tel 081 837 0634, fax 081 837 0918,
www.caprionline.com

Naples
Palazzo Reale, Piazza del Plebiscito, tel 081 252 5711, fax 081 418619, www.inaples.it

Pompei
Via Sacra 1, tel 081 850 7255, fax 081 863 2401,
www.uniplan.it/pompei

Sorrento
Via L. de Maio 35, tel 081 807 4033, fax 081 877 3397,
www.sorrentotourism.it

SICILY AND SARDINIA

Palermo
Piazza Castelnuovo, tel 091 583847, fax 091 605 8351,
www.aapit.pa.it

Siracusa
Via Maestranza 33, tel 0931 464 255, fax 0931 60204,
www.flashcom.it/aatsr

Taormina
Piazza Santa Catarina, Palazzo Corvaja, tel 0942 23243, fax 0942 24941,
www.gate2taormina.com

Cagliari
Piazza Matteotti 9, tel 070 669255 , fax 070 664923,
www.cagliariadascoprire.it

PLANNING

FILMS AND BOOKS

FILMS

● Mussolini's Cinecittà studios came into their own after World War II, when they began to make neorealist films, like *Ladri di Biciclette* (*The Bicycle Thief,* 1948). A winner of both a BAFTA and a Golden Globe, it was shot entirely in Rome, using non-professional actors.
● In the 1950s there was a resurgence in film-making in Rome, encouraged by the much-acclaimed *Roman Holiday* (1953), which thrust Audrey Hepburn into the limelight. You'll recognize many of the landmarks the stars visit, including the Bocca della Verità (p.177).
● *Three Coins in a Fountain* (1954) followed closely behind. Although the storyline now seems old-fashioned, it's still a great travelogue for Rome.
● Probably the most famous film image of Rome is Anita Ekberg's dip in the Trevi Fountain in *La Dolce Vita* (1960), which was also filmed in Tivoli (p. 189) and Viterbo (p. 187).
● More recently, *The Talented Mr. Ripley* (1999) was filmed all over Italy, including Rome, Isola d'Ischia and Isola di Procida near Naples, Palermo, Positano and Venice. *Ripley's Game* (2002), also based on the novels by Patricia Highsmith, is shot predominantly in the north of Italy and captures the slightly shabby classical architecture of Asolo and Vicenza in the Veneto.
● *Gladiator* (2000) is set, in part, in Rome, although much of it was filmed elsewhere.
● There are some great car chases around the streets of Turin and classic lines in *The Italian Job* (1969), an action-packed comedy where Michael Caine and others steal a gold shipment with the aid of a fleet of Minis.
● Nanni Moretti's drama *La Stanza del Figlio* (*The Son's Room*), which won the Palme D'Or at the 2001 Cannes Film Festival, tells the story of a family coming to terms with a devastating loss. Moretti also stars in this film (which he directed, co-wrote and co-produced) as Giovanni, a psychoanalyst who enjoys running through the streets of Ancona in the Marche with his son.

Anthony Hopkins (seated) in Piazza Signoria in Florence filming Hannibal

● *Hannibal* (2001), the grisly sequel to *The Silence of the Lambs*, contains some serene scenes shot in Florence, along the banks of the River Arno.
● To get a feel for the rolling Tuscan countryside, watch Kenneth Branagh's film adaptation of Shakespeare's *Much Ado About Nothing* (1993). Starring Branagh as Benedict and Emma Thompson as Beatrice, this classic play is brought to life in the hilltop Villa Vignamaggio, with its knot gardens and vineyards, typical of Greve in Chianti.
● Set in 1930s Italy and shot in Terni in Umbria and Arezzo in Tuscany, *La Vita e Bella* (*Life is Beautiful,1997*) is a dark yet heart-warming tale of a Jewish bookkeeper who struggles to hold his family together during German occupation and help his son survive the horrors of a Jewish concentration camp.
● *Il Postino* (*The Postman, 1994*) is the story of an island postman who wins over the local beauty with poetry. The film is shot against the backdrop of the lush mountainous coastal scenery of Pollara on Salina Island in Sicily and Isola di Procida near Naples.
● *Cinema Paradiso* (1988), shot in Palermo in Sicily, traces a film-makers childhood love affair with cinema and the friendship he develops with the local movie-theatre projectionist.

BOOKS

Apart from your guidebook, there are many good books available covering Italy's long, vibrant and eventful history.

● By far the most in-depth is Edward Gibbon's *The History of the Decline and Fall of the Roman Empire* , published in six volumes—abridged versions are available (1776–1788).
● Biographies of Rome's major historical players, such as Garibaldi and Mussolini, will help fill in the gaps if you are interested in later periods.
● For history in novel form, try *I, Claudius* (1934), by Robert Graves, or Irvine Stone's *The Agony and the Ecstasy* (1965), which was also made into a film starring Charlton Heston.
● Anyone interested in Italian politics and society should read *The Dark Heart of Italy* (2003) by Tobias Jones, which discusses Italian life under Berlusconi's administration.
● For younger readers, Caroline Lawrence's *Roman Mysteries* series is set in the Roman Empire, and *The Rotten Romans,* part of the cartoon-filled *Horrible Histories* series, takes a more light-hearted look at ancient times.
● Donna Leon's crime novels are set in Venice and follow the investigations of Commissario Brunetti. Her latest titles include *A Sea of Troubles (2001), Willful Behaviour (2002) and Uniform Justice (2003)*
● Classics set in Italy include E. M. Forster's *A Room with a View* (1908), a critique of 19th-century middle class Britons abroad in Florence, and Henry James's *Wings of a Dove* (1902), where the story unfolds in the drawing rooms of London and the gilded palazzi of Venice.
● There are a huge number of travel biographies on the shelves, but particularly good is *Vanilla Beans and Brodo: Real Life in the Hills of Tuscany* (2002) by Isabella Dusi, which provides an insight into rural Tuscan life and the challenges of integrating into a local community.
● A good travel companion is *Desiring Italy* (1997) compiled by Susan Cahill, a collection of stories by women writers such as George Elliot and Edith Wharton that takes you on a cultural journey, from the richness of the North to the unspoilt treasures of the South.

WEBSITES

TOURISM

Abruzzo and Molise
www.laquila.com
www.moliseweb.com
Basilicata
www.aptbasilicata.it
Calabria
www.turismo.regione.calabria.it
Campania
www.ept.napoli.it
Emilia-Romagna
www.apt.emilia-romagna.it
Florence
www.firenze.net
www.firenzeturismo.it
Friuli-Venezia Giulia
www.regione.fvg.it
Lazio
www.apt.rieti.it
www.apt.viterbo.it
Liguria
www.regione.liguria.it
Lombardy
www.inlombardia.it
Marche
www.turismo.marche.it
Piemonte
www.regione.piemonte.it/
turismo
Puglia
www.comune.bari.it
Rome
www.comune.roma.it
www.enit.it
www.enjoyrome.com
www.romaturismo.com
www.romaturismo.it
www.vatican.va
Sicily
www.apt.sicilia.it
Sardinia
www.regione.sardegna.it
Trentino-Alto Adige
www.trentino.to
Tuscany
www.turismo.toscana.it
Umbria
www.umbria-turismo.it
Val d'Aosta
www.regione.vda.it/turismo

Veneto
www.regione.veneto.it
Venice
www.turismovenezia.it
www.comune.venezia.it

GENERAL

www.estateolie.it
www.firenzemusei.it
www.fodor.com
www.vitaliansrus.com
www.italiantourism.com
www.itwg.com
www.museionline.it
www.parks.it
www.theaa.com
www.travel-guide.com
www.vtourist.com

HOTELS

www.florencehotelsnetwork.com
www.1stvenicehotels.com
www.italyhotels.it
www.iturg.com
www.allitalianhotels.com

WEATHER

www.weather.com

TELEPHONE NUMBERS

Italian Yellow Pages
www.paginegialle.it

TRANSPORTATION

www.atac.roma.it
www.trenitalia.it

AIRPORTS

www.adr.it

NEWS

www.onlinenewspapers.com
La Repubblica
www.repubblica.it
Il Messaggero
www.ilmessaggero.it
Corriere della Sera
www.corriere.it
UK and world news
www.bbc.co.uk
USA and world news
www.cnn.com

MAJOR SIGHTS QUICK WEBSITE FINDER		
Sight	**Website**	**Page**
Basilica di San Pietro	www.vatican.va	158–159
Dolomites	www.infodolomiti.it	107
Duomo (Florence)	www.operaduomo.firenze.it	116–119
Duomo (Pisa)	www.opapisa.it	149
Etna	www.aast-nicolosi.it	213
Foro Romano	www.capitolium.org	164–165
Galleria dell'Accademia (F)	www.sbas.firenze.it/accademia	121
Galleria dell'Accademia (Venice)	www.galleriaaccademia.org	88–89
Galleria Borghese	www.galleriaborghese.it	166
Gargano Peninsula	www.parks.it	195
Lago di Como	www.lakecomo.com	69
Musei Capitolini	www.museicapitolini.org	167
Museo dei Ragazzi	wwww.museoragazzi.it	130
Musei Vaticani	www.vaticani.va	168–171
Ostia Antica	www.itnw.roma.it/ostia/scavi	185
Palazzo Doria Pamphilj	www.doriapamphilj.it	172
Parco del Cornero	www.en.conero.it/parco	185
Parco Nazionale Gran Paradiso	www.parks.it/parco.nazionale.gran.paradiso/	76
Parco Nazionale Monti Sibillini	www.sibillini.net	147
Parco Nazionale delo Stelvio	www.stelviopark.it	109
Pompeii	www.pompei.biz	204–207
Santa Maria Gloriosa dei Frari	www.basilicadeifrari.it	101
Santa Maria Immacolata della Concezione		
	www.cappucciniviaveneto.it	177
Santa Maria Maggiore	www.prtour.it	178
Santa Maria Sopra Minerva	www.basilicaminerva.it	177
Vesuvio	www.vvolcanoworld.it	204–207

PLANNING

ITALIAN WORDS AND PHRASES

Once you have mastered a few basic rules, Italian is an easy language to speak: It is phonetic, and unlike English, particular combinations of letters are always pronounced the same way. The stress is usually on the penultimate syllable, but if the word has an accent, this is where the stress falls.

Vowels are pronouned as follows:

a	casa	as in	mat short 'a'
e	vero closed	as in	base
e	sette open	as in	vet short 'e'
i	vino	as in	mean
o	dove closed	as in	bowl
o	otto open	as in	not
u	uva	as in	book

Consonants as in English except:
c before **i** or **e** becomes **ch** as in **ch**urch
ch before **i** or **e** becomes **c** as in **c**at
g before **i** or **e** becomes **j** as in **J**ulia
gh before **i** or **e** becomes **g** as in **g**ood
gn as in onion
gli as in million
h is rare in Italian words, and is always silent
r usually rolled
z is pronounced **tz** when it falls in the middle of a word

All Italian nouns are either masculine (usually ending in o when singular or i when plural) or feminine (usually ending in a when singular or e when plural). Some nouns, which may be masculine or feminine, end in e (which changes to i when plural). An adjective's ending changes to match the ending of the noun.

MONEY

Is there a bank/currency exchange office nearby?
C'è una banca/un ufficio di cambio qui vicino?

Can I cash this here?
Posso incassare questo?

I'd like to change sterling/dollars into euros
Vorrei cambiare sterline/dollari in euro

Can I use my credit card to withdraw cash?
Posso usare la mia carta di credito per prelevare contanti?

CONVERSATION

What is the time?
Che ore sono?

I don't speak Italian
Non parlo italiano

I only speak a little Italian
Parlo solo un poco italiano

Do you speak English?
Parla inglese?

I don't understand
Non capisco

Please repeat that
Può ripetere?

Please speak more slowly
Può parlare più lentamente?

Write that down for me, please
Lo scriva, per piacere

Please spell that
Come si scrive?

My name is
Mi chiamo

What's your name?
Come si chiama?

Hello, pleased to meet you
Piacere

This is my friend
Le presento il mio amico/la mia amica

This is my wife/husband/daughter/son
Le presento mia moglie/mio marito/mia figlia/mio figlio

Where do you live?
Dove abiti?

I live in …
Vivo in …

I'm here on holiday
Sono qui in vacanza

Good morning
Buongiorno

Good afternoon/evening
Buonosera

Goodbye
Arrivederci

How are you?
Come sta?

Fine, thank you
Bene, grazie

I'm sorry
Mi dispiace

USEFUL WORDS

yes **sì**	thank you **grazie**	where **dove**	when **quando**	why **perchè**
no **no**	you're welcome **prego**	here **qui**	now **adesso**	who **chi**
please **per piacere**	excuse me! **scusi!**	there **là**	later **più tardi**	may I/can I **posso**

Could you help me, please?
Può aiutarmi, per favore?

How much is this?
Quanto costa questo?

I'm looking for …
Cerco …

Where can I buy…?
Dove posso comprare…?

How much is this/that?
Quanto costa questo/quello?

When does the shop open/close?
Quando apre/chiude il negozio?

I'm just looking, thank you
Sto solo dando un'occhiata

This isn't what I want
Non è quel che cerco

I'll take this
Prendo questo

Do you have anything less expensive/smaller/larger?
Ha qualcosa di meno caro/più piccolo/più grande?

Are the instructions included?
Ci sono anche le istruzioni?

Do you have a bag for this?
Può darmi una busta?

I'm looking for a present
Cerco un regalo

Can you gift wrap this please?
Può farmi un pacco regalo?

Do you accept credit cards?
Accettate carte di credito?

I'd like a kilo of …
Vorrei un chilo di …

Do you have shoes to match this?
Ha delle scarpe che vadano con questo?

This is the right size
Questa è la taglia (misura—for shoes) giusta

Can you measure me please?
Può prendermi la misura, per favore?

This doesn't suit me
Questo non mi sta bene

Do you have this in …?
Avete questo in …?

Should this be dry cleaned?
Questo è da lavare a secco?

Is there a market?
C'è un mercato?

NUMBERS

0 zero	6 sei	12 dodici	18 diciotto	40 quaranta	100 cento
1 uno	7 sette	13 tredici	19 diciannove	50 cinquanta	1000 mille
2 due	8 otto	14 quattordici	20 venti	60 sessanta	million milione
3 tre	9 nove	15 quindici	21 ventuno	70 settanta	quarter quarto
4 quattro	10 dieci	16 sedici	22 ventidue	80 ottanta	half mezza
5 cinque	11 undici	17 diciassette	30 trenta	90 novanta	three quarters tre quarti

IN TROUBLE

Help!
Aiuto!

Stop, thief!
Al ladro!

Can you help me, please?
Può aiutarmi, per favore?

Call the fire brigade/police/an ambulance
Chiami i pompieri/la polizia/un'ambulanza

I have lost my passport/wallet/purse
Ho perso il passaporto/il portafogllio/il borsellino

Where is the police station?
Dov'è il commissariato?

I have been robbed
Sono stato/a derubato/a

I need to see a doctor/dentist
Ho bisogno di un medico/dentista

Where is the hospital?
Dov'è l'ospedale?

I am allergic to …
Sono allergico/a a…

I have a heart condition
Ho disturbi cardiaci

COLOURS

black **nero**	green **verde**
brown **marrone**	light blue **celeste**
pink **rosa**	sky blue **azzuro**
red **rosso**	purple **viola**
orange **arancia**	white **bianco**
yellow **giallo**	grey **grigio**

AROUND THE TOWN

English	Italian	English	Italian	English	Italian	English	Italian
on/to the right	a destra	near	vincino a	west	ovest	castle	castello
town hall	municipio	lake	lago				

on/to the right
a destra

near
vincino a

west
ovest

castle
castello

town hall
municipio

lake
lago

on/to the left
a sinistra

cross over
attraversi

free
gratis

museum
museo

boulevard
corso

bridge
ponte

around the corner
all'angolo

in front of
davanti

donation
donazione

monument
monumento

square
piazza

no entry
vietato l'accesso

opposite
di fronte a...

behind
dietro

open
aperto

palace
palazzo

street
via

push
spingere

at the bottom (of)
in fondo (a)

north
nord

closed
chiuso

gallery
galleria

avenue
viale

pull
tirare

straight on
sempre dritto

south
sud

cathedral
cattedrale

town
città

island
isola

entrance
ingresso

east
est

church
chiesa

old town
centro storico

river
fiume

exit
uscita

GETTING AROUND

Where is the train/bus station?
Dov'è la stazione ferroviaria/ degli autobus (dei pullman – long distance)?

Does this train/bus go to …?
È questo il treno/l'autobus (il pullman—long distance) per…?

Where are we?
Dove siamo?

Do I have to get off here?
Devo scendere qui?

When is the first/last bus to …?
Quando c'è il primo/l'ultimo autobus per …?

Please can I have a single/ return ticket to …
Un biglietto di andata/andata e ritorno per …

I would like a standard/first class ticket to…
Un biglietto di seconda/ prima classe per…

Where is the timetable?
Dov'è l'orario?

Do you have a subway/bus map?
Ha una piantina della metropolitana/degli autobus?

Where can I find a taxi?
Dove sono i tassi?

Please take me to …
Per favore, mi porti a …

How much is the journey?
Quanto costerà il viaggio?

Please turn on the meter
Accenda il tassametro, per favore

I'd like to get out here please
Vorrei scendere qui, per favore

Is this the way to…?
È questa la strada per…?

Excuse me, I think I am lost
Mi Scusi, penso di essermi perduto/a

TOURIST INFORMATION

Where is the tourist information office/tourist information desk, please?
Dov'è l'ufficio turistico/il banco informazioni turistiche, per favore?

Do you have a city map?
Avete una cartina della città?

Can you give me some information about…?
Puo darmi delle informazioni su …?

What sights/hotels/restaurants can you recommend?
Quali monumenti/alberghi/ristoranti mi consiglia?

Please could you point them out on the map?
Me li può indicare sulla cartina?

What is the admission price?
Quant'è il biglietto d'ingresso?

Is there a discount for senior citizens/students?
Ci sono riduzioni per anziani/studenti?

Is there an English-speaking guide?
C'è una guida di lingue inglese?

Are there organized excursions?
Ci sono escursioni organizzate?

Do you have a brochure in English?
Avete un opuscolo in inglese?

Could you reserve tickets for me?
Mi può prenotare dei biglietti?

Can we make reservations here?
Possiamo prenotare qui?

TIMES/DAYS/MONTHS

Monday **lunedì**	Friday **venerdì**	week **settimana**	January **gennaio**	May **maggio**	September **settembre**
Tuesday **martedì**	Saturday **sabato**	today **oggi**	February **febbraio**	June **giugno**	October **ottobre**
Wednesday **mercoledì**	Sunday **domenica**	yesterday **ieri**	March **marzo**	July **luglio**	November **novembre**
Thursday **giovedì**	day **giorno**	tomorrow **domani**	April **aprile**	August **agosto**	December **dicembre**

RESTAURANTS

Waiter/waitress
Cameriere/cameriera

I'd like to reserve a table for … people at …
Vorrei prenotare un tavolo per … persone a …

A table for …, please
Un tavolo per …, per favore

Could we sit there?
Possiamo sederci qui?

Is this table taken?
Questo tavolo è occupato?

Are there tables outside?
Ci sono tavoli all'aperto?

We would like to wait for a table
Aspettiamo che si liberi un tavolo

Could we see the menu/wine list?
Possiamo vedere il menù/la lista dei vini?

Do you have a menu/wine list in English?
Avete un menù/una lista dei vini in inglese?

What do you recommend?
Cosa consiglia?

What is the house special?
Qual è la specialità della casa?

I can't eat wheat/sugar/salt/pork/beef/dairy
Non posso mangiare grano/zucchero/sale/maiale/manzo/latticini

I am a vegetarian
Sono vegetariano/a

I'd like…
Vorrei…

May I have an ashtray?
Può portare un portacenere?

I ordered …
Ho ordinato …

Could we have some salt and pepper?
Può portare del sale e del pepe?

The food is cold
Il cibo è freddo

The meat is overcooked/too rare
La carne è troppo cotta/non è abbastanza cotta

This is not what I ordered
Non ho ordinato questo

Can I have the bill, please?
Il conto, per favore?

Is service included?
Il servizio è compreso?

The bill is not right
Il conto è sbagliato

We didn't have this
Non abbiamo avuto questo

HOTELS

I have made a reservation for … nights
Ho prenotato per … notti

Do you have a room?
Avete camere libere?

How much per night?
Quanto costa una notte?

Double/single room
Camera doppia/singola

Twin room
Camera a due letti

With bath/shower
Con bagno/doccia

May I see the room?
Posso vedere la camera?

I'll take this room
Prendo questa camera

Could I have another room?
Vorrei cambiare camera

Is there a lift in the hotel?
C'è un ascensore nell'albergo?

Is the room air-conditioned/heated?
C'è aria condizionata/riscaldamento nella camera?

Is breakfast included in the price?
La colazione è compreso?

When is breakfast served?
A che ora è servita la colazione?

The room is too hot/too cold/dirty
La camera è troppo calda/troppo fredda/sporca

I am leaving this morning
Parto stamattina

Please can I pay my bill?
Posso pagare il conto?

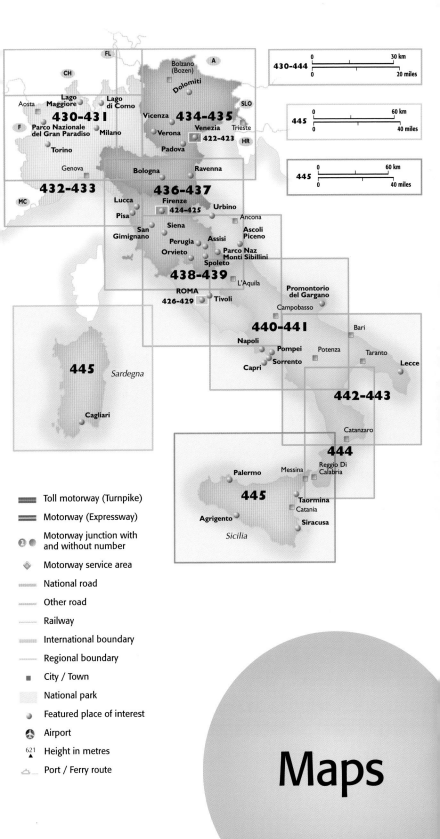

| 430-444 | 0 ——————— 30 km |
| | 0 ——————— 20 miles |

| 445 | 0 ——————— 60 km |
| | 0 ——————— 40 miles |

| 445 | 0 ——————— 60 km |
| | 0 ——————— 40 miles |

FL

CH

A

Bolzano
(Bozen)

Dolomiti

SLO

Aosta

Lago
Maggiore

Lago
di Como

430-431

Vicenza

434-435

Trieste

F

Parco Nazionale
del Gran Paradiso

Milano

Verona

Venezia

422-423

HR

Torino

Padova

Genova

Bologna

Ravenna

432-433

436-437

MC

Lucca

Firenze

424-425

Urbino

Pisa

Ancona

San
Gimignano

Siena

Ascoli
Piceno

Perugia

Assisi

Orvieto

Parco Naz
Monti Sibillini

Spoleto

438-439

ROMA
426-429

Tivoli

L'Aquila

Promontorio
del Gargano

Campobasso

440-441

Bari

Napoli

Pompei

Potenza

Taranto

Capri

Sorrento

Lecce

445   *Sardegna*

442-443

Cagliari

Catanzaro

444

Reggio Di
Calabria

Palermo

Messina

Taormina

445

Catania

Agrigento

Siracusa

Sicilia

▬▬▬ Toll motorway (Turnpike)

▬▬▬ Motorway (Expressway)

② ● Motorway junction with
and without number

◈ Motorway service area

▭▭▭ National road

▭▭▭ Other road

———— Railway

▬▬▬ International boundary

———— Regional boundary

■ City / Town

▒ National park

◉ Featured place of interest

✈ Airport

621
▲ Height in metres

⛴ Port / Ferry route

Maps

VENICE

0 — 200 m
0 — 200 yds

CANNAREGIO

Tre Archi
Fond Contarini
Rio di S Alvise
Rio di San Girolamo
Rio del Battello
Madonna dell 'Orta
Rio Mad dell'Orto
Rio della Sensa
Rio della Misericordia
Calle d Cereria
Canale di Cannaregio
Calle de S Girobbe
Rio di S Giobbe
Rio della Crea
Calle Riello
Rio della Crea
Guglie
Rio Terra Farsetti
Rio d'Noale
Fondamen Nuov
Gesuiti
Canale d Misericordia
Rio di S Caterina
Rio dei Gesuiti
Rio Terra Leonardo
Campo S Geremia
San Marcuola
Rio d Noale
Rio d Felice
SS11
SANTA LUCIA
Riva de Biasio
Rio Terra lista di Spagna
San Stae
Ca' d'Oro
Ca' d'Oro
Ferrovia
Fond S Lucia
Rio di S Zan Degola
Rio Ca' Tron
Rio di S Stae
Rio S Pergola
Rio di S S Apostoli
Piazzale Roma
Fond San Simeon Piccolo
Rio Marin
Rio di S Cassiano
Santa Maria degli Miracoli
Ponte d Liberta
Rio Nuovo
Rio d S Zuane
Rio di S Zuane
Rio dei due Torri
Beccari
Rialto
Piazzale Roma
SANTA CROCE
Muneghette
Santa Maria Gloriosa dei Frari
SAN POLO
Rio del Madonetta
Campo S Polo
Rialto
Rio d Burchielle
Rio Terra dei Pensieri
Scuola Grande di San Rocco
Frescada
Rio di S Polo
San Silvestro
Grande
Calle d Fabbri
Rio d S Salvador
Rio d S M Maggiore
Rio Nuovo
Rio di Ca' Foscari
Sant' Angelo
Rio d S Luca
Basili San M
Rio d Tintor
Scuola Grande dei Carmini
Campo S Margherita
San Toma
SAN MARCO
Fuseri
Piazza San Mar
Ca' Rezzonico
Ca' Rezzonico
San Samuele
Campo Santo Stefano
Museo Civico Correr
Pa D
Rio di S Barnaba
Rio di Duca Vidal
Rio d Santissimo
Rio d S Maurizio
Vallaresso (san Marco)
DORSODURO
Rio di San Nicolo
Rio d A Raffaele
Rio Malpaga
Accademia
Rio di S Trovaso
Rio di S Vio
Giglio
Rio di S Moisè
Salute
MARITTIMA
Rio Ognissanti
Galleria dell'Accademia
Santa Maria della Salute
San Basilio
Fond Zattere ai Ponte Lungo
Collezione Peggy Guggenheim
Rio della Fornace
Zattere
Fond Zattere allo Spirito Santo
Zitelle
Canale della Giudecca
Calle dei Lanzieri
Fond San Biagio
S Eufemia
Fond S Eufemia
Redentore
Fond San Giacomo
Fond della Croce
Calle del Stauri
Canale dei Scali
Rio di San Biagio
Fond d convertite
Giudecca
LA GIUDECCA
C delle scuole
Calle S Giacomo
Rio del P Lungo
Rio d Croce

A   B   C

422

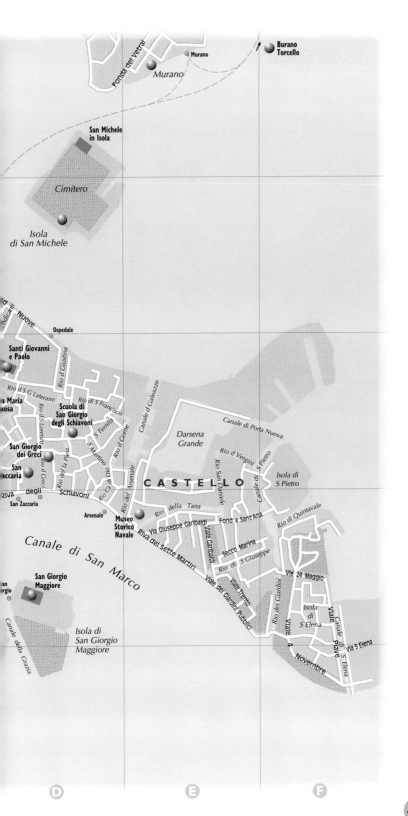

Burano
Torcello

Murano

Fonda del Verrat

Murano

San Michele
in Isola

Cimitero

Isola
di San Michele

dicanti Nuove

Ospedale

Santi Giovanni
e Paolo

Rio d S G Laterano

Rio d I Giustina

Rio di S Francisco

a Maria
osa

Rio d'S Lorenzo

Scuola di
San Giorgio
degli Schiavoni

S Ternita

Canale d Galeazze

Canale di Porta Nuova

San Giorgio
dei Greci

Rio d Greci

Rio de la Pieta

S Martino

Rio d Corte

Rio Ca di Dio

Darsena
Grande

Rio d Vergini

Rio San Daniele

Canale di S Pietro

Isola di
S Pietro

San
accaria

CASTELLO di

iva degli

Schiavoni

Rio del Arsenale

Rio della Tana

Fond a Sant'Ana

Rio di Quintavale

San Zaccaria

Arsenale

Museo
Storico
Navale

Via Giuseppe Garibaldi

Viale Garibaldi

Secco Marina

Riva dei Sette Martiri

Rio di S Giuseppe

Canale di San Marco

Viale Trento

Viale dei Giardini Pubblici

Vle 24 Maggio

Rio dei Giardini

San Giorgio
Maggiore

an
rgio

Viale

Isola
di
S Elena

Viale

Canale di S Elena

Via S Elena

Canale della Grazia

Isola di
San Giorgio
Maggiore

4 Novembre

Plave

D

E

F

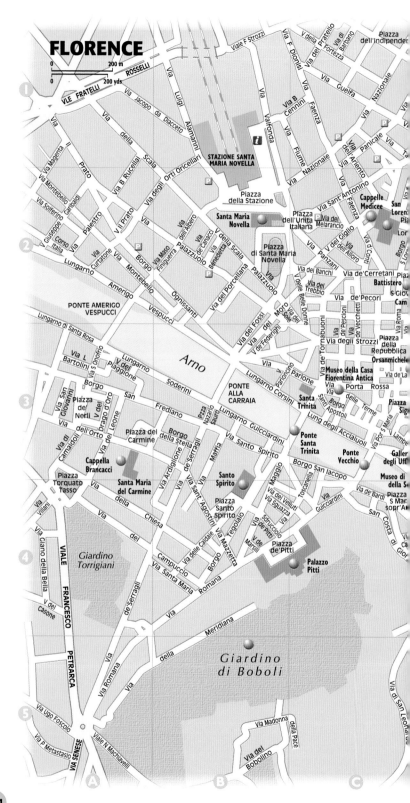

FLORENCE

0 ——— 200 m
0 ——— 200 yds

VLE FRATELLI ROSSELLI

Via Jacopo da Diacceto
Viale F Strozzi
Via F Dionisi
Via della Fortezza
Via del Pratello
Via di Barbano
Piazza dell'Indipenden

Via Luigi Alamanni
Via B Cennini
Via B Faenza
Via Guelfa
Via Nazionale

Via Magenta
Via della Scala
Via degli Orti Oricellari
Vaifonda
Via Flume
Via dell'Ariento
Via Sant'Antonino

Via Montebello
Via B Rucellai
Prato
STAZIONE SANTA MARIA NOVELLA
Via Nazionale

Via Solferino
Via il Prato
Piazza della Stazione
Cappelle Medicee
San Loren
Pia

Giuseppe Corso Italia
Palestro
Via
Via Maso Finiguerra
Santa Maria Novella
Piazza dell'Unità Italiana
Via del Melarancio
Lor
Borgo

Via Curtatone
Borgo
Via dell'Albero
Via de Canacci
Via della Scala
Piazza di Santa Maria Novella
Via del Giglio
Via dell'Amorino
Via de'Conti

Lungarno Amerigo
Montebello
Via del Porcellana
Via del Palazzuolo
Via del Moro
Via Panzani
Via de'Cerretani
Pia
Battistero
S Gio

PONTE AMERIGO VESPUCCI
Vespucci
Via del Fossi
Via delle Belle Donne
Via del Trebbio
Via de'Pecori
Via de'Vecchietti
Cam

Lungarno di Santa Rosa
Arno
Via de'Federighi
Via de'Sole
Via degli Strozzi
Piazza della Repubblica

Via L Bartolini
Lungarno
V del Piaggione
Soderini
Lungarno Corsini
Via
Via de'Tornabuoni
Orsanmichele
Museo della Casa Fiorentina Antica
Via de'La

V di San Onofrio
Borgo San Frediano
PONTE ALLA CARRAIA
Lungarno Guicciardini
Pza Nazario Sauro
Lungarno Corsini
Santa Trinita
Via Porta Rossa
Via delle Terme
Piazza Sig

Piazza de'Nerli
Via dell'Orto
Via Drago d'Oro
Via del Leone
Piazza del Carmine
Borgo della Stella
Maffia
Via Santo Spirito
Ponte Santa Trinita
Borgo Santi Apostoli
Lambe

Via di Camaldoli
Cappella Brancacci
Santa Maria del Carmine
Via Ardiglione
Via Sant'Agostini
Santo Spirito
Ponte Vecchio
Borgo San Iacopo
Galler degli Uff

Piazza Torquato Tasso
Via Villani
della
Chiesa
Piazza Santo Spirito
Via del Velluti
Via Sguazza
Via de'Pitti
Museo di
Via de'Bardi
Piazza S Mar sopr'A

VIALE FRANCESCO
Giardino Torrigiani
Campuccio
Via Santa Maria
Via delle Caldaie
Via Mazzetta
Via del Presto
Piazza de'Pitti
Palazzo Pitti
Via Costa di Gio

V del Casone
Via Romana
Via Chiano della Bella
della
Meridiana

PETRARCA
Via Romana
Via
della
Giardino di Boboli

Via Ugo Foscolo
Via P Metastasio
VIA SENESE
Viale N Machiavelli
Via Madonna della Pace
Via del Bobolino
Via di San Leonar

A   B   C

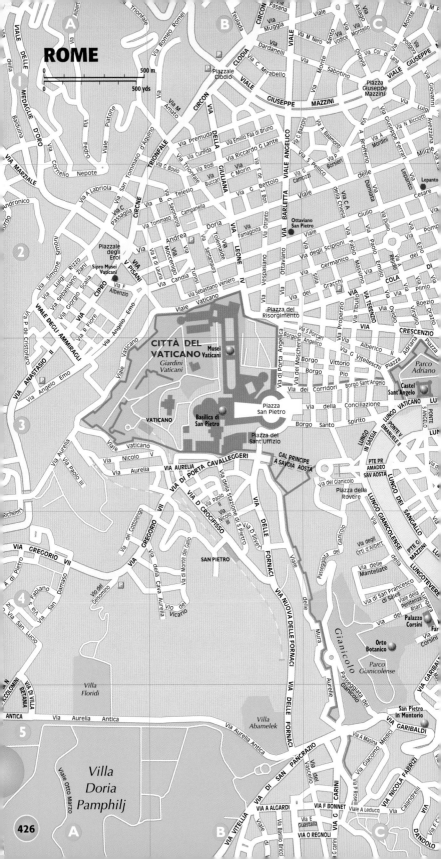

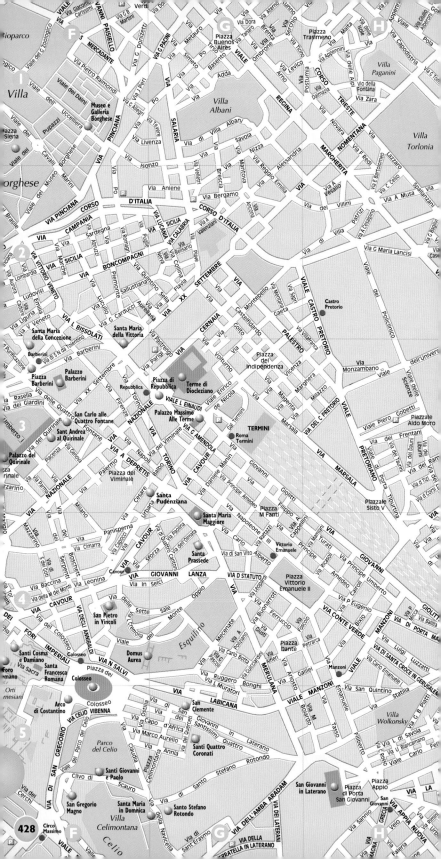

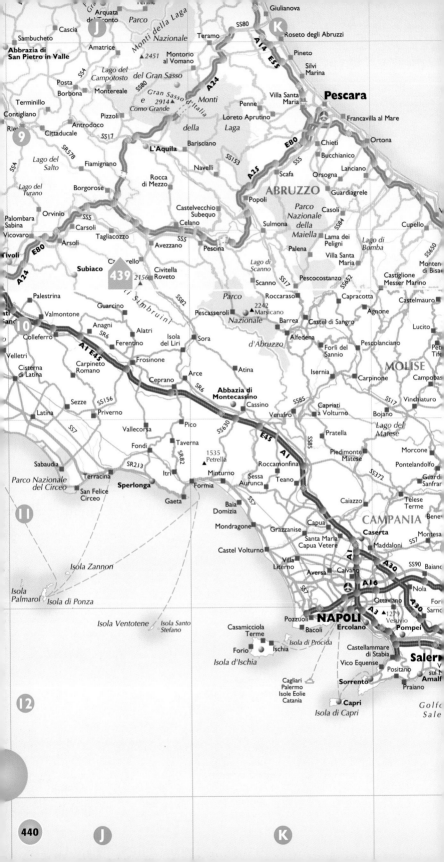

P

Q

R

ARI

SS16 Mola di Bari
Capurso
ifia Rutigliano Polignano a Mare
amassima Conversano Monopoli
Turi
Putignano Castellana Savelletri
Grotte Torre Canne
Fasano
Gioia
del Colle Noci **Alberobello** SS379
Locorotondo Ostuni
Martina Franca San Vito
stellaneta Ceglie Messapica dei Normanni
Mottola SS379 E55 Brindisi
Massafra **PUGLIA** SS16
Palagiano Grottaglie SS613
Latiano Mesagne
Francavilla Fontana San Pietro
Oria Vernotico
TARANTO Manduria San Donaci Squinzano San Cataldo
Marina di Ginosa San Pancrazio Campi
Salentino Salentina **Lecce**
Campomarino Copertino Martano
Porto SS16
Cesareo Nardo **Otranto**
Galatina
Galatone Maglie SS16

Golfo di **Gallipoli** Parabita Santa Cesarea
Terme
Taranto Casarano

Ugento SS274

Gagliano del Capo

Marina
di Leuca

Cariati
ampana SS106
Ciro Marina
E90
li Strongoli

SS107
E846

ilia
castro Crotone

Cutro

SS106 E90 Isola di
Capo Rizzuto

P

Q

R

Map of Sicily (top):

H | J | K | L | M

Golfo di Sant'Eufemia

Isola di Ustica

Cagliari
Genova
Livorno
Napoli
Salerno

Isola Stromboli

ISOLE EOLIE

Isola Filicudi *Isola Panarea*

Isola Salina

Isola Alicudi *Isola Lipari*

Isola Vulcano

15

Mileto

Rosarno

Cagliari

San Vito
lo Capo

Erice

PALERMO

Bagheria

Torre
Faro

Milazzo

Palmi

MESSINA Bo

*ISOLE
EGADI*
sola di Levanzo

Trapani

Monreale

Termini
Imerese

Cefalu

Capo
d'Orlando

Ucria

Reggio
di Calabria

16

*Isola
Marettimo Isola
Favignana*

Segesta
Salemi

Alcamo

Castelbuono

Randazzo

Ali Terme

Brancaleo
Marina

Marsala
Mazara del Vello

Corleone

Prizzi

Alia

Nicosia

Bronte

3323
Etna

Adrano

Taormina

Selinunte

Castelvetrano

Bivona

Caltanissetta

Enna

Paterno

CATANIA

17

SS115

Ribera

Sciacca

Agrigento

Canicatti

**Piazza
Armerina**

SS417

Caltagirone

Grammichele

Golfo di Catania

Augusta

SICILIA

Licata

Gela

Palazzolo
Acreide

Siracusa

18

Isola di Pantelleria

Ragusa

SS11

Noto

Modica

Pachino

Pozzallo

Capo Passero

Map of Sardinia (bottom):

B | C | D | E

*Parco Nazionale
della Maddalena*

Civitavecchia
Livorno

Santa Teresa Gallura

Isloa Asinara

Genova

Palau

C d'Orso

Porto Cervo

Piombino
Livorno
Genova
La Spezia
Civitavecchia

I1

*Golfo
dell'Asinara*

Arzachena

Costa Smeralda

Stintino

Castelsardo

Tempio
Pausania

Olbia

Golfo Aranci

Porto Torres

Sedini

SS199

Monti

San Teodoro

Sassari

Martis

Oschiri

Budoni

Alghero

Ittiri

Ozieri

Ala dei
Sardi

Siniscola

I2

Mores

Bonorva

Bitti

SS131 dcm

Bono

Bosa

Macomer

SS129

Nuoro

Orosei

Cuglieri

Ghilarza

Ottana
Gavoi

**Cala
Gonone**

*Golfo di
Orosei*

SARDEGNA

Dorgali

Oristano

Simaxis

Fonni

*Parco Naz del
Gennargentu*

Baunei

I3

*Golfo di
Oristano*

Sorgono

Aritzo

Arbatax

Laconi

Seui

**Giara di
Gesturi**

Barumini

Jerzu

Bari Sardo

Terralba

Guspini

Sanluri

Escalaplano

Senorbi

Ballao

Fluminimaggiore

Villacidro

SS131

Dolianova

Muravera

Iglesias

SS130

Siliqua

SS125

I4

Portoscuso

Carbonia

*Isola di
S Pietro*

Sarroch

CAGLIARI

*Golfo di
Cagliari*

Capo Carbonara

Giba

*Isola di
S Antioco*

Teulada

Pula

Nora

Civitavecchia, Genova,
Livorno, Napoli,
Palermo, Trapani

445

Marotta 437 J7
Marradi 436 G6
Marsala 445 H17
Marsciano 438 H8
Marsico Nuovo 442 M12
Martigny 430 B2
Martina Franca 443 P12
Martis 445 D11
Massa 436 E6
Massa Marittima
 436 F8
Massafra 443 P12
Matelica 437 J8
Matera 442 N12
Mazara del Vello
 445 H17
Medicina 437 G5
Mel 435 H3
Melegnano 431 E4
Melfi 441 M11
Melito di Porto Salvo
 444 M16
Menaggio 431 D3
Merano 434 G2
Mesola 435 H5
Messina 445 M16
Mestre 435 H4
Metaponto 442 P12
Migliarino 434 H5
Migliarino 436 F7
Miglionico 442 N12
Milano 431 D4
Milano Marittima
 437 H6
Milazzo 445 M16
Mileto 444 N15
Minervino Murge
 441 N11
Minozzo 436 F6
Minturno 440 K11
Mira 435 H4
Mirandola 433 E4
Mirandola 434 G5
Missanello 442 N12
Modena 436 F5
Modica 445 L18
Modigliana 437 G6
Moena 434 G2
Moglia 434 F5
Mola di Bari 443 P11
Molare 433 D5
Molfetta 441 N11
Molinella 437 G5
Moliterno 442 M12
Molveno 434 F3
Moncalieri 432 C4
Mondolfo 437 J7
Mondovi 432 C5
Mondragone 440 K11
Moneglia 433 E6
Monfalcone 435 J3
Monguelfo 435 H2
Monopoli 443 P11
Monreale 445 J16
Monselice 434 G4
Monsummano Terme
 436 F6
Montagnana 434 G4
Montalcino 436 G8

Montalto delle Marche
 439 K8
Monte Argentario
 438 F9
Monte San Savino
 437 G7
Monte Sant'Angelo
 441 M10
Montebelluna 435 H3
Montecchio Maggiore
 434 G4
Montecchio 438 H8
Montecchio 431 D3
Montecorvino Rovella
 442 L12
Montefalco 438 H8
Montefiascone 438 H9
Montefiorino 436 F6
Montegrotto Terme
 434 G4
Montella 441 L12
Montenero di Bisaccia
 439 L10
Montepulciano 437 G8
Montereale 439 J9
Monteriggioni 436 G7
Monterotondo 438 H10
Montesano sulla Marcellana
 442 M12
Montesarchio 440 L11
Montevarchi 436 G7
Monti 445 D11
Montichiari 434 F4
Monticiano 436 G8
Montorio al Vomano
 439 K9
Monza 431 D4
Morano Calabro 442 N13
Morbegno 431 E3
Morciano di Romagna
 437 H6
Morcone 440 L11
Mores 445 D12
Moretta 432 B5
Morgex 430 B3
Mormanno 442 N13
Mortara 433 D4
Motta di Livenza 435 H3
Mottola 443 P12
Muccia 437 J8
Muggia 435 K4
Muravera 445 D14
Muro Lucano 442 M12

Napoli 440 K12
Narni 438 H9
Naturno 434 G2
Navelli 439 K9
Nepi 438 H9
Nereto 439 K8
Nervi 433 D5
Nettuno 438 H10
Nicastro 444 N15
Nice 432 B7
Nicosia 445 L17
Nizza Monferrato
 432 C5
Nocera Umbra 438 J8

Noceto 433 E5
Noci 443 P12
Noepoli 442 N13
Nogara 434 G4
Nola 440 L11
Noli 432 C6
Nora 445 D14
Norcia 439 J8
Noto 445 L18
Nova 441 M11
Nova Levante 434 G2
Novafeltria 437 H6
Novara 431 D4
Novellara 434 F5
Noventa Vicentina
 434 G4
Novi Ligure 433 D5
Numana 439 K7
Nuoro 445 D12

Occhiobello 434 G5
Oderzo 435 H3
Offida 439 K8
Ogliastro Cilento 442 L12
Olbia 445 D11
Oleggio 431 D3
Omegna 431 C3
Oppido Lucano 442 N12
Oppido Mamertina
 444 N16
Ora 434 G2
Orbassano 432 B4
Oria 431 D3
Oriolo 442 N13
Oristano 445 C13
Ormea 432 C6
Orosei 445 E12
Orsogna 439 K9
Orta 441 M11
Ortisei 434 G2
Ortona 439 K9
Orvieto 438 H8
Orvinio 439 J9
Oschiri 445 D12
Osimo 439 J7
Ospedaletti 432 B6
Ostiglia 434 G4
Ostra 437 J7
Otranto 443 R12
Ottana 445 D12
Ottaviano 440 L11
Ottone 433 D5
Oulx 432 B4
Ovada 433 D5
Ozieri 445 D12

Pachino 445 M18
Padova 434 G4
Paesana 432 B5
Paestum 442 L12
Palagiano 443 P12
Palau 445 D11
Palazzo San Gervasio
 441 N11
Palazzolo Acreide 445 L18
Palena 439 K10
Palermo 445 J16

Palestrina 440 J10
Palinuro 442 M13
Palmanova 435 J3
Palmi 444 M16
Palombara Sabina
 438 H9
Paluzza 435 J2
Pandino 431 E4
Paola 444 N14
Papasidero 442 M13
Parabita 443 Q13
Parma 434 F5
Passignano sul Trasimeno
 437 H8
Paterno 442 M12
Paterno 445 L17
Paternopoli 441 L11
Pavia 433 D4
Pavullo nel Frignano
 436 F6
Pedraces 434 H2
Pegli 433 D5
Pejo 434 F2
Pellaro 444 M16
Pellegrino Parmense
 433 E5
Pennabilli 437 H7
Penne 439 K9
Pergola 437 J7
Perugia 437 H8
Pesaro 437 J6
Pescara 439 K9
Pescasseroli 440 K10
Peschici 441 M10
Peschiera del Garda
 434 F4
Pescia 436 F6
Pescina 439 K10
Pescocostanzo 439 K10
Pescolanciano 440 K10
Pescopagano 441 M12
Petilia Policastro 444 P14
Petrella Tifernina 440 L10
Piacenza 433 E4
Piadena 434 F4
Piana Crixia 432 C5
Pianoro 436 G6
Piazza al Serchio 436 F6
Piazza Armerina 445 L17
Picerno 442 M12
Pico 440 J11
Piedimonte Matese
 440 K11
Pienza 437 G8
Pietra Ligure 432 C6
Pietrasanta 436 E6
Pieve di Teco 432 C6
Pieve di Cadore
 435 H2
Pieve Santo 437 H7
Pievepelago 436 F6
Pila 435 H5
Pinerolo 432 B5
Pineto 439 K9
Pinzolo 434 F3
Piobbico 437 H7
Piombino 436 F8
Piove di Sacco
 435 H4

Italy's main attractions, described in The Sights and Out and About sections, are highlighted in **bold type.**

ACKNOWLEDGMENTS

Abbreviations for the credits are as follows:
AA = AA World Travel Library, **t** (top), **b** (bottom), **c** (centre), **l** (left), **r** (right), **bg** (background)

UNDERSTANDING ITALY

4cl AA/Clive Sawyer; **4cc** AA/Max Jourdan; **4cr** AA/Terry Harris; **5cr** AA/Ken Paterson; **6cl** AA/Max Jourdan; **6cc/cr** AA/Clive Sawyer; **8tl** AA/Max Jourdan; **8tr** AA/Clive Sawyer; **8cc** AA/Simon McBride; **8br** AA/Clive Sawyer; **8br** AA/Eric Meacher; **9tl** AA/Ken Paterson; **9cl** AA/Jerry Edmanson; **9cl** AA/Tony Souter; **9bl** AA/Simon McBride; **10tr** AA/Clive Sawyer; **10tc** AA/Max Jourdan; **10cl/cr/br** AA/Clive Sawyer.

LIVING ITALY

11 AA/Max Jourdan; **12bg** AA/Clive Sawyer; **12cl** AA/Ken Paterson; **12tr** AA/Ken Paterson; **12cr** AA/Tony Souter; **12cc** AA/Clive Sawyer; **12br** Ingo Arndt/Nature Picture Library; **13tl** AA/Ken Paterson; **13tr** AA/Ken Paterson; **13cl** Asgeir Helgestad/Nature Picture Library; **13cc** AA/Max Jourdan; **13cr** AA/Clive Sawyer; **14bg/cl** AA/Clive Sawyer; **14tr** AA/Clive Sawyer; **14cl** Lamalfafoto/Team/Grazia Neri; **14cr** AA/Clive Sawyer; **14br** Alex Kouprianoff; **14 vertical strip** AA/Clive Sawyer; **15tc** Franco Origlia/Getty Images; **15cl** AA/Clive Sawyer; **15cc** AA/Max Jourdan; **15cr** AA/Dario Miterdiri; **15bc** AA/Alex Kouprianoff; **16bg** AA/Max Jourdan; **16tc** AA/Simon McBride; **16cl** AA/Simon McBride; **16cr** AA/Max Jourdan; **16cc/r** AA/Simon McBride; **16br** AA/Simon McBride; **17tl** Marco Galbiati/Grazia Neri; **17tr** AA/Tony Souter; **17cr** AA/Max Jourdan; **17 horizontal strip** AA/Simon McBride; **18bg** AA/Simon McBride; **18tl** AA/Clive Sawyer; **18tr** Giulio Andreini/Marka; **18cr** AA/Max Jourdan; **18cl** AA/Clive Sawyer; **19tl** AA/Clive Sawyer; **19tr** AA/Simon McBride; **19cc** AA/Tony Souter; **19cl** AA/Dario Miterdiri; **19cr** Giulio Andreini/Marka; **20bg** AA/Clive Sawyer; **20tl** AA/Clive Sawyer; **20tc** AA/Jim Holmes; **20cc** AA/Alex Kouprianoff; **20b** AA/Simon McBride; **21tl** AA/Simon McBride; **21tr** SIPA/Rex; **21cl** AA/Alex Kouprianoff; **21cc** AA/Jim Holmes; **21cr** AA/Alex Kouprianoff; **21cl** AA/Ken Paterson; **22bg** AA/Alex Kouprianoff; **22tr** AA/Pete Bennett; **22c** AA/Clive Sawyer; **22br** Clive Rose/Getty Images; **22 vertical strip** AA/Max Jourdan; **23tl** AA/Terry Harris; **23tr** AA/Max Jourdan; **23cl** Michael Steele/Getty Images; **23cc** Luca Lozzi/Getty Images; **24bg** AA/Max Jourdan; **24tl** AA/Ken Paterson; **24tc** AA/Dario Miterdiri; **24tr** AA/Simon McBride; **24cl** AA/Max Jourdan; **24cc** AA/Dario Miterdiri; **24cr** Allstar/Cinetext Collection; **24cl** AA/Ken Paterson.

THE STORY OF ITALY

25 AA/Dario Miterdiri; **26bg** AA/Clive Sawyer; **26cc** AA/Ken Paterson; **26cr** AA/The Story of the Nations - Carthage; **26bl** AA/Ken Paterson; **26br** AA/Clive Sawyer; **27cl** AA/Pat Aithie; **27cc** AA/The Story of the Nations - Carthage; **27cr** AA; **27cc** AA/Tony Souter; **27cr** AA/Clive Sawyer; **27bc** AA/Jim Holmes; **28bg** AA/Max Jourdan; **28cc** AA/Story of the Nations - Rome; **28cr** AA; **28bl** AA/Max Jourdan; **28br** AA/Clive Sawyer; **29cl** AA/Max Jourdan; **29cc** AA; **29cr** AA; **29bc** AA/Alex Kouprianoff; **29br** Giraudon/Bridgeman Art Library; **30bg** AA/The Story of the Nations - The Goths; **30cr** AA; **30bl** Mary Evans Picture Library; **30bc** Giraudon/Bridgeman Art Library; **31cl** AA/The Story of the Nations - The Goths; **31cc** AA/James Tims; **31cr** AA; **31cl/cl/c** AA/Clive Sawyer; **31bl** Bridgeman Art Library; **31bc** Bridgeman Art Library; **31br** AA/Tony Souter; **32bg/br** AA/Ken Paterson; **32cl** Roger-Viollet, Paris; **32bl** AA/Max Jourdan; **32bc** AA/Clive Sawyer; **33cl** AA; **33cc** AA; **33cr** AA; **33bc** AA/Clive Sawyer; **33br** AA/Simon McBride; **34bg/br** AA/Jim Holmes; **34cc** AA/Simon McBride; **34cr** AA; **34bl** Giraudon/Bridgeman Art Library; **35cl** Biblioteca Marucelliana, Florence/Bridgeman Art Library/Alinari; **35cc both** AA; **35cr** AA/Simon McBride; **35cr** AA; **35bc** AA/Dario Miterdiri; **35br** AA/Clive Sawyer; **36bg** AA;

36cl AA; **36cc** AA; **36bl** AA/Clive Sawyer; **36bc** AA; **36br** AA; **37cl** Mary Evans Picture Library; **37cc** AA; **37cc** Mary Evans Picture Library; **37cr** AA; **37bc** AA/Peter Wilson; **37br** AA/The Story of the Nations - Venice; **38bg/br** Illustrated London News; **38cc** Mary Evans Picture Library; **38cr** Illustrated London News; **38bl** Mary Evans Picture Library; **39cl** Mary Evans Picture Library; **39cr** AA/Clive Sawyer; **39bc** Mary Evans Picture Library; **39br** Mary Evans Picture Library; **40bg** AA/Simon McBride; **40cl** SIPA/Rex; **40 all others** AA/Clive Sawyer.

ON THE MOVE

41 AA/Clive Sawyer; **42-47t** Pierfabrizio di Marco/Trieste Airport; **42cl** Pierfabrizio di Marco/Trieste Airport; **44c** Aeroporto di Venezia Marco Polo; **46c** AA/Simon McBride; **48-55t** AA/Simon McBride; **48c** AA/Simon McBride; **50cr** AA/Simon McBride; **50cc** AA/John Miller; **50bl** Alessio Pedretti; **51c** AA/Simon McBride; **51bl** EsseBi Italia; **52c** AA/Terry Harris; **52** Tunnel Sign - Automobile Club d'Italia; **52 Other Signs** - EsseBi Italia; **54c** AA/Jim Holmes; **56-59t** AA/Simon McBride; **56c** AA/Simon McBride; **57/58** AA/Simon McBride; **60-61t** Pierfabrizio di Marco/Trieste Airport; **60c** Air One; **61cr** Turrin Fotografia/Trieste Airport; **61b** Aeroporto di Venezia Marco Polo; **62-63t** AA/Dario Miterdiri; **62c** AA/Max Jourdan; **63c** AA/Max Jourdan; **64t** AA/Robert Holmes; **64b** Regency San Marino.

THE SIGHTS

65 AA/Clive Sawyer; **p66-219bg** AA/Richard Ireland; **67tl** AA/Tony Souter; **67tr** AA/Max Jourdan; **68tl** AA/Tony Souter; **68tr** World Pictures; **69** AA/Max Jourdan; **70** AA/Max Jourdan; **71** AA/Max Jourdan; **72tc** AA/Pete Bennet; **72cl** AA/Clive Sawyer; **72cr/bc** AA/Max Jourdan; **73** AA/Clive Sawyer; **75cl** AA/Max Jourdan; **75cr** AA/Clive Sawyer; **76** Italian Tourist Board; **77tl** AA/Clive Sawyer; **77tr** AA/Tony Souter; **78tc** Carlo Cerchioli/Grazia Neri; **78cl** Fiat Auto; **78cc** Claudio Penna/Marka; **78cr** John Heseltine; **79** Ermes Lasagni/Marka; **80tl** Pictures Colour Library; **80tr** AA/Clive Sawyer; **82tc/cl/cc** AA/Clive Sawyer; **82cr** AA/Dario Miterdiri; **82b** AA/Clive Sawyer; **83tl** AA/Peter Wilson; **83cr** AA/Clive Sawyer; **84** AA/Simon McBride; **85tl/cr** AA/Simon McBride; **85b** AA/Clive Sawyer; **86tl** AA/Clive Sawyer; **86tr** AA/Simon McBride; **87** AA/Simon McBride; **88tc/cl** AA/Simon McBride; **88cr** Bridgeman Art Library; **88b** Giraudon/Bridgeman Art Library/Alinari; **89** Bridgeman Art Library; **90** AA/Simon McBride; **91** AA/Clive Sawyer; **92** AA/Rich Newton; **93tc** AA/Rich Newton; **93cl** AA/Simon McBride; **93cr** AA/Clive Sawyer; **94** AA/Clive Sawyer; **95** AA/Simon McBride; **96t** AA/Simon McBride; **96cl** AA/Clive Sawyer; **97** AA/Simon McBride; **98** AA/Simon McBride; **99t** AA/Simon McBride; **99cr** AA/Rich Newton; **100tl** AA/Clive Sawyer; **100tc** AA/Simon McBride; **100tr** AA/Clive Sawyer; **101** AA/Dario Miterdiri; **102tl** AA/Simon McBride; **102tr** AA/Clive Sawyer; **104tl** Italian Tourist Board; **104tr** James Davis Worldwide; **105** AA/Clive Sawyer; **106tl** AA/Clive Sawyer; **106tr** World Pictures; **107** World Pictures; **108** Italian Tourist Board; **109tl** AA/Tony Souter; **109tr** World Pictures; **110** AA/Tony Souter; **111tl** AA/Clive Sawyer; **111tr** Pierfabrizio di Marco/Trieste Airport; **112** AA/Clive Sawyer; **113** AA/Pete Bennett; **114** AA/Clive Sawyer; **116tc/cl** AA/Simon McBride; **116cc** AA/Clive Sawyer; **116cr** AA/Ken Paterson; **117** AA/Simon McBride; **118** AA/Simon McBride; **119** AA/Simon McBride; **120tl** AA/Clive Sawyer; **120tc/tr** AA/Simon McBride; **121** AA/Simon McBride; **122tc** AA/Barrie Smith; **122cl** AA/Jerry Edmanson; **122cr/bl** AA/Simon McBride; **123** AA/Simon McBride; **124tl** AA/Simon McBride; **124tc/tr** AA/Clive Sawyer; **125** AA/Simon McBride; **126tl** AA/Simon McBride; **126tr** AA/Simon McBride;

Abbreviations for the credits are as follows:
AA = AA World Travel Library, **t** (top), **b** (bottom), **c** (centre), **l** (left), **r** (right)

127 AA/Simon McBride; **128tc** AA/Clive Sawyer; **128cl** AA/Jerry Edmanson; **129t** AA/Clive Sawyer; **129bc** AA/Simon McBride; **130t** AA/Simon McBride; **130cl** AA/Barrie Smith; 131 AA/Simon McBride; 132 AA/Simon McBride; 133 AA/Clive Sawyer; **134tl** AA/Barrie Smith; **134tc/tr** AA/Clive Sawyer; 136 AA/Ken Paterson; **137t** AA/Peter Davies; **137tr** AA/Terry Harris; **138tl** AA/Simon McBride; **138tr** AA/Terry Harris; 139 AA/Ken Paterson; **140tl** AA/Clive Sawyer; **140tr** AA/Terry Harris; **141tl** AA/Ken Paterson; **141tr** AA/Terry Harris; **142t** AA/Clive Sawyer; **142cl** AA/Ken Paterson; **143tl** AA/Simon McBride; **143tr** AA/Ken Paterson; **144tl** AA/Terry Harris; **144tc** AA/Simon McBride; **144tr** AA/Ken Paterson; **145tl** AA/Ken Paterson; **145tr** AA/Simon McBride; 146 AA/Terry Harris; 147 World Pictures; **148t** AA/Ken Paterson; **148cl** AA/Terry Harris; 149 AA/Clive Sawyer; **150tl** AA/Clive Sawyer; **150tc** AA/Ken Paterson; **150tr** AA/Clive Sawyer; **151t** AA/Ken Paterson; **151cr** AA/Simon McBride; **152tc** AA/Jerry Edmanson; **152cl** AA/Clive Sawyer; **152cc** AA/Simon McBride; **152cr** AA/Clive Sawyer; **152cb** AA/Clive Sawyer; 153 AA/Clive Sawyer; 154 AA/Terry Harris; **155tl** AA/Terry Harris; **155tr** AA/Ken Paterson; **156tl** AA/Ken Paterson; **156tc** AA/Terry Harris; **156tr** AA/Ken Paterson; **158tc** AA/Dario Miterdiri; **158cl** AA/Dario Miterdiri; **158cr** AA/Peter Wilson; **158bl** AA/Alex Kouprianoff; **158bc** AA/Dario Miterdiri; **159tl** AA/Simon McBride; **159cr** AA/Clive Sawyer; **159b** AA/Peter Wilson; **160tl** Alex Kouprianoff; **160tc/tr** AA/Simon McBride; 161 AA/Jim Holmes; **162tc** AA/Simon McBride; **162cl/cc** AA/Jim Holmes; **162cr** AA/Simon McBride; **162b** AA/Alex Kouprianoff; 163 AA/Jim Holmes; **164tc/cl** AA/Simon McBride; **164cr** AA/Peter Wilson; **164bl** AA/Simon McBride; **165c** AA/Clive Sawyer; **165b** AA/Peter Wilson; 166 AA/Peter Wilson; **167tl** AA/Simon McBride; **167tr** AA/Jim Holmes; **168** AA/Simon McBride; 169 AA/Jim Holmes; **170t** AA/Jim Holmes; **170b** AA/Tony Souter; **171c** AA/Dario Miterdiri; **171b** AA/Simon McBride; **172tl** AA/Peter Wilson; **172tc** AA/Simon McBride; **172tr** AA/Simon McBride; **173t** AA/Simon McBride; 174 AA/Jim Holmes; 175 AA/Jim Holmes; 176 AA/Simon McBride; **177tl** AA/Jim Holmes; **177tr** AA/Simon McBride; **178t** AA/Dario Miterdiri; **179tl** AA/Jim Holmes; **179tc** AA/Simon McBride; **179tr** AA/Dario Miterdiri; **180tl** AA/Simon McBride; **180tc** AA/Dario Miterdiri; **180tr** AA/Peter Wilson; 182 AA/Clive Sawyer; **183tl** AA/Clive Sawyer; **183tc/tr** AA/Tony Souter; **184tl** AA/Simon McBride; **184tr** AA/Clive Sawyer; **185tl** AA/Clive Sawyer; **185tr** AA/Tony Souter; **186t** AA/Tony Souter; **187tl** AA/Clive Sawyer; **187tr** AA/Tony Souter; 188 AA/Simon McBride; 189 AA/Simon McBride; 190 AA/Tony Souter; **192tl** AA/Clive Sawyer; **192tc** AA/Max Jourdan; **192tr** AA/Clive Sawyer; 193 World Pictures; 194 World Pictures; **195t** AA/Clive Sawyer; 196 AA/Clive Sawyer; 197 AA/Tony Souter; 198 AA/Max Jourdan; 199 AA/Max Jourdan; 201 AA/Max Jourdan; **202tl** AA/Tony Souter; **202tr** AA/Clive Sawyer; 203 AA/Clive Sawyer; 204 AA/Max Jourdan; 205 AA/Max Jourdan; 206 AA/Clive Saywer; **207tl** AA/Max Jourdan; **207cr** AA/Clive Sawyer; **208tl** AA/Tony Souter; **208tr** AA/Clive Sawyer; **209t** AA/Clive Sawyer; **209cr** AA/Max Jourdan; **210tl** AA/Clive Sawyer; **210tr** AA/Tony Souter; 212-219 AA/Clive Sawyer; **220tl** AA/Clive Sawyer; **220tr** John Miller.

WHAT TO DO

221 AA/Max Jourdan; **222-224t** AA/Jim Holmes; 222 AA/Clive Sawyer; 223 AA/Max Jourdan; 224 AA/Max Jourdan; **225-226t & 226bl** Archivio Teatro del Maggio Musicale Fiorentino/Gianluca Moggi/New Press Photo Firenze; **225br** AA/Clive Sawyer; 226 Archivio Teatro del Maggio Musicale Fiorentino; **226br** AA/Clive Sawyer; **227t** Brand X Pictures; **227bl** Matilda Club, Sorrento; **228-232t** AA; **230cl** AA/Simon McBride; **230cr** Corbis; 231 Nazionale Turismo Equistre; **233t/b** Time Elevator, Rome; **234t** AA/Dario Miterdiri; **234cl** AA/Simon McBride; **235-239t** AA/Max Jourdan; 235 AA/Max Jourdan; **236cc** Vittoriale Archivio; **236br** AA/Clive Sawyer; **238bl** Image 100; **240-244t** AA/Dario Miterdiri; **241cl/cr** AA/Clive Sawyer; **242cl** AA/Dario Miterdiri; **242bl** AA/Simon McBride; **243cl** El Suk; **244cl** AA/Clive Sawyer; **245-246** AA/Clive Sawyer; **245cc** AA/Clive Sawyer; **246cr** AA/Clive Sawyer; **247-251t** AA/Simon McBride; **247bc** AA/Clive Sawyer; **247br** AA/Simon McBride; **248br** Archivio Teatro del Maggio Musicale Fiorentino; **249cr** AA/Clive Sawyer; **251bl/br** AA/Simon McBride; **252-260t** AA/Simon McBride; 253 AA/Ken Paterson; 258 AA/Ken Paterson; **261-267t** Flavio Raimondo/Fabriano; **262cl** AA/Clive Sawyer; **263cl** AA/Alex Kouprianoff; **263bl** AA/Jim Holmes; **263cr** AA/Clive Sawyer; **264cl** AA/Clive Sawyer; **264cr** AA/Jim Holmes; **265cl/cr** AA/Jim Holmes; **267br** Simon McBride; **268/269t** AA/Clive Sawyer; **268cl** AA/Clive Sawyer; **270-273t** Brand X Pictures; **273br** AA/Max Jourdan; **274-276t** AA/Simon McBride; **276cl** AA/Clive Sawyer.

OUT AND ABOUT

277 AA/Tony Souter; 279 AA/Tony Souter; 280 Pictures Colour Library; 281 AA/Tony Souter; 282 AA/Tony Souter; 283 AA/Tony Souter; 284 AA/Max Jourdan; **285tl/tr** AA/Pete Bennet; **285bl** AA/Max Jourdan; **285br** AA/Clive Sawyer; 286 AA/Max Jourdan; 287 AA/Max Jourdan; 288 AA/Max Jourdan; **289t** AA/Max Jourdan; **289br** AA/Clive Sawyer; 290 Sally Roy; **291t** World Pictures; **291b** Travel Ink/Andrew Watson; 292 Sally Roy; 293 Sally Roy; **294c** AA/Ken Paterson; **294b** Rebecca Ford; 295 AA/Ken Paterson; 296 AA/Ken Paterson; 297 1990, Photo Scala, Florence; 298 AA/Ken Paterson; **299tl/tr** AA/Simon McBride; **299b** AA/Ken Paterson; **301tr** AA/Simon McBride; **301cr** AA/Ken Paterson; **301b** AA/Jerry Edmanson; 302 AA/Simon McBride; **303t** AA/Clive Sawyer; **303c/b** AA/Simon McBride; **304t** AA/Ken Paterson; **304b** AA/Simon McBride; **307tl** AA/Ken Paterson; **307tr/br** AA/Terry Harris; 309 AA/Terry Harris; **311tl/tr/cr** AA/Clive Sawyer; **311b** AA/Tony Souter; 312 AA/Terry Harris; 313 AA/Terry Harris; 314 AA/Clive Sawyer; 315 AA/Clive Sawyer; 316 AA/Clive Sawyer; 317 AA/Clive Sawyer; 318 AA/Clive Sawyer; **319t** AA/Clive Sawyer; **319cc** AA/Max Jourdan; **319cr/b** AA/Max Jourdan; 320 AA/Max Jourdan; 321 AA/Clive Sawyer; 322 AA/Tony Souter; **323tl** AA/Tony Souter; **323tr/b** AA/Clive Sawyer; 324 AA/Tony Souter; **325tl** AA/Clive Sawyer; **325tr/b** AA/Tony Souter; 326 AA/Clive Sawyer; **327t** John Heseltine; **327br** Fausto Giaccone/Marka; **328t** Maurilio Mazzola/Marka; **328b** Danilo Donadoni/Marka; 329 Jenny Squillaci; **330tl** AA; **330tr** AA/Max Jourdan.

EATING AND STAYING

331 AA/Jim Holmes; **332cl** AA/Jim Holmes; **332cc** Isla Love; **332cr** AA/Ken Paterson; 333 AA/Max Jourdan; **334cl** AA/Tony Souter; **334cc** AA/Max Jourdan; **334cr** AA/Jerry Edmanson; **335cl** AA/Tony Souter; **335cc** AA/Ken Paterson; **335cr** AA/Tony Souter; **336cl** AA/Jim Holmes; **336cc** AA/Barrie Smith; **336cr** AA/Clive Sawyer; 365 Photodisc; 374, **375tr**, **376c/cr/bl**, **377tl/tc/cr**, 378, 379, **380cr/bl/bc** all Clive Sawyer; 385/394 Photodisc.

PLANNING

399 AA/Max Jourdan; 404 AA/Clive Sawyer; 405 ECB; 406 AA/Clive Sawyer; 407 AA/Max Jourdan; 408 AA/Clive Sawyer; 409 AA/Max Jourdan; 410 AA/Max Jourdan; 412 AA/Clive Sawyer; 414 AA/Clive Sawyer; 415 AA/Simon McBride; 416 Stockbyte.

Project editor
Nicola Lancaster

Interior design
David Austin, Glyn Barlow, Alan Gooch, Kate Harling, Bob Johnson,
Nick Otway, Carole Philp, Keith Russell

Picture research
Liz Allen, Alice Earle, Debbie Ireland, Charlotte Lippmann, Vivien Little, Serena Mellish

Cover design
Tigist Getachew

Internal repro work
Susan Crowhurst, Ian Little, Michael Moody

Production
Lyn Kirby, Helen Sweeney

Mapping
Maps produced by the Cartography Department of AA Publishing

Main contributors
Sally Roy (consultant), Jack Altman, Anna Maria d'Angelo, The Content Works, Charlotte Eager,
Rebecca Ford, Alex Johnson, Simona Marchetta, Lee Marshall,
Jenny Squillaci, Vittorio Squillaci, Nicky Swallow

Copy editors
Sue Gordon, Janet Tabinski

See It Italy
ISBN-13: 978-1-4000-1383-8
ISBN-10: 1-4000-1383-6

Published in the United States by Fodor's Travel, and simultaneously in Canada by
Random House of Canada Limited, Toronto.
Published in the United Kingdom by AA Publishing.

Color separation by Keenes
Printed and bound by Leo, China
10 9 8 7 6 5

This book is available for special discounts for bulk purchases for sales promotions or premiums.
Special editions, including personalized covers, excerpts of existing books, and corporate imprints,
can be created in large quantities for special needs. For more information, write to Special
Markets/Premium Sales, 1745 Broadway, MD 6-2, New York, NY 10019 or e-mail
specialmarkets@randomhouse.com.

A03041
Mapping in this title produced from:
Map data © 1997–2003 Navigation Technologies BV. All rights reserved.
Mapping © ISTITUTO GEOGRAFICO DE AGOSTINI, Novara - 2005

Relief map images supplied by Mountain High Maps ® Copyright © 1993 Digital Wisdom, Inc
Weather chart statistics supplied by Weatherbase © Copyright 2003 Canty and Associates, LLC
Communicarta assistance with distance/time charts gratefully acknowledged

Important Note: Time inevitably brings changes, so always confirm prices, travel facts, and
other perishable information when it matters. Although Fodor's cannot accept responsibility
for errors, you can use this guide in the confidence that we have taken every care to ensure
its accuracy.

Fodor's Key to the Guides

AMERICA'S **GUIDEBOOK LEADER** PUBLISHES GUIDES FOR **EVERY KIND OF TRAVELER**. CHECK OUT OUR MANY SERIES AND FIND YOUR **PERFECT MATCH**.

FODOR'S GOLD GUIDES

America's favorite travel-guide series offers the most detailed insider reviews of hotels, restaurants, and attractions in all price ranges, plus great background information, smart tips, and useful maps.

COMPASS AMERICAN GUIDES

Stunning guides from top local writers and photographers, with gorgeous photos, literary excerpts, and colorful anecdotes. A must-have for culture mavens, history buffs, and new residents.

FODOR'S CITYPACKS

Concise city coverage in a guide plus a foldout map. The right choice for urban travelers who want everything under one cover.

FODOR'S WHERE TO WEEKEND

A fresh take on weekending, this series identifies the best places to escape outside the city and details loads of rejuvenating activities as well as cool places to stay, great restaurants, and practical information.

FODOR'S AROUND THE CITY WITH KIDS

Up to 68 great ideas for family days, recommended by resident parents. Perfect for exploring in your own backyard or on the road.

FODOR'S TRAVEL HISTORIC AMERICA

For travelers who want to experience history firsthand, this series gives in-depth coverage of historic sights, plus nearby restaurants and hotels. Themes include the Thirteen Colonies, the Old West, and the Lewis and Clark Trail.

FODOR'S FLASHMAPS

Every resident's map guide, with 60 easy-to-follow maps of public transit, parks, museums, zip codes, and more.

FODOR'S LANGUAGES FOR TRAVELERS

Practice the local language before you hit the road. Available in phrase books, cassette sets, and CD sets.

THE COLLECTED TRAVELER

These collections of the best published essays and articles on various European destinations will give you a feel for the culture, cuisine, and way of life.

FODOR'S HOW TO GUIDES

Get tips from the pros on planning the perfect trip. Learn how to pack, fly hassle-free, plan a honeymoon or cruise, stay healthy on the road, and travel with your baby.

KAREN BROWN'S GUIDES

Engaging guides—many with easy-to-follow inn-to-inn itineraries—to the most charming inns and B&Bs in the U.S.A. and Europe.

OTHER GREAT TITLES FROM FODOR'S

Baseball Vacations, The Complete Guide to the National Parks, Family Vacations, Golf Digest's Places to Play, Great American Drives of the East, Great American Drives of the West, Great American Vacations, Healthy Escapes, National Parks of the West, Skiing USA.

At bookstores everywhere.   www.fodors.com/books

Dear Traveler

From buying a plane ticket to booking a room and seeing the sights, a trip goes much more smoothly when you have a good travel guide. Dozens of writers, editors, designers, and cartographers have worked hard to make the book you hold in your hands a good one. Was it everything you expected? Were our descriptions accurate? Were our recommendations on target? And did you find our tips and practical advice helpful? Your ideas and experiences matter to us. If we have missed or misstated something, we'd love to hear about it. Fill out our survey at www.fodors.com/books/feedback/, or e-mail us at seeit@fodors.com. Or you can snail mail to the See It Editor at Fodor's, 1745 Broadway, New York, New York 10019. We'll look forward to hearing from you.

Tim Jarrell
Publisher